Lecture Notes in Artificial Intelligence   3808

Edited by J. G. Carbonell and J. Siekmann

Subseries of Lecture Notes in Computer Science

T0188811

Carlos Bento   Amílcar Cardoso
Gaël Dias (Eds.)

Progress in
Artificial Intelligence

12th Portuguese Conference
on Artificial Intelligence, EPIA 2005
Covilhã, Portugal, December 5-8, 2005
Proceedings

 Springer

Series Editors

Jaime G. Carbonell, Carnegie Mellon University, Pittsburgh, PA, USA
Jörg Siekmann, University of Saarland, Saarbrücken, Germany

Volume Editors

Carlos Bento
Amílcar Cardoso
University of Coimbra, Center for Informatics and Systems
Department of Informatics Engineering, 3030 Coimbra, Portugal
E-mail: {bento, amilcar}@dei.uc.pt

Gaël Dias
University of Beira Interior
Centre of Human Language Technology and Bioinformatics
Department of Computer Science
Rua Marquês de Ávila e Bolama, 6201-001 Covilhã, Portugal
E-mail: ddg@di.fct.unl.pt

Library of Congress Control Number: 2005936461

CR Subject Classification (1998): I.2, H.2, F.1, H.3, D.1.6

ISSN   0302-9743
ISBN-10   3-540-30737-0 Springer Berlin Heidelberg New York
ISBN-13   978-3-540-30737-2 Springer Berlin Heidelberg New York

Springer is a part of Springer Science+Business Media

springeronline.com

© Springer-Verlag Berlin Heidelberg 2005
Printed in Germany

Typesetting: Camera-ready by author, data conversion by Scientific Publishing Services, Chennai, India
Printed on acid-free paper   SPIN: 11595014   06/3142   5 4 3 2 1 0

Preface

With this edition, EPIA, the Portuguese Conference on Artificial Intelligence, celebrates its 20th anniversary. Like all its previous editions, it has been run under the auspices of the Portuguese Association for Artificial Intelligence (APPIA), which was established in 1984 and is also celebrating 20 years of activity.

The first edition of EPIA was held in Porto, in October 1985, organised by Pavel Brazdil, Miguel Filgueiras, Luís Damas and Armando Campos e Matos. EPIA soon evolved to an international conference by adopting in its fourth edition English as the official language and having its proceedings published by Springer, in the LNAI series. In recent years, the conference gradually progressed from a plenary organisation to a workshop-based structure. The conference has steadily assumed high-quality standards, both in its scientific management and in the scientific program, with the aim of progressively broadening its audience and improving its impact over young researchers.

EPIA 2005 was the 12th edition of the conference. With the above-mentioned celebrations in mind, we decided to work towards the involvement of several generations of AI researchers in the organisation of the event. As a result, EPIA 2005 involved for the first time an Advisory Committee, composed of all the founders of APPIA that are still working in AI, and also the Co-chairs of the last EPIAs, as listed elsewhere in these proceedings. We want to express to them our gratitude for all the support, advice and confidence.

When we set about organising the event, we committed ourselves to the objective of expanding the thematic range of the conference by attracting emerging and boundary areas, while still including areas with an already consolidated research history. This led us to adopt from previous issues a conference structure based on a set of Thematic Workshops, to provide the participants with the opportunity to focus on specific thematic and unique application areas.

EPIA 2005 was innovative in this matter by issuing a public Call for Workshops and setting up a refereed selection process, held by the new Advisory Committee, which increased the number and diversity of themes in discussion. As a result, eight thematic workshops were approved, with a diversity of scopes, including novel proposals (AC, BAOSW, CMB, IROBOT and TEMA) as well as progressions of workshops held in previous EPIAs (ALEA, MASTA and EKDB&W). We must acknowledge the key importance of these workshops in the success of the event. Particular thanks are due to the Workshop Chairs, listed elsewhere in these proceedings, for their invaluable proposals and collaboration.

This edition also included, for the first time, a General AI workshop (GAIW), with its own organising structure, which aimed to address all the AI topics not covered by the remaining workshops. This wide-scope workshop complemented the remaining ones by allowing any AI researcher to participate without compromising the overall coherence of the conference structure.

EPIA 2005 reconfirmed the international status of the conference and the high standard of accepted papers. A total of 167 contributions were received from 29 countries (65 from Portugal, 17 from Brazil, 15 from Spain, 10 from Netherlands, 9 from the UK, 4 from France, Iran and the USA, 3 from Belgium and Germany, and the remaining ones from diverse origins, from Algeria to Canada, from China to Mexico, from Korea to India, and many others). All submissions were anonymous. All of them were subject to an IJCAI-style triple-blind peer review. Common guidelines, tools and procedures were adopted for all the workshops. From the submitted contributions, 58 were selected for publication in this volume as full papers and are organised in chapters, by workshop.

The EPIA 2005 Workshops could count on highly qualified Program Committees, which included many internationally distinguished researchers covering a wide range of AI areas. These committees involved 213 researchers from 24 countries (74 from Portugal, 20 from Germany, 18 from the USA, 15 from Spain and the UK, 14 from France, 13 from Brazil, just to mention the most representative). Our special thanks go to them and also to the reviewers, listed elsewhere in these proceedings, for their excellent work.

The participation as invited speakers of the distinguished researchers Richard Benjamin (University of Amsterdam, The Netherlands), Gregory Grefenstette (Commissariat à l'Energie Atomique, France), Auke Ijspeert (École Polytechnique Fédérale de Lausanne, Switzerland), Andrew Phillips (Microsoft Research, UK) and Push Singh (Media Lab, MIT, USA) greatly contributed to broadening the thematic spectrum of the conference.

We are honoured to announce that this conference was organised in cooperation with the following prestigious European and American scientific associations: ECCAI, AAAI, IEEE-SMC and ACM.

The Research to Industry Day, held in Parkurbis, the incubator associated to the University of Beira Interior, was another innovation of this EPIA. It was devoted to the challenging process of going from pre-competitive research to successful commercial projects, and involved specialists on the settlement of new enterprises and on relevant legal and financial aspects of the process. This initiative also comprised an Intelligent Systems Demonstration event, which contributed to the diffusion of the AI achievements, particularly among young students.

Several people gave us invaluable help in several stages of this process of preparing EPIA 2005. Special thanks go to Gabriel Pereira Lopes, Sónia Vaz, João Cunha, Jorge Tavares and Penousal Machado. We are also grateful to the authors and presenters, as well as to all those who participated in EPIA in some way. An acknowledgement is also due to the institutions and companies that sponsored this event. We list them elsewhere in these proceedings. The final thanks go to Springer for their help and assistance in producing this book.

December 2005   Carlos Bento, Amílcar Cardoso, Gaël Dias

EPIA 2005 Conference Organization

Program and Conference Co-chairs

Carlos Bento	Universidade de Coimbra, Portugal
Amílcar Cardoso	Universidade de Coimbra, Portugal
Gaël Harry Dias	Universidade da Beira Interior, Portugal

Advisory Committee

Salvador Abreu	Universidade de Évora, Portugal
Pavel Brazdil	Universidade do Porto, Portugal
Helder Coelho	Universidade de Lisboa, Portugal
Ernesto Costa	Universidade de Coimbra, Portugal
Luís Damas	Universidade do Porto, Portugal
Miguel Filgueiras	Universidade do Porto, Portugal
Alípio Jorge	Universidade do Porto, Portugal
Ernesto Morgado	Instituto Superior Técnico, Portugal
José Carlos Maia Neves	Universidade do Minho, Portugal
Arlindo Oliveira	Instituto Superior Técnico, Portugal
Eugénio Oliveira	Universidade do Porto, Portugal
João Pavão Martins	Instituto Superior Técnico, Portugal
Luís Moniz Pereira	Universidade Nova de Lisboa, Portugal
António Porto	Universidade Nova de Lisboa, Portugal

Workshops Chairs

AC 2005

Ana Paiva	Instituto Superior Técnico, Portugal
Carlos Martinho	Instituto Superior Técnico, Portugal
Eugénio Oliveira	Universidade do Porto, Portugal

ALEA 2005

Luís Correia	Universidade de Lisboa, Portugal
Ernesto Costa	Universidade de Coimbra, Portugal

BAOSW 2005

H. Sofia Pinto	Instituto Superior Técnico, Portugal
Andreia Malucelli	Universidade do Porto, Portugal
Fred Freitas	Universidade Federal de Alagoas, Maceió, Brazil
Christoph Tempich	Universität Karlsruhe, Germany

CMB 2005

Rui Camacho	Universidade do Porto, Portugal
Alexessander Alves	Universidade do Porto, Portugal
Joaquim Pinto da Costa	Universidade do Porto, Portugal
Paulo Azevedo	Universidade do Minho, Portugal

EKDB&W 2005

João Gama	Universidade do Porto, Portugal
João Moura-Pires	Universidade Nova de Lisboa, Portugal
Margarida Cardoso	ISCTE, Portugal
Nuno Marques	Universidade Nova de Lisboa, Portugal
Luís Cavique	Instituto Politécnico de Lisboa, Portugal

GAIW 2005

Carlos Bento	Universidade de Coimbra, Portugal
Amílcar Cardoso	Universidade de Coimbra, Portugal
Gaël Harry Dias	Universidade da Beira Interior, Portugal

IROBOT 2005

Luís Paulo Reis	Universidade do Porto, Portugal
Nuno Lau	Universidade de Aveiro, Portugal
Carlos Carreto	Instituto Politécnico da Guarda, Portugal
Eduardo Silva	Instituto Politécnico do Porto, Portugal

MASTA 2005

João Balsa da Silva	Universidade de Lisboa, Portugal
Luís Moniz	Universidade de Lisboa, Portugal
Luís Paulo Reis	Universidade do Porto, Portugal

TEMA 2005

Gabriel Pereira Lopes	Universidade Nova de Lisboa, Portugal
Joaquim Ferreira da Silva	Universidade Nova de Lisboa, Portugal
Vítor Rocio	Universidade Aberta, Portugal
Paulo Quaresma	Universidade de Évora, Portugal

Program Committee

Salvador Abreu (Portugal)	Paulo Azevedo (Portugal)
Jesus Aguilar (Spain)	Franz Baader (Germany)
Paulo Alexandrino (Portugal)	Ricardo Baeza-Yates (Spain)
Jonas Almeida (USA)	João Balsa da Silva (Portugal)
José Miguel Almeida (Portugal)	Jacky Baltes (Canada)
Alexessander Alves (Portugal)	Pedro Barahona (Portugal)
Elisabeth André (Germany)	Ana Lúcia Bazzan (Brazil)
Helder Araújo (Portugal)	Frederic Benhamou (France)

Carlos Bento (Portugal)
Estela Bicho (Portugal)
Timothy W. Bickmore (USA)
Guido Boella (Italy)
Stefano Borgo (Italy)
Luís Botelho (Portugal)
Jean-Francois Boulicaut (France)
Philip Bourne (USA)
António Branco (Portugal)
Jürgen Branke (Germany)
Agnès Braud (France)
Christopher Brewster (UK)
Virginia Brilhante (Brazil)
Vladimir Brusic (Singapore)
Hans-Dieter Burkhard (Germany)
Chris Bystroff (USA)
Rui Camacho (Portugal)
Luís Camarinha-Matos (Portugal)
Lola Cañamero (UK)
Amílcar Cardoso (Portugal)
Margarida Cardoso (Portugal)
Walter Carnielli (Brazil)
Carlos Carreto (Portugal)
André Carvalho (Brazil)
Cristiano Castelfrachi (Italy)
Marco Castellani (Portugal)
Leandro de Castro (Brazil)
Luís Cavique (Portugal)
An Chen (China)
Ning Chen (China)
Xiaoping Chen (China)
Philipp Cimiano (Germany)
Helder Coelho (Portugal)
Oscar Corcho (UK)
Luís Correia (Portugal)
Ernesto Costa (Portugal)
Vítor Costa (Brazil)
Maria dos Remédios Cravo (Portugal)
Walter Daelemans (Belgium)
Eric de la Clergerie (France)
Luc Dehaspe (Belgium)
Yves Demazeau (France)
Fiorella di Rosis (Italy)
Gaël Harry Dias (Portugal)
Jorge Dias (Portugal)

Rose Dieng-Kuntz (France)
Virginia Dignum (The Netherlands)
Ying Ding (Austria)
Mark d'Inverno (UK)
John Domingue (UK)
Marco Dorigo (Belgium)
Edmund Durfee (USA)
Inês Dutra (Brazil)
Andreas Eisele (Germany)
Tomaz Erjavec (Slovenia)
Mariano Fernandez-Lopez (Spain)
Joaquim Ferreira da Silva (Portugal)
Mário Figueiredo (Portugal)
Miguel Filgueiras (Portugal)
Marcelo Finger (Brazil)
Klaus Fischer (Germany)
Michael Fisher (UK)
Carlos Fonseca (Portugal)
Ana Freitas (Portugal)
João Gama (Portugal)
Pablo Gamallo (Spain)
Aldo Gangemi (Italy)
Graça Gaspar (Portugal)
Hector Geffner (Spain)
Michael Gelfond (USA)
David Gilbert (UK)
Jonathan Gratch (USA)
Gregory Grefenstette (France)
Michael Gruninger (USA)
David Hales (Italy)
Siegfried Handschuh (Germany)
Melanie Hilario (Switzerland)
Owen Holland (UK)
Tan Hongxing (China)
Andreas Hotho (Germany)
Inaki Inza (Spain)
Jose Iria (UK)
Hasan Jamil (USA)
Pieter Jonker (The Netherlands)
Alípio Jorge (Portugal)
Heiki-Jaan Kaalep (Estonia)
Alexandros Kalousis (Switzerland)
Walter Kasper (Germany)
Ross King (UK)
Jelle Kok (The Netherlands)

Vijay Kumar (USA)
Nuno Lau (Portugal)
Mark Lee (UK)
João Leite (Portugal)
Israel Lerman (France)
Dayou Li (UK)
Pedro Lima (Portugal)
Christine Lisetti (France)
Fernando Lobo Pereira (Portugal)
Fernando Lobo (Portugal)
Ramon Lopez de Mantaras (Spain)
José Machado (Portugal)
Henrique Madeira (Portugal)
José Maia Neves (Portugal)
Andreia Malucelli (Portugal)
Nuno Marques (Portugal)
Stacy Marsella (USA)
Ernestina Menasalvas (Spain)
Juan Merelo (Spain)
Pedro Meseguer (Spain)
John-Jules Meyer (The Netherlands)
Zbigniew Michalewicz (Australia)
Peter Mika (The Netherlands)
Luís Moniz Pereira (Portugal)
Luís Moniz (Portugal)
Miguel Monteiro (Portugal)
António Paulo Moreira (Portugal)
Boris Motik (Germany)
João Moura Pires (Portugal)
Susana Nascimento (Portugal)
Mohammad Nejad Sedaghat (Iran)
Junji Nishino (Japan)
Veska Noncheva (Bulgaria)
Leo Obrst (USA)
Eugénio Oliveira (Portugal)
Michael O'Neil (Ireland)
Michael Packianather (UK)
Ana Paiva (Portugal)
H. Van Parunak (USA)
Gabriel Pereira Lopes (Portugal)
Francisco Pereira (Portugal)
José Pereira (Portugal)
Paolo Petta (Austria)
Rolf Pfeifer (Switzerland)
Irene Pimenta Rodrigues (Portugal)

Joaquim Pinto da Costa (Portugal)
Helder Pita (Portugal)
Enric Plaza (Spain)
André Ponce de Carvalho (Brazil)
Bhanu Prasad (USA)
Mikhail Prokopenko (Australia)
Paulo Quaresma (Portugal)
Marie-Laure Reinberger (Belgium)
Luís Paulo Reis (Portugal)
António Ribeiro (Italy)
Fernando Ribeiro (Portugal)
Maria Isabel Ribeiro (Portugal)
Martin Riedmiller (Germany)
José Riquelme (Spain)
Antonio Rocha Costa (Brazil)
Ana Paula Rocha (Portugal)
Luís Rocha (USA)
Vítor Rocio (Portugal)
Thomas Rofer (Germany)
Marta Sabou (The Netherlands)
Kunihiko Sadakane (Japan)
Marie-France Sagot (France)
Ziad Salem (Syria)
Antonio Sanfilippo (USA)
Jorge Santos (Portugal)
Tobias Scheffer (Germany)
Marc Schoenauer (France)
Steffen Schulze-Kremer (Germany)
Luís Seabra Lopes (Portugal)
Frédérique Segond (France)
Jaime Sichman (Brazil)
Carles Sierra (Spain)
Alberto Silva (Portugal)
Eduardo Silva (Portugal)
Mário G. Silva (Portugal)
Jorge Simão (Portugal)
Armando Sousa (Portugal)
Ashwin Srinivasan (India)
Steffen Staab (Germany)
Leon Sterling (Australia)
Ljiljana Stojanovic (Germany)
Heiner Stuckenschmidt
    (The Netherlands)
York Sure (Germany)
Tomoichi Takahashi (Japan)

João Tasso Sousa (Portugal)
Michael Thielscher (Germany)
Luís Torgo (Portugal)
Alfonso Valencia (Spain)
Maria Vargas-Vera (UK)
Jorge Vieira (Portugal)
Renata Vieira (Brazil)
Manuel Vilares Ferro (Spain)
Aline Villavicencio (UK)

Spela Vintar (Slovenia)
Ubbo Visser (Germany)
Nikos Vlassis (The Netherlands)
Maria das Graças Volpe Nunes (Brazil)
Christel Vrain (France)
Christopher Welty (USA)
Mohammed Zaki (USA)
Pierre Zweigenbaum (France)

Additional Reviewers

Nittka Alexander
José Júlio Alferes
Luis Antunes
Jorge Batista
Gerd Brewka
Henrique Cardoso
Marco Costa
Paulo Sousa Dias
Brian Duffy
Peter Eggenber
Mário Florido
Nuno A. Fonseca
Paulo Gomes

Aleem Hossain
Carlos Leão
Jos Lehmann
Jorge Louçã
Luís Macedo
Yves Martin
Alfredo Martins
Claudio Masolo
Truszczynski Mirek
Nelma Moreira
Dulce Mota
João Neto
Eric Pacuit

Antonio Pereira
Josep Puyol-Gruart
Francisco Reinaldo
Gross Roderich
Pedro Rodrigues
Raquel Ros
Luigi Sauro
Alexandre Sousa
Jorge Tavares
José Manuel Torres
Paulo Urbano
Jurriaan van Diggelen
Jesús Vilares Ferro

Local Organization Committee

Elsa Alves
Isabel Marcelino

Universidade Nova de Lisboa, Portugal
Instituto Superior Técnico, Portugal

Local Organization Team

Ricardo Campos
João Paulo Cordeiro

Rumen Moraliyski
Raycho Mukelov

Cláudia Santos
Hugo Veiga

Organizing Institutions

APPIA - Associação Portuguesa para a Inteligência Artificial
DIUBI - Departamento de Informática, Universidade da Beira Interior
CISUC - Centro de Informática e Sistemas da Universidade de Coimbra

Sponsors

Microsoft Research
FCT - Fundação para a Ciência e Tecnologia
Câmara Municipal da Covilhã
Parkurbis - Parque de Ciência e Tecnologia da Covilhã, S.A.
IMB-Hotéis
Caixa Geral de Depósitos
AUTO JARDIM Automóveis, SA
TAP Air Portugal
SEMMAIS.com, Programação e Design Interactivo
OmniSys - Tecnologias de Informação, Lda.
Regisfundão - Máquinas de Escritório, Lda.
Costa e Costa - Topografia e Informática, Lda.
Eurobit - Sistemas Informáticos e Manutenção, Lda
Óptica S.Vicente
webChairing - Scientific Management

In Collaboration With

IEEE - Institute of Electrical and Electronics Engineers
ECCAI - European Coordinating Committee for Artificial Intelligence
AAAI - American Association for Artificial Intelligence
ACM - Association for Computing Machinery

Table of Contents

Chapter 3 – Artificial Life and Evolutionary Algorithms (ALEA 2005)

Chapter 4 – Building and Applying Ontologies for the Semantic Web (BAOSW 2005)

Chapter 5 – Computational Methods in Bioinformatics (CMB 2005)

Chapter 6 – Extracting Knowledge from Databases and Warehouses (EKDB&W 2005)

Chapter 7 – Intelligent Robotics (IROBOT 2005)

Chapter 8 – Multi-agent Systems: Theory and Applications (MASTA 2005)

Chapter 9 – Text Mining and Applications (TEMA 2005)

Chapter 1

GAIW 2005: General Artificial Intelligence

Introduction

Carlos Bento[1], Amílcar Cardoso[1], and Gaël Dias[2]

[1] Universidade de Coimbra, Portugal
{bento, amilcar}@dei.uc.pt
[2] Universidade da Beira Interior, Covilhã, Portugal
ddg@di.ubi.pt

Along the various editions of EPIA the scientific program comprised invited lectures, tutorials, parallel workshops, and paper presentations. The success of the workshop format, since it was adopted by the conference, motivated the organizers of the previous and current editions to generalize the adoption of this model for scientific presentations, leaving the plenary sessions for invited lectures, tutorials, posters and panels.

As expected, although a significant number of workshops are accepted in each edition of EPIA, they do not cover all areas of AI. Another peculiarity of the workshop format is that the areas that are addressed differ substantially from one edition to another.

The General Artificial Intelligence Workshop (GAIW 2005) appears in this context. It shares many aspects with the previous plenary scientific sessions, with the advantage of using a structure similar to the other workshops. This guarantees that all areas of Artificial Intelligence, not covered by the remaining workshops, including theoretical areas, foundational areas, and applications have space in the event.

For GAIW 2005 we received 19 submissions from 8 countries with Portugal, Brazil and Spain being the most contributing countries. The topics addressed by the papers included in these proceedings are: Automated Reasoning, Case-based Reasoning, Common Sense Reasoning, Computer Vision, Knowledge Representation, Logic Programming, Machine Learning, Natural Language Generation, Non-monotonic Reasoning, and Perception.

Each paper was blindly reviewed by three senior program committee members. From the 19 submitted papers, 8 high quality full papers were selected for publication in the Springer LNCS main volume of the conference proceedings, while 5 papers were selected for the local UBI/IEEE proceedings. We would like to thank all the authors who submitted their work to the workshop, giving a strong reason for the realization of GAIW 2005. We would also like to give special thanks to all the members of the Program Committee who guaranteed the high quality of the workshop.

C. Bento, A. Cardoso, and G. Dias (Eds.): EPIA 2005, LNAI 3808, p. 3, 2005.
© Springer-Verlag Berlin Heidelberg 2005

Reducing Propositional Theories in Equilibrium Logic to Logic Programs

Pedro Cabalar[1], David Pearce[2], and Agustín Valverde[3]

[1] Dept. of Computation, Univ. of Corunna, Spain
cabalar@dc.fi.udc.es
[2] Dept. of Informatics, Statistics and Telematics,
Univ. Rey Juan Carlos,
(Móstoles, Madrid), Spain
d.pearce@escet.urjc.es
[3] Dept. of Applied Mathematics,
Univ. of Málaga, Spain
a_valverde@ctima.uma.es

Abstract. The paper studies reductions of propositional theories in equilibrium logic to logic programs under answer set semantics. Specifically we are concerned with the question of how to transform an arbitrary set of propositional formulas into an equivalent logic program and what are the complexity constraints on this process. We want the transformed program to be equivalent in a strong sense so that theory parts can be transformed independent of the wider context in which they might be embedded. It was only recently established [1] that propositional theories are indeed equivalent (in a strong sense) to logic programs. Here this result is extended with the following contributions. (i) We show how to effectively obtain an equivalent program starting from an arbitrary theory. (ii) We show that in general there is no polynomial time transformation if we require the resulting program to share precisely the vocabulary or signature of the initial theory. (iii) Extending previous work we show how polynomial transformations can be achieved if one allows the resulting program to contain new atoms. The program obtained is still in a strong sense equivalent to the original theory, and the answer sets of the theory can be retrieved from it.

1 Introduction

Answer set programming (ASP) is fast becoming a well-established environment for declarative programming and AI problem solving, with several implemented systems and advanced prototypes and applications. Though existing answer set solvers differ somewhat in their syntax and capabilities, the language of disjunctive logic programs with two negations, as exemplified in the DLV system [11] under essentially the semantics proposed in [7], provides a standard reference point. Many systems support different extensions of the language, either through direct implementation or through reductions to the basic language. For example weight constraints are included in smodels [24], while a system called nlp [22]

C. Bento, A. Cardoso, and G. Dias (Eds.): EPIA 2005, LNAI 3808, pp. 4–17, 2005.

for compiling nested logic programs is available as a front-end to DLV. Though differently motivated, these two kinds of extensions are actually closely related, since as [6] shows, weight constraints can be represented equivalently by nested programs of a special kind.

Answer set semantics was already generalised and extended to arbitrary propositional theories with two negations in the system of *equilibrium logic*, defined in [17] and further studied in [18,19,20]. Equilibrium logic is based on a simple, minimal model construction in the nonclassical logic of here-and-there (with strong negation), and admits also a natural fixpoint characterisation in the style of nonmonotonic logics. In [20,13] it was shown that answer set semantics for nested programs [12] is also captured by equilibrium models.

While nested logic programs permit arbitrary boolean formulas to appear in the bodies and heads of rules, they do not support embedded implications; so for example one cannot write in `nlp` a rule with a conditional body, such as

$$p \leftarrow (q \leftarrow r).$$

In fact several authors have suggested the usefulness of embedded implications for knowledge representation (see eg [3,8,23]) but proposals for an adequate semantics have differed. Recently however Ferraris [5] has shown how, by modifying somewhat the definition of answer sets for nested programs, a natural extension for arbitrary propositional theories can be obtained. Though formulated using program reducts, in the style of [7,12], the new definition is also equivalent to that of equilibrium model. Consequently, to understand propositional theories, hence also embedded implications, in terms of answer sets one can apply equally well either equilibrium logic or the new reduct notion of [5]. Furthermore, [5] shows how the important concept of *aggregate* in ASP, understood according to the semantics of [4], can be represented by rules with embedded implications. This provides an important reason for handling arbitrary theories in equilibrium logic and motivates the topic of the present paper.

We are concerned here with the question how to transform a propositional theory in equilibrium logic into an equivalent logic program and what are the complexity constraints on this process. We want the transformed theory to be equivalent in a strong sense so that theory parts can be translated independent of the wider context in which they might be embedded. It was only recently established [1] that propositional theories are indeed equivalent (in a strong sense) to logic programs. The present paper extends this result with the following contributions. (i) We present an alternative reduction method which seems more interesting for computational purposes than the one presented in [1], as it extends the unfolding of nested expressions shown in [12] and generally leads to simpler logic programs. (ii) We show that in general there is no polynomial transformation if we require the resulting program to share precisely the vocabulary or signature of the initial theory. (iii) Extending the work of [15,16] we show how polynomial transformations can be achieved if one allows the resulting program to contain new atoms. The program obtained is still in a strong sense equivalent to the original theory, and the answer sets of the latter can be retrieved from the answer sets of the former.

2   Equilibrium Logic

We assume the reader is familiar with answer set semantics for disjunctive logic programs [7]. As a logical foundation for answer set programming we use the nonclassical logic of here-and-there, denoted here by **HT**, and its nonmonotonic extension, *equilibrium logic* [17], which generalises answer set semantics for logic programs to arbitrary propositional theories (see eg [13]). We give only a very brief overview here, for more details the reader is referred to [17,13,19] and the logic texts cited below.[1]

Given a propositional signature V we define the corresponding propositional language $\mathcal{L}_V$ as the set of formulas built from atoms in V with the usual connectives $\top, \bot, \neg, \wedge, \vee, \rightarrow$. A *literal* is any atom $p \in V$ or its negation $\neg p$. Given a formula $\varphi \in \mathcal{L}_V$, the function $subf(\varphi)$ represents the set of all subformulas of φ (including φ itself), whereas $vars(\varphi)$ is defined as $subf(\varphi) \cap V$, that is, the set of atoms occurring in φ. By $degree(\varphi)$ we understand the number of connectives $\neg, \wedge, \vee, \rightarrow$ that occur in the formula φ. Note that $|subf(\varphi)|$ would be at most[2] $degree(\varphi) + |vars(\varphi)|$ plus the number of occurrences of $\top$ and $\bot$ in φ.

As usual, a set of formulas $\Pi \subseteq \mathcal{L}_V$ is called a *theory*. We extend the use of $subf$ and $vars$ to theories in the obvious way. The degree of a theory, $degree(\Pi)$, is defined as the degree of the conjunction of its formulas.

The axioms and rules of inference for **HT** are those of intuitionistic logic (see eg [2]) together with the axiom schema:

$$(\neg \alpha \rightarrow \beta) \rightarrow (((\beta \rightarrow \alpha) \rightarrow \beta) \rightarrow \beta)$$

The model theory of **HT** is based on the usual Kripke semantics for intuitionistic logic (see eg [2]), but **HT** is complete for Kripke frames $\langle W, \leq \rangle$ (where as usual W is the set of points or worlds and $\leq$ is a partial-ordering on W) having exactly two worlds say h ('here') and t ('there') with $h \leq t$. As usual a *model* is a frame together with an assignment i that associates to each element of W a set of *atoms*, such that if $w \leq w'$ then $i(w) \subseteq i(w')$; an assignment is then extended inductively to all formulas via the usual rules for conjunction, disjunction, implication and negation in intuitionistic logic. It is convenient to represent an **HT** model as an ordered pair $\langle H, T \rangle$ of sets of atoms, where $H = i(h)$ and $T = i(t)$ under a suitable assignment i; by $h \leq t$, it follows that $H \subseteq T$.

A formula φ is true in an **HT** model $\mathcal{M} = \langle H, T \rangle$, in symbols $\mathcal{M} \models \varphi$, if it is true at each world in $\mathcal{M}$. A formula φ is said to be *valid* in **HT**, in symbols $\models \varphi$, if it is true in all **HT** models. Logical consequence for **HT** is understood as follows: φ is said to be an **HT** consequence of a theory Π, written $\Pi \models \varphi$, iff for all models $\mathcal{M}$ and any world $w \in \mathcal{M}$, $\mathcal{M}, w \models \Pi$ implies $\mathcal{M}, w \models \varphi$. Equivalently this can be expressed by saying that φ is true in all models of Π.

---

[1] As in some ASP systems the standard version of equilibrium logic has two kinds of negation, intuitionistic and strong negation. For simplicity we deal here with the restricted version containing just the first negation and based on the logic of here-and-there. So we do not consider here eg logic programs with strong or explicit negation.

[2] It would be strictly lower if we have repeated subformulas.

Clearly **HT** is a 3-valued logic (usually known as Gödel's 3-valued logic) and we can also represent models via interpretations I that assign to every atom p a value in $\mathbf{3} = \{0, 1, 2\}$, where 2 is the designated value. Given a model $\langle H, T \rangle$, the corresponding 3-valued interpretation I would assign, to each atom p, the value: $I(p) = 2$ iff $p \in H$; $I(p) = 1$ iff $p \in T \setminus H$ and $I(p) = 0$ iff $p \notin T$. An assignment I is extended to all formulas using the interpretation of the connectives as operators in $\mathbf{3}$. As a result, conjunction becomes the minimum value, disjunction the maximum, and implication and negation are evaluated by:

$$I(\varphi \to \psi) = \begin{cases} 2 & \text{if } I(\varphi) \leq I(\psi) \\ I(\psi) & \text{otherwise} \end{cases} \qquad I(\neg\varphi) = \begin{cases} 2 & \text{if } I(\varphi) = 0 \\ 0 & \text{otherwise} \end{cases}$$

For each connective $\bullet \in \{\wedge, \vee, \to, \neg\}$, we will denote the corresponding 3-valued operator as $f^{\bullet}$.

Equilibrium models are special kinds of minimal **HT**-models. Let Π be a theory and $\langle H, T \rangle$ a model of Π. $\langle H, T \rangle$ is said to be *total* if $H = T$. $\langle H, T \rangle$ is said to be an *equilibrium model* if it is total and there is no model $\langle H', T \rangle$ of Π with $H' \subset H$. The expression $Eq(V, \Pi)$ denotes the set of the equilibrium models of theory Π on signature V. *Equilibrium logic* is the logic determined by the equilibrium models of a theory. It generalises answer set semantics in the following sense. For all the usual classes of logic programs, including normal, disjunctive and nested programs, equilibrium models correspond to answer sets. The 'translation' from the syntax of programs to **HT** propositional formulas is the trivial one, eg. a ground rule of a disjunctive program of the form

$$q_1 \vee \ldots \vee q_k \leftarrow p_1, \ldots, p_m, not\ p_{m+1}, \ldots, not\ p_n$$

where the p_i and q_j are atoms, corresponds to the **HT** sentence

$$p_1 \wedge \ldots \wedge p_m \wedge \neg p_{m+1} \wedge \ldots \wedge \neg p_n \to q_1 \vee \ldots \vee q_k$$

Proposition 1 ([17,20,13]). *For any logic program Π, an **HT** model $\langle T, T \rangle$ is an equilibrium model of Π if and only if T is an answer set of Π.*

Two theories, Π_1 and Π_2 are said to be *logically equivalent*, in symbols $\Pi_1 \equiv \Pi_2$, if they have the same **HT** models. They are said to be *strongly equivalent*, in symbols $\Pi_1 \equiv_s \Pi_2$, if and only if for any Π, $\Pi_1 \cup \Pi$ is equivalent to (has the same equilibrium models as) $\Pi_2 \cup \Pi$. The two notions are connected via:

Proposition 2 ([13]). *Any two theories, Π_1 and Π_2 are strongly equivalent iff they are logically equivalent, ie. $\Pi_1 \equiv_s \Pi_2$ iff $\Pi_1 \equiv \Pi_2$.*

Strong equivalence is important because it allows us to transform programs or theories to equivalent programs or theories independent of any larger context in which the theories concerned might be embedded. Implicitly, strong equivalence assumes that the theories involved share the same vocabulary, a restriction that has been removed in [21]. Here, in §4 below, we use a slight generalisation of strong equivalence, where we allow one language to include the other.

3   Vocabulary-Preserving Transformations

We first show how to transform an arbitrary theory into a strongly equivalent logic program in the same signature. [1] explores a similar aim but uses a transformation motivated by obtaining a simple proof of the existence of a translation, rather than the simplicity of the resulting programs or the final number of steps involved. To give an example, using the translation in [1], a simple program rule like $\neg a \to b \lor c$ would be first transformed to remove negations and disjunctions and then converted into a (nested) logic program via a bottom-up process (starting from subformulas) which eventually yields the program:

$$\neg a \to b \lor c \lor \neg b, \quad (b \lor \neg c) \land \neg a \to b, \quad \neg a \to b \lor c \lor \neg c, \quad (c \lor \neg b) \land \neg a \to c$$

The result would further require applying the unfolding rules of [12] to yield a non-nested program. Note that the original formula was already a non-nested program rule that did not need any transformation at all.

The transformation we present here adopts the opposite approach. It is a top-down process that relies on the successive application of several rewriting rules that operate on sets (conjunctions) of implications. A rewriting takes place whenever one of those implications does not yet have the form of a (non-nested) program rule.

Two sets of transformations are described next. A formula is said to be in *negation normal form* (NNF) when negation is only applied to literals. As a first step, we describe a set of rules that move negations inwards until a NNF is obtained:

$$\neg\top \Leftrightarrow \bot \quad (1) \qquad \neg(\varphi \land \psi) \Leftrightarrow \neg\varphi \lor \neg\psi \quad (4)$$

$$\neg\bot \Leftrightarrow \top \quad (2) \qquad \neg(\varphi \lor \psi) \Leftrightarrow \neg\varphi \land \neg\psi \quad (5)$$

$$\neg\neg\neg\varphi \Leftrightarrow \neg\varphi \quad (3) \qquad \neg(\varphi \to \psi) \Leftrightarrow \neg\neg\varphi \land \neg\psi \quad (6)$$

Transformations (1)-(5) were already used in [12] to obtain the NNF of so-called *nested expressions* (essentially formulas without implications). Thus, we have just included the treatment of a negated implication (6) to obtain the NNF in the general case.

In the second set of transformations, we deal with sets (conjunctions) of implications. Each step replaces one of the implications by new implications to be included in the set. If φ is the original formula, the initial set of implications is the singleton $\{\top \to \varphi\}$. Without loss of generality, we assume that any implication $\alpha \to \beta$ to be replaced has been previously transformed into NNF. Furthermore, we always consider that α is a conjunction and β a disjunction (if not, we just take $\alpha \land \top$ or $\beta \lor \bot$, respectively), and that we implicitly apply commutativity of conjunction and disjunction as needed.

Left side rules:

$$\top \land \alpha \to \beta \Leftrightarrow \{\alpha \to \beta\} \tag{L1}$$

$$\bot \land \alpha \to \beta \Leftrightarrow \varnothing \tag{L2}$$

$$\neg\neg\varphi \land \alpha \to \beta \Leftrightarrow \{\alpha \to \neg\varphi \lor \beta\} \tag{L3}$$

$$(\varphi \vee \psi) \wedge \alpha \to \beta \;\Leftrightarrow\; \left\{ \begin{array}{l} \varphi \wedge \alpha \to \beta \\ \psi \wedge \alpha \to \beta \end{array} \right\} \tag{L4}$$

$$(\varphi \to \psi) \wedge \alpha \to \beta \;\Leftrightarrow\; \left\{ \begin{array}{l} \neg\varphi \wedge \alpha \to \beta \\ \psi \wedge \alpha \to \beta \\ \alpha \to \varphi \vee \neg\psi \vee \beta \end{array} \right\} \tag{L5}$$

Right side rules

$$\alpha \to \bot \vee \beta \;\Leftrightarrow\; \{\, \alpha \to \beta \,\} \tag{R1}$$

$$\alpha \to \top \vee \beta \;\Leftrightarrow\; \varnothing \tag{R2}$$

$$\alpha \to \neg\neg\varphi \vee \beta \;\Leftrightarrow\; \{\, \neg\varphi \wedge \alpha \to \beta \,\} \tag{R3}$$

$$\alpha \to (\varphi \wedge \psi) \vee \beta \;\Leftrightarrow\; \left\{ \begin{array}{l} \alpha \to \varphi \vee \beta \\ \alpha \to \psi \vee \beta \end{array} \right\} \tag{R4}$$

$$\alpha \to (\varphi \to \psi) \vee \beta \;\Leftrightarrow\; \left\{ \begin{array}{l} \varphi \wedge \alpha \to \psi \vee \beta \\ \neg\psi \wedge \alpha \to \neg\varphi \vee \beta \end{array} \right\} \tag{R5}$$

As with NNF transformations, the rules (L1)-(L4), (R1)-(R4) were already used in [12] for unfolding nested expressions into disjunctive program rules. The additions in this case are transformations (L5) and (R5) that deal with an implication respectively in the antecedent or the consequent of another implication. In fact, an instance of rule (L5) where we take $\alpha = \top$ was the main tool used in [1] to provide the first transformation of propositional theories into logic programs. Note that rules (L5) and (R5) are the only ones to introduce new negations and that they both result in $\neg\varphi$ and $\neg\psi$ for the inner implication $\varphi \to \psi$. Thus, if the original propositional formula was in NNF, the computation of NNF in each intermediate step is needed for these newly generated $\neg\varphi$ and $\neg\psi$.

Proposition 3. *The set of transformation rules (1)-(6), (L1)-(L5), (R1)-(R5) is sound with respect to* **HT**, *that is,* $\models \varphi \leftrightarrow \psi$ *for each transformation rule* $\varphi \Leftrightarrow \psi$.

Of course, these transformations do not guarantee the absence of redundant formulas. As an example, when we have $\beta = \bot$ in (R5), we would obtain the pair of rules $\varphi \wedge \alpha \to \psi$ and $\neg\psi \wedge \alpha \to \neg\varphi$, but it can be easily checked that the latter follows from the former. A specialised version is also possible:

$$\alpha \to (\varphi \to \psi) \;\Leftrightarrow\; \{\, \varphi \wedge \alpha \to \psi \,\} \tag{R5'}$$

Example 1. Let φ be the formula $(\neg p \to q) \to \neg(p \to r)$. Figure 1 shows a possible application of rules (L1)-(L5),(R1)-(R5). Each horizontal line represents a new step. The reference on the right shows the transformation rule that will be applied next to the corresponding formula on the left. From the final result we can remove[3] trivial tautologies and subsumed rules to obtain: $\{q \wedge \neg p \to \bot, q \to \neg r, \neg r \vee \neg p\}$.   □

---

[3] In fact, the rule $q \to \neg r$ is redundant and could be further removed, although perhaps not in a directly automated way.

$$\frac{(\neg p \to q) \to \neg(p \to r) \quad \text{(NNF)}}{(\neg p \to q) \to \neg\neg p \land \neg r \quad \text{(L5)}}$$
$$q \to \neg\neg p \land \neg r$$
$$\frac{\neg\neg p \to \neg\neg p \land \neg r \quad \text{(L3)}}{\neg p \lor \neg q \lor \neg\neg p \land \neg r}$$
$$\frac{q \to \neg\neg p \land \neg r \quad \text{(R4)}}{\neg\neg p \land \neg r \lor \neg p}$$
$$\neg p \lor \neg q \lor \neg\neg p \land \neg r$$
$$\frac{q \to \neg\neg p \quad \text{(R3)}}{q \to \neg r}$$
$$\neg\neg p \land \neg r \lor \neg p$$
$$\frac{\neg p \lor \neg q \lor \neg\neg p \land \neg r}{q \land \neg p \to \bot}$$
$$q \to \neg r$$

$$\frac{\neg\neg p \land \neg r \lor \neg p \quad \text{(R4)}}{\neg p \lor \neg q \lor \neg\neg p \land \neg r \quad \text{(R4)}}$$
$$q \land \neg p \to \bot$$
$$q \to \neg r$$
$$\frac{\neg\neg p \lor \neg p \quad \text{(R3)}}{\neg r \lor \neg p}$$
$$\frac{\neg p \lor \neg q \lor \neg\neg p \quad \text{(R3)}}{\neg p \lor \neg q \lor \neg r}$$
$$\frac{q \land \neg p \to \bot}{q \to \neg r}$$
$$\neg p \to \neg p$$
$$\neg r \lor \neg p$$
$$\neg p \to \neg p \lor \neg q$$
$$\neg p \lor \neg q \lor \neg r$$

Fig. 1. Application of transformation rules in example 1

3.1 Complexity

Perhaps the main drawback of the method presented above is the exponential size of the generated program and the number of steps to obtain it. In fact, it was already observed in [16] that the set of rules (R1)-(R4) and (L1)-(L5) originally introduced in [12] (that is, when we do not consider nested implications) also leads to an exponential blow-up. The main reason is the presence of the "distributivity" laws (R4) and (L4). To give an example, just note that the successive application of (R4) to a formula like $(p_1 \land q_1) \lor (p_2 \land q_2) \lor \cdots \lor (p_n \land q_n)$ eventually yields 2^n disjunctions of n atoms. In this section we show, however, that this drawback is actually inherent to *any* transformation that preserves the vocabulary of the original theory.

A recent result, presented in Theorem 2 in [1], shows that it is possible to build a strongly equivalent logic program starting from the set of countermodels of any arbitrary theory. The method for obtaining such a program is quite straightforward: it consists in adding, per each countermodel, a rule that refers to all the atoms in the propositional signature in a way that depends on their truth assignment in the countermodel. This result seems to point out that the complexity of obtaining a strongly equivalent program mostly depends on the generation of the countermodels of the original theory. Now, it is well-known that in classical logic this generation cannot be done in polynomial time because the validity problem is coNP-complete. This also holds for several finite-valued logics, and in particular for the family of Gödel logics (which includes **HT**) as shown in:

Proposition 4 (Theorem 5 in [9]). *The validity problem for Gödel logics for an arbitrary theory has a coNP-complete time complexity.*   □

The keypoint for our complexity result comes from the observation that validity of a logic program rule can be checked in polynomial time. To see why, let us consider for instance an arbitrary program rule like:

$$a_1 \wedge \cdots \wedge a_m \wedge \neg b_1 \wedge \cdots \wedge \neg b_n \rightarrow c_1 \vee \cdots \vee c_s \vee \neg d_1 \vee \cdots \vee \neg d_t \qquad (7)$$

with $m, n, s, t \geq 0$ and let us define the sets[4] of atoms $A = \{a_1, \ldots, a_m\}$, $B = \{b_1, \ldots, b_n\}$, $C = \{c_1, \ldots, c_s\}$ and $D = \{d_1, \ldots, d_t\}$.

Lemma 1. *An arbitrary rule like* (7) *(with A, B, C, D defined as above) is valid in* **HT** *iff $A \cap B \neq \varnothing$ or $A \cap C \neq \varnothing$ or $B \cap D \neq \varnothing$.*

Proof. For the left to right direction, assume that (7) is valid but $A \cap B = \varnothing$, $A \cap C = \varnothing$ and $B \cap D = \varnothing$. In this situation, it is possible to build a 3-valued assignment I where $I(a) = 2$, $I(b) = 0$, $I(c) \neq 2$ and $I(d) \neq 0$ for each a, b, c, d in A, B, C, D respectively. Note that for any atom in any of the remaining three possible intersections $A \cap D$, $B \cap C$ or $C \cap D$, assignment I is still feasible. Now, it is easy to see that I assigns 2 to the antecedent of (7) whereas it assigns a value strictly lower than 2 to its consequent. Therefore, I is a countermodel for the rule, which contradicts the hypothesis of validity.

For the right to left direction, when $A \cap B \neq \varnothing$, it suffices to note that $p \wedge \neg p \wedge \alpha \rightarrow \beta$ is an **HT** tautology. Similarly, the other two cases are consequences of the **HT** tautology $\alpha \wedge \beta \rightarrow \alpha \vee \gamma$. $\qquad \square$

Since checking whether one of the intersections $A \cap B$, $A \cap C$ or $B \cap D$ is not empty can be done by a simple sorting of the rule literals, we immediately get that validity for an arbitrary program rule has a polynomial time complexity.

Theorem 1. *There is no polynomial time algorithm to translate an arbitrary propositional theory in equilibrium logic into a strongly equivalent logic program in the same vocabulary (provided that $coNP \neq P$).*

Proof. Assume we had a polynomial algorithm that translates the theory into a strongly equivalent logic program. Checking whether this program is valid can be done by checking the validity of all its rules one by one. As validity of each rule can be done in polynomial time (by Lemma 1), the validity of the whole program is polynomial too. But then, the translation first plus the validity checking of the resulting program afterwards becomes altogether a polynomial time method for validity checking of an arbitrary theory. This contradicts Proposition 4, if we assume that $coNP \neq P$. $\qquad \square$

4   Polynomial Transformations

Let I be an interpretation for a signature U and let $V \subset U$. The expression $I \cap V$ denotes the interpretation I restricted to signature V, that is, $(I \cap V)(p) = I(p)$ for any atom $p \in V$. For any theory Π, $subf(\Pi)$ denotes the set of all subformulas of Π.

---

[4] We can use sets instead of multisets without loss of generality, since **HT** satisfies the idempotency laws for conjunction and disjunction.

Definition 1. *We say that the translation* $\sigma(\Pi) \subseteq \mathcal{L}_U$ *of some theory* $\Pi \subseteq \mathcal{L}_V$ *with* $V \subseteq U$ *is* strongly faithful *if, for any theory* $\Pi' \subseteq \mathcal{L}_V$:

$$Eq(V, \Pi \cup \Pi') = \{J \cap V \mid J \in Eq(U, \sigma(\Pi) \cup \Pi')\}$$

The translations we will consider use a signature $V_{\mathbf{L}}$ that contains an atom (a label) for each non-constant formula in the original language $\mathcal{L}_V$, that is:

$$V_{\mathbf{L}} = \{\mathbf{L}_\varphi \mid \varphi \in \mathcal{L}_V \smallsetminus \{\bot, \top\}\}$$

For convenience, we use $\mathbf{L}_\varphi \overset{\text{def}}{=} \varphi$ when φ is $\top$, $\bot$ or an atom $p \in V$. This allows us to consider $V_{\mathbf{L}}$ as a superset of V. For any non-atomic formula $\varphi \bullet \psi$ built with a binary connective $\bullet$, we call its *definition*, $df(\varphi \bullet \psi)$, the formula:

$$\mathbf{L}_{\varphi \bullet \psi} \leftrightarrow \mathbf{L}_\varphi \bullet \mathbf{L}_\psi$$

Similarly $df(\neg\varphi)$ represents the formula $\mathbf{L}_{\neg\varphi} \leftrightarrow \neg\mathbf{L}_\varphi$.

Definition 2. *For any theory* Π *in* $\mathcal{L}_V$, *we define the translation* $\sigma(\Pi)$ *as:*

$$\sigma(\Pi) \overset{\text{def}}{=} \{\mathbf{L}_\varphi \mid \varphi \in \Pi\} \cup \bigcup_{\gamma \in subf(\Pi)} df(\gamma)$$

That is, $\sigma(\Pi)$ collects the labels for all the formulas in Π plus the definitions for all the subformulas in Π.

Theorem 2. *For any theory* Π *in* $\mathcal{L}_V$: $\{I \mid I \models \Pi\} = \{J \cap V \mid J \models \sigma(\Pi)\}$.

Proof. Firstly note that $I \models \varphi$ iff $I(\varphi) = 2$ and $I \models \varphi \leftrightarrow \psi$ iff $I(\varphi) = I(\psi)$.

'$\subseteq$' direction: Let I be a model of Π and J the assignment defined as $J(\mathbf{L}_\varphi) = I(\varphi)$ for any formula $\varphi \in \mathcal{L}_V$. Note that as $J(\mathbf{L}_p) = J(p) = I(p)$ for any atom $p \in V$, $J \cap V = I$. Furthermore, $J \models \mathbf{L}_\varphi$ for each formula $\varphi \in \Pi$ too, since $I \models \Pi$. Thus, it remains to show that $J \models df(\gamma)$ for any $\gamma \in subf(\Pi)$. For any connective $\bullet$ we have $J \models \mathbf{L}_{\varphi \bullet \psi} \leftrightarrow \mathbf{L}_\varphi \bullet \mathbf{L}_\psi$ because:

$$J(\mathbf{L}_{\varphi \bullet \psi}) = I(\varphi \bullet \psi) = f^\bullet(I(\varphi), I(\psi)) = f^\bullet(J(\mathbf{L}_\varphi), J(\mathbf{L}_\psi)) = J(\mathbf{L}_\varphi \bullet \mathbf{L}_\psi)$$

This same reasoning can be applied to prove that $J \models df(\neg\varphi)$.

'$\supseteq$' direction: We must show that $J \models \sigma(\Pi)$ implies $J \cap V \models \Pi$, that is, $J \models \Pi$. First, by structural induction we show that for any subformula γ of Π, $J(\mathbf{L}_\gamma) = J(\gamma)$. When the subformula γ has the shape $\top$, $\bot$ or an atom p this is trivial, since $\mathbf{L}_\gamma = \gamma$ by definition. When $\gamma = \varphi \bullet \psi$ for any connective $\bullet$ then:

$$J(\mathbf{L}_{\varphi \bullet \psi}) \overset{*}{=} J(\mathbf{L}_\varphi \bullet \mathbf{L}_\psi) = f^\bullet(J(\mathbf{L}_\varphi), J(\mathbf{L}_\psi)) \overset{**}{=} f^\bullet(J(\varphi), J(\psi)) = J(\varphi \bullet \psi)$$

In $(*)$ we have used that $J \models df(\varphi \bullet \psi)$ and in $(**)$ we apply the induction hypothesis. The same reasoning holds for the unary connective $\neg$. Finally, as J is a model of $\sigma(\Pi)$, in particular, we have that $J \models \mathbf{L}_\varphi$ for each $\varphi \in \Pi$. But, as we have seen, $J(\mathbf{L}_\varphi) = J(\varphi)$ and so $J \models \varphi$. $\quad\square$

γ	$df(\gamma)$	$\pi(\gamma)$	γ	$df(\gamma)$	$\pi(\gamma)$
$\varphi \wedge \psi$	$\mathbf{L}_{\varphi \wedge \psi} \leftrightarrow \mathbf{L}_\varphi \wedge \mathbf{L}_\psi$	$\mathbf{L}_{\varphi \wedge \psi} \rightarrow \mathbf{L}_\varphi$ $\mathbf{L}_{\varphi \wedge \psi} \rightarrow \mathbf{L}_\psi$ $\mathbf{L}_\varphi \wedge \mathbf{L}_\psi \rightarrow \mathbf{L}_{\varphi \wedge \psi}$	$\neg\varphi$	$\mathbf{L}_{\neg\varphi} \leftrightarrow \neg\mathbf{L}_\varphi$	$\neg\mathbf{L}_\varphi \rightarrow \mathbf{L}_{\neg\varphi}$ $\mathbf{L}_{\neg\varphi} \rightarrow \neg\mathbf{L}_\varphi$
$\varphi \vee \psi$	$\mathbf{L}_{\varphi \vee \psi} \leftrightarrow \mathbf{L}_\varphi \vee \mathbf{L}_\psi$	$\mathbf{L}_\varphi \rightarrow \mathbf{L}_{\varphi \vee \psi}$ $\mathbf{L}_\psi \rightarrow \mathbf{L}_{\varphi \vee \psi}$ $\mathbf{L}_{\varphi \vee \psi} \rightarrow \mathbf{L}_\varphi \vee \mathbf{L}_\psi$	$\varphi \rightarrow \psi$	$\mathbf{L}_{\varphi \rightarrow \psi} \leftrightarrow (\mathbf{L}_\varphi \rightarrow \mathbf{L}_\psi)$	$\mathbf{L}_{\varphi \rightarrow \psi} \wedge \mathbf{L}_\varphi \rightarrow \mathbf{L}_\psi$ $\neg\mathbf{L}_\varphi \rightarrow \mathbf{L}_{\varphi \rightarrow \psi}$ $\mathbf{L}_\psi \rightarrow \mathbf{L}_{\varphi \rightarrow \psi}$ $\mathbf{L}_\varphi \vee \neg\mathbf{L}_\psi \vee \mathbf{L}_{\varphi \rightarrow \psi}$

Fig. 2. Transformation $\pi(\gamma)$ generating a generalised disjunctive logic program

Clearly, including an arbitrary theory $\Pi' \subseteq \mathcal{L}_V$ in Theorem 2 as follows:

$$\{I \mid I \models \Pi \cup \Pi'\} = \{J \cap V \mid J \models \sigma(\Pi) \cup \Pi'\}$$

and then taking the minimal models on both sides trivially preserves the equality. Therefore, the following is straightforward.

Corollary 1. *Translation $\sigma(\Pi)$ is strongly faithful.*

Modularity of $\sigma(\Pi)$ is quite obvious, and the polynomial complexity of its computation can also be easily deduced. However, $\sigma(\Pi)$ does not have the shape of a logic program: it contains double implications where the implication symbol may occur nested. Fortunately, we can unfold these double implications in linear time without changing the signature $V_{\mathbf{L}}$ (in fact, we can use transformations in Section 3 for this purpose). For each definition $df(\gamma)$, we define the strongly equivalent set (understood as the conjunction) of logic program rules $\pi(\gamma)$ as shown in Figure 2. The fact $df(\gamma) \equiv_s \pi(\gamma)$ can be easily checked in here-and-there. The main difference with respect to [16] is of course the treatment of the implication. In fact, the set of rules $\pi(\varphi \rightarrow \psi)$ was already used in [15] to unfold nested implications in an arbitrary theory, with the exception that, in that work, labelling was exclusively limited to implications. The explanation for this set of rules can be easily outlined using transformations in Section 3. For the left to right direction in $df(\varphi \rightarrow \psi)$, that is, the implication $\mathbf{L}_{\varphi \rightarrow \psi} \rightarrow (\mathbf{L}_\varphi \rightarrow \mathbf{L}_\psi)$, we can apply (R5') to obtain the first rule shown in Figure 2 for $\pi(\varphi \rightarrow \psi)$. The remaining three rules are the direct application of (L5) (being $\alpha = \top$) for the right to left direction $(\mathbf{L}_\varphi \rightarrow \mathbf{L}_\psi) \rightarrow \mathbf{L}_{\varphi \rightarrow \psi}$.

The program $\pi(\Pi)$ is obtained by replacing in $\sigma(\Pi)$ each subformula definition $df(\varphi)$ by the corresponding set of rules $\pi(\varphi)$. As $\pi(\Pi)$ is strongly equivalent to $\sigma(\Pi)$ (under the same vocabulary) it preserves strong faithfulness with respect to Π. Furthermore, if we consider the complexity of the direct translation from Π to $\pi(\Pi)$ we obtain the following result.

Theorem 3. *Translation $\pi(\Pi)$ is linear and its size can be bounded as follows:* $|vars(\pi(\Pi))| \leq |vars(\Pi)| + degree(\Pi)$, $\quad degree(\pi(\Pi)) \leq |\Pi| + 12\, degree(\Pi)$.

$df(\neg\varphi)$	$\pi'(\neg\varphi)$		$df(\varphi \to \psi)$	$\pi'(\varphi \to \psi)$
$\mathbf{L}_{\neg\varphi} \leftrightarrow \neg\mathbf{L}_\varphi$	$\neg\mathbf{L}_\varphi \to \mathbf{L}_{\neg\varphi}$		$\mathbf{L}_{\varphi\to\psi} \leftrightarrow (\mathbf{L}_\varphi \to \mathbf{L}_\psi)$	$\mathbf{L}_{\varphi\to\psi} \wedge \mathbf{L}_\varphi \to \mathbf{L}_\psi$
	$\mathbf{L}_{\neg\varphi} \wedge \mathbf{L}_\varphi \to \bot$			$\neg\mathbf{L}_\varphi \to \mathbf{L}_{\varphi\to\psi}$
				$\mathbf{L}_\psi \to \mathbf{L}_{\varphi\to\psi}$
				$\mathbf{L}_\varphi \vee \mathbf{L}_{\neg\psi} \vee \mathbf{L}_{\varphi\to\psi}$
				$\neg\mathbf{L}_\psi \to \mathbf{L}_{\neg\psi}$
				$\mathbf{L}_{\neg\psi} \wedge \mathbf{L}_\psi \to \bot$

Fig. 3. Transformation $\pi'(\gamma)$ generating a disjunctive logic program

Proof. As we explained before, we use a label in $\pi(\Pi)$ per each non-constant subformula in Π (including atoms). We can count the subformulas as the number of connectives[5], $\leq degree(\Pi)$, plus the number of atoms in Π, $|vars(\Pi)|$.

As for the second bound, note that $\pi(\Pi)$ consists of two subtheories. The first one contains a label $\mathbf{L}_\varphi$ per each formula φ in Π. The amount $|\Pi|$ counts implicit conjunction used to connect each label to the rest of the theory. The second part of $\pi(\Pi)$ collects a set of rules $\pi(\gamma)$ per each subformula γ of Π. The worst case, corresponding to the translation of implication, uses eight connectives plus four implicit conjunctions to connect the four rules to the rest of the theory. $\square$

A possible objection to $\pi(\Pi)$ is that it makes use of negation in the rule heads, something not usual in the current tools for answer sets programming. Although there exists a general translation [10] for removing negation in the head, it is possible to use a slight modification of $\pi(\Pi)$ to yield a disjunctive program in a direct way. To this end, we define a new $\pi'(\gamma)$ for each subformula γ of T that coincides with $\pi(\gamma)$ except for implication and negation, which are treated as shown in Figure 3. As we can see, the use of negation in the head for $\pi(\neg\varphi)$ can be easily removed by just using a constraint $\mathbf{L}_{\neg\varphi} \wedge \mathbf{L}_\varphi \to \bot$. In the case of implication, we have replaced negated label $\neg\mathbf{L}_\psi$ by the labeled negation $\mathbf{L}_{\neg\psi}$ in the resulting disjunctive rule. The only problem with this technique is that $\neg\psi$ need not occur as subformula in the original theory Π. Therefore, we must include the definition for the newly introduced label $\mathbf{L}_{\neg\psi}$, that leads to the last two additional rules, and we need a larger signature, $V_{\mathbf{L}} = \{\mathbf{L}_\varphi, \mathbf{L}_{\neg\varphi} \mid \varphi \in \mathcal{L}_V \setminus \{\bot, \top\}\}$. If we consider now the translation $\pi'(\Pi)$ it is not difficult to see that modularity and strong faithfulness are still preserved, while its computation can be shown to be polynomial, although using slightly greater bounds $|vars(\pi(\Pi))| \leq 2\,|vars(\Pi)| + 2\,degree(\Pi)$ and $degree(\pi(\Pi)) \leq |\Pi| + 22\,degree(\Pi)$.

5   Concluding Remarks

Equilibrium logic provides a natural generalisation of answer set semantics to propositional logic. It allows one to handle embedded implications, in particular to write programs containing rules with conditional heads or bodies. As [5] has

---

[5] Note that $degree(\Pi)$ also counts the implicit conjunction of all formulas in T.

recently shown, such rules can be used to represent aggregates in ASP under the semantics of [4].

In this paper we have explored different ways in which arbitrary propositional theories in equilibrium logic can be reduced to logic programs and thus implemented in an ASP solver. First, we presented rules for transforming any theory into a strongly equivalent program in the same vocabulary. Second, we showed that there is no polynomial algorithm for such a transformation. Third, we showed that if we allow new atoms or 'labels' to be added to the language of a theory, it can be reduced to a logic program in polynomial time. The program is still in a strong sense equivalent to the original theory and the theory's equilibrium models or answer sets can be be retrieved from the program.

We have extended several previous works in the following way. In [12] several of the reduction rules of §3 were already proposed in order to show that nested programs can be reduced to generalised disjunctive programs. In [1] it is shown for the first time that arbitrary propositional theories have equivalent programs in the same vocabulary; but complexity issues are not discussed. In [16] a reduction is proposed for nested programs into disjunctive programs containing new atoms. The reduction is shown to be polynomial and has been implemented as a front-end to DLV called nlp. Following the tradition of structure-preserving normal form translations for nonclassical logics, as illustrated in [14], the reduction procedure of [16] uses the idea of adding labels as described here. Our main contribution has been to simplify the translation and the proof of faithfulness as well as extend it to the full propositional language including embedded implications. The formulas we have added for eliminating implications were previously mentioned in [15]. However that work does not provide any details on the complexity bounds of the resulting translation, nor does it describe the labelling method in full detail.

Many issues remain open for future study. Concerning the transformation described in §3, for example, several questions of efficiency remain open. In particular the logic program obtained by this method is not necessarily 'optimal' for computational purposes. In the future we hope to study additional transformations that lead to a minimal set of program rules. Concerning the reduction procedure of §4, since, as mentioned, it extends a system nlp [22] already available for nested programs, it should be relatively straightforward to implement and test. One area for investigation here is to see if such a system might provide a prototype for implementing aggregates in ASP, an issue that is currently under study elsewhere.

Another area of research concerns the language of equilibrium logic with an additional, strong negation operator for expressing explicit falsity. The relation between intermediate logics and their least strong negation extensions has been well studied in the literature. From this body of work one can deduce that most of the results of this paper carry over intact to the case of strong negation. However, the reductions are not as simple as the methods currently used for eliminating strong negation in ASP. In particular, for the polynomial translations of propositional theories additional defining formulas are needed. We postpone the details for a future work.

References

1. P. Cabalar & P. Ferraris. Propositional Theories are Strongly Equivalent to Logic Programs. Unpublished draft, 2005, available at
   http://www.dc.fi.udc.es/~cabalar/pt2lp.pdf.
2. D. van Dalen. Intuitionistic logic. In *Handbook of Philosophical Logic, Volume III: Alternatives in Classical Logic*, Kluwer, Dordrecht, 1986.
3. P. M. Dung. Declarative Semantics of Hypothetical Logic Programing with Negation as Failure. in *Proceedings ELP 92*, 1992, 99. 45-58.
4. W. Faber, N. Leone & G. Pfeifer. Recursive Aggregates in Disjunctive Logic Programs: semantics and Complexity. in J.J. Alferes & J. Leite (eds), *Logics In Artificial Intelligence. Proceedings JELIA'04*, Springer LNAI 3229, 2004, pp. 200-212.
5. P. Ferraris. Answer Sets for Propositional Theories. In *Eighth Intl. Conf. on Logic Programming and Nonmonotonic Reasoning* (LPNMR'05), 2005 (to appear).
6. P. Ferraris & V. Lifschitz. Weight Constraints as Nested Expressions. *Theory and Practice of Logic Programming* (to appear).
7. M. Gelfond & V. Lifschitz. Classical negation in logic programs and disjunctive databases. *New Generation Computing*, 9:365–385, 1991.
8. L. Giordano & N. Olivetti. Combining Negation-as-Failure and Embedded Implications in Logic Programs. *Journal of Logic Programming* 36 (1998), 91-147.
9. R. Hähnle. Complexity of Many-Valued Logics. In Proc. 31st International Symposium on Multiple-Valued Logics, IEEE CS Press, Los Alamitos (2001) 137–146.
10. T. Janhunen, I. Niemelä, P. Simons & J.-H. You. Unfolding Partiality and Disjunctions in Stable Model Semantics. In A. G. Cohn, F. Giunchiglia & B. Selman (eds), *Principles of Knowledge Representation and Reasoning (KR-00)*, pages 411424. Morgan Kaufmann, 2000.
11. N. Leone, G. Pfeifer, W. Faber, T. Eiter, G. Gottlob, S. Perri & F. Scarcello. The dlv System for Knowledge Representation and Reasoning. CoRR: cs.AI/0211004, September 2003.
12. V. Lifschitz, L. R. Tang & H. Turner. Nested Expressions in Logic Programs. *Annals of Mathematics and Artificial Intelligence*, 25 (1999), 369–389.
13. V. Lifschitz, D. Pearce & A. Valverde. Strongly Equivalent Logic Programs. *ACM Transactions on Computational Logic*, 2(4):526–541, 2001.
14. G. Mints. Resolution Strategies for the Intuitionistic Logic. In B. Mayoh, E. Tyugu & J. Penjaam (eds), *Constraint Programming* NATO ASI Series, Springer, 1994, pp.282-304.
15. M. Osorio, J. A. Navarro Pérez & J. Arrazola Safe Beliefs for Propositional Theories *Ann. Pure & Applied Logic* (in press).
16. D. Pearce, V. Sarsakov, T. Schaub, H. Tompits & S. Woltran. Polynomial Translations of Nested Logic Programs into Disjunctive Logic Programs. In Proc. of the 19th Int. Conf. on Logic Programming (ICLP'02), 405–420, 2002.
17. D. Pearce. A New Logical Characterisation of Stable Models and Answer Sets. In *Non-Monotonic Extensions of Logic Programming, NMELP 96*, LNCS 1216, pages 57–70. Springer, 1997.
18. D. Pearce. From Here to There: stable negation in logic programming. In D. Gabbay & H. Wansing, eds., *What is Negation?*, pp. 161–181. Kluwer Academic Pub., 1999.
19. D. Pearce, I. P. de Guzmán & A. Valverde. A Tableau Calculus for Equilibrium Entailment. In *Automated Reasoning with Analytic Tableaux and Related Methods, TABLEAUX 2000*, LNAI 1847, pages 352–367. Springer, 2000.

20. D. Pearce, I.P. de Guzmán & A. Valverde. Computing Equilibrium Models using Signed Formulas. In *Proc. of CL2000*, LNCS 1861, pp. 688–703. Springer, 2000.
21. D. Pearce & A. Valverde. Synonymous Theories in Answer Set Programming and Equilibrium Logic. in R. López de Mántaras & L. Saitta (eds), *Proceedings ECAI 04*, IOS Press, 2004, pp. 388-392.
22. V. Sarsakov, T. Schaub, H. Tompits & S. Woltran. nlp: A Compiler for Nested Logic Programming. in *Proceedings of LPNMR 2004*, pp. 361-364. Springer LNAI 2923, 2004.
23. D. Seipel. Using Clausal Deductive Databases for Defining Semantics in Disjunctive Deductive Databases. *Annals of Mathematics and Artificial Intelligence* 33 (2001), pp. 347-378.
24. P. Simons, I. Niemelä & T. Soininen. Extending and implementing the stable model semantics. *Artificial Intelligence*, 138(1–2):181–234, 2002.

Preference Revision Via Declarative Debugging

Pierangelo Dell'Acqua[1,2] and Luís Moniz Pereira[2]

[1] Department of Science and Technology - ITN,
Linköping University, 601 74 Norrköping, Sweden
pier@itn.liu.se
[2] Centro de Inteligência Artificial - CENTRIA,
Departamento de Informática, Faculdade de Ciências e Tecnologia,
Universidade Nova de Lisboa, 2829-516 Caparica, Portugal
lmp@di.fct.unl.pt

Abstract. Preference criteria are rarely static. Often they are subject to modification and aggregation. The resulting preference criteria may not satisfy the properties of the original ones and must therefore be revised. This paper investigates the problem of revising such preference criteria by means of declarative debugging techniques.

1 Motivation

Preference criteria are subject to be modified when new information is brought to the knowledge of the individual, or aggregated when we need to represent and reason about the simultaneous preferences of several individuals. As motivating example, suppose you invite three friends Karin, Leif and Osvald to go and see a movie. Karin prefers thrillers to action movies. Leif, on the other hand, prefers action movies to thrillers. Finally, Osvald is like Leif and prefers action movies to thrillers. Suppose you need to buy the tickets. Which movie do you choose?

Preference aggregation is an important problem and potential applications of this work include those where preference reasoning plays a role, e.g., in artificial intelligence, political science, and economics (cf. social choice and multi-criteria decision).

Typically, preference criteria must satisfy certain properties, e.g., those of strict partial order. When aggregating or updating preference criteria such properties might not be preserved, and therefore the need arises for a revision. In this paper, we consider any preference criteria expressible in the language of logic programs (LP), and investigate the problem of revising them by means of declarative debugging techniques for LP. In particular, we employ an adapted version of the contradiction removal method defined for the class of normal logic programs plus integrity constraints proposed in [10]. The resulting framework is flexible and general, and tailored neither to any specific preference criteria nor any specific method for preference aggregation, but rather to any method expressible in LP. The ability to express meta-information on the diagnoses of a revision problem gives us a further level of abstraction permitting to select the best diagnosis for the problem at hand.

C. Bento, A. Cardoso, and G. Dias (Eds.): EPIA 2005, LNAI 3808, pp. 18–28, 2005.
© Springer-Verlag Berlin Heidelberg 2005

2   Background

In this section we provide some logic programming fundamentals and few basic definitions regarding preference relations.

2.1   Language

Let $\mathcal{L}$ be a first order language. A literal in $\mathcal{L}$ is an atom A in $\mathcal{L}$ or its default negation *not* A. A normal logic program P over $\mathcal{L}$ (sometimes simply called program) is a set of rules and integrity constraints of the form:

$$A \leftarrow L_1, \ldots, L_n \quad (n \geq 0)$$

where A is an atom, $L_1, \ldots, L_n$ are literals in $\mathcal{L}$, where in integrity constraints A is $\perp$ (contradiction). A rule stands for all its ground instances with respect to $\mathcal{L}$. When $n = 0$ we write the rule as A. $\mathcal{L}_P$ denotes the language of P.

For normal logic programs we consider the Well Founded Semantics [7]. We write $P \models L$ whenever a literal L belongs to the well-founded model of a program P. P is contradictory if $P \models \perp$. Programs are liable to be contradictory because of the integrity constraints.

Example 1. Let $P = \{a \leftarrow not\ b; \perp \leftarrow a\}$. Since we have no rules for b, by Closed World Assumption (CWA), it is natural to accept *not* b as true and therefore conclude a. Because of the integrity constraint, we conclude $\perp$ and thus engender a contradiction.   ⫠

2.2   Preference Relation

Given a set N, a preference relation $\succ$ is any binary relation on N. Given two elements a and b in N, $a \succ b$ means that a is preferred to b. We assume that N contains at least two elements.

We do not assume any property of $\succ$, although in many situations it will satisfy the properties of a strict partial order. Typical properties of $\succ$ include:

- irreflexivity: $\forall x.\ x \not\succ x$
- asymmetry: $\forall x\, \forall y.\ x \succ y \Rightarrow y \not\succ x$
- transitivity: $\forall x\, \forall y\, \forall z.\ (x \succ y \wedge y \succ z) \Rightarrow x \succ z$
- negative transitivity: $\forall x\, \forall y\, \forall z.\ (x \not\succ y \wedge y \not\succ z) \Rightarrow x \not\succ z$
- connectivity: $\forall x\, \forall y.\ x \succ y \vee y \succ x \vee x = y$

The relation $\succ$ is:

- a strict partial order if it is irreflexive and transitive (thus also asymmetric);
- a weak order if it is a negatively transitive strict partial order;
- a total order if it is a connected strict partial order.

Every preference relation $\succ$ induces an indifference relation $\sim$. Two elements a and b in N are indifferent $a \sim b$ if neither is preferred to the other one, that is, $a \not\succ b$ and $b \not\succ a$.

3   Diagnosis

In this section we present the notion of diagnosis adapted from [10] to handle preference relations. We illustrate the use of diagnoses with a number of examples. Given a contradictory program P, to revise its contradiction ($\perp$) we have to modify P by adding and removing rules. In this framework, the diagnostic process reduces to finding such rules. To specify which rules in P may be added or removed, we assume given a set C of predicate symbols in $\mathcal{L}_P$. C induces a partition of P into two disjoint parts: a changeable one P_c and a stable one P_s. P_c contains the rules in P defining predicate symbols in C, while P_s contains the rules in P defining predicate symbols not belonging to C. P_c is the part subject to the diagnosis process.

Definition 1. Let P be a program and C a set of predicate symbols in $\mathcal{L}_P$. Let D be a pair $\langle U, I \rangle$ where U is a set of atoms, whose predicate symbols are in C, and $I \subseteq P_c$. Then D is a *diagnosis* for P iff $(P - I) \cup U \not\models \perp$. The pair $\langle \{\}, \{\} \rangle$ is called *empty diagnosis*.

Intuitively, a diagnosis specifies the rules to be added and removed from the changeable part of P to revise its contradiction $\perp$. In order to minimize the number of changes we consider minimal diagnoses.

Definition 2. Let P be a program and $D = \langle U, I \rangle$ a diagnosis for P. Then, D is a *minimal diagnosis* for P iff there exists no diagnosis $D_2 = \langle U_2, I_2 \rangle$ for P such that $(U_2 \cup I_2) \subseteq (U \cup I)$.

Preference relations can be composed in several ways, or updated to reflect changes in user preference criteria. Following [3] we distinguish between unidimensional and multidimensional composition. In unidimensional composition, a number of preference relations over the same domain are composed, producing another preference relation over the same domain. In contrast, in multidimensional composition, a number of preference relations defined over several domains are composed, producing a preference relation defined over the Cartesian product of those relations.

When composing preference relations, it is often the case (see [3] for a discussion) that the resulting preference relation does not satisfy some required property, and therefore needs revising.

Example 2. Consider a framework where preference relations are required to satisfy the properties of strict partial orders. Let $\succ_1$ and $\succ_2$ be two preference relations defined as: $a \succ_1 b$, and $b \succ_2 c$ and $b \succ_2 a$. Consider the boolean composition $\succ$ of $\succ_1$ and $\succ_2$ defined as $\succ \ = \ \succ_1 \cup \succ_2$. Clearly, $\succ$ is not a strict partial order being antisymmetric and transitivity not preserved. To revise $\succ$, we formalize both $\succ$ and the properties of strict partial order with program P. Assume we want to revise only the rules in P encoding $\succ_1$ and $\succ_2$.

$$P_s = \left\{ \begin{array}{l} \bot \leftarrow p(x,x) \\ \bot \leftarrow p(x,y),\, p(y,x) \\ \bot \leftarrow p(x,y),\, p(y,z),\, not\ p(x,z) \\ p(x,y) \leftarrow p_1(x,y) \\ p(x,y) \leftarrow p_2(x,y) \end{array} \right\} \quad and \quad P_c = \left\{ \begin{array}{l} p_1(a,b) \\ p_2(b,c) \\ p_2(b,a) \end{array} \right\}.$$

The integrity constraints in P_s state that if the preference relation $\succ$ (represented by p) is reflexive, symmetric or not transitive, then the program is contradictory. The last two rules in P_s define $\succ$ as the union of $\succ_1$ and $\succ_2$ (represented by p_1 and p_2). The rules in P_c formalizing the two original preference relations ($\succ_1$ and $\succ_2$) are those subject to diagnosis (that is, $C=\{p_1,p_2\}$).

P is contradictory because its well-founded model $M_P=\{p_1(a,b),\ p_2(b,c),\ p_2(b,a),\ p(a,b),\ p(b,c),\ p(b,a),\ \bot\}$ contains $\bot$. According to Def. 1, P affords four minimal diagnoses:

$$D_1 = \langle\{p_2(a,c)\}, \{p_2(b,a)\}\rangle \qquad D_2 = \langle\{p_1(a,c)\}, \{p_2(b,a)\}\rangle$$
$$D_3 = \langle\{\}, \{p_2(b,a),\, p_2(b,c)\}\rangle \qquad D_4 = \langle\{\}, \{p_1(a,b)\}\rangle$$

E.g., D_1 is a diagnosis since the well-founded model of $(P-\{p_2(b,a)\})\cup\{p_2(a,c)\}$ is $M = \{p_1(a,b),\ p_2(b,c),\ p_2(a,c),\ p(a,b),\ p(b,c),\ p(a,c)\}$ and $M \not\models \bot$.   ⬛

This example illustrates the prioritized composition of conditional preference relations:

Example 3. Given the two preference relations $\succ_1$ and $\succ_2$, the prioritized composition $\succ$ of $\succ_1$ and $\succ_2$ is defined as: $x \succ y \equiv x \succ_1 y \lor (x \sim_1 y \land x \succ_2 y)$ where $\sim_1$ is the indifference relation induced by $\succ_1$, that is: $x \sim_1 y \equiv x \not\succ_1 y \land y \not\succ_1 x$. Let $\succ_1$ and $\succ_2$ be two preference relations defined as $a \succ_1 b$, and $b \succ_2 c$, $c \succ_2 a$ *if cond*, and $b \succ_2 a$. Conditional preference $c \succ_2 a$ *if cond* states c is preferred to a if *cond* holds. Suppose $\succ$ is required to be a strict partial order. Let *cond* denote some condition that cannot be revised, and assume *cond* true. This situation can be formalized with a program $P = P_s \cup P_c$. Suppose we wish to revise only preference relation $\succ_2$ (and not $\succ_1$) because $\succ_1$ has priority over $\succ_2$. To do so, we place the rules defining $\succ_1$ in P_s and the rules defining $\succ_2$ in P_c.

$$P_s = \left\{ \begin{array}{l} \bot \leftarrow p(x,x) \\ \bot \leftarrow p(x,y),\, p(y,x) \\ \bot \leftarrow p(x,y),\, p(y,z),\, not\ p(x,z) \\[4pt] p(x,y) \leftarrow p_1(x,y) \\ p(x,y) \leftarrow ind_1(x,y),\, p_2(x,y) \\[4pt] ind_1(x,y) \leftarrow not\ p_1(x,y),\, not\ p_1(y,x) \\[4pt] p_1(a,b) \\[4pt] cond \end{array} \right\} \quad and \quad P_c = \left\{ \begin{array}{l} p_2(b,c) \\ p_2(c,a) \leftarrow cond \\ p_2(b,a) \end{array} \right\}.$$

It is easy to see that $\succ$ is not a strict partial order. The well-founded model of P is $M_P = \{p_1(a,b),\ p_2(b,c),\ p_2(c,a),\ p_2(b,a),\ p(a,b),\ p(b,c),\ p(c,a),\ \bot\}$. P admits three minimal diagnoses:

$$D_1 = \langle \{p_2(a,c)\}, \{p_2(c,a) \leftarrow cond\} \rangle \qquad D_2 = \langle \{p_2(c,b)\}, \{p_2(b,c)\} \rangle$$
$$D_3 = \langle \{\}, \{p_2(b,c), p_2(c,a) \leftarrow cond\} \rangle$$

◻

The next example exhibits a situation of multidimensional composition.

Example 4. Given the two preference relations $\succ_1$ and $\succ_2$, the Pareto composition $\succ$ of $\succ_1$ and $\succ_2$ is defined as:

$$(x, x_2) \succ (y, y_2) \equiv x \succeq_1 y \wedge x_2 \succeq_2 y_2 \wedge (x \succ_1 y \vee x_2 \succ_2 y_2)$$

where $\quad x \sim_i y \equiv x \not\succ_i y \wedge y \not\succ_i x \quad$ and $\quad x \succeq_i y \equiv x \succ_i y \vee x \sim_i y$
with $i = 1, 2$. Let $\succ_1$ and $\succ_2$ be:

$$a \succ_1 b$$
$$a_2 \succ_2 b_2 \quad b_2 \succ_2 c_2 \quad a_2 \succ_2 c_2$$

The Pareto composition $\succ$ does not preserve the properties of total order. In fact, the tuples (b, a_2) and (a, b_2) are indifferent to one another, and hence $\succ$ does not preserve connectivity.

The Pareto composition of $\succ_1$ and $\succ_2$ can be formalized by the program $P = P_s \cup P_c$:

$$P_s = \begin{cases}
\perp \leftarrow p(x,x) \\
\perp \leftarrow p(x,y), p(y,x) \\
\perp \leftarrow p(x,y), p(y,z), not\ p(x,z) \\
\\
\perp \leftarrow notConnected \\
\\
p((x,x_2),(y,y_2)) \leftarrow p_1(x,y), peq_2(x_2,y_2) \\
p((x,x_2),(y,y_2)) \leftarrow peq_1(x,y), p_2(x_2,y_2) \\
\\
peq_1(x,y) \leftarrow p_1(x,y) \\
peq_1(x,y) \leftarrow ind_1(x,y) \\
ind_1(x,y) \leftarrow not\ p_1(x,y), not\ p_1(y,x) \\
\\
peq_2(x,y) \leftarrow p_2(x,y) \\
peq_2(x,y) \leftarrow ind_2(x,y) \\
ind_2(x,y) \leftarrow not\ p_2(x,y), not\ p_2(y,x) \\
\\
notConnected \leftarrow not\ p((x,x_2),(y,y_2)), not\ p((y,y_2),(x,x_2))
\end{cases}$$

and

$$P_c = \begin{cases}
p_1(a,b) \\
p_2(a_2,b_2) \\
p_2(b_2,c_2) \\
p_2(a_2,c_2)
\end{cases}.$$

P is contradictory because there exist two tuples that are not connected (being indifferent to one another), i.e. the tuples (b,a_2) and (a,b_2). Thus, by the last rule in P_s notConnected holds and by the last integrity constraint $\bot$ holds as well. The following property generalizes this specific example by stating that the Pareto composition $\succ$ cannot be a total order.

Property 1. Let $\succ_x$ and $\succ_y$ be two preference relations whose domains contain at least two elements. If $\succ_x$ and $\succ_y$ are strict partial orders, then the Pareto composition $\succ$ of $\succ_x$ and $\succ_y$ cannot be a total order.

Proof. Let $N_x = \{x_1, x_2\}$ and $N_y = \{y_1, y_2\}$ be the domains of $\succ_x$ and $\succ_y$. Consider the tuples (x_1, y_1) and (x_1, y_2), and suppose that the first one is preferred to the second, i.e. $(x_1, y_1) \succ (x_1, y_2)$. Then, by definition of Pareto composition it must hold that $y_1 \succ_y y_2$. Consider now the tuples (x_1, y_1) and (x_2, y_1), and assume that $(x_1, y_1) \succ (x_2, y_1)$. Clearly, we must have that $x_1 \succ_x x_2$. Since $\succ_x$ and $\succ_y$ are strict partial orders, it follows that $(x_2, y_1) \sim (x_1, y_2)$. Hence, $\succ$ cannot be a total order.

The impossibility of $\succ$ of being a total order is reflected in the fact that there exists no diagnosis that makes P non-contradictory. ⬚

4 Computing Minimal Diagnosis

To compute minimal diagnoses of a contradictory program, we employ the contradiction removal method presented in [10], adapted here to handle preference relations. Consider again Example 1. It is arguable that CWA may not hold of atom b as it leads to contradiction. The contradiction removal method is based on the idea of revising (to false) some of the default atoms *not A* true by CWA. A default atom *not A* can be revised to false by simply adding A to P. According to [10] the default literals *not A* true by CWA that are allowed to change their truth value are those for which there exists no rule in P defining A. Such literals are called revisable.

Definition 3. The *revisables* of a program P is a subset of that set of atoms A (with $A \neq \bot$) for which there are no rules defining A in P.

Definition 4. Let P be a program and V a set of revisables of P. A set $Z \subseteq V$ is a *revision* of P wrt. V iff $P \cup Z \not\models \bot$.

Example 5. Consider the contradictory program $P = P_s \cup P_c$:

$$P_s = \left\{ \begin{array}{l} \bot \leftarrow a, a' \\ \bot \leftarrow b \\ \bot \leftarrow d, not\ f \end{array} \right\} \quad \text{and} \quad P_c = \left\{ \begin{array}{l} a \leftarrow not\ b, not\ c \\ a' \leftarrow not\ d \\ c \leftarrow e \end{array} \right\}$$

with revisables $V = \{b, d, e, f\}$. Intuitively the literals *not b*, *not d* and *not e* are true by CWA, entailing a and a', and hence $\bot$ via the first integrity constraint. The revisions of P are $\{e\}$, $\{d, f\}$, $\{e, f\}$ and $\{d, e, f\}$, where the first two are minimal. ⬚

The following transformation maps programs into equivalent programs that are suitable for contradiction removal.

Definition 5. Let P be a program and C a set of predicate symbols in $\mathcal{L}_P$. The transformation Γ that maps P into a program P' is obtained by applying to P the following two operations:

-   Add $not\ incorrect(A \leftarrow Body)$ to the body of each rule $A \leftarrow Body$ in P_c.
-   Add the rule $p(x_1, \ldots, x_n) \leftarrow uncovered(p(x_1, \ldots, x_n))$ for each predicate p with arity n in C.

We assume the predicate symbols *incorrect* and *uncovered* do not belong to the language of P. The transformation Γ preserves the truths of program P.

Property 2. Let P be a program and L a literal. Then $P \models L$ iff $\Gamma(P) \models L$.

Proof. The claim follows immediately by noting that $not\ incorrect(.)$ and $uncovered(.)$ are true and false in $\Gamma(P)$ because *incorrect* and *uncovered* do not belong to $\mathcal{L}_P$.

Example 6. Let P be the program of Example 2. Then, the program $\Gamma(P)$ is:

$$\Gamma(P) = \left\{ \begin{array}{l} \bot \leftarrow p(x,x) \\ \bot \leftarrow p(x,y),\ p(y,x) \\ \bot \leftarrow p(x,y),\ p(y,z),\ not\ p(x,z) \\ \\ p(x,y) \leftarrow p_1(x,y) \\ p(x,y) \leftarrow p_2(x,y) \\ \\ p_1(a,b) \leftarrow not\ incorrect(p_1(a,b)) \\ p_2(b,c) \leftarrow not\ incorrect(p_2(b,c)) \\ p_2(b,a) \leftarrow not\ incorrect(p_2(b,a)) \\ \\ p_1(x,y) \leftarrow uncovered(p_1(x,y)) \\ p_2(x,y) \leftarrow uncovered(p_2(x,y)) \end{array} \right\}$$

The minimal revisions of $\Gamma(P)$ wrt. the revisables of the form $incorrect(.)$ and $uncovered(.)$ are:

$$\begin{array}{l} Z_1 = \{uncovered(p_2(a,c)),incorrect(p_2(b,a))\} \\ Z_2 = \{uncovered(p_1(a,c)),incorrect(p_2(b,a))\} \\ Z_3 = \{incorrect(p_2(b,a)),incorrect(p_2(b,c))\} \\ Z_4 = \{incorrect(p_1(a,b))\} \end{array}$$

It is easy to see that Z_1, for instance, is a revision since the well-founded model M of $P \cup Z_1$ is $M = \{p_1(a,b),\ p_2(b,c),\ p(a,b),\ p(b,c),\ p_2(a,c),\ p(a,c),\ uncovered(p_2(a,c)),\ incorrect(p_2(b,a))\}$ and $M \not\models \bot$. ▫

The following result relates the minimal diagnoses of a program P with the minimal revisions of $\Gamma(P)$.

Property 3. Let P be a program. The pair $D = \langle U, I \rangle$ is a diagnosis for P iff

$$Z = \{uncovered(A) : A \in U\} \cup \{incorrect(A \leftarrow Body) : A \leftarrow Body \in I\}$$

is a revision of $\Gamma(P)$, where the revisables are all the literals of the form $incorrect(.)$ and $uncovered(.)$. Furthermore, D is a minimal diagnosis iff Z is a minimal revision.

Proof. It follows immediately by noting that the programs $P - I \cup U$ and $P \cup Z$ are equivalent, that is, for every literal L with $L \neq uncovered(.)$ and $L \neq incorrect(.)$ it holds that $P - I \cup U \models L$ iff $P \cup Z \models L$.

To compute the minimal diagnosis of a program P we consider the transformed program $\Gamma(P)$ and compute its minimal revisions. An algorithm for computing minimal revisions is given in [10].

5   Selecting Minimal Diagnosis

Typically in a preference revision problem, we only consider minimal diagnoses (wrt. set inclusion) and the problem that naturally arises is how to select the best ones. In some situations, we may ask the user for more information about his or her preferences in order to narrow down the alternatives. In other situations, we require a completely automatized approach. Thus, we need a selection function $f(X) \subseteq X$ where X is a set of minimal diagnoses. Ideally $f(X)$ is a singleton, otherwise we must arbitrarily choose one diagnosis from it. The selection function can be defined by using meta-preference information:

- Temporal information: in case of conflict keep more recent/older preferences.
- Weights can be associated to preferences so that one can compute the total weight of a diagnosis.
- The preference relation can be revised for each minimal diagnosis and shown to the user. The user by choosing one answer over others makes the system infer the preferred diagnosis. Thus, consequences of preferences can be used to revise the preferences themselves. (Typically, preferences are revisable.)
- One may want to make the smallest number of changes. Thus, one will prefer D_4 in Example 2 to the other minimal diagnoses. In contrast, one may prefer adding preferences rather than removing them. In this case, one prefers D_2 to D_3.
- In multi-agent scenarios, it is often the case that one wants to select a fair revision, for example, and not to reject all the preferences of one agent while maintaining the preferences of another agent.
- Preferences can be associated with a domain that can be employed to select diagnoses. For instance, regarding wine one gives priority to the preferences of Carlo, who is a wine producer, rather than to the preferences of John.
- Diagnoses containing more specific preferences can be selected. For example, given the two diagnoses $\langle \{\}, \{moscato \succ chianti\} \rangle$ and $\langle \{\}, \{redWine \succ whiteWine\} \rangle$ the first is selected since moscato is a white wine and chianti is a red wine.

6   Related Work

Recently, several approaches have been proposed in literature for aggregating preference criteria. These approaches tackle the problem from different perspectives. One line of research studies which properties are preserved by different methods of preference criteria aggregation. In contrast, another line investigates how to reconcile (a posteriori) preference criteria once they are aggregated.

In [3, 9], the authors consider preference relations definable by first-order formulas, and study the preservation of properties by different composition operators. For example, Chomicki [3] shows that prioritized composition preserves the properties of weak orders, while it does not preserve the ones of strict partial orders. Furthermore, he studies the problem of preference refinement [4], a special case of preference revision in which the original preferences are augmented with new preferences. In this working paper the authors do not consider conflicting preferences, but instead assume the old and new preference relations are compatible.

A new method for preference aggregation is studied in [8] by Grosof. This method generalizes the lexicographic combination method and is applicable to conflict management problems as a qualitative "weak method".

The problem of fairness of preference aggregation systems is studied by Rossi et al [11]. They generalize Arrow's impossibility theorem for combining total orders [2] to the case of partial orders.

Yager [13] and Rossi et al [12] investigated the problem of preference aggregation in the context of multi-agent systems. The approach outlined by Yager supports different types of relationship with respect to the importance of the interacting agents (e.g., total and weak order). He studied also the aggregation of fuzzy sets representing individual agent preferences. Rossi et al proposed mCP nets, a formalism that extends CP nets to handle preferences of several agents. They provided a number of different semantics for reasoning with mCP nets based on the notion of voting.

In contrast to the above mentioned approaches, we followed the second line of research. Basically, two distinct approaches have been proposed in literature to tackle the problem of amalgamating distributed data:

– paraconsistent formalisms, in which the amalgamated data may remain inconsistent. The idea is to answer queries in a consistent way without computing the revision of the amalgamated data.
– coherent methods, in which the amalgamated data is revised to restore consistency.

We have considered a coherent method to handle the problem of revising (a posteriori) preference criteria. Our approach is flexible and general, and is tailored neither to any specific preference criteria nor to any specific method for preference aggregation. Furthermore, the ability to express meta-information on the diagnoses of a revision problem gives us a further level of abstraction allowing us to select the best diagnosis for the problem at hand. Our approach shares the principle of minimal change with classical belief revision [6]. However, the basic theoretical setting is different belief revision being concerned with the revision of finite theories.

We have implemented an algorithm to compute minimal diagnoses by using a version of ABDUAL [1] for constructive negation with abducibles. ABDUAL extends Well-Founded semantics with abducibles and integrity constraints. By means of the latter it can also compute Stable Models, where default literals are envisaged as constrained abducibles. Alternatively, ABDUAL is implemented in XSB-Prolog and so, by means of its XASP version that connects it to the Smodels implementation, stable models can be computed where relevant abducibles for a query are coded into even loops over default negation. The role of the ABDUAL is then to identify the relevant abducibles and send the residue program plus the so coded abducubles to Smodels.

Furthermore, when there exist no abducubles, ABDUAL is polynomial on the size of the program. When there are abducibles, because of its program transformation, ABDUAL computes abductive solutions depth-first, one at a time, via backtracking. So, if solution minimality is not required, a satisfying solution for preferences revision may found with no need to compute them all first. A study of the complexity of ABDUAL can be found in [1].

In the near future, we plan to combine our work on preference updating [5] with preference revision.

References

1. J. J. Alferes, L. M. Pereira, and T. Swift. Abduction in Well-Founded Semantics and Generalized Stable Models via Tabled Dual Programs. *Theory and Practice of Logic Programming*, 4(4):383–428, 2004.
2. K. Arrow. *Social Choice and Individual Values*. John Wiley and Sons, 1951.
3. Jan Chomicki. Preference Formulas in Relational Queries. *ACM Transactions on Database Systems*, 28(4):427–466, 2003.
4. Jan Chomicki and Joyce Song. On Preference Refinement. Paper in progress, 2004.
5. P. Dell'Acqua and L. M. Pereira. Preferring and updating in logic-based agents. In O. Bartenstein, U. Geske, M. Hannebauer, and O. Yoshie (eds.), *Web-Knowledge Management and Decision Support. Selected Papers from the 14th Int. Conf. on Applications of Prolog (INAP)*, LNAI 2543, pp. 70–85, 2003.
6. P. Gärdenfors and H. Rott. Belief Revision. In D. M Gabbay, C. J. Hogger, and J. A. Robinson (eds.), *Handbook of Logic in Artificial Intelligence and Logic Programming*, volume 4, pp. 35–132. Oxford University Press, 1995.
7. A. V. Gelder, K. A. Ross, and J. S. Schlipf. The Well-Founded Semantics for General Logic Programs. *J. ACM*, 38(3):620–650, 1991.
8. B. N. Grosof. New Prioritization Methods for Conflict Management. In M. Klein (ed.), *Proc. IJCAI-93 W. on Computational Models of Conflict Management in Cooperative Problem-Solving*. Int. Joint Conf. on Artificial Intelligence, 1993.
9. Andréka H., M. Ryan, and P. Y. Schobbens. Operators and Laws for Combining Preference Relations. *J. of Logic and Computation*, 12(1):13–53, 2002.
10. L. M. Pereira, C. Damásio, and J. J. Alferes. Debugging by Diagnosing Assumptions. In P. Fritzson (ed.), *1st Int. Ws. on Automatic Algorithmic Debugging, AADEBUG'93*, LNCS 749, pp. 58–74. Preproceedings by Linköping Univ., 1993.

11. F. Rossi, K. B. Venable, and T. Walsh. Aggregating Preference Cannot be Fair. Preprint n. 12-2004, Dept. of Pure and Applied Mathematics, Univ. of Padova, Italy, 2004.
12. F. Rossi, K. B. Venable, and T. Walsh. mCP nets: Representing and Reasoning with Preferences of Multiple Agents. In D. L. McGuinness and G. Ferguson (eds.), *Proc. 19th Conf. on Artificial Intelligence, 16th Conf. on Innovative Applications of Artificial Intelligence*, LNCS 749, pp. 729–734. AAAI Press, 2004.
13. Ronald R. Yager. Fusion of Multi-Agent Preference Ordering. *Fuzzy Sets and Systems*, 117:1–12, 2001.

Revised Stable Models – A Semantics for Logic Programs

Luís Moniz Pereira and Alexandre Miguel Pinto

Centro de Inteligência Artificial – CENTRIA,
Universidade Nova de Lisboa, 2829-516 Caparica, Portugal
{lmp, amp}@di.fct.unl.pt

Abstract. This paper introduces an original 2-valued semantics for Normal Logic Programs (NLP), which conservatively extends the Stable Model semantics (SM) to all normal programs. The distinction consists in the revision of one feature of SM, namely its treatment of odd loops, and of infinitely long support chains, over default negation. This single revised aspect, addressed by means of a *Reductio ad Absurdum* approach, affords a number of fruitful consequences, namely regarding existence, relevance and top-down querying, cumulativity, and implementation.

The paper motivates and defines the Revised Stable Models semantics (rSM), justifying and exemplifying it. Properties of rSM are given and contrasted with those of SM. Furthermore, these results apply to SM whenever odd loops and infinitely long chains over negation are absent, thereby establishing significant, not previously known, properties of SM. Conclusions, further work, terminate the paper.

Keywords: Logic program semantics, Stable Models, *Reductio ad absurdum*.

1 Introduction

The paper introduces a new 2-valued semantics for Normal Logic Programs (NLP), called Revised Stable Models semantics (rSM), cogent in the properties it enjoys. Its name intends to draw attention to being inspired by, and actually revising, Stable Model semantics (SM) [2]. Indeed SMs are just particular rSM models, and the definition of the SM is a specific instance or specialization of the rSM one. But its name also draws attention to that the definitional distinction between the two consists in the *revision* of one feature of SM, namely its treatment of odd loops over negation, as well as of infinite support chains over negation. Finally, this single revised aspect is addressed by means of a *Reductio ad Absurdum* approach, a form of belief *revision*, and affords a number of fruitful consequences, not shared by SM, the present 'de facto' standard for 2-valued semantics for NLP.

For one, rSM are guaranteed to *exist* for all NLP. The concrete examples below show that odd loops may be required to model knowledge. Moreover, this guarantee is crucial in program composition (say from knowledge originating in divers sources) so that the result has a semantics. It is also important to warrant the existence of semantics after external updating, or even SM based self-updating languages [1]. Two, rSM is *relevant*, meaning that there may exist purely top-down, program call-graph based, query driven methods to determine whether a literal belongs to some model or other. These methods can thus simply return a partial model, guaranteed

C. Bento, A. Cardoso, and G. Dias (Eds.): EPIA 2005, LNAI 3808, pp. 29–42, 2005.

extendable to a complete one, there existing no need to compute all models or even to complete models in order to answer a query. Relevance is also crucial for modelling abduction, it being query driven. Three, rSM is cumulative (and two kinds of cumulativity will be considered), so that lemmas may be stored and reused. These and other properties shall be examined in the sequel. These results apply to SM whenever odd loops over negation (OLONs) and infinitely long chains over default negation (ICONs), are absent, thereby establishing significant, not previously known, properties of SM.

Odd Loops Over Negation (OLONs)

In SM, programs such as a ← ~a, where '~' stands for default negation, do not have a model. One can easily perceive that the Odd Loop Over Negation is the trouble-maker. The single rSM model however is {a}. The reason is that if assuming '~a' leads to an inconsistency, namely by implying 'a', then in a 2-valued semantics 'a' should be true instead by *Reductio ad Absurdum*.

Example 1: The president of Morelandia is considering invading another country. He reasons thus: if I do not invade them now they are sure to deploy Weapons of Mass Destruction (WMD) sometime; on the other hand, if they shall deploy WMD I should invade them now. This is coded by his analysts as:

deploy_WMD ← ~ invade_now   invade_now ← deploy_WMD

Under the SM semantics this program has no models. Under the rSM semantics invasion is warranted by the single model M={invade_now}, and no WMD will be deployed.

It is an apparently counter-intuitive idea to permit such loops to support a literal's truth value, because it means the truth of the literal is being supported on its own negation, and this seems self-inconsistent. SM does not go a long way in treating such OLON. It simply decrees there is no model (throwing out the baby along with the bath water), instead of opting for taking the next logical step: reasoning by absurdity or *Reductio ad Absurdum* (RAA). That is, if assuming a literal false (i.e. its default negation is true) leads to an inconsistency, then, in a 2-valued semantics, the literal must be true if that's consistent. SM does not do this – it requires a true literal to be supported by its rules, i.e. by a rule with true body. The solution proffered by rSM is to extend the notion of support to include reasoning by absurdity, i.e. one supported indeed by those rules creating the odd loop. That is why the single rSM of a ← ~a is {a}.

Example 2: During elections, the prime minister of Italisconia promises to lower taxes as soon as possible, justifying it as inevitable. Indeed, if taxes are not lowered the rich do not invest, the economy cools down, and the country is all the poorer. People thus cannot afford to pay taxes, and these must be lowered anyway:

no_investment ← ~ lower_taxes   cool_economy ← no_investment
unaffordable_taxes ← cool_economy   lower_taxes ← unaffordable_taxes

Under SM this program has no models. Under rSM lowering taxes is warranted by the single model M={lower_taxes}, and the economy does not cool, etc. These two examples are typical of political *reductio ad absurdum* inevitability arguments.

<u>Example 3</u>: A murder suspect not preventively detained is likely to destroy evidence, and in that case the suspect shall be preventively detained:

likely_to_destroy_evidence(murder_suspect)←~preventively_detain(murder_suspect)
preventively_detain(murder_suspect)← likely_to_destroy_evidence(murder _suspect)

There is no SM, and a single rSM={ preventively_detain(murder_suspect) }. This jurisprudential reasoning is carried out without need for a murder_suspect to exist now. Should we wish, rSM's *cumulativity* (cf. below) allows adding the model literal as a fact.

<u>Example 4</u>: Some friends are planning their joint vacation. They separately express preference rules Q ← ~R, meaning "I want to go to Q if I cannot go to R", resulting in program P={mountain ← ~beach; beach ← ~travel; travel ← ~mountain}. P has no SMs, but affords three rSMs: {mountain, beach}, {beach, travel}, {travel, mountain}, so all of the friends will be happy if they jointly go on any of these three combination trips.

In a NLP, we say we have a *loop* when there is a rule dependency call-graph path that has the same literal in two different positions along the path – meaning that the literal depends on itself. An *OLON* is a loop such that the number of default negations in the rule dependency graph path connecting the same literal at both ends is odd.

It may be argued that SM employs OLON as integrity constraints (ICs), and so they should not be resolved; and moreover that the problem remains, in program composition or updating, that unforeseen OLON may appear. We will see below how ICs are dealt with under rSM, separated from the OLONs issue, and so having it both ways, i.e. dealing with OLON *and* ICs.

SM envisages default literals as assumptions that should be maximally true (the Closed World Assumption – CWA), on the proviso of *stability*, that is, that the conclusions following from the assumptions do not go against these. To the contrary, the whole model is confirmed by them, through its support by program rules. rSM takes this reasoning all the way, but relies on RAA to lend support to the model atoms (minimally) introduced to resolve odd loops and infinitely long support chains.

Whereas in the Well-Founded Semantics (WFS) the truth of literals, be they positive or default, may be interpreted as provability justified by a well-founded derivation, the lack of provability does not result in their falsity, since a third logical value is available: *'undefined'*. In SM, though it's 2-valued, no notion of provability is used, and one resorts to interpreting default negations as assumptions. The rSM view is that assumptions be revised (and hence its name too), in a 2-valued way, if they would otherwise lead to self-inconsistency through odd loops or infinitely long chains.

That rSM resolves the inconsistencies of odd loops of SM (and note these are not contradictions, for there is no explicit negation) does not mean rSM should resolve contradictions. That's an orthogonal problem, whose solutions can be added to different semantics, including rSM.

Infinite chains over negation (ICONs)
It is well-known [5] that SM does not assign semantics either to programs with infinite chains over default negation. We illustrate next that rSM does so.

<u>Example 5</u>: Let P be $\qquad$ p(X) ← p(s(X)) $\qquad$ p(X) ← ~p(s(X))
P has no SM, but there is one rSM, consisting of p(X) for every X. To see this
assume, reasoning by absurd, that p(X) was false for some X; then the two bodies of
each clause above would have to be false, meaning that p(s(X)) would be true by the
second one; but then, by the first one, p(X) would be true as well, thereby
contradicting the default assumption. Hence, by *Reductio ad Absurdum* reasoning,
p(X) must be true, for arbitrary X.

The paper's remaining structure: a section on the definition of Revised Stable Models,
justification and examples; forthwith, a section on properties of rSM and their contrast
with SM's; the last section addresses conclusions, future work, and potential use.

2 Revised Stable Models

A Normal Logic Program (NLP) is a finite set of *rules* of the form H ←B1, B2, ...,
Bn, not C1, not C2, ..., not Cm (n, m ≥ 0) comprising positive literals H, and Bi, and
default literals not Cj. Often we use '~' for 'not'.

Models are 2-valued and represented as sets of those positive literals which hold in
the model. The set inclusion and set difference mentioned below are with respect to
these positive literals. Minimality and maximality too refer to this set inclusion. We
will often write S – T to represent the set difference between sets S and T, i.e., S \ T.

<u>Definition 1 (Gelfond-Lifschitz Γ_P operator [2])</u>: Let P be a NLP and I a 2-valued
interpretation. The GL-transformation of P modulo I is the program P/I, obtained
from P by performing the following operations:

- remove from P all rules which contain a default literal not A such that A ∈ I
- remove from the remaining rules all default literals

Since P/I is a definite program, it has a unique least model J: Define $\Gamma_P(I) = J$.
Stable Models are the fixpoints of Γ_P, and they do not always exist.

As a shorthand notation, let WFM(P) denote the positive atoms of the Well-
Founded Model of P, that is WFM(P) is the least fixpoint of operator Γ_P^2 [6], ie. Γ_P
applied twice.

<u>Definition 2 (Sustainable Set)</u>: Intuitively, we say a set S is sustainable in P iff any
atom 'a' in S does not go against the well-founded consequences of the remaining
atoms in S, whenever, S\{a} itself is a sustainable set. The empty set by definition
is sustainable . Not going against means that atom {a} cannot be false in the WFM
of P∪S\{a}, i.e., 'a' is either true or undefined. That is, it belongs to set
$\Gamma_{P∪S\{a\}}(WFM(P ∪ S\{a\}))$. Formally, we say S is sustainable iff

$$\forall_{a∈S} \; S\{a\} \text{ is sustainable} \Rightarrow a∈\Gamma_{P∪S\{a\}}(WFM(P ∪ S\{a\}))$$

If S is empty the condition is trivially true.

<u>Definition 3 (Revised Stable Models and Semantics)</u>: Let $RAA_P(M) ≡ M – \Gamma_P(M)$. M
is a Revised Stable Model of a NLP P, iff:

- M is a minimal classical model, with '~' interpreted as classical negation
- $\exists \; \alpha ≥ 2$ such that $\Gamma_P^{\alpha}(M) ⊇ RAA_P(M)$
- $RAA_P(M)$ is sustainable

The Revised Stable Models semantics is the intersection of its models, just as the SM semantics is. Next we explain the function of, and justify, each condition above.

<u>First Condition</u>: *M is a minimal classical model* – A classical model of a NLP is one that satisfies all its rules, where '~' is seen as classical negation and '←' as material implication. Satisfaction means that for every rule body true in the model its head must be true in the model too. Minimality of classical models is required to ensure maximal supportedness (i.e., any true head is supported on a necessarily true body), compatible with model existence.

SMs are supported minimal classical models, and we keep them as a specific case of rSMs. In fact SMs are the special case when there are no inconsistent OLON or ICON. However, not all rSMs are SMs since inconsistent OLON or ICON of an atom are allowed in rSM to be resolved for the positive value of the atom. Nevertheless, this is to be achieved in a minimal way, i.e. resolving a minimal set of such atoms, and justified through the logical "support" on a specific application of *Reductio Ad Absurdum* (RAA) to that effect.

<u>Example 6</u>: Let P be $\{a \leftarrow \sim a \; ; \; b \leftarrow \sim a\}$. The only candidate minimal model is $\{a\}$, since $\{\}$ and $\{b\}$ are not models in the classical sense and $\{a, b\}$ is not minimal. The need for RAA reasoning comes from the requirement to resolve OLON – an issue not dealt with in the traditional SM semantics. In P, $\Gamma_P(\{a\}) = \{\}$ and so $RAA_P(\{a\}) = \{a\} - \{\} = \{a\}$. The truth-value of 'a' is supported by a specific RAA on '~a' just in case it leads inexorably to 'a'. The first rule forces 'a' to be in any possible model under the new semantics. I.e., assuming 'a' is not in a model, i.e. '~a' is true, then the first rule insists that 'a' is in the model – an inconsistency. But if '~a' cannot be true, and since the semantics is 2-valued, then '~a' must be false, and therefore 'a' must be true. So, the only model of this program must be $\{a\}$, since $\{b\}$ is not a model, and $\{a, b\}$ is not a minimal classical model with respect to model $\{a\}$.

The second condition, explained below, aims at testing the inexorability of a default literal implying its positive counterpart, given the context of the remaining default literals assumed in the candidate model. The $\Gamma_P(M) \subseteq M$ proviso, verified by all minimal models, allows atoms to be minimally added to M over and above those of SMs, since these are defined as $\Gamma_P(SM) = SM$. The additional candidate model atoms are specified by the next condition, i.e. those in $RAA_P(M) = M - \Gamma_P(M)$.

<u>Second Condition</u>: $\exists \alpha \geq 2 \; \Gamma_P^\alpha(M) \supseteq RAA_P(M)$ – For the sake of explanation, let us first start with a more verbose, but also more intuitive version of this condition:

$$\exists \; \alpha \geq 0 \; \Gamma_P^\alpha(\Gamma_P(M - RAA_P(M))) \supseteq RAA_P(M) \quad \text{where } \Gamma_P^0(X) = X \text{ for any X}$$

Since $RAA_P(M) = M - \Gamma_P(M)$, the $RAA_P(M)$ set can be understood as the subset of literals of M whose defaults are self-inconsistent, given the rule-supported literals in $\Gamma_P(M)$, the SM part of M. The $RAA_P(M)$ atoms are not obtainable by $\Gamma_P(M)$. The condition states that successively applying the Γ_P operator to $M - RAA_P(M)$, i.e. to $\Gamma_P(M)$, which is the "non-inconsistent" part of the model or Γ_P rule-supported context of M, we will get a set of literals which, after α iterations of Γ_P, if needed, will get us the $RAA_P(M)$. $RAA_P(M)$ is thus verified as the set of self-inconsistent literals, whose defaults actually RAA-support their positive counterparts, given the $\Gamma_P(M)$ context.

This is intuitively correct: by assuming the self-inconsistent literals as false, they later appear as true Γ_P consequences. We can simplify this expression to $\exists \ \alpha \geq 0$ $\Gamma_P^\alpha(\Gamma_P(\Gamma_P(M))) \supseteq RAA_P(M)$. And then to $\exists \ \alpha \geq 2 \ \Gamma_P^\alpha(M) \supseteq RAA_P(M)$, to obtain the original one. Of course, all SMs comply with this condition because in their case $RAA_P(SM)=\{\}$. So, for SMs all three rSM conditions particularize to the usual definition of $\Gamma_P(SM)=SM$.

The approach to this condition has been inspired by the use of Γ_P and Γ_P^2, in one definition of the Well-Founded Semantics (WFS) [4], to determine the undefined literals. We want to test that the atoms in $RAA_P(M)$ introduced to resolve odd loops and infinite chains, actually lead to themselves through repeated (at least 2) applications of Γ_P, noting that Γ_P^2 is the consequences operator appropriate for odd loop detection (as seen in the WFS), whereas Γ_P is appropriate for even loop SM stability. Since odd loops can have an arbitrary length, repeated (ordinal) applications may be required. Because even loops are stable in just one application of Γ_P, they do not need iteration, which is the case with SMs.

The non-monotonic character of Γ_P, when coupled with the existence of odd loops, may produce temporary spurious elements not in M in the second application of Γ_P in Γ_P^2, and hence the use of set inclusion in the condition. No matter, because the test is just to detect that introduced atoms additional to $\Gamma_P(M)$ actually are supported by RAA on themselves, given the initial $\Gamma_P(M)$ context. On the other hand, such spurious atoms do not persist: they disappear in the next Γ_P application.

Example 7: $a \leftarrow \sim a, \sim b$ $d \leftarrow \sim a$ $b \leftarrow d, \sim b$

$M_1=\{a\}$, $\Gamma_P(M_1)=\{\}$, $RAA_P(M_1)=\{a\}$, and $M_2=\{b, d\}$, $\Gamma_P(M_2)=\{d\}$, $RAA_P(M_2)=\{b\}$ are the rSMs. Let us see why. $\Gamma_P^2(M_1) = \Gamma_P(\Gamma_P(M_1)) = \Gamma_P(\{\}) = \{a,b,d\} \supseteq \{a\} = RAA_P(M_1)$. Also, $\Gamma_P^2(M_2) = \Gamma_P(\Gamma_P(M_2)) = \Gamma_P(\{d\}) = \{a,b,d\} \supseteq \{b\} = RAA_P(M_2)$; so, both M_1 and M_2 respect the second condition. Since both Models have RAA sets with just one atom and both are undefined in the WFM of the program, the third condition is trivially satisfied for both M_1 and M_2.

Example 8: $a \leftarrow \sim b$ $t \leftarrow a, b$ $k \leftarrow \sim t$
                        $b \leftarrow \sim a$ $i \leftarrow \sim k$

$M_1=\{a,k\}$, $\Gamma_P(M_1)= \{a,k\}$, $RAA_P(M_1)=\{\}$, $\Gamma_P(M_1) \supseteq RAA_P(M_1)$. M_1 is a rSM and a SM.
$M_2=\{b,k\}$, $\Gamma_P(M_2)= \{b,k\}$, $RAA_P(M_2)=\{\}$, $\Gamma_P(M_2) \supseteq RAA_P(M_2)$. M_2 is a rSM and a SM.
$M_3=\{a,t,i\}$, $\Gamma_P(M_3)= \{a,i\}$, $RAA_P(M_3)=\{t\}$, $\not\exists \ \alpha \geq 2 \ \Gamma_P^\alpha(M_3) \supseteq RAA_P(M_3)$. M_3 is no rSM.
$M_4=\{b,t,i\}$, $\Gamma_P(M_4)= \{b,i\}$, $RAA_P(M_4)=\{t\}$, $\not\exists \ \alpha \geq 2 \ \Gamma_P^\alpha(M_4) \supseteq RAA_P(M_4)$. M_4 is no rSM.

Although M_3 and M_4 are minimal models, the 't' atom in their respective RAA sets is not obtainable by iterations of Γ_P. Simply because '$\sim t$', implicit in both $\Gamma_P(M_3)$ and $\Gamma_P(M_4)$, is not conducive to 't' through Γ_P. This is the purpose of the second condition. The attempt to introduce 't' into $RAA_P(M)$ fails because RAA cannot be employed to justify 't'. Indeed, the second condition of the rSM definition is intended to detect negative self-dependencies of atoms in the RAA set. This is clearly not the case of atom 't': it does not depend on itself, let alone on its own negation. For this reason 't' is not a "legitimate" atom to appear in any RAA set.

Example 9: $a \leftarrow \sim b$ $b \leftarrow \sim a$ $c \leftarrow a, \sim c$
                  $x \leftarrow \sim y$ $y \leftarrow \sim x$ $z \leftarrow x, \sim z$

$M_1 = \{b, y\}$, $M_2 = \{a, c, y\}$, $M_3 = \{b, x, z\}$, $M_4 = \{a, c, x, z\}$, are its rSMs.
$\Gamma_P(M_1) = \{b, y\}$, $\Gamma_P(M_2) = \{a, y\}$, $\Gamma_P(M_3) = \{b, x\}$, $\Gamma_P(M_4) = \{a, x\}$.
$RAA_P(M_1) = \{\}$, $RAA_P(M_2) = \{c\}$, $RAA_P(M_3) = \{z\}$, $RAA_P(M_4) = \{c, z\}$.

In this program we have two even loops (one over 'a' and 'b', and the other over 'x' and 'y'), creating the four possible combinations $\{a,x\}$, $\{a,y\}$, $\{b,x\}$, and $\{b,y\}$. Moreover, whenever 'a' is present in a model, the odd loop over 'c' becomes 'active' and so, by RAA we need 'c' to be also present in that model. The same happens for 'x' and 'z'. So the four Minimal Models are $\{a,c,x,z\}$, $\{a,c,y\}$, $\{b,x,z\}$, $\{b,y\}$. Since 'c' and 'z' are involved in odd loops, their negations lead to their positive conclusions. It is easy to see that these are the rSMs of P, satisfying the third condition too – there is no dependency on 'z' nor on 'c' and so each of them remains undefined in the Well-Founded Model of P even when the other atom ('c' or 'z') is added as a fact. Note that $RAA_P(M_4)$ is a proper superset of $RAA_P(M_2)$ and of $RAA_P(M_3)$; hence, minimality of RAA sets is *not* a requirement for a rSM.

Example 10: $a \leftarrow \sim b$ $b \leftarrow \sim c$ $c \leftarrow \sim a$

$M_1 = \{a,b\}$, $\Gamma_P(M_1) = \{b\}$, $RAA_P(M_1) = \{a\}$, $\Gamma_P^2(M_1) = \{b,c\}$, $\Gamma_P^3(M_1) = \{c\}$, $\Gamma_P^4(M_1) = \{a,c\} \supseteq RAA_P(M_1)$. Since M_1 has an RAA set with just one atom and all of 'a', 'b', and 'c' are undefined in the WFM, the third condition is trivially satisfied. The remaining rSMs, $\{a,c\}$ and $\{b,c\}$, are similar, by symmetry.

Note: In Example 10, it took us 4 iterations of Γ_P to get a superset of $RAA_P(M)$ in a program with an OLON of length 3. In general, a NLP with an OLON of length α will require $\alpha+1$ iterations of the Γ_P operator. Let us see why. First we need to obtain the supported subset of M, which is $\Gamma_P(M)$. The $RAA_P(M)$ set is precisely the subset of M that does not intersect $\Gamma_P(M)$, so under $\Gamma_P(M)$ all literals in $RAA_P(M)$ have truth-value 'false'. Now we start iterating the Γ_P operator over $\Gamma_P(M)$. Since the odd loop has length α, we need α iterations of Γ_P to finally make arise the set $RAA_P(M)$. Hence we need the first iteration of Γ_P to get $\Gamma_P(M)$ and then α iterations over $\Gamma_P(M)$ to get $RAA_P(M)$ leading us to $\alpha+1$. In general, if the odd loop lengths can be decomposed into the primes $\{N_1,...,N_m\}$, then the required number of iterations, besides the initial one, is the product of all the N_i.

The other possible way for a NLP to have no SMs is by having an infinitely long support chain over negation (ICON) even without having any OLONs. An example of such a program first appeared in [5]. It illustrates well the general case for such chains.

Example 11 (François Fage's [5]): $p(X) \leftarrow p(s(X))$ $p(X) \leftarrow \sim p(s(X))$

The grounded version of this program is:

        $p(0) \leftarrow p(s(0))$
        $p(0) \leftarrow \sim p(s(0))$

$$p(s(0)) \leftarrow p(s(s(0)))$$
$$p(s(0)) \leftarrow \sim p(s(s(0)))$$
...

Although P has no Odd-Loop Over Negation, its unique Minimal Classical Model is $M = \{p(0), p(s(0)), p(s(s(0))), ...\}$, and complies with the second condition of the definition of rSM. In fact, $\Gamma_P(M) = \{\}$, and $\Gamma_P^2 (M) = \Gamma_P(\Gamma_P(M)) = \Gamma_P(\{\}) = M \supseteq RAA_P(M)$. So, $M = RAA_P(M)$. Also, M also complies with the third rSM condition for as soon as one atom $p(s^i(0))$ of $RAA_P(M)=M$ is added as a fact, all the other $p(0)$, $p(s(0))$, ..., $p(s^{i-1}(0))$ become true in the Well-Founded Model of the resulting program due to the '$p(X) \leftarrow p(s(X))$' rules. Moreover, all the other $p(s^j(0))$ – where j>i – atoms remain undefined in the WFM of the resulting program. Hence all atoms in $RAA_P(M)=M$ will be elements of $\Gamma_{P\cup R}$ (WFM($P\cup R$)), for every $R\subseteq RAA_P(M)$, and $RAA_P(M)$ turns out to be sustainable.

Third Condition: $RAA_P(M)$ is sustainable

Let us explain this condition in detail. In a Stable Model there are no elements in the RAA set. This is because there are no actual active OLON or ICON in the program. The only elements we want to admit in any RAA set are those strictly necessary to resolve some actual active OLON or ICON.

The first two conditions of the rSM definition cope with the guarantee that every atom in a rSM is supported, according to a generalized conception of support. There is, however, one additional necessary third condition: the elements in $RAA_P(M)$ must be compatible with each other for $RAA_P(M)$ to be sustainable, in the sense that each of its elements respects the well-founded model obtained by adding to P the remaining elements as facts. That is, every element 'a' of the $RAA_P(M)$ is either true or undefined in the context of all the other atoms of $RAA_P(M)$, but only if the $RAA_P(M)\setminus\{a\}$ set, in turn, verifies the same sustainability condition.

Intuitively, an $RAA_P(rSM)$ set can be incrementally constructed by means of a sequence of sets as follows:

- The first element E_1 in the sequence of sets contains the intersection (which may be empty) of all RAA_P of Minimal Models which respect the second condition of the definition. These are the inevitable and deterministically necessary atoms in any $RAA_P(rSM)$.
- The second element E_2 of the sequence is a singleton set containing one RAA_P atom not in E_1, non-deterministically chosen from some RAA_P of the step before, and which respects all the atoms in the previous set E_1 – i.e., the atom in this singleton set is either true or undefined in the Well-Founded Model of the program in the context of the atoms of the first set (when we add the atoms of the first set to the program as facts).
- The third element E_3 of the sequence contains the intersection of all RAA_P of Minimal Models of $P \cup S$ which respect the second condition of the RSM definition – where P stands for the original program, and $S = E_1 \cup E_2$. E_3 contains the inevitable and deterministically necessary atoms in any $RAA_P(rSM)$, given the choice in E_2.

- The fourth element E_4 of the sequence is again a singleton set with another non-deterministically chosen atom which, as for the second set, respects the Well-Founded Model of the program in the context of $S = E_1 \cup E_2 \cup E_3$
- Etc.

The sequence construction continues until a Minimal Model is achieved. The $RAA_P(rSM)$ obtained by such sequences comply with the sustainability condition.

<u>Example 12</u>: $a \leftarrow \sim a$ $b \leftarrow \sim a$ $c \leftarrow \sim b$ $d \leftarrow \sim c$ $e \leftarrow \sim e$

With this example we will show how the sequence process can be used to calculate the RAA sets. This program has two Minimal Models: $M_1=\{a,c,e\}$ and $M_2=\{a,b,d,e\}$. It is easy to verify that both M_1 and M_2 comply with the second condition of the rSM definition. $\Gamma_P(M_1)=\{c\}$, $RAA_P(M_1)=\{a,e\}$; and $\Gamma_P(M_2)=\{d\}$, $RAA_P(M_2)=\{a,b,e\}$. So now we will start the process of creating the acceptable RAA sets. The first element E_1 of the sequence is the intersection of $RAA_P(M_1)$ and $RAA_P(M_2)$ which is $\{a,e\}$. Now we add the atoms in $E_1=\{a,e\}$ to the program as facts and calculate the WFM of the resulting program: $WFM(P\cup\{a,e\})=\{a,c,e\}$. The resulting program $P\cup\{a,e\}$ has two Minimal Models which coincide with M_1 and M_2, but now, under $P\cup\{a,e\}$, M_2 no longer satisfies the second condition of the rSM definition. In fact, both 'b' and 'd' now become 'false' in the $WFM(P\cup\{a,e\})$. So the only Minimal Model respecting the second condition, after adding 'a' and 'e' as facts to P is just M_1. $RAA_P(M_1)$ is the only acceptable RAA set (which is sustainable by construction) and hence the unique rSM is M_1.

<u>Example 13</u>: $a \leftarrow \sim b$ $b \leftarrow \sim c,e$ $c \leftarrow \sim a$ $e \leftarrow \sim e, a$

We saw that in a rSM, every atom 'a' in RAA must be either true of undefined in the context of $RAA_P(M)\backslash\{a\}$ if $RAA_P(M)\backslash\{a\}$ in turn complies with the same requirement. This happens for any atom 'a' when it does not have only negative dependencies on other $RAA_P(M)$ atoms. Let us see this example in detail. This program has three Minimal Models $M_1 = \{b,c\}$, and $M_2 = \{a,c,e\}$, and $M_3 = \{a,b,e\}$. 'a', 'b', and 'c' and involved in an OLON; and so is 'e'. But the OLON in 'e' is only active when we also have 'a'. So, if we do not have 'a' in a Model we also do not need 'e'; hence the Minimal Model $M_1=\{b,c\}$. $\Gamma_P(M_1)=\{c\}$, $RAA_P(M_1)=\{b\}$, and $\Gamma_P^4(M_1)=\{a,b,e\}\supseteq\{b\}=RAA_P(M_1)$, so M_1 respects the second condition. Since all the atoms of the program are undefined in the Well-Founded Model, $\{b\}$ is sustainable.

$M_2=\{a,c,e\}$, $\Gamma_P(M_2)=\{a\}$, $RAA_P(M_2)=\{c,e\}$, $\Gamma_P^4(M_2)=\{a,b,c,e\}\supseteq\{c,e\}=RAA_P(M_2)$. $\{c\}$ and $\{e\}$ are sustainable because both 'c' and 'e' are undefined in the WFM of the program. Since 'e'$\in\Gamma_{P\cup\{c\}}(WFM(P\cup\{c\}))$ and 'c'$\in\Gamma_{P\cup\{e\}}(WFM(P\cup\{e\}))$ we conclude that $\{c,e\}$ is sustainable and M_2 is also a rSM.

$M_3=\{a,b,e\}$, $\Gamma_P(M_3)=\{\}$, $RAA_P(M_3)=\{a,b,e\}$, $\Gamma_P^2(M_3)=\{a,b,c,e\}\supseteq\{a,b,e\}=RAA_P(M_3)$.

In this example, the atom 'a' depends just on '$\sim$b', and 'b' is also an element of $RAA_P(M_3)$. This means that if $RAA_P(M_3)\backslash\{a\}$ is sustainable then $RAA_P(M_3)$ is not sustainable and, therefore, M_3 is not a rSM. However, $RAA_P(M_3)\backslash\{a\}=\{b,e\}$ is not a sustainable set, and this does not imply $RAA_P(M_3)$ non-sustainability. On the other hand, we have one atom 'b' which is in the $RAA_P(M_3)$ set because it has only positive dependencies on atoms of the $RAA_P(M_3)$ set.

M_3 is a more complex example concerning the third condition. But a quick way of finding out that it also complies with the sustainability requisite is by checking that since 'a' depends negatively on 'b', as soon as we add 'b' as a fact to the program both 'a' and 'e' become immediately false in the $WFM(P\cup\{b\})$. Hence neither $\{b,e\}$ nor $\{a,b\}$ are sustainable. Since $\{a,e\}$ is sustainable and 'b'$\in\Gamma_{P\cup\{a,e\}}(WFM(P\cup\{a,e\}))$ we conclude $\{a,b,e\}=RAA_P(M_3)$ is sustainable.

<u>Example 14:</u>   c $\leftarrow$ a, ~c   a $\leftarrow$ ~b   b $\leftarrow$ ~a

$M_1=\{b\}$ is a minimal model. $\Gamma_P(M_1)=M_1$, and $RAA_P(M_1)=\{\}$. $M_2=\{a,c\}$ is a minimal model. $\Gamma_P(M_2)=\{a\}$, and $RAA_P(M_2)=\{c\}$. We have as rSMs $\{b\}$, the only SM, but also M_2. In fact, 'c' is involved in an odd loop which becomes active when 'a' is true. $\Gamma_P^2(M_2) = \Gamma_P(\Gamma_P(M_2)) = \Gamma_P(\{a\}) = \{a,c\} \supseteq RAA_P(M_2) = \{c\}$. So M_2 respects the second condition. Since the $RAA_P(M_2)$ set consists of just one atom which is undefined in the WFM of the program, and there are no other atoms depending on 'c', adding it to the program as a fact cannot produce any impact one any other atoms of the $RAA_P(M_2)$ set – there are none – and so $RAA_P(M_2)$ is sustainable.

<u>Example 15:</u>   a $\leftarrow$ ~b   b $\leftarrow$ ~a   c $\leftarrow$ a, ~ c   c $\leftarrow$ b, ~ c   d $\leftarrow$ b, ~d

There are two Minimal Models for this NLP: $M_1 = \{a, c\}$ and $M_2 = \{b, c, d\}$. They both are Revised Stable Models. Let us see why.

$$M_1 = \{a, c\}, \Gamma_P(M_1) = \Gamma_P(\{a, c\}) = \{a\}, RAA_P(M_1) = M_1 - \Gamma_P(M_1) = \{a,c\} - \{a\} = \{c\}$$

$\Gamma_P^2(M_1) = \Gamma_P(\Gamma_P(M_1)) = \Gamma_P(\{a\}) = \{a,c\}$, so $\Gamma_P^2(M_1) \supseteq RAA_P(M_1)$. The second condition is satisfied by M_1. The only atoms involved in odd loops are 'c' and 'd'. There are no atoms depending on 'c', so, adding 'c' as a fact to the program will not produce any impact on any other atom of $RAA_P(M_1)$, also because $RAA_P(M_1)$ has just one atom. Let us look now into M_2:

$$M_2 = \{b, c, d\}, \Gamma_P(M_2) = \Gamma_P(\{b, c, d\}) = \{b\}$$
$$RAA_P(M_2) = M_2 - \Gamma_P(M_2) = \{b, c, d\} - \{b\} = \{c, d\}$$

$\Gamma_P^2(M_2) = \Gamma_P(\Gamma_P(M_2)) = \Gamma_P(\{b\}) = \{b, c, d\}$, so $\Gamma_P^2(M_2) \supseteq RAA(M_2)$. The second condition is satisfied by M_2. Similarly to as explained for M_1, no atoms depend on 'c' nor on 'd'; so we conclude that adding any of 'c' or 'd' to the program as a fact will have no impact on the other atom of the RAA set. But let us see it thoroughly. Since both 'c' and 'd' are undefined in the WFM of the program, both $\{c\}$ and $\{d\}$ are sustainable. Consider now $R = \{c\} \subset RAA_P(M_2) = \{c,d\}$. The set of positive atoms of $P \cup R$ is $WFM(P\cup R) = \{c\}$, and $\Gamma_{P\cup R}(WFM(P\cup R)) = \Gamma_{P\cup R}(\{c\}) = \{a,b,c,d\}$, and 'd'$\in\{a,b,c,d\}$. Which means that adding 'c' as a fact to the program does not render 'd' as 'false' in the Well-Founded Model of the resulting program. Doing the same with R=$\{d\}$ we will get the same result for 'c', i.e., 'c'$\in\Gamma_{P\cup R}(WFM(P\cup R))=\{a,b,c,d\}$. Hence $\{c,d\}$ is sustainable and M_2 is a rSM.

3   Integrity Constraints (ICs)

It may be argued that SM needs to employ OLON for expressing denial ICs, but the problem remains that in program composition unforeseen odd loops may appear, so that not all OLON refer to ICs. rSM can mimic the SM denial ICs by means of OLON involving a programmer chosen reserved literal such as *'falsum'*, or simply by means of adding a rule of the form *'falsum* ← IC'. One can then prefer only those rSMs without the *'falsum'* atom. Thus, rSM semantics separates the two issues, having it both ways (cf. Example 13, where one can substitute 'c' for *'falsum'*).

<u>Definition 3 (Integrity Constraints)</u> Incorporating denial ICs in a NLP under the Revised Stable Models semantics consists in adding, similarly to SM, a rule in the OLON form

falsum ← an_IC, ~falsum   or, more simply,   falsum ← an_IC

for each IC, where 'falsum' is a reserved atom chosen by the programmer. The 'an_IC' in the rule stands for a conjunction of literals, which must not be true, and form the IC.

   In the case of the OLON introduced this way it results that, whenever 'an_IC' is true, 'falsum' must be in the model. Consequently one can retain only models where 'an_IC' is false, that is those without 'falsum'. Whereas in SM odd loops are used to express ICs, in rSM they can too, but by using the reserved 'falsum' predicate. Or, more simply, by just having the 'an_IC' implying 'falsum'. The OLON form is used by the SMs community to prevent 'an_IC' becoming true, due to the Γ-'instability' of the OLON.

<u>Example 16</u>: In a Middle Region two factions are at odds, and use two sets of reasoning rules. One believes that if terrorism does not stop then oppression will do it and hence become unnecessary. The other believes that if oppression does not stop then terror will do it and hence become unnecessary. Combining them requires two integrity constraints.

oppression_on ← ~ terror_off   terror_on ← ~ oppression_off
terror_off ← oppression_on   oppression_off ← terror_on

falsum ← oppression_on, oppression_off, ~falsum
falsum ← terror_on, terror_off, ~falsum

So far so good, there is a single joint rSM={oppression_off, terror_off}, and no SM. But introducing either or both of the next two rules, makes it impossible to satisfy the ICs:

oppression_on ← ~ terror_on   terror_on ← ~ oppression_on

In this case all the rSMs will contain the atom 'falsum'. Note the difference between rSM and SM semantics concerning this case: under rSM there are still models, they just do not comply with our requirements of not having 'falsum'; whereas under SM semantics there are no models.

4 Properties of the Revised Stable Models Semantics

Theorem 3 – Existence: Every NLP has at least one Revised Stable Model.

Theorem 4 – Stable Models extension: Every Stable Model of an NLP is also a Revised Stable Model of it.

SM does not deal with Odd Loops Over Negation nor ICONs, except to prohibit them, and that unfortunately ensures it does not enjoy desirable properties such as *Relevance*. For example, take a program such as:

$$c \leftarrow a, {\sim}c \qquad a \leftarrow {\sim}b \qquad b \leftarrow {\sim}a$$

Although it has a SM={b} it is non-relevant, e.g. in order to find out the truth-value of literal 'a' we cannot just look below the rule dependency call-graph for 'a', but need also to look at all other rules that depend on 'a', namely the first rule for 'c'. This rule in effect prohibits any SM containing 'a' because of the odd loop in 'c' arising when 'a' is true, i.e. 'c $\leftarrow$ ~c'. Hence, as the example illustrates, no top down call-graph based query method can exist for SM, because the truth of a literal potentially depends on all of a program's rules.

Relevance [3] is the property that makes it possible to implement a top-down call-directed query-derivation proof-procedure – a highly desirable feature if one wants an efficient theorem-proving system that does not need to compute a whole model to answer a query. The non-relevance of Stable Models, however, is caused exclusively by the presence of OLONs or ICONs, as these are the ones that may render unacceptable a partial model compatible with the call-graph below a literal. In contradistinction, the even loops can accommodate a partial solution by veering in one direction or the other.

rSM enjoys relevance, by resolving odd loops – and ICONS – in favour of their heads, thus effectively preventing their constraining hold on literals permitting the loop, and so it is potentially amenable to top-down call-graph based query methods. These methods are designed to try and identify whether a query literal belongs to some rSM, and to partially produce an rSM supporting a positive answer. The partial solution is guaranteed extendable to a full rSM because of relevance.

Theorem 5 – Relevancy: The Revised Stable Models semantics is Relevant.

Theorem 6 – Cumulativity: The Revised Stable Models semantics is Cumulative.

Example 17: $a \leftarrow {\sim}b \qquad b \leftarrow {\sim}a, c \qquad c \leftarrow a$

The single stable model is SM_1={a, c}, $\Gamma_P(SM_1)=SM_1$, and $RAA_P(SM_1)$={ }. If 'c $\leftarrow$' is added, then there is an additional SM_2={b, c}, and cumulativity for SM fails because 'a' no longer belongs to the intersection of SMs. There exists also rSM_2={b}, with $\Gamma_P(rSM_2)$={ } and $RAA_P(rSM_2)$={b}; so 'c $\leftarrow$' cannot be added as it does not belong to the intersection of all rSMs. This ensures cumulativity for rSMs.

To see why {b} is a rSM note that 'c' in the rule for 'b' partially evaluates into '~b' through the rule for 'a', and that since 'a' is false the rule for 'b' provides an odd loop on 'b'. rSM_2 respects the second condition. In fact, $\Gamma_P^2(rSM_2) = \Gamma_P(\Gamma_P(rSM_2)) = \Gamma_P(\{\}) = \{a,b,c\} \supseteq RAA_P(rSM_2) = \{b\}$. Again, in $RAA_P(rSM_2)$ there is no other atom besides 'b', so there are no dependencies of other atoms of $RAA_P(rSM_2)$ on 'b'. rSM_2 thus respects the third condition since 'b' is undefined in the WFM(P).

Cumulativity [3] pertains to the intersection of models, which formally defines the SM and the rSM semantics. But seldom is this intersection used in practice, and SM implementations are focused instead on computing the set of models.

Another, but similar, second notion of cumulativity pertains to storing lemmas as a proof develops, giving rise to the techniques of memoizing and tabling in some Prolog and WFS systems. This is a nice property, which ensures one can use old computation results from previous steps in a query-oriented derivation to speed up the computation of the rest of the query by avoiding redundant computations. This type of cumulativity is common in top-down call-graph oriented query derivation methods, which can exist for rSM because it enjoys relevance, but not for SM.

For this second type of cumulativity, relevance is again essential because it guarantees that the truth of a literal depends only on the derivational context provided by the partial rSM supporting the derivation, namely those default literals which are true in it. Consequently, if a positive literal A is found true in (finite) context not_C (standing for the conjunction of default literals true in it), then a rule may be added to that effect, namely A ← not_C or, better still for efficiency, entered into a table.

5 Conclusions and Future Work

Having defined a new 2-valued semantics for normal logic programs, and having proposed more general semantics for several language extensions, much remains to be explored, in the way of properties, complexity analysis, comparisons, implementations, and applications, contrasting its use to other semantics employed heretofore for knowledge representation and reasoning.

The fact that rSM includes SMs and the virtue that it always exists and admits top-down querying is a novelty that may make us look anew at the use of 2-valued semantics of normal programs for knowledge representation and reasoning.

Having showed that the rSM semantics is equivalent to the SM semantics for programs without OLONs and without ICONS, it is proven that the SM semantics, for these specific "well-behaved" kinds of programs exhibits the Relevancy property as well as guarantee of Model Existence, and Cumulativity. This is, to the best of our knowledge, a new important result about the Stable Models semantics which has never before appeared in the literature.

Another avenue is using rSM, and its extension to default negation in heads, in contrast to SM based ones, as an alternative base semantics for updatable and self-evolving programs [1] so that model *inexistence* after an update may be prevented in a variety of cases. It may be of significance to Semantic Web reasoning, a context where programs may be being updated and combined dynamically from a variety of sources.

rSM implementation, in contrast to SM's ones, because of its relevance property can avoid the need to compute whole models and all models, and hence the need for complete groundness and the difficulties it begets for problem representation.

Finally, rSM has to be put the test of becoming a usable and useful tool. First of all, by persuading researchers that it is worth using, and worth pursuing its challenges.

Acknowledgements. P. Dell'Acqua, J. Alferes, F. Banti, C. Caleiro, M. Gelfond, M. Knorr, N. Leone, L. Soares, anonymous referees.

References

1. J. J. Alferes, A. Brogi, J. A. Leite, L. M. Pereira. Evolving Logic Programs. In S. Flesca et al. (eds.), 8th European Conf. on Logics in AI (JELIA'02), pp. 50–61, Springer, LNCS 2424, 2002.
2. M. Gelfond, V. Lifschitz. The stable model semantics for logic programming. In R. Kowalski, K. A. Bowen (eds.), 5th Intl. Logic Programming Conf., pp. 1070–1080. MIT Press, 1988.
3. J. Dix. A Classification Theory of Semantics of Normal Logic Programs: I. Strong Properties, II. Weak Properties. *Fundamenta Informaticae* XXII(3)*227—255, 257–288, 1995.
4. A. van Gelder, K. A. Ross, J. S. Schlipf. The Well-Founded Semantics for General Logic Programs. In J. ACM, 38(3):620–650, 1991.
5. F. Fages. Consistency of Clark's Completion and Existence of Stable Models. In Methods of Logic in Computer Science, vol. 1, pp. 51–60, 1994.
6. A. van Gelder 1993. The Alternating Fixpoint of Logic Programs with Negation. Journal of computer and system sciences 47:185–221.

Operational Semantics for DyLPs[*]

F. Banti[1], J.J. Alferes[1], and A. Brogi[2]

[1] CENTRIA, Universidade Nova de Lisboa, Portugal
[2] Dipartimento di Informatica, Università di Pisa, Italy

Abstract. Theoretical research has spent some years facing the problem of how to represent and provide semantics to updates of logic programs. This problem is relevant for addressing highly dynamic domains with logic programming techniques. Two of the most recent results are the definition of the refined stable and the well founded semantics for dynamic logic programs that extend stable model and well founded semantic to the dynamic case. We present here alternative, although equivalent, operational characterizations of these semantics by program transformations into normal logic programs. The transformations provide new insights on the computational complexity of these semantics, a way for better understanding the meaning of the update programs, and also a methodology for the implementation of these semantics. In this sense, the equivalence theorems in this paper constitute soundness an completeness results for the implementations of these semantics.

1 Introduction

In recent years considerable effort was devoted to explore the problem of how to update knowledge bases represented by logic programs (LPs) with new rules. This allows, for instance, to better use LPs for representing and reasoning with knowledge that evolves in time, as required in several fields of application. The LP updates framework has been used, for instance, as the base of the MINERVA agent architecture [14] and of the action description language EAPs [4].

Different semantics have been proposed [1, 2, 5, 6, 8, 15, 18, 19, 23] that assign meaning to arbitrary finite sequences $P_1, \ldots, P_m$ of logic programs. Such sequences are called *dynamic logic programs* (DyLPs), each program in them representing a supervenient state of the world. The different states can be seen as representing different time points, in which case P_1 is an initial knowledge base, and the other $P_i s$ are subsequent updates of the knowledge base. The different states can also be seen as knowledge coming from different sources that are (totally) ordered according to some precedence, or as different hierarchical instances where the subsequent programs represent more specific information. The role of the semantics of DyLPs is to employ the mutual relationships among different states to precisely determine the meaning of the combined program comprised of all individual programs at each state. Intuitively, one can add at the end of

---

[*] This work was supported by project POSI/40958/SRI/01, FLUX, and by the European Commission within the 6th Framework P. project Rewerse, no. 506779.

C. Bento, A. Cardoso, and G. Dias (Eds.): EPIA 2005, LNAI 3808, pp. 43–54, 2005.

the sequence, newer rules or rules with precedence (arising from newly acquired, more specific or preferred knowledge) leaving to the semantics the task of ensuring that these added rules are in force, and that previous or less specific rules are still valid (by inertia) only as far as possible, i.e. that they are kept as long as they are not rejected. A rule is rejected whenever it is in conflict with a newly added one (*causal rejection of rules*). Most of the semantics defined for DyLPs [1, 2, 5, 6, 8, 15] are based on such a concept of causal rejection.

With the exception of the semantics proposed in [5], these semantics are extensions of the stable model semantics [10] to DyLPs and are proved to coincide on large classes of programs [8, 11, 13]. In [1] the authors provide theoretical results which strongly suggest that the refined semantics [1] should be regarded as the proper stable model-like semantics for DyLPs based on causal rejection. In particular, it solves some unintuitive behaviour of the other semantics in what regards updates with cyclic rules.

As discussed in [5], though a stable model-like semantics is the most suitable option for several application domains[1] other domains exist, whose specificities require a different approach. In particular, domains with huge amount of distributed and heterogenous data require an approach to automated reasoning capable of quickly processing knowledge, and of dealing with inconsistent information even at the cost of losing some inference power. Such areas demand a different choice of basic semantics, such as the well founded semantics [9]. In [5] a well founded paraconsistent semantics for DyLPs (WFDy) is defined. The WFDy semantics is shown to be a skeptical approximation of the refined semantic defined in [1]. Moreover, it is always defined, even when the considered program is inconsistent, and its computational complexity is polynomial w.r.t. the number of rules of the program. For these reasons we believe that the refined and the well founded semantics for DyLPs are useful paradigms in the knowledge representation field and hence implementations for computing both semantics are in order.

The existing definitions of both semantics are purely declarative, a feature that provides several advantages, like the simplicity of such definitions and the related theorems. However, when facing computational problem like establishing computational complexity and programming implementations, a more operational approach would have several advantages. For providing an operational definition for extensions of normal LPs, a widely used technique is that of having a transformation of the original program into a normal logic program and then to prove equivalence results between the two semantics. In logic programs updates this methodology has been successfully used several times (see, for instance, [2, 8]). Once such program transformations have been established (and implemented), it is then an easy job to implement the corresponding semantics by applying existing software for computing the semantics of normal LPs, like DLV [7] or smodels [20] for the stable model semantics, or XSB-Prolog [22] for the well founded semantics. Following this direction, we provide two transfor-

---

[1] In particular, the stable model semantics has been shown to be a useful paradigm for modelling NP-complete problems.

mations of DyLPs into normal LPs (namely the *refined* and the *well founded transformation*), one for each semantics and provide equivalence results.

The shape of the transformations proposed for the refined and well founded semantics for DyLPs is quite different from the ones proposed for the other semantics (see for instance [2, 3, 12]). These differences are partially related to the different behavior of the considered semantics (none of the existing program transformation is sound and complete w.r.t. the refined and the well founded semantics) but they are also related to peculiar properties of the presented program transformations. One of such properties is the minimum size of the transformed program. Since the size of the transformed program significantly influences the cost of computing the semantics (especially in case of the stable model semantics), this topic is quite relevant. A drawback of the existing program transformations is that the size of the transformed program linearly depends on the size of the language times the number of performed updates. This means that, when the number of updates grows, the size of the transformed program grows in a way that linearly depends on the size of the language. This happens even when the updates are empty. On the contrary, in our approach the size of the transformed programs has an upper bound that does not depend on the number of updates, but solely (and linearly) on the number of rules and the size of the original language (see Theorems 2 and 4).

Prototypical implementations that use the theoretical background of this paper are available at http://centria.di.fct.unl.pt/~banti/Implementation.htm. These implementations take advantage of DLV, smodels, and XSB-Prolog systems to compute the semantics of the transformed programs.

Due to their simplicity, the proposed transformations are also interesting beyond the scope of implementation. They give new insights on how the rejection mechanism works and how it creates new dependencies among rules. The transformed programs provide an alternative, more immediate description of the behaviour of the updated program.

The rest of the paper is structured as follows. Section 2 establishes notation and provides some background and the formal definition of the refined and well founded semantics for DyLPs. Section 3 illustrates the refined transformation, describes some of its properties and makes comparisons to related transformations for other semantics. The well founded transformation is defined and studied in Section 4 . Finally, Section 5 draws conclusions and mentions some future developments. For lack of space, proofs cannot be presented here, but they can be obtained from the authors.

2   Background: Concepts and Notation

In this section we briefly recall the syntax of DyLPs, and the refined and well founded semantics defined, respectively, in [1] and [5].

To represent negative information in logic programs and their updates, DyLP uses generalized logic programs (GLPs) [16], which allow for default negation *not* A not only in the premises of rules but also in their heads. A language $\mathcal{L}$ is any set literals of the form A or *not* A such that $A \in \mathcal{L}$ iff *not* $A \in \mathcal{L}$. A GLP defined over a propositional language $\mathcal{L}$ is a (possibly infinite) set of ground rules of the form $L_0 \leftarrow L_1, \ldots, L_n$, where each L_i is a literal in $\mathcal{L}$, i.e., either a propositional atom A in $\mathcal{L}$ or the default negation *not* A of a propositional atom A in $\mathcal{L}$. We say that A is the *default complement* of *not* A and viceversa. With a slight abuse of notation, we denote by *not* L the default complement of L (hence if L is the *not* A, then *not* L is the atom A). Given a rule τ as above, by $hd(\tau)$ we mean L_0 and by $B(\tau)$ we mean $\{L_1, \ldots, L_n\}$.

In the sequel an *interpretation* is simply a set of literals of $\mathcal{L}$. A literal L is *true* (resp. *false*) in I iff $L \in I$ (resp. *not* $L \in I$) and *undefined* in I iff $\{L, not\ L\} \cap I = \{\}$. A conjunction (or set) of literals C is true (resp. false) in I iff $C \subseteq I$ (resp. $\exists\ L \in C$ such that L is false in I). We say that I is *consistent* iff $\forall\ A \in \mathcal{L}$ *at most* one of A and *not* A belongs to I, otherwise we say I is *paraconsistent*. We say that I is *2-valued* iff for each atom $A \in \mathcal{L}$ *exactly* one of A and *not* A belongs to I.

A *dynamic logic program* with length n over a language $\mathcal{L}$ is a finite sequence $P_1, \ldots, P_n$ (also denoted $\mathcal{P}$, where the P_is are GLPs indexed by $1, \ldots, n$), where all the P_is are defined over $\mathcal{L}$. Intuitively, such a sequence may be viewed as the result of, starting with program P_1, updating it with program P_2, $\ldots$, and updating it with program P_n. For this reason we call the singles P_is *updates*. Let P_j and P_i be two updates of $\mathcal{P}$. We say that P_j is *more recent* than P_i iff $i < j$. We use $\rho(\mathcal{P})$ to denote the multiset of all rules appearing in the programs $P_1, ..., P_n$.

The *refined stable model semantics* for DyLPs is defined in [1] by assigning to each DyLP a set of stable models. The basic idea of the semantics is that, if a later rule τ has a true body, then former rules in conflict with τ should be *rejected*. Moreover, any atom A for which there is no rule with true body in any update, is considered false by default. The semantics is then defined by a fixpoint equation that, given an interpretation I, tests whether I has exactly the consequences obtained after removing from the multiset $\rho(\mathcal{P})$ all the rules rejected given I, and imposing all the default assumptions given I. Formally, let:

$$Default(\mathcal{P}, I) = \{not\ A \mid \nexists\ A \leftarrow body \in \rho(\mathcal{P}) \wedge body \subseteq I\}$$
$$Rej^S(\mathcal{P}, I) = \{\tau \mid \tau \in P_i \mid \exists\ \eta \in P_j\ i \le j,\ \tau \bowtie \eta \wedge\ B(\eta) \subseteq I\}$$

where $\tau \bowtie \eta$ means that τ and η are conflicting rules, i.e. the head of τ is the default complement of the head of η.

Definition 1. *Let $\mathcal{P}$ be any DyLP of length n, $i \le n$ over language $\mathcal{L}$ and M a two valued interpretation and let $\mathcal{P}^i$ be the prefix of $\mathcal{P}$ with length i. Then M is a refined stable model of $\mathcal{P}$, at state i, iff M is a fixpoint of $\Gamma_{\mathcal{P}^i}^S$:*

$$\Gamma_{\mathcal{P}^i}^S(M) = least\left(\rho\left(\mathcal{P}^i\right) \setminus Rej^S(\mathcal{P}^i, M) \cup Default(\mathcal{P}^i, M)\right)$$

where $least(P)$ denotes the least Herbrand model of the definite program obtained by considering each negative literal not A in P as a new atom[2].

---

[2] Whenever clear from the context, we omit the $\mathcal{P}$ in the above defined operators.

The definition of dynamic stable models of DyLPs [2] is as the one above, but where the $i \leq j$ in the rejection operator is replaced by $i < j$. I.e., if we denote this other rejection operator by $Rej(\mathcal{P}, I)$, and define $\Gamma_{\mathcal{P}}(I)$ by replacing in $\Gamma_{\mathcal{P}}^{S}$ Rej^{S} by Rej, then the stable models of $\mathcal{P}$ are the interpretations I such that $I = \Gamma_{\mathcal{P}}(I)$.

The *well founded semantics for DyLPs* is defined through the two operators Γ and Γ^{S}. We use the notation $\Gamma\Gamma^{S}$ to denote the operator obtained by first applying Γ^{S} and then Γ. The well founded model of a program is defined as the least fix point of such operator. Formally:

Definition 2. *The well founded model $WFDy(\mathcal{P})$ of a DyLP $\mathcal{P}$ at state i is the (set inclusion) least fixpoint of $\Gamma_{\mathcal{P}^{i}}\Gamma_{\mathcal{P}^{i}}^{S}$ where $\mathcal{P}^{i}$ is the prefix of $\mathcal{P}$ with length i.*

Since the operators Γ and Γ^{S} are anti-monotone (see [5]) the composite operator $\Gamma\Gamma^{S}$ is monotone and, as it follows from the Tarski-Knaster Theorem [21], it always has a least fixpoint. In other words, $WFDy$ is uniquely defined for every DyLP. Moreover, $WFDy(\mathcal{P})$ can be obtained by (transfinitely) iterating $\Gamma\Gamma^{S}$, starting from the empty interpretation. As already mentioned, the refined and well founded semantics for DyLPs are strongly related. In particular, they share analogous connections to the ones shared by the stable model and the well founded semantics of normal LPs, as we see from the following proposition.

Proposition 1. *Let M be any refined stable model of $\mathcal{P}$. The well founded model $WFDy(\mathcal{P})$ is a subset of M. Moreover, if $WFDy(\mathcal{P})$ is a 2-valued interpretation, it coincides with the unique refined stable model of $\mathcal{P}$.*

This property does not hold if, instead of the refined semantics, we consider any of the other semantics based on causal rejection [2, 6, 8, 15].

Example 1. Let $\mathcal{P}$: P_1, P_2, P_3 be the as follows:

$$P_1 : a \leftarrow b. \qquad P_2 : b. \quad c. \qquad P_3 : not\ a \leftarrow c.$$

The well founded model of $\mathcal{P}$ is $M = \{b, c, not\ a\}$. Moreover, M is a two valued interpretation and so, by Proposition 1, M is also the unique refined model.

3   A Program Transformation for the Refined Semantics

The refined transformation defined in this section turns a DyLP $\mathcal{P}$ in the language $\mathcal{L}$ into a normal logic program $\mathcal{P}^{R}$ (called the *refined transformational equivalent of $\mathcal{P}$*) in an extended language. We provide herein a formal procedure to obtain the transformational equivalent of a given DyLP.

Let $\mathcal{L}$ be a language. By $\mathcal{L}^{R}$ we denote the language whose elements are either atoms of $\mathcal{L}$, or atoms of one of the following forms: u, A^{-}, $rej(A, i)$, $rej(A^{-}, i)$, where i is a natural number, A is any atom of $\mathcal{L}$ and no one of the atoms above belongs to $\mathcal{L}$. Intuitively, A^{-} stands for "A is false", while $rej(A, i)$ (resp. $rej(A^{-}, i)$), stands for: "all the rules with head A (resp. *not* A) in the update P_i are rejected". For every literal L, if L is an atom A, then $\overline{L}$ denotes A itself, while if L is a negative literal *not A* then $\overline{L}$ denotes A^-. Finally, u is a new atom not belonging to $\mathcal{L}$ which is used for expressing integrity constraints of the form $u \leftarrow not\ u, L_1, \ldots, L_k$ (which has the effect of removing all stable models containing $L_1, \ldots, L_k$).

Definition 3. *Let $\mathcal{P}$ be a Dynamic Logic Program whose language is $\mathcal{L}$. By the refined transformational equivalent of $\mathcal{P}$, denoted $\mathcal{P}^R$, we mean the normal program $P_1^R \cup \ldots \cup P_n^R$ in the extended language $\mathcal{L}^R$, where each P_i^R exactly consists of the following rules:*

Default assumptions. *For each atom A of $\mathcal{L}$ appearing in P_i, and not appearing in any other P_j, $j \leq i$ a rule:*
$$A^- \leftarrow not\ rej(A^-, 0)$$

Rewritten rules. *For each rule $L \leftarrow body$ in P_i, a rule:*
$$\overline{L} \leftarrow \overline{body},\ not\ rej(\overline{L}, i)$$

Rejection rules. *For each rule $L \leftarrow body$ in P_i, a rule:*
$$rej(\overline{not\ L}, j) \leftarrow \overline{body}$$

where $j \leq i$ is either the largest index such that P_j has a rule with head not L or. If no such P_j exists, and L is a positive literals, then $j = 0$, otherwise this rule is not part of P_i^R. Moreover, for each rule $L \leftarrow body$ in P_i, a rule:
$$rej(\overline{L}, j) \leftarrow rej(\overline{L}, i)$$

where $j < i$ is the largest index such that P_j also contains a rule $L \leftarrow body$. If no such P_j exists, and L is a negative literal, then $j = 0$, otherwise this rule is not part of P_i^R.

Totality constraints. *For each pair of conflicting rules in P_i, with head A and not A, the constraint:*
$$u \leftarrow not\ u,\ not\ A,\ not\ A^-$$

Let us briefly explain the intuition and the role for each of these rules. The *default assumptions* specify that a literal of the form A^- is true (i.e. A is false) unless this initial assumption is rejected. The *rewritten rules* are basically the original rules of the sequence of programs with an extra condition in their body that specifies that in order to derive conclusions, the considered rule must not be rejected. Note that, both in the head and in the body of a rule, the negative literals of the form *not A* are replaced by the corresponding atoms of the form A^-. The role of *rejection rules* is to specify whether the rules with a given head in a given state are rejected or not. Such a rule may have two possible forms. Let $L \leftarrow body$ be a rule in P_i. The rule of the form $rej(\overline{L}, j) \leftarrow \overline{body}$ specifies that all the rules with head *not L* in the most recent update P_j with $j \leq i$ must be rejected. The rules of the form $rej(\overline{L}, j) \leftarrow rej(\overline{L}, i)$ "propagate" the rejection to the updates below P_j. Finally, *totality constraints* assure that, for each literal A, at least one of the atoms A, A^- belongs to the model. This is done to guarantee that the models of transformed program are indeed two valued.

The role of the atoms of the extended language $\mathcal{L}^R$ that do not belong to the original language $\mathcal{L}$ is merely auxiliary, as we see from the following theorem. Let $\mathcal{P}$ be any Dynamic Logic Program and P_i and update of $\mathcal{P}$. We use $\rho(\mathcal{P})^{Ri} = P_0^R \cup \ldots \cup P_i^R$.

Theorem 1. *Let $\mathcal{P}$ be any Dynamic Logic Program in the language $\mathcal{L}$, P_i an update of $\mathcal{P}$, and let $\rho(\mathcal{P})^{Ri}$ be as above. Let M be any interpretation over $\mathcal{L}$. Then M is a refined stable model of $\mathcal{P}$ at P_i iff there exists a two valued interpretation M^R such that M^R is a stable model of $\rho(\mathcal{P})^{Ri}$ and $M \equiv_{\mathcal{L}} M^R$. Moreover, M and M^R satisfy the following conditions:*

$$A \in M \Leftrightarrow A \in M^R \qquad\qquad not\ A \in M \Leftrightarrow A^- \in M^R$$
$$not\ A \in Default(\mathcal{P}^i, M)) \Leftrightarrow rej(A^-, 0) \notin M^R$$
$$\tau \in rej^S(M, \mathcal{P}^i) \wedge \tau \in P_i \Leftrightarrow rej(\overline{hd(\tau)}, i) \in M^R$$

For illustration, we present an example of the computation of the refined transformational equivalent of a DyLP.

Example 2. Let $\mathcal{P}: P_1$, P_2 be the as in example 1. The transformational equivalent of $\mathcal{P}$ is the following sequence P_1^R, P_1^R, P_2^R:

$$P_1^R: \quad a^- \leftarrow not\ rej(a^-, 0). \qquad b^- \leftarrow not\ rej(b^-, 0).$$
$$a \leftarrow b,\ not\ rej(a, 1). \qquad rej(a^-, 0) \leftarrow b.$$
$$P_2^R \quad c^- \leftarrow not\ rej(c^-, 0).$$
$$rej(b^-, 0). \qquad\qquad rej(c^-, 0).$$
$$b \leftarrow not\ rej(b, 2). \qquad c \leftarrow not\ rej(c, 2).$$
$$P_3^R: \quad a^- \leftarrow c,\ not\ rej(a, 3). \quad rej(a, 1) \leftarrow c.$$

For computing the refined semantics of $\mathcal{P}$ at P_2 we just have to compute the stable model semantics of the program $P_1^R \cup P_2^R$. This program has a single stable model M^R consisting of the following set[3].

$$M^R = \{a^-,\ b,\ c, rej(a,1),\ rej(a^-,0),\ rej(b^-,0),\ rej(c^-,0)\}$$

We conclude that, $\mathcal{P}$ has $M = \{b, c\}$ as the unique refined model. To compute the refined semantics of $\mathcal{P}$ we have to compute, instead, the stable model semantics of the program $P^R = P_1^R \cup P_2^R \cup P_3^R$. Let us briefly examine the transformed program P^R and see how it clarifies the meaning of the related DyLP. Since there exist no rules with head $rej(b, 2)$ and $rej(c, 2)$, we immediately infer b and c. Then we also infer $rej(a, 0)$, $rej(b, 0)$ and $rej(c, 0)$, and so that all the default assumptions are rejected. The last rule of P_3^R implies $rej(a, 1)$, thus the rule $a \leftarrow b$ in P_1 is rejected and we do not infer a. In fact, we infer a^- by the first rule of P_3^R. Hence, the program has the single stable model M^R which means $\mathcal{P}$ as the unique refined model $\{b, c\}$.

To compute the refined semantics of a given DyLP $P_1, \ldots, P_n$ at a given state, it is sufficient to compute its refined transformational equivalent $P_1^R, \ldots P_n^R$, then

---

[3] As usual in the stable model semantics, hereafter we omit the negative literals.

to compute the stable model semantics of the normal logic program $\rho(\mathcal{P})^{Ri}$ and, finally, to consider only those literals that belong to the original language of the program. A feature of the transformations in this papers, is that of being incremental i.e., whenever a new update P_{n+1} is received, the transformational equivalent of the obtained DyLP is equal to the union of P_{n+1}^R and the refined transformational equivalent of the original DyLP. The efficiency of the implementation relies largely on the size of the transformed program compared to the size of the original one. We present here a theoretical result that provides an upper bound for the number of clauses of the refined transformational equivalent of a DyLP.

Theorem 2. *Let* $\mathcal{P} = P_1, \ldots P_m$ *be any finite ground DyLP in the language* $\mathcal{L}$ *and let* $\rho(\mathcal{P})^{Rn}$ *be the set of all the rules appearing in the refined transformational equivalent of* $\mathcal{P}$. *Moreover, let* m *be the number of clauses in* $\rho(\mathcal{P})$ *and* l *be the cardinality of* $\mathcal{L}^4$. *Then, the program* $\rho(\mathcal{P})^{Rn}$ *consists of at most* $2m + l$ *rules.*

The problem of satisfiability under the stable model semantics (i.e. to find a stable model of a given program) is known to be NP-Complete, while the inference problem (i.e. to determine if a given proposition is true in all the stable models of a program) is co-NP-Complete [17]. Hence, from the fact that DyLPs extends the class of normal LPs and from Theorems 1 and 2 it immediately follows that such problems are still NP-Complete and co-NP-Complete also under the refined semantics for DyLPs. The size of the refined transformational equivalent of a DyLP depends linearly and solely on the size of the program and of the language. It has an upper bound which does not depend on the number of updates performed. Thus, we gain the possibility of performing several updates of our knowledge base without losing too much on efficiency.

The refined transformation presents some similarities with the one presented in [2] and [8]. The three transformations use new atoms to represent rejection of rules. A fundamental difference between these transformations is that they are not semantically equivalent. The transformation in [2] is defined for implementing the *dynamic stable model semantics of DyLPs* of [2], while the one in [8] implements the *Update semantics* [8]. These semantics are not equivalent to the refined one, which was, in fact, introduced for solving some counterintuitive behaviours of the previously existing semantics for DyLPs (cf. [1]). In particular, it is proved in [1] that every refined stable model is also a dynamic stable model and an update stable model but the opposite is not always true. Moreover, the size of the transformation defined in [2] is $2m + l(n + 2)$ where l and m are as in Theorem 2 and n is the number of updates of the considered DyLP. Hence, a single (even empty or single rule) update add at least l rules to the transformed program. A similar result also holds when considering the transformation of [8] (here the size of the transformed program is $2m + nl$). The size of the refined transformational equivalent is instead independent from n. Hence, for DyLPs with many updates, the transformed programs of these transformation become

---

^{4} Since $\mathcal{L}$ contains the positive and the negative literals, l is equal to two times the number of predicates appearing in $\mathcal{P}$.

considerably larger then the ones of the refined transformation, especially in cases where each of these updates has few rules.

Moreover, the transformations of [2] and [8] approach the problem of computing the semantics at different states by introducing an extra index on the body of the transformed program. On the contrary, when using the refined transformation, it is sufficient to ignore the rules of the transformed program that are related to the updates after P_i. Apart from computational aspect, the use of extra indexes and the proliferation of rules make these semantics unsuitable for the purpose of understanding the behaviour of the updated program.

4 Transformational Well Founded Semantics

The well founded transformation turns a given DyLP $\mathcal{P}$ in the language $\mathcal{L}$ into a normal logic program $\mathcal{P}^{TW}$ in an extended language $\mathcal{L}^W$ called the *well founded transformational equivalent of* $\mathcal{P}$.

Let $\mathcal{L}$ be a language. By $\mathcal{L}^W$ we denote the language whose atoms are either atoms of $\mathcal{L}$, or are atoms of one of the following forms: A^S A^{-S}, $rej(A, i)$, $rej(A^S, i)$, $rej(A^-, i)$, and $rej(A^{-S}, i)$, where i is a natural number, A is any atom of $\mathcal{L}$ and no one of the atoms above belongs to $\mathcal{L}$. Given a conjunction of literals C, use the notation C^S for the conjunction obtained by replacing any occurrence of an atom A in C with A^S.

Definition 4. *Let $\mathcal{P}$ be a Dynamic Logic Program on the language $\mathcal{L}$. By the well founded transformational equivalent of $\mathcal{P}$, denoted $\mathcal{P}^{TW}$, we mean the normal program $P_1^W \cup \ldots \cup P_n^W$ in the extended language $\mathcal{L}^W$, where each P_i exactly consists of the following rules:*

Default assumptions. *For each atom A of $\mathcal{L}$ appearing in P_i, and not appearing in any other P_j, $j \leq i$ the rules:*
$$A^- \leftarrow not\ rej(A^{-S}, 0) \qquad A^{-S} \leftarrow not\ rej(A^-, 0)$$

Rewritten rules. *For each rule $L \leftarrow body$ in P_i, the rules:*
$$\overline{L} \leftarrow \overline{body},\ not\ rej(\overline{L}^S, i) \qquad \overline{L}^S \leftarrow \overline{body}^S,\ not\ rej(\overline{L}, i)$$

Rejection rules. *For each rule $L \leftarrow body$ in P_i, a rule:*
$$rej(\overline{not\ L}, j) \leftarrow \overline{body}$$

where $j < i$ is the largest index such that P_j has a rule with head not L. If no such P_j exists, and L is a positive literals, then $j = 0$, otherwise this rule is not part of P_i^W.

Moreover, for each rule $L \leftarrow body$ in P_i, a rule:
$$rej(\overline{not\ L}^S, k) \leftarrow \overline{body}^S.$$

where $k \leq i$ is the largest index such that P_k has a rule with head not L. If no such P_j exists, and L is a positive literals, then $j = 0$, otherwise this rule is not part of P_i^W.

Finally, for each rule $L \leftarrow body$ in P_i, the rules:

$$rej(\overline{L}^S, j) \leftarrow rej(\overline{L}^S, i) \qquad rej(\overline{L}, j) \leftarrow rej(\overline{L}, i)$$

where $j < i$ is the largest index such that P_j also contains a rule $L \leftarrow body$. If no such P_j exists, and L is a negative literal, then $j = 0$, otherwise these rules are not part of P_i^W.

As the reader can see, the program transformation above resembles the one of Definition 3. The main difference is that the transformation of Definition 4 duplicates the language and the rules. This is done for simulating the alternate application of two different operators, Γ and Γ^S used in the definition of $WFDy$. The difference between these two operators is on the rejection strategies: the Γ^S operator allows rejection of rules in the same state, while the Γ operator does not. In the transformation above this difference is captured by the definition of the rejection rules. Let $L \leftarrow body$ be a rule in the update P_i. In the rules of the form $rej(\overline{L}, j) \leftarrow \overline{body}^S$ and $rej(\overline{L}^S, j) \leftarrow \overline{body}^S$, j is *less* than i, in the first case, and *less or equal* than i in the second one. A second difference is the absence of the *totality constraints*. This is not surprising since the well founded model is not necessarily a two valued interpretation. Note however, that the introduction of any rule of the form $u \leftarrow not\ u, body$ would not change the semantics. As for the refined transformation, the atoms of the extended language $\mathcal{L}^W$ that do not belong to the original language $\mathcal{L}$ are merely auxiliary. Let $\mathcal{P}$ be any Dynamic Logic Program, P_i and update of $\mathcal{P}$, and let $\rho(\mathcal{P})^{Wi} = P_0^W \cup \ldots \cup P_i^W$.

Theorem 3. *Let $\mathcal{P}$ be any Dynamic Logic Program in the language $\mathcal{L}$, P_i and update of $\mathcal{P}$, and let $\rho(\mathcal{P})^{Wi}$ be as above. Moreover, Let W_i be the well founded model of the normal logic program $\rho(\mathcal{P})^{Wi}$ and $WFDy(\mathcal{P}^i)$ be the well found model of $\mathcal{P}$ at P_i. Then $WFDy(\mathcal{P}^i) = \{A \mid\ \in W_i\} \cup \{not\ A \mid A^- \in W_i\}$.*

To compute the well founded semantics of a given DyLP $P_1, \ldots, P_n$ at a given state, it is hence sufficient to compute its well founded transformational equivalent $P_1^W, \ldots P_n^W$, then to compute the well founded model of the normal logic program $\rho(\mathcal{P})^{Wn}$ and, finally, to consider only those literals that belong to the original language of the program.

We present here a result analogous that of Theorem 2 that provides an upper bound to the size of the well founded transformational equivalent.

Theorem 4. *Let $\mathcal{P} : P_1, \ldots P_m$ be any finite ground DyLP in the language $\mathcal{L}$ and let $\rho(\mathcal{P})^{Wn}$ be the set of all the rules appearing in the transformational equivalent of $\mathcal{P}$. Moreover, let m be the number of clauses in $\rho(\mathcal{P})$ and l be the cardinality of $\mathcal{L}$. Then, the program $\rho(\mathcal{P})^{Wn}$ consists of at most $5m + l$ rules.*

The problem of computing the well-founded model of a normal LP has a polynomial complexity [9]. Hence, from Theorems 3 and 4, it follows that such a problem is polynomial also under the well founded semantics for DyLPs.

Other program transformations for the computation of a well founded-like semantics for DyLPs (see [2, 3, 12]), do not compute the well founded semantics of DyLPs, as shown in [5]. Moreover, they suffer from the same drawbacks on the size of the transformed program that have been discussed in Section 3.

5   Concluding Remarks and Future Works

Dynamic Logic Programs is a framework for representing knowledge that evolves with time. The purpose of this paper was to illustrate operational characterizations of the refined and well founded semantics for DyLPs defined by program transformations that convert a DyLP into a semantically equivalent normal LP. This directly provides a way to implement these semantics, by relying on software like DLV, smodels (for the refined semantics) and XSB-Prolog (for the well founded one). Moreover, we have shown that the size of the transformed programs is linearly bound by the size of the original program. Moreover, especially in case of the refined semantics, the transformed program is usually readable and may help to better understand the meaning of the considered DyLP.

The close relationships between the two semantics rise the question whether an approach to the implementation based on a *single* program transformation would have been possible instead. Indeed, the answer is positive. The program transformation of Definition 4 for computing the $WFDy$ semantics can be adapted for the refined semantics. This is done by adding proper integrity constraints of the form $u \leftarrow not\ u, body$ to the transformed program. Recall that, as noted in section 4, the addition of such constraints does not change the well founded model of the program, and hence the new program transformation would still compute the $WFDy$ semantics.

We opted for presenting two separate transformations for a matter of optimization. Indeed, the size of the transformed program after the transformation of Definition 3 is less than half the size that the unique transformation would require. Moreover, the transformed program can be used also for "reading" a DyLP as a normal logic program, a task for which a program transformation with many more auxiliary rules and predicates would not be suitable.

As mentioned in the introduction there are several works on possible usage of DyLPs. Other possible usages can be found in any application areas where evolution and reactivity are a primary issue. We believe it is the time for the research on DyLPs to realize practical applications of the framework, to provide implementations for such applications and face real world problems. One of the most obvious things to do is to transform the existing prototypical implementation into a real system and test its performance. In this perspective the paper presented here is a, still preliminary, but fundamental step.

References

1. J. J. Alferes, F. Banti, A. Brogi, and J. A. Leite. The refined extension principle for semantics of dynamic logic programming. *Studia Logica*, 79(1), 2005.
2. J. J. Alferes, J. A. Leite, L. M. Pereira, H. Przymusinska, and T. C. Przymusinski. Dynamic updates of non-monotonic knowledge bases. *The Journal of Logic Programming*, 45(1–3):43–70, 2000. A preliminary version appeared in KR'98.
3. J. J. Alferes, L. M. Pereira, H. Przymusinska, and T. Przymusinski. LUPS: A language for updating logic programs. *Artificial Intelligence*, 132(1 & 2), 2002.

4. J.J. Alferes, F. Banti, and A. Brogi. From logic programs updates to action description updates. In *CLIMA V*, 2004.
5. F. Banti, J. J. Alferes, and A. Brogi. The well founded semantics for dynamic logic programs. In Christian Lemaître, editor, *Proceedings of the 9th Ibero-American Conference on Artificial Intelligence (IBERAMIA-9)*, LNAI, 2004.
6. F. Buccafurri, W. Faber, and N. Leone. Disjunctive logic programs with inheritance. In D. De Schreye, editor, *Proceedings of the 1999 International Conference on Logic Programming (ICLP-99)*, Cambridge, November 1999. MIT Press.
7. DLV. The DLV project - a disjunctive datalog system (and more), 2000. Available at http://www.dbai.tuwien.ac.at/proj/dlv/.
8. T. Eiter, M. Fink, G. Sabbatini, and H. Tompits. On properties of update sequences based on causal rejection. *Theory and Practice of Logic Programming*, 2002.
9. A. Van Gelder, K. A. Ross, and J. S. Schlipf. The well-founded semantics for general logic programs. *Journal of the ACM*, 38(3):620–650, 1991.
10. M. Gelfond and V. Lifschitz. The stable model semantics for logic programming. In R. Kowalski and K. A. Bowen, editors, *5th International Conference on Logic Programming*, pages 1070–1080. MIT Press, 1988.
11. M. Homola. Dynamic logic programming: Various semantics are equal on acyclic programs. In J. Leite and P. Torroni, editors, *5th Int. Ws. On Computational Logic In Multi-Agent Systems (CLIMA V)*. Pre-Proceedings, 2004. ISBN: 972-9119-37-6.
12. J. A. Leite. Logic program updates. Master's thesis, Dept. de Informática, Faculdade de Ciências e Tecnologia, Universidade Nova de Lisboa, November 1997.
13. J. A. Leite. *Evolving Knowledge Bases*, volume 81 of *Frontiers in Artificial Intelligence and Applications*. IOS Press, 2003.
14. J. A. Leite, J. J. Alferes, and L. M. Pereira. Minerva - a dynamic logic programming agent architecture. In J. J. Meyer and M. Tambe, editors, *Intelligent Agents VIII — Agent Theories, Architectures, and Languages*, volume 2333 of *LNAI*, pages 141–157. Springer-Verlag, 2002.
15. J. A. Leite and L. M. Pereira. Iterated logic program updates. In J. Jaffar, editor, *Proceedings of the 1998 Joint International Conference and Symposium on Logic Programming (JICSLP-98)*, pages 265–278, Cambridge, 1998. MIT Press.
16. V. Lifschitz and T. Woo. Answer sets in general non-monotonic reasoning (preliminary report). In B. Nebel, C. Rich, and W. Swartout, editors, *Proceedings of the 3th International Conference on Principles of Knowledge Representation and Reasoning (KR-92)*. Morgan-Kaufmann, 1992.
17. W. Marek and M. Truszczynski. Autoepistemic logics. *Journal of the ACM*, 38(3):588–619, 1991.
18. C. Sakama and K. Inoue. Updating extended logic programs through abduction. In M. Gelfond, N. Leone, and G. Pfeifer, editors, *Proceedings of the 5th International Conference on Logic Programming and Nonmonotonic Reasoning (LPNMR-99)*, volume 1730 of *LNAI*, pages 147–161, Berlin, 1999. Springer.
19. J. Sefranek. A kripkean semantics for dynamic logic programming. In *Logic for Programming and Automated Reasoning(LPAR'2000)*. Springer Verlag, LNAI, 2000.
20. SMODELS. The SMODELS system, 2000. Available at http://www.tcs.hut.fi/Software/smodels/.
21. A. Tarski. A lattice-theoretic fixpoint theorem and its applications. *Pacific Journal of Mathematics*, 5:285–309, 1955.
22. XSB-Prolog. The XSB logic programming system, version 2.6, 2003. xsb.sourceforge.net.
23. Y. Zhang and N. Y. Foo. Updating logic programs. In Henri Prade, editor, *Proceedings of the 13th European Conference on Artificial Intelligence (ECAI-98)*, 1998.

Case Retrieval Nets for Heuristic Lexicalization in Natural Language Generation

Raquel Hervás and Pablo Gervás

Departamento de Sistemas Informáticos y Programación,
Universidad Complutense de Madrid, Spain
raquelhb@fdi.ucm.es, pgervas@sip.ucm.es

Abstract. In this paper we discuss the use of Case Retrieval Nets, a particular memory model for implementing case-base reasoning solutions, for implementing a heuristic lexicalisation module within a natural language generation application. We describe a text generator for fairy tales implemented using a generic architecture, and we present examples of how the Case Retrieval Net solves the Lexicalization task.

1 Introduction

Natural Language Generation (NLG) is divided into various specific tasks [1], each one of them operating at a different level of linguistic representation (discourse, semantics, lexical,...). NLG can be applied in domains where communication goals and features of generated texts are diverse, from transcription into natural language of numerical contents [2] to literary texts generation [3].

Each kind of NLG application may need a different division into modules [4]. Given a specific organization (or *architecture*) of the system, it may occur that diverse classes of application require different solutions when facing each of the specific tasks involved in the generation process. For a particular task, in processes where a quick answer is required (for instance, in interactive communication between user and machine in real time) it can be useful to use simple solutions based on heuristics, that provide quick answers even if the achieved quality is poor. On the other hand, in situations where long texts of high quality are needed with no constraints on response time it would be better to draw on knowledge-based techniques that exhaustively consider more possibilities.

The present paper proposes a case-based approach to decide which words should be used to pick out or describe particular domain concepts or entities in the generated text. The idea is that people do not create new words each time they need to express an idea not used before, but rather they appeal to the lexicon they have acquired throughout time looking for the best way to express the new idea, always taking into account existing relations between the elements of the lexicon they already know.

The paper starts with a revision of the Case-Based Reasoning and Lexicalization fields. Then we expose the fairy tale text generator where the work presented in this paper is implemented, and we consider the performance of the CBR module. Finally, the obtained results and future research lines are discussed.

C. Bento, A. Cardoso, and G. Dias (Eds.): EPIA 2005, LNAI 3808, pp. 55–66, 2005.

2 Lexicalization and Case Based Reasoning

Lexicalization is the process of deciding which specific words and phrases should be chosen to express the domain concepts and relations which appear in the messages [1]. The most common model of lexicalisation is one where the lexicalisation module converts an input graph whose primitives are domain concepts and relations into an output graph whose primitives are words and syntactic relations. Lexicalization researchers have developed powerful graph-rewriting algorithms which use general "dictionaries" that relate domain primitives and linguistic primitives. Graph-rewriting lexical choice is most useful in multilingual generation, when the same conceptual content must be expressed in different languages. The technique handles quite naturally some kinds of lexical divergences between languages. This scheme can be valid for most applications where the domain is restricted enough in order that direct correspondence between the content and the words to express it is not a disadvantage. In general, thinking on more expressive and versatile generators, this model requires some improvement. Cahill [5] differentiates between "lexicalization" and "lexical choice". The first term is taken to indicate a broader meaning of the conversion of something to lexical items, while the second is used in a narrower sense to mean deciding between lexical alternatives representing the same propositional content. Stede [6] proposes a more flexible way of attaching lexical items to configurations of concepts and roles, using a lexical option finder that determines the set of content words that cover pieces of the message to be expressed. These items may vary in semantic specificity and in connotation, also including synonyms and nearsynonyms. From this set, the subsequent steps of the generation process can select the most preferred subset for expressing the message.

Machine learning techniques have been shown to significantly reduce the knowledge engineering effort for building large scale natural language processing (NLP) systems: they offer an automatic means for acquiring robust solutions for a host of lexical and structural disambiguation problems. A good review of how they have been applied in the past to specifical NLP tasks is available in [7]. Among the learning algorithms that have been used successfully for natural language learning tasks are case based learning methods where the natural language system processes a text by retrieving stored examples that describe how similar texts were handled in the past. Case based approaches have been applied to stress acquisition [8], word sense disambiguation [9] and concept extraction [10], among others.

Case-based Reasoning (CBR) [11] is a problem solving paradigm that uses the specific knowledge of previously experienced problem situations. Each problem is considered as a domain case, and a new problem is solved by retrieving the most similar case or cases, reusing the information and knowledge in that cases to solve the problem, revising the proposed solution, and retaining the parts of this experience likely to be useful for future problem solving. General knowledge, understood as general domain-dependent knowledge, usually plays a part in this cycle by supporting the CBR processes.

Case Retrieval Nets (CRNs) [12] are a memory model developed to improve the efficiency of the retrieval tasks of the CBR cycle. They are based on the idea that humans are able to solve problems without performing an intensive search process, but they often start from the given description, consider the neighbourhood, and extend the scope of considered objects if required.

As its name indicates, CRNs organize the case base as a net. The most fundamental item in the context of the CRNs are so-called Information Entities (IEs). These represent any basic knowledge item in the form of an attribute-value pair. A case then consist of a set of such IEs, and the case base is a net with nodes for the entities observed in the domain and additional nodes denoting the particular cases. IE nodes may be connected by similarity arcs, and a case node is reachable from its constituting IE nodes via relevance arcs. Different degrees of similarity and relevance are expressed by varying arcs weights. Given this structure, case retrieval is carried out by activating the IEs given in the query case, propagating this activation according to similarity through the net of IE nodes, and collecting the achieved activation in the associated case nodes.

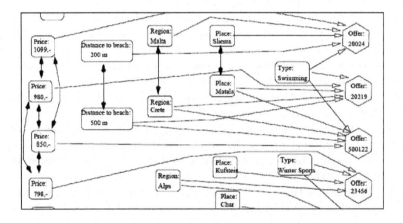

Fig. 1. An Example Case Retrieval Net in the domain of travel agencies

An example of a Case Retrieval Net applied to the domain of travel agencies is shown in Figure 1. Rectangles represent entity nodes, with their corresponding attribute-value pairs. Hexagons are case nodes, with the description that identifies them univocally. Entity nodes are related among themselves with arcs with black arrowheads, and they are related with cases by arcs with white arrowheads. Weights associated to arcs are not represented in the figure, and arcs with weight zero are ommitted.

Case Retrieval Nets present the following important features:

- CRNs can handle partially specified queries without loss of efficiency, in contrast to most case retrieval techniques that have problems with partial descriptions.

- Case retrieval can be seen as case completion. Given only a part of a case, the net can complete the rest of its content.
- The net can express different similarity and relevance values at run time by simply changing the related arc weights, while most other techniques need a new compilation to do the same.
- Cases do not need to be described by attribute vectors. There are features that would be relevant for some cases but not for the others.
- Insertion of new cases (even with new attributes) can be performed incrementally by injecting new nodes and arcs.

3   Text Generation for Fairy Tales

ProtoPropp [13] is a system for automatic story generation that reuses existing stories to produce a new story that matches a given user query. ProtoPropp receives a query from the user with the features the generated story must fulfill from the point of view of main characters, some important events that may occur, etc. The system uses this information to look for in its case base of analyzed and annotated fairy tales by means of Case-Based Reasoning (CBR). A plot plan is generated by the CBR module, structured in terms of specific instances of concepts in the ontology (characters and their attributes, scenarios where the action takes place, events that occurs,...). From this plot plan, the NLG subsystem builds the textual rendition of the story.

The specific architecture of the NLG module presented here is implemented using cFROGS [14], a framework-like library of architectural classes intended to facilitate the development of NLG applications. It is designed to provide the necessary infrastructure for developing NLG applications, minimising the implementation effort by means of schemas and generic architectural structures commonly used in this kind of systems.

cFROGS identifies three basic design decisions when designing the architecture of any NLG system: (1) what set of modules or tasks compound the system, (2) how control should flow between them, deciding the way they are connected and how the data are transferred from one to another, and (3) what data structures are used to communicate between the modules. Our solutions for these three decisions in the NLG module of ProtoPropp are the following.

3.1   Data Structures

Abstract classes provided by the library allow us to create the data structures we need in our system, always taking into account that all modules must be able to work with them when necessary. A generic data structure is defined for the text that is being created, where all obtained information during system operation is stored. Any module can access all the information accumulated during the processing of the tale being treated.

Three particular inputs to the NLG module are relevant to the work described here: the knowledge base, the vocabulary and the plot plan.

The knowledge base contains all the domain information about tales the generator can consult and use, organized as a tree. This information includes characters, locations, objects, relations between them and their attributes.

The vocabulary contains all the lexical information essential to write the final text. It is structured as a tree as well, very similar to the knowledge base one, with the difference that each fact or relation has a lexical tag associated to its eventual realization in the final text.

The plot plan is the structure of the tale that is to be rendered as text. Each line of this input corresponds to a paragraph sized portion of the story, containing information about a sequence of actions, the place where they take place, the characters involved, and the objects used in them.

3.2   Set of Modules

The NLG system is composed of five different modules:

- **ContentDeterminationStory.** Decides what facts of the original plot plan are going to be included in the final text. Taking into account the "historical register" of the information already mentioned we can decide what information is redundant and erase it.
- **DiscoursePlanningStory.** The discourse planning stage has to organise all the information that has been selected as relevant into a linear sequence, establishing the order in which it is going to appear in the final text. The output of this module is the rhetorical structure of the tale the module is processing.
- **ReferringExpressionStory.** This stage takes the decision of what must be the reference for each concept that appears in the tale, avoiding lexical redundancies and ambiguity.
- **LexicalizationStory.** This stage selects words from the vocabulary to describe the concepts involved in the current draft, using lexical tags for static concepts, as characters and scenarios, and templates for actions and verbs, providing structure to the sentences. Templates partly solve the need for having an explicit grammar, but the knowledge base provides the required information to solve issues like number and gender agreement.
- **SurfaceRealizationStory.** This stage is in charge of using the terms selected in the previous stage to fill in the templates. Additionally, it carries out a basic orthographic transformation of the resulting sentences. Templates are converted into strings formatted in accordance to the orthographic rules of English - sentence initial letters are capitalized, and a period is added at the end.

3.3   Flow of Control Information

The generation module of ProtoPropp implements the flow of control information among the modules as a simple pipeline, with all the modules in a sequence in such a way that the output of each one is the input for the next. From the plot plan generated by the CBR module, the text generator carries out the mentioned tasks of Content Determination, Discourse Planning, Referring Expression Generation, Lexicalization and Surface Realization, each one of them in an independent module.

4 Case Based Solutions for Lexicalization

Lexicalization based on templates is an acceptable method when operating in restricted domains, but results can be poor if complex actions have to be expressed. Complex actions require the introduction of lexical chains that are employed exclusively for a specific verb in some tale. This introduces an unwanted rigidity in the system, because it makes the task of extending the vocabulary an arduous one. This solution also implies that the vocabulary holds no semantic information about actors or objects involved in an action.

As an alternative, we have implemented a case-based lexicalisation module. When human beings talk or write, they do not invent new words whenever they need to express a specific idea that they have never before put into words. Instead, they search for relations between the new idea to be expressed and other ideas expressed previously, taking the same vocabulary and adapting it as required. They reuse previous experience to solve a new case.

4.1 Representation of Cases

The new module operates with the same vocabulary for domain concepts and attributes as the original lexicalisation module. A lexical tag is assigned to each one of them, made up of one or more words. The vocabulary for actions or verbs becomes more complex: it is stored in the form of cases, where each case stores not only the corresponding lexical tag but also additional information concerning the type of case, the elements involved in the action, and the role that those elements play in the action.

The domain of tales is restricted, and so is the type of actions that can appear in them. The types of actions that appear in this module are:

- **Move.** Actions that result in a change of location, whether of a character or an object.
- **Atrans.** Actions where there is a transfer of possession, whether of a character or an object.
- **Fight.** Actions involving physical confrontations between characters.
- **Ingest.** Actions where a character ingests something (either another character or an object).
- **Propel.** Actions where a physical force is applied to an object.
- **State.** Actions representing a change of state of a character or an object.
- **Use.** Actions where an element of the domain participates in the action.
- **Feel.** Actions that involve feelings, both positive or negative.
- **Speak.** Actions where a character or an object express an idea out loud.

Examples of cases for the different types of action are given below:

```
FIGHT:attack, ACTOR:witch, OBJECT:Hansel
FEEL:envy, ACTOR:stepsisters, OBJECT:Cinderella, FEELING:bad
STATE:marry, ACTOR1:knight, ACTOR2:princess, INI:single, FINAL:married
```

It is important to take into account that the structure of each one of these types is not rigid. They will not always have the same elements, nor in the same order. A clear example is provided by the verbs 'leave' and 'go', both of type Move. The first one has an attribute From to indicate where the character is coming from, whereas the second one has an attribute To that indicates his destination.

Cases have been extracted from the formalised tales that were already available. A case is not an abstract instance of a verb or action, but rather a concrete instance in which specific characters, places and objects appear. These elements are stored in the module's knowledge base. This allows the establishment of relations between them when it comes to retrieving or reusing the cases.

4.2   The Case Base

Cases are stored in a Case Retrieval Net. This model is appropriate for the problem under consideration, because on one hand our cases consist of attribute-value pairs that are related with one another, and on the other hand the queries posed to the module will not always be complete. When the system asks for the appropriate lexical tag for a new action, the module looks for related verbs based on their type and the class of elements that are involved in them.

The vocabulary of the module is built from the case base. For each attribute-value pair in the cases an information entity is created. For each case, a node is created which holds references to the information entities that make it up. When introducing an IE, if that entity has already appeared in another case it is not duplicated. Instead, another association is created between the new case and the existing information entity.

As IEs are inserted to form the net, it is necessary to establish a measure of similarity between them. This is done by reference to the module's knowledge base, in which the different concepts of the domain are organised into a taxonomy. The similarity between two entities is calculated by taking into account the distance between them in the knowledge base and using Formula 1.

$$similarity(c1, c2) = 1 - (1 + distance(c1, c2))/10 \qquad (1)$$

The distance between two concepts is calculated by finding their first shared ancestor, and adding up the distance between this ancestor and each of the concepts. It can be seen as the number of nodes we have to pass when going from one of the concepts to the other. It is also necessary to have a similarity value for each entity with itself. This value is always 1, the maximum possible.

Each of the IEs is related to the cases to which it belongs with a certain value of relevance. In the implemented module, the maximum relevance within a case corresponds to the attribute Type with value 1, and the rest of the elements have relevance 0.5. This is because when retrieving cases we are mainly interested in the type of action that we are looking for, more than which elements are involved in it. However, it can occur that the module retrieves a case of a different type, if the similarity weights of the attributes of the case are high enough.

4.3   The CBR Cycle

The module described in this paper executes each of the processes of the CBR cycle in the following way.

Case Retrieval. The retrieval task starts with a partial or complete problem description, and ends when a matching previous case has been found. In our module, the retrieval of cases is directly handled by the Case Retrieval Net and its method of similarity propagation. Starting from a partial description of the action we need to lexicalise, formed by the information available in the input plot plan, the retrieval of the more similar cases is done by calculating an activation value for each case in the case base. The ones with higher activation are the more similar ones to the given query. This calculation is performed in three steps:

1. The IE nodes that correspond to the query are activated. If they are not in the net because they did not belong to any case in the case base, the correspondent nodes are inserted at the time of querying, calculating the similarity and relevance weights using the knowledge base. The nodes corresponding to the query are assigned an activation value of 1, and the rest a value of 0.
2. The activation is propagated according to the similarity values of the arcs. This is performed by looking over all the entity nodes of the net and by calculating for each one its activation value using its own activation and its similarity with the rest of IE nodes. This is achieved by using Formula 2 (where N is the total number of IE nodes).

$$activation(e) = \sum_{i=1}^{N}(sim(e_i, e) * activation(e_i)) \qquad (2)$$

3. The achieved activations in the previous step are collected in the associated case nodes, calculating the final activations of the cases also considering the relevance weights of the arcs that connect the cases with their entities. This final activation value of the cases is calculated with Formula 3.

$$activation(c) = \sum_{i=1}^{N}(rel(e_i, c) * activation(e_i)) \qquad (3)$$

Once we have the final activation in the cases, the one with the higher value is returned by the net. It would be possible to take not only the most similar one, but a set with the most similar cases to the query.

Case Reuse. Each retrieved case has an associated template from the vocabulary for the verb or action it represents. In the process of reusing the case we have obtained from the net, we have to substitute the attribute values of the past case with the query values. Here we have tree different possibilities:

- If the attributes of the retrieved and the query cases are the same, the values of the past case are simply changed for the values of the query one. The template of the past case would be filled with the new values.
- If the attributes of the retrieved case are a subset of the query, then the attributes of the past case are filled with the correspondent query values, and the rest of the query attributes are ignored. The template of the past case would be filled with the new values, although we may have lost some important data of the query.
- If there are more attributes in the retrieved case than in the query, there are spaces in the corresponding template that the system does not know how to fill in. The easiest solution is to keep the values of the past case in the slots for which the query does not specify any value.

At the end of the reuse process the query has an assigned template to pass the message it is supposed to express into text.

Case Revision and Retainment. When a case solution generated by the reuse task is identified as correct or incorrect, an opportunity for learning from success or failure arises. At the moment, this task is not implemented in our CBR module. Due to the constraints associated with language use, the contribution of an expert in the domain is required to revise the achieved results of the module, retaining and refining them if possible.

5   Experiments and Results

The method described here has been tested over a set of formalised fairy tales that had been originally used as input data for ProtoPropp. They were constructed manually as simplified conceptual representations of existing renditions of the corresponding texts. This involved removing those sentences of the original tales with a meaning too complex to be expressed in terms of simple attribute-value pairs, such as *"The stepsisters envied Cinderella"*. The current corpus consists of five tales: the Lioness, Hansel & Gretel, Cinderella, the Merchant, and the Dragon.

To test the validity of the approach, several experiments have been carried out, using in each experiment part of the available material as case base and the remainder as test case. In each experiment, the conceptual representation of the test tale is used as input to the system, using the actions that appear in the other four formalised tales as case base. The resulting lexicalisation is then compared manually with the original lexicalisation available for the test tale. Each lexical choice is evaluated according to the scale presented in Table 1.

Table 1. Evaluation scale

Score	Observed lexicalisation	Relative Meaning
4	Matches original tale	
3	Equivalent to original	no loss of meaning
2	Valid	with slight loss of meaning
1	Acceptable	with significant loss of meaning
0	Unaceptable	radical departure from meaning

Some retrieval examples are shown in Table 2.

Table 2. Examples

Query	Cases retrieved	Associated template	Score
TYPE: MOVE, ACTOR: princess, FROM: castle	TYPE: MOVE, MOVE: leaveInHurry, ACTOR: Cinderella, FROM:palace	_ left _ in a hurry	3
	TYPE: MOVE, MOVE: comeout, ACTOR: Hansel, FROM: house	_ came out of _	3
TYPE:STATE, ACTOR: knight, OBJECT:princess, FINAL:alive	TYPE: STATE, STATE: release, ACTOR: Gretel, OBJECT: Hansel, INI:jailed, FINAL: free	_ released _	1
	TYPE: STATE, STATE: find, ACTOR: boatmen, OBJECT: son, INI:lost FINAL:found	_ found _	0

Table 3. Average Score for the Five Experiments

Tale	Av. Score	# Sent.	CB Size	Precision
Lioness	2.60	10	76	0.60
Hansel & Gretel	2.55	11	57	0.55
Cinderella	2.91	11	65	0.73
Dragon	3.50	6	81	1.00
Merchant	2.80	5	81	0.60

Results in the first example are acceptable. In the second one the meaning of the retrieved cases does not match the meaning of the query. This is due to the fact that the system stores no case for which the final state is 'alive', so it returns cases of type State that are not related.

The experiments are repeated for all possible partitions of the available material into pairs of test tale / sources for the necessary case base of actions. In each one two different features are evaluated: the average score of the test tale and the precision, that shows the relation between the number of retrieved cases with 3 or 4 score values and the total number of retrieved cases. The results for simple syntactic structures - presented in Table 3 - are positive, providing valid and similar cases for the queries.

6   Conclusions and Future Work

Once again, the bottleneck for this type of system lies in the process of knowlege acquisition. The use of the case-based reasoning paradigm for the task of lexicalisation is a good approximation whenever enough information is available in the case base to express in an acceptable form any new request. With a larger case base, the module would have more chances of finding a case that matches the system's need.

The main advantage of this method instead of other lexicalisation approaches is that the system does not need an exhaustive lexicon, as CRNs work by approximation and can retrieve similar cases for unknown queries due to the automatic semantic relations attained in the net.

An important point to take into account in future work is the formalisation of actions appearing in the tales. In the implemented module, the actions considered are quite simple, so they could be organised according to a simple type system. Enriching the language the system can use would slowly lead to the need for more complex actions that may be difficult to classify with simple types. For this reason, we are considering the use of primitives to build complex actions from simple ingredients. A possible starting point is Schank's Conceptual Dependency theory [15]. This has already been used for story generation in Tale-Spin [16]. Schank proposes an open set of primitives to express the meaning of any sentence. These meanings are built up from primitive using a complex system for representing states and relationships. Some such mechanism would be very useful when extending the system to deal with complex actions. A possible solution is the use of not only attribute-value pairs, but also attribute-case pairs, where the value for some attribute may be also a whole case.

Another improvement of the module's operation would be to implement *lazy spreading activation* [17] in the Case Retrieval Net. Instead of propagating activation to all entity nodes, and then to all case nodes, propagation takes place progressively from most similar nodes to not so similar nodes. Once enough case nodes have been activated to reply to the query, propagation stops.

References

1. Reiter, E., Dale, R.: Building Natural Language Generation Systems. Cambridge University Press (2000)
2. Goldberg, E., Driedger, N., Kittredge, R.: Using natural-language processing to produce weather forecasts. IEEE Expert: Intelligent Systems and Their Applications **9** (1994) 45–53

3. Callaway, C., Lester, J.: Narrative prose generation. In: Proceedings of the 17th IJCAI, Seattle, WA (2001) 1241–1248
4. DeSmedt, K., Horacek, H., Zock, M.: Architectures for natural language generation: Problems and perspectives. In Ardoni, G., Zock, M., eds.: Trends in natural language generation: an artificial intelligence perspective. LNAI 1036. Springer Verlag (1995) 17–46
5. Cahill, L.: Lexicalisation in applied NLG systems. Technical Report ITRI-99-04 (1998)
6. Stede, M.: Lexical options in multilingual generation from a knowledge base. In Adorni, G., Zock, M., eds.: Trends in natural language generation: an artificial intelligence perspective. Number 1036. Springer-Verlag (1996) 222–237
7. Daelemans, W.: Introduction to the special issue on memory-based language processing. J. Exp. Theor. Artif. Intell. **11** (1999) 287–296
8. Daelemans, W., Gillis, S., Durieux, G.: The acquisition of stress: a data-oriented approach. Comput. Linguist. **20** (1994) 421–451
9. Ng, H.T., Lee, H.B.: Integrating multiple knowledge sources to disambiguate word sense: an exemplar-based approach. In: Proceedings of the 34th annual meeting on Association for Computational Linguistics, Morristown, NJ, USA, Association for Computational Linguistics (1996) 40–47
10. Cardie, C.: A case-based approach to knowledge acquisition for domain-specific sentence analysis. In: National Conference on Artificial Intelligence. (1993) 798–803
11. Aamodt, A., Plaza, E.: Case-based reasoning : Foundational issues, methodological variations, and system approaches (1994)
12. Lenz, M., Burkhard, H.D.: Case retrieval nets: Basic ideas and extensions. In: KI - Kunstliche Intelligenz. (1996) 227–239
13. Gervás, P., Díaz-Agudo, B., Peinado, F., Hervás, R.: Story plot generation based on CBR. In Macintosh, A., Ellis, R., Allen, T., eds.: 12th Conference on Applications and Innovations in Intelligent Systems, Cambridge, UK, Springer, WICS series (2004)
14. García, C., Hervás, R., Gervás, P.: Una arquitectura software para el desarrollo de aplicaciones de generación de lenguaje natural. Procesamiento de Lenguaje Natural **33** (2004) 111–118
15. Schank, R.: A Conceptual Dependency Representation for a Computer-Oriented Semantics. PhD thesis, University of Texas, Austin (1969)
16. Meehan, J.: Tale-spin, an interactive program that writes stories. In: Proceedings of the 5th International Joint Conference on Artificial Intelligence. (1977)
17. Lenz, M., Burkhard, H.: Case Retrieval Nets: Foundations, properties,implementation, and results. Technical report, Humboldt University, Berlin (1996)

Partially Parametric SVM

José M. Matías

Dpto. de Estadística, Universidad de Vigo, 36310 Vigo, Spain
jmmatias@uvigo.es

Abstract. In this paper we propose a simple and intuitive method for constructing partially linear models and, in general, partially parametric models, using support vector machines for regression and, in particular, using regularization networks (splines). The results are more satisfactory than those for classical nonparametric approaches. The method is based on a suitable approach to selecting the kernel by relaying on the properties of positive definite functions. No modification is required of the standard SVM algorithms, and the approach is valid for the ε-insensitive loss. The approach described here can be immediately applied to SVMs for classification and to other methods that use the kernel as the inner product.

1 Introduction

The support vector machine (SVM) approach ([10], [7]) is one of the most relevant non-parametric curve-smoothing methods of recent years. Based on essentially linear techniques, its formal elegance and the intuition lying behind the concepts of margin (ε-insensitive loss in regression), support vectors, feature space and kernel as inner product in the feature space, all make this family of techniques a highly attractive option, not to mention the unique solution to the optimization problem in hand and the sparsity of its final expression.

However, the SVMs, like many techniques arising in the machine learning field, have one major drawback in terms of modeling, and that is the difficulty in interpreting their final expression. Yet the SVMs do permit difficult points to be identified (support vectors), and these are undoubtedly of relevance to the analyst. That said, interpretative capacity is still restricted to this set of important points, and fails to identify the relationships between input and output variables.

This paper is intended to palliate this problem by means of the construction of partially linear models ([6], [9]) based on the SVMs (PL–SVMs) and, with greater generality, partially parametric SVMs (PP–SVMs), which include as particular cases, partially polynomial SVMs.

Recently, Espinoza et al. [3] proposed the PL–LSSVMs as an adaptation of SVMs with quadratic loss (LSSVM), in order to implement a partially linear model.

Unlike the PL–LSSVMs, our method results in a standard SVM, and so it exploits two of the most powerful elements of the SVMs, namely, the feature space and associated kernel, and the concept of the support vector.

C. Bento, A. Cardoso, and G. Dias (Eds.): EPIA 2005, LNAI 3808, pp. 67–75, 2005.

The method is thus valid for the ε-insensitive loss (linear or quadratic) and can be used immediately since none of the SVM algorithms need modification – all that is needed is a suitably intuitive selection of the kernel.

Moreover, our approach not only enables partially linear models to be formulated, like the PL–LSSVMs, but also enables more general models to be formulated for the parametric part, and in particular, polynomials of any degree.

2 Partially Parametric SVM

Let the model be as follows:

$$Y_i = h(\mathbf{Z}_i; \beta) + g(\mathbf{T}_i) + \varepsilon_i, \ i = 1, ..., n \qquad (1)$$
$$= \psi(\mathbf{X}_i; \beta) + \varepsilon_i, \ i = 1, ..., n \qquad (2)$$

where for $i = 1, ..., n$, ε_i is i.i.d. zero-mean random noise, $\mathbf{Z}_i$ is the ith observation of the random vector $\mathbf{Z} = (\mathsf{Z}_1, ..., \mathsf{Z}_{d_1})^t$, $h(\cdot; \beta) : \mathbb{R}^{d_1} \to \mathbb{R}$ is a known and predetermined function (which will serve as the parametric term in the model), parameterized by a vector $\beta \in \mathbb{R}^m$ of parameters to be estimated, $g : \mathbb{R}^{d_2} \to \mathbb{R}$ is an unknown function, and $\mathbf{T}_i$ is the ith observation of the random vector $\mathbf{T} = (\mathsf{T}_1, ..., \mathsf{T}_{d_2})^t$. Likewise, we denote as $\mathbf{X} = (\mathbf{Z}^t \ \mathbf{T}^t)^t$ the vector for all the covariables (where t denotes transpose), with observations $\mathbf{X}_i = (\mathbf{Z}_i^t \ \mathbf{T}_i^t)^t \in \mathcal{S} \subset \mathbb{R}^d$, with $d = d_1 + d_2$, $i = 1, ..., n$, and with ψ as the regression function $\mathbb{E}(\mathsf{Y}|\mathbf{X} = \mathbf{x})$.

The model in (1) includes as a particular case the partially linear model:

$$Y_i = \mathbf{Z}_i^t \beta + g(\mathbf{T}_i) + \varepsilon_i, \ i = 1, ..., n \qquad (3)$$

– requiring only a definition of $h(\mathbf{Z}_i; \beta) = \mathbf{Z}_i^t \beta$, – but also other parametric models (e.g. higher degree polynomials).

The model in (2) is a typical application of SVM to regression. Thus, by means of a transformation $\phi : \mathcal{S} \subset \mathbb{R}^d \to \mathbb{R}^r$ in which r may be infinite, a feature space is defined $\mathcal{F} = \{\phi(\mathbf{x}) : \mathbf{x} \in \mathcal{S} \subset \mathbb{R}^d\}$ as equipped with an inner product (defined in turn by means of a positive definite function (kernel)[1] $\langle \phi(\mathbf{x}_i), \phi(\mathbf{x}_j) \rangle_{\mathcal{F}} = k(\mathbf{x}_i, \mathbf{x}_j)$) in which the problem is posed of determining the optimum hyperplane $f_{\mathbf{w},b}(\mathbf{x}) = \langle \mathbf{w}, \phi(\mathbf{x}) \rangle + b$ for the problem:

$$\min_{\mathbf{w},b} \{ \frac{1}{2} \|\mathbf{w}\|^2 + C \sum_{i=1}^{n} \ell_p(y_i, f(\mathbf{x}_i)) \}$$

where $\ell_p(y, f(\mathbf{x})) = |y - f(\mathbf{x})|_\varepsilon^p = \max\{0, (|y - f(\mathbf{x})| - \varepsilon)^p\}$ is the Vapnik ε-insensitive loss in which $p = 1$ or 2.

---

[1] Henceforth, wherever we consider it superfluous, we will omit any reference to the space $\mathcal{F}$ in its inner product $\langle \cdot, \cdot \rangle_{\mathcal{F}}$ and in its norm.

For example, if $p = 1$ the above problem is equivalent to the problem ([10], [7]):

$$\min_{\mathbf{w},b,\xi,\xi'} \{ \tfrac{1}{2} \|\mathbf{w}\|^2 + C \sum_{i=1}^{n} (\xi_i + \xi'_i) \}$$

$$\text{s.t.} \begin{cases} \langle \mathbf{w}, \phi(\mathbf{x}_i) \rangle + b - y_i \leq \varepsilon + \xi_i \\ y_i - (\langle \mathbf{w}, \phi(\mathbf{x}_i) \rangle + b) \leq \varepsilon + \xi'_i \quad i = 1, \ldots, n \\ \xi_i, \xi'_i \geq 0 \end{cases} \tag{4}$$

a quadratic program with a unique solution taking the form $\mathbf{w} = \sum_{SV} \alpha_i \phi(\mathbf{x}_i)$, and so:

$$f_{\mathbf{w},b}(\mathbf{x}) = \sum_{i \in SV} \alpha_i \langle \phi(\mathbf{x}_i), \phi(\mathbf{x}) \rangle + b = \sum_{i \in SV} \alpha_i k(\mathbf{x}_i, \mathbf{x}) + b \tag{5}$$

where the abbreviation SV represents the set of support vectors (for which $\alpha_i \neq 0$).

The solution in (5) is based on a non-parametric philosophy and so is difficult to interpret in terms of the covariables. Without further refinement, therefore, it is not very useful for problems of the type in (1).

Our approach to dealing with this drawback is to make use of the following results ([1],[2]):

1. If k is a positive definite function in $\mathbb{R}^s \times R^s$, and $\varphi : \mathbb{R}^d \to \mathbb{R}^s$, then it can be verified that the function $\bar{k}$ defined as $\bar{k}(\mathbf{x}, \mathbf{x}') = k(\varphi(\mathbf{x}), \varphi(\mathbf{x}'))$ is positive definite.
2. If $\bar{k}_i$ defined in $\mathbb{R}^d \times \mathbb{R}^d$, are positive definite, then $\bar{k}(\mathbf{x}, \mathbf{x}') = \bar{k}_1(\mathbf{x}, \mathbf{x}') + \bar{k}_2(\mathbf{x}, \mathbf{x}')$ is positive definite.

Consequently, if the functions k_i, $i = 1, 2$ defined in $\mathbb{R}^{d_i} \times \mathbb{R}^{d_i}$, $i = 1, 2$ are positive definite functions, and the transformations $\varphi_1(\mathbf{x}) = \mathbf{z} \in \mathbb{R}^{d_1}$ and $\varphi_2(\mathbf{x}) = \mathbf{t} \in \mathbb{R}^{d_2}$ are used, where $\mathbf{x} = (\mathbf{z}\ \mathbf{t})$, then – applying the above two properties – the function $k : \mathbb{R}^d \times \mathbb{R}^d \to \mathbb{R}$ defined as:

$$k(\mathbf{x}, \mathbf{x}') = \bar{k}_1(\mathbf{x}, \mathbf{x}') + \bar{k}_2(\mathbf{x}, \mathbf{x}') = k_1(\varphi_1(\mathbf{x}), \varphi_1(\mathbf{x}')) + k_2(\varphi_2(\mathbf{x}), \varphi_2(\mathbf{x}'))$$
$$= k_1(\mathbf{z}, \mathbf{z}') + k_2(\mathbf{t}, \mathbf{t}')$$

is a positive definite function and can be used as the kernel in an SVM.

As for the feature space and its inner product, the above can be interpreted as the choice of a transformation $\phi : \mathbb{R}^d \to \mathbb{R}^r$, with two components $\phi^{(i)} : \mathbb{R}^d \to \mathbb{R}^{r_i}$, with $\mathcal{F}_i = \{\phi^{(i)}(\mathbf{x}) : \mathbf{x} \in \mathcal{S} \subset \mathbb{R}^d\}$, $i = 1, 2$, such that $\mathcal{F} = \mathcal{F}_1 \oplus \mathcal{F}_2$, where $\phi^{(1)}(\mathbf{x}) = \phi_1(\mathbf{z})$ and $\phi^{(2)}(\mathbf{x}) = \phi_2(\mathbf{t})$, with $\phi_i : \mathbb{R}^{d_i} \to \mathbb{R}^{r_i}$, $i = 1, 2$. In other words:

$$\phi(\mathbf{x}) = (\phi^{(1)}(\mathbf{x}), \phi^{(2)}(\mathbf{x})) = (\phi_1(\mathbf{z}), \phi_2(\mathbf{t}))$$

such that:

$$\langle \phi(\mathbf{x}), \phi(\mathbf{x}') \rangle_{\mathcal{F}} = \left\langle \left(\phi^{(1)}(\mathbf{x}), \phi^{(2)}(\mathbf{x}) \right), \left(\phi^{(1)}(\mathbf{x}'), \phi^{(2)}(\mathbf{x}') \right) \right\rangle_{\mathcal{F}}$$
$$= \langle (\phi_1(\mathbf{z}), \phi_2(\mathbf{t})), (\phi_1(\mathbf{z}'), \phi_2(\mathbf{t}')) \rangle_{\mathcal{F}}$$
$$= \langle \phi_1(\mathbf{z}), \phi_1(\mathbf{z}') \rangle_{\mathcal{F}_1} + \langle \phi_2(\mathbf{t}), \phi_2(\mathbf{t}') \rangle_{\mathcal{F}_2}$$
$$= k_1(\mathbf{z}, \mathbf{z}') + k_2(\mathbf{t}, \mathbf{t}')$$

In order to deal with partially linear problems of the type in (3), it is sufficient to select $\phi^{(1)}(\mathbf{x}) = \phi_1(\mathbf{z}) = \mathbf{z}$ with an inner product:

$$\langle \phi_1(\mathbf{z}), \phi_1(\mathbf{z}') \rangle_{\mathcal{F}_1} = k_1(\mathbf{z}, \mathbf{z}') = \langle \mathbf{z}, \mathbf{z}' \rangle$$

and $\phi^{(2)}(\mathbf{x}) = \phi_2(\mathbf{t})$ with an inner product in $\mathcal{F}_2$ defined by a kernel $k_2(\mathbf{t}, \mathbf{t}')$ with sufficient approximating properties to represent the complexity of the function g.

The above approach can be generalized to other functions $h(\cdot; \beta) : \mathbb{R}^{d_1} \to \mathbb{R}$ parameterized by β. For example, if h is a polynomial of degree a in $\mathbf{z}$, suffice it to choose:

$$\langle \phi_1(\mathbf{z}), \phi_1(\mathbf{z}') \rangle_{\mathcal{F}_1} = k_1(\mathbf{z}, \mathbf{z}') = (\langle \mathbf{z}, \mathbf{z}' \rangle + c)^a$$

Consequently, the solution in (5) becomes:

$$
\begin{aligned}
f_{\mathbf{w},b}(\mathbf{x}) &= \langle \mathbf{w}, \phi(\mathbf{x}) \rangle_{\mathcal{F}} + b = \sum_{i \in SV} \alpha_i \langle \phi(\mathbf{x}_i), \phi(\mathbf{x}) \rangle_{\mathcal{F}} + b \\
&= \sum_{i \in SV} \alpha_i \left(\langle \phi_1(\mathbf{z}_i), \phi_1(\mathbf{z}) \rangle_{\mathcal{F}_1} + \langle \phi_2(\mathbf{t}_i), \phi_2(\mathbf{t}) \rangle_{\mathcal{F}_2} \right) + b \\
&= \sum_{i \in SV} \alpha_i (\mathbf{z}^t \mathbf{z}_i + c)^a + \sum_{i \in SV} \alpha_i k_2(\mathbf{t}_i, \mathbf{t}) + b
\end{aligned}
\tag{6}
$$

And if, for example, $a = 1$ and $c = 0$, then it takes the form:

$$f_{\mathbf{w},b}(\mathbf{x}) = \mathbf{z}^t \sum_{i \in SV} \alpha_i \mathbf{z}_i + \sum_{i \in SV} \alpha_i k_2(\mathbf{t}_i, \mathbf{t}) + b = \mathbf{z}^t \hat{\beta} + \hat{g}(\mathbf{t})$$

$$\text{with:} \begin{cases} \hat{\beta} = \sum_{i \in SV} \alpha_i \mathbf{z}_i = Z^t \alpha \\ \hat{g}(\mathbf{t}) = \sum_{i \in SV} \alpha_i k_2(\mathbf{t}_i, \mathbf{t}) + b \end{cases}$$

where Z is the matrix with elements Z_{ij} (the ith observation of the jth variable), where i is such that $\mathbf{x}_i$ is a support vector.

The above formulation admits variations that can be adapted to each specific problem. Thus, if the model in (3) has a constant term β_0 to be estimated: $Y_i = \beta_0 + \mathbf{Z}_i^t \beta + g(\mathbf{T}_i) + \varepsilon_i$, $i = 1, ..., n$, then several alternatives can be evaluated for each situation, among them:

1. use $k_1(\mathbf{z}, \mathbf{z}') = \langle \mathbf{z}, \mathbf{z}' \rangle$ with an SVM with a constant term b;
2. use an SVM without a constant term b and $k_1(\mathbf{z}, \mathbf{z}') = \langle \mathbf{z}, \mathbf{z}' \rangle + 1$;
3. consider the extended covariable vector $\bar{\mathbf{z}} = (1\ \mathbf{z})$ with $k_1(\mathbf{z}, \mathbf{z}') = \langle \mathbf{z}, \mathbf{z}' \rangle$ without a constant term;
4. center the variables beforehand.

For the second-degree partially polynomial model:

$$Y_i = \theta_0 + \mathbf{Z}_i^t \theta + \mathbf{Z}_i^t \Theta \mathbf{Z}_i + g(\mathbf{T}_i) + \varepsilon_i, \ i = 1, .., n$$

if, for example, we set $c = 1$, $b = 0$ in (6) we obtain:

$$
\begin{aligned}
f_{\mathbf{w},b}(\mathbf{x}) &= \sum_{\text{s.v.}} \alpha_i (\mathbf{z}^t \mathbf{z}_i + 1)^2 + \sum_{\text{s.v.}} \alpha_i k_2(\mathbf{t}_i, \mathbf{t}) \\
&= \sum_{\text{s.v.}} \alpha_i (\sum_{j=1}^{d_1} z_{ji} z_j + 1)^2 + \sum_{\text{s.v.}} \alpha_i k_2(\mathbf{t}_i, \mathbf{t}) \\
&= \sum_{j=1}^{d_1} \hat{\theta}_{jj} z_j^2 + \sum_{j,l=1}^{d_1} \hat{\theta}_{jl} z_j z_l + \sum_{j=1}^{d_1} \hat{\theta}_j z_j + \hat{\theta}_0 + \sum_{\text{s.v.}} \alpha_i k_2(\mathbf{t}_i, \mathbf{t}) \\
&= \mathbf{z}^t \hat{\Theta} \mathbf{z} + \mathbf{z}^t \hat{\theta} + \hat{\theta}_0 + \sum_{\text{s.v.}} \alpha_i k_2(\mathbf{t}_i, \mathbf{t})
\end{aligned}
$$

where $(\hat{\Theta})_{jl} = \hat{\theta}_{jl}$, $(\hat{\theta})_j = \hat{\theta}_j$, $j, l = 1, ..., d_1$ and $\hat{\theta}_0$ are the estimations of the true parameters expressed in terms of the observations $\mathbf{z}_i$ and of their coefficients α_i, $i \in$SV in the optimal vector $\mathbf{w}$:

$$
\hat{\theta}_{jl} = \sum_{i \in \text{SV}} \alpha_i z_{ji} z_{li}
$$

$$
\hat{\theta}_j = 2 \sum_{i \in \text{SV}} \alpha_i z_{ji}
$$

$$
\hat{\theta}_0 = \sum_{i \in \text{SV}} \alpha_i
$$

2.1   Relationship Between the PL-SVM and the PL-LSSVM

At this stage it is of interest to analyze the relationships between the proposed method and the PL-LSSVM method formulated by [3] for the partially linear case with quadratic loss ($p = 2$ and $\varepsilon = 0$ in the ε-insensitive loss). At a new point $\mathbf{x} = (\mathbf{z}^t \ \mathbf{t}^t)^t$, the PL-LSSVM solution takes the form:

$$
f_E(\mathbf{x}) = \mathbf{z}^t \beta_E + \sum_{i=1}^{n} (\alpha_E)_i k_2(\mathbf{t}_i, \mathbf{t}) + b = \mathbf{z}^t \bar{\beta}_E + \mathbf{k}_2^t \alpha_E + b_E
$$

where $\mathbf{k}_2 = (k_2(\mathbf{t}_1, \mathbf{t}), ..., k_2(\mathbf{t}_n, \mathbf{t}))^t$ and the coefficients β_E, α_E, b_E are obtained as a solution to the problem:

$$
\min_{\mathbf{w}, \beta, b, \xi,} \{ \tfrac{1}{2} \|\mathbf{w}\|^2 + C \sum_{i=1}^{n} \xi_i^2 \} \tag{7}
$$
$$
\text{s.t. } y_i - (\mathbf{z}_i^t \beta + \langle \mathbf{w}, \phi_2(\mathbf{t}_i) \rangle + b) = \xi_i, \ i = 1, \ldots, n
$$

It can be shown that the solution to this problem is given by:

$$
\alpha_E = \bar{K}_2^{-1} \mathbf{y} - \bar{K}_2^{-1} Z \beta_E \tag{8a}
$$
$$
\beta_E = (Z^t \bar{K}_2^{-1} Z)^{-1} Z^t \bar{K}_2^{-1} \mathbf{y} \tag{8b}
$$

where $\beta_E = (b_E, \bar{\beta}_E^t)^t$, $\bar{K}_2 = (K_2 + C^{-1}I_{n \times n})$ with K_2 the matrix with elements $(K_2)_{ij} = k_2(\mathbf{t}_i, \mathbf{t}_j)$, Z is the matrix with rows $\mathbf{z}_i^t = (1, z_{1i}, ..., z_{d_1 i})$, $i = 1, ..., n$ (which henceforth in this text is assumed to have a maximum range), and $\mathbf{y} = (y_1, ..., y_n)^t$ is the vector of observations of the dependent variable. Note that in the above, we have homogenized the notation, assuming that for the covariables $\mathbf{T}$ the same kernel k_2 as in the PP-SVM case is used.

Meanwhile, our method applied to the partially linear case ($a = 1$), with quadratic loss ($p = 2$ and $\varepsilon = 0$) and using the inner product $k_1(\mathbf{z}, \mathbf{z}') = \langle \mathbf{z}, \mathbf{z}' \rangle$, produces a solution of the form:

$$f_M(\mathbf{x}) = \mathbf{z}^t \beta_M + \sum_{i=1}^{n} (\alpha_M)_i k_2(\mathbf{t}_i, \mathbf{t}) + b_M = \mathbf{z}^t \beta_M + \mathbf{k}_2^t \alpha_M + b_M$$

Like the previous case, the constant b_M can be ignored if the covariables vector $\mathbf{Z}$ is considered to include a constant variable equal to 1. The solution provided by this method is:

$$\alpha_M = (ZZ^t + \bar{K}_2)^{-1} \mathbf{y} \tag{9a}$$

$$\beta_M = Z^t \alpha_M = Z^t (ZZ^t + \bar{K}_2)^{-1} \mathbf{y} \tag{9b}$$

where, as previously, $\bar{K}_2 = K_2 + C^{-1}I_{n \times n}$.

Analysing the equations in (8) and (9) from a Bayesian perspective, in which a priori, $\beta \sim \mathcal{N}(\mathbf{0}_{d_1}, \tau I_{d_1 \times d_1})$, it can be demonstrated that:

1. On the one hand, $\hat{\beta}_E$ is obtained for $\tau \to 0$, which implies a frequentist approach equivalent to giving full credit to the data with a maximum bias penalty. (Note that, unlike the PL–SVM, in (7) the norm of the vector β is not penalized in the objective function, only that of the vector $\mathbf{w}$ – in this problem, $\mathbf{w}$ only affects $\phi_2(\mathbf{t}_i)$ and, therefore, has a different meaning than in the problem in (4)).
2. On the other hand, $\hat{\beta}_M$ is obtained with $\tau = 1$, in other words, assuming that the coefficients have an initial uncertainty of variance unity. This value for the variance corresponds to the interest in minimizing the MSE (mean squared error) in regularized kriging [5], thereby balancing bias and variance. Hence, the PL–SVMs are, in theory, more suitable for circumstances in which there is a higher level of noise in the data.

That said, the presence of the constant C^{-1} in the matrix $\bar{K}_2 = K_2 + C^{-1}I_{n \times n}$ means that if C is large (and more so if the covariables $\mathbf{Z}$ are centered or standardized), the results produced by either of the estimators will be similar.

3   Simulations

The performance of the proposed method was studied in different partially linear and nonlinear test models with very satisfactory results. With a view to comparing the method with the Espinoza et al's PL-LSSVM and the partially linear Nadaraya-Watson (PL-NW) estimator we used the following linear models taken from [3]:

I. $y_t = a_1 z_t + 2\mathrm{sinc}(x_t) + \varepsilon_t$ with $a_1 = 1.5$, z_t and x_t are drawn from a uniform distribution over $[0, 2.5]$ and $[0, 1.5]$ respectively, and $\varepsilon_t \sim \mathcal{N}(0, 0.02)$ that is, it is drawn from a Gaussian distribution of variance 0.02.

II. $y_t = a_1 y_{t-1} + a_2 y_{t-2} + 2\mathrm{sinc}(x_t) + \varepsilon_t$, with $a_1 = 0.6$ and $a_2 = 0.3$, $x_t \sim \mathcal{N}(0, 5)$ and $\varepsilon_t \sim \mathcal{N}(0, 0.02)$.

III. $y_t = a_1 y_{t-1} + a_2 y_{t-2} + \mathrm{sinc}(y_{t-3}) + \varepsilon_t$, with $a_1 = 0.6$, $a_2 = 0.3$ and $\varepsilon_t \sim \mathcal{N}(0, 0.02)$.

IV. $y_t = a_1 y_{t-1} + a_2 y_{t-2} + a_3 y_{t-3} + b_1 \mathrm{sinc}(u_{t-1}) + b_2 \mathrm{sinc}(u_{t-2}) + \varepsilon_t$ with $a_1 = 0.6$, $a_2 = 0.2$, $a_3 = 0.1$, $b_1 = 0.4$, $b_2 = 0.2$, $u_t \sim \mathcal{N}(0, 2)$ and $\varepsilon_t \sim \mathcal{N}(0, 0.1)$.

These test models possess little dimensionality, and this is a terrain in which the classic models (e.g. PL-NW) perform better. For problems of greater dimensionality, it is anticipated that their performance would deteriorate in comparison with the SVM with $\varepsilon \neq 0$, which combat this difficulty with the support vectors.

One hundred samples were generated for each model, and with a view to comparing the efficiency of the different techniques, relatively small sample sizes were used ($n = 50$). The model was selected using 5-fold cross-validation.

Table 1 shows the results of these simulations for the test models mentioned above. Here we show only the results of the PL-SVMs in the squared version ($p = 2$) and with $\varepsilon = 0$ (regularization networks or splines). The following comments are in order:

1. In terms of estimating the parameters, all the methods produced similar results in these tests, although with slight improvements in the mean (and with a lower standard deviation) for the PL-SVM. Of note is the fact that, in Case IV, the proposed PL-SVM method is the only method that adequately approximates the second parameter ($a_2 = 0.2$).
2. In terms of the squared error and absolute error, the improvements in the PL-LSSVM and PL-SVM - both very similar - are the most significant.

4   Conclusions

In this work we propose a simple and effective method for constructing partially parametric models using support vector machines. The method produces results comparable to those produced by the recently proposed PL-LSSVMs [3]. However, unlike the PL–LSSVMs our method is a standard SVM, and so it exploits two of its most powerful elements, namely, the feature space and associated kernel concept, and the concept of the support vector.

The method is thus valid for the ε-insensitive loss (linear or quadratic) and can be used immediately since none of the SVM algorithms need modification – all that is needed is a suitably intuitive selection of the kernel.

Moreover, our approach not only enables partially linear models to be formulated, like the PL–LSSVMs, but also enables more general models to be formulated for the parametric part, and in particular, polynomials of any degree.

In the simulations performed, the proposed method in its linear version (PL–SVM) and with $\varepsilon = 0$ has demonstrated itself to produce frequently better

Table 1. Results of the simulations for Cases I, II,III and IV as described in the text. Shown are: the parameter estimates and standard deviations, as also the mean and standard deviation, for 100 samples, of the sum of the squared errors (SSE) and the sum of the absolute errors (SAE) for the data left out for validation.

Case	Method	$\hat{a}_1$	$\hat{a}_2$	$\hat{a}_3$	CV-SSE	CV-SAE
I	PL-NW	1.502 (0.036)			0.1295 (0.0271)	0.6419 (0.0763)
	PL-LSVM	1.502 (0.034)	–	–	0.1077 (0.0239)	0.5859 (0.0702)
	PL-SVM	1.498 (0.034)	–	–	0.1077 (0.0238)	0.5863 (0.0701)
II	PL-NW	0.604 (0.036)	0.298 (0.039)		0.2489 (0.1212)	0.8360 (0.1273)
	PL-LSVM	0.604 (0.030)	0.297 (0.034)	–	0.1567 (0.1103)	0.6593 (0.1178)
	PL-SVM	0.603 (0.029)	0.298 (0.033)	–	0.1566 (0.1100)	0.6593 (0.1176)
III	PL-NW	0.601 (0.089)	0.284 (0.133)		0.1206 (0.0470)	0.6147 (0.0915)
	PL-LSVM	0.604 (0.087)	0.278 (0.127)	–	0.1071 (0.0465)	0.5786 (0.0855)
	PL-SVM	0.600 (0.085)	0.278 (0.124)	–	0.1068 (0.0462)	0.5784 (0.0858)
IV	PL-NW	0.661 0.172	0.133 (0.202)	0.108 (0.158)	0.5529 (0.1144)	1.3562 (0.1615)
	PL-LSVM	0.660 0.152	0.139 (0.177)	0.100 (0.151)	0.5063 (0.1091)	1.2975 (0.1588)
	PL-SVM	0.552 (0.120)	0.195 (0.131)	0.128 (0.120)	0.5016 (0.1085)	1.2943 (0.1587)

results than the partially linear models based on Nadaraya-Watson and local linear regression (not shown here). But the PL-SVM's (with $\varepsilon \neq 0$) are naturally better suited for problems of greater dimension thanks to the support vectors.

Moreover, given that the SVMs are a generalization of the splines (regularization networks (RN) in general) resulting from the use of the quadratic loss (ε-insensitive loss with $p = 2$ and $\varepsilon = 0$), the method is perfectly valid and produces equally satisfactory results in these cases.

Given the relationship between RN/splines and kriging [4], the method enables partially parametric kriging to be formulated if the spatial variables are accompanied by other variables on which the response depends parametrically. In this case it will be necessary to fit the empirical covariogram to a covariogram model with two components as has been done here: one of these components (polynomial or another model of interest) will give rise to the parametric expression of the final predictor; the other component, based on a model with good approximating properties (e.g. spherical, Gaussian, exponential, etc.) will give rise to the non-parametric part. We are unaware of the existence of techniques for this kind of fitting, and so would consider this to be an interesting avenue for further research.

The PP–SVMs should not be confused with the semi-parametric SVMs ([8], also [4]), whose solution takes the form:

$$f_{\mathbf{w},\mathbf{c}}(\mathbf{x}) = \sum_{i=1}^{n} \alpha_i k(\mathbf{x}, \mathbf{x}_i) + \sum_{j=0}^{m} c_j q_j(\mathbf{x})$$

where $q_j : \mathbb{R}^d \to \mathbb{R}$, $j = 0, ..., m$ are known functions. Despite the fact that these SVMs may also include linear (or, in general, parametric) terms that affect any given reduced subset of covariables, these covariables are also present in the non-parametric term unless techniques like those described here are used. Thus the semi-parametric SVMs cannot be applied to the estimation of models of the type in (1) nor, consequently, can they be interpreted.

The method described here can be extended in an analogous manner to the problem of classification, as also to other methods that use the kernel as inner product, such as [7]: kernel principal component analysis (KPCA), kernel discriminant (KD), kernel canonical correlation (KCC), etc.

References

1. Aronszajn, N. Theory of Reproducing Kernels. *Transactions of the American Mathematical Society*, **68** (1950) 337–404.
2. Cristianini N., Shawe-Taylor J. Kernel Methods for Pattern Analysis. (2004). Cambridge University Press.
3. Espinoza M., Pelckmans K., Hoegaerts L., Suykens J., De Moor B. A comparative study of LS-SVMs applied to the Silver box identification problem. *Proceedings of the 6th IFAC Nonlinear Control Systems (NOLCOS)*, Stutgartt, Germany (2004).
4. Matías J. M., Vaamonde A., Taboada J., González-Manteiga W. Support Vector Machines and Gradient Boosting for Graphical Estimation of a Slate Deposit. *Journal of Stochastic Environmental Research and Risk Assessment*, **18** (2004) 309–323.
5. Matías J. M., González-Manteiga, W. *Proceedings of the Joint 13th International Conference on Artificial Neural Networks and 10th International Conference on Neural Information Processing. Istambul, Turkey.* LCNS 2714, (2003) 209-216. Springer.
6. Robinson, P.M. Root-n-consistent semiparametric regression. *Econometrica*, **56** (1988) 931–954.
7. Schölkopf, B., Smola, A. J. *Learning with Kernels.* (2002). MIT Press.
8. Smola A, Frieβ J., Schölkopf B. Semiparametric support vector and linear programming machines. *Advances in Neural Information Processing Systems 11.* MIT press (1999) 585–591.
9. Speckman, P. Kernel smoothing in partial linear models. *Journal of the Royal Statistical Society, Series B*, **50** (1988) 413–436.
10. Vapnik, V. Statistical Learning Theory. (1998). John Wiley & Sons.

Adapting Hausdorff Metrics to Face Detection Systems: A Scale-Normalized Hausdorff Distance Approach

Pablo Suau

Departamento de Ciencia de la Computación e Inteligencia Artificial,
Universidad de Alicante, Ap. de correos 99, 03080, Alicante, Spain
pablo@dccia.ua.es

Abstract. Template matching face detection systems are used very often as a previous step in several biometric applications. These biometric applications, like face recognition or video surveillance systems, need the face detection step to be efficient and robust enough to achieve better results. One of many template matching face detection methods uses Hausdorff distance in order to search the part of the image more similar to a face. Although Hausdorff distance involves very accurate results and low error rates, overall robustness can be increased if we adapt it to our concrete application. In this paper we show how to adjust Hausdorff metrics to face detection systems, presenting a scale-normalized Hausdorff distance based face detection system. Experiments show that our approach can perform an accurate face detection even with complex background or varying light conditions.

1 Introduction

Several human machine interface systems and biometric applications need to be built over a reliable face detection system. Results of these applications will not be robust enough to be useful if a correct face localization is not performed; an automated system will not be able to fully recognize a facial expression, for instance, if this fundamental step is not correct and some essential information such as eyebrows position or upper face wrinkles are not properly recognized. However, although face detection significance, several complex systems avoid this step, due to the fact that their designers consider that is not so important, and manual techniques are used to know in a quite simple way where a face is in an image [11].

Recent research surveys [1] reveal the existence of several simplified facial detection systems that could be useful as a first step of more complex systems. These systems are based on *face localization* [2], that aims to determine the image position of a single face, with the assumption that the input image only includes one.

In the case of face localization, these surveys [1] indicate that the method based on template matching and Hausdorff distance is one of the most robust.

C. Bento, A. Cardoso, and G. Dias (Eds.): EPIA 2005, LNAI 3808, pp. 76–86, 2005.

In template matching approaches, a standard face pattern (usually frontal) is predefined, and the part of the image more similar to this pattern is searched in an image, by correlation. In [3], Jesorsky et al. describe a face localization system based on template matching, using Hausdorff distance to calculate correlation. Their method allows to find a face in an image at different scales, and gives better detection results that other face detction systems ysing differente distance metrics. However, results of this proposal and related ones are strongly affected if complex backgrounds are present. Other approaches are based on previous steps before using Hausdorff metrics, like skin color segmentation [8], but using color images is not always possible.

In this work, we present an improved face detection system based on a scale-normalized Hausdorff distance and template matching. We have chosen a face localization method because we will use it as a first step of a more complex facial expression recognition system. In section 2, we define Hausdorff distance metrics and how it can be used to find objects in an image. Then, in section 3, we explain how our face detection system works, remarking changes we have made to improve it. Finally, in section 4 we show some experimental results.

2   Hausdorff Distance for Template Matching

Hausdorff distance is a technique for comparing sets of points; for each point of a model set, it measures how near they lie from any point of another image set and vice versa. It is used in pattern recognition to determine the degree of resemblance between two objects ([4],[5]).

Hausdorff distance can be defined as the maximum distance from a point set to the nearest point in other point set. If $A = \{a_1, ..., a_m\}$ and $B = \{b_1, ..., b_n\}$ are two point sets, the Hausdorff distance between A and B is defined as

$$H(A, B) = \max(h(A, B), h(B, A)) \tag{1}$$

where

$$h(A, B) = \max_{a \in A} \min_{b \in B} \|a - b\| \tag{2}$$

is called the *directed Hausdorff distance* from set A to set B with some underlying norm $\| \cdot \|$ on the points of A and B, and

$$h(B, A) = \max_{b \in B} \min_{a \in A} \|b - a\| \tag{3}$$

is called the *reverse Hausdorff distance*. As we can see, Haussdorff distance is not symmetric. It gives an interesting measure of the mutual proximity of two set of points, by indicating the maximal distance between any point of one set to other set.

Two main problems exist when we use Hausdorff distance for image processing: scale (which will be discussed in section 3) and outlier points. The experiments in [7] have proven that outlier points effect can be reduced using an average version of the Hausdorff distance, based on taking the average of the single point distances. In fact, this Hausdorff variant gives better results than other known Hausdorff metrics ([7]). The average Hausdorff distance is defined as:

$$h_{avg}(A, B) = \frac{1}{|A|} \sum_{a \in A} \min_{b \in B} \|a - b\| \tag{4}$$

$$h_{avg}(B, A) = \frac{1}{|B|} \sum_{b \in B} \min_{a \in A} \|b - a\| \tag{5}$$

As we have said before, Hausdorff distance is very useful to detect a single object in an image. Let A be a representation of the image where we want to look for an object, and B a representation of the object itself. Let also $T = (t_x, t_y, s_x, s_y)$ be our transformation space, where t_x and t_y represent translation, and s_x and s_y scale, and P a set containing all possible values for T (so, if $b = (b_x, b_y)$ is a point of B and $p \in P$, then $T_p(b) = (s_x \cdot b_x + t_x, s_y \cdot b_y + t_y)$. Allowed transformations and their parameter space P depend on the application). Figure 1 shows the process to find a model B in an image A using transformations.

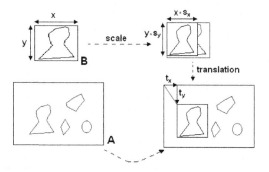

Fig. 1. Applying transformations to detect a model in an image

In order to find B inside A, we need to search for transformation parameters values $p \in P$ such that the Hausdorff distance between the transformed model $T_p(B)$ and A is minimized. The Hausdorff distance to be minimized is:

$$d_{\hat{p}} = \min_{p \in P} H(A, T_p(B)) \tag{6}$$

where $\hat{p}$ is the set of values $p \in P$ for the transformation space parameters T that minimize the Hausdorff distance between the image A and the transformed model B.

So, $f_B(T_p) = h(T_p(B), A)$ is called the *forward distance* and will be used to find the object in the image, and $f_A(T_p) = h(A, T_p(B))$ is called the *reverse distance* and will allow the system to detect a false positive. We must note that only the part of the image that is covered by the model must be considered.

3   System Description

We expect to use our face detection approach as part of a more complex facial expression recognition system. Therefore, as in [3], our method is based on face localization: only one face is present in test images at any time, and the part of the image more similar to a face is searched. As a consequence, we can have a complete system including face detection, and focus more on our main goal.

Figure 2 shows the complete face localization process, which is divided in a segmentation step and a localization step. The segmentation step transforms the input image into a binary edge image, so a template matching search can be performed on it. Once the segmentation is finished, the localization step uses Eq.(6) as a distance metrics to compute a template matching algorithm using a face template, in order to detect the exact position and size of the face in the image. These two steps are described in detail in the following sections.

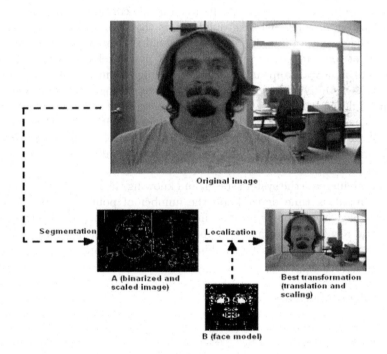

Fig. 2. A summary of the face localization system

3.1   Segmentation Phase

The input image must be transformed into a binary edge image prior to starting the localization step. This binary image should contain enough information to get correct localization results.

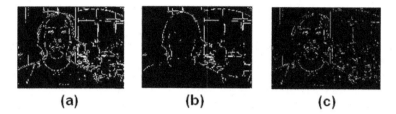

Fig. 3. a) Sobel edge detection using threshold = 0.04. b) Sobel edge detection using threshold = 0.09. c) Edge detection combining multiple Sobel operators.

To extract edges from the input image, we could use several edge operators, like Canny, Sobel, and so on, being the Sobel operator the most used in template matching systems combined with Hausdorff distance metrics ([3], [4], [5]). However, as we can see in Figure 3a and Figure 3b, using a simple Sobel operator in an image with complex background can be inappropriate. Sobel edge detection with a low threshold (Figure 3a) results in an image containing too much edges, including a high amount of background points that can affect the localization step. Sobel edge detection with a higher threshold (Figure 3b) slightly decreases the number of edges detected, but it also makes points related to facial features like eyes and mouth disappear; furthermore, points from complex background still are present. Our system solves this problem combining two Sobel edge detections with different thresholds (Figure 3c). We calculate the difference between the edge image obtained after a Sobel edge detection with a low threshold and another obtained using a high threshold. This operation makes most of background points disappear, while points obtained from facial features segmentation still remain.

In order to increase the system speed, and knowing the fact that the Hausdorff distance computing time depends on the number of points of sets A and B, the input image is scaled *before* the image segmentation process starts. Our experimental results show that the input image could be scaled up to a 40% of its original size without affecting the final outcome and decreasing considerably the computation time.

3.2   Localization Phase

After the segmentation step, we obtain a scaled binary image where some patterns of points representing a face could be found. The template we will use is the same as in [3] (Figure 4). As shown in [6], this point template is created from genetic algorithms as an average of a set of faces. Almost all points represent facial features like eyes, mouth and nose, while some other points represent face boundaries.

Using the face model B and the segmented binary image A, we try to find the face in the image using Eq.(6), testing different scales and translations for B. The values for the transformation set $\hat{p}$ that minimizes $H(A, T_p(B))$ gives us the position and size of the face in the image.

Fig. 4. Face template

As discussed before, the scale is one of the main practical problems of Hausdorff distance when it is used for image processing. Due to the fact that the size of faces could be highly variable, we must try a high range of scale values (s_x, s_y) for the model B during the search. The problem is that Hausdorff distance values are lower for smaller template sizes; which means that if the face in the image is large, although correct template transformations for scale and translation results in a low Hausdorff distance, the smallest values of scale applied to the template generate even smaller distance values. The consequences can be seen in Figure 5a. It seems that a normalization factor is needed to adapt the Hausdorff distance metrics to different template sizes. It must be chosen carefully, since modifying the distance substantially can result in the opposite effect: smaller faces would be very difficult to detect.

After completing the experimentation process (that will be discussed in next section), we found that dividing $h(T_p(B), A)$, and $h(A, T_p(B))$ by $\sqrt{\frac{s_x + s_y}{2}}$, allows the system to detect exactly the size and position of faces, without any scale effect. Figure 5b shows how this normalization factor solves the scale issue.

A correct combination of the forward and reverse Hausdorff distance can be very useful to avoid false positives. In [3], authors use the product of the two distances to help in a face/non-face decision. Figure 6a shows some examples of incorrect face localization when only forward distance is used. The point is to find the transformation set $\hat{p}$ that minimizes the product of the forward

Fig. 5. Scale issue. a) face detection without normalization factor. b) face detection with normalization factor. Normalization factor is flexible enough to allow detection of any size faces.

Fig. 6. Using the reverse distance to discard false positives. a) Face detection without reverse distance. b) Face detection with reverse distance. Reverse distance, in combination with forward distance, helps in discarding parts in an image that are not faces.

distance $h(A, T_{\hat{p}}(B))$ and the reverse distance $h(T_{\hat{p}}(B), A)$. Figure 6b shows face localization results for the same images but using the reverse distance to discard false positives.

4   Experimental Results

This section is divided in two subsections. In section 4.1 we will demonstrate that our normalization factor improves the Hausdorff metrics results for face detection. In section 4.2 we will show our system results.

The test set used in experiments was the BioID database[1], that is available for free on the Internet and includes 1521 gray level images, having all of them a size of 384x288 pixels. This complete database contains images of 23 different people, having a wide variety of light conditions, face sizes, and complex backgrounds. The binary template associated to this database is shown in Figure 4 and its size is 81x86 pixels.

The search region is restricted to a centered square in the image, covering the whole image height. Before the process, we scale the input image to a 40% of its original size. In the segmentation phase, the two edge images created from the two different Sobel operators (with thresholds 0.04 and 0.09, respectively) are subtracted. The scaling parameter range for the template is between 55% and 120%.

4.1   Normalization Factor

Face localization based on Hausdorff distance needs a template to compare with. This template is scaled so faces with different sizes can be detected. To demonstrate that distance and template scale are related, we calculated, for every image in the BioID database, the minimum distance obtained for every template scale. As we can see in Figure 7a, distance increases in a quadratic way with template scale, so bigger faces (Figure 5a) are not correctly detected because although

---

[1] http://www.humanscan.de/support/downloads/facedb.php

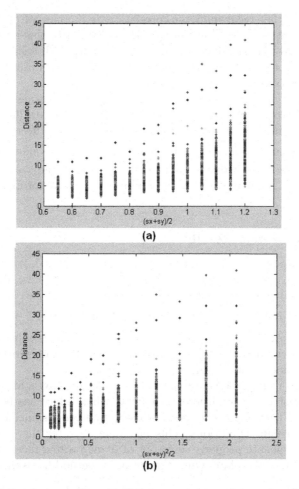

Fig. 7. Correlation between Hausdorff distance and template scale. a) Distance versus scale. b) Distance versus $scale^2$.

correct template transformations for scale and translation result in a low distance, the smallest values of scale applied to the template generate even smaller values.

A more formal demonstration can be performed using the Pearson's correlation coefficient, that is a measure of the strength of the association between two variables, used quite often in statistics. Pearson's correlation coefficient value ranges from -1 to +1, being this value higher when a strong relationship exists. The Pearson's correlation coefficient value for our two variables (Hausdorff distance and template scale) is $p = 0.795$ with a significance level of 99%; it means that there is a strong lineal relationship.

However, Figure 7a shows that relationship between these two variables seems more quadratic than linear. When a correlation is strong but clearly non linear, it is common to transform one or both of the variables in order to remove the curvilinearity and then recalculate the correlation. In our case we created a graph where distance versus $[\frac{s_x+s_y}{2}]^2$ is shown (Figure 7b). After this transformation, the Pearson's correlation coefficient value is $p = 0.8278$ with a significance level of 99%. Therefore, quadratic relationship between these two variables is stronger than lineal relationship.

Thus, we must be aware of this quadratic dependance when we define the normalization factor. If we use $\frac{s_x+s_y}{2}$ as normalization factor, distance will be substantially modified, and it will result in the opposite effect: smaller faces will be quite difficult to detect. However, using $\sqrt{\frac{s_x+s_y}{2}}$ as normalization factor reduces the distance value significantly for larger scale values, and more slightly for smaller templates, resulting in a lower error rate for face localization (Figure 5b).

4.2   Face Localization Results

If we draw a bounding box where the face has been detected, we consider that a face is correctly detected when it contains all important facial features (eyes, nose, mouth, etc.) and when the face fills at least 80% of this bounding box. The error rate of our system was 7.3%, using BioID database and $\sqrt{\frac{s_x+s_y}{2}}$ as normalization factor. In the case that we use $\frac{s_x+s_y}{2}$ as normalization factor, the error rate is increased to 23.73%, due to the fact that Hausdorff distance is strongly affected for low scale values.

Other systems using BioID database to test its results have a higher error rate [9], or use less restrictive conditions to indicate when a face has been correctly detected [10]. In Figure 8a we can see some correct detections, including different scales, poses and light conditions. This fact demonstrates that our system is flexible enough to locate properly some out of plane rotated faces, even using a standard frontal face template. Our segmentation method helps in finding faces

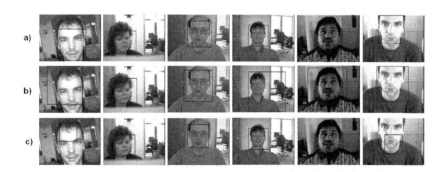

Fig. 8. a) Some examples of correct face detection, including not frontal faces and complex backgrounds, using $\sqrt{\frac{s_x+s_y}{2}}$ as normalization factor. b) Results for the same images using $\frac{s_x+s_y}{2}$ as normalization factor. c) Results for the same images without any normalization factor.

in images where a complex background exists, with varying light conditions, as we can see in Figure 8a, as well.

In Figure 8 we can see also how the normalization factor affects the face localization. Figure 8a shows correct face localization using the $\sqrt{\frac{s_x+s_y}{2}}$ as normalization factor. In Figure 8b the results for the same images using $\frac{s_x+s_y}{2}$ as normalization factor can be seen. Finally, Figure 8c shows the results for the same images, but without using any normalization factor. Thus, Figure 8 illustrates how large faces are correctly detected with our normalization factor, without affecting small faces localization.

5   Conclusions and Future Work

We have presented a face detection system based on template matching in an edge image using a scale-normalized Hausdorff distance. Results are better in robustness than in previous similar works. Our system is flexible enough to detect faces in images with complex backgrounds under varying light conditions, and can detect some not frontal faces.

We have introduced a normalization factor in the Hausdorff distance calculation, so this metric is not affected by template size. We have also proven that is possible to highly reduce the input image's size without affecting facial detection and resulting in a much faster process. Our segmentation method allows not interesting background points to be removed.

Future work could focus on study how some Hausdorff distance improvements can affect our detection results. It could be interesting to test if there is any gain in using a multiresolution Hausdorff distance. It could be also interesting to check if it is possible to combine several templates to try to find faces in different orientations. Finally, our face detection system would be used as a part of an automated facial expression recognition system, which is currently being developed.

References

[1] Yang, M. H., Kriegman, D., Ahuja, N., Detecting Faces in Images: A Survey, *IEEE Transactions on Pattern Analysis and Machine Intelligence (PAMI)*, vol. 24, no. 1, pp. 34-58, 2002.

[2] Lam, K., Yan, H., Fast Algorithm for Locating Head Boundaries, *J. Electronic Imaging*, vol.3, no.4, pp. 351-359, 1994.

[3] Jesorsky, O., Kirchberg, K. J., Frischholz, R. W., Robust Face Detection Using the Hausdorff Distance, *Third International Conference on Audio and Video-based Biometric Person Authentication*, Springer Lecture Notes in Computer Science, LNCS-2091, pp. 90-95, Halmstad, Sweden, 2001.

[4] Huttenlocher, D. P., Klanderman, G. A., Rucklidge, W. J., Comparing Images Using the Hausdorff Distance, *IEEE Transactions on Pattern Analysis and Machine Intelligence*, vol. 14, no. 9, pp. 850-853, 1993.

[5] Huttenlocher, D. P., Rucklidge, W. J., A multi-resolution technique for comparing images using the Hausdorff distance, *Technical Report 1321, Cornell University, Department of Computer Science*, 1992.

[6] Kirchberg, K. J., Jesorsky, O., Frischholz, R. W., Genetic Model Optimization for Hausdorff Distance-Based Face Localization, *International ECCV 2002 Workshop on Biometric Authentication*, Springer Lecture Notes in Computer Science, LNCS-2359, pp. 103-111, Copenhagen, Denmark, 2002.

[7] Shapiro, M. D., Blaschko, M. B., On Hausdorff Distance Measures, *Technical Report UM-CS-2004-071, Department of Computer Science, University of Massachusetts Amherst*, 2004.

[8] S. Srisuk, W. Kurutach and K. Limpitikeat, A Novel Approach for Robust, Fast and Accurate Face Detection, *International Journal of Uncertainty, Fuzziness and Knowledge-Based Systems (IJUFKS)*, Vol. 9, No. 6, pp. 769-779, December 2001, World Scientific Publishing Company.

[9] V. Manian, A. Ross, A Texture-based Approach to Face Detection, *Biometric Consortium Conference (BCC)*, (Crystal City, VA), September 2004.

[10] B. Frba, C. Kblbeck, Robust Face Detection at Video Frame Rate Based on Edge Orientation Features, *Fifth IEEE International Conference on Automatic Face and Gesture Recognition (FGR 2002)*, pp. 342-347, Washington, USA, 2002.

[11] M. Rosenblum, Y. Yacoob, L. Davis, Human Expression Recognition from Motion using a Radial Basis Function Network Architecture, *IEEE Transactions on Neural Networks*, Vol. 7, no. 5, pp. 1121-1138, 1996.

Robust Real-Time Human Activity Recognition from Tracked Face Displacements*

Paul E. Rybski and Manuela M. Veloso

The Robotics Institute and Computer Science Department,
Carnegie Mellon University, USA
{prybski, mmv}@cs.cmu.edu

Abstract. We are interested in the challenging scientific pursuit of how to characterize human activities in any formal meeting situation by tracking people's positions with a computer vision system. We present a human activity recognition algorithm that works within the framework of CAMEO (the Camera Assisted Meeting Event Observer), a panoramic vision system designed to operate in real-time and in uncalibrated environments. Human activity is difficult to characterize within the constraints that the CAMEO must operate, including uncalibrated deployment and unmodeled occlusions. This paper describes these challenges and how we address them by identifying invariant features and robust activity models. We present experimental results of our recognizer correctly classifying person data.

1   Introduction

Recognizing human activity is a very challenging task, ranging from low-level sensing and feature extraction from sensory data to high-level inference algorithms used to infer the state of the subject from the dataset. We are interested in the scientific challenges of modeling simple activities of people who are participating in formal meeting situations. We are also interesting in recognizing activities of people as classified by a computer vision system.

In order to address these challenges, our group is developing a physical awareness system for an agent-based electronic assistant called CAMEO (Camera Assisted Meeting Event Observer) [1]. CAMEO is an omni-directional camera system consisting of four FireWire cameras mounted in a 360° configuration, as shown in Figure 1. The individual data streams extracted from each of the cameras are merged into a single panoramic image of the world. The cameras are connected to a Small Form-Factor 3.0GHz Pentium 4 PC that captures the video data and performs image processing.

---

* This research was supported by the National Business Center (NBC) of the Department of the Interior (DOI) under a subcontract from SRI International. The views and conclusions contained in this document are those of the authors and should not be interpreted as necessarily representing the official policies or endorsements, either expressed or implied, by the NBC, DOI, SRI, or the US Government.

C. Bento, A. Cardoso, and G. Dias (Eds.): EPIA 2005, LNAI 3808, pp. 87–98, 2005.

Fig. 1. The CAMEO system consists of a set of FireWire cameras arranged in a panoramic fashion and a small-form-factor PC

The panoramic video stream is scanned for human activity by identifying the positions of human faces found in the image. We make the assumption that people can be recognized in the image based on the location of their face. To be able to recognize people's activities within any meeting scenario, the challenge is to find appropriate features in terms of face positions without a global coordinate system. Low-level features are extracted from the raw dataset and are modeled as the observations for the recognition methods. The range of all possible human activities is reduced to a small discrete set.

We successfully solve this problem by two main contributions: (i) the identification of robust meeting features in terms of relative displacements; and (ii) the application of Dynamic Bayesian Networks (DBNs) to this problem, extending their use from other signal-understanding tasks.

2   Related Work

We use DBNs [2] to model the activities of people in the meetings. DBNs are directed acyclic graphs that model stochastic time series processes. They are a generalization of both Hidden Markov Models (HMM) [3] and linear dynamical systems such as Kalman Filters. DBNs are used by [4] to recognize gestures such as writing in different languages on a whiteboard, as well as activities such as using a Glucose monitor. Our system infers body stance and motion by tracking the user's face in a cluttered and general background rather than attempting to track the hands, which is difficult to do in general.

In [5], finite state machine models of gestures are constructed by learning spatial and temporal information of the gestures separately from each other. However, it is assumed that the gestures are performed directly in front of the camera and that the individual features of the face and hands can be recognized and observed without error.

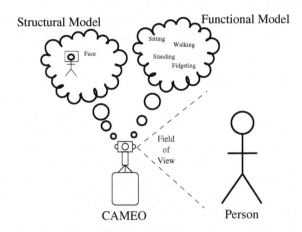

Fig. 2. CAMEO maintains both an image and activity model of people in the environment. The image model is a representation off the person from CAMEO's sensors (e.g. the detected face). The activity model represents how the person is expected to move about and what those movements mean in terms of actions.

Fig. 3. A frame of video from a typical meeting as annotated by CAMEO

An extension to the HMM formalism called the Abstract Hidden Markov mEmory Model (AHMEM) [6] is used to represent a hierarchy of both state-dependent and context-free behaviors. However, this work uses a network of cameras set up throughout the entire office space to view hand-labeled locations.

A system for using stereo cameras to infer deictic information through torso and arm position tracking is described in [7]. Our system is essentially monocular and is not intended to be addressed directly where it could observe the full torso and arm positions of everyone attending the meeting.

Recognizing the behaviors of individual robotic (non-human) agents has been studied in [8]. Robots playing soccer against other robots [9] would greatly benefit by being able to classify the different behavioral patterns observed by their opponents. In this work, robots are tracked by an overhead camera and their actions are classified by a series of hand-crafted modified hidden Markov models (called Behavior HMMs).

Much of the related work in activity modeling relies upon fixed cameras with known poses with respect to the objects and people that they are tracking. Our efforts focus very heaviliy on activity models that can be tracked and observed by uncalibrated vision systems which do not have the luxury of knowing their absolute position in the environment. This approach is attractive because it minimizes the cost for setting up the system and increases its general utility.

3 The CAMEO System

CAMEO is part of a larger effort called CALO (Cognitive Agent that Learns and Organizes) to develop an enduring personalized cognitive assistant that is capable of helping humans handle the many daily business/personal activities in which they engage. In order to be useful in a general set of environments, CAMEO must operate in many different meeting room configurations and should not require any lengthy calibration for distance or lighting conditions.

Raw visual data from the multi-camera system is captured and merged into a single consistent image mosaic [1]. People in the image are located by identifying their faces using the detector in Intel's OpenCV[1] computer vision library. Faces are matched between subsequent video frames by computing a distance metric between sets of tracked faces and the new faces. Matches are those that have the smallest distance. The metric is computed by taking the SVD of the image sets and computing the weighted sum of the most significant eigenvectors. CAMEO is capable of recording mpeg movies of meetings for archival purposes and off-line analysis. All of CAMEO's detection/inference algorithms can be run on either live or recorded video. Finally, streams of tracked facial information are fed into a DBN classifier that identifies the state of each person. The following sections describe the details of CAMEO's state inference mechanisms.

4 Meeting State Inference

As mentioned previously, CAMEO must be able to operate in uncalibrated environments and infer the activities of people in real time. Additionally, activity models that are used in one meeting must be transferable to other meetings with different attendees. This enforces a number of constraints on CAMEO's data processing, the most significant of these are shown in Figure 4. Because the environment contains objects that are unknown and unmodeled, detecting people's bodies is very challenging and difficult to do properly. As a result, the most robust feature for detecting a person becomes their face. Faces are very unique and distinguishing features which greatly simplify the task of determining whether an object is a person or not. The face detection algorithms that we use are a compromise between the need for accurate and robust person detection and the needs for CAMEO to operate in real-time. The decision to process facial data only directly affects the selection of specific features for activity recognition. For instance, the absolute Y positions of people's faces are not very meaningful because CAMEO is not aware of the positions of people in the environment, nor is it aware of its own relative distance to those people.

---

[1] http://www.intel.com/research/mrl/research/opencv/

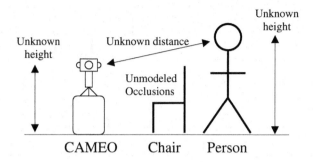

Fig. 4. Unknown spatial quantities that the CAMEO activity recognition system must contend with when attempting to infer activities from observed people

In order to operate within these constraints, a number of simplifying assumptions are made about the structure of the environments and the behaviors of the participants in the meetings. These assumptions are:

1. CAMEO will be in the center of a meeting and can see all the participants
2. When performing an action, a person is likely to remain doing that action and not rapidly switch from one action to another
3. People's activities are first-order Markovian (the current state can be inferred by only considering the previous state and the current data).

4.1 Observation Model – Features

At every frame of video, all of the faces that have been found return an (x, y) position in image coordinates. The CAMEO software tracks each face from frame to frame and stores a history of the face positions. Because relying on absolute (x, y) positions will be brittle due to the above constraints, we instead look at the difference of the face positions between subsequent frames of video, e.g. $(\Delta x, \Delta y)$, where $\Delta x = x_t - x_{t-1}$ and $\Delta y = y_t - y_{t-1}$.

As an illustrative example, a single person's face was tracked by CAMEO and the resulting raw displacements in the horizontal and vertical direction are shown in Figure 5. In practice, this particular choice of features has proven to be quite robust.

4.2 Observation Model and States

In order to define a DBN, the model states must be identified and observation probabilities distributions must be assigned to those states. Initially, we were interested in the following activities: "Standing," "Walking," "Fidgeting," and "Sitting". The observation features as previously introduced consist of real-valued 2D vectors of face *displacements* (to address the challenges of general meeting processing). To correctly define this model, we needed to perform some empirical studies to find out how our observation features were related for these activities that we wanted to track.

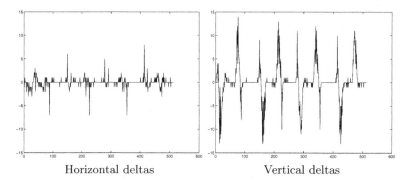

Horizontal deltas   Vertical deltas

Fig. 5. Raw data from a tracked person. The left graph shows ΔX (horizontal displacement) of the face in pixels over time while the right shows ΔY (vertical displacement) over time. The horizontal axis is time in seconds.

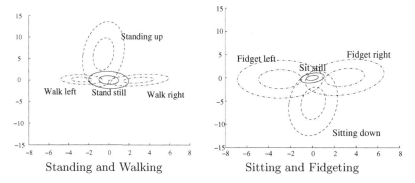

Standing and Walking   Sitting and Fidgeting

Fig. 6. Learned Gaussian distributions for the real-valued observation vectors corresponding to the four hidden states associated with standing and walking on the left and sitting and fidgeting on the right. The first and second standard deviations are shown for each distribution.

Several meetings were recorded and the actions of the people in them were hand-annotated to generate class labels to train the DBN's observation probability distributions. Interestingly, some of our general states could not be distinguished from one another. The stationary standing and sitting states are indistinguishable because the face displacements $(\Delta x, \Delta y)$ are identical given that the person is generally immobile. To address this problem, we refined our model to include states "Sitting down," "Standing up," "Stand still," and "Sit still". Fidgeting and walking left or right could also not be distinguished. In our model, the transitions through intermediate states also resolved this problem. The final observation empirically-defined distributions are shown in Figure 6.

Note the symmetry between the observations in the states associated with "Standing up" and "Sitting down" in Figure 6. The "Walking" and "Fidgeting" states have very similar means, as do the "Stand still" and "Sit still" states. This directly illustrates the uncertainties associated with the CAMEO's observation models, particularly because absolute values in the Y dimension are not directly meaningful.

4.3 Person States

We have used these constraints and assumptions to define a finite state machine which encapsulates a coarse level of possible activities that can be detected in the image data stream. This state machine is illustrated in Figure 7.

The "Sit still" state represents instances when a person is sitting in a chair and is stationary. The "Fidget left" and "Fidget right" states represent motion of those people in their chairs, such as if they look around or lean to one side to talk to someone. The "Standing up" and "Sitting down" states represent the transitions from a "Sit still" and "Stand still" state. These are the actual activities involved with getting up from one's chair and taking one's seat, respectively. Finally, once a person is in the "Stand still" state, they can "Walk left" and "Walk right".

Conceptually, the "Standing up" and "Sitting down" states could be modeled as transitions rather than as actual states, but from observing meeting records, we have seen that people spend anywhere from 3-10 frames in each of these states. This, we feel, warrants that they be treated as states of the system rather than as some sort of transition condition.

Several of our assumptions about how people move in their environment directly dictate the structure for the DBN model. For instance, we have to assume that once people start a particular motion, they will continue doing that motion for a few frames until the observations dictate otherwise. This is done by manually setting the state probability transitions $P(X_t = i | X_{t-1} = j)$, or the probability that state X at time t is i given that the state at time $t - 1$ is j, to:

$$P(X_t = i | X_{t-1} = i) = 0.999999 \qquad (1)$$
$$P(X_t = i | X_{t-1} = j) \approx 0.000001 (\text{where } i! = j) \qquad (2)$$

This probability distribution represents the shortcoming of the standard HMM formalism for modeling timeseries data where the states may have explicit state

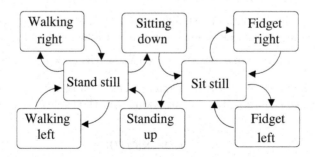

Fig. 7. Example finite state machine for a single person in a meeting

durations. Without these probabilities, the state transitions are much more likely to change states and to do so very quickly. While the state transition probabilities are set manually in this fashion, the probability of making an observation given a particular state, $P(Y|X)$, is learned from real data.

4.4 The Viterbi Algorithm for State Estimation

The activity recognition system models the human activity framework using a DBN. A layer of hidden nodes represents the discrete set of activities shown previously in Figure 7. The observed output nodes are continuous-value Gaussian distributions over the Δx and Δy signal values returned from the CAMEO system (note that lower-case x and y refer to image coordinates, while upper-case X and Y refer to the state and observation probabilities for a DBN as described next).

Traditionally, the Forward algorithm [3] is used to return the most likely state given an observation sequence. The Forward algorithm computes the most likely state at each timestep by summing the probabilities of the previous states. However, if the state transition $P(X_t = i|X_{t-1} = j) = 0$ at a given timestep, the Forward algorithm can still return that the most likely state at time $t-1$ is j and the most likely state at time t is state i. This is a problem for our model since there are numerous states that do not link to each other.

An algorithm which addresses this shortcoming and provides a more accurate estimate of the model's state sequence is the Viterbi algorithm [3]. Viterbi is a dynamic programming algorithm which takes into account the state transition probabilities to generate the most likely state sequence that could have generated the observation sequence. This is more formally defined as:

$$q_{1:t} = arg \max_{q_1:t} P(q_{1:x}|y_{1:t}) \tag{3}$$

where q_t is the most likely state at time t. Thus, for each timestep, Viterbi computes a term $\delta_t(j)$, defined as:

$$\delta_t(j) = \max_i \left[\delta_{t-1}(i) P(X_t = j|X_{t-1} = i) \right] P(y_t|X_t = j) \tag{4}$$

which is initialized as:

$$\delta_0(i) = P(X_0 = i) P(y_0|X_0 = i) \tag{5}$$

Additionally, the index of the most likely state at time $t-1$ to transition into each state at time t is computed and stored in a table $\psi_t(j)$ as follows:

$$\psi_t(j) = arg \max_i \left[\delta_{t-1}(i) P(X_t = j|X_{t-1} = i) \right] \tag{6}$$

Finally, after the entire observation sequence has been analyzed in this fashion, the state sequence is obtained by backtracking over the table of ψ values ranging from $t = 0$ to $t = T$:

$$q_T = arg \max_i \left[\delta_T(i) \right]$$

$$q_t = \psi_{t+1}(q_{t+1}) \tag{7}$$

4.5   Fixed-Length Backtracking Extension to Viterbi

Viterbi is a very powerful algorithm because it is able to employ the entire observation sequence at once to correct for noise that might corrupt the observation sequence. However, because of this, Viterbi requires the full observation sequence to be obtained before it is able to backtrack to resolve the complete state sequence. This will not work with CAMEO when it performs inference in real-time.

In order to achieve the benefits of Viterbi while not requiring that CAMEO wait for the entire state sequence, we have defined a hybrid approach by which backtracking is only done on the latest k states. Thus, when the observation at time t is received, the state at $t - k$ is inferred. In a real-time system, this fixed-window approach will cause a delay in the state estimate, but as long as the delay is not too long, the estimate may still be useful to act upon. Thus, the value of k represents a tradeoff in accuracy and estimation lag in a real-time system. This relationship will be explored further in the experimental results section.

5   Experimental Results

Figure 8 shows some results from the dynamic Bayesian network action recognition system as compared to hand-labeled ground truth. Data was collected from a short sequence of video that showed a single person standing up and then sitting down again.

In this figure, the solid line shows the hand-labeled ground truth of the person's activities, the dashed line shows the estimated activities, and the circles indicate states that were misclassified. Of the 315 images encoded with person tracked data, only 29 of the states were misclassified. Most of these occurred during the transitions from the "stand" state through the "sitting down" state to the "sit" state. This is primarily due to variances in the way that people

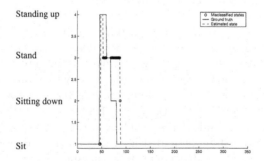

Fig. 8. Classified actions of a person standing up and sitting down. Of the 315 timesteps in this dataset, only 29 of the states were misclassified. The Y-axis represents the state where, 1="Sit", 2="Sitting down", 3="Stand", and 4="Standing up". The X-axis is the frame count. The data was captured at 15 fps.

move around. However, while the alignments of the activities were slightly off from ground truth (their starting and stopping times), the fact that the person stood up and sat down was not missed.

The performance of the fixed-window Viterbi algorithm with different values of k was evaluated. Figure 9 shows the effect of the window size on the accuracy of the inferred state sequence (the larger the window size, the more accurate the results are). Compare this with the Forward algorithm alone which scored only 67.95% correct. This high error rate of the Forward algorithm is caused primarily by the inference algorithm making illegal state transitions.

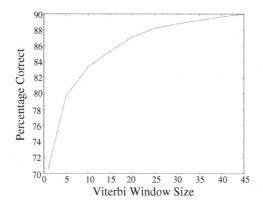

Fig. 9. Plot of the effect that the amount of backtracking in the fixed-window Viterbi algorithm has on the accuracy of the state inference. The larger the window size, the more accurate the state sequence from the ground truth. As a comparison, the Forward algorithm alone was only 67.95% correct on this dataset.

For each frame of video the Viterbi algorithm uses to improve its inference, the longer the time lag between the observation and the state inference. The full CAMEO system, which includes face detection, tracking, and face recognition, typically can track 5-6 people while running in real-time at approximately 3-4 frames per second. This means that each frame of video adds between 0.25-0.3 seconds of latency to the state inference. Any decision process that makes use of CAMEO's state estimation must always take this lag into account.

Finally, the images shown in Figure 10 graphically illustrate the state estimation algorithm running on data captured from CAMEO. The panoramic images have been truncated to only show the areas of interest. In this image sequence, two people enter a room and sit down. Their states are successfully tracked as transitioning through walking, stand still, sitting down, and sit still.

The activity recognizer is dependent upon the ability for CAMEO to successfully track people. If the tracker loses a person due to occlusions, or because the person left the room, then the data stream for the activities will be truncated or possibly erroneous. Additionally, if the person moves very slowly, their relative displacements will be lost in the noise model for the states which represent

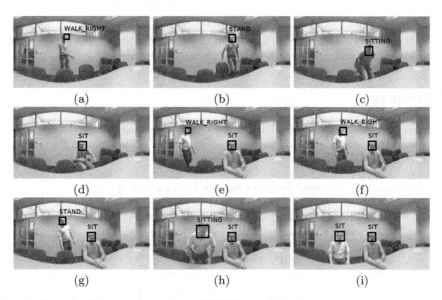

Fig. 10. Sample video captured from CAMEO in which the people's motions are captured by the face detector and classified by the Viterbi algorithm

stationary positions. Because of this, the activity recognizer might not classify a transition from standing to sitting (or vice versa). In this case, the activity recognizer will be out of alignment with the person's true position and will not catch up until another transition occurs that the recognizer successfully detects. Such "missed" transitions could be addressed by adding additional features to the classifier, such as using the motions of others in the environment to disambiguate the current state of a person. We are currently looking at ways to enhance our recognition algorithms to use this additional information.

6   Summary

CAMEO is designed to observe and infer state information about people in meetings. To do so, it requires minimal room instrumentation and calibration to operate. Because very little *a priori* information is known about the position (and possible occlusions) of people in the meeting, CAMEO makes use of a robust identification scheme to find and track people's faces in the environment. CAMEO tracks motions of faces and feeds their displacements into a Dynamic Bayesian Network-based classification system used to infer the tracked person's state. This classifier uses a model of human behavior which is encoded into the Bayesian Network's hidden state's conditional probability distribution. The parameters for the observed states are learned from labeled data. A fixed-sized backtracking implementation of Viterbi was implemented to recover the most likely state information from the data. We have shown experimental results from a state model illustrating how CAMEO is able to infer the state of individual people in the meeting. We have also discussed the tradeoffs of this approach between accuracy and real-time operation as well as describing some limitations of the algorithm and future directions of the research.

References

1. Rybski, P.E., de la Torre, F., Patil, R., Vallespi, C., Veloso, M.M., Browning, B.: Cameo: The camera assisted meeting event observer. In: International Conference on Robotics and Automation, New Orleans (2004)
2. Murphy, K.: Dynamic Bayesian Networks: representation, Inference and Learning. PhD thesis, UC Berkeley, Computer Science Division (2002)
3. Rabiner, L.R.: A tutorial on Hidden Markov Models and selected applications in speech recognition. Proceedings of the IEEE **77** (1989) 257–286
4. Hamid, R., Huang, Y., Essa, I.: ARGMode – activity recognition using graphical models. In: Conference on Computer Vision and Pattern Recognition Workshop. Volume 4., Madison, WI (2003) 38–44
5. Hong, P., Turk, M., Huang, T.S.: Gesture modeling and recognition using finite state machines. In: Proceedings of the Fourth IEEE International Conference and Gesture Recognition, Grenoble, France (2000)
6. Nguyen, N., Bui, H., Venkatesh, S., West, G.: Recognizing and monitoring high level behaviours in complex spatial environments. In: Proceedings of the IEEE International Conference on Computer Vision and Pattern Recognition. (2003)
7. Darrell, T., Gordon, G., Harville, M., Woodfill, J.: Integrated person tracking using stereo, color, and pattern detection. International Journal of Computer Vision **37** (2000) 175–185
8. Han, K., Veloso, M.: Automated robot behavior recognition applied to robotic soccer. In Hollerbach, J., Koditschek, D., eds.: Robotics Research: the Ninth International Symposium. Springer-Verlag, London (2000) 199–204 Also in the Proceedings of IJCAI-99 Workshop on Team Behaviors and Plan Recognition.
9. Bruce, J., Bowling, M., Browning, B., Veloso, M.: Multi-robot team response to a multi-robot opponent team. In: Proceedings of ICRA'03, the 2003 IEEE International Conference on Robotics and Automation, Taiwan (2003)

Chapter 2

AC 2005: Affective Computing: Towards Affective Intelligent Systems

Introduction

Ana Paiva[1], Carlos Martinho[1], and Eugénio de Oliveira[2]

[1] Departamento de Engenharia Informática, IST and INESC-ID
[2] LIACC, Faculdade de Engenharia do Porto

Almost forty years ago, Herbert Simon emphasised the role of emotions in problem solving. Nevertheless, until recently, research on intelligent systems has traditionally been focused on the development of theories and techniques mostly inspired on what was considered the "rational" aspects of human behaviour.

But findings from neuroscience (such as by Damásio and LeDoux's) and psychology suggesting that emotions are a leading part of what is considered intelligent behaviour, has brought the role of emotions into the limelight. Furthermore, the work by R. Picard, and the creation of the area of Affective Computing, has provided the right frame for research and develop new intelligent systems. Emotions can further be considered, not only as essential for problem solving techniques in intelligent systems but also allow for the construction of systems that interact with humans in more natural and human-like manner. Also, the increasing attention given to Agent-oriented programming makes it more relevant the enhancement of agent deliberation on the grounds of both rationality and emotionality.

This workshop combines a set of papers where the role of affect in the construction of intelligent systems is discussed, and techniques for building such systems are provided. Furthermore, one of the goals of the workshop is to bring together not only researchers from AI and agents, but also from different disciplines such as psychology, robotics, graphics and animation, in a forum to discuss the creation of emotional systems. Focusing on areas such as Emotion theories and their impact on computational models of intelligence, on Affective reasoning and affective planning among others, we expect that this workshop will contribute for the area of Affective Computing to be placed as one of the emerging subfields of AI.

C. Bento, A. Cardoso, and G. Dias (Eds.): EPIA 2005, LNAI 3808, p. 101, 2005.
© Springer-Verlag Berlin Heidelberg 2005

Adaptation and Decision-Making Driven
by Emotional Memories

Luís Morgado[1,2] and Graça Gaspar[2]

[1] Instituto Superior de Engenharia de Lisboa,
Rua Conselheiro Emídio Navarro, 1949-014 Lisboa, Portugal
lm@isel.ipl.pt
[2] Faculdade de Ciências da Universidade de Lisboa,
Universidade de Lisboa, Campo Grande, 1749-016 Lisboa, Portugal
gg@di.fc.ul.pt

Abstract. The integration between emotion and cognition can provide an important support for adaptation and decision-making under resource-bounded conditions, typical of real-world domains. The ability to adjust cognitive activity and to take advantage of emotion-modulated memories are two main aspects resulting from that integration. In this paper we address those issues under the framework of the *agent flow model*, describing the formation of emotional memories and the regulation of their use through attention focusing. Experimental results from simulated rescue scenarios show how the proposed approach enables effective decision making and fast adaptation rates in completely unknown environments.

1 Introduction

Growing experimental evidence from neurosciences indicates that emotion plays a fundamental role in human reasoning and decision-making (e.g. [7, 11]). On the other hand, the importance of emotional phenomena in learning and adaptive behavior is also well documented (e.g. [17]). This evidence of an encompassing role of emotion in cognitive activity has stimulated the development of cognitive models that incorporate emotional modeling (e.g. [3, 13]). Even traditional decision research has begun to incorporate emotion in models, as is the case of *decision affect theory* [18], and of some authors that propose emotion as an integral part of bounded rationality (e.g. [12, 9]).

However, two main problems are recognized underlying this emotion-based approach: (i) the tightly intertwined relation between emotion and cognition, which is hardly compatible with patching emotional phenomena as an addition to the cognitive mechanisms of an agent [1]; (ii) the dynamic and continuous nature of emotional phenomena, which is highly constrained by the classical notion of a discrete emotional state and its assessment via verbal labels [24].

In our view, to address these issues we must go beyond the classical separation between emotion and cognition and recognize their symbiotic relation. That is, emotion is a result of cognitive activity and cognitive activity is modulated by emotion, in a dynamic process that unfolds through time according to agent-environment

C. Bento, A. Cardoso, and G. Dias (Eds.): EPIA 2005, LNAI 3808, pp. 102–114, 2005.

interaction. We concretized this view by developing an agent model where emotion and cognition are modeled as two integrated aspects of intelligent behavior. Two main aspects are involved in this relation between emotion and cognition: (i) the regulation of cognitive activity due to the present achievement conditions; and (ii) the modulation of the changes in the cognitive structure due to past experiences (i.e. the formation of emotional memories). In this paper we will focus on this second aspect, that is, how can emotional memories enhance the adaptation and decision-making under time-limited conditions.

The paper is organized as follows: in sections 2 and 3 we present an overview of the emotion and agent models that support the proposed approach; in section 4 we further detail the agent model regarding emotional memory formation and activation and its use in decision-making; in section 5 experimental results from a simulation of a rescue environment are presented; in section 6 we establish comparisons with related work and draw some conclusions and directions for future work.

2 The Flow Model of Emotion

In the proposed model we adopt a view where emotional phenomena result from the dynamics of cognitive activity. This view is in line with emotional models proposed by some authors (e.g. [6, 24]).

However, a distinctive aspect of the proposed model is the fact that those dynamics are rooted on the dynamics of energy exchange between the agent and the environment. This is possible due to conceiving an agent as an open system that maintains itself in a state far from equilibrium, yet keeping an internally stable overall structure. This kind of systems is known as dissipative structures [15]. Adopting this view, the agent-environment relation is determined by the relation between the agent's internal potential, its *achievement potential*, and the agent-environment coupling conductance, the *achievement conductance*. The achievement potential represents the potential of change that the agent is able to produce in the environment to achieve the intended state-of-affairs. The achievement conductance represents the degree of the environment's conduciveness or resistance to that change, which can also mean the degree of environment change that is conducive, or not, to the agent intended state-of-affairs. In a dissipative system the achievement potential can be viewed as a force (P) and the achievement conductance as a transport property (C). The behavioral dynamics of an agent can therefore be characterized as a relation corresponding to a flow, called *achievement flow* (F), which results from the application of potential P over a conductance C. These behavioral dynamics, expressed as energy flows, are considered the root of emotional phenomena, underlying and modulating cognitive activity. They are described as a vectorial function *ED*, called *emotional disposition*, defined as:

$$ED \equiv (\delta P, \delta F) \quad \text{where} \quad \delta P = \frac{dP}{dt} \quad \text{and} \quad \delta F = \frac{dF}{dt} \tag{1}$$

As can be seen in figure 1.a, at a given instant $t = \tau$ an emotional disposition vector has a quality, defined by its orientation (or argument) and an intensity defined by its module. Each quadrant of the two dimensional space $\delta P \times \delta F$ can be directly related to a specific kind of *emotional disposition quality* as indicated in figure 1.b, although

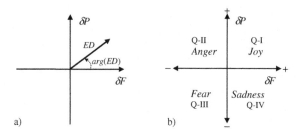

Fig. 1. Vector *ED* as a function of *δP* and *δF* (a); relation between *ED* quadrants and emotional quality tendency (b)

the tag associated to each quadrant (joy, anger, fear, sadness) is only indicative of its main nature, since the quality of the emotional disposition is continuous [19]. As an example, quadrant Q–III (*δP* < 0 and *δF* < 0) corresponds to situations where the agent does not have capacity to handle the "adversities", which is typical of fear situations.

We will not discuss the aspects related to emotional modeling, however it is important to note that *emotional disposition* is defined as an action regulatory disposition or tendency, but it does not constitute in itself an emotion. Emotions are considered emergent phenomena that result from agents' cognitive dynamics.

3   The Agent Flow Model

By defining a foundational framework where emotional phenomena result from the dynamics of cognitive activity, the *flow model of emotion* provides the support for an agent model where the base notions of potential and flow can be rendered concrete and cognitive structure and mechanisms can be defined. We called that model *agent flow model*. In this section we will present its overall structure.

3.1   Agent Cognitive Structure

Energy flows generate energetic signals called *cognitive potentials*. Cognitive potentials result both from agent-environment interaction and from agent internal activity. In both cases they express aspects of the environment (internal and external) that the agent is able to discriminate and perceive, commonly called quality dimensions [10]. Formally, cognitive potentials $p(t)$ are modeled as a composition of two types of signals: a base signal $\varphi(t)$ with a specific angular frequency ω that identifies the discriminated aspect or quality; and a quantitative signal $\rho(t)$ corresponding to the actual value of the discriminated quality, expressed as a frequency shift $\Delta\omega$ that modulates the base signal $\varphi(t)$. That is:

$$p(t) = \rho(t).\varphi(t) \tag{2}$$

Through superposition, cognitive potentials form aggregates that are the base cognitive elements of an agent's cognitive structure. Superposition occurs without loss of information because the base signals $\varphi(t)$ are orthogonal among each other. Therefore a *cognitive element* $\sigma(t)$ is modeled as a composition of cognitive potentials:

$$\sigma(t) = \sum_{i=1}^{K} p_i(t) \tag{3}$$

where K is the number of potentials in the aggregate.

3.2 Cognitive Space and Cognitive Dynamics

The base signals that compose potentials and cognitive elements form a signal space underlying the cognitive structure of an agent, which we call a *cognitive space*. Formally, a cognitive space CS_K is defined by a set of K orthonormal basis functions $\Phi = \{\varphi_i: i = 1, 2, \ldots, K\}$ with $K \in \aleph$. Each basis function φ_i corresponds to a base signal $\varphi_i(t)$ with a specific quality $\omega = \Omega_i$.

Cognitive elements correspond to specific positions in the cognitive space. Since cognitive elements change with time, at successive time instants they occupy different positions, describing trajectories that reflect the behavior of an agent. At some instant $t = \tau$, a cognitive element $\sigma(t)$ is represented in a cognitive space CS_K as a vector σ, defined as:

$$\sigma = (\rho_1, \rho_2, \ldots, \rho_k) \tag{4}$$

where the dimensional factors $\rho_i \in \mathbb{C}$ convey the intensity and frequency shift of quality Ω_i in the cognitive element.

Besides enabling a concise description of agents' cognitive structure, the cognitive space also enables a concise description of cognitive dynamics as movement of cognitive elements, as will be discussed next.

One of the main characteristics of intelligent behavior is the orientation towards the achievement of motivations. Cognitive elements play different roles in this process: *motivators* represent intended situations, acting as forces driving agent's behavior; *observations* represent the current situation, resulting from inward flows associated to activities like perception; *mediators* represent the media for action, forming an interface between cognitive processes and concrete action. Cognitive activity is consequently guided by the maximization of the achievement flows that lead to the reduction of the distance between observations and motivators. This process can be described as movement in the cognitive space, where motivators and observations correspond to specific positions and mediators define directions of movement, as illustrated in figure 2.

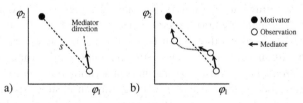

Fig. 2. Elements participating in the achievement of a motivator in a two-dimensional cognitive space

As shown in figure 2.a, the direction of the selected mediators may not be the exact direction towards the motivator. Besides that, motivators can change and the dynamics of the environment (either internal or external) can influence the movement of the observations. Figure 2.b shows a possible trajectory resulting from the adjustment of agent's behavior by switching to different mediators. Independently of the specific processes that generated the new mediators, the forces that led to that change underlie the cognitive dynamics of an agent. Emotional phenomena are considered the expression of those forces, characterized as emotional dispositions.

In the cognitive space, emotional dispositions are defined by the evolution of the distance s between an observation σ_{obs} and a motivator σ_{mot}, and by the velocity v of the movement towards the motivator. That is:

$$ED \equiv (\delta s, \delta v) \quad \text{where} \quad \delta s = -\frac{ds}{dt} \quad \text{and} \quad \delta v = \frac{dv}{dt} \tag{5}$$

These emotional disposition tendencies are behavioral forces that constrain the cognitive processes of an agent. Therefore, the dynamics resulting from these forces are, at the same time, a result of the cognitive activity and a constraint that influences it, reflecting the symbiotic relation between emotion and cognition, as we proposed initially.

4   Supporting Adaptation and Decision-Making

In order to support adaptation to uncertain and dynamic environments and to enable real-time decision-making, two main aspects must be considered: (i) the ability to take advantage of past experiences in order to adapt to the changing conditions and to anticipate future situations; and (ii) the ability to regulate cognitive activity according to the achievement conditions [20].

4.1   Emotional Memory

As cognitive elements change with time they describe trajectories in the cognitive space that reflect past experiences. These trajectories can be assimilated into the cognitive structure of an agent, forming autobiographic memories.

The cognitive elements that constitute those trajectories have an integrated emotional disposition, therefore they form *emotional disposition memories*, which can be related to what is referred by other authors as *emotional memories* (e.g. [4, 7]).

Cognitive potentials and cognitive elements were previously described as evolving in time. However time can be viewed as a special dimension in cognitive space. In this way, autobiographic memories are organized according to the time of formation, which is expressed as a specific spatial frequency. In the same way that the quality-representation frequencies ω allow for qualitative discrimination, a time-representation frequency v allows for memory discrimination (that is, discrimination between different occurrence instants). Considering an abstract spatial dimension x, the memory mechanisms generate a time-reference signal $\phi_v(x)$ whose spatial frequency v continuously and monotonically changes with time.

In agents with memory, this signal is used to modulate each cognitive element $\sigma(t)$ to produce a cognitive element $\sigma(t,x)$, which can be incorporated into the memory or just be used to interact with the memory. That is:

$$\sigma(t, x) = \sigma(t)\phi_v(x) \tag{6}$$

In the cognitive space this new representation of a cognitive element can be related to the previous one (4) as follows. Considering some instant $t = \tau$, a cognitive element $\sigma(t,x)$ is represented in a cognitive space CS_K as a vector σ, defined as:

$$\sigma = \rho_v \cdot (\rho_0, \rho_1, ..., \rho_k) \tag{7}$$

where the dimensional factor $\rho_v \in \mathbb{C}$ conveys the intensity and frequency v of signal $\phi_v(x)$ at time $t = \tau$. From this expression it is clear that time is not represented as just another qualitative dimension. Rather, time has an effect on each quality dimension representation.

Due to its signal-based nature, the memory field of the cognitive structure of an agent acts as a resonant structure where cognitive elements are activated by qualitative and temporal contact [14]. Therefore, a trigger cognitive element σ interacting with the memory field will produce multiple recalled memory elements. Given a memory element σ_M previously assimilated, a recalled memory element σ_R is formed as follows:

$$\sigma_R = \langle \sigma, \sigma_M \rangle \cdot \sigma_M \tag{8}$$

where $\langle x, y \rangle$ denotes the scalar product of vectors x and y. In this way, the recalled memory elements are modulated images of the original memory elements, whose intensity depends on the correlation (expressed by the scalar product) between the trigger element and the memory elements.

4.2 Integrating Memory and Attention Mechanisms

Given the possibly large number of memory elements that can be recalled, the agent must decide on what to focus or decision-making in due time will not be possible.

The attention focusing mechanism allows to deal with this problem by restricting the attention of the cognitive processes to specific cognitive elements, namely recalled memory elements, according to their emotional disposition content. This mechanism acts like a depletion barrier, producing an *attention field* formed by the cognitive elements able to bypass the barrier. Only the elements in the attention field are considered by the high-level cognitive processes, such as reasoning and deliberation. Figure 3 illustrates the relation between the different mechanisms involved.

Besides producing the emotional disposition potentials p_s and p_v, the emotional disposition mechanisms also generate two regulatory signals λ^+ and λ^- that convey the affective character underlying those cognitive potentials (the intensity of positive and negative valences). Together with the emotional disposition potentials p_s and p_v, these signals are the main source for the regulation of cognitive activity, including the regulation of the attention field depletion barrier.

The depletion barrier is characterized by a depletion intensity and by a permeability [20]. The depletion intensity ε, is regulated by the affective signals λ^+ and λ^-, expressing their cumulative effect. The permeability μ determines the intensity ε^σ of the interaction between a cognitive element σ and the depletion barrier. Given a certain

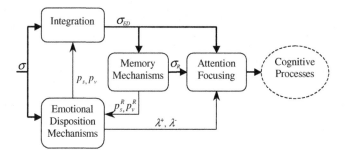

Fig. 3. Emotion-based mechanisms supporting adaptation and decision-making

depletion intensity ε, a cognitive element σ bypasses the barrier and is included in the attention field if $\varepsilon^{\sigma} > \varepsilon$.

At the same time, the emotional disposition content associated with the recalled memories (the p_s^R and p_v^R cognitive potentials shown in figure 3) is fed back to the emotional disposition mechanisms, producing an anticipatory regulatory effect. This kind of mechanism can play a key role in highly dynamic environments where the time available for reasoning is limited, as will be discussed next.

4.3 Influence of Emotional Memories on Reasoning and Decision-Making

The influence of emotional memories on cognitive activity can occur at multiple levels. For instance, at a reactive level the emotional dispositions that result from recalled emotional memories can directly trigger the activation of specific behavioral patterns such as a fight or flight response. However, particularly interesting is the influence of emotional memories on reasoning and decision-making, where they can significantly contribute to make those processes practical under time-limited conditions.

In the proposed model, decision-making occurs through the evaluation of the available options for action. These options are mediators that define directions of movement in the cognitive space, as shown in figure 4.

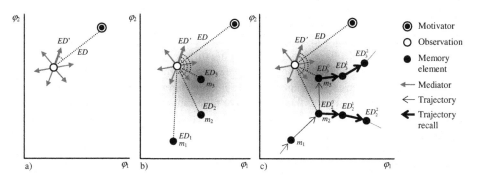

Fig. 4. Levels of influence on decision-making (two-dimensional cognitive space): (a) perceived situation; (b) direct memory recall; (c) trajectory recall

For each mediator an emotional disposition (*ED'*) will be determined depending on three kinds of influencing elements: (i) *perceived situation* (relation between the agent motivators and the current observations); (ii) *direct memory recall*; (iii) *trajectory recall*. The resulting emotional disposition is a weighted sum of the emotional disposition of each one of the influencing elements. The weights are the correlation between the direction of the mediator and the direction of that element (relative to the current observation). The mediator with the more favorable emotional disposition is selected as the current mediator and the corresponding action is activated.

Figure 4.a illustrates the first level of influence, perceived situation, in which the decision-making will depend only on the emotional dispositions resulting from the interaction of each observation (resulting from the perception processes) and each motivator. Therefore the mediator selected is the mediator whose direction is more correlated with the direction of the motivator.

The next level of influence occurs through the direct memory recall of emotional memories, as shown in figure 4.b. At this level the decision-making will depend not only on the emotional dispositions resulting from the current observations, but also from the emotional dispositions (*ED$_i$*) resulting from the recalled memories (*m$_i$*). These memories are triggered by current observations and filtered through the attention focusing mechanisms, previously discussed (see figure 3).

As an example, figure 4.b illustrates the influence of memories resulting from past experience possibly overriding the influence of current observations. Memory influence (gray color) depends on the distance between the memory and the observation (qualitative and temporal). Therefore recalled elements have a local scope of influence.

At the third level of influence, reasoning processes play the key role by exploring possible trajectories in the cognitive space, providing in this way a wider scope for decision-making. This kind of influence is illustrated in figure 4.c.

This prospective reasoning process starts from the directly recalled memory elements and explores the cognitive space guided by the trajectories of those elements, as illustrated in figure 4.c. In this way, trajectory exploration corresponds to a chained recall of memories. The extent of that exploration is controlled by a temporal focusing mechanism [20], which is regulated by the emotional disposition mechanisms through the affective signals λ^+ and λ^-. Since the emotional disposition content associated to the recalled memories (the p_s^R and p_v^R cognitive potentials shown in figure 3) are fed back to the emotional disposition mechanisms, the emotional memories provide not only the starting point for prospective reasoning, but also provide a regulatory effect through the recalled emotional dispositions, which limits the extent of that exploration.

At this prospective level, instead of using directly the emotional disposition of the recalled memory element, as explained previously, an emotional disposition is generated that is a function of the explored trajectory elements. For instance, in the experience that we will report in the next section the agent estimated, for each of the explored trajectory elements, what would be its emotional disposition, relative to the current motivator, given the trajectory step that led to that element, and then considers the cumulative effect of those emotional dispositions (in this example the average).

Therefore, the influence of emotional memories on decision-making occurs at two levels: (i) at a base *associative level*, where emotional memories are triggered by current observations and filtered through attention focusing mechanisms; and (ii) at a *prospective level*, where the cognitive space is explored guided by recalled trajectories.

5 Experimental Results

We implemented and tested the proposed model in simulated rescue scenarios. This kind of scenarios was selected due to its strict requirements regarding time and information available for adaptation and decision-making.

The experimental framework is a simulation of rescue environments where a rescue agent must move targets to a safe position. The environments represent houses, where the targets are located, with different room configurations and different target positions. Targets emit a distress signal that the rescue agent is able to detect.

Minimum sensing ability is considered, that is, the agent is only able to detect distress signals and derive from it the direction and some measure of proximity of the target. The agent is also unable to detect the walls of the rooms unless by direct contact (collision). Environments are modeled as continuous, in the sense that all their characteristics are real-valued. At the start of each run the environment is completely unknown to the agent. The agent has a limited time to perform the rescue, therefore no training phase is possible. That is, the agent must act directly in the unknown environment and learn on-line how to move in it.

Figure 5 shows the behavior of the agent in one of the test environments with two differently positioned targets (represented by gray circles). The starting and safe positions are the same (represented by a dotted circle). When the agent begins moving to the first target it is guiding its actions only by the position of the target (the motivator) and by the agent's current position, therefore multiple collisions with the walls occur. Whenever a collision occurs the agent turns $180°$ and moves forward. However, during this walk to the first target, emotional memories are formed that lead to improved effectiveness as the agent goes on. This is especially visible in the return path (figure 5.a, in bold) and in the second rescue operation (figure 5.b).

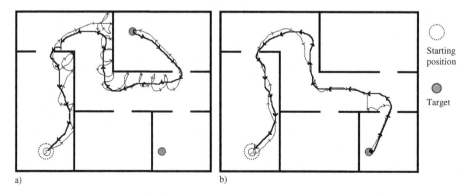

Fig. 5. Behavior of the agent in one of the test environments: (a) rescue of the first target; (b) rescue of the second target

Notice that when the agent reaches the target and initiates the return path, the motivator now changes to the starting position. Therefore, when the agent tries to explore a trajectory from a recalled memory element, it should not use the recalled emotional disposition but rather estimate what it would be in reference to the new motivator. This is why the influence of memory trajectories upon decision-making requires prospective reasoning and not merely trajectory recall.

To test the agent performance over time, the rescue task was repeated for different environments with 10 targets at the same position. The performance indicator considered was the time taken to rescue each target. Figure 6 shows the results (average values over 10 different environments).

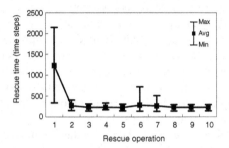

Fig. 6. Agent performance over time

As can be observed, significant improvement in decision making and adaptation to the specific environment occurs during the first rescue, since in the second rescue operation the agent already reaches a good performance independent of the environment. Thereafter, the agent's performance continues to improve but in a smaller scale, with some variations due to exploratory behavior. The difference between minimum and maximum values in the first rescue operation corresponds to the different types of environment used in the experiments that were chosen with different levels of complexity.

6 Discussion and Conclusions

Three main aspects underlie the experimental scenario just presented: (i) the environment is continuous; (ii) there are severe restrictions on the time available for action; (iii) the environment is unknown to the agent and no training phase is possible, therefore learning must be online. Any of these constraints poses important problems to classical learning approaches, namely to reinforcement learning approaches (e.g. [16, 30]). On the other hand, approaches based on classical planning methods are also problematic to address this kind of problems, namely due to the severe time constraints (e.g. [2, 8]).

The proposed approach addresses these problems through a tight integration between emotional phenomena and cognition, supported on a signal based modeling of the agent cognitive structure and activity. One main result is the fast adaptation rate. Underlying this result is the implicit ability to generalize from previous experiences and to generate expectations, resulting from modulated recall of memory elements and prospective trajectory recall.

A related work has been done by Ventura & Pinto-Ferreira [29], where the *"movie-in-the-brain"* concept proposed by Damásio [7] is used to implement a mechanism that allows an agent to establish and learn causal relationships between its actions and the responses obtained from the environment. A key difference from their work is that in our approach there is no need for discrete affective/emotional labeling, instead the emotional disposition notion expresses the continuous dynamics that result from cognitive activity.

Our approach differs from a main line of emotion research centered on appraisal-based models (e.g. [23]). Appraisal theories emphasize the structural aspects of emotion elicitation, but don't say much about the underlying processes [27]. On the other hand, the aspects of adaptation and learning are not addressed. To overcome these problems, some authors have explored alternative ways to model the dynamic aspects of emotional phenomena in the context of appraisal theories (e.g. [22, 28]), however they maintain an emphasis on discrete sets of emotional labels, which restricts the integration between emotion and cognition.

A complementary line of research addresses these limitations by adopting a "design-based" approach (e.g. [26]) where emotional mechanisms are embedded within an overall architecture in a resource-bounded agent. However, a sharp line is drawn between cognitive and emotional processing, where emotion plays essentially an interruptive role [21, 25], shifting the attention of the cognitive processes due to environmental contingencies.

Our proposal departs from these approaches by modeling emotion and cognition as two symbiotically integrated aspects of agent cognitive activity. This means that the relation between emotion and cognition occurs not only at a functional specialization level. Instead it is intrinsic to all cognitive activity and to the nature of the involved cognitive elements. On the other hand, the relation between emotional phenomena, adaptive behavior and reasoning and decision-making, which is a main characteristics of our model, have remained almost unexplored in cognitive models due to the strong emphasis on functional division. However, as some authors have proposed (e.g. [5]), it is a fundamental aspect that enables effective intelligent behavior in concrete environments.

Future research will aim at exploring the aspects of mood congruence in emotional memory recall, and the role of emotional mechanisms in long-term memory consolidation. We also consider important to further study the relation between our approach and other approaches such as classical approaches to learning and adaptive control mechanisms.

Acknowledgments

This research has been partially supported by the program PRODEP III 5.3/2/2001.

References

1. Z. Arzi-Gonczarowski, 'AI Emotions: Will One Know Them When One Sees Them?', *Proc. 16th European Meeting on Cybernetics and Systems Research,* 2002.
2. E. Atkins, T. Abdelzaher, K. Shin, E. Durfee, 'Planning and Resource Allocation for Hard Real-time, Fault-Tolerant Plan Execution', *Autonomous Agents and Multi-Agent Systems,* 4:57-78, 2001.
3. L. Botelho, H. Coelho, 'Machinery for Artificial Emotions', *Cybernetics and Systems,* 32(5):465-506, 2001.
4. G. Bower, 'Some Relations Between Emotions and Memory', in *The Nature of Emotion: Fundamental Questions,* eds. P. Ekman, R. Davidson, 303-305, Oxford Univ. Press, 1994.
5. L. Cañamero, 'Designing Emotions for Activity Selection in Autonomous Agents', *Emotions in Humans and Artifacts,* eds. R. Trappl, P. Petta, S. Payr, MIT Press, 115-148, 2003.
6. C. Carver, M. Scheier, 'Control Processes and Self-organization as Complementary Principles Underlying Behavior', *Personality and Social Psychology Review,* 6:304-315, 2002.
7. A. Damásio, 'A Second Chance for Emotion', *Cognitive Neuroscience of Emotion,* eds. R. Lane, L. Nadel, 12-23, Oxford Univ. Press, 2000.
8. T. Dean, L. Kaelbling, J. Nicholson, 'Planning with Deadlines in Stochastic Domains', *Proc. of the 11th National Conference on Artificial Intelligence,* 1993.
9. P. Doshi, P. Gmytrasiewicz, 'Towards Affect-based Approximations to Rational Planning: A Decision-Theoretic Perspective to Emotions', *AAAI Spring Symposium,* ed. E. Hudlicka, L. Cañamero, Technical Report SS-04-02, 33-36, 2004.
10. P. Gärdenfors, *Conceptual Spaces: The Geometry of Thought,* MIT Press, 2000.
11. J. Gray, T. Braver, M. Raichle, 'Integration of Emotion and Cognition in the Lateral Prefrontal Cortex', *Proc. of the National Academy of Sciences USA,* 99:4115-4120, 2002.
12. Y. Hanoch, 'Neither an Angel nor an Ant: Emotion as an Aid to Bounded Rationality', *Journal of Economic Psychology, 23,* 1-25, 2002.
13. E. Hudlicka, 'Two Sides of Appraisal: Implementing Appraisal and Its Consequences within a Cognitive Architecture', *AAAI Spring Symposium,* ed. E. Hudlicka, L. Cañamero, Tech. Rep. SS-04-02, 70-78, 2004.
14. T. Kohonen, *Content-Addressable Memories,* Springer-Verlag, 1980.
15. D. Kondepudi, I. Prigogine, *Modern Thermodynamics: From Heat Engines to Dissipative Structures,* J. Wiley & Sons, 1998.
16. R. Kühn, R. Menzel, W. Menzel, U. Ratsch, M.Richter, I. Stamatescu, *Adaptivity and Learning: An Interdisciplinary Debate,* Springer, 2003.
17. J. LeDoux, 'Cognitive-Emotional Interactions: Listen to the Brain', *Cognitive Neuroscience of Emotion,* eds. R. Lane, L. Nadel, 129-155, Oxford Univ. Press, 2000.
18. B. Mellers, 'Choice and the Relative Pleasure of Consequences', *Psychological Bulletin,* 126, 910-924, 2000.
19. L. Morgado, G. Gaspar, 'Emotion in Intelligent Virtual Agents: The Flow Model of Emotion', in *Intelligent Virtual Agents,* eds. T. Rist et al., LNAI 2792, 31-38, Springer-Verlag, 2003.
20. L. Morgado, G. Gaspar, 'Emotion Based Adaptive Reasoning for Resource Bounded Agents', *Proc. of the 4th International Joint Conference on Autonomous Agents and Multi-Agent Systems,* 2005.
21. K. Oatley, P. Johnson-Laird, 'Emotion and Reasoning to Consistency', in *Emotional Cognition,* eds. S. Moore, M. Oaksford, John Benjamins, 2002.

22. E. Oliveira, L. Sarmento, 'Emotional Advantage for Adaptability and Autonomy', *Proc. of the 2nd International Joint Conference on Autonomous Agents and Multi-Agent Systems*, 2003.

23. A. Ortony, G. Clore, A. Collins, *The Cognitive Structure of Emotions*. Cambridge Univ. Press, 1988.

24. K. Scherer, 'Emotions as Episodes of Subsystem Synchronization Driven by Nonlinear Appraisal Processes', in *Emotion, Development, and Self-Organization*, eds. M. Lewis, I. Granic, 70-99, Cambridge Univ. Press, 2000.

25. H. Simon, 'Motivational and Emotional Controls of Cognition', *Psychological Review*, 74:29-39, 1967.

26. A. Sloman, 'What Are Emotion Theories About?', *AAAI Spring Symposium*, ed. E. Hudlicka, L. Cañamero, Technical Report. SS-04-02, 128-134, 2004.

27. C. Smith, L. Kirby, 'Affect and Cognitive Appraisal Processes', in *Affect and Social Cognition*, ed. J. Forgas, 75-92, L. Erlbaum, 2001.

28. J. Velásquez, 'Modeling Emotion-Based Decision-Making', *Proc. of the 1998 AAAI Fall Symposium Emotional and Intelligent: The Tangled Knot of Cognition*, 164-169, 1998.

29. R. Ventura, C. Pinto-Ferreira, 'Generating and Refining Causal Models for an Emotion-based Agent', *AAAI Spring Symposium*, ed. E. Hudlicka, L. Cañamero, Technical Report SS-04-02, 146-149, 2004.

30. S. Whitehead, L. Lin, 'Reinforcement Learning of non-Markov Decision Processes', *Artificial Intelligence*, 73:271-306, 1995.

Affective Revision

César F. Pimentel and Maria R. Cravo

Instituto Superior Técnico, Dep. Eng. Informática, GIA,
Av. Rovisco Pais, 1049-001 Lisboa — Portugal
cesar.pimentel@dei.ist.utl.pt, mrcravo@gia.ist.utl.pt

Abstract. Moods and emotions influence human reasoning, most of the
time in a positive way. One aspect of reasoning is the revision of beliefs,
i.e., how to change a set of beliefs in order to incorporate new information
that conflicts with the existing beliefs. We incorporate two influences of
affective states on belief maintenance identified by psychologists, in a AI
belief revision operation. On one hand, we present an alternative operation to conventional Belief Revision, Affective Revision, that determines
the preference between new and old information based on the mood of
the agent revising its beliefs. On the other, we show how beliefs can be
automatically ordered, in terms of resistance to change, based on (among
other aspects) the influence of emotion anticipations on the strength of
beliefs.

1 Introduction

The influence of emotions in reasoning has been recognized by philosophers since
Aristotle. Generally, this influence was believed to be negative, i.e., emotions
were seen as an impairment to rational thought.

Given this state of affairs, it is no wonder that AI researchers did not think of
emotions as a useful component of AI systems. Exceptions to this are the views
of Simon and Minsky: Simon [17] says that "a general theory of reasoning and
problem solving must incorporate the influences of motivation and emotion";
and Minsky [11] says that "the question is not whether intelligent machines can
have emotions, but whether machines can be intelligent without emotions".

In the last years, work done in neuroscience and psychology has shown that,
more often than not, emotions are essential to rational reasoning, decision making and social interactions.

As a consequence, AI researchers started to show a growing interest in the
possible benefits that the study of emotions can bring to AI systems. This led
to the birth of a new area known as *Affective Computing*, defined by Rosalind
Picard as the study of "computing that relates to, arises from or deliberately
influences emotions" [15].

In this paper we focus on the benefits of considering the influences of affective states in a particular aspect of AI reasoning, belief revision. The aim of
belief revision theories is to define how a rational agent should change its set
of beliefs, in order to incorporate a new belief, which is inconsistent with this

C. Bento, A. Cardoso, and G. Dias (Eds.): EPIA 2005, LNAI 3808, pp. 115–126, 2005.

set. Psychologists have by now identified several ways in which affective states in general, i.e., moods and emotions, do influence the maintenance of beliefs in people. In this paper we model the incorporation of some of these influences in a belief revision theory.

This paper is organized as follows. In the next section we describe the main aspects of the work we built upon: belief revision theories developed in AI, and influences of affective states on the maintenance of beliefs (as identified by psychologists). In this section, we also briefly mention a system of emotion generation that will be needed for the present work. In Section 3, we show how two such influences can be modelled in AI. In Section 4, we present an illustrative example. Finally, in Section 5 we present some conclusions and point directions in which this work will be continued.

2   Background

2.1   Belief Revision and Permissive Belief Revision

An essential aspect of commonsense reasoning is the ability to revise one's beliefs, i.e., change one's beliefs when a new belief is acquired, that is not consistent with the existing beliefs.

In AI, *belief revision* theories decide which of the previous belief(s) should be abandoned in order to incorporate the new belief, and keep the set of beliefs consistent. All belief revision theories try to keep the change as small as possible, according to what is called the *minimal change principle* [10]. The reason for this principle is that beliefs are valuable, and we do not easily give them up. However, this principle is not enough to determine, in a unique way, the change to be made, and so belief revision theories assume the existence of an order among beliefs, which states that some beliefs are less valuable than others, and should more easily be abandoned.

A number of belief revision theories have been developed since the seminal work of Alchourrón, Gärdenfors and Makinson [1]. These theories assume that beliefs are represented by formulas of the language $\mathcal{L}$ of some logic, and represent the revision of a set of beliefs β with a belief F by $(\beta * F)$. This represents the new set of beliefs and must be such that: 1) It contains F; 2) It is consistent, unless of course, F is a contradiction. To ensure that the result is a unique set of beliefs these theories either assume the existence of a total order among beliefs, or allow for a partial order, and abandon all beliefs whose relative value is not known, thus abandoning more beliefs than necessary.

In this paper, we consider a particular belief revision theory [2], based on a non-monotonic extension of First Order Logic. For the purpose at hand, it is enough to say that this theory allows for any number of partial orders among beliefs, and that its result is a set of sets of beliefs, instead of a unique set of beliefs. For instance, suppose that the initial set of beliefs β contains the formulas A and $A \rightarrow B$, and that nothing is known about the relative value of these formulas. Then $(\beta * \neg B) = \{\{A, \neg B\}, \{A \rightarrow B, \neg B\}\}$. Note that if a single result is required, then we can not do better than $\{\neg B\}$, unless an arbitrary choice is made. On the other hand, if we had the order $A \leq_\beta A \to B$ [1], then the result would be unique: $(\beta * \neg B) = \{\{A \to B, \neg B\}\}$.

In [3] permissive belief revision is presented. This operation takes the beliefs abandoned by a belief revision theory, and adds a weakened version of these beliefs to the final result. In order to do this, permissive revision uses the function $Weaken$ [2] that takes a formula and a set of formulas and returns a weakened version of the first that is consistent with the second. A formula A is considered weaker than a formula B if whatever is derivable from A is also derivable from B.

Let β_F be the (a) result of revising β with F. Then the permissive revision of β with F, $(\beta \otimes F)$, is defined by:

$$(\beta \otimes F) = \beta_F \cup Weaken(\bigwedge(\beta \setminus \beta_F), \beta_F).$$

Typically, with permissive revision, the weakening function is able to keep some part of what is abandoned in classical revision. This is advantageous because it implies that there is less loss of information (the same criterion behind the *minimal change principle*).

2.2   Affective Influences on the Maintenance of Beliefs

In [7], an extensive description of influences of affective states on the maintenance of beliefs can be found. In this section, we briefly describe the two influences that are modelled in the present work.

First, we consider the influence of affective states on the relative strength of beliefs. Humans are known to cling to some belief (deny some fact), not because of any objective reason, like the high credibility/authority of its source, but simply because the abandonment of that belief (acceptance of that fact) would cause a negative emotional state. In general, the *anticipation* of emotions can support or prevent, depending on the emotion, the acceptance or rejection of information [8]. If the potential acceptance or abandonment of a belief leads to the anticipation of a negative emotion, such as *distress*, such process of acceptance or abandonment is "discouraged". Analogously, if it leads to a positive emotion, such as *joy*, such process is "encouraged". In this sense, emotion anticipations are an important source of belief strength.

Second, we consider how affects can influence the individual's tendency to either rely on his current beliefs or actively search for new information.

Let us start by considering the work presented by Fiedler and Bless in [4]. The authors cite Piaget [14], who distinguishes two modes of cognitive behavior, that can be summarized as follows:

Assimilation. In this mode, one assimilates the stimuli into one's own structures. One actively elaborates, relying on one's knowledge. One is curious and not cautious and makes active inferences under uncertainty.

---

[1] Note that the meaning of $F_1 \leq_\beta F_2$ and $F_2 \not\leq_\beta F_1$ is that if we have to choose between abandoning F_1 and abandoning F_2, we should abandon F_1.

[2] The definition of this function can be found in [3], and [16].

Accommodation. In this mode, one reacts reliably to external demands or threats. One "sticks to the stimulus facts" and updates one's own structures to accommodate external requirements.

Fiedler and Bless claim that positive affective states (in particular, positive moods) facilitate active generation (input transformation; inference; productive thinking; creativity), and trigger assimilation. On the other hand, negative affective states (in particular, negative moods) facilitate conservation (to keep record of input from outside or from memory), and trigger accommodation. The authors explain that these effects do not correspond to superficial response tendencies, but rather to genuine effects on memory and internal beliefs.

If we restrict ourselves to the matter that concerns us in this paper, the revision of beliefs, we can summarize this influence as follows. Positive moods trigger the assimilation behavior mode, which in turn promotes reliance and use of current beliefs. Negative moods trigger the accommodation behavior mode, which in turn supports the updating and correction of existing beliefs in order to accommodate the new belief.

In consonance with this is Forgas [6], who explains that, while negative moods facilitate questioning and weakening of beliefs, positive moods facilitate reliance on existing beliefs. If these negative and positive moods are caused by failures and successes (respectively) in the performance of tasks, this mechanism may lead us to more promptly keep beliefs related to successes and reject those related to failures.

The two influences described in this section bias humans towards believing: a) what is more pleasant and b) what is related to more successful achievements. These two tendencies are potentially "useful" in the sense that the first acts as a mechanism of mood enhancement and eventually *mood control* (see, e.g. [4] and [6]) and the second may help one to achieve one's goals. There are, of course, many other sources of belief strength that may support or compete with those approached in this paper.

2.3   Generation of Emotions from Descriptions of Situations

To model the influence of emotion anticipation on the strength of beliefs, we need a way of generating emotions from descriptions of situations.

A system which does this generation is now under development. It is based on the *OCC* theory of emotions [12], and consists of two sub-systems. One that generates the appraisal of a situation, described by a set of percepts of the agent, and another (which is finished by now) that generates a set of pairs emotion/intensity from the appraisal of a situation. The percepts of an agent can be of different kinds, e.g. observations of facts in the world, observation of actions of other agents, communications from other agents, etc.

3   Modelling Affective Maintenance in AI

In this section we show a way of incorporating the two influences of affective states on the maintenance of beliefs discussed in the previous section, in an existing belief revision theory. For now our work considers only affective influences of "joy" and "distress". Consequently, this paper approaches only the aspects of valence and intensity of moods and emotions.

If we think of the influence of moods on biasing us either towards keeping existing beliefs and rejecting new information, or accepting new information and changing previous beliefs, it is clear that no revision operation captures these two modes of behavior, since, by definition, the result of revision *has to contain the new belief.* Operations of revision that do not always accept the new information are known as *non-prioritized revision* [9]. These are more realistic, since, in general, there is no reason why new information should automatically be accepted, even if it means changing previous beliefs. Furthermore, they allow us to model the two modes of behavior mentioned before, accommodation and assimilation. In Section 3.1, we present the affective revision operation, that models this influence.

In the previous section we also saw how emotion anticipations are used by humans to encourage/discourage the acceptance/rejection of both old and new beliefs. This influence is modelled in Section 3.2, through the generation of orders among beliefs, that result from emotion anticipations.

3.1   Affective Revision

We present a non-prioritized revision operation, called *Affective Revision*, that uses syntectic affects in the determination of what kind of change should occur when new information contradicts the existing beliefs. Henceforth, we will refer to the set of basic (in the sense that they were not derived) beliefs of an agent, as a *context.*

As we discussed in Section 2.2, someone in a significantly low mood has a tendency for a behavior of accommodation and, on the other hand, someone in a significantly high mood has a tendency for a behavior of assimilation. While in accommodation, a person tends to give more value to new information and less value (and resistance to change) to previously existing beliefs. While in assimilation, a person tends to give more value (and resistance to change) to previous beliefs and often "molds" the new information in order to "fit" in what was previously believed.

We consider mood as having a valence, positive or negative, and a numerical absolute value, that represents the intensity of the mood. The influence of mood on the way the agent is going to maintain its beliefs is modelled by distinguishing three different functional modes: 1) *Negative moods trigger the accommodation mode*: The new information is accepted, and existing beliefs are changed to allow this acceptance; 2) *Positive moods trigger the assimilation mode*: The existing beliefs are kept as they are, and the new information is rejected (or, at least, not totally accepted); 3) *Neutral moods correspond to the neutral mode*: There is no a-priori preference between the new information and the existing beliefs.

Apart from the fact that moods will have to have an intensity (absolute value) that is bigger than a given threshold[3], the selection of the above modes

---

[3] That may vary from agent to agent.

only depends on the valence of the mood. However, it is reasonable to assume that the intensity of the mood influences the radicalness of the change the agent performs on its beliefs: The higher the intensity of the mood, the bigger, i.e., more radical, the change performed. Radical changes can be modelled by non-permissive revision, i.e., each belief is either totally kept or utterly rejected. On the other hand, less radical changes can be modelled by permissive revision, i.e., beliefs can be partially accepted/rejected.

We start by defining the function $ResistantCtxs$ that captures the influence of the valence of mood on the selection of mode. Basically, for moods whose intensity is not bigger than a given threshold, the selected mode is neutral. For other moods, accommodation or assimilation mode will be selected, for negative and positive moods, respectively.

Definition 1. *Let:*

- $\beta \subset \mathcal{L}$ *be a consistent context;*
- $F \in \mathcal{L}$ *be the formula that represents the new information;*
- *mood* $\in \mathbb{R}$ *represent the valence and intensity of the agent's mood;*
- $t_{accom0} \in \mathbb{R}^-$ *be the threshold for basic accommodation behavior;*
- $t_{assim0} \in \mathbb{R}^+$ *be the threshold for basic assimilation behavior;*
- $*$ *be a classical revision operator;[4]*

$$ResistantCtxs(\beta, F, mood, t_{accom0}, t_{assim0}) =$$

$$= \begin{cases} (\beta * F), & \text{if } mood \leq t_{accom0} \\ ((\beta \cup \{F\}) * \top), & \text{if } t_{accom0} < mood < t_{assim0} \ [5] \\ \{\beta\}, & \text{if } mood \geq t_{assim0} \end{cases}$$

Note that the function $ResistantCtxs$ returns a set of context(s). This is because the revision operation we are considering may return more than one context (see Section 2.1).

Finally, we define the Affective Revision operation, that in addition to using the function $ResistantCtxs$, reflects the influence of the intensity of mood in the radicalness of change. As we said before, the higher the intensity of the mood, the more radical should be the change of beliefs. For this purpose, two more thresholds are used by AR, in order to determine the radicalness of the change.

Definition 2. *Let:*

- $\beta \subset \mathcal{L}$ *be a consistent context;*
- $F \in \mathcal{L}$ *be the formula that represents the new information;*
- *mood* $\in \mathbb{R}$ *represent the valence and intensity of the agent's mood;*
- $t_{accom0}, t_{accom1} \in \mathbb{R}^-$ *and* $t_{assim0}, t_{assim1} \in \mathbb{R}^+$ *be the two accommodation thresholds and two assimilation thresholds, respectively, such that* $t_{accom1} \leq t_{accom0} < 0 < t_{assim0} \leq t_{assim1}$;

---

[4] Classical in the sense that it is prioritized and not permissive.

[5] $((\beta \cup \{F\}) * \top)$ is just a way of using revision to make $(\beta \cup \{F\})$ consistent.

– *Weaken be the weakening function (see Section 2.1);*
– $\phi = \bigcap ResistantCtxs(\beta, F, mood, t_{accom0}, t_{assim0})$;
– *Rejected* $= (\beta \cup \{F\}) \setminus \phi$

The affective revision of β with F, $(\beta \heartsuit F)$, is defined by
$(\beta \heartsuit F) =$

$$= \begin{cases} \beta \cup \{F\}, & \text{if } F \text{ is consistent with } \beta \\ \phi \cup Weaken(\bigwedge Rejected, \phi), & \text{if } t_{accom1} < mood < t_{assim1} \\ \phi, & \text{if } (mood \leq t_{accom1}) \text{ or } (mood \geq t_{assim1}) \end{cases}$$

Note that while the first branch of the operation corresponds to the case where there is no contradiction, the other two branches correspond to *Permissive* and *Radical* change, in this order. Whether this change gives preference to the previous context (assimilation), to the new information (accommodation) or to none of them (neutral), is reflected in ϕ which is the intersection of the contexts returned by *ResistantCtxs*. Figure 1 shows, in a schematic way, how the different types of change are determined by the valence and intensity of the mood.

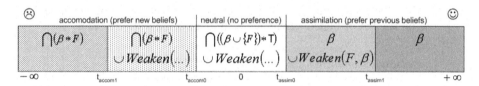

Fig. 1. The Affective Revision operation in each interval of mood values

3.2   Generation of Orders Among Beliefs

In the last section we used the classical revision operation $*$, in the definition of function *ResistantCtxs*. In Section 2.1, we said that this operation accepts any number of partial orders, that are used in the decision of which beliefs to abandon. This operation was developed to be used by a reasoning system, and the orders could only come from outside the system (the user).

Now that we are thinking of agents using the Affective Revision operation defined in the last section, it is no longer reasonable to assume that these orders will come from the outside. So, in this section we describe how an agent can generate orders among its beliefs.

These orders are generated from the *strength of beliefs* (a numerical value) in an straightforward way. For any two formulas, F_1 and F_2: $F_1 \leq_\beta F_2$ iff $Strength(F_1) \leq Strength(F_2)$.

The strength of a belief F, $Strength(F)$, may have two different origins: 1) It may come from emotions anticipations, as described in Section 2.2; we represent this component by $EmotionalStrength(F)$; 2) It may come from non-emotional considerations, like the credibility/authority of the source of the belief; we represent this component by $SourceStrength(F)$. The relative weight of the these components will depend on how much the agent is influenceable by emotions. This factor is represented by the numerical parameter $emotiveness \in [0, 1]$, and may vary from agent to agent. A simple formula that captures this idea is:

$$Strength(F) =$$
$$(1 - emotiveness) \times SourceStrength(F) + emotiveness \times EmotionalStrength(F)$$

Let us now see how $EmotionalStrength$ and $SourceStrength$ can be defined. Since the emotional strength is relative to emotion anticipations, we must consider which emotion(s) would result from adding/removing a belief to/from the current beliefs of the agent. The intensities of such emotions can be added (or subtracted) in order to determine the overall emotional positiveness or negativeness associated with the anticipation of adding/removing the belief. To this end, let us consider the following functions: $AnticipateRemoval(F)$ returns the intensities of the emotions that the agent would feel if it no longer believed in F; $AnticipateAddition(F)$ returns the intensities of the emotions that the agent would feel if it came to believe in F. These values of intensity are accompanied by signs representing the valence of the correspondent emotions. These two functions use the generation of emotions from situation descriptions mentioned in Section 2.3, which takes into account the current internal state of the agent.

Let β be the set of beliefs of the agent under consideration. Then

$$EmotionalStrength(F) = \begin{cases} \sum_{i \in AnticipateAddition(F)} i, & \text{if } F \notin \beta \\ -\sum_{i \in AnticipateRemoval(F)} i, & \text{if } F \in \beta \end{cases}$$

Finally, we present a way of determining the source strength of a belief. To this end, we assume that each agent associates a credibility to every other agent, represented by a numerical value, in the interval $]0, 1[$. This value may be a default value, or may have been determined from previous interactions of the agent under consideration *self*, with the other agent *other*, and is part of the agent's (*self*) internal state. For the purpose at hand, we represent this value by $credibility(other)$.

Before we define the function $SourceStrength$, we point out some aspects that the behavior of that function should exhibit. The source strength of an observed belief should always be higher than that of a communicated one ("seeing is believing"). The strength of a belief that was only communicated should increase with the number of agents that communicated it, and with the credibility of those agents.

If we see the credibility of an agent as the probability that that agent speaks the truth, then the probability that a piece of information F which was told by agents $ag_1, ..., ag_n$ is true, that is the combined credibility of these agents, is[6]

$$CombCredib(ag_1, ..., ag_n) = 1 - \prod_{i=1}^{n} (1 - credibility(ag_i))$$

---

[6] We used probability calculus to determine the expression for the probability that at least one event (from a set of independent events) is true.

Let $Obs \in \mathbb{R}^+$ be the strength of observed beliefs, i.e., the maximal strength a belief can possibly have. Then

$$SourceStrength(F) = \begin{cases} Obs & \text{if } F \text{ was observed} \\ Obs \times CombCredib(ag_1, ..., ag_n) & \text{if } F \text{ was communi-} \\ & \text{cated by } ag_1, ..., ag_n \end{cases}$$

This is a first approach to the computation of the strength of beliefs. Besides the source strength and emotional strength, the strength of a belief can be influenced by other factors, as, e.g., those mentioned in [13].

4   An Example

To illustrate the ideas presented in the last section, we now present an example.

Consider that the agent under consideration, henceforth referred to simply by "the agent" (female), is a student and believes that if one does not know the subject matter of an exam, then one does not pass the exam. She believes it because her colleagues *Bruno* and *Mary* told her so. Suppose that the agent did an exam and that, not having studied for it, she did not know the subject matter.

Let $F_1 = \forall(x)\neg Studied(x) \rightarrow \neg PassedExam(x)$, and $F_2 = \neg Studied(Self)$. Then, the beliefs of the agent can be represented by the context $\beta = \{F_1, F_2\}$, where *Self* represents the agent.

Now suppose another agent, *Smith*, tells our agent that she has passed the exam. *Smith* adds that he always considered the agent very intelligent. Let us say that the agent models this new information by formula $F_3 = PassedExam(Self) \wedge Intelligent(Self)$. The agent "would be happy" to believe in this, but F_3 cannot be straightforwardly added to β because it would cause an inconsistency. We now apply the ideas of the last section. Let us consider that Obs (the strength of an observation) is 100, and that the credibility that the agent attributes to agents *Bruno*, *Mary* and *Smith* is 0.5, 0.6 and 0.5, respectively. Then $SourceStrength(F_1) = 100 \times (1 - (1 - 0.5) \times (1 - 0.6)) = 80$, $SourceStrength(F_2) = 100$, and $SourceStrength(F_3) = 100 \times (1 - (1 - 0.5)) = 50$. Suppose that $AnticipateAddition(F_3) = \{60\}$. Then, $EmotionalStrength(F_3) = 60$. Assuming that the emotiveness of the agent is 0.4: $Strength(F_1) = 0.6 \times 80 + 0.4 \times 0 = 48$, $Strength(F_2) = 0.6 \times 100 + 0.4 \times 0 = 60$, and $Strength(F_3) = 0.6 \times 50 + 0.4 \times 60 = 54$. So, $F_1 \leq_\beta F_3 \leq_\beta F_2$. The preferred belief is F_2 and the least preferred is F_1. Notice how observations (i.e., F_2) are usually preferred to communicated beliefs. Notice also how F_3 is preferred to F_1, even having less source strength, only because the agent would like to believe in it (i.e., because of the positive emotion anticipation).

Now that beliefs have an order of preference, let us see how affective revision (see Section 3.1) deals with the arrival of the contradictory belief F_3. Given the above order, we have $(\beta * F_3) = ((\beta \cup \{F_3\}) * \top) = \{F_2, F_3\}$.

Assume the values -5, -2, 2 and 5 for the four mood thresholds, t_{accom1}, t_{accom0}, t_{assim0} and t_{assim1}, respectively. As an intermediate step, let us calculate the preferred context, ϕ, and the rejected formulas, *Rejected*, according to the abbreviations used in Definition 2. For this, let us consider the three possible situations:

In accommodation moods ($mood \leq -2$): $\phi = \{F_2, F_3\}$, $Rejected = \{F_1\}$
In neutral moods ($-2 < mood < 2$): $\phi = \{F_2, F_3\}$, $Rejected = \{F_1\}$
In assimilation moods ($mood \geq 2$): $\phi = \{F_1, F_2\}$, $Rejected = \{F_3\}$

The function $Weaken$, defined in [16], returns the following results:

- $Weaken(F_1, \{F_2, F_3\}) = \{\bigtriangledown(x)\neg Studied(x) \rightarrow \neg PassedExam(x)\}$
- $Weaken(F_3, \{F_1, F_2\}) = \{Intelligent(Self)\}$

In the first case, the universal rule is transformed into a default rule ($\bigtriangledown(x)$ $\neg Studied(x) \rightarrow \neg PassedExam(x)$ states that "Usually, if an individual does not study for an exam, he/she does not pass the exam", so it is a rule that allows exceptions). In the second case, the conjunction looses the conjunct that is causing the inconsistency, and the other conjunct remains.

Finally, let us observe the result of affective revision in the five possible cases of mood:

$mood = -8$ (**radical accommodation**):
    $(\beta \heartsuit F_3) = \{F_2, F_3\}$
$mood = -3$ (**permissive accommodation**):
    $(\beta \heartsuit F_3) = \{F_2, F_3, \bigtriangledown(x)\neg Studied(x) \rightarrow \neg PassedExam(x)\}$
$mood = 0$ (**neutral**):
    $(\beta \heartsuit F_3) = \{F_2, F_3, \bigtriangledown(x)\neg Studied(x) \rightarrow \neg PassedExam(x)\}$
$mood = 3$ (**permissive assimilation**):
    $(\beta \heartsuit F_3) = \{F_1, F_2, Intelligent(Self)\}$
$mood = 8$ (**radical assimilation**):
    $(\beta \heartsuit F_3) = \{F_1, F_2\}$

Analyzing the behavior of affective revision, we can see that:

- In accommodation mode the agent automatically accepts the new information told by $Smith$. The belief F_1 is abandoned (radical change) or just weakened into a default rule (permissive change).
- In neutral mode there is no a priori preference between old and new information. The result is equal to that of permissive accommodation because the order among formulas states that F_1 is the weakest.
- In assimilation mode the agent does not change anything in his previous beliefs. What $Smith$ says is either completely rejected (radical change) or simply weakened (permissive change).

Note that, in this example, the results of affective revision in assimilation mode are not intuitive, because the agent rejects a belief that would make her happy. In fact, the results follow the influences described in Section 2.2 and one should not expect "usefulness" in every situation. In a real situation it is perhaps more probable that the agent would be, a priori, in a negative mood thinking she would not pass the exam, so she would unlikely be in assimilation mode.

5   Conclusions and Future Work

We present an alternative operation to conventional belief revision: affective revision. It is a non-prioritized type of revision since it does not necessarily accept the new information, which is also the case in human belief maintenance. Affective revision models the fact that, in humans: Negative moods bias us towards questioning our present beliefs, and more easily accepting (and even search for) new information; Positive moods, on the other hand, bias us towards strongly relying on our present beliefs, and being more skeptical about new information that contradicts our beliefs.

Affective revision also models another affective influence on belief maintenance, namely how emotion anticipations can affect the strength of beliefs. We use this influence, as well as non-emotional factors, to order beliefs in terms of their resistance to change. This is an important aspect when we move from reasoning systems to systems based on agents, which have goals, plans, emotions, etc. In this context it is neither plausible nor desirable to consider that the orders among the beliefs of an agent come from outside the agent.

We approached problems in AI belief maintenance by drawing inspiration from affective influences on human reasoning. The usefulness of considering affective influences in AI belief maintenance is still to be assessed. However, since that is the case in humans, we believe that it may potentially be the case in AI.

The contribution of this work is a small part of what can be done in the study of the influence of affective states in reasoning, including the maintenance of beliefs. Even the maintenance of beliefs, that we tackled in this paper, can be completed with other influences, known in psychology such as, e.g., *mood congruency* (see, e.g. [4] and [6]). We are currently attempting to model this influence as a contribution to the calculation of belief strength.

According to Forgas' *Affect Infusion Model* [5], [6], one may be more or less influenceable by affects (i.e., under more or less affect infusion) depending on one's undergoing processing strategy (i.e., the cognitive task one is pursuing). In this sense, we plan to "regulate" the weight of emotional aspects in the calculation of belief strength, based on the agent's undergoing processing strategy.

References

1. Alchourrón C.E., Gärdenfors P., and Makinson D., "On the logic of theory change: partial meet functions for contraction and revision" in *The Journal of Symbolic Logic*, 50(2), pp 510-530, 1985.
2. Cravo M.R., "A Belief Revision Theory based on SWMC", Technical Report GIA 93/03, Lisbon, Portugal: Instituto Superior Técnico, Departamento de Engenharia Mecânica, 1993.
3. Cravo M.R., Cachopo J.P., Cachopo A.C. e Martins J.P., "Permissive Belief Revision", *Progress in Artificial Intelligence, Proc. of the 10th Portuguese Conference in AI*, Brazdil P. and Jorge A. (eds), pp 335-348, Lecture Notes in Artificial Intelligence 2258, Heidelberg, Germany: Springer-Verlag, 2001.

4. Fiedler K., and Bless H., "The formation of beliefs at the interface of affective and cognitive processes", in *Emotions and Beliefs - How Feelings Influence Thoughts*, Frijda N.H., Manstead A.S.R., and Bem S. (eds), pp 144-170, Cambridge, UK: Cambridge University Press, 2000.

5. Forgas J.P., "Mood and judgment: The affect infusion model (AIM)", in *Psychological Bulletin*, 117(1), pp 39-66, 1995.

6. Forgas J.P., "Feeling is believing? The role of processing strategies in mediating affective influences on beliefs", in *Emotions and Beliefs - How Feelings Influence Thoughts*, Frijda N.H., Manstead A.S.R., and Bem S. (eds), pp 108-143, Cambridge, UK: Cambridge University Press, 2000.

7. Frijda N.H., Manstead A.S.R., and Bem S. (eds) *Emotions and Beliefs - How Feelings Influence Thoughts*, Cambridge, UK: Cambridge University Press, 2000.

8. Frijda N.H., and Mesquita B., "Beliefs through emotions", in *Emotions and Beliefs - How Feelings Influence Thoughts*, Frijda N.H., Manstead A.S.R., and Bem S. (eds), pp 45-77, Cambridge, UK: Cambridge University Press, 2000.

9. Hansson S.O., "Ten philosophical problems in belief revision", in *Journal of Logic and Computation*, 13(1), pp 37-49, 2003.

10. Harman. G.H., *Change in View: Principles of Reasoning*, MIT Press, Cambridge, MA, USA, 1986.

11. Minsky M., *The Society of Mind*, New York, N.Y.: Simon and Schuster, 1985.

12. Ortony A., Clore G.L., and Collins A., *The Cognitive Structure of Emotions*, New York, N.Y.: Cambridge University Press, 1988.

13. Paglieri F., "See what you want, believe what you like: Relevance and likeability in belief dynamics", in *Proceedings AISB 2005 Symposium 'Agents that want and like: Motivational and emotional roots of cognition and action'*, L. Cañamero (ed), pp. 90-97, Hatfield, AISB, 2005.

14. Piaget J., *The origins of intelligence in children*, New York: International University Press, 1952.

15. Picard R., "Affective Computing", Cambridge, MA: The MIT Press, 1997.

16. Pimentel C.F., and Cravo M.R., "Extending SNePSwD with Permissive Belief Revision", in *Conceptual Structures: Integration and Interfaces, Proc. of the 10th International Conference on Conceptual Structures, ICCS 2002*, Priss U., Corbett D., and Angelova G. (eds), pp 271-284, Lecture Notes in Artificial Intelligence 2393, Heidelberg, Germany: Springer-Verlag, 2002.

17. Simon H.A., "Motivational and Emotional Controls of Cognition", in *Psychological Review*, 74(1), pp 29-39, 1967.

Feeling and Reasoning: A Computational Model for Emotional Characters

João Dias and Ana Paiva

GAIPS Grupo de Agentes Inteligentes e Personagens Sintéticas,
INESC-ID and IST, Tagus Park,
Av. Prof. Cavaco Silva, 2780-990 Porto Salvo, Portugal
joao.assis@tagus.ist.utl.pt, ana.paiva@inesc-id.pt

Abstract. Interactive virtual environments (IVEs) are now seen as an engaging new way by which children learn experimental sciences and other disciplines. These environments are populated by synthetic characters that guide and stimulate the children activities. In order to build such environments, one needs to address the problem of how achieve believable and empathic characters that act autonomously. Inspired by the work of traditional character animators, this paper proposes an architectural model to build autonomous characters where the agent's reasoning and behaviour is influenced by its emotional state and personality. We performed a small case evaluation in order to determine if the characters evoked empathic reactions in the users with positive results.

1 Introduction

The art of creating engaging and believable characters is well studied among traditional animators [22]. Traditional characters like *Mickey Mouse*, or more recent 3D characters like *Shrek*, are able to create the illusion of life and allow for the establishment of emotional relations by the viewers. The viewer feels sad when they are sad, angry when something unfair is done to them and so on. These emotional relations are named empathic relations. Empathy can be defined in broad terms as "an observer reacting emotionally because he perceives that another is experiencing or about to experience an emotion" [6].

The use of such empathic characters in virtual learning environments has obvious advantages. Children's didactic software usually uses animated characters (3D or not) to guide the child trough the application and activities. They stimulate the child interaction with the environment, enrich the child experience and captivate their attention. However, such animated characters, like in traditional animation, are scripted for each possible scenario when the application is designed. When the child presses a given button, the character will just play the corresponding scripted behaviour. This does not only forces to create such scripted animations for each possible situation, but also limits the possibilities of the child's interaction.

Ideally, one would like to have Intelligent Virtual Environments (IVEs) inhabited by autonomous agents, which "think" and act on their own. Such

C. Bento, A. Cardoso, and G. Dias (Eds.): EPIA 2005, LNAI 3808, pp. 127–140, 2005.

autonomous agents make the environment neither predictable nor completely controlled, and thus it is not possible to prescript animations for each situation. The narrative can then emerge from the individual performance of each character. However, making autonomous agents believable and empathic it's a quite difficult problem. This paper presents an agent architecture that aims at achieving such empathic autonomous characters, inspired by some of the elements present in traditional animation.

To illustrate our approach, we will look at one particular example of a pedagogical system. FearNot![5] is a computer application developed to tackle and eventually help to reduce bullying problems in schools. Bullying has associated with it a wide variety of behaviours such as hitting, or kicking, in the case of direct bullying, or, in relational bullying, social exclusion or malicious rumour spreading. Thus, the overall objective of the development of FearNot!, was to build an anti-bullying demonstrator in which children age 8 to 12 experience a virtual scenario where they can witness (from a third-person perspective) bullying situations. The child acts as an invisible friend to a victimized character, discussing the problems that arise and proposing coping strategies.

Note that in bullying situations there are quite clear identifiable roles: the bully, the victim, bully-victim (a child that is sometimes the victim and sometimes the bully) and bystander. Therefore it is necessary to build an agent architecture that not only supports believability, but also offers an easy process of building characters with particular behaviours. In sum, the architecture aims at achieving synthetic characters with the following characteristics:

- **Believability and Empathy:** The characters must be believable and be able to produce empathic reactions with users.
- **Reactive and Cognitive Capabilities:** Given the scope of possible domains, characters should react as quickly as necessary in a rapidly changing environment. However, reactive behaviour is too predictable for a truly autonomous character. Believable characters should display motivations, goals and desires, which is only possible if they have cognitive capabilities.
- **User Interaction:** The characters should be able to interact with an external user and receive suggestions. However, any influence the user may perform cannot be direct, because the character cannot take the user suggestions blindly without taking the risk of not acting in character and thus loosing believability.
- **Generality:** The agent architecture should be domain independent, i.e. it must allow the easy creation of different characters with different personalities for different domains.

To determine if the developed architecture is able to achieve believable characters a small evaluation was performed with eleven-year old children. In order to determine the effects of the user's interaction in the story, we compared our results with the results obtained from a scripted version, where the children could not influence the outcome of the story.

The rest of the paper is organized as follows: in section two we present some related work that led us to the final design of our architecture; next we define some of the most relevant concepts used in our model and depict the architecture. Afterwards an illustrative example is presented to explain how the internal mechanisms achieve the overall behaviour; finally we analyse the results obtained from the evaluation and draw some final remarks.

2   Related Work

In order to achieve believable characters, our work focuses mainly on two characteristics early pointed out by traditional animators and often explored by researchers working in synthetic characters: emotional expressivity and personality. Characters that are unable to express their feelings and cannot react emotionally to events are lifeless. As Thomas and Johnston put it: "... it has been the portrayal of emotions that has given the Disney characters the illusion of life" [22]. They define three major requisites to successfully express emotions with characters: (1) the emotional state of the character should be undoubtedly perceived by the audience; (2) emotions can be accentuated or exaggerated to be better understood; and (3) emotions affect the reasoning process and consequences should be noticeable in the actions of the characters.

Together with emotional expressivity, personality plays a very important role in believability. Thomas and Johnston state that if the process of thought reveals the feeling, it should also reveal the character's personality. This means that like the emotions, personality also influences the reasoning process. Two different characters may act differently in the same situation because of their personality, and the viewers must perceive such differences. Furthermore, a well defined role and personality is crucial to achieve emergent narrative.

Realizing the importance of emotions in reasoning, several psychologists developed emotion theories that model the generation of emotions in human beings. One of the most important, especially for the computer science community, is the OCC theory of emotions (named after its creators Ortony, Clore and Collins) because it is an appraisal theory that is easily implemented by a computer program [16]. OCC defines emotions as a valenced (good or bad) reaction to an event, which is triggered by a subjective evaluation of the event according to the character's goals, standards and beliefs.

Several researchers used OCC to explore the role of emotions in behaviour. For instance, Joseph Bates realized the importance of believable characters (a term introduced by him [3]) in Virtual Reality applications [2] and together with Reilly [18] used OCC to model emotions in the Oz project [1]. Elliott was also one of the first ones to use OCC in his Affective Reasoner [7]. Another researcher that has further explored the use of OCC theory, Jonathan Gratch, introduced the concept of emotional planners in the Émile system [10]. Gratch argues that planning algorithms have several properties that ease cognitive appraisal. Instead of using domain specific rules to determine the appraisal, Émile takes advantage of explicitly storing the agent plans into memory to reason about future possible outcomes and to automatically generate the character's emotional state. As plans grow and change, so changes the emotional state.

Looking at a different perspective, emotions can also play a significant role in coping strategies. Usually, characters act in the environment to solve their problems (problem-focused coping). Stacy Marsella introduced a new coping concept in Carmen Bright's Ideas (CBI) [14]. The characters can change their interpretation of the world to discharge negative emotions and to reinforce positive ones, which enables a mental coping mechanism guided by emotions (emotion-focused coping). For example, a problem-focused way to attempt to deal with a loved one's illness, is to take action that gets them medical attention. On the other hand, emotion-focused strategies may include avoiding thinking about it, focusing on the positive or denying the seriousness of an event. Gratch and Marsella further extended and integrated their ideas to create EMA which is used in the Mission Rehearsal Exercise system [11].

Our proposed architecture uses a multi-layered approach similar to TABASCO architecture [21]. The cognitive layer is mainly inspired by Gratch and Marsella's work. A emotional planner builds up the core of the cognitive layer and emotional-focused coping differentiates behaviours according to the characters' personality. The reactive layer is based on the emotional rules used in Martinho's work [15].

3   Emotion and Dynamics of Emotion

Our concept of emotion steams from OCC cognitive theory of emotions. The OCC structure of emotions defines a hierarchical organization for emotion types. An emotion type represents a family of related emotions differing in terms of their intensity and manifestation. Thus, when an emotion type is referred, such as Fear, it does not specify the particular emotion associated with the word fear. Instead, it references the possible set of emotions resulting from appraising the prospect of a goal expected to fail, with varying degrees of intensity - concern, fright, petrified. Therefore, the attributes considered in the proposed model for the description of an emotion are:

- *Type:* The type of the emotion being experienced
- *Valence:* Denotes the basic types of emotional response. Positive or negative value of reaction
- *Target:* The name of the agent/object targeted by the emotion
- *Cause:* The event/action that caused the emotion
- *Intensity:* The intensity of the emotion
- *Time-stamp:* The moment in time when the emotion was created or updated

Every emotion has associated an Intensity attribute which is assigned with different values depending on the different situations that generated the particular emotion. Basically, it assesses how strong the emotion is. However, the intensity of an emotion does not remain constant during its life cycle in the system. Since the moment it is generated, the intensity of an emotion must be attenuated through time in order to reflect the dynamics of the emotional system itself. This characteristic reflects the notion that an emotion does not last forever and does not affect the evaluation of the subsequent emotional states in the same way. According to this concept, the model uses a decay function for emotions proposed by Picard [17], which characterizes intensity as a function of time. At any time (t), the value for the intensity of an emotion (em) is given by:

$$Intensity\,(em, t) = Intensity\,(em, t_0) \times e^{-b.t} \qquad (1)$$

The constant b determines how fast the intensity of this particular emotion will decrease over time. This value can be controlled in order to reflect the short or long duration of the emotion types. The value $Intensity(em, t0)$, refers to the value of the intensity parameter of the emotion (em) when it was generated. When after some time t, the value of $Intensity(em,t)$ reaches a defined threshold near zero, the emotion (em) must be removed from the system's repository, meaning that that specific emotion will no longer be part of the agent's emotional state.

In addition to emotions, the proposed model represents arousal and mood. Arousal represents the degree of excitement of the character. Aroused characters will feel more intense emotions. FearNot! only models psychological arousal, so whenever the character experiences a high intensity emotion (positive or negative), his arousal level will rise. Just like ordinary emotions, the arousal decays over time. Therefore, if nothing happens for a while, the character will "calm down". Mood represents an overall valence of the character's emotional state and is also used to influence the intensity of emotions. The idea, based on Picard, is that characters with a bad mood will tend to experience more negative emotions, and characters with a good mood will experience more positive emotions. Mood is represented as an internal variable that increases when positive emotions are created and decreases with negative emotions. This variable also decays over time until it reaches its neutral value (using a linear decay function).

4   Personality

In our model, the character's personality is also strongly based in OCC and is defined by: a set of goals; a set of emotional reaction rules; the character's action tendencies; emotional thresholds and decay rates for each of the 22 emotion types defined in OCC.

Our model uses two of OCC goal types, active-pursuit goals and interest goals. Active-pursuit goals are goals that the characters actively try to achieve, like going to a dentist appointment. Interest goals represent goals that a character has but does not pursue, as for instance wanting his favourite team to win a match, or avoiding getting hurt.

The emotional reaction rules assess how generic events are appraised and represent the character's standards and attitudes. Since the appraisal process is clearly subjective, these rules must be very dependent on personality. Action tendencies represent the character's impulsive actions which he performs without thinking (reactive actions). This labelling of reactive actions as action tendencies is due to Lazarus [12], which states that action tendencies are innate biological impulses, while coping is "a much more complex, deliberate and often planful psychological process". However, note that other psychological theorists may have distinct notions for the concept of action tendencies (ex: Frijda [8]). Specifying action tendencies for characters is very important to convey the viewer a well defined personality. Loyall [13] pointed out that in order to achieve believability, characters must have very particular details of movements, mannerisms and reactions. As example, in FearNot!, when the victim is very sad it will tend to cry, while the bully will express his sadness in a completely different way.

OCC specifies for each emotion type an emotional threshold and decay rate. An emotional threshold specifies a character's resistance towards an emotion type, and the decay rate assess how fast does the emotion decay over time. When an event is appraised, the created emotions are not necessarily "felt" by the character. The appraisal process determines the potential of emotions. However such emotions are added to the character's emotional state only if their potential surpasses the defined threshold (the threshold is specific for each emotion). And even if they do overcome the threshold, the final emotion intensity is given by the difference between the threshold and the initial potential.

So, in addition to goals, standards and attitudes, these emotional thresholds and decay rates are used to complement a character's personality. For example, a peaceful character will have a high threshold and a strong decay for the emotion type of Anger, thus its anger emotions will be short and low. Thus, it is possible to have two characters with the same goals, standards and behaviours that react with different emotions to the same event (by having different thresholds). In order to model the decay rate, each emotion type has a different decay function (1), which differs in the constant value b. This value is given by the character's decay rate for each emotion.

5   Architecture

Figure 1 shows the complete model for our architecture. Taking into account the requirements depicted in the beginning of the paper, it presents two layers for the appraisal and coping processes. The reactive layer is responsible for the character's action tendencies, while the deliberative layer achieves the agent planful behaviour.

Action tendencies represent hardwire reactions to emotions and events that must be rapidly triggered and performed. Thus, the character must be able to react to an event and execute an action tendency almost immediately. Since the action tendencies depend on the character's emotional state, such assessment can only be made after the appraisal process. However, the cognitive appraisal depends on the agent's plans and can take some time: when an event is received, the continuous planner has to update all active plans (according to the event) even before the start of the generation of emotional reactions. For that reason, we applied the same two-level distinction to the appraisal process. Note that the planner will not extend (develop) any plan at this stage, it will just remove executed actions and update the plan probabilities accordingly.

While the deliberative level generates prospect-based emotions (hope, fear, satisfaction) based on the agent's plans and goals, the reactive level generates

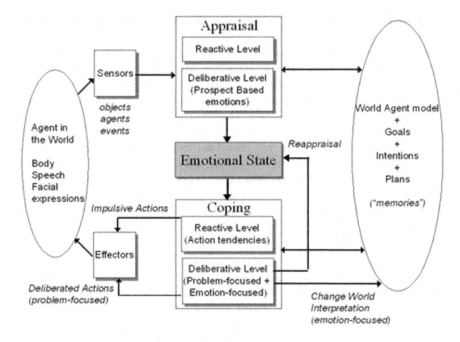

Fig. 1. Architecture Diagram

all other types of OCC emotions (fortune of others, well being, attribution, attraction) using a set of domain dependent emotional reaction rules as used by Martinho in S3A [15]. When an event is perceived, the reactive appraisal matches the event against the set of defined emotional rules, generating the corresponding emotions.

5.1 Cognitive Appraisal (Focus and Attention)

A continuous planner [19] that uses partial-ordered-plans builds up the core of the deliberative layer. However, the planner was extended to include probability information about actions and to perform emotion-focused coping strategies. The probability of a given action is biased by the character's personal interpretation and can be changed by emotion-focused strategies. More details about how the plans are represented, how a plan's probability of success is determined and how the planner works can be found in [5].

Each character has defined a set of active-pursuit goals that are triggered upon certain conditions. Thus, every time the agent receives a new perception from the environment, the deliberative layer checks all deactivated goals to determine if any of them has become active. If so, an intention to achieve the goal is added to the intention structure. The intention represents the agent's commitment to achieve the goal and stores all plans created for it. Initial hope and fear emotions based on the goal's importance are created in this process (and are stored inside the intention). After this initial process, the deliberative layer must choose between the existing intentions/goals to continue deliberation (and planning).

The OCC theory of emotions does not specify how do emotions affect reasoning/cognition and action selection. Thus, we had to look at the work of researchers that explored the influence of emotion in behaviour. For instance, according to Sloman [20], emotions are an efficient control mechanism used to detect situations or motives that need urgent response from the agent, and to trigger the appropriate redirection of processing resources. Applying the same idea in our architecture, we can use emotions to determine the most relevant intention: the ones generating the strongest emotions are the ones that require the most attention from the agent, and thus are the ones selected by the planner to continue deliberation.

After selecting the strongest intention, the best plan built so far is brought into consideration. This process is named focus and generates the following prospect based emotions:

- **Hope of success:** Hope to achieve the intention. The emotion intensity is determined from the goal's importance of success and the plan's probability of success.
- **Fear of failure:** Fear for not being able to achieve the intention. The emotion intensity is determined from the importance of failure and the plan's probability of failing.
- **Inter-goal fear:** Fear for not being able to preserve an interest goal. This emotion is generated if the plan contains any inter-goal threat.

In addition to active-pursuit goals, a character also has interest goals that specify protection constraints. These allow the modelling of conditions that the character wishes to protect/maintain. Whenever an action is added to a plan, a conflict between the action's effects and existing protected conditions may arise. This conflict is named an inter-goal threat. When the best plan is brought into focus, if it has any inter-goal threat, in addition to the normal emotions, it also generates a inter-goal fear emotion according to the respective interest goal that is being threatened. This emotion's intensity depends on the likelihood of the threat succeeding and on the interest goal's importance.

In the final phase of the deliberative appraisal, all active goals are checked to determine whether they succeed or fail. When such events occur or if the planner is unable to make a plan, more prospect based emotions will be generated, such as *Satisfaction*, *Disappointment*, *Relief* and *Fears-Confirmed*.

5.2   Coping

The coping strategies performed over the selected plan depends on the character's emotional state and personality. Inspired by CBI[14], the proposed model uses two types of coping: problem focused coping and emotional focused coping. The first one focuses on acting on the environment to cope with the situation, thus it consists on planning a set of actions that achieve the pretended final result and executing them. The second works by changing the agent's interpretation of circumstances (importance of goals, effect's probability), thus lowering strong negative emotions. When the planner analyses a plan, it applies every coping

Table 1. Applying coping strategies

Activation condition	Strategy	Effect
Plan probability very low	Acceptance	Drop the plan
Inter-goal threat detected, current goal's emotion stronger than interest goal's emotion	Acceptance or Wishful thinking	Accept the failure of the interest goal (ignore the threat) or lower the threat's probability
Inter-goal threat detected, interest goal stronger than goal's emotion	Acceptance	Drop the plan
Acceptance strategy applied	Mental Disengagement	Lower the goal's importance
Causal Conflict detected	Planning or Wishful thinking	Use promotion, demotion, or lower the conflict probability
Open Precondition	Planning	Add a step that achieves the precondition
Consistent plan without open preconditions	Execution	Execute an action

strategy that satisfies its conditions (with a specific order). Table 1 presents the several coping strategies.

Acceptance is the recognition that something is not possible to achieve or protect/maintain. If the selected plan's probability is lower than a given threshold, the character thinks that it's not worth the time to try to improve the plan, since adding more actions will not increase its probability of success, and drops the plan.

Whenever an acceptance strategy is applied, mental disengagement is also applied. Mental disengagement works by reducing the goal's importance. Since acceptance will frequently lead to goal failure, lowering the goal's importance reduces the intensity of the negative emotions triggered when the goal fails. This does not mean that to fail is ok, in fact the character will feel distressed about failing. Mental disengagement just slightly mitigates his distress.

If the planner detects an inter-goal threat in the plan, it can use additional coping strategies. If the threatened condition generates emotions stronger than the goal's emotions, the current plan is dropped. In the opposite situation, the character can either accept the interest goal's failure (by removing the protected condition) or use wishful thinking to cope with the fear emotion. Wishful thinking works by denying the reality of an event or by thinking that something bad will not happen. This strategy lowers the threat's probability by lowering the probability of the effect that threatens the condition.

Finally, when the planner achieves a consistent plan with no open preconditions it has reached a solution. This solution that corresponds to a partial ordered plan is then executed by repeatedly choosing and performing any of the next possible actions.

It is important to point out that since part of the coping strategies are triggered by emotions, the emotional state and personality influence the strategies applied and hence the overall reasoning performed by the characters. For instance, a fearful character has much more chances to drop an active pursuit goal if it presents threats to other goals.

6   Illustrative Example

This section presents an illustrative example that helps the reader understand how the mechanisms described in the previous section achieve a believable behaviour. In FearNot!'s first episode, John, the victim is studying in the classroom when Luke (the bully) enters. Luke does not like John and so when sees John he starts insulting him. As a result, John has an active pursuit goal of fighting back that is triggered when he is insulted by other characters. So, he tries to build a plan in order to fight back. However all the actions that John considers to fight back have some likelihood of getting hit back. So, when such plans are selected, a threat to John's interest goal of not getting hurt is detected and thus John feels frightened. Due to the victim's fearful nature, his inter-goal fear is much stronger than the hope of succeeding in fighting back and so he gives up the goal and does not do anything.

At the same time John is thinking, Luke notices the book over the table and realizes a bullying opportunity. So he makes a plan to push John's books to the floor. Luke moves towards the books and pushes them away. This event matches an emotional reaction that generates a gloating emotion, which triggers an action tendency. Luke performs a tease speech act that corresponds to saying something along the lines: "Come and get them you Muppet!" When the victim realizes that the books are on the floor he activates the goal of picking them, and thus walks towards them and picks them up. As if it was not enough, when the bully sees John picking up the books he decides to push him. So Luke goes behind John and pushes him (see Fig. 2-a).

When John falls, he appraises this event as very undesirable and activates an action tendency to start crying. At the same time, Luke appraises the same event as very desirable and starts to gloat about John by saying something along the lines of "What a wimp, I've hardly touched you". When John cries, Luke finds it very blameworthy and thus threatens him to stop crying and to not tell anyone.

At this point, the episode ends and the application changes to the interaction mode (Fig. 2-b) where the child user talks with the victim (John) and advises him on what to do next. The agent perceives three suggestions: fight back, ignore the bully or tell someone. These strategies correspond to goals that the character already has but is unable to achieve because they usually threaten other interest goals. Suppose that the user types something containing "hit" or "kick" or "punch", the language system recognizes such utterances as fightback suggestions. The agent remembers his goal's results and knows that he has not actually tried to fight back before, so he accepts the suggestion and increases the fight back goal's importance.

Therefore, on the next episode, when John is insulted once more, he will activate his goal of fighting back. However, since the goal's importance is much higher now, the emotions created by the goal are stronger than the ones created

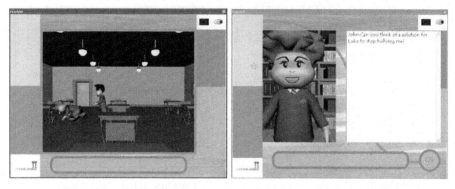

(a) Paul pushes John   (b) The user interacts with John

Fig. 2. FearNot! application

by the threat of getting hurt. So, instead of giving up fighting, John decides to confront Luke.

In the victim's perspective, both user and character's actions are perceived equally. Therefore, the victim can experience emotional reactions triggered by the user's interaction. For instance, the victim feels satisfied whenever he receives a suggestion from the user.

7   Evaluation

In order to obtain some results concerning the believability of the characters created and the emotional reactions be the children, we performed a preliminary evaluation with the goal of determine whether the architecture is capable of achieving similar results as the scripted version concerning believability and empathy felt by the children.

The scripted version used the same characters as the emergent one, but all the behaviours were predefined for each episode. After each episode, the victim appears to the user like in the emergent version, however the interaction is different: the child just has to select between different strategies (by pressing a button).

Experiments made with the scripted version in Portuguese, English and German schools showed that the children found the characters believable and felt empathy for them [4]. Although we have not yet made a similar cross-cultural evaluation with the emergent version, the preliminary evaluation gave us some insights on how children react to the autonomous characters. For the experiment, we chose eleven children aged between eight and eleven from third and fourth year, male and female from a Portuguese school.

The results obtained were similar to the scripted version. As expected, Luke (the bully) is the most disliked character, while John (the victim) is the favourite one. This means that children really create an empathic bond with the victim

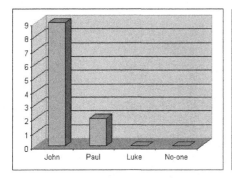   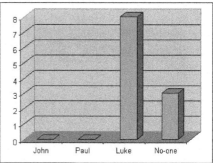

(a) Whom did you feel sorry for?   (b) Whom did you feel angry at?

Fig. 3. Emotional reactions from the users

Table 2. Scripted Vs. Emergent version

	Scripted	Emergent
Did the conversations seem real? (yes-1;no-5)	2.4	1.9
Where the conversations (interesting-1;boring-5)	2	1.64
Did the victim understand the conversation? (yes-1;no-5)		1.36
Did the victim follow the advice? (yes-1;no-5)	2.3	1.7
Did you help the victim? (helped a lot-1;no-5)	1.8	1.27

character just like in the scripted version. In order to assess if children felt any emotional reactions to the situations created with the characters we tested two reactions: (1) did they feel sorry for any character? And (2) did they feel angry at any character? Figure 3 shows that children did feel sorry at John (the victim), and reported feeling angry at the bully character, as expected. The additional character, Paul (a friend of John), appears in one of the episodes when John asks for help. These results show that the architecture's emergent behaviour can also elicit emotional reactions from the users.

In addition, we asked children if they felt in control of the story and if they liked to interact with the victim. These questions were evaluated using a Likert scale (1-5; 1 - Very good; 5 - Very Bad). Table 2 shows the questions and the results obtained with both versions.

We believe that the conversation with the victim, and the fact that the victim follows the children suggestions, makes children find the overall dialogue and narrative seem more real and interesting. For example, when the victim accepts the fight back strategy, it seems more real to see him threatening the bully on the next episode than to behave like in the first episode.

8   Final Remarks

The results attained, although very limited, do however suggest that the use of autonomous synthetic characters can lead to believable situations that do evoke empathy in users, and that like in traditional animation, emotions and personality are key to achieve this goal. Furthermore, the results also suggest that the use of the characters is an advantage as far as building a conversational interaction with the users. The fact that the children help the victim by giving him suggestions creates a stronger bond between the character and them. For instance, if the victim succeeds in coping with the situation both the victim and the child will feel satisfied. The child feels satisfied not only as an empathic response but also because she took an active role in the situation's success.

In the future, we expect to perform more tests, in particular with more parameterizations, and for relational bullying scenarios. Indeed, the use of the agent architecture poses no problems to building and configuring those new episodes.

References

1. Bates, J.: The Nature of Character in Interactive Worlds and The Oz Project. Technical Report CMU-CS-92-200, School of Computer Science, Carnegie Mellon University, Pittsburgh, 1992.
2. Bates, J.: Virtual Reality, Art, and Entertainment. Presence: The Journal of Teleoperators and Virtual Environments, 1(1), 133-138, 1992.
3. Bates, J.: The Role of Emotion in Believable Agents. In Communications of the ACM, Volume 37, Issue 7, 122-125, July 1994.
4. Zoll, C., Enz, S., Schaub, H., Woods, S., Hall, L.: Deliverable 7.2.1 Evaluation of Demonstrator in Schools, VICTEC Project, 2005
5. Dias, J.: FearNot!: Creating Emotional Autonomous Synthetic Characters for Empathic Interactions. Universidade Técnica de Lisboa, Instituto Superior Técnico, Lisboa, MSc Thesis, 2005.
6. Eisenberg, N., Strayer J.: Critical issues in the study of empathy. In N. Eisenberg and J. Strayer, editors, Empathy and its Development. Cambridge University Press, 1987.
7. Elliott, C.: The Affective Reasoner: A process model of emotions in a multi-agent system. Northwestern University, PhD Thesis, Illinois, 92.
8. Frijda N.: The Emotions. Cambridge University Press, UK, 1986.
9. Gadanho, S.: Learning Behavior-Selection by Emotions and Cognition in Multi-Goal Robot Task. In Journal of Machine Learning Research 4, pages 385-412, 2003
10. Gratch, J.: Émile: Marshalling Passions in Training and Education. In 4th International Conference on Autonomous Agents, ACM Press, June 2000.
11. Gratch, J., Marsella, S.: A Domain-independent Framework for Modeling Emotion. Appears in Journal of Cognitive Systems Research, Volume 5, Issue 4, pages 269-306, 2004.
12. Lazarus, R.: Emotion and Adaptation. Oxford University Press, New York, 1991.
13. Loyall, B.: Believable Agents: Building Interactive Personalities. Technical Report CMU-CS-97-123, School of Computer Science, Carnegie Mellon University, Pittsburgh, 1997.
14. Marsella, S., Johnson, L, LaBore, C.: Interactive Pedagogical Drama. In proceedings of the Fourth International Conference on Autonomous Agents, pp. 301-308, ACM Press, 2000
15. Martinho C.: Emotions in Motion: short time development of believable pathematic agents in intelligent virtual environments. Universidade Técnica de Lisboa, Instituto Superior Técnico, Lisboa, MSc Thesis, 1999.

16. Ortony, A., Clore, G., Collins, A.: The Cognitive Structure of Emotions. Cambridge University Press, UK, 1988.
17. Picard, R.: Affective computing. MIT Press, Cambridge, 1997.
18. Reilly, S.: Believable Social and Emotional Agents. Ph.D. Thesis. Technical Report CMU-CS-96-138, School of Computer Science, Carnegie Mellon University, Pittsburgh, 1996.
19. Russel, S., Norvig, P.: Artificial Intelligence: A Modern Approach. 2 Edition Englewood-Cliff, N.J.: Prentice-Hall, 2002.
20. Sloman, A.: Damasio, descartes, alarms, and metamanagement, In Proceedings of the IEEE International Conference on Systems, Man, and Cybernetics (SMC '98), pages 2652-7, San Diego, CA, USA, 1998
21. Staller, A., Petta, P.: Towards a Tractable Appraisal-Based Architecture for Situated Cognizers. In Grounding Emotions in Adaptive Systems, Workshop Notes, Fifth International Conference of the Society for Adaptive Behaviour (SAB98), Zurich, 1998.
22. Thomas, F., Johnston, O.: Disney Animation: The Illusion of Life. Abbeville Press, New York (1981)

Chapter 3

ALEA 2005: Artificial Life and

Evolutionary Algorithms

Introduction

Luís Correia[1] and Ernesto Costa[2]

[1] Universidade de Lisboa, Portugal
[2] Universidade de Coimbra, Portugal
Luis.Correia@di.fc.ul.pt, ernesto@dei.uc.pt

In this part we present accepted communications to ALEA'05, which took place at University of Covilhã, Portugal, on 5-8 December 2005. ALEA'05 was the second workshop on Artificial Life and Evolutionary Algorithms, organised as part of EPIA'05 (Portuguese Conference on Artificial Intelligence). ALEA is an event targeted at Artificial Life (ALife) community, Evolutionary Algorithms (EA) community and researchers working in the crossing of these two areas.

To a certain extent, ALife and EA aim at similar goals of classical Artificial Intelligence (AI): to build computer based intelligent solutions. The path, however, is diverse since ALife and EA are more concerned with the study of simple, bottom-up, biologically inspired modular solutions. Therefore, research on computer based bio-inspired solutions, possibly with emergent properties, and biology as computation, may be the global characterisation of this workshop.

In ALEA'05 we received an interesting set of good quality international contributions. The papers herein presented have been selected, by rigorous double-blind peer-review, for oral presentation and they represent less than 1/3 of the total submissions. The spectrum covered by the papers reflects well the broad approach of the field.

The paper by Silva et al. presents an interesting comparison of different EA approaches to the problem of synthesising 3D object models. It succeeds in applying both Genetic Algorithms (GA) and Genetic Programming (GP) to the same problem. Redou and co-authors describe a multi-agent system to simulate biological chemical kinetics in an interactive way. The fact that the model is asynchronous, for which a proof of convergence is supplied, is distinctive in this paper. An hybrid approach for a classification system, using Neural Networks (NN) and Decision Trees (DT) is described in the paper by Kim et al. This work may also be considered in a bridge to bioinformatics, since it applies the classification method to a health diagnosis problem. In the contribution of Hog-yun et al. a modified Particle Swarm Optimization model is presented. It is oriented towards multiobjective optimisation. Specific operators such as competition and clonal selection, inspired in artificial life models are applied in this model. Yet a different perspective of ALife research is provided by Meshoul and co-authors. Their contribution presents an application of a quantum based EA also to a multi-objective optimization problem. Its main focus is on the representation necessary to encompass a multi-objective problem and in extending evolutionary operators with quantum specific ones.

We feel this set of papers shows the many facets of ALife and EA which constitute one of their main positive features. Their potential in cross-fostering new research and new results has not ceased to be explored.

C. Bento, A. Cardoso, and G. Dias (Eds.): EPIA 2005, LNAI 3808, p. 143, 2005.
© Springer-Verlag Berlin Heidelberg 2005

Evolutionary Computation Approaches for Shape Modelling and Fitting

Sara Silva[1], Pierre-Alain Fayolle[2], Johann Vincent[3], Guillaume Pauron[3], Christophe Rosenberger[3], and Christian Toinard[4]

[1] Centro de Informática e Sistemas da Universidade de Coimbra,
Polo II - Pinhal de Marrocos, 3030 Coimbra, Portugal
`sara@dei.uc.pt`
[2] University of Aizu, Software Department, AizuWakamatsu,
Fukushima ken 965-8580, Japan
`d8052103@u-aizu.ac.jp`
[3] Laboratoire Vision et Robotique, UPRES EA 2078, ENSI de Bourges - Université
d'Orléans, 10 boulevard Lahitolle, 18020 Bourges, France
`{johann.vincent, guillaume.pauron,`
`christophe.rosenberger}@ensi-bourges.fr`
[4] Laboratoire d'informatique Fondamentale d'Orléans, CNRS FRE 2490, ENSI de
Bourges - Université d'Orléans, 10 boulevard Lahitolle, 18020 Bourges, France
`christian.toinard@ensi-bourges.fr`

Abstract. This paper proposes and analyzes different evolutionary computation techniques for conjointly determining a model and its associated parameters. The context of 3D reconstruction of objects by a functional representation illustrates the ability of the proposed approaches to perform this task using real data, a set of 3D points on or near the surface of the real object. The final recovered model can then be used efficiently in further modelling, animation or analysis applications. The first approach is based on multiple genetic algorithms that find the correct model and parameters by successive approximations. The second approach is based on a standard strongly-typed implementation of genetic programming. This study shows radical differences between the results produced by each technique on a simple problem, and points toward future improvements to join the best features of both approaches.

1 Introduction

Shape modelling is a mature technology, extensively used in the industry for various applications (rapid prototyping, animation, modelling of cherubical prothesis, *etc*) [4]. Our purpose is to ease shape modelling of objects from the real world by fitting template shape models, defined by a functional representation (FRep) [17], to point data sets. The resulting model can later be modified and reused to fit the requirements of an application. An approach for modelling human body with template parameterized models was recently proposed [19]. Such a work underlines, in a different context, the importance to be able to later process and modify models from the real world.

C. Bento, A. Cardoso, and G. Dias (Eds.): EPIA 2005, LNAI 3808, pp. 144–155, 2005.
© Springer-Verlag Berlin Heidelberg 2005

The traditional methods used in reverse engineering and shape recovery of constructive solids rely on a segmentation of scan data and fitting of some mathematical models. Usually, these mathematical models are parametric or algebraic surface patches [3,7]. They are then converted to a boundary representation model. In [3,7], the need of relations between parameters or objects is introduced. These relations intend to guarantee symmetry or alignment in the object, thus enforcing the accuracy of the recovery procedure. Fitting parametric and algebraic surfaces, using relations between the parameters and objects, is a difficult problem of non-linear constrained optimization. Robertson *et al.* [18] proposes an evolutionary method based on GENOCOP III [14,15] to efficiently resolve this hard problem. The drawback of such methods in shape recovery is that they suit only boundary representation with segmented point sets. Adding new primitives would require a corresponding segmentation of the point sets, which is difficult or even impossible in the case of complex blends or sweeps. Furthermore, it may be difficult for the resulting model available only as a BRep (*i.e.* Boundary Representation) to be reused in extended modelling, analysis or animation.

We have extended [5] the general idea of knowledge-based recovery (*i.e.* the use of relations between parameters and primitives) with a different interpretation and a different model, the function representation of objects [17]. In this approach, standard shapes and relations are interpreted as primitives and operations of a constructive model. The input information provided by the user is a template (sketch) model, where the construction tree contains only specified operations and types of primitives while the parameters of operations and primitives are not required and are recovered by fitting. Template models may exist in dedicated library for each domain of applications, available to be reused, or else they need to be created by the user. In [5], a method based on a genetic algorithm is proposed for fitting the template FRep model to point sets. The main problem of this method is that the FRep model has to be defined by the user.

In this paper, we propose different Evolutionary Computation (EC) [1] approaches to automatically determine both the model (shape modelling) and its best parameters (shape fitting). We use both Genetic Algorithm (GA) [10,8] and Genetic Programming (GP) [12,2] methodologies, and discuss the results, pros and cons, and possible improvements of each approach.

2   The FRep Model

In general, the shape recovery of objects follows a sequence of different steps, shown in Fig. 1. This paper is focused on the methods used to derive the FRep model and its parameters (modelling and model estimation).

2.1   The Function Representation

The function representation (FRep) [17] follows a constructive approach for modelling multidimensional objects. In the constructive modelling approach, a com-

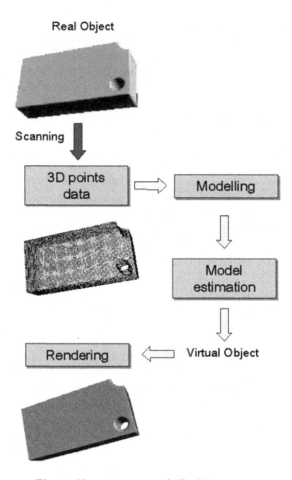

Fig. 1. Shape recovery of 3D objects

plex object is decomposed into a set of simple ones, called primitives, that are then combined by different operations. The data structure describing the combination of primitives is called a construction tree. In the FRep model, the primitives are any continuous real valued functions, for example skeletal implicit surfaces, or algebraic surfaces. The operations themselves are defined analytically in such a manner that they yield continuous real valued functions as output, ensuring the closure property of the representation. Figure 2 represents the FRep model of the simple object illustrated in Fig. 1. Figure 3 represents the corresponding construction tree.

In the FRep model, a multidimensional object is defined by a single continuous real valued function f. The points x for which $f(x) \geq 0$ belong to the object, whereas the points for which $f(x) < 0$ are outside. In the construction tree, only specified operations and primitives are included, along with the parameters of each primitive, which must be tuned according to some modelling criteria.

Fig. 2. Representation of the object in Fig. 1 by a FRep model

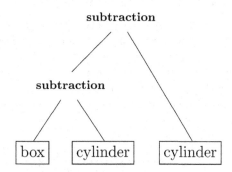

Fig. 3. Construction tree of the object shown in Fig. 2

2.2   Finding the Model

A FRep model classically uses 5 different primitives (sphere, box, cylinder in X, Y and Z) and 3 operations (intersection, union, subtraction). Even if we have a low number of primitives and operations, if we try to determine the FRep model of a simple object with 2 operators in its construction tree, we have $5 \times 3 \times 5 \times 3 \times 5 = 1125$ possible combinations. This is a very computationally expensive problem. This task is usually performed by a user but, depending on the object complexity, it may be too difficult to do. Once the model is determined, it is possible to find the best parameters [5] but, wanting to find an automatic approach to do both at the same time, we are dealing with an even more complex problem.

In the rest of the paper, the notation $f(\mathbf{x}, \mathbf{a})$ is used for a parameterized FRep, where $\mathbf{x} = (x, y, z) \in \mathbb{R}^3$ is a point in 3D space and $\mathbf{a} = (a_1, \ldots, a_m) \in \mathbb{R}^m$ is a vector of m parameters.

2.3   Tuning the Parameters

Tuning the parameters is based on a set of 3D points, $S = \{\mathbf{x_1}, \ldots, \mathbf{x_N}\}$, scattered on the surface of the object. Given S, the task is to find the best configuration for the set of parameters $\mathbf{a}^* = (a_1, \ldots, a_m)$ so that the parameterized FRep model $f(\mathbf{x}, \mathbf{a}^*)$ closely fits the data points. The FRep model $f(\mathbf{x}, \mathbf{a})$, built in a constructive way, approximates the shape of the solid being reverse engineered. The vector of parameters $\mathbf{a}$ controls the final location and shape of the solid and thus the best fitted parameters should give the closest possible model according to the information provided by S.

The sphere primitive requires 4 parameters (a 3D point indicating the center, plus the radius), while the box primitive requires 5 parameters (3D center point, width, height and depth). Each cylinder primitive requires only 3 parameters (because each cylinder is infinite in its respective direction, a 2D center plus the radius is enough to completely define it).

2.4   Evaluating the Parameterized Model

In order to evaluate the mismatch between the discrete representation of the solid, given by S, and the surface of the solid for the current vector of parameters, implicitly defined by f, a fitness function is needed. The function f defines an algebraic distance between the current point of evaluation $\mathbf{x}$ and the surface it implicitly defines [17]. The fitness error thus becomes the square of the defining function values at all points of S (the surface of the solid being the set of points with zero function value):

$$error(\mathbf{a}) = \frac{1}{2} \sum_{i=1}^{N} f^2(\mathbf{x_i}, \mathbf{a}) \tag{1}$$

Our goal is to search for both the function f and the vector of parameters $\mathbf{a}^*$ minimizing (1). This is the fitness function used by the different approaches described next.

3   Evolutionary Computation Approaches

Given the characteristics of the FRep model described in the previous section, we realize that our goal is just a particular case of the general problem of evolving both a structure and its parameters at the same time. Different Evolutionary Computation (EC) approaches can be tried in order to find an efficient and reliable method to solve this task.

3.1   Genetic Algorithms Within Genetic Programming

GP is known to be very good at evolving variable-length structures, while GAs are most appropriate for optimizing a fixed-length set of parameters. The first idea to tackle the problem of doing both at the same time is very obvious: use a GP to evolve the construction tree, where the evaluation of each individual is preceded by the optimization of its parameters performed by a GA.

However, we have abandoned this approach for being too computationally demanding. A single run of standard GP evolving 500 individuals during 50 generations would launch a GA as many as $50 \times 500 = 25000$ times! Although this could be the ultimate and most appropriate solution for the problem, we quickly moved to other less demanding techniques.

3.2   Multiple Genetic Algorithms

Using a single GA to evolve both the construction tree and its parameters was not a promising option. Due to its typical fixed-length representation, the usage of a single GA would require the prior information regarding how many levels the construction tree should have. It would also require distinct genes for the structure and for the parameters, as well as the consequent additional care in terms of the genetic operators used in the evolution.

So, we have decided to try an automatic approach where multiple GAs are used to iteratively determine each level of the FRep construction tree. We try by this approach to reproduce the methodology of a sculptor for a real object. At each step, the object is refined until the desired level of precision. In our approach, at the first level, we determine the geometric primitive that best approximates the 3D points by launching 5 GAs, one for each primitive. Each GA only has to optimize the fixed set of parameters of the corresponding primitive by minimizing the fitness function (1) where f is already determined by the primitive. The GA achieving the lowest fitness determines the primitive to be used in the first level.

To determine the second level, we assume the primitive defined previously is correct and try to determine the operation and the other primitive. For this we must launch 15 GAs, one for each possible combination (3 operations $\times$ 5 primitives). These new GAs optimize the parameters of both the first and second primitives. An option could be made to always use the parameters found in the previous level, but recalculating them is more correct in terms of optimization.

After determining the best operation and primitive for the second level of the construction tree, 15 GAs are once again launched to determine the third level, and so on until the fitness reaches the minimum value of zero, or the user decides that the approximation is sufficiently good. The task of the GAs becomes more complex as more levels are determined. The results obtained with this approach are described in Sect. 4.1.

3.3   Strongly-Typed Genetic Programming

Using only GP to automatically evolve the construction tree and its parameters at the same time appeared to be a viable and promising option from the very beginning. GP typically uses variable-length representations, and its enormous flexibility make it easily adaptable to almost any type of problem.

However, standard GP [12] is not particularly suited for evolving structures where the closure property is not present. This is the case in our problem where, for instance, the only valid arguments of an operation are primitives or other operations, and the only valid arguments of a primitive are the parameters. So, instead of standard GP, we have used strongly-typed GP [16], a much suitable option for this type of problem.

We have defined two types in our strongly-typed system. The first type includes all the primitives (sphere, box, cylinder in X, Y and Z) and operations (intersection, union, subtraction) mentioned earlier. The second type refers to the parameters, and includes terminals and simple arithmetic functions. Elements of the first type can be further differentiated in two subtypes, because primitives can only accept parameters as input arguments, while operations can only accept primitives or other operations.

Two standard genetic operators are used in our system: tree crossover and tree mutation. We do not use different genetic operators for each type, but we do ensure that both crossover and mutation are type-aware, meaning that any two parents always create type-valid offspring. In crossover, the crossing point in the first tree is chosen randomly, and then the crossing point in the second tree is chosen such that swapping the subtrees creates a type-valid individual. In mutation, the crossing point is also chosen randomly, and the new replacing subtree is created such that the mutated individual is valid. A description of the results obtained with the strongly-typed GP approach can be found in Sect. 4.2.

4   Experimental Results

In all our experiments, we have tested the different approaches with the object used in figures 1 through 3, modelled for testing purposes using HyperFun [9], a set of tools for FRep geometric modelling. The surface of the object has been sampled to create a data set of 10714 3D points, represented in Fig. 4. This data set is used for calculating the fitness function (1) described in Sect. 2.4.

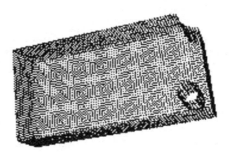

Fig. 4. Data set of 3D points used for the virtual modelling of the object

The FRep defining function F shown below has been determined as a parameterized model for the recovery process:

$$F(\mathbf{x}, \mathbf{a}) := subtraction(subtraction(box(\mathbf{x}, \mathbf{a}), cylinder Z(\mathbf{x}, \mathbf{a})),$$
$$cylinder Z(\mathbf{x}, \mathbf{a})); \qquad (2)$$

This FRep model consists of three simple primitives: one box and two infinite cylinders oriented along the Z axis, each primitive defined by its parameterized model. For example, in the case of the cylinderZ, the defining function is: $cylinder(x, a) := a[1]^2 - (x[1] - a[2])^2 - (x[2] - a[3])^2$, where $a[1]$, $a[2]$, and $a[3]$ are parameters meaning the radius, and the center (X,Y) of the cylinder, respectively. All the primitives are combined together using the subtraction operator ($\backslash$), which is itself defined analytically as discussed in [17] (see Fig. 3 for the associated constructive tree).

4.1   Multiple Genetic Algorithms

The GA system used was the GAOT [11], implemented in ©MATLAB [22], with the main running parameters indicated in Table 1. Unspecified parameters were used with the default values.

Table 1. Main running parameters of the GA system used

Chromosome Type	real-valued
Population Size	1000
Mutation	non-uniform, probability 0.8
Crossover	arithmetic, 20 tries
Selection for Reproduction	normalized geometric ranking
Stop Criteria	100 generations

Table 2 shows the values of the fitness function achieved for each possible primitive at the first level of the construction tree. The lowest (best) fitness value was achieved for the box primitive, clearly the one that best fits the point data set. This successfully concludes the first iteration of the multiple GA approach.

Table 2. Value of the fitness function at the first level of the construction tree for each possible primitive

Sphere	CylinderZ	CylinderY	CylinderX	Box
717449.8	47747.2	749123.7	756618.1	**534.1**

Table 3 shows the values of the fitness function achieved for each possible combination of operation and primitive at the second level of the construction tree. The lowest value corresponds to the cylinderZ and subtraction pair, which can be verified in Fig. 3 to be correct. Although the best fitness is not even close to zero, the structural elements chosen for the construction tree are correct. This means that, after finishing this iterative process, a single GA can be used to perform the full optimization of all the parameters of the structure, thus achieving high quality shape fitting.

Table 3. Value of the fitness function at the second level of the construction tree for each possible combination of primitive and operation

	Sphere	CylinderZ	CylinderY	CylinderX	Box
Intersection	230247.1	24756.7	712364.5	1502950.5	775.3
Union	749166.7	46059.7	31695.3	10156.8	78192.8
Substraction	176985.1	**544.2**	1827.9	1493.0	3463.3

At each subsequent iteration we adopt the same methodology, comparing 15 values of the fitness function derived by the multiple GAs. We always choose the operation and primitive pair that achieves the lowest fitness value.

4.2 Strongly-Typed Genetic Programming

The strongly-typed GP system used was an adaptation of GPLAB [20], a GP toolbox for ©MATLAB [22], with the main running parameters indicated in Table 4. Unspecified parameters were used with the default values.

Table 4. Main running parameters of the GP system used

Function Set	$\{intersection, union, subtraction\}$ (type 1, subtype 1) $\{sphere, box, cylinder X \dots Z\}$ (type 1, subtype 2) $\{+, -\}$ (type 2)
Terminal Set	$\{rand, 0, 1\}$ (type 2)
Population Initialization	Ramped Half-and-Half [12]
Population Size	500
Maximum Tree Depth	initial: 3-6, final: 6-10 [21]
Operator Rates	crossover/mutation: 0.5/0.5
Reproduction Rate	0.1
Selection for Reproduction	tournament [13], size 2-50
Selection for Survival	replacement (no elitism)
Stop Criteria	100 generations

The function set contains all the elements indicated in the three sets of the table. Their types are described in Sect. 3.3. *rand* is a random constant between 0 and 1, created once and then used like the other constants. We have adopted some parsimony pressure measures in our GP system, namely the Lexicographic Parsimony Pressure tournament [13] and the Heavy Dynamic Limit [21] on tree depth, along with the traditional static limit [12]. We have used a range of values for the maximum tree depth and tournament size in different GP runs.

Figure 5(left plot) shows the results of a typical GP run obtained with a tournament of size 50 (10% of the population) and an initial tree depth of 6 with maximum value 10. It is immediately apparent that GP is able to easily achieve

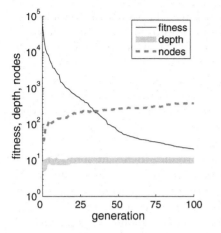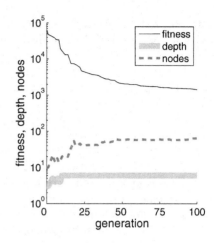

Fig. 5. Results of typical GP runs, with high selective pressure and low parsimony pressure *(left)*, and with low selective pressure and high parsimony pressure *(right)*

good fitness values, and keep improving them as the evolution proceeds (best value of this run was 20.7). However, the typical GP solution is not parsimonious at all, obtaining good approximations only thanks to an extensive and creative combination of primitives, one that does not reflect the simplicity of the object being modelled. For instance, the run illustrated in the left plot produces a solution containing 46 operations, 47 primitives, and 76+218 parameter elements (arithmetic constants and constants), totalling 387 nodes in the construction tree. The first primitive used in this tree was not the box.

On the attempt to produce shorter and more realistic solutions, we have increased the parsimony pressure by using an initial tree depth of only 3, with maximum value 6. We have also decreased the selective pressure to allow a larger exploration of the search space, by reducing the tournament size to 2. Figure 5 (right plot) illustrates a typical run obtained with these parameters. The convergence to better fitness values was much more difficult (best value of this run was 1434.4), and the solution produced was much smaller, but still far from expected, containing 8 operations, 9 primitives, and $10 + 37$ parameter elements (operators and constants), totalling 64 nodes in the construction tree. Once again, the first primitive used was not the box.

5 Conclusions and Future Work

We have extended the work presented in [6] for determining and fitting a parameterized FRep model to a 3D point data set. We have proposed different EC approaches and shown that they produce radically different results when applied to a simple problem of shape modelling and fitting.

The multiple GA approach produces the correct construction tree, simple and compact as a human user would do. The process can be performed in two phases, first iteratively deriving the tree and later fine tuning its parameters with a final single GA. The disadvantage of this approach is that launching so many GAs is computationally expensive, especially when we consider that each level of the construction tree demands more from each GA. Another problem with the approach is its user dependence, at least in its current implementation where the system is not autonomous enough to decide when to add more levels to the construction tree, and when to stop. However, this can also be regarded as an advantage, because no one better than the user can decide which level of detail is necessary for the current application.

The strongly-typed GP approach is able to produce highly fit solutions in a totally automatic manner. However, the construction trees generated suffer from the extreme lack of parsimony that usually plagues GP evolution, even when parsimony pressure measures are applied. The creative solutions produced by GP do not please the practitioners of the field. Further work should be performed in order to make GP operate more like the iterative generation of the construction trees. Starting from very small trees and regular genetic operators to optimize the parameters, other genetic operators could be used to specifically add primitives to the tree, producing a similar behavior to the multiple GA approach.

Real-world objects of higher complexity should be used to test both approaches, reflecting the more realistic conditions where the shape modelling and fitting problem is too difficult to be performed by the user. Under such conditions, the multiple GA approach may not be able to produce such simple and clear-cut solutions in a feasible amount of time, and the creativeness and flexibility of the GP approach may become essential in producing acceptable results.

Regardless of what we may expect from future results, we believe that somewhere among the proposed approaches are already the necessary ingredients to achieve a fully automatic EC solution for the shape modelling and fitting problem, hopefully readily applicable to other problems dealing with the same issue of optimizing a model and its parameters at the same time.

Acknowledgements

This work was partially financed by grant SFRH/BD/14167/2003 from Fundação para a Ciência e a Tecnologia, Portugal. We would like to thank the members of the ECOS – Evolutionary and Complex Systems Group (Universidade de Coimbra), in particular group leader Ernesto Costa, for the valuable ideas and suggestions provided regarding this work. The authors would also like to thank the financial support provided by the Conseil Général du Cher, France.

References

1. Back, T., Fogel, D.B., Michalewicz, Z. (eds.): Handbook of Evolutionary Computation. IOP Publishing and Oxford University Press, New York and Bristol (1997)
2. Banzhaf, W., Nordin, P., Keller, R.E., Francone, F.D.: Genetic Programming - An Introduction. Morgan Kaufmann, San Francisco (1998)

3. Benko, P., Kos, G., Varady, T., Andor, L., Martin, R.: Constrained Fitting in Reverse Engineering. Computer Aided Geometric Design **19** (2002) 173–205
4. Costantini, F., Toinard, C.: Collaboration and Virtual Early Prototyping Using the Distributed Building Site Metaphor. In: Rahman, S.M.M. (ed.): Multimedia Networking: Technology, Management and Applications (2002) 290–332
5. Fayolle, P.-A., Rosenberger, C., Toinard, C.: Shape Recovery and Functional Modeling Using Genetic Algorithms. In: Proceedings of IEEE LAVAL VIRTUAL (2004) 227–232
6. Fayolle, P.-A., Pasko, A., Kartasheva, E., Mirenkov, N.: Shape Recovery Using Functionally Represented Constructive Models. In: Proceedings of SMI 2004 (2004) 375–378
7. Fisher, R.: Applying Knowledge to Reverse Engineering Problems. In: Proceedings of Geometric Modeling and Processing. IEEE Computer Society (2002) 149–155
8. Goldberg, D.E.: Genetic Algorithms in Search, Optimization and Machine Learning. Addison-Wesley, Boston, MA (1989)
9. HyperFun project (2005) http://cis.k.hosei.ac.jp/~F-rep/HF_proj.html
10. Holland, J.H.: Adaptation in Natural and Artificial Systems. The University of Michigan Press, Ann Arbor (1975)
11. Houck, C., Joines, J., Kay, M.: A Genetic Algorithm for Function Optimization: A Matlab Implementation. Technical Report NCSU-IE TR 95-09 (1995)
12. Koza, J.R.: Genetic Programming –On the Programming of Computers by Means of Natural Selection. MIT Press, Cambridge, MA (1992)
13. Luke, S., Panait, L.: Lexicographic Parsimony Pressure. In: Langdon, W.B. *et al.* (eds.): Proceedings of GECCO-2002. Morgan Kaufmann (2002) 829–836
14. Michalewicz, Z.: Genetic Algorithms + Data Structures = Evolution Programs. Springer-Verlag, Berlin (1996)
15. Michalewicz, Z., Fogel, D.B.: How to Solve It: Modern Heuristics, 2nd edn. Springer, Berlin (2004)
16. Montana, D.J.: Strongly Typed Genetic Programming. BBN Technical Report #7866 (1994)
17. Pasko, A., Adzhiev, V., Sourin, A., Savchenko, V.: Function Representation in Geometric Modeling: Concepts, Implementation and Applications. The Visual Computer **11** (1995) 429–446
18. Robertson, C., Fisher, R., Werghi, N., Ashbrook, A.: An Evolutionary Approach to Fitting Constrained Degenerate Second Order Surfaces. EvoWorkshops (1999) 1–16.
19. Seo, H., Magnenat-Thalmann, N.: An Example-Based Approach to Human Body Manipulation. Graphical Models **66** (2004) 1–23
20. Silva, S.: GPLAB – A Genetic Programming Toolbox for MATLAB (2005) http://gplab.sourceforge.net
21. Silva, S., Costa, E. Dynamic Limits for Bloat Control - Variations on Size and Depth. In: Deb, K., Poli, R., Banzhaf, W. *et al.* (eds.): Proceedings of GECCO-2004. Springer (2004) 666–677
22. The MathWorks – MATLAB and Simulink for Technical Computing (2005) http://www.mathworks.com/

Reaction-Agents: First Mathematical Validation of a Multi-agent System for Dynamical Biochemical Kinetics

Pascal Redou[1], Sébastien Kerdelo[1], Christophe Le Gal[1], Gabriel Querrec[1], Vincent Rodin[1], Jean-François Abgrall[2], and Jacques Tisseau[1]

[1] CERV, European Center for Virtual Reality, BP 38, F-29280 Brest, France
`Pascal.Redou@enib.fr`
[2] Hematology Laboratory, CHU Brest, Bd Tanguy Prigent, 29609, Brest, France

Abstract. In the context of multi-agent simulation of biological complex systems, we present a reaction-agent model for biological chemical kinetics that enables interaction with the simulation during the execution. In a chemical reactor with no spatial dimension -e.g. a cell-, a reaction-agent represents an autonomous chemical reaction between several reactants : it reads the concentration of reactants, adapts its reaction speed, and modifies consequently the concentration of reaction products. This approach, where the simulation engine makes agents intervene in a chaotic and asynchronous way, is an alternative to the classical model -which is not relevant when the limits conditions change- based on differential systems. We establish formal proofs of convergence for our reaction-agent methods, generally quadratic. We illustrate our model with an example about the extrinsic pathway of blood coagulation.

1 Introduction

Simulation in biology makes use of algorithms for the numerical resolution of differential systems. These algorithms, though they give precise results, do not fit well with the study of complex systems [At1]. Indeed, complex systems are *a priori* open (dynamical appearance/disappearance of components), heterogenous (various morphology and behaviours) and made of entities that are composite, mobile and distributed in space ; their number changes during time, and they interact with each other. Describing the evolution of such systems by means of deterministic methods like differential systems is uneasy, for limits conditions and number of processus fluctuate. As an alternative, the multi–agent approach [Fe1, WC1], already used in several biochemical models [HX1, JS1, WW1], provides a conceptual, methodological and experimental framework well-fitted for imagination, modelisation and experimentation of complexity. In this context, our work applies to the simulation of biological chemical kinetics phenomenons taking into account the variability of the number of implied reactants.

In a dimensionless chemical reactor -e.g. a cell-, a reaction-agent represents a chemical reaction which loops into a perception/decision/action cycle : it reads the concentration of reactants, adapts its reaction speed, and modifies consequently the concentration of reaction products. Each agent independently executes a classical ordinary differential system algorithm [CL1]. For each of these classical methods, we build the matching reaction-agent method.

C. Bento, A. Cardoso, and G. Dias (Eds.): EPIA 2005, LNAI 3808, pp. 156–166, 2005.

The simulation engine evolves reaction-agents asynchronously and chaotically (see section 2), in order to avoid the typical inflexibility of synchronous systems, as well as bias in numerical results.

From a more general point of view, we set up agents autonomy as a basic principle [TH1] : firstly autonomy is characteristic of living organisms, from the cell to the man (they are *essentially autonomous*); secondly the model should be able, at runtime, to sense changes in environment and thus the limits conditions, especially if the man is part of the system (*necessarily autonomous*); lastly, they are *autonomous by ignorance* since we are for now unable to report the behaviour of complex systems by the way of analysis reductionist method.

Therefore we gain the ability to interact with a running simulation, opening the path to a new way of experimenting : the *in virtuo* experimentation [Ti1]. *In virtuo* experimentation makes it possible to interfere with a chemical kinetics model by adding or removing reactions. The main interest of such an experimentation is that these alterations are possible without having to stop the progress of the simulation : experimental conditions of the *in virtuo* way are therefore very close to the *in vivo* and *in vitro* (with "man in the loop") ones, and fundamentally different from the *in silico* one (without "man in the loop").

In section 2 of this paper, we present the reaction-agent model for numerical computation of differential systems for chemical kinetics. In section 3 we formalize our model and state the main results about convergence of one step reaction-agent methods. In section 4 we describe how we adapt reaction-agent point of view for multistep methods, in the special case where the number of reactions is constant. Section 5 shows an illustrating example of our approach for a blood coagulation simulation. For the sake of concision, we will not expose the detailed demonstrations of mathematical results. Please contact first author to obtain proofs.

2   Reaction-Agent Model

2.1   Principle

The reaction-agents based methods are numerical methods for computation of differential systems which permit to take into account, at runtime, the evolvingness of these systems. Chemical kinetics is a natural application context for these methods : a classical example is given by cancer, since chromosomic instability [HW1] implies on a regular basis modifications or creations of new reactions [Bo1]. We have also used our reaction agent model for simulation of MAPK pathway [QR1]. We propose here (see section 5) an example about the extrinsic pathway of blood coagulation [LB1].

To achieve modelisation of such a processus we propose to reify chemical reactions. These reified reactions should be able, independently of each other, to carry out or not. Since it's the reactions that are reified in our model, we called it *reaction-agent*. Each reaction-agent matches a reaction of the system we want to modelize. Each agent behaviour loops in the following cycle :

- **Perception:** sensing of concentration of all reactions components (*i.e.* reactants and products),

- **Decision:** computation of the amount of consumed reactants (and thus of the amount of formed products),
- **Action:** writing the new concentrations of the reaction components.

Reaction-agents act by the way of chaotic and asynchronous iterations, as described below.

2.2 Chaotic and Asynchronous Iterations

At each step, the scheduler [HT1] makes one reaction-agent carry out its perception/decision/action cycle. Reaction-agents act one after the other following the scheduler cycle whose length equals the number of agents. The reaction-agents each act once and only once in a sheduler cycle, but the order in which they do so is randomly chosen. Let's precise these notions:

- **Asynchronous Iterations:** a fundamental statement is that in the classical approach, time discretisation induces the hypothesis that all reaction occur simultaneously during the same time-step. Indeed, classically used differencial systems numerical resolution algorithms *a priori* do this hypothesis based upon the choice of infinitesimal time-step. *A contrario*, reaction-agent model does the asynchronic hypothesis for chemical reactions. We claim that this hypothesis is not only more realistic, but moreover allows the user to interfere at runtime with the reactions by adding or removing a reaction-agent, at any time of the simulation. Time is then divided into scheduler cycles inside of which each reaction-agent acts once and only once, considering the state of the system at the moment it acts. From a physical point of view, each scheduler cycle corresponds to one time-step of the classical approach.
- **Chaotic Iterations:** an unalterable arrangement for reaction-agents operations at each cycle might introduce a bias -we proved some mathematical results that confirm it- in the simulation. In order to avoid this bias the scheduler makes each reaction-agent operate in a random order, which changes for each iteration step. This is what we call chaotic iterations.

Figure 1 illustrates this scheduling strategy.

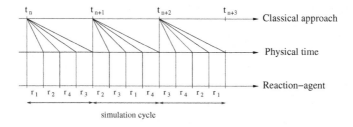

Fig. 1. Classical and reaction-agent points of view for reactions scheduling. Case of 4 reaction-agents r_i, $1 \leq i \leq 4$.

2.3   Illustration

Let's illustrate our views, and consider a medium with no spatial dimension containing several reactants. Let $[C(t)]$ be the concentrations vector at instant t. In this medium m chemical reactions occur. Their respective speeds are given by vectorial functions f_i, $1 \leq i \leq m$, whose arguments are time and concentrations vector. The evolution in time of reactants concentrations are classicaly described by the differential system

$$\frac{d}{dt}[C(t)] = (f_1 + f_2 + \cdots + f_m)(t, C[t]), \tag{1}$$

under conditions $C[t_0]$ for concentrations at initial instant. Such systems are numericaly solved by the mean of very precises algorithms [CL1, HN1], which allows computation of all concentrations at each instant of the discretised time : for one step methods, the concentrations vector C_{n+1} at instant t_{n+1} is computed from the same vector at instant t_n, named C_n. This leads to a computation algorithm such as below :

$$\begin{aligned} C_0 &= C[t_0] \\ C_{n+1} &= C_n + h_n \Phi_{f_1 + \cdots + f_m}(t_n, C_n, h_n) \end{aligned} \tag{2}$$

where $h_n = t_{n+1} - t_n$, $\Phi_{f_1 + \cdots + f_m}$ is a function dependent on the sum of f_i speeds, and which characterizes the chosen algorithm. As we stated, here reactions are supposed to be simultaneous and the main drawback of this modelisation is its staticness : adding or removing a reaction at runtime implies rewriting the system and reruning the program, which is unsuitable for complex system simulation and runtime modification of these systems. Our method also uses a classical resolution algorithm but applies it for each reaction during the same time-step. Let's consider an elementary example with two reactions, whose speeds are f_1 and f_2. As an alternative to the numerical computation of the system (1) (when $m = 2$) using algorithm (2), that is,

$$C_{n+1} = C_n + h_n \Phi_{f_1 + f_2}(t_n, C_n, h_n), \tag{3}$$

we propose a *reaction-agent version* of this algorithm :

$$\begin{aligned} C_\star &= C_n + h_n \Phi_{f_1}(t_n, C_n, h_n) \\ C_{n+1} &= C_\star + h_n \Phi_{f_2}(t_n, C_\star, h_n) \end{aligned} \tag{4}$$

or, equiprobably,

$$\begin{aligned} C_\star &= C_n + h_n \Phi_{f_2}(t_n, C_n, h_n) \\ C_{n+1} &= C_\star + h_n \Phi_{f_1}(t_n, C_\star, h_n) \end{aligned} \tag{5}$$

Thus, in a single time-step, the algorithm is here applied two times : once for each reaction. Each application takes into account the state of the system at the current time. In order to avoid bias, at each time step a random arrangement of reaction-agents operations is performed.

3   Formalization and Principal Results

We now give the mathematical formalization of our reaction-agent model, and the validating results we have obtained. The natural integers ring is called $\mathbb{N}$, $\mathbb{R}$ is the reals field, and S_m the permutations of order m group [Ca1]. For the sake of simplicity we only consider differential systems of a single equation; however definitions and results are easily generalizable. More details about numerical resolution of ordinary differential equations can be found in [HN1].

Remark 1. We have also adapted this autonomous agents point of view for classical multiple steps methods, or for implicits methods [HN2] : we develop this point in section 4. Convergence and stability features are better for these methods than for single step methods. However these methods not only conflict with principles of multi agents systems whose behaviour is markovian; but moreover they rule out the ability to modify the number of agents at runtime.

3.1   General Definition

Definition 1. *Let*

$$y_{n+1} = y_n + h_n \Phi_f(t_n, y_n, h_n) \tag{6}$$

be a one step method for Cauchy problem resolution

$$\begin{cases} y(t_0) = y_0 \\ y'(t) = f(t, y(t)). \end{cases} \tag{7}$$

Let $m \in \mathbb{N}^*$. We call reaction-agent version of method (6), *for resolution of problem*

$$\begin{cases} y'(t) = (f_1 + f_2 + \cdots + f_m)(t, y(t)) \\ y(t_0) = y_0 \end{cases} \tag{8}$$

the method given by

$$y_{n+1} = y_n + h_n \Phi_{\sigma_n}(t_n, y_n, h_n) \tag{9}$$

defined by an equiprobable choice, at each time step $n \to n+1$, of $\sigma_n \in S_m$, and by relations

$$y_{\star 1} = y_n + h_n \Phi_{f_{\sigma_n(1)}}(t_n, y_n, h_n)$$
$$\forall i, \ 1 \le i \le m-1, \qquad y_{\star i+1} = y_{\star i} + h_n \Phi_{f_{\sigma_n(i+1)}}(t_n, y_{\star i}, h_n) \tag{10}$$
$$y_{n+1} = y_{\star m}$$

Example 1. We remind the reader that for Cauchy problem resolution (7), order 2 Runge-Kutta method is given by

$$y_{n+1} = y_n + h_n \Phi_f(t_n, y_n, h_n)$$

where

$$\Phi_f(t, y, h) = f(t + \frac{h}{2}, y + \frac{h}{2} f(t, y)).$$

The matching reaction-agent version for resolution of problem (8) is given by definition 1, where $\forall i, \ 1 \le i \le m$,

$$\Phi_{f_i}(t, y, h) = f_i(t + \frac{h}{2}, y + \frac{h}{2} f(t, y)).$$

For instance, two reaction-agents case leads to

$$y_{n+1} = y_n + h_n \Phi_{\sigma_n}(t_n, y_n, h_n)$$

with, equiprobably,

$$
\begin{aligned}
&\Phi_{\sigma_n}(t,y,h) \\
&= f_1(t + \tfrac{h}{2}, y + \tfrac{h}{2} f_1(t,y)) \\
&+ f_2\Big(t + \tfrac{h}{2}, y + h f_1(t + \tfrac{h}{2}, y + \tfrac{h}{2} f_1(t,y)) \\
&\qquad\qquad + \tfrac{h}{2} f_2(t, y + h f_1(t + \tfrac{h}{2}, y + \tfrac{h}{2} f_1(t,y))) \Big)
\end{aligned}
$$

if $\sigma_n = \mathrm{Id}$

or

$$
\begin{aligned}
&\Phi_{\sigma_n}(t,y,h) \\
&= f_2(t + \tfrac{h}{2}, y + \tfrac{h}{2} f_2(t,y)) \\
&+ f_1\Big(t + \tfrac{h}{2}, y + h f_2(t + \tfrac{h}{2}, y + \tfrac{h}{2} f_2(t,y)) \\
&\qquad\qquad + \tfrac{h}{2} f_1(t, y + h f_2(t + \tfrac{h}{2}, y + \tfrac{h}{2} f_2(t,y))) \Big)
\end{aligned}
$$

if $\sigma_n(1) = 2$.

3.2 Average Order of a Reaction-Agent Method

Acoording to definition 1, the computation of y_{n+1} in function of y_n depends upon the choice of the permutation σ_n. Thus we have to keep this in mind to characterize the convergence. With the same notations as above, the average evolution on one step is given by

$$
\begin{aligned}
y_{n+1} &= y_n + \bar{\Phi}(t_n, y_n, h_n), \\
\bar{\Phi} &= \frac{1}{m!} \sum_{\sigma_n \in S_m} \Phi_{\sigma_n}
\end{aligned}
\tag{11}
$$

Definition 2. *The order (in the usual sense) of the method given by (11) is called the average order of the method given by definition 1.*

Remark 2. This definition is consistent, for during the execution of reaction-agent algorithm, all elements of S_m intervene with the same probability, even though only one of these elements is chosen at each time step. As we consider the average of $m!$ algorithms, each one bound to one permutation, a reaction-agent method of average order p will in fact be less efficient than a method of order p in the classical sense. Actually, we prove that its efficiency is intermediate between two methods of order $p-1$ and p, respectively. Example in section 5 illustrates this fact.

3.3 Main Results

We enounciate here our main results about convergence of reaction-agent methods. We just provide the main ideas of the proofs, detailed ones can be asked to first author.

Theorem 1.   *1. Reaction-agent version of Euler's method is convergent of average order 1.*
  2. *Reaction-agent version of order 2 Runge-Kutta method is convergent of average order 2.*
  3. *Consider a one step method, convergent of order $p \geq 3$. Thus its reaction-agent version is convergent of average order 2.*

Theorem 1 claims in substance that there is no point in using reaction-agent's version of a Runge-Kutta method of order ≥ 3.

One can regret that the efficiency of our reaction-agent model is not better. However, we stress again the point that it is the only model -to our knowledge- that enables *in virtuo* experimentation.

Proof. We now give a few elements about the proof of theorem 1, which comprises two parts : we first prove the stability of a given reaction-agent method, then we evaluate the consistency error. We keep the same notations as in definitions 1 and 2.

1. Stability.
   We suppose that functions Φ_{f_i} are lipschitzian in y. Thus there are $(\lambda_1, \lambda_2, \ldots, \lambda_m) \in \mathbb{R}^m$ such that :

   $$|\Phi_{f_i}(t, y_2, h) - \Phi_{f_i}(t, y_1, h)| \leq \lambda_i |y_2 - y_1| \tag{12}$$

   This implies the following lemma, proved by induction :

   $$\begin{aligned}
   |\Phi_{\sigma_n}(t, y_2, h) &- \Phi_{\sigma_n}(t, y_1, h)| \\
   &\leq \sum_{i=1}^{m} \lambda_i |y_2 - y_1| \\
   &+ h \sum_{i<j}^{m} \lambda_i \lambda_j |y_2 - y_1| \\
   &+ \cdots \\
   &+ h^{m-1} \lambda_1 \lambda_2 \cdots \lambda_m |y_2 - y_1|.
   \end{aligned} \tag{13}$$

   As Φ_{σ_n} is lipschitzian, the stability is proved for reaction-agent version of any classical method.
2. Consistency.
   According to the following lemma :
   Lemma 1. *The algorithm*

   $$y(t_0) = y_0, \quad y_{n+1} = y_n + h_n \Phi_f(t_n, y_n, h_n) \tag{14}$$

   is consistent of order p if and only if

   $$\Phi_f(t, y, h) = \sum_{k=1}^{p} \frac{h^{k-1}}{k!} f^{[k-1]}(t, y) + O(h^p),$$

   $$\text{where } f^{[n]}(t, z(t)) = \frac{d^n}{dt^n} \Big(f(t, z(t)) \Big). \tag{15}$$

   Thus, we end by establishing the following equality :

   $$\begin{aligned}
   \frac{1}{m!} \sum_{\sigma_n \in S_m} \Phi_{\sigma_n}(t, y, h) \\
   = \sum_{k=1}^{p} \frac{h^{k-1}}{k!} (\sum_{i=1}^{m} f_i)^{[k-1]}(t, y) + O(h^p),
   \end{aligned} \tag{16}$$

   which is true if and only if $p \leq 2$.   □

4 Multistep and Implicit Methods

Simulation of systems submitted to constant perturbations *a priori* empeaches the use of implicit or multistep methods [HN1, HN2], since the number of constituants of the system can change from one time step to the other. However, in the case where, during the simulation, the system is stable, involving for instance a constant number of chemical reactions, we wish to keep the efficiency of such methods. We can keep the point of view of autonomous agents and use implicit and multisteps methods in this case, where reaction-agent model is unprofitable.

4.1 Description

Recall that if we want to solve the Cauchy problem (1), Adams $k + 1$-step classical methods [HN1] are based on algorithms like :

$$C_{n+1} = C_n + h_n \sum_{i=-1}^{k-1} \beta_i (f_1 + \cdots + f_m)(t_{n-i}, C_{n-i}), \qquad (17)$$

where the sum $\beta_i (f_1 + \cdots + f_m)(t_{n-i}, C_{n-i})$ is the interpolation polynomial of function $f_1 + \cdots + f_m$ at points (t_l, C_l), $n - k + 1 \leq l \leq n + 1$. Or, this can also be written, for any permutation σ_n in S_m,

$$
\begin{aligned}
C_{\star 1} &= C_n + h_n \sum_{i=-1}^{k-1} \beta_i f_{\sigma_n(1)}(t_{n-i}, C_{n-i}) \\
C_{\star 2} &= C_{\star 1} + h_n \sum_{i=-1}^{k-1} \beta_i f_{\sigma_n(2)}(t_{n-i}, C_{n-i}) \\
&\vdots \\
C_{\star m} &= C_{\star(m-1)} + h_n \sum_{i=-1}^{k-1} \beta_i f_{\sigma_n(m)}(t_{n-i}, C_{n-i}) \\
C_{n+1} &= C_{\star m}.
\end{aligned}
\qquad (18)
$$

The algorithm described above enables one to keep the point of view of autonomous agents carrying their own execution of implicit and multistep algorithm.

4.2 Simulation Strategy

Hence, simulation of chemical kinetics phenomenons using reaction-agents can be summarized the following way :

– If, during the simulation, the system is perturbed by a new phenomenon (e.g. a new chemical reaction), a one step reaction-agent method is embraced, to take this perturbation into account.
– During a long non-perturbation period, we embrace a multistep Adams method, however keeping the autonomy principiæ for our multi-agent system.

5 Example

Recall that our reaction-agent model is not intented to simulate chemical kinetics phenomenons when the number of reactions is constant. However, in order to illustrate results of section 3, we consider such a case.

We take, as an example of application of our method, the mathematical model of the extrinsic pathway of blood coagulation published by [LB1], see figure 2. In their study, they used a kinetic model based on ordinary differential equations in order to show that factor IXa could be a major product of the extrinsic pathway. We have implemented this model and solved it using either our reaction-agent (here denoted RA) methods, either classical methods. When the system is solved using our reaction-agent methods, a Euler or an order 2 Runge-Kutta or an order 4 Runge-Kutta method is embedded in each reaction-agent. When the system is solved using classical methods, a euler or an order 2 Runge-Kutta or an order 4 Runge-Kutta is used. We focus solely on factor Xa generation (*i.e.* only on the solution of one equation). We have compared the local error obtained on 6 points with each method (RA euler, RA rk2, RA rk4, ODE euler, ODE rk2, ODE rk4) to the solution given when the system is solved using an adaptative step size Runge-Kutta-Fehlberg method (here denoted ODE rk4 and supposed to be the exact solution). Results are shown in table 1.

Table 1. Results. The set of ODE of the kinetic model is solved using either our reaction agent (RA) method, either classical methods. Local errors (obtained with a constant step size of 1.0 s) on 6 points are reported. We intentionally use a huge step size, in order to get a significant error.

time (s)	RA euler	RA rk2	RA rk4
50	2.77 %	0.30 %	0.54 %
100	3.26 %	0.33 %	0.62 %
150	3.67 %	0.41 %	0.68 %
200	4.10 %	0.50 %	0.58 %
250	4.75 %	0.55 %	0.47 %
300	5.65 %	0.86 %	0.48 %

time (s)	ODE euler	ODE rk2	ODE rk4
50	2.93 %	0.05 %	0.00 %
100	2.59 %	0.04 %	0.00 %
150	2.39 %	0.04 %	0.00 %
200	2.16 %	0.04 %	0.00 %
250	1.90 %	0.04 %	0.00 %
300	1.61 %	0.04 %	0.00 %

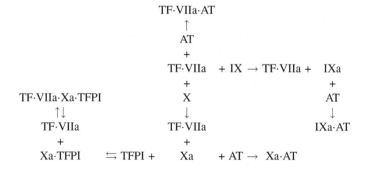

Fig. 2. Kinetic model of blood coagulation extrinsic pathway proposed by [LB1]

As expected, when classical methods are used, the higher the order of the method, the smaller the local error. This table confirms that the local error obtained using the RA Euler method is approximatively of the same order than the classical one. The RA order 2 Runge-Kutta method gives a smaller error than the Euler one but the classical order 2 Runge-Kutta is a bit more precise. The RA order 4 Runge-Kutta method shows a local error similar to the RA order 2 Runge-Kutta one, which confirms that the precision of the reaction-agent method could not exceed order 2.

6   Conclusion

We have exposed the proof of efficiency of reaction-agent based methods for the *in virtuo* simulation of biological chemical kinetics phenomenons. We have chosen to autonomize reactions. This leads to a lesser convergence than the one obtained by one step classical methods, since this order is at best quadratic, even if superior order classical method is chosen. Nevertheless, as far as we know, reaction-agent model is the only one which allows *in virtuo* simulation of a true dynamic chemical kinetics, as can be found only in life.

References

[At1]   Atlan, H. : The Living Cell as a Paradigm for Complex Natural Systems. ComplexUs. **1** (2003) 1-3

[Bo1]   Bos J.L. : Ras oncogene in human cancer : a review. Cancer Research. **50** (1989) 1352-1361

[Ca1]   Cameron, P. : Permutation Groups. New York : Cambridge University Press (1999)

[CL1]   Ciarlet, P.G., Lions, J.L. : Handbook of Numerical Analysis. North Holland (1990)

[Fe1]   Ferber J. : Multi-agent systems : An introduction to distributed artificial intelligence. Addison Wesley (1999)

[HN1]   Hairer,E., Nørsett, S.P., Wanner, P. : Solving Ordinary Differential Equations I. Nonstiff Problems. Springer Series in Comput. Mathematics.**8** (1993)

[HN2]   Hairer,E., Nørsett, S.P., Wanner, P. : Solving Ordinary Differential Equations II. Stiff and differential-algebraic problems. Springer Series in Comput. Mathematics. (1996)

[HT1]   Harrouet F., Tisseau J., Reignier P., Chevaillier P. : oRis : un environnement de simulation interactive multi-agents. RSTI-TSI. **21(4)** (2002) 499-524

[HW1]   Hanahan, D., Weinberg, J.A. : The hallmarks of cancer. Cell. **100** (2000) 57-70

[HX1]   Huang, Y, Xiang, X, Madey, G. and Cabaniss, S.E. : Agent-Based Scientific Simulation, Computing in Science and Engineering. **07(1)** (2005) 22-29

[JS1]   Jonker, C.M., Snoep, J.L., Treur, J., Westerhoff, H.V., and Wijngaards, W.C.A. : BDI-Modelling of Intracellular Dynamics. In: *A.B. Williams and K. Decker (eds.), Proceedings of the First International Workshop on Bioinformatics and Multi-Agent Systems,* BIXMAS'02, (2002) 15-23

[LB1]   Lu, G., Broze, G.J. and Krishnaswamy, S. : Formation of factors IXa and Xa by the extrinsic pathway. Differential regulation by tissue factor pathway inhibitor and antithrombin III. The journal of biological chemistry. **279(17)** (2004) 17241-17249

[QR1]   Querrec, G., Rodin, V., Abgrall, J.F., Kerdelo, S.,Tisseau, J. : Uses of Multiagents Systems for Simulation of MAPK Pathway. In *Third IEEE Symposium on BioInformatics and BioEngineering.*(2003) 421-425

[Ti1]   Tisseau, J. : Virtual Reality -in virtuo autonomy-, *accreditation to Direct Research.* (2001)

[TH1]   Tisseau, J., Harrouet, F. : Autonomie des entités virtuelles. in Le traité de la réalité virtuelle, 2nd édition, vol. 2. Les Presses de l'Ecole des Mines de Paris. **4** (2003)

[WC1]   Wooldridge, M. and Ciancarini, P. : Agent-Oriented Software Engineering: The State of the Art in P. Ciancarini and M. Wooldridge, editors, Agent-Oriented Software Engineering. Springer-Verlag Lecture Notes in AI. (2001)

[WW1]   Webb, K, White, T : Cell Modeling using Agent-based Formalisms *AAMAS'04, July 19-23, 2004, New York, New York, USA.* Copyright 2004 ACM 1-58113-864-4/04/0007 (2004)

A Hybrid Classification System for Cancer Diagnosis with Proteomic Bio-markers

Jung-Ja Kim[1], Young-Ho Kim[2], and Yonggwan Won[1],*

[1] Department of Electronics and Computer Engineering, Chonnam National University,
300 Yongbong-Dong Buk-Gu Kwangju, Republic of Korea
{j2kim, ykwon}@chonnam.ac.kr
[2] Doul Info. Technology, 1412-8 Yongbong-Dong Buk-Gu,
Gwang-ju, Republic of Korea
melchi@grace.chonnam.ac.kr

Abstract. A number of studies have been performed with the objective of applying various artificial intelligence techniques to the prediction and classification of
cancer specific biomarkers for use in clinical diagnosis. Most biological data, such
as that obtained from SELDI-TOF (Surface Enhanced Laser Desorption and Ioni-
zation-Time Of Flight) MS (Mass Spectrometry) is high dimensional, and therefore requires dimension reduction in order to limit the computational complexity
and cost. The DT (Decision Tree) is an algorithm which allows for the fast classification and effective dimension reduction of high dimensional data. However, it
does not guarantee the reliability of the features selected by the process of dimension reduction. Another approach is the MLP (Multi-Layer Perceptron) which is
often more accurate at classifying data, but is not suitable for the processing of
high dimensional data. In this paper, we propose on a novel approach, which is
able to accurately classify prostate cancer SELDI data into normal and abnormal
classes and to identify the potential biomarkers. In this approach, we first select
those features that have excellent discrimination power by using the DT. These
selected features constitute the potential biomarkers. Next, we classify the selected features into normal and abnormal categories by using the MLP; at this
stage we repeatedly perform cross validation to evaluate the propriety of the selected features. In this way, the proposed algorithm can take advantage of both the
DT and MLP, by hybridizing these two algorithms. The experimental results
demonstrate that the proposed algorithm is able to identify multiple potential biomarkers that enhance the confidence of diagnosis, also showing better specificity,
sensitivity and learning error rates than other algorithms. The proposed algorithm
represents a promising approach to the identification of proteomic patterns in serum that can distinguish cancer from normal or benign and is applicable to clinical
diagnosis and prognosis.

1 Introduction

The improvements in technologies to detect, identify, and characterize proteins, particularly two-dimensional electrophoresis and mass spectrometry, coupled with

---

* To whom all correspondences should be addressed.
This work was supported by grant No. RTI04-03-03 from the Regional Technology Innovation Program of the Ministry of Commerce, Industry and Energy(MOCIE).

C. Bento, A. Cardoso, and G. Dias (Eds.): EPIA 2005, LNAI 3808, pp. 167–177, 2005.
© Springer-Verlag Berlin Heidelberg 2005

development of bioinformatics database and analysis tool, makes proteomics a powerful approach to succeed in identifying new tumor markers.

The recent advances made in proteomic profiling technologies, such as SELDI-TOF MS, have enabled the preliminary profiling and identification of tumor markers in biological fluids in several cancer types and the establishment of clinically useful diagnostic computational models. Several studies using serum have now been published, in which the combination of SELDI profiling with artificial intelligence techniques, such as genetic algorithms, clustering, neural networks or decision tree classification algorithms, has produced extremely promising results [1][2].

SELDI-TOF MS has the potential to improve clinical diagnostics tests for cancer pathologies. The goal of this technique is to select a reduced set of measurements or "features" that can be used to distinguish between cancer and control patients. These features are essentially ion intensity levels at specific mass/charge values. However, analyses using SELDI-TOF MS are susceptible to contain thousands of data points. In such cases, because of the computational complexity and cost overhead associated with the processing of this high dimensional data, it is necessary to reduce the dimensionality by selecting useful features. Furthermore, it is important to select those features which are most likely to lead to an accurate classification. Feature selection can also be reinforced by classification. Randomized feature selection generates random subsets of features and assesses their quality independently.

The DT and MLP algorithms have been successfully applied to a wide range of pattern classification problems [3]. The DT generally runs significantly faster in the training stage and gives better expressiveness. The MLP is often more accurate at classifying novel examples in the presence of noisy data. In previous studies, these two techniques were successfully applied to the classification of human cancers and the identification of the potential biomarker proteins using SELDI-TOF mass spectrometry [1][4][5].

In this paper, we describe a novel approach that was used to find cancer specific biomarkers in prostate cancer SELDI-TOF MS data, and to accurately separate the normal and abnormal classes. These biomarkers or marker proteins are features by means of which the abnormal cases (patients) can be potentially distinguished from the normal cases (healthy men). In this approach, we first selected those features that had excellent discrimination power using the DT and found a number of potential biomarkers. As a result, the problem of dimension reduction could be solved, but the reliability of the selected features could not be guaranteed. To solve this problem, as a second step, we accurately classified the selected features into the normal and abnormal categories by using the MLP, and performed repeated cross validation to evaluate the propriety of the selected features.

The proposed algorithm takes advantage of both the DT and MLP, by hybridizing these two algorithms. The experimental results show that, with this technique, it is possible to determine the optimal number of features, and that this algorithm outperforms the other methods in terms of the specificity, sensitivity and confidence.

2 Cancer Diagnosis Using SELDI-TOF MS and Artificial Intelligence Technique

SELDI –TOF MS is a relatively new protein analysis method which was developed by Hutchens and Yip in the 1990's, and many studies have since been conducted in which this method was applied to cancer diagnosis. The advantage of this technique is that it is able to analyze the MS data on the basis of the molecular weights of the proteins more rapidly than MALDI-TOF MS, and can identify biomarkers without preprocessing.

On the other hand, SELDI-TOF MS data can contain thousands of data points originating from the mass/intensity spectra, with the molecular weight (mass) and intensity being presented on the x-axis and y-axis, respectively. Due to the high dimensionality of the data that is generated from a single analysis, it is essential to use algorithms that can detect expression patterns correlating to a given biological phenotype from large volume of data originating from multiple samples.

In clinical studies, considerable potential has also been shown in combining SELDI-TOF MS with the use of various computational models that, irrespective of the knowledge of the peak identities, can generate diagnostic predictions based on the peak profiles, with promising results being obtained in studies using serum samples from patients. In the field of bioinformatics, a new algorithm was developed to enhance the confidence of the diagnosis.

In previous studies, in cases of ovarian cancer that frequently occur in women, they classify normal case or patient by using SOM (Self Organized Map) and genetic algorithm to SELDI-TOF MS data of patients [2]. Another example involves the investigation of the clinical utility of the SELDI profiling of urine samples, in conjunction with neural-network analysis to either detect renal cancer or to identify proteins of potential use as markers, using samples and examining the critical technical factors affecting the potential utility of this approach [6]. Another study involved the discrimination of prostate cancer from non-cancer cases by using a boosted DT [7]. We conducted a study in which we identified renal cell cancer specific biomarkers which classified the subjects into BPH(Benign Prostate Cancer), healthy or cancer cases(PCA) by using a DT [8].

In solving problems in the biomedical domain, we need to develop bioinformatic tools that increase the sensitivity and specificity of the diagnosis. Moreover, the development of algorithm that can determine the optimal solution by examining the characteristic of the problem domain using various methodologies is important.

3 A Hybrid Classification System for Prostate Cancer Diagnosis

In this study, we identified a significant biomarker that can classify prostate cancer sample data into normal, cancer and BPH cases, using a diagnostic algorithm that exactly classifies each subject into the appropriate class.

We found potential biomarkers by using the DT as the feature selection system. The DT has a faster learning rate than the other classification models, but has lower reliability. Therefore, we cannot immediately affirm that a potential biomarker, which is found using the DT at once, induces disease. To solve this problem, the number of potential biomarker candidates can be increased by repeatedly performing the DT. However, although multiple biomarkers increase the reliability of the diagnosis, questions such as, "What is the optimal number of features?", "How good are the features that were selected?" cannot be answered by the DT alone.

Therefore, we propose a novel approach involving a hybrid of the MLP and DT algorithms to solve the above-mentioned problem. Neural networks have high confidence in terms of classification, but their time complexity is proportional to $O(n^2)$ for high dimensional data such as SELDI-TOF MS data. In the proposed algorithm, we overcame the shortcoming of the DT by hybridizing it, with the MLP acting as the backend processor of the DT.

3.1   Feature Selection by Using the Decision Tree

In this paper, we used the DT as a technique for performing biomarker identification. DT classifies a pattern through a sequence of questions, in which the next question asked depends upon the answer to the current question. Such a sequence of questions forms a node connected by successive links or branches downward to other nodes. Each node selects the best feature with which heterogeneity of the data in the next descendent nodes is as pure as possible. The DT was based on the C4.5. The biomarker identification algorithm developed using C4.5 is composed of forward feature selection and backward elimination. Forward feature selection is the process that calculates the entropy of the features and finds the optimal featured biomarkers while the backward elimination step performs the elimination process, which reduces meaningless features to minimize cross validation error [9].

Here, entropy refers to the purity for intensity for relation of intensity in each protein molecular weight between normal and abnormal patients. As shown in equation 1, the entropy impurity can be expressed as the probability that the intensity (j) is included in the normal case or patient category (ω_j) for molecular weight (node N). When the impurity, i(N), is close to 0, it means that the involved molecular weight is a biomarker that is able to distinguish between normal cases and patients. In other words, it can be used as a biomarker.

$$i(N) = -\sum_j P(\omega_j) \log_2 P(\omega_j) \tag{1}$$

Forward feature selection using entropy impurity has the benefit of selecting features faster than a fitness-evaluated selection. However, although the DT model is constructed using equation (1), it cannot provide answer to the questions "Is this model optimal?", "Is the result of test estimated from entire population data?", "How many features should be included in the feature selection?". If the constructed model is over-fitted, it cannot be generalized to the entire population dataset. The problem of over-fitting is more pronounced with models that have a very high dimensionality.

The identification of biomarkers using the DT is based on the selection of those features that have the lowest impurity. This prevents the extraction of unnecessary candidates by cross validation. The use of the DT alone resulted in an average of 29.2 biomarkers being selected for a testing error rate of 13.44%. A test error rate of 13.44% is not good, as compared to those of many pattern classification systems [1].

3.2   Prostate Cancer Diagnosis by Using the MLP Neural Network

As mentioned above, in this paper, we hybridize the MLP and DT to enhance their classification power. Multi-layer perceptron neural networks have one input layer, one output layer, and one or more hidden layers between the input and output layers. Each layer has several processing units, called nodes, neurons, or units which are generally non-linear units except the input units that are simple bypass buffers. Due to its sensitivity and specificity, the neural network is best used for disease diagnosis measurements. Therefore, it is employed for the classification and estimation of high dimensional data. We used neural network for those biomarkers found by the DT which resulted from an over-fitting estimation. Literally, the features selected by the DT were used as the input of the MLP. The MLP performed the training and test stages, with the learning stage either being terminated when the sensitivity and specificity came within a certain tolerance limit, or otherwise repeated.

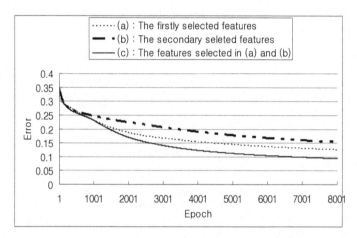

Fig. 1. The classification error when using the features selected in the first DT loop (a), the features selected in the second DT loop (b), and (c) the features selected in both DT loops, as the input of the MLP

To prove that the repeated feature selection by the DT shows better results, we performed the following experiments. First, we performed the MLP immediately after the first feature selection loop of the DT and calculated the error rate. Next, we performed the second loop of the DT and entered only the newly selected features into the MLP and calculated the error rate. Finally, we performed the MLP by inputting the features that were selected during both the first and second feature selection loops of the DT and calculated the error rate. Figure 1 shows the result of these experiments. However, those biomarker candidates in figure 1 that were selected iteratively may not show good results in terms of diagnosis. This is why, after those biomarkers that are the most effective in terms of diagnosis are first selected; other biomarkers that are less effective are likely to be selected. However, repeatedly selected biomarkers don't always show good results. This is why cross validation (evaluation) should be performed on the selected features to obtain the optimal result. To accomplish this, we accurately classified the selected features as corresponding to either the normal cases or patients by using the MLP, and performed repeated cross validation to evaluate the propriety of the selected features.

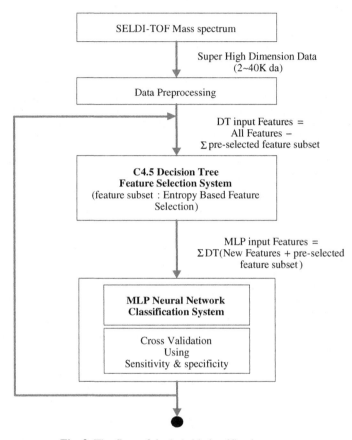

Fig. 2. The flow of the hybrid classification system

3.3 System Overview

The procedure of the proposed system is shown in figure 2. The first step involves the preprocessing of the prostate cancer SELDI-data, such as baseline subtraction, peak detection, and peak alignment. The details of the biological/chemical processes and the pre-processing procedure are described in [1]. Then, feature selection is performed by the DT to detect the potential biomarkers, followed by classification by the MLP to diagnose the normal and cancer patients. In this way, the features selected by the DT become the input of the MLP. The system then repeats the whole procedure, with the new input to the DT in each stage being the features identified by the DT, with the exception of those selected in the previous stage. The input to the MLP in each step is reconstructed by repeatedly adding the previously selected features to the new features selected by the DT, except during the first stage. In the classification by the MLP, it performs repeatedly cross validation to evaluate propriety of selected features. The entire process is terminated when a predefined certain value comes within certain tolerance limits.

4   Experiments and Analysis of the Results

4.1   Data Acquisition

We used SELDI-TOF MS data obtained from the Virginia Prostate Cancer Center for this study, which is available at http://www.evms.edu/vpc/seldi. There are two sets of SELDI-TOF MS data: one is the training set used for constructing a classification model and the other is the test set used for validating the model. We experimented with 326 sample data, which each are composed of 779 feature vectors through preprocessing. As shown in table 1, the number of patterns in each class made 10 learning data groups which consisted of 80% training data (262) and 20% test data (64), which were extracted randomly from the 326 sample data. Table 1 shows the number of patterns in each class.

Table 1. Number of training and test data sets for each class

	BPH	PCA	Healthy	No. Samples
Training set	62	134	66	262
Test set	15	33	16	64

4.2   Experimental Results

The results of the experiments represent the averaged results obtained after repeating each experiment 10 times for the 10 learning data groups.

In figure 3, the number of biomarker candidates increases with each application of the DT.

Figure 3(a) shows that the number of newly selected features increases in each step of the DT. The C 4.5 system uses the method of entropy based feature selection.

Therefore, the number of features inevitably increases, because the proposed algorithm performs feature selection on the data remaining after the exclusion of the previously selected features. One of the objectives of this study is to overcome the problem of significant features being missed, because feature selection is only performed once, thereby increasing the number of biomarker candidates. Figure 3(b) shows the total number of features which were input to the MLP.

In this study, we performed cross validation for the training and test results of the MLP. As shown in figure 4, the training error rate continuously decreased, whereas the test error rate continuously increased after the 4'R biomarker selection loop.

Strictly speaking, from the viewpoint of information engineering, the SELDI-TOF MS technique provides too much data without meaning. However, in terms of identifying biomarkers, it is able to determine the optimal number of biomarker candidates.

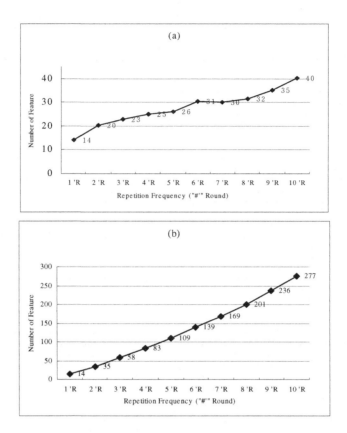

Fig. 3. Figure 3 (a) shows the number of newly selected features obtained in each step of the DT. Figure 3 (b) shows the total number of features that were input to the MLP.

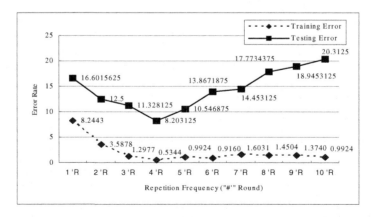

Fig. 4. The training and test error rates of the system obtained during 10 loops

4.3 Performance Analysis

In this section, we show the results of the cross tabulated performance evaluation. It is the number of patterns mapped in each class. Table 2 shows the results of the classification process using the DT only. The classification in this table is similar to the composition ratio of the test data shown in table 1, however the proportion of wrong diagnoses in each class is higher, possibly including normal cases that were classified as cancer and vice versa.

Table 2. The result of the classification process using only the DT

	BPH	PCA	Healthy	Unknown
BPH	11	4	0	0
PCA	1	27	5	0
Healthy	2	2	12	0
total	14	33	17	64

Table 3 shows the results of the classification process using Fisher's Linear Discriminator. As shown in table 3, the proportion of cases classified as PCA is lower than that of the other methods. The number of cancer cases misclassified as normal is lower than that of those methods that use the DT only. However, since the sensitivity to PCA is low, there may nevertheless be some cancer cases that are misclassified as normal.

Table 3. The result of classification process using Fisher's Linear Discriminator

	BPH	PCA	Healthy	Unknown
BPH	15	1	0	0
PCA	5	26	1	0
Healthy	2	0	14	0
total	22	27	15	64

Table 4 shows the good results obtained by using the 5 top ranked candidates resulting from the entropy based DT. However, as the selection criteria for candidate biomarkers, this technique suffers from the drawback of using a randomly defined number of candidate biomarkers.

Table 4. The results obtained using the DT and the MLP with the 5 top ranked candidates

	BPH	PCA	Healthy	Unknown
BPH	12	2	1	0
PCA	0	32	1	0
Healthy	1	0	15	0
total	13	34	17	64

Table 5 shows the classification result for the method proposed in this paper. The proposed method reduces the percentile of wrong diagnosis. In table 5, "unknown" refers to those cases that were outside of the tolerance limits in the classification result produced by the MLP. This information can be used by the doctor to reduce the possibility of making a wrong diagnosis. As mentioned above, the proposed method produced a diagnosis of BPH, PCA or Healthy when the result was within the tolerance limits and unknown when it was outside of the tolerance limits. This can help the doctor when diagnosing prostate cancer and, from the point of view of the PCA classification, we were able to obtain nearly perfect results.

Table 5. The result of the classification process using the DT and the MLP iteratively

	BPH	PCA	Healthy	Unknown
BPH	13	1	0	1
PCA	0	32	0	1
Healthy	1	0	14	1
total	14	33	14	64

Figure 5 shows the results of the performance analysis, in which the proposed method is compared with the other methods for the same sample data [1][10][11]. As shown in figure 5, our approach outperforms the other methods in terms of specificity and sensitivity. Sensitivity is defined as the ratio of the PCA patients that contained the biomarker to the total number of PCA patients included in the study. Specificity is defined as the ratio of the individuals that do not have the protein peak and do not have PCA, to the total number of individuals without PCA.

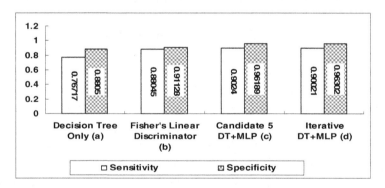

Fig. 5. Sensitivity and specificity: Figure 5(a) corresponds to the case where only the Decision tree is used and figure 5 (b) to the case where fisher's Linear Discriminator is used. Figure 5 (c) corresponds to the case where the MLP is used after 5 candidate features were selected for each node of the DT and figure 5 (d) corresponds to the proposed method.

5 Conclusion

SELDI-TOF MS is a protein analysis method, which is associated with high dimensionality, and requires a high level of confidence because it is used in disease diagnosis. High dimensional data decreases the system performance because of noise, and lowers the classification ability. Therefore, to construct an efficient system, we need to reduce the feature dimensionality of the data, by selecting those features that can provide the most accurate classification. We proposed a novel approach which identified biomarkers satisfying the above-mentioned conditions, and accurately separated the prostate cancer SELDI data into normal and abnormal classes.

The proposed system has the following characteristics. First, the confidence of classification is enhanced by hybridizing the DT and the MLP. Second, new features are selected in each step by repeated iterations of the hybrid system for the purpose of identifying potential biomarker candidates. Third, feature evaluation is performed by repeated cross validation in each step for the purpose of selecting the optimal biomarkers.

Even though it has high dimensionality, SELDI-TOF MS data requires a high level of confidence, because it is used in clinical diagnosis. Many feature vectors need dimensional reduction, because they interfere with the process of classification. In this study, we reduce the number of feature dimensions by using the DT, thereby making it possible to obtain the optimal classification, by inputting the selected features to the MLP. This also validates the propriety of the selected features.

References

1. Adam, B., Qu, Y., Davis, J, et al, " Serum protein fingerprinting coupled with a pattern-matching algorithm distinguishes prostate cancer from benign prostate hyperplasia and healthy men ", Cancer Research, 62 (2002) 3609-3614
2. Petricoin III, E., Ardekani, A., Hitt, B, et al, " Use of proteomic patterns in serum to identify ovarian cancer ", The Lancet, 359 (2002) 572-577
3. Ball, G., Mian, S., Holding, F., et al, " An integrated approach utilizing artificial neural networks and SELDI mass spectrometry for the classification of human tumors and rapid identification of potential biomarkers ", Bioinformatics, Vol. 18, No. 3 (2002) 395-404
4. Duda, R., Hart, P, Stork, D.: Pattern classification. Wiley-interscience, New York (2001)
5. Merchant, M., and Weinberger, S.R., " Recent advancements in surface-enhanced laser desorption/ionization time-of-flight mass spectrometry ", Electrophoresis, 21 (2000) 1164-1177
6. Rogers MA, Clarke P, Noble J, Munro NP, Paul A, Selby PJ, Banks RE, " Proteomic profiling of urinary proteins in renal cancer by surface enhanced laser desorption ionization and neural-network analysis : identification of key issues affecting potential clinical utility", Cancer research, pp.6971-6983, October 2003
7. Qu, Y., Adam, B-L., Yasui, Y., Ward,M. D., Cazares, L. H., Schellhammer, P. F., Feng, Z., Semmes, O.J., and Wright, G.L., " Boosted decision tree analysis of surface-enhanced laser desorption/ionization mass spectral serum profiles discriminates prostate cancer from noncancer patients", Clin. Chem., 48: pp.1835-1843, 2002
8. Y. Won, H. -J Song, T. -W Kang, J. J. Kim, B. D Han, S. W Lee, "Pattern Analysis of Serum Proteome Distinguishes Renal Cell Carcinoma from Other Renal Diseases and Healthy Persons," Proteomics, pp.2310-2316, December 2003
9. Quinlan, J.R.,C4.5: Programs for machine learning, Morgan Kaufmann Publisher (1993)
10. Michael Wagner, Dayanand N Naik, Alex Pothen, Srinivas Kasukurti, Raghu Ram Devineni, Bao-Ling Adam, O John Semmes and George L Wright Jr, "Computational protein biomarker prediction : a case study for prostate cancer", BMC Bioinformatics, May 2004
11. Jung-Ja Kim, Yonggwan Won, Young-ho Kim, "Proteomic Pattern Classification using Bio-markers for Prostate Cancer Diagnosis," Lecture Notes in Computer Science, Vol. 3314, December 2004

Intelligent Multiobjective Particle Swarm Optimization Based on AER Model

Hong-yun Meng[1], Xiao-hua Zhang[2], and San-yang Liu[1]

[1] Dept. of Applied Math., XiDian University, Xian, China
{mhyxdmath, lsy}@hotmail.com
[2] Institute of Intelligent Information Processing, XiDian University, Xian, China
mzhangh@hotmail.com

Abstract. How to find a sufficient number of uniformly distributed and representative Pareto optimal solutions is very important for Multiobjective Optimization (MO) problems. An Intelligent Particle Swarm Optimization (IPSO) for MO problems is proposed based on AER (Agent-Environment-Rules) model, in which competition and clonal selection operator are designed to provide an appropriate selection pressure to propel the swarm population towards the Pareto-optimal Front. An improved measure for uniformity is carried out to the approximation of the Pareto-optimal set. Simulations and comparison with NSGA-II and MOPSO indicate that IPSO is highly competitive.

1 Introduction

Particle Swarm Optimization (PSO) is a relatively recent heuristic algorithm inspired by the choreography of a bird flock developed by Eberhart and Kennedy [1, 2]. It has been found to be successful in a wide variety of single optimization task. Recently, there have been several recent proposals to extend PSO to deal with multi-objective problem [3-8]. Coello[3,4] uses a secondary repository of particles that is later used by other particles to guide their own flight. Hu[5] uses lexicographic ordering to optimize one objective at a time. Moore [6] emphasizes the importance of performing both an individual and a group search, but the author did not adopt any scheme to maintain diversity. Parsopoulos [7] adopts dynamic weights to build up search ability of the algorithm. Ray [8] uses crowding to maintain diversity and a multi-level sieve to handle constraints. In this paper, a new model for PSO is provided, and an Intelligent Particle Swarm Optimization (IPSO) for MO problems is proposed based on AER (Agent-Environment-Rules) model to provide an appropriate selection pressure to propel the swarm population towards the Pareto-optimal Front. Simulations and comparison with MOPSO [4] and NSGA-II [9] show the proposed algorithm can achieve a good convergence and diversity of solutions.

A general minimization MO problem includes n decision variables, l objective functions and m constraints. Objective functions and constraints are functions of the decision variables. The optimization goal is to

C. Bento, A. Cardoso, and G. Dias (Eds.): EPIA 2005, LNAI 3808, pp. 178–189, 2005.

$$\min_{x \in R^n} y = F(x) = (f_1(x), \cdots, f_l(x)) \tag{1}$$

$$s.t. \ g = g(x) = (g_1(x), \cdots, g_m(x)) \le 0$$

$X = \{x \mid x \in R^n, g_i(x) \le 0, i = 1, \cdots, m.\}$ is called feasible solution space. Very often, the objective functions can not be optimized simultaneously, and the decision maker has to accept a compromise solution.

Let $U = (u_1, \cdots, u_l)$, $V = (v_1, \cdots, v_l)$ be two vectors, then U dominates V denoted as $U \preceq V$ if and only if $u_i \le v_i (i = 1, \cdots, l)$ and $u_i < v_i$ for at least one component. This property is known as Pareto Dominance. Thus, a solution x of the MO problem is said to be Pareto Optimal if and only if there does not exist another solution y such that $F(y)$ dominates $F(x)$. The set of all Pareto Optimal solutions of MO problem is called Pareto Optimal Set and we denote it with P^* and the set $PF^* = \{F(x) \mid x \in P^*\}$ is called Pareto Front. $Pareto(I) = \{x \mid x \in I, \nexists y \in I, F(y) \prec F(x)\}$ is defined as the Pareto filter of set $I \subset X$.

2 A Modified Particle Swarm Optimization

It is well-known that the update of particle in the standard PSO is very monotone and invariable, that is to say a new particle is generated only based on the velocity v, the best position *pbest* which the current particle has visited so far and the best position *gbest* which the entire population has found so far. In addition, there exists no sharing of information with other particles in the population, except that the particle can access the global best or *gbest* is replaced by local best particle, but in the first case information sharing is difficult and seldom, and easily gets trapped in local optima; in the second case the velocity of approximation will be reduced. While for MO problem, sharing of information among the individuals or particles in a population or swarm is crucial in order to introduce the necessary selection pressure to propel the population moving towards the true Pareto-optimal Front. Hence, a modified model for PSO is given based on the local perception of each particle in the following.

$$\begin{cases} v = v + c_1 r_1 (pbest - x) + c_2 r_2 (nbest - x) + c_3 r_3 (gbest - x) \\ x = x + wv \end{cases} \tag{2}$$

In this new model, each particle can not only remember its best position *pbest* of the current particle found so far and the best positions *gbest* of the swarm found so far, but also the local best position *nbest* of the current particle's neighbors found. It needs to be pointed out here that *gbest* is used to speed up convergence and the *nbest* is used to escape the local optima. The Constriction factor w depends on the energy of each particle or its distance to the optimal solution *gbest*.

Similar to other evolutionary algorithms, PSO could be a potential method for MO problem. However, basic global or local version PSO algorithm is not suitable because there is no absolute optimum but many incomparable tradeoff Pareto optimums in MO problems. In this paper, two sets PS and GS were taken to record the $pbest$ and $gbest$, respectively. During initial stage of the evolution, when the cardinality of PS exceeds the given threshold, to explore more potential objective point, the particle who is the nearest to the current one is discarded. In contrast, during the final stage, the nearest one is preserved to enhance the process of convergence. While the method for updating GS is similar to that in SPEA [10] for external population.

3   Intelligent Particle Swarm Optimization

AER (Agent-Environment-Rules) model is a multiagent system model [11] based on the theory of artificial life. The word "agent" firstly comes from the book of "Society of Mind" wroten by Minsky, where an agent is a physical or virtual entity that essentially has the following properties: (1)It is able to live and act in the environment. (2)It is able to sense its local and global environment. (3)It is driven by certain purposes. (4)It has some reactive behaviors.

As can be seen, the meaning of an agent is very comprehensive, and what an agent represents is different for different problem. Agent, Environment and Interactive Rules are three main concepts in it. In recent years, AER model has been widely used in NP-hard problem and achieved good performance.

In this paper, all agent particles live in a lattice like environment, with each agent fixed on a lattice-point. In order to survive in the system, they compete or cooperate with their neighbors so that they can gain more resources. Making full use of the interaction between them, multi-agent system realizes the ability of agent to sense and act on the environment they live. Enlightened by it, an algorithm for MO problem is proposed by combining it with our new PSO model, and we call it Intelligent Particle Swarm Optimization (IPSO) in this paper.

3.1   New Rules for Agent Particles

Using the adaptability and cooperation relation between particles in this paper, each particle is taken as an agent particle with the ability of memory, communication, response, cooperation and self-learning. Moreover, each agent particle has not only the power of global sensing but that of local sensing. Based on the above consideration, we design each agent particle with the following properties. (1)It has its initial position, velocity and energy. Here energy is related to fitness. (2)It has the ability of global sensing and that of local sensing. (3)It can remember not only its best position, $pbest$, and the best previous position, $gbest$, of the swarm, but the best one, $nbest$, in its neighborhood. (4)There exists competition between agent particles, and positions of died agent particles will be inhabited by the particle with higher energy in their neighborhood, which is called law of the jungle, or the positions are taken by particle randomly chosen from the swarm and the behavior called mutation. (5)Each particle has self-clone ability, and the scale for it depends on its energy.

Here, the agent particle lattice can be represented as the one in Fig.1. Each rectangle represents an agent particle, and the data in it denotes its relative position in the lattice. Suppose that the agent particle located at (i, j) is represented as $P(i, j)$, define $NP(P(i, j)) = \{P(i-m, j-n) \mid m, n = -d, \cdots, 0, \cdots, d, \mid m \mid + \mid n \mid \neq 0\}$ as the neighborhood of $P(i, j)$, and the radius d shows its local perception range.

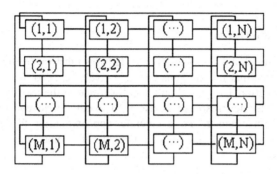

Fig. 1. Model of the agent particle lattice

Accordingly, two behaviors for agent particles are designed based on their ability in sensing and acting in the environment. Contrary to the common particle, agent particles have more behaviors which are driven by its intention. In AER model, in order to increase energies, they compete or cooperate with their neighbors and they can also learn from each other. Hence, competition operator and clonal selection operator are carried out for agent particles.

3.2 Competition Operator

In our AER model, each particle has a local sensing neighbor with radius of $d = 1$, that is to say each of which contains 8 particles. For each agent particle P, it will compare its energy with that of others in its neighborhood. If its energy is not less than the others, then particle P will survive and produce new agent particle by equation (2); else, it will be abandoned or died forcedly, and at the same time its position will be replaced by other agents. Here, two ways are taken to replace the position. If random number $rand$ $(0, 1)$ is less than a given probability, then the first way is chosen, else takes the second one.

Assume the agent $P = (x_1, \cdots, x_n)$ to be died forcedly and $P_{\max} = (y_1, \cdots, y_n)$ be the agent with the maximum energy in its neighborhood. In the first way, new agent $P^{new} = \left(x_1^{new}, \cdots, x_n^{new}\right)$ is given according to the equation $P^{new} = P + rand(0,1)$ $\left(P_{\max} - P\right)$. While in the second way, let $range_i = (u_i - l_i)f(t)$, where $[l_i, u_i]$ is the range of design variable of the problem, and t is the number of generation and $f(t)$ satisfies $1 > f(1) > f(2) > \cdots$. Let

$$l_i' = \begin{cases} x_i - range_i, & if \ x_i - range_i > l_i \\ l_i, & otherwise \end{cases}, \quad u_i' = \begin{cases} x_i + range_i, & if \ x_i + range_i < u_i \\ u_i, & otherwise \end{cases},$$

then the new agent particle $P^{new} = \left(x_1^{new}, \cdots, x_n^{new}\right)$ is produced by: $x_i^{new} = l_i' + rand$ $(0,1)\left(u_i' - l_i'\right)$, $i = 1, \cdots, n$. This aims not only to explore remote regions of the search space, but also tries to ensure that the full range of each decision variable is explored.

3.3 Clonal Selection Operator

The famous antibody clonal selection theory [12] was put forward by Burnet in 1958. It establishes the idea that the antigens can selectively react to the antibodies, which are the native production and spread on the cell surface in the form of peptides. In the standard PSO, the limited resource is assigned averagely to every particle, which always slackens convergence. To accelerate approximation to optimum, Clonal Selection Operator is utilized. The major elements of Clonal Selection Operator are presented in Fig. 2.

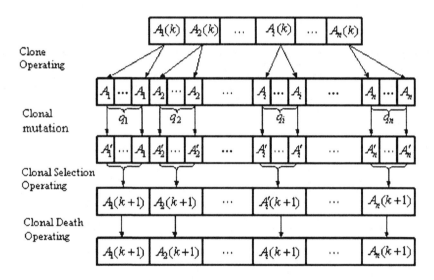

Fig. 2. The flow of Clonal Selection Operator

Clonal Operator. In this paper, general agent particles and latency agent particles will be cloned. Let T^C be clonal operator and for any particle $A_i(k)$, P_{clone} is the outcome of $A_i(k)$ by T^C as $P_{clone} = I_i \times A_i(k)$, where I_i is q_i dimension row vector with entries all as one. Easy to see, P_{clone} is also a q_i-dimension vector with the same component $A_i(k)$, as its element. The scale of P_{clone} is q_i, which is defined as $q_i = g(n_c, F(A_i(k)), p_i)$, in which p_i reflects the affinity with other agent particles, and the higher affinity between particles, the smaller p_i is. Generally speaking, q_i is related to the number of generation. Here

$$q_i = Int\left(n_c * \frac{Energy(A_i(k))}{\sum Energy(A_i(k))} * p_i\right) \qquad (3)$$

where $n_c > MN$ is a constant, p_i is the minimize distance between $A_i(k)$ to other particle in its neighborhood and $Int(x)$ rounds x to the least integer bigger than x. For single agent particle, it is easy to see that the scale of clone is adjusted adaptively according to its affinity and energy. Obviously, the aim of this operator is to increase the competition between particles and improve the convergence of the process. Here, latency agent particles refer to those who have smaller energy but having some characteristics (called vaccine in this paper), operating clone on them will guide particles towards the optimal solutions and maintain the diversity of the swarm. For convenience, the clone size is fixed.

Clonal Mutation. Crossover and Mutation are the main operator in Immune genic operating. According to the information exchanging characters of the Monoclonal and the Polyclonal in biology, Monoclonal Selection Operator (MCSO) is defined as only adopting the mutation in the step of immune genic operating, but the Polyclonal Selection Operator (PCSO) adopting both Crossover and Mutation. It needs to be pointed out here that clonal selection operator in this paper is used only to introduce the mechanism of the immunology, rather than to follow the concepts of the immunology completely. For MO problems, only clonal mutation is adopted in our new model to enhance the diversity of the population. Let T_M be clonal mutation operator, $A_i^{'}(k)$ is produced through T_M by (4), where $Rand(A_i(k))$ denotes an agent particle chosen randomly, p_m is a given threshold and $PSO(A_i(k))$ produced by (2).

$$A_i'(k) = \begin{cases} Rand(A_i(k)), & \eta < p_m \\ PSO(A_i(k)), & otherwise \end{cases} \qquad (4)$$

Clonal Selection T_s^C : denotes $B = \{A_{iq_j}''(k) \mid \max energy(A_{ij}'') \ q_j = 1,2,\cdots q_i\}$ $i = 1,2,\cdots n$ the probability of B taking place of $A_i'(k) \in \bar{A}(k)$ is:

$$\qquad (5)$$

$$p_s^k\{A_i \to B\} = \begin{cases} 1 & F(B) \preceq F(A_i(k)) \\ \exp(-\dfrac{dist(F(A_i(k)) - F(B))}{\alpha}) & else\ if\ A_i(k) \neq A_i^{best} \\ 0 & else\ \ A_i(k) = A_i^{best} \end{cases}$$

where A_i^{best} is the best in the current population and $a>0$ is a value related to the diversity of the population. Generally, the better the diversity is, the bigger α is. Otherwise, α is smaller.

Clonal Death T_d^C : After the clonal selection, the new population is

$$\bar{A}(k+1) = \{A_1(k+1), A_2(k+1), \cdots, A_i'(k+1), \cdots, A_n(k+1)\} \tag{6}$$

If $dist\left(A_i'(k+1), A_j(k+1)\right) < \varepsilon, A_i'(k+1), A_j(k+1) \in \bar{A}(k+1)$ $i \neq j$, $\varepsilon > 0$, one of $A_i(k+1)$ and $A_j(k+1)$ should be canceled according to the probability p_d . The death strategies can be used to either generate a new particle randomly to replace $A'_i(k+1)$ or $A_j(k+1)$, or take mutation strategy to produce a new particle to replace them. After the operation of clonal selection operator, we can obtain the corresponding new populations $\bar{A}(k+1) = \{A_1(k+1), A_2(k+1), \cdots, A_n(k+1)\}$ .Thus we complete the Clonal Slection Operator for the whole swarm.

It is easy to see that Clonal Selection Operator in essence produces a solution set around Pareto Optimal solution, which accordingly expands search range to improve learning capability of the particle.

4   Quality Measure for the Uniformity of the Approximation Set

Different objective functions may have different orders of magnitude. If we adopt Euclidean distance in the objective space, it may be dominated by the objective functions with the largest order of magnitude. To overcome this problem, we normalize each objective function $f_i(x)$ by $g_i(x) = (f_i(x) - L_i)/(U_i - L_i)$ where $U_i = \max\limits_{x \in P^*} f_i(x)$, $L_i = \min\limits_{x \in P^*} f_i(x)$ ($i = 1, \cdots, l$). For convenience, functions normalized are still denoted as $f_i(x)(i = 1, \cdots, l)$. To measure uniformity of a given non-dominated solution set, Schott [13] proposed Spacing (SP) to measure the spread of approximation vectors throughout the non-dominated vectors found so far. In this metric, a value of zero indicates all members of the Pareto Front currently available are equidistantly spaced. However, it is not the usual case, such as Fig.3, and we will specify it in the following.

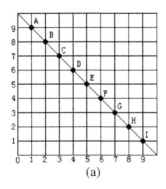
(a)

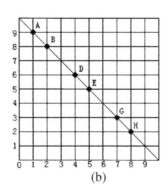
(b)

Fig. 3. Example with two given solution sets. (a) Solution set of P_1. The solutions in P_1 are uniformly scattered over the given portion of Pareto Front. (b) Solution set of P_2. The solutions in P_2 are not uniformly scattered over the given portion of Pareto Front.

In Fig.3, $P_1=\{A,B,C,D,E,F,G,H,I\}$ and $P_2=\{A,B,D,E,G,H\}$ are two approximation sets of the Pareto optimal set. From Fig.3, it is easy to see that set P_1 is uniform or equidistantly spaced, while P_2 is not. However, the Spacing metric for them is equal, i.e., $SP_1=SP_2=0$. Hence, when the Spacing metrics of two solution sets are equal, which can not indicate that the distributions of them are complete same. Furthermore, when the Spacing metric of a given solution set is equal to zero, it is also not able to show the uniformity of approximation set. In a word, if the uniformity of P_1 is superior to that of P_2, it can not assure $SP_1<SP_2$, either. From the point of view of Zitzler [17], this measure is compatible, but not complete. What cause this deficiency is that the only nearest solution is concerned and other solutions in its neighborhood are neglected.

To provide an efficient quality measure for the uniformity of a given algorithm, we firstly define the distance between approximation set P and Q as

$$D(P,Q)= \min_{p\in P,q\in Q} d(p,q) \tag{7}$$

Let $P_1 = \{p_1^1, p_2^1, \cdots, p_N^1\}$, $P_2 = \{p_1^2, p_2^2, \cdots, p_M^2\}$ be two approximation of the Pareto optimal set by two different evolutionary algorithms, respectively. The main steps of our new measure for uniformity are the following.

Step1. Let $k = 1$, and $P_{New}^1 = \{P_1^1 = \{p_1^1\}, P_2^1 = \{p_2^1\}, \cdots, P_N^1 = \{p_N^1\}\}$.
$P_{New}^2 = \{P_1^2 = \{p_1^2\}, P_2^2 = \{p_2^{21}\}, \cdots, P_M^2 = \{p_M^2\}\}$

Step2. Compute $d_i^1 = \min_{\substack{j=1,\cdots,i-1 \\ ,i+1,\cdots,N}} D(P_i^1, P_j^1)$, $\bar{d}_k^1 = \sum_{i=1}^{N} d_i^1 / N$,

$SP_k^1 = \sqrt{\sum_{i=1}^{N}(1 - F(d_i^1, \bar{d}_k^1))^2 /(N-1)}$, here $F(x, y) = \begin{cases} x/y, & if \ x>y \\ y/x, & esle \end{cases}$. Using the

similar method, we can also compute SP_k^2.

Step3. If $SP_k^1 > SP_k^2$, then the uniformity of P_2 is superior to that of P_1; If $SP_k^1 < SP_k^2$, then the uniformity of P_1 is superior to that of P_2; else $SP_k^1 = SP_k^2$, and let $D(P_i^1, P_m^1) = \min\{d_1^1, \cdots, d_N^1\}$ and take the union of P_i^1 and P_m^1, the outcome is $P_{New}^1 = \{P_1^1, P_2^1, \cdots, P_{N-1}^1\}$ and so is P_{New}^2. Let $k = k+1$, $N = N-1$, $M = M-1$. And if $k < \min(N-1, M-1)$, then go to Step2.

Step4. If $SP_k^1 > SP_k^2$, then the uniformity of P_2 is superior to that of P_1; If $SP_k^1 < SP_k^2$, then the uniformity of P_1 is superior to that of P_2; else, let $SP_k^1 = SP_k^2$, then the uniformity of P_1 is as the same as P_2.

By the new measure, we compute the uniformity of two given sets P_1 in Fig.3 (a) and P_2 in Fig.3 (b). $SP_1^1 = SP_1^2 = 0$, while $SP_2^1 = 0, SP_2^2 = 0.3837 > 0$. Thus, P_1 outperforms P_2 in uniformity, which is fit with the fact from Fig.3.

From the above measure, we can compare the uniformity between any two algorithms. It is easy to see that the new measure is in essence the concept of multi-scale from wavelet analysis. When we can not evaluate the uniformity of two algorithms in a certain scale, perhaps, in another scale they can be distinguished.

5   Experiments and Discussion

In order to know how competitive our approach was, we decided to compare it against NSGA-II and MOPSO that are representative of the state-of-the-art, where the source codes of NSGA-II and MOPSO are from URL http://delta.cs.cinvestav.mx/~ccoello/EMOO/EMOOsoftware.html. The four test functions used in this paper are all from [16], and each Pareto Front of them has certain characteristics such as convex, concave or partially convex or non-convexity, discontinuous, and non-uniformity. In addition, the last three cases present the greatest difficulty for the most MO techniques.

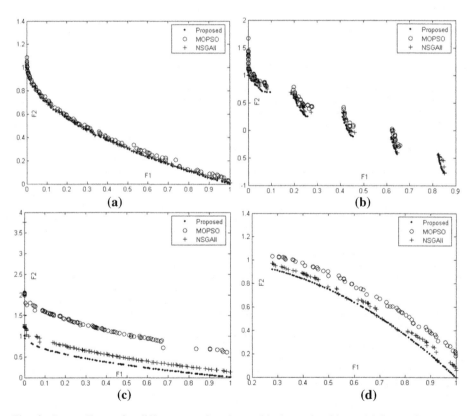

Fig. 4. Pareto Fronts for different test functions with three algorithms. (a) Pareto Fronts for ZDT1 with different algorithms. (b) Pareto Fronts for ZDT3 with different algorithms. (c) Pareto Fronts for ZDT4 with different algorithms. (d) Pareto Fronts for ZDT6 with different algorithms.

In the proposed algorithm, we take population size as 100 and external population size 100, c_1 and c_2 were set to 2.0. w was decreased linearly from 0.6 to 0.2 . The NSGA- II was run using a population size of 100, a crossover rate of 0.8, tournament selection, and a mutation rate of 1/L, where L is the length of chromosome(binary representation was adopted in it). MOPSO used a population of 100 particles, a repository size of 100 particles, a mutation rate of 0.05, and 30 divisions for the adaptive grid. In all the test functions, we report the results obtained from performing 30 independent runs of each algorithm compared. The total number of fitness function evaluations for each function is set to 2500, 2000, 10000 and 7200, respectively. Figure 4 shows the Pareto Front produced by IPSO, NSGA and MOPSO in 30 independent runs. It is easy to see that the Pareto Fronts produced by the proposed algorithm are all below those of others.

Furthermore, performance comparison is also done in this paper. As we known, generational distance (GD) introduced by Van Veldhuizen and Lamont in[14] addresses how far the elements are in the set of nondominated vectors found so far from those in the Pareto optimal set. Error ration(ER) proposed by Veldhuizen [15] is to indicate the percentage of solutions (from the nondominated vectors found so far) that are not members of the true Pareto optimal set. And the Spacing (SP) proposed above is used to measure the spread (distribution) of vectors throughout the nondominated vectors found so far. However, the true Pareto Front is usually unknown, so we take the Pareto filter of the outcomes produced by different algorithms as the true Pareto optimal set approximation.

Tables 1, 2, 3 and Table 4 show the comparison results among the three algorithms considering the metrics previously described. It is easy to see that the average performance of IPSO is the best with respect to the Generational distance (GD). Furthermore, from the definition of GD, we know the approximation set by IPSO is the best for all functions. To Spacing (SP), IPSO does worse (except for ZDT4) than NSGA-II and MOPSO in uniformity. Regarding to Error ration(ER), IPSO outperforms the other ones, and it would mean the percentage of solutions generated by IPSO that are members of the true Pareto optimal set is higher than that of NSGA-II and MOPSO in all test functions, which addresses the IPSO performs well in maximizing the number of elements of the Pareto optimal set found. What makes NSGA-II and MOPSO poor in ER is the Pareto optimal solutions they produced are too superposed. To sum up, NSGA-II performs well in Spacing, i.e., a well-extended Pareto Front can be found by NSGA-II (except ZDT3), followed by the MOPSO and IPSO. With respect to ER, MOPSO outperforms well in ZDT1 than NSGA-II, while NSGA-II outperforms well in ZDT3, ZDT4 and ZDT6 than MOPSO. For Generational distance (GD), the IPSO does well than the other two. In addition, we can also find from the Figure 4 that the performance of the three algorithms are similarity in ZDT1 and ZDT3, while for ZDT4 and ZDT6, IPSO outperforms well than the other two, and in the four test functions, ZDT 4 and ZDT6 are the most difficult to achieve a well distributed non-dominated Front, since ZDT4 contains 21^9 local Pareto-optimal sets and has Pareto Front with multimodality, while ZDT6 has a non-convex and non-uniform Pareto Front. However, IPSO performs well on both of them. Furthermore, we think the approximation and a number of sufficient Pareto optimal solutions are the most important aspects when designing an efficient MO algorithm, and then is Spacing.

Table 1. Comparison Results of metrics for the ZDT1

	IPSO			NSGA-II			MOPSO		
	GD	SP	ER	GD	SP	ER	GD	SP	ER
Worst	1.6e-5	0.2922	0.8614	0.0001	0.3056	1.0000	0.0006	0.2684	0.9800
Best	4.0e-5	0.5981	0.6733	0.0033	0.3059	0.9900	0.0040	0.6077	0.9500
Average	2.7e-5	0.4918	0.7875	0.0013	0.3058	0.9937	0.0015	0.4548	0.9640
Median	2.7e-5	0.5653	0.7921	0.0001	0.3059	0.9900	0.0015	0.4943	0.9800
Std. Dev.	5.0e-6	0.1078	0.9546	0.0015	0.0001	0.9951	0.0008	0.1187	0.9953

Table 2. Comparison Results of metrics for the ZDT3

	IPSO			NSGA-II			MOPSO		
	GD	SP	ER	GD	SP	ER	GD	SP	ER
Worst	2.4e-6	0.3394	0.5100	0.0000	0.3271	1.0000	0.0176	0.0858	1.000
Best	3.4e-6	0.5172	0.2800	8.0348	2.7046	0.2000	15.549	3.7311	0.9910
Average	2.8e-6	0.4377	0.3593	0.6331	0.6820	0.9123	1.2488	0.6976	0.9930
Median	2.4e-6	0.5172	0.2800	0.0319	0.4784	1.0000	0.4635	0.5742	0.9940
Std. Dev.	4.4e-7	0.0873	0.9121	1.8238	0.5881	0.8102	2.8277	0.6358	0.9966

Table 3. Comparison Results of metrics for the ZDT4

	IPSO			NSGA-II			MOPSO		
	GD	SP	ER	GD	SP	ER	GD	SP	ER
Worst	0.000	0.2364	0.0000	0.0003	0.2477	1.0000	0.0053	0.2292	1.0000
Best	3.7e-5	0.4927	0.0000	0.0051	0.4627	0.9687	0.0102	0.4828	09872
Average	2.6e-5	0.4046	0.0000	0.0021	0.3486	0.9835	0.0076	0.3718	0.9992
Median	2.6e-5	0.4462	0.0000	0.0015	0.3246	0.9868	0.0075	0.3840	1.0000
Std. Dev.	4.5e-6	0.0916	1.0000	0.0016	0.0754	0.9870	0.0011	0.0858	0.9968

Table 4. Comparison Results of metrics for the ZDT6

	IPSO			NSGA-II			MOPSO		
	GD	SP	ER	GD	SP	ER	GD	SP	ER
Worst	1.3e-5	0.3966	0.9307	0.0002	0.4401	0.9733	0.0017	0.3107	1.0000
Best	3.8e-5	0.8442	0.7624	0.0151	0.8477	0.9556	0.0470	0.7722	0.9880
Average	2.1e-5	0.6519	0.8399	0.0039	0.6259	0.9636	0.0120	0.5700	0.9993
Median	2.0e-5	0.6258	0.8366	0.0026	0.6072	0.9633	0.0103	0.5261	1.0000
Std. Dev.	6.0e-6	0.1427	0.9508	0.0037	0.1137	0.9961	0.0099	0.1382	0.9971

6　Conclusion

With the aim to improve the diversity and convergence of the standard PSO in multiobjective optimization, this paper has proposed a modified PSO, IPSO. The model can provide a more appropriate selection pressure for the population to approach the true Pareto Front. It has shown that the proposed algorithm performs remarkably well against some difficult test functions (with multimodality or non-uniform Pareto Front) found in the literature, which once again proves that PSO can be used to multiobjective optimization. As to measure the distribution uniformity of vectors throughout the nondominated vectors found so far, improved SP is put forward. However, there are still some theoretical works to be done in PSO, such as number of particles, number of cycles and the effect of parameters to the whole process. In addition, further work will be done on the application of IPSO to the problem with more than two objectives and real-world multiobjective optimization.

References

[1] Eberhart R, Kennedy J. A new optimizer using particle swarm theory. Proc. 6th Int.Symposium on Micro machine and Human Science. Nagoya, 39-43, 1995.
[2] Kennedy J, Eberhart R. Particle swarm optimization. Proc. IEEE Int. Conf. On Neural Networks. Perth, 1942-1948, 1995.
[3] Coello C.C.,Lechunga M.S. A proposal for Multiple Objective Particle Swarm Optimization. In Proceedings of the IEEE World Congress on Computational Intelligence, Hawaii, May 12-17, 2002. IEEE Press.
[4] Coello C.C., Pulido G.T. and Lechuga M.S... Handling Multiple Objectives with Particle Swarm Optimization. IEEE Trans. On Evolutionary Computation, 8(3): 256-279, 2004.
[5] Hu X.,Eberhart R.C, Shi Y., Particle Swarm with extended memory for Multi-Objective Optimization. In Proc. 2003 IEEE Swarm Intelligence Symp. Indianapolis, IN.Apr. 193-197.
[6] Moore J. and Chapman R. Application of Particle Swarm to Multi-Objective Optimization: Dept. Comput.Sci. Software Eng., Auburn Univ., 1999.
[7] Parsopoulos K.E. and Vrahatis M.N. Particle swarm optimization method in multi-objective Problems. In Proceedings of the 2002 ACM Symposium on Applied Computing (SAC2002), 603-607, 2002.
[8] Ray T., Liew K. M. A Swarm Metaphor for Multiobjective design Optimization. Eng. Opt., 34(2): 141-153, 2002.
[9] Deb K, Pratap A, Agrawal S, Meyarivan T. A Fast Elitist Non-Dominated Sorting Genetic Algorithm for Multi-Objective Optimization: NSGA- II. IEEE Trans. On Evolutionary Computation, 6(2): 182-197, 2002.
[10] Zitzler and Thiele. Multi-objective Evolutionary Algorithm☐A Comparative Case Study and the Strength Pareto Approach [J]. IEEE Trans. On EC, 1999, 3(4), 257-271.
[11] Liu JM, Jing H, Tang YY. Multi-Agent oriented constraint satisfaction. Artificial Intelligence, (136)1:101-144, 2002.
[12] Lu D., Ma B.. Modern Immunology (in Chinese). Shanghai: Shanghai Scientific and Technological Education Publishing House, 1998.
[13] J.R.Schott. Fault tolerant design using single and multicriteria genetic algorithm optimization.M.S. thesis,Dept.Aeronautics and Astronautics, Massachusetts Inst.Technol.,Cambridge,MA,May,1995.
[14] D.A.Van Veldhuizen and G.B. lamont. Multiobjective Evolutionary Algorithm Research: history and analysis. Dept. Elec.Comput.Eng.,Graduate School of Eng., Air Force Inst.Technol.,Wright-Patterson AFB, OH.Tech.Rep.TR-98-03,1998.
[15] D.A.Van Veldhuizen. Multiobjective evolutionary algorithms: Classifications, analyzes, and new innovations. Ph.D. dissertation, Dept. Elec. Compt. Eng., Graduate School of Eng., Air Force Inst.Technol., Wright-Patterson AFB,OH,May,1999.
[16] Zitzler E. Evolutionary Algorithms for Multi-objective Optimization: Methods and Applications.Ph.D. Thesis, Swiss Federal Institute of Technology (ETH), Zurich, Switzerland, November, 1999.
[17] Zitzler and Thiele. Performance Assessment of Multiobjective Optimizers: An Analysis and Review. IEEE Trans. On Evolutionary Computation,7(2), 117-132

A Quantum Inspired Evolutionary Framework for Multi-objective Optimization

Souham Meshoul, Karima Mahdi, and Mohamed Batouche

Computer Science Department, PRAI Group, LIRE Laboratory,
University Mentouri of Constantine, 25000 Algeria
{meshoul, mahdi, batouche}@wissal.dz

Abstract. This paper provides a new proposal that aims to solve multi-objective optimization problems (MOP$_s$) using quantum evolutionary paradigm. Three main features characterize the proposed framework. In one hand, it exploits the states superposition quantum concept to derive a probabilistic representation encoding the vector of the decision variables for a given MOP. The advantage of this representation is its ability to encode the entire population of potential solutions within a single chromosome instead of considering only a gene pool of individuals as proposed in classical evolutionary algorithms. In the other hand, specific quantum operators are defined in order to reward good solutions while maintaining diversity. Finally, an evolutionary dynamics is applied on these quantum based elements to allow stochastic guided exploration of the search space. Experimental results show not only the viability of the method but also its ability to achieve good approximation of the Pareto Front when applied on the multi-objective knapsack problem.

1 Introduction

Most of the real world problems either in scientific or engineering fields involve simultaneous optimization of several and often competing objectives that are subject to a set of constraints. These problems are known as multi-objective, multi-criteria or vector optimization problems [1]. Unlike single-objective optimization problems that may have a unique optimal solution, multi-objective optimization problems (MOP$_s$) have a set of alternative solutions known as Pareto optimal solutions. These solutions are optimal in the sense that no other solutions in the space are superior to them when all objectives are considered. Generally, the optimal solution obtained by individual optimization of the objectives is not a feasible solution to a MOP. Generally, a great number of non optimal solutions are obtained when solving a MOP. They don't optimize all objectives of the problem but they are compromise solutions. To identify best compromises, one makes use of relation of order between these solutions. This relation is called Dominance relation. Several dominance relations have been proposed in the literature [2]. The most commonly used is the Pareto Dominance. The set of the solutions that dominate all the others but don't dominate each other is called Pareto Optimal Set. Its image in the objective space is known as Pareto Front. For formal definition of these basic Pareto concepts, one can refer to [2,10]. Hence, obtaining a set of non dominated solutions and selecting a solution from this set are

C. Bento, A. Cardoso, and G. Dias (Eds.): EPIA 2005, LNAI 3808, pp. 190 – 201, 2005.
© Springer-Verlag Berlin Heidelberg 2005

the main tasks of a multi-objective optimization process. Therefore, a decision making process is required.

Several methods have been proposed in the literature to handle MOP_s. A comprehensive state of the art can be found in [2,19]. Some of these methods rely on linear objective function aggregation. They are applied many times in order to find a different solution in each run. Others make use of Pareto dominance. They are known as Pareto-based methods. They allow finding multiple Pareto-optimal solutions in one single run. During the last years, stochastic optimization heuristics have been employed in order to move towards the true Pareto front over time. Among these heuristics, evolutionary algorithms have been widely investigated for two main reasons. In one hand, they allow defining population-based methods. This fact enables finding several members of the Pareto optimal set in a single run of the algorithm instead of having to perform a series of separate runs. In the other hand, evolutionary algorithms have abilities to cope with discontinuous and concave Pareto front. Several variants of evolutionary algorithms for multi-objective optimization have been adopted. They are characterized by two main and common features. The first one concerns the use of the Pareto dominance relation to rank individuals within a population. Non dominated individuals are given the highest rank. The second feature deals with the balance between the exploitation and exploration capabilities of the search process. For this purpose, some form of elitism is used to reward globally non dominated solutions intensifying in this manner the search in their neighbourhood. In the other side, diversity is maintained using appropriate mechanisms. The way these two issues are addressed distinguishes one approach from the other. Generally, designing appropriate fitness functions to capture the characteristics of a MOP and defining the adequate decision making process are among the main issues addressed by an evolutionary algorithm for multi-objective optimization. The first work on using evolutionary algorithms to solve MOP_s goes back to the mid-eighties [3]. Since the mid-nineties, an active and intensive research effort has been conducted in quest to develop powerful and efficient multi-objective evolutionary algorithms ($MOEA_s$) for which several reviews have been proposed. NPGA [4], NSGA-II [5,6], SPEA [7,8] and Micro-genetic algorithm proposed in [9] are notable examples of $MOEA_s$. An other approach concerns the use of artificial immune systems to solve MOP_s. In [10], the clonal selection principle has been tailored to MOP_s leading to a viable alternative.

Independently to multi-objective optimization research field, quantum computing principles have been recently successfully incorporated to evolutionary algorithms resulting in efficient hybrid algorithms [11,12]. Quantum computing is a new proposed paradigm which relies on ideas borrowed from quantum mechanics field. Compared to a purely evolutionary algorithm, a quantum-inspired evolutionary algorithm suggests a new philosophy to encode individuals using states superposition and to define the overall dynamics using in addition to genetic operators quantum gates or operators. Within this issue, we propose in this paper tackling the problem of multi-objective optimization by exploiting such ideas. This issue has not been investigated yet. We show how to suit some quantum concepts to the multi-objective knapsack problem.

Consequently, the rest of the paper is organized as follows. In section 2, we present the basic concepts underlying quantum computing paradigm. In section 3, we describe the method we propose for multi-objective optimization by addressing the problem of multi-objective knapsack problem. In section 4, we present the results obtained during the experiments we have conducted. Finally, conclusions and future work are given.

2   Quantum Computing Paradigm

Quantum computing is a new paradigm which has been proposed as a consequence of applying quantum mechanics to computer science. The underlying motivation is twofold. The first one consists in the observation that the real world follows the laws of quantum mechanics whereas the current computing model relies on the foundations of classical physics. The second is the investigation of the possibilities a computer could have if it follows the laws of quantum mechanics.

According to quantum computing principles, the smallest unit of information being processed is the qubit. A qubit is the quantum counterpart of the classical bit. Contrary to this latter, a qubit represents the superposition of the two binary values 0 and 1. In another way, a qubit can be in state 0 and state 1 simultaneously with complementary probabilities. The state of a qubit can be represented by using the braket notation:

$$|\Psi\rangle = \alpha|0\rangle + \beta|1\rangle \tag{1}$$

where $|\Psi\rangle$ denotes more than a vector $\vec{\Psi}$ in some vector space. $|0\rangle$ and $|1\rangle$ represent respectively the classical bit values 0 and 1. α and β are complex number that specify the probability amplitudes of the corresponding states. When we measure the qubit's state we may have '0' with a probability $|\alpha|^2$ and we may have '1' with a probability $|\beta|^2$. For more theoretical insights of the basic definitions and laws of quantum information theory the reader can refer to [13].

Having k qubits, a quantum system can represent 2^k states at the same time instead of only a single state as in classical systems. All the states present within the superposition are processed in parallel when a quantum operation is performed. This ability suggests an exponential speed up of computation on quantum computers over classical computers. A single state among those states in superposition is derived as a consequence of observing the quantum state.

Historically, by observing that some quantum mechanical effects cannot be efficiently simulated on a computer in the early 80, Richard Feynman is considered as being at the origin of quantum computing. The dynamics of a quantum system are governed by Schrödinger's equation. Any unitary transformation of a quantum space is a legitimate quantum transformation and vice versa. Rotations constitute one among the unitary transformations types. Later on, in 1994, Shor described a polynomial time quantum algorithm for factoring numbers [14]. His work has proven Feynman's speculation. Grover's algorithm [15] is another notable example where quantum computing has been used to perform a search in a database. During the last decade, quantum computing has attracted widespread interest and has induced intensive investigations and researches since it appears more powerful than its classical counterpart. Indeed, the parallelism that the quantum computing provides, reduces obviously the algorithmic complexity. Such an ability of parallel processing can be used to solve combinatorial optimization problems which require the exploration of large solutions spaces.

Quantum computing includes researches on quantum algorithms and quantum mechanical computers. Quantum algorithms are difficult to design. They require quantum gates and quantum circuits. Actually, issues are being investigated in order to build quantum computers. By the time when quantum computers will be part of our life, researches are conducted to get benefit from the quantum computing field. Merging quantum computing and evolutionary algorithms seems to be a productive issue when considering the related major research effort spent since the late 1990 especially the one devoted to quantum inspired evolutionary computing for a digital computer [11]. The first related work goes back to [16]. Like any other evolutionary algorithm, a quantum inspired evolution algorithm relies on the representation of the individual, the evaluation function and the population dynamics. The particularity of quantum inspired evolutionary algorithms stems from the quantum representation they adopt which allows representing the superposition of all potential solutions for a given problem. It also stems from the quantum operators it uses to evolve the entire population through generations [11, 12].

3   The Proposed Quantum Evolutionary Framework

3.1   Problem Statement

In the context of our work, we have considered the multi-objective knapsack problem (MOKP). Although the description of this problem seems to be simple, it still remains difficult to solve. Moreover, due to its relevance, it has been subject to several investigations in various fields. Particularly, several evolutionary algorithms have been developed to cope with MOKP. The MOKP is defined by a set of items. For each item, profits and weights are associated. Furthermore, constraints corresponding to the knapsack capacities are imposed.

Formally the problem is defined in following the way: Given a set of m items and a set of k knapsacks, the problem consists in:

$$\max \quad z^j(x) = \sum_{i=1}^{m} c_i^j x_i, j = 1,...,k \tag{2}$$

$$Where \ \sum_{i=1}^{m} w_i^j x_i \le c_j, j = 1,...,k$$

$$x_i \in \{0,1\}, i = 1,...,m$$

Where m is the number of items, x_i denotes a decision variable, k is the number of objectives, z^j the jth component of the multi-objective function vector z, c_i^j is the profit of item i of knapsack j, w_i^j the weight of item i of knapsack j and c_j the capacity of the knapsack j. The problem consists in finding the decision vector $X = [x_1, x_2, x_3, ..., x_m]^T$ leading to best compromises in optimizing objective functions.

In order to tackle the defined problem using quatum computing concepts, we have to address the following issues:

1. Define an appropriate Qubit representation of the problem.
2. Define the operators that are applied on the representation and the overall dynamics using an evolutionary framework.

3.2 Quantum Representation

A potential solution for a MOKP is given by the decision vector $X = [x_1, x_2, x_3, ..., x_m]^T$. Each variable x_i takes value 1 if the corresponding item i is present in the knapsack and 0 otherwise. Finding a qubit representation for this solution vector requires defining probabilities for an item to be present or absent in the knapsack. Hence, each item can be naturally represented by a pair of numbers (α, β) to define the qubit:

$$|\Psi\rangle = \alpha|0\rangle + \beta|1\rangle \text{ where } |\alpha|^2 + |\beta|^2 = 1 \qquad (3)$$

$|\alpha|^2$ is the probability for the qubit to be in the '0' state that is the decision variable has value 0 and and $|\beta|^2$ is the probability for the qubit to be in the '1' state that is the decision variable has value 1. As a consequence, the decision vector can be encoded in terms of a quantum register q containing m qubits as follows:

$$q = \begin{pmatrix} \alpha_1 \ \alpha_2 ... \alpha_m \\ \beta_1 \ \beta_2 ... \beta_m \end{pmatrix} \qquad (4)$$

This quantum representation has the advantage to represent a linear superposition of states. All possible combinations of values of the decision variables can be derived from this single representation. For more diversity, we maintain a population of solutions using at each generation t of the evolutionary process a quantum matrix $Q(t)$:

$$Q(t) = \{q_1^t, q_2^t, ..., q_n^t\} \qquad (5)$$

Where n is the size of population, and q_j^t is a qubit individual or a quantum chromosome defined as:

$$q_j^t = \begin{pmatrix} \alpha_{j1}^t & \alpha_{j2}^t & ... & \alpha_{jm}^t \\ \beta_{j1}^t & \beta_{j2}^t & ... & \beta_{jm}^t \end{pmatrix} \qquad (6)$$

3.3 Outline of the Proposed Framework

We now describe how the quantum representation defined above has been employed within an evolutionary algorithm to obtain an approximation of the Pareto Front for the MOKP. In addition to the population $Q(t)$, we maintain in our algorithm a temporary population denoted by *Temp(t)* and an external population, denoted by *A(t)*, that stores the non dominated solutions found along the search process. We make use of Pareto Dominance in order to assign scalar fitness values to individuals. For sake of clarity, we first give the general scheme of our algorithm and then we emphasize each of its steps.

INPUT: Problem specification

Begin

$t \leftarrow 0$

  i. Set to empty external non dominated solutions set: $A(t) = \{\}$
  ii. Initialize $Q(t)$
  Repeat

  iii. Make $P(t)$ by observing the states of $Q(t)$.
  iv. Repair $P(t)$ for restoring the feasibility of the solutions in $P(t)$.
  v. Copy non dominated solutions of $P(t)$ and $A(t)$ in $A(t+1)$.
  vi. Compute the fitness value for each individual in $P(t)$ and $A(t+1)$.
  vii. Select individuals from $P(t)$ and $A(t+1)$ and store them in $Temp(t)$.
  viii. Interfere $Q(t)$ toward $Temp(t)$.
  ix. Apply quantum crossover and quantum mutation.

$t \qquad \leftarrow t + 1$

Until Maximum number of generations
End

OUTPUT the set $A(t)$ of non dominated solutions.

Problem specification includes the indication of objective functions, problem constraints and problem parameters like the size m of the decision vector and the number k of profits and weights. In step **ii.** $Q(0)$ is generated by setting to $(1/\sqrt{2})$ all α_i^0 and β_i^0 for $i=1,2,...,m$ of all $q_j^0 = q_j^t|_{t=0}$, $j=1,2,...,n$. It means that one qubit individual q_j^0 represents the linear superposition of all possible states with the same probability:

$$\left|\psi_{q_j^0}\right\rangle = \sum_{k=1}^{2^m} \frac{1}{\sqrt{2^m}} \left|X_k\right\rangle \qquad (7)$$

Where X_k is the kth state represented by the binary string $(x_1 x_2 ... x_m)$ for which each x_i is either 0 or 1 according to the probabilities $\left|\alpha_i^0\right|^2$ or $\left|\beta_i^0\right|^2$. During step **iii.** a quantum operation called measurement is applied. It consists in deriving a binary image of the population $Q(t)$. This binary representation is denoted by $P(t)$ and defined as: $P(t) = \{b_1^t, b_2^t, ..., b_n^t\}$. Each component b_j^t for $j=1,..,n$ is a binary string of length m which is formed by selecting either 0 or 1 for the corresponding qubits in the current $Q(t)$ according to their probabilities $|\alpha_i^0|^2$ and $|\beta_i^0|^2$. $P(t)$ can be viewed as a binary matrix containing a gene pool of specific solutions. In the following step, the feasibility of obtained binary solution is verified. If binary individuals in $P(t)$ violate the capacity constraints as indicated in problem specification, the algorithm attempts to repair them and restore the feasibility of the solutions in $P(t)$. According to step **v.** the external population $A(t)$ initially set to empty is regularly updated using Pareto dominance relation. During each iteration, the new non dominated solutions are added to the external population and the old individuals of this population that are dominated by these new individuals are eliminated. Step **vi** consists in computing the fitness value of individuals of $P(t)$ and $A(t+1)$ following the spirit of SPEA2 described in [8]. For each element i in $P(t)$ and $A(t+1)$, the fitness value is computed as follows:

1. Let S_i the strength of individual i. S_i is the number of individuals dominated by individual i.

$$\forall i \in P(t) \vee A(t+1) \qquad S_i = |\{j \in P(t) \vee A(t+1) / i \text{ dominates } j\}| \qquad (8)$$

2. Compute the Raw Fitness R_i for individual i. It is defined as the sum of strengths of individuals dominating i :

$$R_i = \sum_{\substack{j \in P(t) \vee A(t+1) \\ j \text{ dominates } i}} S_j \qquad (9)$$

3. Compute the density D_i given by:

$$D_i = \frac{1}{\sigma_i^k + 2} \qquad \text{Where} \quad k = \sqrt{|P(t)| + |A(t+1)|} \qquad (10)$$

σ_i^k is the distance between individual i and its kth neighbour which is selected from the ranked list of distances in the objectives space between individual i and the other individuals.

4. Finally, the fitness value of individual I is computed as follows:

$$F_i = R_i + D_i \qquad (11)$$

In step **vii,** the temporary population is formed using best individuals in $P(t)$ and $A(t+1)$. The n best individuals of $A(t+1)$ are selected to be stored in $Temp(t)$. If there are less than n individuals in $A(t+1)$ then the remaining individuals are completed from $P(t)$. $Temp(t)$ and $P(t)$ have the same length N. This temporary population is used to perform interference operation as indicated in step **viii.** Interference is a special rotation operator. This is a quantum operation whose aim is to intensify the search in the neighbourhood of solutions in $Temp(t)$. It is performed by altering qubits in the quantum matrix $Q(t)$ in a way to reward solutions in $Temp(t)$.

Finally quantum individuals in $Q(t)$ are selected to undergo crossover and mutation. Quantum crossover is identical in its principal to the classical crossover. The difference is that it operates on quantum chromosomes. Pairs of quantum chromosomes are selected. A crossing point is chosen randomly and then parts of the chromosomes are swapped leading to new quantum chromosomes. The mutation operator acts on the probability values of a qubit in the chromosome selected for mutation. If the qubit representation is $\alpha|0\rangle+\beta|1\rangle$ then mutation inverts this representation to $\beta|0\rangle+\alpha|1\rangle$ as shown in figure 1.

$$
\begin{pmatrix}
0.2383 & 0.1079 & 0.5057 & 0.8337 \\
0.9712 & 0.9942 & 0.8627 & 0.5522 \\
& & \downarrow & \\
0.2383 & 0.1079 & 0.8627 & 0.8337 \\
0.9712 & 0.9942 & 0.5057 & 0.5522
\end{pmatrix}
$$

Fig. 1. Quantum mutation

All the above steps are applied iteratively and the whole process evolves until maximum number of iterations or generations is reached. The external population is presented as the solution to the tackled problem.

4 Experimental Results

In order to assess the performance of the proposed method, several experiments have been conducted. The present section illustrates some obtained results. As a baseline comparison, we have chosen two quality measures. The first one, given in equ. 12, is the coverage measure C of two approximations of the dominated set. The measure allows relative evaluation of two approximations A and B. It is defined as:

$$
C(A, B) = \frac{\left|\{z'' \in B\} / \exists\, z' \in A : z' \text{ dominates } z''\right|}{|B|}
\tag{12}
$$

The measure $C(A,B)$ takes value 1 if all points in B are dominated or equal to some points in A and takes value 0 if no point in B is covered by any point in A.

The second measure is the ratio RS of the hyper-area covered by an approximation A over the hyper-area covered by the actual non-dominated set S.

An hyper-area H_W for a given set W is calculated as follows:

$$
H_w = \left\{ \bigcup_i a_i / v_i \in A \right\}
\tag{13}
$$

Where a_i is the area occupied by the solution v_i. The hyper-area ratio is then defined as:

$$RS = \frac{H_s}{H_A} \tag{14}$$

For the comparative study, we have chosen SPEA [8] which is one of the state of the art methods. In all runs, the size of the population has been fixed to 10 quantum individuals. The first data set used in our experiments was defined by Eckart Zitzler and Marco Laumanns in [17]. We have a bi-objective MOKP with 2 constraints and 100 items per knapsack.

Figure 2 shows the evolution of our algorithm through iterations. It illustrates the obtained values of two objectives during the search process. It provides a graphical comparison with respect to the true Pareto front. A comparison with SPEA method's results is also provided. We can observe clearly that the proposed method approaches gracefully the theoretical front and can compete with SPEA if we take into account that classical genetic algorithms used to perform this task require an obviously greater number of chromosomes and a lot of iterations are needed to have acceptable solutions. We should notice that a good approximation of the Pareto front is obtained after less than 1000 iterations. To investigate more the performance of the method, we have studied the influence of the population size as we don't operate on a quantum computer but on a conventional one. Figure 3 presents the obtained results for a population size of 10 and 20 individuals and number of iterations equal to 500 and

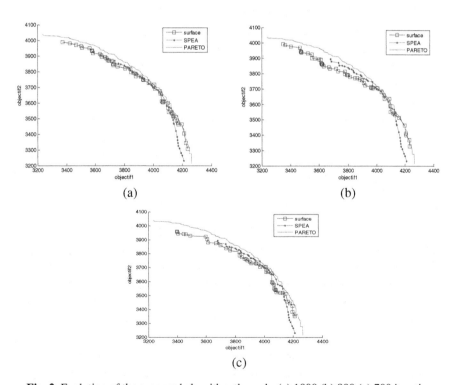

Fig. 2. Evolution of the proposed algorithm through: (a) 1000 (b) 800 (c) 700 iterations

1000. Significant improvement of the method is achieved as can be observed in the figure. In table 1, we present the obtained values for the two measures defined above. In this table symbol S refers to our approach. These results show the competitivity of our method with regard to SPEA.

We have also tested our algorithm with the data set defined in MCDM Numerical Instances Library [18]. We have a bi-objective MOKP, one constraint and 50 items/knapsack. The results were very promising.

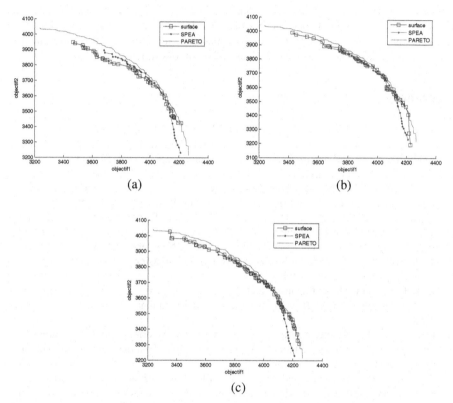

(a)   (b)

(c)

Fig. 3. Evolution of the proposed algorithm through : (a) 500-10 (b) 500-20 and (c) 1000-20

Table 1. Obtained values for coverage and hyperarea measures through iterations

	iterations	N	RH	C(S,SPEA)	C(SPEA,S)
Figure2a	1000	10	1.0200	**0.4681**	0.3645
Figure2b	800	10	1.0247	0.3404	0.5660
Figure2c	700	10	1.0134	0.3191	0.6304
Figure3a	500	10	1.0110	0.2979	0.6000
Figure3b	500	20	1.0245	**0.5745**	0.3300
Figure3c	1000	20	1.0356	**0.4468**	0.3382

5 Conclusion

We have presented in this paper an approach for multi-objective optimization. The main features of the proposed approach consist basically in adopting a probabilistic representation of the entire population using a quantum encoding and in defining specific operators like quantum measurement and interference. Comparing to an evolutionary algorithm, the quantum based approach provides the advantage of giving a greater diversity. All the solutions exist within only one chromosome. The obtained results are very encouraging and show the feasibility and also the effectiveness of the proposed approach. To enhance the performance in both speed and quality, it would be a very interesting attempt to use a clever initialization step to exploit the intrinsic parallelism of the method and to investigate other fitness functions.

References

1. Y. Collette and P. Siarry, *Optimisation multi-objectifs*, Eyrolles Edition 2002.
2. D.A.Van Veldhuizen and G.B Lamont, Multi-objective evolutionary algorithms: Analyzing the state of the art, Evolutionary computation, 8(2): 125-147 2000.
3. J.D. Schaffer, Multi-objectiveoptimization with vector evaluated genetic algorithms, In genetic Algorithms and their Applications: Proc of the first International Conference on genetic algorithms, Lawrence Erlbaum, Hillsdale, new jersey, 93-100, 1985.
4. J. Horn, N. Nafptiolis and D. Goldberg, A Niched Pareto Genetic Algorithm for Multiobjective Optimization, First IEEE Conference on evolutionary Computation, IEEE World Congress on computational Intelligence,1,82-8, New Jersey, 1994.
5. N. Srinivas and K. Deb, Multi-objective optimization using nondominated sorting in genetic algorithms, 2(3): 221-248, 1994.
6. K. Deb, S. Agrawal, A. Pratapand and T. Meyarivan, A Fast and Elitist multiobjective genetic algorithm: NSGA-II, IEEE Transactions on Evolutionary computation, 6(2), April 2002.
7. E. Zitzler and L. Thiele, Multiobjective Evolutionary Algorithms: A Comparative Case Study and the Strength Pareto Approach", IEEE Transactions on Evolutionary Computation, 3(4), 257-271, 1999.
8. E. Zitzler, M. Laumanns, and L. Thiele, SPEA2:Improving the Performance of the Strength Pareto evolutionary Algorithm, Technical Report 103, Computer Engineering and Communication Networks lab(Tik), Swiss Federal Institute of Technology(ETH) Zurith, Gloriastrasse 35, CH-8092 Zurith, May 2001.
9. C.A. Coello Coello and G.Toscano Publido, Multi-objective optimization using a micro-genetic algorithm, in Proceedings of the Genetic and Evolutionary Computation Conference (GECCO'01), Morgan Kaufman, San Fransisco, CA p247-282, 2001.
10. C.A.Coello Coello, N.C Cortes, Solving multi-objective optimization problems using artificial immune system, Genetc Programming and Evolvable Machines, 6, 163-190, 2005.
11. K.H. Han and J.H. Kim, Quantum inspired evolutionary algorithms with a new termination criterion, H_ε gate and two phase scheme, IEEE Transactions on Evolutionary Computation, 8, 156-169, 2004.

12. K. H. Han and J. H Kim, Genetic quantum algorithm and its application to combinatorial optimization problem. *Proc. Congr. Evolutionary Computation,* vol. 2, La Jolla, CA, 1354–1360, 2000.
13. C.P. Williams and S.H. Clearwater, *Explorations in quantum computing.* Springer Verlag, Berlin, Germany, 1998.
14. P.W. Shor, Algorithms for quantum computation: Discrete logarithms and factoring, In *Proc. 35th Annu. Symp. Foundations Computer Science*, Sante Fe, NM, 124–134, 1994.
15. L. K. Grover, A fast quantum mechanical algorithm for database search, In *Proc. 28th ACM Symp. Theory Computing*, 212–219, 1996.
16. A. Narayanan and M. Moore, Quantum-inspired genetic algorithms. *Proc. IEEE Int. Conf. Evolutionary Computation,* 61–66, 1996.
17. E. Zitzler and M. Laumanns, Problems and Test Data for MultiobjectiveOptimizers, http://www.tik.ee.ethz.ch/~zitzler/testdata.html.
18. International Society on Multiple Criteria Decision Making. MCDM Numerical Instances Library, http://www.univ-valencienne.fr/ROAD/MCDM
19. C.A.Coello Coello, D.A. Van veldhuilzen and G.B. Lamot, Evolutionary algorithms for solving multi-objective problems, Kluwer Academic Publishers, New York, May 2002.

Chapter 4

BAOSW 2005: Building and Applying
Ontologies for the Semantic Web

Introduction

H. Sofia Pinto[1], Andreia Malucelli[2], Fred Freitas[3], and Christoph Tempich[4]

[1] INESC-ID/IST, Lisboa, Portugal
sofia@algos.inesc-id.pt
[2] FEUP, Porto, Portugal
malu@fe.up.pt, malu@ppgia.pucpr.br
[3] Universidade Federal de Alagoas, Maceió, Brazil
fred.freitas@tci.ufal.br
[4] AIFB, Universität Karlsruhe, Germany
cte@aifb.uni-karlsruhe.de

The emergence of the Semantic Web has marked another stage in the evolution of the ontology field. According to Berners-Lee, the Semantic Web is an extension of the current Web in which information is given well-defined meaning, better enabling computers and people to work in cooperation. This cooperation can be achieved by using shared knowledge-components. Therefore ontologies have become a key instrument in developing the Semantic Web. They interweave human understanding of symbols with their machine processability.

This workshop addressed the problems of building and applying ontologies in the semantic web as well as the theoretical and practical challenges arising from different applications. We invited and received contributions that enhance the state-of-the-art of creating, managing and using ontologies. The workshop received high quality submissions, which were peer-reviewed by two or three reviewers.

For this chapter we selected the best two papers. *Curé and Squelbut* addresses the problem of mapping between databases and ontologies, which is an important issue for the creation of the semantic web. In particular, an automatic database trigger strategy for maintenance of the Abox of a knowledge base created from a database is proposed. *Sure et all.* describe the publicly available SWRC (Semantic Web for Research Communities) ontology, in which research communities and relevant related concepts are modelled. The SWRC ontology is a very good example for other ontology building efforts making design guidelines explicit and facilitating it reuse.

We would like to express our sincere gratitude to all the people who helped to bring about BAOSW'05. First of all thanks to the contributing authors, for ensuring the high scientific standard of the workshop and for their cooperation in the preparation of this volume.

Special thanks go to the members of the program committee and auxiliary reviewers for their professionalism and their dedication in selecting the best papers for the workshop. Thanks also to the EPIA'05 organizers for their guidance and their continuous support.

Finally, we hope the workshop provided its attendees a lively, fruitful and interesting discussions on building and applying ontologies for the semantic web.

C. Bento, A. Cardoso, and G. Dias (Eds.): EPIA 2005, LNAI 3808, p. 205, 2005.
© Springer-Verlag Berlin Heidelberg 2005

A Database Trigger Strategy to Maintain Knowledge Bases Developed Via Data Migration

Olivier Curé and Raphaël Squelbut

Université de Marne-la-Vallée, Laboratoire ISIS,
77454 Champs-sur-Marne, France

Abstract. The mapping between databases and ontologies is an issue of importance for the creation of the Semantic Web. This is mainly due to the large amount of web data stored in databases. Our approach tackles the consideration of the dynamic aspects of relational databases in knowledge bases. This solution is of particular interest for "ontology-driven" information systems equipped with inference functionality and which require synchronization with legacy database.

1 Introduction

The role of ontologies is foundational in providing semantics to vocabularies used to access and exchange data within the Semantic Web. The creation and maintenance of large scale, concrete and useful ontologies is a major challenge which will drive the success of the next generation Web [6]. Several researches in this direction aim to exploit the databases underlying the "Deep Web" [7] to develop knowledge bases. Different efficient mapping techniques are already available (see section 2) and usually involve a reverse engineering processing. This task can be defined as the analysis of a "legacy" system in order to identify the system's components and their inter-relationships [10]. In the context of the "Deep Web", legacy data is generally stored in (object-) relational database management systems.

The DBOM (DataBase Ontology Mapping) system uses this approach and enables the creation, population and maintenance of expressive and richly axiomatized OWL ontologies from relational database schemata. This paper does not present the global architecture of the DBOM system, which has already been described in [12], but instead focuses on developing maintenance functionalities for knowledge bases. This set of services, called the trigger strategy, handles dynamic aspects of relational databases (triggers, referential actions).

The knowledge bases created and maintained with DBOM belong to the family of Description Logics (DL) systems [4] and we thus make the usual distinction between the description of a domain terminology (called the Tbox) and the actual assertions that make use of the terminology (called the Abox). The trigger strategy is designed to automatically maintain the knowledge base assertional box synchronized as closely as possible to the states of the mapping source database. This approach implies that whenever a database tuple related

C. Bento, A. Cardoso, and G. Dias (Eds.): EPIA 2005, LNAI 3808, pp. 206–217, 2005.

to a DL entity (concept, property) is updated (via a conjunctive query, e.g. SQL query), the Abox is similarly modified to ensure that it remains in a consistent state wrt to its source. With such characteristics, DBOM is designed to be a valuable tool for information-driven and inference enabled applications that are highly dependant on frequently updated data stored in databases. This paper is organized as follows :

- Section 2 presents a survey of the most influencial solutions designed in the field of data migration between databases and ontologies. This section also presents the main characteristics of the DBOM solution.
- Section 3 explains the motivations behind DBOM's trigger strategy and presents its general principle.
- Sections 4 and 5 respectively provide a formal definition of the concepts used in the trigger strategy and detail the implementation, concentrating particularly on the heuristics of this strategy.
- Section 6 concludes this paper with a discussion and hints on DBOM-related future works.

2   Survey of Existing Solutions

This survey is broadened to the study of solutions addressing data migration between databases and ontologies. We have selected eight influencial solutions which pertain to three approaches :

- creation of a knowledge base (Tbox and Abox) from an existing database [3,19,17,8,9].
- creation of a database schema from an existing knowledge base [18].
- creation of a mapping between an existing ontology and database schemata [2,5,16], in order to enable information integration. In this approach, an ontology schema corresponding to the database schema has been manually designed and a mapping is required to enable interoperability.

An evaluation framework has been designed to highlight the main features of these influencial solutions as well as to emphasize the distinctive features of DBOM. These features are :

- an automaticity creation feature which can take two different values:
  - automatic solutions which do not involve user interactions but are limited in terms of providing semantics.
  - semi-automatic solutions which require interactions with human design-ers, for example via the creation of a mapping file (i.e. [19]) or via adjust-ments of the system results [17]. This approach is time-consuming and requires a knowledge of both the source schema and the functionalities of the target application. But these solutions also enable the design of expressive and usually richly axiomatized ontologies.
- data coupling which proposes two solutions: a loose coupling, where the Abox is populated at mapping processing time, and a tight coupling, where the Abox is instanciated on-demand, whenever requested by a query.

- terminological axiomatization which refers to the knowledge base's language (called the target in table 1). This survey also proposes the format in which the mapping files are written.
- possibility to enrich the target ontology with Tbox axioms.

Table 1. Survey of database/ontology solutions (DB: database, KB:Knowledge Base, A:Automatic, SA:Semi-Automatic)

Solutions	Approaches						Coupling		Format		Terminological
	DB to KB		KB to DB		existing DB KB		Loose	Tight	Mapping	Target	Axiomatization
	A	SA	A	SA	A	SA					
[17]InfoSleuth		X									
[19]		X						X	F-logic	RDFS	Yes
[18]			X								
[8]D2R Map		X					X		XML	RDF	
[5] eD2R				X			X		XML	RDF	
[16]						X		X	F-logic	DAML-OIL	
[3]	X						X		F-logic		Yes
[2]Maponto					X						

The survey results are presented in Table 1 and serve to highlight DBOM's features. In a nutshell, DBOM belongs to the semi-automatic category and uses the XML syntax to express the mapping between the existing database and the target ontology. The semi-automatic characteristic is motivated by the fact that DBOM aims to develop light ontologies supporting inferences in domain-specific applications. By light ontologies we mean knowledge bases that only contain data involved in reasoning activities. For example, in the XIMSA (eXtended Interactive Multimedia System for Automedication) system [11], several relation attributes of the source database are not mapped to the ontology as they are not pertinent for the inferences computed in this application. However, these attributes can still be incorporated in the application's user interface via database SQL queries and links with inferred results, i.e. the pharmaceutical attribute of the drug relation is displayed on the drug information web page although it is not present in the ontology.

In terms of the source database, DBOM handles relational and some constructs of object-relational databases. These databases must be in at least third normal form due to the mapping's syntax and semantics. These characteristics make DBOM similar to D2R MAP however an important difference between these two solutions is in the terminological axiomatization possibilities of DBOM which enable the creation of ontologies as expressive as OWL DL. DBOM also proposes additional services one of which, maintenance solutions, is emphasized in the following sections.

3 Principle and Motivation of the DBOM Trigger Strategy

The trigger strategy's goal is to exploit dynamic aspects of the relational source database to maintain an up-to-date Abox. The dynamic aspects considered are triggers and referential actions such as "ON UPDATE" and "ON DELETE". Thus this solution only tackles modifications of instances in relational database tables, meaning that updates of schema through Data Definition Language (DDL) queries are not taken into account. Consequently this approach is related to the view-update problem in which the DL Abox can be considered as a view of the relational database.

A study of the solutions presented in section 2 highlights that the Abox instance maintenance is usually performed via a complete processing of the mapping. Such a solution is inefficient for the following reasons:

- any processing of the mapping implies the creation from scratch of the Tbox and the Abox. These tasks are time-consuming and are unnecessary unless major changes are made to mapping files.
- in practical cases, the number of tuples updated by a single query is relatively small (even in the presence of referential actions such 'ON DELETE CASCADE). A consequence is that the larger the Abox, the less efficient is the in mass re-creation of instances.

Definition 1. *DBOM mapping processing:*
The processing of the mapping is only necessary when the mapping file is changed. Database tuple updates are automatically computed by the trigger strategy.

Potential applications for DBOM are information-driven systems which store their data in relational databases. Usually, these applications are equipped with graphical user interfaces that allow authorized users the ability to maintain the database states. With the trigger strategy, this routine work remains unchanged, keeping end-users within a confortable software environment. This situation also avoids the integration of ontology maintenance tools which would require a training period for the administrator and end-users.

We conclude this section with a concrete example which motivated the development of DBOM and its maintenance solution. The XIMSA system offers self-medication services which are highly dependent on updated drug data. The drug database requires frequent updates due to the rapid evolution of the drug market in most industrial countries (drug addition, deletion, modification). The health care professionals involved in this project are quite familiar with the provided Web interface. This user-friendly application enables end-users to insert, delete and update drugs stored in the database from any computer linked to the World Wide Web. We consider that the efficiency of this maintenance solution is mainly responsible for the motivation of involved health care professionals and thus the quality of the maintained databases. At the time of integrating a knowledge base into XIMSA, it was inconceivable to ask these partners to change their working habit and invest time in the learning of a new software environment.

4   Formal Definition for the Trigger Strategy

This section proposes a formal definition of the trigger strategy. It does not provide a formalization of the mapping between a database and an ontology, as this has already been treated in [15] and [4] (chap.16).

The trigger strategy definition is expressed with the formalization of a translation approach which relates a relational model to DBOM's mapping model. In definition 2, we use an extract of the formal definition of the relational model presented in [1].

Definition 2. *The relational model M is defined has having a 4-tuple (R,A,ra,rk) consisting of:*

- *A finite set R of relations.*
- *A finite set A of attributes.*
- *A function ra : $R \rightarrow 2^A$ that defines attributes contained in a specific relation $r_i \in R$.*
- *A function rk : $R \rightarrow 2^A$ which defines attributes that are primary keys in a given relation. Thus $rk(r_i) \subseteq ra(r_i)$ must hold.*

The next definition desribes the mapping model which proposes concrete and abstract entities (binary object properties and concepts). The terms "concrete" and "abstract" are interpreted in the object oriented programming domain : "concrete" means that individuals can be created, while "abstract" relates to the organization of entities (hierarchy of entities) and not to any kind of instantiations.

Definition 3. *Property definition in DBOM mapping*

- *A finite set P_{dt} of datatype property definitions. The range of these datatype properties are XML built in datatypes. The mapping between database schema datatypes and XML datatypes is the responsibility of the ontology designer.*
- *A finite set P_{cob} of concrete object property definitions, meaning that these properties relate instances.*
- *A finite set P_{aob} of abstract object property definitions, meaning that these properties do not relate instances but participate in the creation of a hierarchy of properties.*

Definition 4. *Concept definition in DBOM mapping*

- *A finite set C_c of concrete concept definitions, meaning that instances of these concepts can be created in the knowledge base.*
- *A finite set C_a of abstract concept definitions, meaning that instances of these concepts are not created., instead they are usually defined to be super concepts of concrete (or abstract) ones and support a class hierarchy.*

Definition 5. *Terminological axiomatization in DBOM mapping*

- *A finite set E of axioms based on a description language equivalent to the expressiveness of OWL DL without nominals.*

- A function $fe : C_c \cup C_a \to E$ which provides sufficient (and necessary) conditions to concept definitions.

The instantiation of the concrete entities is processed via the definition of SQL Data Manipulation Language (DML) queries in the mapping.

Definition 6. *Queries in the DBOM mapping model*
A finite set Q of SQL DML queries involved in the population of the knowledge base. A distinction is made between a finite set Q_p of queries designed in object property definitions and a finite set Q_c of queries designed in concrete concept definitions, so that $Q_p \cup Q_c = Q$ must hold.

We can now propose a definition of the functions used in the trigger strategy.

Definition 7. *Function definitions necessary for the trigger strategy*

- A function $mf: Q \to R$ which provides relations contained in a mapping's specific SQL query FROM clause.
- A function $ms: Q \to R$ which provides relations containing attributes present in a mapping's specific SQL query SELECT clause. Thus for any query q_i, $ms(q_i) \subseteq mf(q_i)$ must hold.
- A function ma whose domain is Q and range is a 2-tuple (attma, relma) with:
  - attma is a non-primary key attribute used to populate the Abox and is present in a mapping's SQL query SELECT clause.
  - relma is the name relation of attma. Thus $ma.relma(q_i) \in ms(q_i)$.
- A function mk whose domain is Q and range is a 2-tuple (attmk, relmk) which is defined as follow:
  - attmk is an attribute used as an identifier of individuals in a specific query.
  - relmk is the relation name of attmk. We have the following properties: $mk.relmk(q_i) \subseteq rk(ms(q_i))$, $mk.relmk(q_i) \in ms(q_i)$ and $mk(q_i) \cap ma(q_i) = \emptyset$.
- A function mc which deals with joins in the WHERE clause. The domain of mc is Q and the range is a set of 2-tuple (attmc, valmc) with:
  - attmc, an attribute name of r_i such that $attmc \in ra(r_i)$.
  - valmc is a value taken by attmc of q_i in the domain of the attribute attmc.

These definitions are used in the following section which presents the implementation and heuristics for Abox maintenance.

5 Implementation and Heuristics

5.1 Trigger Definition

Relational DBMS provide, via the SQL3 standard, varying functionalities to handle dynamic aspects of data. The objective of the trigger strategy is to handle triggers and referential actions.

This first sub-section emphasizes the automatic generation of triggers by the DBOM system. This task is automatic for the following reasons : the non-automatic design of triggers is error-prone and can be bothersome, especially for large schemata where many triggers can be created. The mapping file processing involves the creation of triggers according to the following rules:

- for all relations obtained from $ms(Q_c)$, we create triggers tackling a method concerned with concept operations.
- for all relations obtained from $ms(Q_p) - (ms(Q_c) \cap ms(Q_p))$, we create triggers tackling a method concerned with object property operations.

The triggers automatically created in the RDBMS are based on a simplification of the SQL3 proposal:

```
CREATE TRIGGER trigger-name
{BEFORE | AFTER} { INSERT | DELETE | UPDATE } ON table-name
FOR EACH {ROW | STATEMENT} EXECUTE PROCEDURE procedure-name;
```

The triggers generated by the trigger strategy are defined as "AFTER" triggers, because the system needs to have the data stored in the dababase before processing updates of the Abox, and as "ROW LEVEL" triggers, meaning that the trigger action is executed for every row that is inserted, deleted or updated by the query as opposed to statement level where the trigger is executed only once [13]. This "AFTER/ROW LEVEL" policy allows to consider, when not limited by recursive trigger characteristics, referential actions such as "ON DELETE | ON UPDATE action". The triggers are implemented by two generic Java methods (concept method and property method) defined in the DBOM framework and whose functionality is described in the heuristics section.

5.2   Finding and Processing Candidate Entities

Both the property and object Java methods need to find the candidate entities, respectively object properties and concepts, that can be updated from the trigger. The current policy is to search the mapping file for all the definitions matching the relation updated.

Definition 8. *Let r_i be a relation updated by an SQL DML query. A concept (object property) is a candidate if $r_i \in ms(Q_c)$ ($r_i \in ms(Q_p)$ for an object property).*

The processing of candidate entities is described in Definition 9.

Definition 9. *Let r_i be the relation fired by the trigger and a set T_{r_i} of the 2-tuple (key,val) for all $rk(r_i)$ with:*

- *key_j, an attribute of $rk(r_i)$.*
- *val_j, the value of key_j in the firing trigger query.*

The processing of concept (resp. property) candidates enriches the queries of Q'_c (resp. Q'_p), a sub-set of Q_c (resp. Q_p) containing concept (resp. property) candidates with additional conjuncts of equalities between elements of T_{r_i} in the WHERE clause.

5.3   Example

This example exploits an excerpt of the 'automed' database, which is intensively used in the XIMSA system. The following relational schema, henceforth referered to as the drug relational schema is the source of the mapping file (primary keys are underlined):

drug (drugId, drugName, drugPharmaceutical, rating, systemId,...)
system (systemId, systemName)
therapeuticClass (therapeuticClassId, therapeuticClassName)
therap2Drug (drugId, therapeuticClassId)

A potential DBOM mapping from the drug relational schema to an OWL knowledge base is now proposed. Due to the verbosity of XML and the constraints on page limits, we only present concepts and object properties and their respective queries and omit datatype properties:

- the AntitussiveDrug concept has two datatype properties which are related to the drugId and drugName attributes of the drug relation. Other attributes of the drug relation are not considered in the ontology. Only drugs with a rating greater than 18 and which belong to the 'antitussive' therapeutic class (therapeuticClassId=295) are selected. The SQL query used is:
  - SELECT d.drugId, d.drugName FROM drug d, therap2Drug td WHERE td.idclass=295 AND rating>18 AND td.drugId=d.drugId;.
- the TherapeuticClass concept has two datatype properties which are related to the therapeuticClassId and therapeuticClassName attributes. The goal of this concept is to create instances for all tuples of the therapeuticClass relation that are related to at least one drug. The SQL query is:
  - SELECT tc.therapeuticClassId, tc.therapeuticClassName FROM therapeuticClass tc, therap2Drug tc WHERE
    td.therapeuticClassId = tc.therapeuticClassId;
- the System concept is instantiated via the following query:
  - SELECT systemId, systemName FROM system;
  This concept also has datatype properties for its identifier and name. System names correspond to categories of drugs encountered in the database ('allopathy', 'homeopathy', etc.).
- the values of the therap2Drug object property are defined with the following query:
  - SELECT d.drugId, td.therapeuticClassId FROM drug as d, therap2Drug as td WHERE td.idclass = 295 AND rating > 18 AND td.drugId = d.drugId;
- A last object property needs to be defined to relate Drug objects to System objects. This corresponds to the drugSystem property whose values are processed via the following SQL query:
  - 'SELECT d.drugId, s.systemId FROM drug as d, system as s, therap2Drug as td WHERE td.therapeuticClassId=295 AND rating>18 AND d.systemId = s.systemId AND d.drugId=td.drugId;

– As an example of Tbox axiomatization, we propose in a DL syntax (for
  brevity reasons) a definition of the Drug concept, super concept of the Anti-
  tussiveDrug: $= 1.drugSystem.System \sqcap \exists therap2Drug.TherapeuticClass \sqcap \forall therap2Drug.TherapeuticClass$.

5.4   Heuristics

Several techniques have been chosen to solve the problem of efficiently and accurately mapping an update at the database level to the knowledge base level.
The presentation of these heuristics is decomposed into rules that solve insert,
delete and update trigger events. For each of these three categories, we distinguish between triggers that call the property method and those that call the
concept method. It is important to emphasize that referential actions help to
maintain the Abox's consistency.

   In this section, we refer to q_i as the instantiation query of a candidate entity e_i.

   Concerning the insert-oriented triggers, several rules can be designed according to properties of e_i. For the concept method, we distinguish 2 cases:

– if $mc(q_i) = \emptyset$ or all conditions of $mc(q_i)$ are satisfied then a new instance is
  added to the knowledge base.
– if the set of conditions $mc(q_i)$ is not totally satisfied, the creation of instances
  is postponed. This situation occurs whenever a referential integrity violation
  is detected. In the drug relational schema example, we consider the insertion
  of a new antitussive drug with drugID value 101. Due to referential integrity
  constraints, no tuple exist in the therap2Drug relation with drugId equal to
  101. The conditions in the WHERE clause of the AntitussiveDrug concept
  are not all satisfied and the instance cannot be created. It is necessary to
  wait for the insertion in the therap2Drug relation of a tuple of the form
  101,x, with x an existing therapeuticClassId.

   For the property oriented method, the following situations can be encountered:

– if all instances involved in the object property that is those related by the
  domain and the range, are already present in the Abox then the relation
  between these 2 individuals can be created.
– if any, or both, of the instances involved in the object property is (are) missing then it is necessary to first create the instance(s) and then to relate them.
  In our 101 identified antitussive drug scenario, this rule is activated when the
  tuple 101,295 is inserted in the therap2Drug relation. The 101 instance still
  does not exist, so it is necessary to create it. During the creation of this instance, object properties can also be created, for example a relation between
  instance AntitussiveDrug 101 and its system. This situation is handled with
  the Tbox which enables a search of all properties of a given concept. Using
  the Abox, we can then search for instantiations of these relations.

   With regards to the delete-oriented triggers, we further distinguish between
the following situation:

- firing of the concept method: if the instance corresponding to the deleted tuple is present in the Abox then this instance is deleted. In case of postponing situation, an update of the Abox may not be necessary, i.e. the tuple with drugId 101 is deleted from the drug relation before inserting the corresponding tuple in the therap2Drug relation.
- firing the property method: due to the insert-oriented trigger policy, the system deletes the object property between involved instances.

Concerning the update-oriented triggers, we only consider queries where updated attributes belong to either $mk.attmk(q_i)$, $ma.attma(q_i)$ or $mc.attmc(q_i)$. Otherwise, nothing needs to be done because modified attributes are not present in the knowledge base.

- if a modified attribute is in $ma.attma(q_i)$ then the datatype property value for an existing instance is updated.
- if a modified attribute is in $mk.attmk(q_i)$ then it is necessary to change the value of the identifier for this instance and also to change all the object properties leading to this object. As far as the database is concerned with integrity constraints, this action should not render the knowledge base inconsistent as it has been populated according to those integrity constraints. However, this situation is awkward for the integrity of the mapping as it may involve the modification of the static query of the mapping file and involves the expertise of the ontology administrator who is warned about this situation via a log file.
- if a modified attribute is in $mc.attmc(q_i)$ then several solutions are possible: we can either delete the instance if the (new) condition is not satisfied anywhere else in the mapping file (in a concept definition), e.g. no concept for drugs with a rating lower than 18. If a query exists with this condition satisfied, the system modifies the concept realization for this individual.
- firing of the property method requires that the system deletes the relation between instances corresponding to old values of the tuple. Further if possible is created a new relation between the instances corresponding to the new values. For example, the tuple 101,295 is updated and now becomes 100,295 (drug with identifier 100 becomes an antitussive) then two cases are possible depending on the existence of the drug instance 100:
  - it does not exist and a new relation can not be created. This is a typical postponing situation.
  - it exists and a new relation between drug instance 100 and the therapeutic class 295 is created.

6   Discussion and Future Work

In this paper, we described an automatic maintenance solution for a knowledge base Abox using database triggers. This solution handles the two main limitations of the problem mapping between databases and ontologies; formal ontologies provide more semantics than database schemata and the ontology model is richer than the relational schema. Our approach enables a designer to provide semantic annotation to the database schema in the form of a mapping file. It is usually considered that different interpretations of a given database schema are possible due to differences in what the original designers intended to represent and what the mapping designers understand the database to mean [10]. The most convenient situation is encountered when the mapping designer and database schema designer is the same (group of) person(s). However this scenario is not typical and most of the time the legacy database designer is not available and no valuable documentation exists. DBOM aims to develop light ontologies related to a specific domain (domain-ontologies) and highly correlated to a software application. This vision allows mapping designers to concentrate on the application rather than on the intrinsic database semantics.

The DBOM system creates ontologies in OWL (DL), a language based on Description Logics, and thus handles binary object properties. The issue of n-ary relations (with n>=3) has been studied in [4] (chap. 10,16) and the usage of reification is proposed. The solution adopted by DBOM proposes the creation of a concrete concept C_r for the n-ary relations and the creation of n object properties whose domain is C_r and range is the concept corresponding to the n entities involved in the ER diagram. This method enables the processing of n-ary relations with the proposed heuristics and implementation.

We are actually working on a graphical user interface (implemented as a Protege [14] plug-in) to design mapping files in user-friendly way. Future work on the trigger strategy will concentrate on the evaluation of heuristics with large knowledge bases (tens thousand instances). The current Abox running on the XIMSA system contains around eight thousand instances distributed over more than one hundred concepts and properties. We also would like to experiment server solutions for the management of highly updated knowledge bases.

References

1. Abiteboul, S., Hull, R., Vianu, V. : Foundation of databases. Addison-Wesley Publishing Company, 1995.
2. An Y., Borgida, A., Mylopoulos, J. : Refining Semantic Mappings from Relational Tables to Ontologies. Proceedings of the Semantic Web and Data Bases workshop (2004) 84–90
3. Astrova, I. : Reverse Engineering of Relational Databases to Ontologies. European Semantic Web Symposium (2004) 327–341.
4. Baader, F., Calvanese, D., McGuinness, D., Nardi, D., Patel-Schneider, P. : The Description Logic Handbook: Theory, Implementation and Applications. Cambridge University Press (2003).
5. Barrasa, J., Corcho, O., Gomez Perez, A. : Fund Finder: A case study of database-to-ontology mapping Proceedings of the Semantic Integration Workshop. 2nd International Semantic Web Conference (2003).
6. Bechhofer, S., Gangemi, A., Guarino, N., van Harmelen, F., Horrocks, I., Klein, M., Masolo, C. Oberle, D., Staab, S., Stuckenschmidt, H., Volz, R. : Tackling the Ontology Acquisition Bottleneck: An Experiment in Ontology Re-Engineering. Available on-line at http://citeseer.ist.psu.edu/657698.html

7. Bergman, M. : The deep Web : Surfacing the Hidden Value. Available on-line at : http://www.brightplanet.com/technology/deepweb.asp. (2001).

8. Bizer, C. : D2R MAP - A Database to RDF Mapping Language. The Twelfth International World Wide Web Conference (2003).

9. Borgida, A. : Loading Data into Description Reasoners. Proceedings of ACM SIG-MOD International Conference on Management of Data (1993) 315–333

10. Chiang, R., Barron, T., Storey, V. : A framework for the design and evaluation of reverse engineering methods for relational databases. Data and Knowledge Engineering 21 (1997) 57–77.

11. Curé, O. : XIMSA : eXtended Interactive Multimedia System for Auto-medication. Proceedings of IEEE Computer-Based Medical Systems (2004) 570–575

12. Curé, O. : Semi-automatic data migration in a self-medication knowledge-based system. Proceedings of WM2005: Professional Knowledge Manangement, Experiences and Visions (2005). 323-329

13. Elmasri, R., Navathe, S. : Fundamentals of database systems. Addison-Wesley Publishing Company, (2003).

14. Gennari, J., Musen, M., Fergerson, R., Grosso, W., Crubezy, M., Eriksson, H., Noy, N., Tu, S. : The evolution of protege: an environment for knowledge - based systems development. International Journal of Human - Computer Studies, vol 123 (2003) 58:89.

15. Goni, A., Blanco, J.M., Illaramendi, A. : Connecting konwledge bases with databases : a complete mapping relation. Proceedings of the 8th ERCIM Workshop. (1995).

16. Handschuh, S., Staab, S., Volz, R. : On Deep Annotation. 12th International World Wide Web Conference (2003). 431–438.

17. Kashyap, V. : Design and creation of ontologies for environmental information retrieval. Proceedings of the 12th Workshop on Knowledge Acquisition, Modeling and Management (1999)

18. Moreno Vergara, N., Navas Delgado, I., Francisco Aldana Montes, J. : Putting the Semantic Web to Work with DB Technology. IEEE Data Engineering Bulletin Volume 26, issue 4 (2003) 49–54

19. Stojanovic, L., Stojanovic, N., Volz, R. : Migrating data-intensive web sites into the semantic web. Proceedings of the ACM Symposium on Applied Computing SAC (2002) 1100–1107

The SWRC Ontology – Semantic Web for Research Communities

York Sure, Stephan Bloehdorn, Peter Haase,
Jens Hartmann, and Daniel Oberle

University of Karlsruhe, Institute AIFB, D-76128 Karlsruhe, Germany
{sure, bloehdorn, haase, hartmann, oberle}@aifb.uni-karlsruhe.de
http://www.aifb.uni-karlsruhe.de/WBS

Abstract. Representing knowledge about researchers and research communities is a prime use case for distributed, locally maintained, interlinked and highly structured information in the spirit of the Semantic Web. In this paper we describe the publicly available 'Semantic Web for Research Communities' (SWRC) ontology, in which research communities and relevant related concepts are modelled. We describe the design decisions that underlie the ontology and report on both experiences with and known usages of the SWRC Ontology. We believe that for making the Semantic Web reality the re-usage of ontologies and their continuous improvement by user communities is crucial. Our contribution aims to provide a description and usage guidelines to make the value of the SWRC explicit and to facilitate its re-use.

1 Introduction

One of the driving forces of the Semantic Web is the need of many communities to put machine-understandable data on the Web which can be shared and processed by automated tools as well as by people. Representing knowledge about researchers, research communities, their publications and activities as well as about their mutual interrelations is a prime use case for distributed, locally maintained, interlinked and highly structured information in the spirit of the Semantic Web.

The SWRC ontology – initially phrased *Semantic Web Research Community Ontology* – which we will describe in this paper, generically models key entities in a typical research community and reflects one of the earliest attempts to put this usage of Semantic Web Technologies in academia into practice.

The SWRC ontology initially grew out of the activities in the KA[2] project [1]. By then it was already used in the context of Semantic Community Web Portals [2] and has been ported to various knowledge representation languages including both Semantic Web Standards like RDF(S) or DAML+OIL and other languages like F-Logic consecutively. In the most recent versions, the SWRC ontology has been released in OWL format[1]. Since its initial versions it has

---

[1] The SWRC ontology itself and some of its extensions are available via
http://ontoware.org/projects/swrc/

C. Bento, A. Cardoso, and G. Dias (Eds.): EPIA 2005, LNAI 3808, pp. 218–231, 2005.

been used and adapted in a number of different settings, most prominently for providing structured metadata for web portals. These include the web portal of the authors' institute AIFB and for the portals in the research projects OntoWeb and SemIPort. These and other usages of the ontology in different settings will be described later on.

In this paper, we will focus on describing the SWRC ontology and on making the design considerations explicit that have led to a particular modelling approach. We show a number of typical modelling problems and report on their solutions. While some of the issues that arose in modelling the SWRC ontology are domain specific – sometimes also specific to the chosen modelling language, e.g. OWL– others appear to be more general and may thus serve as a handy reference for knowledge engineers. At the same time this paper aims at providing usage guidelines for the SWRC ontology.

The remainder of this paper is structured as follows. Section 2 gives an initial overview over the ontology itself and the modelled domain. Section 3 reviews the critical design considerations made and discusses alternatives. Section 4 lists a number of guidelines for users and systems working with the SWRC ontology while Section 5 reports on three prototypical usages of the ontology. Finally, Section 6 reviews related schemas and discusses their relation to the SWRC ontology. We conclude in Section 7.

2   Overview of the Ontology

The SWRC ontology generically models key entities relevant for typical research communities and the relations between them. The current version of the ontology comprises a total of 53 concepts in a taxonomy and 42 object properties, 20 of which are participating in 10 pairs of inverse object properties. All entities are enriched with additional annotation information.

SWRC comprises at total of six top level concepts, namely the Person, Publication, Event, Organization, Topic and Project concepts. Figure 1 shows a small portion of the SWRC ontology with its main top-level concepts and relations. The Person concept models any kind of human person and a large number of properties restrict their domain or range to individuals of this concept like studiesAt or author, respectively. The Person concept is specialized by a large number of – not necessarily disjoint – subconcepts, e.g. Employee, Student and the like. The Event concept is meant to model different types of events and is thus specialized by a wide range of concepts including events like Lecture or Conference. The Publication concept subsumes all different types of research publications modelled in close correspondence with the well known BIBTEX publication types like Article or InProceedings. The Organization and Project concepts model more abstract concepts like the subconcepts Department or SoftwareProject, respectively. Both concepts can participate in a large number of relations like for example to the Person concept via the employs or member relations. The Topic captures arbitrary topics of interest which are arranged on the instance level via the subTopic relation.

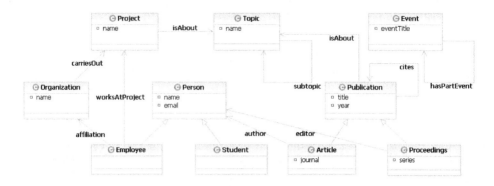

Fig. 1. Main Concepts of the SWRC Ontology

3   Design Considerations

In this section we outline and justify major design decisions that have been made in the development of the SWRC ontology. By making them explicit we facilitate the proper usage of the SWRC but also provide decision support for other modelling efforts.

3.1   Choice of Language

As of today, many different ontology representation languages embodying various paradigms exist, including description logics, frame-based and logic-programming languages etc. Apparently, some of the reasons why there are competing ontology representation languages lie in the differing requirements imposed by the respective application scenarios to which semantic technologies are being applied. Simpler languages are easier and more efficient to deal with but lack the complex modelling facilities of the richer paradigms. Some scenarios may require particular modelling facilities or even tools which are only available for certain paradigms.

For applying semantic technologies, the practitioner is faced with the question, which ontology modelling paradigms should be adopted. For performance reasons, simpler paradigms are often preferable, but equally important is interoperability between different systems and reusability in the future, i.e. compatibility with to be established standards.

When the SWRC ontology was first created, no widely accepted and standardized format for representing ontologies existed. Therefore, the SWRC was initially made available in various formats, including for example F-Logic and DAML+OIL. In 2004, the Web Ontology Language OWL [3, 4] was adopted by the W3C as the standard for representing ontologies on the web. OWL is a very expressive ontology representation language which can be described as a fragment of first-order logic. It comes in three different variants, namely OWL-Lite, OWL-DL and OWL-Full, with differences in expressiveness and reasoning complexity. As compatibility with standards was one of our major design goals, we decided to model the SWRC ontology in an OWL-compliant manner.

In particular, we decided for a subset of the OWL language, called Description Logic Programs (OWL-DLP)[2] [5, 6]. We argue that OWL-DLP provides a basic ontology modelling paradigm which meets most of the requirements above while being a flexible choice for future developments, as it is not only a proper fragment of OWL, but also of logic programming languages such as F-Logic. As for performance, OWL-DLP features polynomial data complexity and exptime combined complexity, which renders it to be far better than the more expressive languages we mentioned. Extensions made for either more general language can be adopted for the fragment in a straightforward manner. Modelling and reasoning tools available for OWL or F-Logic can naturally deal with OWL-DLP, and interoperability is guaranteed to the largest extent possible.

For modelling of the above mentioned domain we found the primitives offered by OWL-DLP sufficiently expressive. However, since some natural support for e.g. sequences of authors we had to find alternative solutions which are explained in the following subsections.

3.2 Representing Entities as Objects or Data Values

A common question that occurs frequently while modeling data is whether certain entities should be modelled as "first class objects" or dependent of some other object, e.g. in the form of an attribute.

This issue also applies to the modelling of ontologies. For example, many bibliographic models simply provide a concept to represent publications, and model all properties of publications, e.g. their authors, corresponding organizations, topic classifications etc. as attributes. While such a model has advantages because of its simplicity, it is not easily extensible and also does not make important relations between entities explicit. We have therefore chosen to introduce explicit concepts wherever possible to make the semantics of the model explicit.

3.3 Representing Sequences of Authors

The choice of OWL-DLP as the ontology languages with its foundation in first order logic provides no native support to model sequences, lists, or any data structure requiring ordering of entities in an extension. Instead, all extensions of concepts and properties have the semantics of sets. However, sometimes it is necessary to capture the ordering of elements, for example the order of authors of a publication is important.

While RDF provides a container model in its data model, which allows to describe bags, sequences and alternatives, this container model is only available in OWL-Full. An alternative would be to model a ternary relation of publication, person, and order. This ternary relation can be reduced to binary relations by introducing a new concept, e.g. Authorship. However, this significantly increases complexity and is not intuitive.

---

[2] see http://logic.aifb.uni-karlsruhe.de.

Here, our design decision was to follow the basic idea of the RDF container model, but to capture it in a way compatible with OWL-DLP. RDF uses the predefined property `<rdf:li>` to denote the membership of a container. The order of the members is defined by subproperties of `<rdf:li>`, i.e. `<rdf:_1>`, `<rdf:_2>`,... to denote the first, second member and so on. Similarly, for applications that need to express the order of authors, we use subproperties of author, i.e. author_1, author_2,... Applications not interested in the order still can use the author property, as it subsumes the newly introduced properties.

3.4 Representation of Topic Classification

A key feature of bibliographic metadata is the classification against established topic hierarchies. In a sense, topic hierarchies can be seen as light-weight ontologies by themselves that complement the SWRC ontology with domain specific models of particular research domains. One example is the ACM topic hierarchy for the Computer Science domain. Further, many other topic hierarchies for other domains exist, for which an integration with the SWRC ontology is desirable. Here, a standard way of representing topics is required. Several options for such a representation exist. Some of these options model topics as concepts in the ontology, others require a feature called meta-modelling in the ontology language, where concepts can also be used as instances (cf. [7] for a detailed comparison), leading to an OWL-Full ontology.

In alignment with the choice of our ontology language, which requires a strict separation between concepts and instances, we model topics as instances of the concept Topic. The instances of Topic are arranged hierarchically by means of the subTopic relation. The relation between publications and a topic is established via the isAbout property. To link a specific topic hierarchy with the SWRC ontology, the topic concept of the topic hierarchy specializes the ResearchTopic concept of the SWRC ontology, e.g. for the ACM topic hierarchy: ACMTopic $\sqsubseteq$ Topic.

3.5 Modularization of OWL Ontologies

In general, it is desirable to have a modularized ontology design for mainly two reasons. First, it facilitates reuse of individual ontology modules. Second, maintenance efforts can be decreased by reuse.

In our case, modularization is of central importance, because the different uses of the SWRC ontology require minor variations in modelling. Particular settings might require the addition of Dublin Core attributes or additional concepts and associations. Thus, we factorized a common core from application-specific extensions like shown in Figure 2. The common core facilitates information integration across different applications.

Modularization is realized by the `owl:imports` statement. An `owl:imports` statement references another OWL ontology containing definitions, whose meaning is considered to be part of the meaning of the importing ontology. Each reference consists of a URI specifying from where the ontology is to be imported.

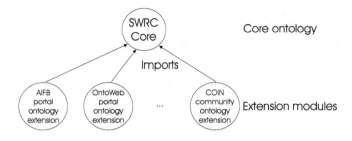

Fig. 2. SWRC modules

Syntactically, `owl:imports` is a property with `owl:Ontology` as its domain and range.[3] In our case, the extension modules import the SWRC core module.

In Section 5 we discuss the different uses of the SWRC ontology. Most of them define their own extension module to specify application-specific idiosyncracies like the AIFB portal ontology module, for instance.

3.6 Pragmatic Versioning

Ontologies are not static entities, but evolve over time. In its history, the SWRC ontology has undergone several changes, and we expect future changes as new requirements arise. With versioning, the old ontologies are kept along with the modified one. It thus provides the ability to relate metadata with a particular version of the ontology. Unfortunately, no standard versioning scheme for ontologies exists yet. We have therefore followed a versioning scheme that has proven practicable for other web data (such as W3C recommendations) already: Identifying versions via namespaces. Here, all versions share a common base URI, appended with a suffix indicating the date of creation. The relation between the versions is established via the OWL annotation property `owl:priorVersion`, which provides a link to the immediate predecessor. The base URI itself refers to the latest version of the ontology. An application not interested in particular versions thus simply relies on the base URI.

4   Guidelines for Usage

In this section we describe guidelines for using the SWRC ontology that evolved out of our experience. First, we elaborate on how to create extensions to the SWRC in order to model the idiosyncracies of particular applications. Second, the generation of identical URIs for identical entities across different SWRC applications requires special care. Finally, we discuss the handling of duplicates.

4.1   How to Create Extensions for SWRC Core

Section 3.5 already discussed the modular design of the SWRC where applications might introduce extension modules for their particular modelling require-

---

[3] http://www.w3.org/TR/owl-ref/

ments. In this subsection we give some guidelines on how to create extensions by means of examples.

A particular variation concerns whether to use the OWL datatype restrictions in the ontology or not. The question here is whether one should model datatypes for attributes such as "year" as xsd:integer or even as xsd:datetime. Often bibliographic metadata is very unclean, such that it may be more appropriate to simply use xsd:string. One example is the AIFB portal where information is coming out of a database. When entering the year for a publication, e.g., users are often sloppy and include additional blanks or non-integers. In this case, defining year as xsd:integer would yield an error in type-checking ontology editors like Protege. However, another usage of the SWRC might require xsd:datetime in order to enable datatype checking. The solution is to omit datatype restrictions in the SWRC and include them on demand in extending modules.

Another example where extensions come in handy are additional concepts and associations which are only required in a particular application. Community portals might extend the SWRC core by COIN which is a set of concepts and associations formalizing communities, user, their interrelationships etc. It is obvious that such information is not required in all uses of the SWRC.

Further extensions might require a more powerful representation formalism. The SWRC core is formalized in OWL-DLP whose expressiveness might not be enough for reasoning in concrete applications. Thus, we can think of extensions in OWL-DL, that import the SWRC core, but add axioms that are beyond the expressiveness of OWL-DLP.

Finally, extensions might define mappings to other ontologies, e.g. the ones mentioned in Section 6. An example would be the associations defined in Dublin Core (DC). We could specify a mapping of dc:author to swrc:author (the author of a publication) via owl:equivalentProperty, for instance.

4.2   URI Generation

Applications of the SWRC ontology such as semantic portals (see Section 5) and interoperability with other applications require sophisticated methods and techniques for identifying not only classes and properties of the ontology but also instances that describe (real-world) entities. Therefore we describe a common mechanism for generating Uniform Resource Identifiers (URI) for such instances.

The underlying idea is to generate *uniform* identifiers which are *identical* for the same entity in all applications. Hence, an instance generated in one application can easily be identified or re-used in another application. The process of comparing and verifying instances can be reduced to comparing and verifying URIs which makes functions such as *integration on-the-fly* and *duplicate detection* more scalable and efficient.

Technically, several mechanisms are available and well-known for standard URI generation. A widely used approach is to generate a hash code of an object and use this hash as URI whereby a change of an object would generate also a new hash.

The benefit of this approach is to ensure interoperability and re-use of instances. The drawback of this uniform identifier generation is the computing time for generating the URIs.

Practical experiences have shown limitations and practical restrictions. Our experiences with common ontology editors and dynamic HTML pages are worth mentioning. Dynamic pages with contents stemming from a database often feature an additional parameter in their URL, e.g. `http://www.aifb.uni-karlsruhe.de/Personen/viewPersonOWL?id=79`. It would be natural to adopt these URLs also for ontology instances URIs when generated dynamically. The OWL specification does not explicitly disallow this usage. However, the current state-of-the-art editor, viz. the OWL plug-in of Protege, forbids URIs with parameters due to internal constraints ("=" is internally used for cardinality and "?" for "someValuesFrom"). It is thus necessary to rewrite such URIs to `http://www.aifb.uni-karlsruhe.de/Personen/viewPersonOWL/id79.owl`, for instance.

Another problem is the lack of a default mechanism for retrieving ontologies describing an instance for given URI. When we have dynamically generated ontologies, each describing one instance, we cannot use the same URI for both the ontology and the instance. The AIFB portal, e.g., features numerous dynamically generated ontologies with inter-linkage between instances. The URIs of the described instance and its corresponding ontology cannot be equal. A crawler cannot easily follow the link and harvest required information. A solution is to establish a forward reference from the URI of the ontology instance to the URI of the ontology itself. This would allow a crawler to follow the link to the ontology. A valid solution (as used in the AIFB portal) is depicted below

```
<rdf:RDF>
 <owl:Ontology rdf:about=
  "http://www.aifb.uni-karlsruhe.de/Personen/viewPersonOWL/id79.owl">
 </owl:Ontology>
 <rdf:Description rdf:about=
  "http://www.aifb.uni-karlsruhe.de/Personen/viewPersonOWL/id79instance">
  ...
 </rdf:Description>
</rdf:RDF>
```

4.3 How to Deal with Duplicates

When dealing with bibliographic metadata, but also in other common usage scenarios, one often encounters duplicate entries, i.e. entries which refer to the same bibliographic item, but which differ in their representation, e.g. by having the first names of authors abbreviated or not.

Duplicate detection is a challenging task in most information systems as well as in our applications. Quality of service and data quality are key successors of current ontology-based systems. Hence, we have come up with an intelligent method for duplicate detection, which will be presented only shortly here.

Avoiding duplicates in the first place is obviously the most efficient method for solving the problem which can be achieved by using the described URI technique above. Furthermore, dealing with existing duplicates is still a challenge. However, the smart combination of existing comparison algorithms applied in a multilayered duplicate detection system using additional domain and world knowledge has shown promising results in our experiments. Specific methods for semantic similarity functions are described in [8].

The semi-automatic system works in an iterative mode in which the user (mainly the administrator of the system) can stop the process at each iteration or continue with a more intensive search. In general, the detection starts with an light-weight comparison of *promising* attributes whereby promising attributes are identified by *statistical properties* or *semantic relevance*. Semantic relevance is given by the occurrence of facts in a domain ontology and corresponding attributes in the analyzed data. Each iteration then takes further attributes into account or uses a more cost-intensive comparison algorithm. In this manner, it is possible to identify a large set of duplicates within the first iterations.

5   Known Usages of SWRC

This section describes some of the different usages of the SWRC ontology. First, there are several portals that apply the SWRC to semantically annotate their resources. All of them follow our SEAL (SEmantic portAL) approach. Second, we introduce Bibster, a semantics-based Peer-to-Peer application, which uses the SWRC to describe bibliographic metadata. Finally, we describe a comprehensive extension of the SWRC, called COIN, that supports the modelling of communities of interest.

5.1   Semantic Portals (SEAL)

SEAL (SEmantic portAL) is a conceptual model that exploits ontologies for fulfilling the requirements set forth by typical community web sites. The requirements are the need to integrate many different information sources and the need for an adequate web site management system. The ontology provides a high level of sophistication for web information integration as well as for web site management. For further information about the general architecture please cf. [9, 10]. We have implemented several portals that conform to our SEAL approach and use the SWRC ontology correspondingly:

AIFB. The portal of the Institute AIFB uses the SWRC to annotate staff, publications, projects and their corresponding interrelationships. The usage of the ontology will be explained below. http://www.aifb.uni-karlsruhe.de

OntoWare. Ontoware is a software development community platform for Semantic Web related software projects. The SWRC ontology is extended for annotating developers and software projects. http://www.ontoware.org

OntoWeb. The community site for the European Union founded project OntoWeb uses the SWRC to facilitate ontology-based information exchange for knowledge management and electronic commerce [10]. `http://www.ontoweb.org`

SEKT. The SEKT project is a European research projects bringing together the communities of knowledge discovery, human language technology and Semantic Web. Its corresponding portal uses the SWRC much like the OntoWeb portal. `http://www.sekt-project.com/`

SemiPort. The SemIPort (Semantic Methods and Tools for Information Portals) project develops innovative methods and tools for creating and maintaining semantic information portals (annotated by the SWRC ontology) for scientific communities. `http://km.aifb.uni-karlsruhe.de/semiport`

In the following we will describe the usage of the SWRC in the AIFB portal in more detail. Besides regular pages for human consumption, the portal of the Institute AIFB also provides annotated pages which contain machine processable content in form of OWL annotations (Figure 3).

The AIFB portal is based on the Zope application server where information about persons, publications or projects are retrieved from a relational database and presented to the user by XHTML. Such sites are also annotated by machine-understandable descriptions according to the SWRC ontology. Both XHTML files and annotations are interlinked by the `<link rel="meta">` tag. In addition, pages about persons, publications or projects feature an "OWL/RDF" button at the bottom to view the automatically generated information.

A typical annotation contains an ontological description about exactly one instance, viz. the person, publication or project regarded. However, there are also bulk annotations, e.g. for sites listing the whole staff or sites listing all publications of a person. In this case the descriptions just contain links to actual publication description (cf. also Section 4.2). We also offer a complete export of the database as 2 MB OWL file.

5.2   Bibster Application

Bibster[4] [11] is an award-winning semantics-based Peer-to-Peer application aiming at researchers who want to benefit from sharing bibliographic metadata, which they usually laboriously maintain manually in BibTeX files. Bibster enables the management of bibliographic metadata in a Peer-to-Peer fashion: it allows to import bibliographic metadata into a local knowledge repository, to share and search the knowledge in the Peer-to-Peer system.

Two ontologies are used to describe properties of bibliographic entries in Bibster, an application ontology and a domain ontology [12]. Bibster makes a rather strong commitment to the application ontology, but the domain ontology can be easily substituted to allow for the adaption to different domains. Bibster uses the SWRC ontology as application ontology while the domain ontology

---

[4] `http://bibster.semanticweb.org/`

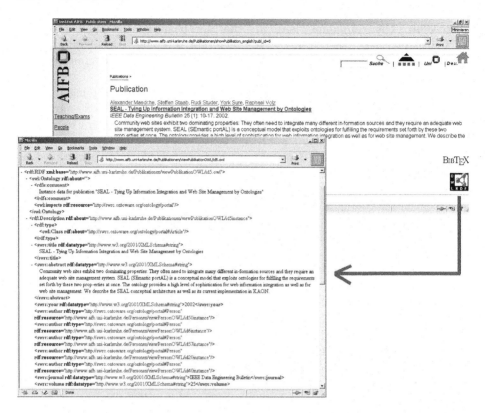

Fig. 3. Every page on Publications, Persons or Projects in the AIFB portal has its OWL annotation

is used for classification of metadata entries, enabling advanced querying and browsing. It describes topic hierarchies using relations such as subTopic, related-Topic, etc. In Bibster, we use the ACM Topic Hierarchy[5] as the default domain ontology. This topic hierarchy describes specific categories of literature for the Computer Science domain. It covers large areas of computer science, containing over 1287 topics ordered using taxonomic relations, e.g.: subTopic(Artificial Intelligence, Knowledge Representation Formalisms). Bibster relies on BibToOnto https://sourceforge.net/bibtoonto to automatically extract an ontology-based representation of the bibliographic metadata from plain BibTeX files. It also automatically classifies bibliographic entries according to the ACM topic hierarchy.

5.3   COIN Community Ontology

While the SWRC ontology itself is directed at modelling the explicit objects and relationships in the academic domain, it does not cover the implicit col-

---
[5] http://www.acm.org/class/1998/

laborations and interests of the researchers – or users – in general. The COIN community ontology is an extension to SWRC to support modelling of *communities of interest* [13] and aims at capturing the membership of users in communities of interest, the knowledge flow within a community and relevant community resources. Together, the SWRC+COIN ontologies provide a flexible means for modelling knowledge communities, their people, individual roles played in the communities, the status of a community in its life cycle and relevant events or publications. SWRC+COIN strictly extends SWRC through additional concepts, subconcepts and additional restrictions on OWL properties and the like.

6   Related Work

BIB TEX is a metadata format for modelling bibliography entries used within the LATEX document preparation system. LATEX which can be used on most every operating system is a well known system for typesetting documents and is used often in the scientific and academia communities or by commercial publishers. LATEX itself is based on TeX an initial typesetting system developed by Donald Knuth. BIBTEX is on the one hand a metadata standard and on the other hand a system for managing bibliographic entries obtaining these data from bibliographic databases. The metadata format and program was developed in 1985 by Oren Patashnik and Leslie Lamport [14]. BIBTEX provides metadata attributes (entry types) for nearly every kind of bibliographic entry which has its own set of attributes describing a reference. The tag-based syntax of BIBTEX is at the moment the most well-known (exchange-) format for bibliography metadata, especially on the World Wide Web.

The *Dublin Core (DC)* metadata standard is an attribute-value based set for describing a wide range of resources. It was developed during 1995 and 1996 as a response to the need to improve retrieval of information resources, especially on the World Wide Web. The DC standard includes two levels: Simple and Qualified. Simple DC comprises fifteen elements; Qualified DC includes an additional element, Audience, as well as a group of element refinements (or qualifiers) that refine the semantics of the elements in ways that may be useful in resource discovery. The semantics of DC have been established by an international, cross-disciplinary group of professionals from librarianship, computer science, text encoding, the museum community, and other related fields of scholarship and practice.

FOAF, or 'Friend of a Friend', provides a way to create machine-readable Web documents, mainly for people (their interests, relationships and activities), groups and companies. Therefore the FOAF project uses a vocabulary to provide a collection of basic terms that can be used in these Web documents and to express relations about things in the world. The initial focus of FOAF has been on the description of people. Founded by Dan Brickley and Libby Miller, FOAF is an open community-lead initiative which is tackling head-on the wider Semantic Web goal of creating a machine processable web of data. Technically, FOAF is an RDF/XML Semantic Web vocabulary. FOAF documents are most commonly used as a way of representing information about people in a way that is easily processed, merged and aggregated.

SIOC (Semantically Interlinked Online Communities)[6] describes discussion forums and posts of online community sites. SIOC is modeled as an ontology in RDFS whereby it reuses terms from DC and FOAF. The main focus of SIOC is to represent information about online communities. Hence, concepts like 'forum' and 'post' has been modelled. This technical oriented representation allows an easy application and integration of many communities and complements very well the SWRC so that we foresee possible future joint applications using SIOC and SWRC.

Closest to the SWRC are the *AKT reference ontology*[7] which is developed by the AKT project and e.g. is used in the CS AKTive Portal and the *Knowledge Web portal ontology*[8] which is developed by the Knowledge Web consortium and e.g. is used in the Knowledge Web portal. Both contain similar concepts and relationships as the SWRC ontology and serve a similar purpose. In fact, as has been shown in [15], it is fairly easy to generate mappings between the Knowledge Web portal and the SWRC (referenced in the deliverable as OntoWeb portal ontology) ontologies.

7   Conclusion

In this paper we have described the SWRC ontology – the Semantic Web Research Community Ontology, which models key entities in research communities. The SWRC ontology has its origin in early research projects in the Semantic Web Community and has been consecutively refined up to the current OWL version of the ontology which we have presented in this paper and is thus a good example for ontology reuse.

We have also presented a set of known usages for the ontology. The benefits of using, reusing and extending SWRC are obvious. On the one hand, the ontology in its current state is mature and has been agreed upon by many parties. It is therefore a good choice for a ready and established out-of-the-box ontology in the research domain, thus e.g. saving time and effort for building a comparable schema. On the other hand, using the SWRC ontology ensures inter-operability and easy data integration between different applications, for example between different portals. Future work may include optional modules for alignment with the related schemas pointed to in Section 6. To conclude, we believe that for making the Semantic Web reality the re-usage of ontologies and their continuous improvement by user communities is crucial. Our contribution aims to provide a description and usage guidelines to make the value of the SWRC explicit and to facilitate its re-use.

---

[6] http://rdfs.org/sioc/
[7] http://www.aktors.org/publications/ontology/
[8] http://knowledgeweb.semanticweb.org/

Acknowledgements. Research reported in this paper has been partially financed by EU in the IST projects OntoWeb (FP5-29243), SWAP (FP5-34103), Knowledge Web (FP6-507482) and SEKT (FP6-506826) and by the German Ministry for Education and Research (bmb+f) in the project SemiPort.

References

1. Benjamins, V.R., Fensel, D.: Community is knowledge! $(KA)^2$. In: Proceedings of the 11th Workshop on Knowledge Acquisition, Modeling, and Management (KAW '98), Banff, Canada. (1998)
2. Staab, S., Angele, J., Decker, S., Hotho, A., Maedche, A., Schnurr, H.P., Studer, R., Sure, Y.: Semantic community web portals. In: Proc. of Int. Conf. WWW9, Amsterdam, NL, May, 15-19, 2000, Elsevier (2000)
3. : Web ontology language (OWL). www.w3.org/2004/OWL/ (2004)
4. Antoniou, G., van Harmelen, F.: Web Ontology Language: OWL. In Staab, S., Studer, R., eds.: Handbook on Ontologies. Springer (2004) 67–92
5. Hitzler, P., Studer, R., Sure, Y.: Description logic programs: A practical choice for the modelling of ontologies. In: 1st Workshop on Formal Ontologies Meet Industry, FOMI'05, Verona, Italy, June 2005. (2005)
6. Grosof, B., Horrocks, I., Volz, R., Decker, S.: Description logic programs: Combining logic programs with description logics. In: Proc. of WWW 2003, Budapest, Hungary, May 2003, ACM (2003) 48–57
7. Noy, N.: Representing classes as property values on the semantic web. Technical report, W3C (2005) http://www.w3.org/TR/swbp-classes-as-values/.
8. Ehrig, M., Haase, P., Stojanovic, N., Hefke, M.: Similarity for ontologies - a comprehensive framework. In: 13th European Conference on Information Systems. (2005)
9. Maedche, A., Staab, S., Studer, R., Sure, Y., Volz, R.: SEAL – tying up information integration and web site management by ontologies. IEEE Computer Society Data Engineering Bulletin, Special Issue on Organizing and Discovering the Semantic Web **25** (2002) 10–17
10. Hartmann, J., Sure, Y.: An infrastructure for scalable, reliable semantic portals. IEEE Intelligent Systems **19** (2004) 58–65
11. Haase, P., et al.: Bibster – a semantics-based bibliographic peer-to-peer system. In: Proc. of the 3rd Int. Semantic Web Conference, Hiroshima, Japan, 2004. Volume 3298 of LNCS., Springer (2004) 122–136
12. Guarino, N.: Formal ontology in information systems. In Guarino, N., ed.: Formal Ontology in Information Systems. Proceedings of FOIS'98, Trento, Italy, June 6-8, 1998, Amsterdam, IOS Press (1998) 3–15
13. Bloehdorn, S., Haase, P., Hefke, M., Sure, Y., Tempich, C.: Intelligent community lifecycle support. In: Proceedings of the 5th International Conference on Knowledge Management (I-KNOW 05). (2005)
14. Lamport, L.: LaTeX: A Document Preparation System. Addison-Wesley (1986)
15. Suárez-Figueroa, M.C., Gómez-Pérez, A., López-Cima, A.: Portal ontology. Knowledge Web Deliverable 1.6.2, UPM (2005)

Chapter 5

CMB 2005: Computational Methods in Bioinformatics

Introduction

Rui Camacho[1], Alexessander Alves[1], Joaquim Pinto da Costa[1],
and Paulo Azevedo[2]

[1] Universidade do Porto, Portugal
rcamacho@fe.up.pt, alves@ieee.org, jpcosta@fc.up.pt
[2] Universidade do Minho, Portugal
pja@di.uminho.pt

The Workshop on Computational Methods in Bioinformatics was held in Covilhã between the 5th and 8th December 2005, as part of the 12th Portuguese Conference on Artificial Intelligence.

The success of bioinformatics in recent years has been prompted by research in molecular biology and molecular medicine in initiatives like the human genome project. These initiatives gave rise to an exponential increase in the volume and diversification of data, including protein and gene data, nucleotide sequences and biomedical literature. The accumulation and exploitation of large-scale data bases prompts for new computational technology and for research into these issues. In this context, many widely successful computational models and tools used by biologists in these initiatives, such as clustering and classification methods for gene expression data, are based on artificial intelligence (AI) techniques. Hence, this workshop brought the opportunity to discuss applications of AI with an interdisciplinary character, exploring the interactions between sub-areas of AI and Bioinformatics.

This year we had ten accepted papers focusing on up-to-date and highly relevant topics of Computational Bioinformatics. Papers reporting interesting work in progress were also accepted to be presented as posters.

The full papers address the following themes: Classification of protein sequences, Functional Genomics, Quantum Evolutionary Algorithms, and Text Mining and Database Integration. All of the above mentioned themes are of the out-most importance in the field of Bioinformatics. We hope the reader considers the work reported in the papers as useful contributions in Bioinformatics.

Our special thanks to the members of the Program Committee for their work in the reviewing process allowing us to have three reviewers per paper. We would like to thank Marco Costa and Nuno Fonseca for helping us in the review process.

Finally, our word of appreciation to all the authors who have submitted papers to the workshop, without whom none of this would have been possible.

C. Bento, A. Cardoso, and G. Dias (Eds.): EPIA 2005, LNAI 3808, p. 235, 2005.
© Springer-Verlag Berlin Heidelberg 2005

Protein Sequence Classification Through Relevant Sequence Mining and Bayes Classifiers

Pedro Gabriel Ferreira* and Paulo J. Azevedo**

University of Minho,
Department of Informatics,
Campus of Gualtar, 4710-057 Braga, Portugal
{pedrogabriel, pja}@di.uminho.pt

Abstract. We tackle the problem of sequence classification using relevant subsequences found in a dataset of protein labelled sequences. A subsequence is *relevant* if it is frequent and has a minimal length. For each query sequence a vector of features is obtained. The features consist in the number and average length of the relevant subsequences shared with each of the protein families. Classification is performed by combining these features in a Bayes Classifier. The combination of these characteristics results in a multi-class and multi-domain method that is exempt of data transformation and background knowledge. We illustrate the performance of our method using three collections of protein datasets. The performed tests showed that the method has an equivalent performance to state of the art methods in protein classification.

1 Introduction

Concerning data where an order relation between atomic elements occurs, sequence data appears as a natural representation. An important and very useful operation to be done over sequence data is classification. The problem of classifying sequence data is to take a given set of class labelled sequences and build up a procedure to *a posteriori* assign labels to unlabelled sequences (queries). Many examples of the application of this task can be found in a variety of domains. Consider the case of biology/bioinformatics field where given a database of nucleotide sequences (DNA/RNA) or amino-acids sequences. Portions of the former sequences code for the latter through two mechanisms: *transcription* and *translation* [12, 6]. A sequence of amino-acids constitute a protein and is hereafter called as a protein sequence. A possible scenario would be the case where a biologist wants to find the respective family/domain or function of an unclassified sequence, for example a new synthesized protein. This problem is of critical

---

* Supported by a PhD Scholarship from Fundação para Ciência e Tecnologia, Ministério da Ciência e Ensino Superior of Portugal.
** Supported by POSI/2001/CLASS project, sponsored by Fundação Ciência e Tecnologia and European program FEDER.

C. Bento, A. Cardoso, and G. Dias (Eds.): EPIA 2005, LNAI 3808, pp. 236–247, 2005.
© Springer-Verlag Berlin Heidelberg 2005

importance due to the exponential growth of newly generated sequence data in the last years, which demands for automatic methods for sequence classification. In the problem of sequence categorization/classification three types of methods can be distinguished:

- The *Direct Sequence Classifiers*, that exploit the sequential nature of data by directly comparing the similarity between sequences. Example of these type of classifiers is the k-Nearest Neighbour. In this method the class label of the k most similar sequences in respect to the query sequence are used to vote on a decision. Sequence similarity can be assessed through a method like FASTA [17] or BLAST [1].
- The *Feature based Sequence Classifiers*, that work by first extracting and model a set of features from the sequences and then adapt those features to accomplish with the traditional techniques, like decision trees, rule based classifiers, SVM's and many others. In [15, 16, 5, 4, 21] we have examples of these type of methods.
- The *Probabilistic Model Classifiers*, that work by simulating the sequence family under consideration. Typical probabilistic classifiers are the simple and k-order Markov Chain [19], Hidden Markon Models [14] and Probabilistic Suffix Trees [11].

Recently Probabilistic Suffix Trees (PSTs) [11] and Sparse Markov Transducers (SMTs) [8] have been applied in the protein classification problem, and have shown superior performance. A PST is essentially a variable length Markov Model, where the probability of a symbol in a sequence depends on the previous symbols. The number of previous considered symbols is variable and context dependent. The prediction of an input sequence is done symbol by symbol. The probability of a symbol is obtained by finding the longest subsequence that appears in the tree and ends just before the symbol. These probabilities are then combined to determine the overall probability of the sequence in respect to a database of sequences. One of the disadvantages of the PSTs is that the conditional probabilities of the symbols rely on exact subsequence matches. In protein family classification this becomes a limitation since substitutions of symbols by equivalent ones is often very frequent. SMTs are a generalization of PSTs that support wild-cards. A wild-card is a symbol that denotes a gap of size one and matches any symbol on the alphabet. In [11] an experimental evaluation has shown that PSTs perform much better than a typical BLAST search and as good as HMM. This is very interesting since the latter approach makes use of multiple alignments and the families are usually defined based on an HMM [9]. Additionally PSTs are a totally automotive method without prior knowledge (multiple alignments or score matrices) or any human intervention. In [8], SMTs have shown to outperform PSTs.

Our motivation to this work is to suggest a robust and adaptable classification method using a straightforward algorithm. We propose a multi-class sequence classification method which can be applied to data in many different domains, in particular to protein sequence data without requiring any type of data transformation, background knowledge or multiple alignment. Our proposal fits under the *direct sequence classifiers* type described before.

2   Preliminaries

Our method exploits global and local similarity of the sequences by extracting common subsequence patterns of different sizes that occur along the query sequence and the sequence families. These same patterns can then be used to interpret and understand the classification results.

Since our main concern is protein datasets we are only considering the alphabet of amino-acids. Each symbol of the sequence is generically called as an *event* and the distance between consecutive events as *gaps*. Considering the definition of a pattern as $A_1 - x(p_1, q_1) - A_2 - x(p_2, q_2) - \ldots - A_n$ where A_i are amino-acids and $-x-$ gaps greater than p_i and smaller than q_i, then two types of patterns can be distinguished:

- **Rigid Gap Patterns** only contain gaps with a fixed length, i.e. $p_i = q_i, \forall i$ The symbol "." is a wild-card symbol used to denote a gap of size one and it matches any symbol of the alphabet. Ex: $MN..A.CA$
- **Flexible Gap Patterns** allow a variable number of gaps between events of the sequence, i.e. $p_i \leq q_i, \forall i$. Ex: A-x(1,3)-C-x(4,6)-D.

The idea behind our method is that a sequence can be classified based on its *relevant* subsequences. A (sub)sequence is *relevant* if it is:

- *Frequent*, i.e. appears in at least an user defined number (*minimum support*) of database sequences.
- Has a *non trivial length*, i.e. satisfies a minimal defined length.

The problem that we address in this work can be formulated as follows: *Given a collection D of previously classified sequences, an unclassified query sequence, a minimum support (σ) and a minimal sequence length, determine the similarity of the query sequence w.r.t all the classes present in D.*

2.1   Sequence Patterns

Protein sequences of the same family typically share common subsequences, also called motifs. These subsequences are possibly implied in a structural or biological function of the family and have been preserved through the protein evolution. Thus, if a sequence shares patterns with other sequences it is expected that the sequences are biologically related.

Since the protein alphabet is small, many small patterns that express trivial local similarity may arise. Therefore, longer patterns are expected to express greater confidence in the sequences similarity.

Considering the two types of patterns, rigid gap patterns reveal better conserved regions of similarity. On the other hand, flexible gap patterns have a greater probability of occur by chance, having a smaller biological significance.

3   Method

Sequence pattern mining [20, 18, 2, 13] is the task of finding frequent patterns along the sequence data. A pattern is considered to be frequent if it occurs in the data sequences a number of times greater than a pre-determined threshold, called *support*. Besides providing valuable information about the data, these patterns have application in many areas like clustering or classification.

In this work we will make use of a method that consists in an adaptation of a sequence pattern mining algorithm [10] designed for the task of protein mining. The method reports all the frequent patterns occurring in a query sequence in respect to a user defined database. The query sequence is used to drive the mining process ensuring containment of the reported patterns. The algorithm allows a refined analysis by enumerating frequent patterns that eventually occur in a small subset of the database sequences. Two types of patterns (described in section 2), with variable or fixed length spacing between events, satisfying the user restrictions and associated options can be identified. The restrictions or constraints that the algorithm supports are:

- *Item Constraints*: restricts the set of the events (*excludedEventsSet*) that may appear in the sequence patterns,
- *Gap Constraints*: defines the (*minGap*) minimum distance or the maximum distance (*maxGap*) that may occur between two adjacent events in the sequence patterns,
- *Duration or Window Constraints*: defines the maximum distance (*window*) between the first and the last event of the sequence patterns.

Given a query sequence S and a collection of protein families D, applying the above algorithm, two parameters are obtained: *number of relevant patterns* and *average length of the patterns*. This information is then combined to determine the probability of S belonging to one of the families in D.

3.1   Bayes Classifier

The naïve Bayes Classifier is a simple probabilistic classifier. It is based on a probabilistic model that requires strong independence assumptions of the variables involved. Nevertheless, even in the cases where the independence assumption is not strictly satisfied the classifier performs well on a variety of situations, including complex real world situations [7]. The goal of the classifier is to assign a probability to one of the classes in $\{C_1, C_2, \ldots, C_n\}$, based on a d-dimensional vector of observed parameters, $\overrightarrow{f} = f_1 \ldots f_m$. This can be expressed through a conditional probability relation in the form $P(C_i | \overrightarrow{f})$. Using the Bayes Theorem this can be written as:

$$P(C_i | \overrightarrow{f}) = \frac{P(C_i) \times P(\overrightarrow{f} | C_i)}{P(\overrightarrow{f})} \tag{1}$$

$P(C_i)$ is known as the apriori probability of the class and can be obtained through the relative occurrence of C_i in the data. Since $P(\overrightarrow{f})$ is class independent its value can be expressed as a constant value. Thus, equation 1 can be rewritten as:

$$P(C_i|\overrightarrow{f}) = \alpha_i \times \prod_{j=1}^{n} P(f_j|C_i) \tag{2}$$

where α_i is a constant value for the respective class C_i. For our classification problem, the vector consist only of two parameters: total number and average length of the extracted relevant subsequences. We assume that they are statistically independent, although this is not entirely the case.

In our work three different models are studied and compared. These models are slightly variations of the model in 2. In the first model (A), the apriori probability of the class is not taken into account, thus in equation 2: $\alpha_i = 1\ \forall_i$.

When a query sequence S is analyzed against a database D, it is naturally expected that the number of extracted patterns is proportional to the number of sequences in D. To avoid the bias due to the different databases length the probability is normalized by the length of the class. In equation 2, $\alpha_i = \frac{N}{|C_i|}$ where $N = \sum_{i=1}^{n} C_i$, i.e. it corresponds to the inverse of the apriori probability of C_i. Finally, in model C, the parameter "average length" is given a greater relative weight than the parameter "number of patterns" and in equation 2, $P(f = avgLength|C_i)$ is raised to a power of three.

Now for the three models, and given the feature vector $\overrightarrow{f}$ of a sequence S, the classification is simply given by:

$$max\{P(\overrightarrow{f}|C_i)\ \forall_i\} \tag{3}$$

4   Results and Discussion

To evaluate our method, we configured our query driven miner to extract rigid gap patterns. Only two types of constraints were applied: maxGap and Window, with a value of 15 and 20, respectively. These constraints allow a confinement of the search space and make possible the mining in interactive time. The minimal length of the extracted patterns is two. We used three collections of protein families. A smaller collection was obtained from Pfam [9] version 17.0. Most of the proteins in this collection were taken from the top twenty list of April 2005. This collection gave us the first insights in the performance of the method. The second collection is composed of 50 sequences, obtained from Pfam version 1.0, and can be downloaded from [9]. This set of families was already used in [8] and will allow a direct comparison with the PSTs and SMTs. Due to the constant refinement in the topology of the PFam database we should note that there are significant differences in the families common to the two collections. The third dataset consist on 27 families from the receptors group entries on the Prosite [3] database.

All the methods are assessed based on the precision rate (PR) measure:

$$PR = \frac{NumCorrect}{NumTested} \times 100\% \tag{4}$$

The method was evaluated using the "leave-one-out" methodology[1]. The classification result is determined by equation 4. The evaluation in [11] and [8] was different from ours. They used 4/5 of the family sequences to build a model for the respective family and evaluated the model with the remaining 1/5 of the sequences. Unfortunately, since there is no indication on how the folds were created, their experiment could not be totally recreated.

The only parameter required by our model is the support value. Since we do not have a way to apriori define this value, it was determined empirically. For each family we measured the average time to mine the largest, the smallest and two medium size sequences of the respective family. If the average time was approximately below one minute than that support value was used for that family. The reason for the use of this criterion is that the performance of the mining process directly depends on the support value and on the density (similarity between the sequences) of the family. Thus, if the support is set to low values in the more dense families the mining process becomes very time consuming.

All the experiments were performed on 1.5GHz Intel Centrino machine with 512MB of main memory, running windows XP Professional. The mining application was written in C++ language.

In table 1 we present the classification results for the collection of 26 protein families. In the left columns we have the name, the number and the average length of the sequences in the family. The intra similarity of the family is also presented (see [9]). The fifth column shows the support used to mine the respective family. In the right side of the table, the precision rate for the three probabilistic models of our method is presented. The last column shows the average time that it takes to mine each sequence of the family. This value has to be multiplied by the total number of families to give the total amount of time spent mining the sequence against all the families. From the presented results we can see that the prediction rate is around or above the 80%, except for the PPR and the TPR-1 family. In these cases, the number of missed sequences is extremely large. These results can be explained due to a combination of small intra-similarity, low average length and a large family size, resulting in a relative small number of common patterns shared by the sequences of the family. On the other hand, the small length of the sequences leads the query sequences to share more patterns with the families with a greater average length. Model B gives particularly bad results for these cases since the multiplication factor imposes a big penalty in the classification probability. Table 2 shows the average classification results for table 1, when all the families are considered (row 2), when the family PPR is left out (row 3) and when PPR and TPR are both left out of the classification (row 4).

In table 3 we compare the three probabilistic models with the results from the PSTs and SMTs published in [11, 8]. In the last row of the table we present the average classification results. We can see that the precision rates of all classifiers are above the 90% threshold and that SMT ranks at the top. We should remind that this is a raw comparison since different evaluation methods were used.

---

[1] The complete set of the results and the datasets can be obtained from the authors.

Table 1. Classification results of the three models, for the collection of 26 sequences from Pfam 17.0

Name	Size	AvgLen	Intra-Sim	Supp.	A(%)	B(%)	C(%)	Time(secs)
7tm-1	64	269	19	2	100.0	100.0	100.0	0.18
7tm-2	33	263	25	2	100.0	100.0	100.0	2.65
7tm-3	30	256	27	2	100.0	100.0	100.0	3.34
AAA	245	194	25	2	95.3	88.4	97.7	0.26
ABC-tran	65	191	26	2	100.0	100.0	100.0	0.22
ATP-synt-A	30	162	52	2	78.6	96.4	89.3	0.20
ATP-synt-ab	157	232	54	6	98.9	98.9	98.9	1.29
ATP-synt-C	35	69	49	2	93.9	97.0	97.0	0.09
c2	409	76	23	2	89.2	46.7	91.3	0.13
CLP-protease	88	182	41	2	91.8	85.9	94.1	0.14
COesterase	129	541	27	2	86.5	58.7	87.3	1.73
cox1	24	461	48	2	90.9	90.9	90.9	0.41
cox2	32	117	60	2	96.7	100.0	100.0	0.43
Cys-knot	24	103	37	2	95.5	100.0	100.0	0.09
Cytochrom-B-C	9	101	74	2	100.0	100.0	100.0	1.61
Cytochrom-B-N	8	199	69	2	85.7	100.0	85.7	0.15
HCV-NS1	10	347	51	2	100.0	100.0	100.0	6.90
Oxidored-q1	33	284	28	2	90.3	93.5	93.5	0.26
Pkinase	54	274	24	2	98.1	90.4	96.2	0.21
PPR	558	36	20	2	11.9	0.0	22.6	0.03
RuBisCO-large	17	310	79	10	81.3	87.5	81.3	0.72
rvt-1	164	219	74	4	76.5	75.5	79.6	0.23
RVT-thumb	42	71	89	4	88.2	97.1	91.2	2.84
TPR-1	569	35	18	2	43.6	10.5	54.9	0.04
zf-C2H2	196	25	37	2	83.6	64.0	88.4	0.03
zf-CCHC	208	19	51	2	100.0	100.0	100.0	0.04

For our method all the sequences were evaluated, in this sense our evaluation provides more confidence on the presented results. Besides, at the cost of an extra computational work, the precision of a class can be increased by setting the support of that class to a lower value.

We applied a two-tailed signed rank test [22] to study if the medians of the classifiers C, PST and SMT are statistically equal. It was tested as a null hypothesis that medians for the pairs of classifiers C and PST, C and SMT are equal. For the first pair, the null hypothesis is rejected, thus the medians of the

Table 2. Average classification results for the collection of 26 proteins from Pfam 17.0

PrecisionRate	A(%)	B(%)	C(%)
All	87.6	83.9	90.0
without PPR	90.6	87.3	92.7
without PPR and TPR	92.5	90.5	94.3

Table 3. Classification results of the three models, PSTs and SMTs, for the collection of 50 sequences from Pfam 1.0

Name	Supp	Size	A(%)	B(%)	C(%)	PST(%)	SMT(%)	Time(secs)
7tm-1	14	530	90.2	41.3	90.4	93.0	97.0	0.34
7tm-2	3	36	97.2	97.2	97.2	94.4	97.2	1.32
7tm-3	3	12	100.0	100.0	100.0	83.3	100.0	0.57
AAA	15	79	87.3	89.9	89.9	87.9	94.9	0.37
ABC-tran	20	330	92.1	62.7	94.8	83.6	93.3	0.43
actin	100	160	86.3	86.3	86.9	97.2	97.5	0.80
ATP-synt-A	7	79	82.3	82.3	83.5	92.4	94.9	0.09
ATP-synt-ab	12	183	88.5	84.2	90.7	91.9	96.8	15.68
ATP-synt-C	14	62	96.8	98.4	100.0	96.7	100.0	0.10
c2	15	101	95.0	95.0	94.1	92.3	96.0	0.08
COesterase	5	62	91.9	93.5	88.7	91.7	90.3	0.35
cox1	4	80	100.0	100.0	100.0	83.8	97.5	0.17
cox2	10	114	91.2	91.2	93.0	98.2	95.6	1.27
Cys-Knot	2	61	86.9	91.8	91.8	93.4	100.0	0.07
Cys-protease	4	95	94.7	94.7	94.7	87.9	95.1	4.94
DAG-PE-bind	2	108	97.2	97.2	99.1	89.7	95.4	5.82
DNA-methylase	2	57	86.0	100.0	89.5	83.3	91.2	0.71
DNA-pol	4	51	88.2	98.0	94.1	80.4	88.2	0.35
E1-E2-ATPase	20	117	94.9	80.3	94.0	93.1	94.0	0.18
EGF	2	676	99.6	97.8	99.6	89.3	98.8	0.05
FGF	7	39	100.0	100.0	100.0	97.4	100.0	2.53
GATase	2	69	94.2	100.0	95.7	88.4	94.2	0.12
GTP-EFTU	40	184	91.3	82.6	92.4	91.8	98.4	0.23
HLH	3	133	97.7	95.5	98.5	94.7	98.5	0.05
HPS70	25	171	88.9	80.7	94.7	95.7	98.2	0.35
HSP20	40	132	97.0	95.5	97.0	94.6	96.2	0.14
HTH-1	2	101	100.0	100.0	100.0	84.2	85.1	0.11
HTH-2	2	65	89.2	93.8	90.8	85.7	81.5	0.09
KH-domain	2	51	88.2	90.2	88.2	88.9	84.0	2.30
Kunitz-BPTI	2	79	98.7	100.0	100.0	90.9	92.3	7.30
MCP-signal	7	24	100.0	100.0	100.0	83.3	100.0	0.20
MHC-I	125	151	97.4	96.7	98.0	98.0	100.0	0.60
NADHdh	3	61	96.7	98.4	96.7	93.0	98.4	0.18
PGK	10	51	90.2	98.0	98.0	94.1	98.0	0.46
PH	5	77	93.5	94.8	96.1	93.3	83.1	4.36
Pribosyltran	4	45	86.7	93.3	88.9	88.9	95.6	0.11
RIP	3	37	86.5	91.9	89.2	94.6	91.9	0.13
RuBisCO-large	250	311	99.7	98.7	99.7	98.7	99.7	9.79
RuBisCO-small	20	107	98.1	97.2	99.1	97.0	99.1	4.86
s4	28	54	87.0	92.6	90.7	92.6	96.3	0.12
s12	12	60	85.0	90.0	90.0	96.7	100.0	1.20
SH2	3	150	100.0	98.0	100.0	96.1	98.7	0.10
SH3	2	161	98.8	98.1	98.8	88.3	96.9	12.31
STphosphatase	15	88	100.0	100.0	100.0	94.2	97.7	6.37
TGF-beta	15	79	92.4	92.4	92.4	92.4	98.7	0.14
TIM	4	42	95.2	100.0	97.6	92.5	100.0	0.15
TNFc6	2	91	79.1	89.0	81.3	86.2	93.4	0.04
UPAR-c6	2	18	94.4	100.0	94.4	85.7	94.4	0.68
Y-phosphatase	8	122	87.7	83.6	89.3	91.3	96.7	0.04
Zn-clus	2	54	96.3	100.0	96.3	81.5	90.7	0.05
Avg. PR(%)			93.1	93.3	94.5	91.0	95.4	

Table 4. Identifier of the Prosite entries (Dataset), number of sequences in the Swiss-Prot database that match the respective entry and the relative support value used for sequence classification

Dataset	Size	support(%)	Dataset	Size	support(%)
ps00236	772	0.03	ps00790	101	0.2
ps00237	8522	0.017	ps00950	121	0.2
ps00238	862	0.03	ps00952	52	0.35
ps00239	157	0.05	ps00969	89	0.05
ps00240	119	0.06	ps00979	82	0.12
ps00242	170	0.03	ps01026	36	0.08
ps00243	116	0.3	ps01156	417	0.025
ps00244	22	0.99	ps01212	82	0.15
ps00419	521	0.18	ps01352	104	0.11
ps00421	226	0.05	ps01353	66	0.03
ps00458	20	0.5	ps01354	48	0.05
ps00538	44	0.2	ps01355	71	0.08
ps00649	233	0.04	ps01356	33	0.2
ps00652	372	0.014			

classifiers are significantly different. In the second case the null hypothesis is accepted, consequently there is no significant difference between the medians for the classifiers C and SMT, with a level of significance of 0.05 and a p-value of 0.34.

In terms of computational demands, our method has low requirements. Since the mining algorithm only counts and does not collect the frequent patterns, it required a maximum of 5 MB of memory usage. This is in contrast with HMMs, PSTs and SMTs which are known to have high memory requirements.

As a last experiment we selected a set of proteins that match the patterns in the group of Receptors from the PROSITE [3] database. This group contains 27 entries matching a total of 13458 protein sequences. Table 4 contains the name and the size of each group of sequences and the respective support used. Next, we randomly selected 30% of the sequences of each group. Based on the percentage of the true positives (main diagonal) and false negatives we built a similarity matrix for the 27 groups of sequences. Figure 1 displays the similarity matrix, where each row and column represent the entries listed in table 4. Dark areas represent a higher number of class hits.

4.1   Factors That Affect the Performance of the Method

Although we do not have the exact values, we verified that all the protein families in the second dataset, have a high intra-similarity. This explains the high precision values of the three methods in the second evaluation.

From the three probabilistic models of our method, the one with higher precision in the performed evaluations is model C. It seems that the average length of the patterns has a bigger impact in the sequence classification. As naturally expected, the lower it is the support value the higher the precision rate of the

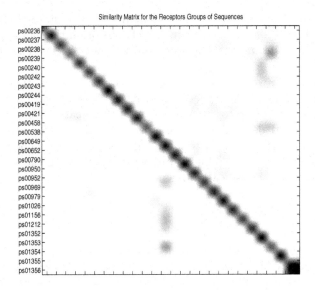

Fig. 1. Similarity Matrix for the classification performed on the 27 families of the set of sequences that match the entries in the Prosite Database

models is. Lower support values allow finding more common patterns between the query sequence and smaller subsets of families sequences. The support values used for the two evaluations establish a reasonable trade-off between the performance and the precision of the method. A very important aspect of this method is that the extracted motifs reveal local and global similarity. One of the aspects pointed in [8] for the success of SMTs is the use of common short subsequences patterns that contain wild-cards. These wild-cards allow to describe the positions of the patterns that can be occupied by two or more amino-acids. Our method incorporates this feature through the rigid gap patterns. We do not include any type of biological information. We believe that the introduction of Equivalent/ Substitution sets of amino-acids can further improve the precision of the method. These sets will permit that during the mining process an event can be substituted by another event belonging to the same set without lost of equivalence. Additionally, the introduction of a discrimination score for the most biological or statistical relevant patterns may result in another improvement.

5   Conclusions and Future Work

In this article we presented a method of straightforward implementation to perform multi-class and multi-domain sequence classification. The method does not require background knowledge or any change in the sequence representation. It extracts two features, number and average length of the frequent patterns, which the query sequence has in relation to the sequences families. These features are then combined through a Bayesian classifier. We present three probabilistic models based on this classifier. When compared to two state-of-the-art methods, PSTs and SMTs, for protein sequence classification the method shows very promising results. Our method performs better than PSTs and has an equivalent performance to SMTs.

As a future work, we plan to evaluate and compare our method with collections of protein families with lower homology. We believe that our method may have superior performance to other methods in those cases. We are also seeking for a way to apriori determine the support value to be used for each family. Finally, we aim to extend our pattern mining process to determine the biological significance of the patterns. This will allow discriminating the weight of each pattern in the overall classification results.

References

1. Stephen F. Altschul, Thomas L. Madden, Alejandro A. Schaeffer, Jinghui Zhang, Zheng Zhang, Webb Miller, and David J. Lipman. Gapped BLAST and PSI-BLAST: a new generation of protein database search programs. *Nucleic Acids Research*, 25:3389–3402, 1997.
2. J. Ayres, J. Flannick, J. Gehrke, and T. Yiu. Sequential pattern mining using a bitmap representation. In *Proceedings of the 8th International Conference of Knowledge Discovery and Data Mining SIGKDD, S. Francisco, July 2002.*, pages 429–435, 2002.
3. A. Bairoch. Prosite: a dictionary of sites and patterns in proteins. *Nucleic Acids Res*, 25(19):2241–2245, 1991.
4. A. Ben-Hur and D. Brutlag. Remote homology detection:a motif based approach. *Bioinformatics*, 19(1):26–33, 2003.
5. A. Ben-Hur and D. Brutlag. Sequence motifs: highly predictive features of protein function. In *In Proceeding of Workshop on Feature Selection, NIPS - Neural Information Processing Systems*, December 2003.
6. Necia Grant Cooper. *The Human Genome Project, Dechiphering the blueprint of heredity*, volume 1. University Science Books, 1994.
7. P. Domingos and M. Pazzani. Beyond independence: Conditions for the optimality of the simple bayesian classifier. In *International Conference on Machine Learning*, pages 105–112, 1996.
8. E. Eskin, W. N. Grundy, and Y. Singer. Biological sequence analysis: Probabilistic models of proteins and nucleic acids. *Journal of Computational Biology 10(2)*, pages 187–214, 2003.
9. A. Bateman et al. The pfam protein families database. *Nucleic Acids Research*, vol 32, Database issue, October 2003.
10. Pedro Ferreira and Paulo Azevedo. Protein sequence pattern mining with constraints. In *Proceedings of 9th European Conference on Principles and Practice of Knowledge Discovery in Databases (PKDD)*, Porto, October 2005.
11. Bejerano G. and Yona G. Modeling protein families using probabilistic suffix trees. In ACM press, editor, *In the proceedings of RECOMB1999*, pages 15–24, 1999.
12. Lawrence Hunter. Molecular biology for computer scientists (artificial intelligence & molecular biology).
13. A.Floratos I. Rigoutsos. Combinatorial pattern discovery in biological sequences: the teiresias algorithm. *Bioinformatics*, 1(14), January 1998.

14. Mian Sojlander Krogh, Brown and Haussler. Hidden markov models in computational biology: applications to protein modeling. *Journal of Molecular Biology*, (235):1501–1531, 1994.
15. Daniel Kudenko and Haym Hirsh. Feature generation for sequence categorization. In *AAAI/IAAI*, pages 733–738, 1998.
16. Neal Lesh, Mohammed J. Zaki, and Mitsunori Ogihara. Mining features for sequence classification. In *Proceedings of the fifth ACM SIGKDD international conference on Knowledge discovery and data mining*, pages 342–346. ACM Press, 1999.
17. R.W. Pearson and D.J. Lipman. Improved tools for biological sequence comparison. *Proceedings Natl. Academy Sciences USA*, 5:2444–2448, 1998.
18. J. Pei, J. Han, B. Mortazavi-Asl, H. Pinto, Q. Chen, U. Dayal, and M.-C. Hsu. PrefixSpan mining sequential patterns efficiently by prefix projected pattern growth. In *Proceedings Int. Conf. Data Engineering (ICDE'01), Heidelberg, Germany, April 2001*, pages 215–226, 2001.
19. Durbin R. and Eddy S. R. Biological sequence analysis: Probabilistic models of proteins and nucleic acids. *Cambridge University Press*, 1998.
20. Ramakrishnan Srikant and Rakesh Agrawal. Mining sequential patterns: Generalizations and performance improvements. In Peter M. G. Apers, Mokrane Bouzeghoub, and Georges Gardarin, editors, *Proc. 5th Int. Conf. Extending Database Technology, EDBT*, volume 1057, pages 3–17. Springer-Verlag, 25–29, 1996.
21. N.M. Zaki, R.M. Ilias, and S. Derus. A comparative analysis of protein homology detection methods. *Journal of Theoretics*, 5-4, 2003.
22. J. H. Zar. *Biostatistical Analysis 3rd Edition*. Prentice Hall, 1999.

CONAN: An Integrative System for Biomedical Literature Mining

Rainer Malik and Arno Siebes

Universiteit Utrecht, Institute for Information and Computing Sciences,
PO Box 80.089, 3508TB Utrecht, The Netherlands
rainer@cs.uu.nl

Abstract. The amount of information about the genome, transcriptome
and proteome, forms a problem for the scientific community: how to find
the right information in a reasonable amount of time. Most research aiming to solve this problem, however, concentrate on a certain organism or
a very limited dataset. Complementary to those algorithms, we developed CONAN, a system which provides a full-scale approach, tailored
to experimentalists, designed to combine several information extraction
methods and connect the outcome of these methods to gather novel information. Its methods include tagging of gene/protein names, finding
interaction and mutation data, tagging of biological concepts, linking to
MeSH and Gene Ontology terms, which can all be found back by querying the system. We present a full-scale approach that will ultimately
cover all of PubMed/MEDLINE. We show that this universality has no
effect on quality: our system performs as well as existing systems.

1 Introduction

It is an often quoted fact that the number of articles in MEDLINE and PubMed
is growing exponentially [1]. The problem for the scientist is that interesting
and useful information, like interaction data and mutation data, could appear
in papers they have not read. Therefore, important facts might get overlooked
and the scientific work might be affected. To overcome these problems, many
systems have been developed that search the literature automatically for the
relevant information [2]. Most systems, however, focus only on a very specific
aspect of literature, on a very limited dataset or on a certain organism.

Complementary to those systems, we want to address - as completely as
possible - the problem of experimentalists to find certain information "hidden"
in the abstracts of biomedical literature. We present here the first release of
CONAN, a system which is as complete as possible, offering a wide range of
information. This information is also combined to construct new information, e.g.
the output of a protein name tagging method is used as input for a method which
finds Protein-Protein-Interaction Data and as input to find protein synonyms.
Our system can be regarded as the "right-hand" of a scientist: given a query, it
hands the researcher back a set of essential results.

C. Bento, A. Cardoso, and G. Dias (Eds.): EPIA 2005, LNAI 3808, pp. 248–259, 2005.
© Springer-Verlag Berlin Heidelberg 2005

Our goal is not to find new algorithms, but to integrate interesting and important algorithms into one system. The system can be installed locally or accessed via a web-service.

The road map of this paper is as follows: In the next section, we describe the general architecture of CONAN and its components. In Section 3, we show the performance evaluation, and we discuss the results. In Section 4, we draw the conclusion and give future directions.

2   Approach

The general architecture is shown in Figure 1. It shows that MEDLINE XML Files, containing abstracts, serve as input for several processing steps, namely BLAST-searching and the tagging of Gene and Protein names. These Gene and Protein names serve as input for the detection of Protein-Protein-Interaction Data. Mutation Data is also extracted from the abstracts. MeSH- and Gene Ontology (GO)-terms serve as additional input, the data is combined and integrated in the Data Integrator-Step (see Section 2.4), before it gets stored in an XML-File. This XML-File can be queried directly by XPath-queries or via a Web-Interface, using pre-defined queries.

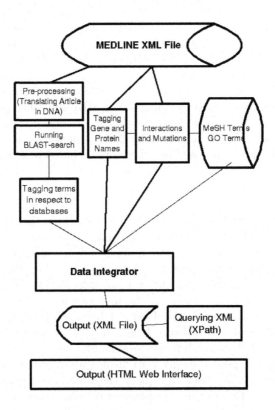

Fig. 1. Flow Diagram of CONAN

2.1   Input

MEDLINE. The basis of all the tagging and information extraction are the MEDLINE files released by the National Library of Medicine. The database contains over 12 million citations dating back to the mid-1960's. PubMed is the system which provides access to bibliographic information that includes MED-LINE [3]. Via a licensing system, users are allowed to download MEDLINE files or are able to get the files wanted on tape sent to them by the NCBI. These files are in the MEDLINE XML format. For this experiment, only articles were taken into account which are completed, meaning that it is the final version of articles which have an abstract and were written in English.

MeSH. The second source of information are the MeSH (Medical Subject Headings)-terms. MeSH (http://www.nlm.nih.gov/mesh) is the National Library of Medicine's controlled vocabulary thesaurus. It consists of sets of terms naming descriptors in a hierarchical structure that permits searching at various levels of specificity. MeSH terms are part of NCBI's MEDLINE distribution.

Gene Ontology. The third source of information is the Gene Ontology (GO) Database [4] and, more specifically, the current annotation of Uniprot terms by GO (GOA) [5]. The concept of GO is to develop three structured ontologies, namely Biological Processes, Cellular Components and Molecular Functions. Protein names found in text have a certain synonym in UniProt [6]. These synonyms again are annotated by the EBI, assigning GO-terms to Uniprot-terms.

ENSEMBL. As an additional source of information, for each gene/protein name found in text, the corresponding ENSEMBL-identifier is retrieved. EN-SEMBL [7] provides complete and consistent annotation across the human genome as well as other genomes. ENSEMBL identifiers are used as cross-references to other identifiers and are therefore included in our system.

2.2   Output

We designed our system to give scientists a tool to help them find and process valuable information in abstracts. What we want the system to achieve is to combine several sources of input, thereby finding "novel" knowledge in biomedical literature and presenting this knowledge to the user. The "novel" information should be accessible as easily as the original information. The data available consists of information per abstract. The user can use several entry points to gather information. Specific PubMed ID numbers (PMIDs), Protein and Gene Names, Protein-Protein-Interactions, Gene Ontology (GO) identifiers, UniProt identifiers or EnSeMBL codes, but also specific biological concepts like Cell, Cell Component or Cell Type can be given to display all information extracted from a particular abstract. The user can query the database in two different ways, discussed in the next two sections. Dependent on which way the researcher used the system, several of those questions can be combined to one query.

XML-Output. The basic output of CONAN is an XML file which holds all information about a certain abstract. For this XML file, a DTD (Document Type Definition) file was constructed which defines the legal building blocks of the XML document. This means that only specific types of data can be entered in the XML document. XML was chosen because it offers several benefits in regard to storing data, a major advantage being its platform-independency. The XML-file can be queried with several XML Query Languages (XQuery, XPath, XSLT). Using the query language, the researcher can combine several of the questions mentioned above.

HTML-Output. A web-server has been set up which allows users to query our results. The web-server was built using HTML, the XML database has been made accessible for querying via a web-server by using the server-side scripting language Perl. The querying of the XML-file is done via XPath (http://www.w3.org/TR/xpath) which allows to refine the query while still being fast enough. The overall goal of this server is to generate reliable results of biological information in biomedical abstracts, given user-defined input terms. This web-server is an internet-based application.

There are two main query systems: Quick Search and Advanced Search.

- When starting a Quick-Search session, the user has the option to give two different types of data as input: the PMID of an article, or the name of a gene or protein. The logical operators (AND,OR) can be used to combine several terms to one search term. When giving a PMID, the result page shows all information found in the specific abstract and all "novel knowledge" found by combining the different data sources.
- In an Advanced Search, the input can be a Gene name, a Protein name, an arbitrary keyword,a PMID or a gene ontology number. When giving a protein name, there is a possibility to search for an interaction or mutation where this protein is involved.
- In neither of these search-methods, it is currently possible to combine several questions to one query.

In both Search Methods, the results itself are links to different pages again.

There is no graphical visualization of the results yet, but there are plans to make this happen in the future.

2.3   Algorithms

In this section, we show the algorithms used in this system. For details about these methods, please refer to the original publications and to Table 1.

BLAST-Searching. The first method implemented is a BLAST-searching method first published by Krauthammer et al. [8]. It uses the BLAST-algorithm [9] to discover relevant biological information in text. In the original method, only gene and protein names were used.

Table 1. Overview of Methods and Algorithms used (derived from original publications)

Name	Measure
BLAST-Searching	Recall: 78.8%
	Precision: 71.7%
Gene/Protein-Tagging	Prediction correct: 77%
Mutation-Tagging	Sensitivity: 87.1%
	Specificity: 87.9%
Protein Tagging	Precision: 75%
	Recall: 76%

Table 2. Sample of Databases used in keyword search

Database	No. of Terms included
Gene	737801
Protein	41733
Organic Chemical	38258
Disease or Syndrome	36999
Therapeutic or Preventive Procedure	8328
Neoplastic Process	7791
Species	14121
Body Part, Organ or Organ Component	6555
Cell Component	818
Cell Function	456

In our approach, the original method was improved to extract even more information from an abstract. The UMLS Metathesaurus [10] is used by us to retrieve lists of biological relevant terms. These terms were split up into different databases, specified by their so-called Semantic Type. An example of this would be the terms "Cell Differentation" and "Endocytosis" which have the Semantic Type "Cell Function" assigned. The system includes now 90 different databases (Table 2 shows a selection of some databases used). The terms in the databases are translated to DNA using a specific translation table which can be found in the original publication. The abstract itself is translated following the same schema. To adjust the search process,the BLAST-parameters e-value and Word Size had to be adjusted (see Table 3). After fine-tuning these parameters, the BLAST-algorithm can be used to extract biological concepts from text in a quick manner.

Gene-Tagging. The second method implemented is a Gene/Protein-tagging method called AbGene first published by Tanabe [11]. It uses a combination of statistical and knowledge-based strategies. It does not make a distinction between Gene and Protein Names. This method incorporates automatically generated rules from a transformation-based part-of-speech tagger, and manually gen-

Table 3. Parameters used in BLAST-search

Term length (characters)	e-value	Word Size	mismatch penalty
3	$1e^{-15}$	12	6
4-5	$1e^{-15}$	16	6
6-10	$1e^{-20}$	20	3
11-20	$1e^{-25}$	40	3
20 or more	$1e^{-25}$	80	3

erated rules from morphological clues, low frequency trigrams, indicator terms, suffixes and part-of-speech information. The original source code was taken and altered slightly to suit the needs of CONAN.

Mutation-Tagging. The third method implemented is based on the MuText application [12]. It takes several regular expressions to detect mutations mentioned in an abstract. The pattern usually starts with one amino-acid in one- or three-letter-code, followed by a number and another amino-acid abbreviation. The result of these regular expressions are verified or falsified by the surrounding elements in the text. While there is still a chance of false positives (e.g. the pattern of one-letter/number/one-letter is frequently found in names of cell lines), comparing it to data obtained by the other methods lowers the false positive ratio. As an example, if the BLAST-searching method finds the words "mutation" or "mutagenesis" in the abstract, there is a high probability that the mutation found is really a mutation.

Protein-Tagging. Another method to find protein names and information about these proteins in the text comes from the so called NLProt method [13,14]. It automatically extracts protein names from the literature and links those to associated entries in a sequence database. It uses rule-based filtering and Support Vector Machines (SVMs) to tag protein names in PubMed abstracts. It also gives the corresponding UniProt entries of the protein names as well as the organism this protein belongs to.

Interaction-Finding. The last method implemented is used to extract interaction data from text. The basis of this method are again regular expressions as used in the PreBIND and BIND system [15,16]. Some regular expressions have been deleted by us from the set due to redundant results. There are several categories of possible interactions:

- positive interactions
- negative interactions (inhibitions)
- positive/negative complex building / subunit / association
- positive binding
- negative binding
- activation

- (de-)phosphorylation
- (co)precipitation
- conjugation
- mutation

It is very important to notice that not only positive interactions are found by this method.

2.4   Data Integrator

Having different methods to obtain data, the main focus is to combine this data to gather new information. There are two major ways in CONAN to join data.

- The first way is to combine data before storing it in the Output-XML-file. This is done in the case of Interaction Data. The output of the NLProt-method serves as input for the Interaction-Tagging method. The list of protein names found by NLProt is passed through to the Regular Expressions which give Protein-Protein-Interactions as a result. Additionally, the output of the NLProt method is used to find the related UniProt, ENSEMBL and GO-identifiers.

  Another example of this type of integration of data is the validation of those protein names found by NLProt. NLProt offers a reliability-score (ranging from 0 to 1), assigning a score to each protein-name found in text. Given this score, a list is constructed which holds each occurrence of a protein name in text and its score. The list is compared to the list of protein names found by the BLAST-searching-method and the list of Gene- and Protein-names found by the Gene/Protein-Tagging-method. If certain terms are found by the other methods as well, the reliability score increases (+0.1 for each additional method) and it decreases, if the name is not found by the other methods (-0.1 for each method). If a protein-term is not found by NLProt, but by the BLAST-searching method or the Gene/Protein-tagging method,a score of +0.1 per method is also added.

  The methods can be compared because they all give the exact position of the term in the text. In this way, the number of false-positives and false-negatives is minimized.
- The second way is to combine data at the time when the Output-XML-file is queried. This is done with the mutation data. As explained above, to filter out false positives, the co-occurrence of the mutation and a term related to "mutation" is looked for. This mutation-related term has to be a result of the BLAST-searching method, also stored in the Output-XML-file. Specific XPath-Queries have been created to verify this co-occurrence. When searching for interactions between proteins, the XML file is again searched through by an XPath Query.

  Let N_p be the number of abstracts where the interaction of two proteins is shown to be positive, N_n the number of abstracts where it is shown to be negative (e.g. inhibition). N_a is the total number of abstracts found where two specific proteins are found to participate in an interaction. The number and type of interaction is computed by $W_t = N_p/N_a$, $W_f = N_n/N_a$. If $W_t > W_f$, it is more likely that the interaction is positive than negative.

Although the probability that an interaction is positive is more likely if $W_t > W_f$, it is not impossible that the interaction is negative (e.g. inhibition) or that, under certain circumstances, both kinds of interactions can occur. Due to this fact, all results are displayed with their respective weights (W_t, W_f).

3   Results and Discussion

In this section we show how we evaluated the system in terms of performance and discuss the results.

3.1   Performance Evaluation

Overview. The big problem in most literature-mining systems is the large amount of false-positives in their results. In CONAN, the sheer amount of data rules out a large number of these false positives. When looking at different abstracts about the same topic, we assume that the underlying information should be the same. This means that, if one false-positive result is obtained by computing one abstract and several other true-positive results are acquired, the false-positive is overruled by the true-positives. A perfect example are interaction data in literature. Automatic extraction of interaction data is difficult, especially dealing with false positive results. If abstract A shows that proteins P1 and P2 inhibit each other, abstracts B, C and D on the other hand show that proteins P1 and P2 interact positively, the probability that abstract A is wrong is quite high. The same strategy can be applied for abstracts which have the right information, but this information is extracted wrongly (false-positive). In CONAN, such a false-positive remains in the data, but is overruled by true-positives.

Experiment Design. All experiments that are shown, were conducted on an Intel Pentium 4, 2 GHz, 512MB RAM, running SuSE Linux 8.3.

In a first test of the reliability, stability and speed of the system, the latest 100,000 articles published on PubMed were processed. These files were medline04n0576.xml - medline04n0594.xml, including articles from every field. The whole collection of articles is approximately 745 Megabytes big. The computation of the details of all those articles took about two weeks. The resulting XML files have been merged and used as a basis of analysis. The result was that CONAN is stable enough and fast enough to cope even with a large amount of data. For the final version, quicker and larger machines will be used to cover the whole of MEDLINE.

Test Set Construction. Unfortunately, there are no benchmark databases against which the accuracy of CONAN could be measured. With no well-annotated dataset at the moment, in order to analyze interaction data, a dataset of 1,765 abstracts has been created, all of these containing one or more interactions. This was done because a high percentage of MEDLINE abstracts does not contain interactions at all and we only wanted articles including interactions in our set. These 1,765 abstracts are a combination of available lists of PMIDs from BIND [16] and DIP [17], ensuring that the abstracts contained at least one interaction. As these test-datasets are not or only partially annotated, there was a need to annotate a test set by hand, resulting in a more precise annotation. One hundred of those 1,765 abstracts have been selected completely at random by us to ensure that no organism or protein family is overrepresented and those interactions have been manually annotated. This annotation was done by one person only, resulting in no inter-annotator difficulties.

The 100 abstracts is a quite small number compared to the 100,000 abstracts originally processed by our system, but the effort of manually annotating 100,000 abstracts or even 1,765 abstracts would have been too high. This set of 100 manually annotated abstracts is considered by us of being the test-set. Not only interactions were manually annotated in this set, but also biologically interesting keywords (see Section BLAST Searching) and Gene/Protein names (see Section Protein Tagging) have been annotated.

This test-set of 100 abstracts was run by CONAN to give us data to evaluate. We used this test-set of 100 abstracts for all three following evaluations (see Sections BLAST Searching, Protein Tagging and Interactions), thus giving a coherent evaluation of the whole method.

BLAST Searching. Firstly, the BLAST searching algorithm was evaluated. Both Precision, defined as the fraction of retrieved relationships that are relevant, and Recall, defined as the fraction of relevant relationships retrieved, have been computed. When analyzing the BLAST-searching method, we see that we get recall and precision comparable to the original method, even though we are using more and much more extensive dictionaries, containing not only Protein and Gene names, as in the original publication, but also more "real language"-terms, like the terms in the "Therapeutic Procedure"-database. Those "real language"-terms cannot be evaluated, because there is overlap between terms and there are no sharp term-boundaries, so we concentrated on Gene and Protein Names. We used the manually-annotated test-set of 100 abstracts (see Section Test Set Construction). By being very strict in our cut-offs, especially with the e-value, we get a higher precision than in the original publication, namely 80%, the recall of our implementation of the method still is 71%.

Protein Tagging. When analyzing the different Protein-name-tagging methods, we see that the Data-Integrator-Step boosts the performance of those methods. We again used the same test-set of 100 manually annotated articles (see Section Test Set Construction) as in the evaluation of the BLAST searching. The original NLProt method shows a Precision of 75% and a Recall of 76%, the Protein/Gene-Tagging methods shows a correctness of 77%. Manual annotation showed 480 protein names in the abstracts, whereas CONAN found 504 protein names. When integrating the Protein-Tagging-data with the data found by the BLAST-search and the Gene/Protein-Tagging method, as described in Section 2.4 , we see an increase of Precision to 80.9% (408/504) and of Recall to 85%(408/480), when evaluating Protein names.

The same articles were used as in the evaluation of the Protein-Interaction-Tagging. It has to be said that most articles in this set are Yeast (Saccharomyces cerevisiae)-related articles and Protein-Tagging-Methods usually perform better on Yeast-articles than on articles related to Drosophila, a fact that is also mentioned in [13]. This result is also supported by the good result of the Interaction-Tagging method (see Section Interactions), because the tagging of interaction data is highly dependent on the tagging of Protein Names in text.

Interactions. Finally, the protein-protein interactions were evaluated. In this analysis, no distinction was made between different groups of interactions. Positive interactions have been counted as well as negative interactions (e.g. inhibitions). In the 100 manually-annotated abstracts, a total of 427 interactions are documented. Those 427 interactions were manually annotated. CONAN found 477 interactions in total, compared to the 427 interactions which were annotated manually in the abstracts, this yields a number of 50 or more false positives. Analyzing those abstracts achieved a precision of 81.55% (389/477) and a recall of 91.10% (389/427).

Here we see that, by using our system, we get very good results in a fast and easy way, detecting almost all available interactions mentioned in the abstracts.

The main reason why CONAN did not detect the remaining 38 interactions is the failure to recognize certain generalized protein names. Although we use three different methods for tagging Gene/Protein names, we still get false-positives and false-negatives. This is why the regular expressions used for finding interactions cannot give back all results.

But, Does it Scale ? In Section 3.1, we describe the design of the experiment. We ran the latest 100,000 articles of PubMed with our system, using a single-processor machine. This calculation took 17 days. After indexing the output files with the freely-available XML-indexing software Gnosis (`http://gnosis.cx`), we determined the speed of the queries used in the system. A simple query of those 100,000 articles takes 90 seconds on the same single-processor machine. There are already plans for using a multi-processor, high-memory cluster for this system which will definitely improve speed in processing the articles and querying the results, respectively.

This indicates that CONAN can handle big amounts of data in a fast and reliable way, showing reproducible results. On a reasonably powerful machine, the method can be applied to the whole of MEDLINE, giving the user a tool which shows him all available information.

4   Conclusion

Our goal is to address, as completely as possible, the problem of experimentalists to find certain information "hidden" in the abstracts of biomedical literature. Most systems available at the moment either focus on a very small dataset, a specific organism or specific information (e.g. only interaction data, only Gene Ontology identifiers). We constructed CONAN, which is as complete as possible, offering a wide range of information, from Gene and Protein Names to Mutation Data, Interaction Data and tagging of distinct biomedical entities The big plus of our approach is that we integrate different sources of information to build one system useful for experimentalists.

The results we are obtaining are encouraging. We are performing better or at least as good in the methods we are using (Protein-Interaction Data, Protein/Gene-Name-Tagging), compared to similar systems like Chilibot [18] and present much needed information, like Mutation Data or reliable Interaction Data. The approach presented here provides good methods for all the problems addressed, putting everything into a bigger perspective.

The system itself is currently under consideration of several biologists. Their experience will give us new insights for improving the system and finally putting it accessible to everyone.

Future directions include generating interaction networks from our data, and graphical representation of those networks. Time is required to cover all of MED-LINE, but the ultimate goal is to cover every article published.

Acknowledgements

This work was supported by the Dutch Ministry of Economic Affairs through the Innovation Oriented Research Program on Genomics, grant IGE01017.

References

1. Rebholz-Schuhmann, D., Kirsch, H., Couto, F.: Facts from text–is text mining ready to deliver? PLoS Biol. **3** (2005) e65
2. Krallinger, M., Valencia, A.: Text-mining and information-retrieval services for molecular biology. Genome Biol. **6** (2005) 224
3. Canese, K., Jentsch, J., Myers, C.: The NCBI Handbook. National Center for Biotechnology Information. (2003)
4. Ashburner, M., Ball, C., Blake, J., Botstein, D., Butler, H., Cherry, J., Davis, A., Dolinski, K., Dwight, S., Eppig, J., Harris, M., Hill, D., Issel-Tarver, L., Kasarskis, A., Lewis, S., Matese, J., Richardson, J., Ringwald, M., Rubin, G., Sherlock, G.: Gene ontology: tool for the unification of biology. The Gene Ontology Consortium. Nat Genet **25** (2000) 25–29
5. Camon, E., Magrane, M., Barrell, D., Lee, V., Dimmer, E., Maslen, J., Binns, D., Harte, N., Lopez, R., Apweiler, R.: The Gene Ontology Annotation (GOA) Database: sharing knowledge in Uniprot with Gene Ontology. Nucleic Acids Res. **32** (2004) 262–266

6. Apweiler, R., Bairoch, A., Wu, C.H., Barker, W.C., Boeckmann, B., Ferro, S., Gasteiger, R., Huang, H., Lopez, R., Magrane, M., Martin, M.J., Natale, D.A., O'Donovan, C., Redaschi, N., Yeh, L.S.: UniProt: the Universal Protein knowledgebase. Nucleic Acids Res **32** (2004) D115–D119

7. Birney, E., Andrews, T.D., Bevan, B., Caccamo, M., Chen, Y., Clarke, L., Coates, G., Cuff, J., Curwen, V., Cutts, T., Down, T., Eyras, E., Fernandez-Suarez, X., Gzane, P., Gibbins, B., Gilbert, J., Hammond, M., Hotz, H., Iyer, V., Jekosch, K., Kahari, A., Kasprzyk, A., Keefe, D., Keenan, S., Lehvaslaiho, H., McVicker, G., Melsopp, C., Meidl, P., Mongin, E., Pettett, R., Potter, S., Proctor, G., Rae, M., Searle, S., Slater, G., Smedley, D., Smith, J., Spooner, W., Stabenau, A., Stalker, J., Storey, R., Ureta-Vidal, A.: An Overview of Ensembl. Genome Res. **14** (2004) 925–928

8. Krauthammer, M., Rzhetsky, A., Morozov, P., Friedman, C.: Using BLAST for identifying gene and protein names in journal articles. Gene **259** (2000) 245–252

9. Altschul, S., Gish, W., Miller, W., Myers, E., Lipman, D.: Basic local alignment search tool. J Mol Biol. **215** (1990) 403–410

10. Bodenreider, O.: The Unified Medical Language System (UMLS): integrating biomedical terminology. Nucleic Acids Res. **32** (2004) 267–270

11. Tanabe, L., Wilbur, W.: Tagging gene and protein names in biomedical text. Bioinformatics **18** (2002) 1124–1132

12. Horn, F., Lau, A., Cohen, F.: Automated extraction of mutation data from the literature: application of MuteXt to G protein-coupled receptors and nuclear hormone receptors. Bioinformatics. **20** (2004) 557–568

13. Mika, S., Rost, B.: Protein names precisely peeled off free text. Bioinformatics. **20** (2004) I241–I247

14. Mika, S., Rost, B.: NLProt: extracting protein names and sequences from papers. Nucleic Acids Res. **32** (2004) W634–W637

15. Donaldson, I., Martin, J., de Bruijn, B., Wolting, C., Lay, V., Tuekam, B., Zhang, S., Baskin, B., Bader, G., Michalickova, K., Pawson, T., Hogue, C.: PreBIND and Textomy–mining the biomedical literature for protein-protein interactions using a support vector machine. BMC Bioinformatics. **4** (2003)   11

16. Bader, G., Betel, D., Hogue, C.: BIND: the Biomolecular Interaction Network Database. Nucleic Acids Res. **31** (2003) 248–250

17. Xenarios, I., Salwinski, L., Duan, X., Higney, P., Kim, S., Eisenberg, D.: DIP, the Database of Interacting Proteins: a research tool for studying cellular networks of protein interactions. Nucleic Acids Res. **30** (2002) 303–305

18. Chen, H., Sharp, B.: Content-rich biological network constructed by mining PubMed abstracts. BMC Bioinformatics **5** (2004) 147

A Quantum Evolutionary Algorithm for Effective Multiple Sequence Alignment

Souham Meshoul, Abdessalem Layeb, and Mohamed Batouche

Computer Science Department, PRAI Group, LIRE Laboratory,
University Mentouri of Constantine, 25000 Algeria
{meshoul, layeb, batouche}@wissal.dz

Abstract. This paper describes a novel approach to deal with multiple sequence alignment (MSA). MSA is an essential task in bioinformatics which is at the heart of denser and more complex tasks in biological sequence analysis. MSA problem still attracts researcher's attention despite the significant research effort spent to solve it. We propose in this paper a quantum evolutionary algorithm to improve solutions given by CLUSTALX package. The contribution consists in defining an appropriate representation scheme that allows applying successfully on MSA problem some quantum computing principles like qubit representation and superposition of states. This representation scheme is embedded within an evolutionary algorithm leading to an efficient hybrid framework which achieves better balance between exploration and exploitation capabilities of the search process. Experiments on a wide range of data sets have shown the effectiveness of the proposed framework and its ability to improve by many orders of magnitude the CLUSTALX's solutions.

1 Introduction

Bioinformatics is an interdisciplinary field which borrows techniques from many disciplines like biology, computer science and applied mathematics. It aims to model, to analyze, to compare and to simulate biological information including sequences, structures, functions and phylogeny [1]. Computer science takes a prominent part in bioinformatics as it is extensively used to address several information processing problems in many areas of computational molecular biology. One of such areas is sequence analysis where sequence alignment is the most common task. Sequence alignment is generally needed for sequence comparison purposes in an attempt to discover evolutionary, structural or functional relationships within a set of DNA, protein or biological macromolecule sequences. Practically, it is performed by studying sequences similarity. This is motivated by the fact that proteins or genes that have similar sequences are likely to perform the same function. Sequence alignment may concern two sequences or more. The latter case is known as Multiple Sequence Alignment (MSA). A comprehensive review of the related principle, uses and methods can be found in [2]. The areas where MSA is needed range from detecting homology between sequences and known protein/gene, to phylogenetic trees

C. Bento, A. Cardoso, and G. Dias (Eds.): EPIA 2005, LNAI 3808, pp. 260 – 271, 2005.

computation going through predicting secondary and tertiary structures of proteins, and identifying motifs preserved by evolution. MSA methods can be viewed as different combinations of choices for the following components: the set of sequences, the objective function and the optimization scheme. Indeed, aligning a set of sequences appropriately chosen is generally performed by optimizing a defined objective function. This latter is the mathematical tool used to measure the extent to which two or more sequences are similar. Hence, the definition of an adequate objective function is basically a biological problem and represents in its own an active research area.

The value of the objective function reflects the biological relevance of an alignment and indicates the structural or the evolutionary relation that exists among the aligned sequences. Sequence alignment allows mismatches and insertion/deletion which represent biological mutations. The weighted sum of pairs (WSP) [3] and COFFEE function [4] are notable examples of objective functions that are most commonly used for sequence alignment.

By another hand, optimizing an objective function is typically a computational problem. It consists in searching for the best alignment of sequences which maximizes a similarity measure or minimizes a cost function. Several optimization methods have been proposed in the literature to tackle this problem [2]. They can be loosely divided into the following classes depending on the search strategy used to perform the optimization task: progressive methods, exact methods and iterative methods.

In progressive methods, alignment is achieved by starting with the most related sequences and then gradually adding sequences one by one according to a pre-established order. Speed and simplicity are the main aspects of these methods. Most of them make use of dynamic programming. Clustalw is the example of the most widely used package which relies on this principle. The main drawback with the progressive methods can be explained by their greedy nature which can lead to sub-optimal solutions. To align all the sequences simultaneously, exact methods have been developed as a generalization of the Needlman and Wunsch algorithm [5]. The detection of the best alignment from the number of all potential alignments is at the heart of these methods. Their main shortcoming is their complexity which becomes even more critical with the increase of the number of sequences. To face the huge dimensionality of the combinatorial search space, iterative methods seem to be an interesting alternative. The key idea is to produce initial alignment and to refine them through a series of modification steps called iterations. The refinement can be performed in a deterministic way or stochastic one. During the last decade, several stochastic methods have been proposed to control the computational burden of the optimization process.

At first attempt to solve MSA, simulated annealing (SA) has been used [6] because it offers a sophisticated way to enhance the quality of a given alignment. It proposes to move from the current alignment to one of its neighbors, accepting with a certain probability to move also when the quality of the new solution is worst than previous ones. Other stochastic heuristic have been investigated like Genetic algorithm [7], Tabu Search [8] and Evolutionary algorithms [9]. Evolutionary algorithms adapt nature optimizing principles like mechanics of natural selection and natural genetics. They allow guided search that samples the search space. In [10], their implicit parallelism is exploited in order to achieve better speed and quality convergence.

Recently and far from bioinformatics field, a growing theoretical and practical interest is devoted to researches on merging evolutionary computation and quantum computing [11, 12]. The aim is to get benefit from quantum computing capabilities to enhance both efficiency and speed of classical evolutionary algorithms. This has led to the design of quantum inspired evolutionary algorithms that have been proved to be better than conventional EAs. Quantum computing (QC) is a new research field that encompasses investigations on quantum mechanical computers and quantum algorithms. QC relies on the principles of quantum mechanics like qubit representation and superposition of states. QC is capable of processing huge numbers of quantum states simultaneously in parallel. QC brings new philosophy to optimization due to its underlying concepts.

Within this issue, we propose in this paper a new algorithm to solve MSA problem. The aim is twofold. In one way, we show how quantum computing concepts can be appropriately exploited to handle MSA problem. In another way, we show that the resulting framework which we name QEAMSA (Quantum Evolutionary Algorithm for Multiple Sequence Alignment) improves notably the results provided by CLUSTALX. The features of the proposed method consist in adopting a representation scheme that takes into account all potential alignments for a given set of sequences instead of considering only a gene pool of individuals. The other feature of the method is the application of quantum operators to govern the dynamics of the population that aims to optimize a defined objective function. In the context of our work, we have used the weighted sum of pairs as objective function and we have tested our approach on datasets taken from BAliBASE (Benchmark Alignment Database).

The remainder of the paper is organized as follows. In section 2, a formulation of the tackled problem is given. Section 3 presents some basic concepts of quantum computing. In section 4, the proposed method is described. Experimental results are discussed in section 5. Finally, conclusions and future work are drawn.

2   Problem Statement

Let $S = \{s_1, s_2, ..., s_n\}$ a set of n sequences with $n \geq 2$. Each sequence s_i is a string defined over an alphabet A. The lengths of the sequences are not necessarily equal. The problem of MSA can be defined by specifying implicitly a pair (Ω, C) where Ω is the set of all feasible solutions that is potentials alignments of sequences of and C is a mapping $\Omega \rightarrow R$ called score of the alignment. Each potential alignment is viewed as a set $S' = \{s'_1, s'_2, ..., s'_n\}$ satisfying the following criteria:

1. Each sequence s'_i is an extension of s_i. It is defined over the alphabet $A' = A \cup \{-\}$. The symbol "–" is a dash denoting a gap. Gaps are added to s_i in a way when deleted from s'_i, s_i and s'_i are identical.

2. For all i, j, $length (s'_i) = length (s'_j)$.

Let us now define the optimum value of C as $C_{best} = \{\max C(S')/ S' \in \Omega\}$ and the set of optima $\Omega_{best} = \{S' \in \Omega / C(S') = C_{best}\}$. The optimal alignment can be then defined by S'_* such that:

$$S'_* = \arg\max_{s' \in \Omega}(C(S')) \qquad (1)$$

The addressed task is obviously a combinatorial optimization problem. As the required computation grows exponentially with the size of the problem, it is often desirable to find near optimal solutions to these problems. Efficient heuristic algorithms offer a good alternative to reach this goal. Exploitation of the optimization philosophy and the parallel great ability of quantum computing is an attractive way to probe complex problems like MSA.

3   Quantum Computing Principles

The current computing model takes its origins from the foundations of classical physics whereas the world follows the laws of quantum mechanics. Quantum computing is a new theory which has emerged as a result of merging computer science and quantum mechanics. Its main goal is to investigate all the possibilities a computer could have if it follows the laws of quantum mechanics.

The origin of quantum computing goes back to the early 80 when Richard Feynman observed that some quantum mechanical effects cannot be efficiently simulated on a computer. Later on, in 1994, Shor described a polynomial time quantum algorithm for factoring numbers [13]. Grover's algorithm [14] is another notable example where quantum computing has been used to perform a search in a database. During the last decade, quantum computing has attracted widespread interest and has induced intensive investigations and researches since it appears more powerful than its classical counterpart. Indeed, the parallelism that the quantum computing provides reduces obviously the algorithmic complexity. Such an ability of parallel processing can be used to solve combinatorial optimization problems which require the exploration of large solutions spaces. The basic definitions and laws of quantum information theory are beyond the scope of this paper. For in-depth theoretical insights, one can refer to [15].

The qubit is the smallest unit of information stored in a two-state quantum computer. Contrary to classical bit which has two possible values, either 0 or 1, a qubit can be in the superposition of those two values at the same time. The state of a qubit can be represented by using the bracket notation:

$$|\Psi\rangle = \alpha|0\rangle + \beta|1\rangle \qquad (2)$$

Where: $|\Psi\rangle$ denotes a function wave in Hilbert space. $|0\rangle$ and $|1\rangle$ represent respectively the classical bit values 0 and 1. α and β are complex number that specify the probability amplitudes of the corresponding states. When we measure the qubit's state we may have '0' with a probability $|\alpha|^2$ and we may have '1' with a probability $|\beta|^2$.

A system of m-qubits can represent 2^m states at the same time. Quantum computers can perform computations on all these values at the same time. It is this exponential growth of the state space with the number of particles that suggests exponential speed-up of computation on quantum computers over classical computers. Each quantum operation will deal with all the states present within the superposition in parallel. When observing a quantum state, it collapses to a single state among those states.

Quantum Algorithms consist in applying successively a series of quantum operations on a quantum system. Quantum operations are performed using quantum gates and quantum circuits. It should be noted that designing quantum algorithms is not easy at all. Yet, there is not a powerful quantum machine able to execute the developed quantum algorithms. By the time when a powerful quantum machine would be constructed, researches are conducted to get benefit from the quantum computing field. Since the late 1990s, merging quantum computation and evolutionary computation has been proven to be a productive issue when probing complex problems. The first related work goes back to [11]. Like any other evolutionary algorithm, a quantum inspired evolution algorithm relies on the representation of the individual, the evaluation function and the population dynamics. The particularity of quantum inspired evolutionary algorithms stems from the quantum representation they adopt which allows representing the superposition of all potential solutions for a given problem. It also stems from the quantum operators it uses to evolve the entire population through generations. QEA has been successfully applied on the knapsack problem and others [12, 16].

4   Quantum Evolutionary Algorithm for MSA

4.1   Quantum Representation

To successfully apply quantum principles on MSA, we need to map potential solutions into a quantum representation that could be easily manipulated by quantum operations. According to the problem formulation given in section II, a potential solution is an alignment given by the set S' of sequences derived from the initial set of sequences S by adding gaps. This alignment is viewed as a binary matrix BM where each row represents a sequence s'_i. The value 1 of an element of BM denotes the presence of a basis (nucleotide or amino acid) that is a letter in alphabet A and the value 0 denotes the presence of a gap. In terms of quantum computing, each sequence is represented as a quantum register as shown in figure 1. The register contains superposition of all possible combinations in the sequence. Each column in this register represents a single qubit and corresponds to an element of A'. The probability amplitudes a_i and b_i are real values satisfying $|a_i|^2 + |b_i|^2 = 1$. For each qubit, a binary value is computed according to its probabilities $|a_i|^2$ and $|b_i|^2$. $|a_i|^2$ and $|b_i|^2$ are interpreted as the probabilities to have respectively an element of A or a gap.

Consequently, all feasible alignments can be represented by a quantum matrix QM (see figure 1) that contains the registers associated to the sequences in S'.

$$\begin{bmatrix} \begin{pmatrix} \left|a_{11}\right| & \left|a_{12}\right| & \cdots & \left|a_{1m}\right| \\ \left|b_{11}\right| & \left|b_{12}\right| & & \left|b_{1m}\right| \end{pmatrix} \\ \begin{pmatrix} \left|a_{21}\right| & \left|a_{22}\right| & \cdots & \left|a_{2m}\right| \\ \left|b_{21}\right| & \left|b_{22}\right| & & \left|b_{2m}\right| \end{pmatrix} \\ \vdots \\ \begin{pmatrix} \left|a_{n1}\right| & \left|a_{n2}\right| & \cdots & \left|a_{nm}\right| \\ \left|b_{n1}\right| & \left|b_{n2}\right| & & \left|b_{nm}\right| \end{pmatrix} \end{bmatrix}$$

Fig. 1. Quantum matrix: quantum representation of a set of sequences

This quantum matrix can be viewed as a probabilistic representation of all potential alignments. All alignment configurations are superposed within this representation. When embedded within an evolutionary framework, it plays the role of the chromosome. Only one chromosome is needed to represent the entire population.

4.2 Quantum Operations

We define now the following operations we apply on the quantum representation.

Measurement operation: This operation allows extracting from the quantum matrix one solution among all those present in superposition without destroying all other configurations as it is done in pure quantum systems. This has the advantage to preserve the superposition for the next iterations knowing that we operate on a conventional computer. The result of this operation is a binary matrix BM. The binary values for a qubit are computed according to its probabilities $\left|a_i\right|^2$ and $\left|b_i\right|^2$ and by taking into account the number of non gap elements (basis) in the corresponding sequence. For example the following quantum matrix can give by measurement the following binary matrix:

$$\begin{bmatrix} \begin{pmatrix} \left|0.70\right| \left|0.90\right| \left|-0.90\right| \left|0.77\right| \\ \left|0.70\right| \left|0.44\right| \left|0.40\right| \left|0.63\right| \end{pmatrix} \\ \begin{pmatrix} \left|0.77\right| \left|0.77\right| \left|0.70\right| \left|0.90\right| \\ \left|0.60\right| \left|0.63\right| \left|0.70\right| \left|0.40\right| \end{pmatrix} \\ \begin{pmatrix} \left|0.63\right| \left|0.44\right| \left|0.99\right| \left|1.00\right| \\ \left|0.77\right| \left|0.90\right| \left|-0.14\right| \left|0.00\right| \end{pmatrix} \\ \begin{pmatrix} \left|0.70\right| \left|0.63\right| \left|0.77\right| \left|0.99\right| \\ \left|0.70\right| \left|0.77\right| \left|0.63\right| \left|0.14\right| \end{pmatrix} \end{bmatrix} \rightarrow \begin{pmatrix} 1 & 0 & 1 & 1 \\ 0 & 1 & 0 & 1 \\ 1 & 1 & 1 & 1 \\ 0 & 0 & 1 & 1 \end{pmatrix}$$

Fig. 2. Result of a measurement operation

The binary matrix of figure 3 encodes for example the alignment of the sequences: *AGA*, *AA*, *AGCA*, and *AA*. Figure 4 shows how it is translated to an alphabetic matrix to get a potential alignment.

$$\begin{pmatrix} 1 & 0 & 1 & 1 \\ 0 & 1 & 0 & 1 \\ 1 & 1 & 1 & 1 \\ 0 & 0 & 1 & 1 \end{pmatrix} \leftrightarrow \begin{pmatrix} A & - & G & A \\ - & A & - & A \\ A & G & C & A \\ - & - & A & A \end{pmatrix}$$

Fig. 3. Equivalence between binary and alphabetic matrices

***Quantum interference*:**   This operation aims to increase the probability for a good alignment to be extracted as a result of the measurement operation. It consists mainly in shifting each qubit of *QM* in the direction of the corresponding bit value in the best binary matrix. This is practically performed by applying a unitary quantum operation which achieves a rotation whose angle is function of a_i and b_i and the corresponding binary value (see figure 4).

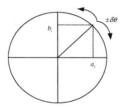

Fig. 4. Quantum Interference

The value of the rotation angle $\delta\theta$ is chosen so that to avoid premature convergence. It is set experimentally and its direction is determined as a function of the values of a_i, b_i and the corresponding element's value in the binary matrix as shown in Table 1. Doing so, interference operation intensifies the search around the best alignment found during the search process.

Mutation operation: This operation allows exploring new solutions and thus enhances the diversification capabilities of the search process. It consists to alter some qubits in *QM*. Taking inspiration from the mutation operations adopted in SAGA [7] and in MSAEA [3] several kinds of quantum mutation operations can be defined:

1. **Single qubit shift:** it consists to select randomly a qubit corresponding to a basis and to swap it with a row neighbor qubit corresponding to a gap.
2. **Set of qubit shift:** It consists to select randomly a set of consecutive qubits of a selected row all corresponding to either gaps or basis and to move it to the left or to the right.
3. **Bloc of qubits shift:** It consists to move a randomly selected bloc of qubits.

Table 1. Lookup table of the rotation angle

Angle	Reference bit value	a_i	b_i
$+\delta\theta$	1	> 0	> 0
$-\delta\theta$	0	> 0	> 0
$-\delta\theta$	1	> 0	< 0
$+\delta\theta$	0	> 0	< 0
$-\delta\theta$	1	< 0	> 0
$+\delta\theta$	0	< 0	> 0
$+\delta\theta$	1	< 0	< 0
$-\delta\theta$	0	< 0	< 0

4.3 Outline of the Proposed Framework

Now, we describe how the representation scheme including quantum representation and quantum operations has been embedded within an evolutionary algorithm and resulted in a hybrid stochastic algorithm performing multiple sequence alignment. At initialization, a quantum matrix is first constructed according to the input set of sequences to be aligned. The CLUSTALX solution for the same input is set as the current best alignment and its corresponding score as the current best score. A binary matrix is derived from the CLUSTALX solution. It is used to apply the first quantum interference of the whole process allowing in this manner a shift of each qubit in the quantum matrix in the direction of the corresponding bit value in the current binary matrix. This can be viewed as the initialization of the quantum matrix with a quantum representation of the CLUSTALX solution. During the optimization process, the algorithm evolves through iterations where quantum operations are applied according to the general scheme given below. At each iteration, we need to evaluate the current obtained solution. For this purpose, the corresponding binary matrix is first translated to its alphabetic equivalent matrix. Then, we make use of the Weighted Sum of Pairs (WSP) objective function because it has been recommended to reduce the bias induced by using the classical Sum of Pairs (SP) score function [3]. Each pair wise alignment is multiplied by a weight which is inversely proportional to the relatedness of the sequences. The score is computed according to the following formulae:

$$C(S') = \sum_{i=1}^{m-1} \sum_{j=i+1}^{m} W_{ij} * M(s_i', s_j') - Penalty\,(gaps) \qquad (3)$$

Where W_{ij} is the weight of the pair (s_i', s_j') and M is a substitution score. To score the gaps penalties, we have considered the affine-gap-penalty model. The gap penalty scoring function is defined as follows:

$$Penalty\,(gaps) = GOP + NG*GEP \qquad (4)$$

Where GOP is the penalty to open a gap, GEP is the penalty to extend an existing gap and NG the number of gaps.

Input: A set of sequences S

(1) Quantum matrix construction. Let QM be this matrix.
(2) Generate an initial alignment S' using CLUSTALX. Let BM be the corresponding binary matrix.
(3) Set $S_{best} = S'$ and $C_{best} = C(S')$.
Repeat
(4) Apply an interference operation on QM according to the best solution.
(5) Apply mutation operation on QM according to a permutation probability p_m.
(6) Apply a measurement operation on QM to derive a new binary matrix BM.
(7) Evaluate the current alignment S' corresponding to BM
(8) if $C(S_{best}) < C(S')$ then $S_{best} = S'$ and $C_{best} = C(S')$
Until a termination-criterion is reached

Output: S_{best} and $C(S_{best})$.

5 Experiments and Performance Evaluation

We now present some practical issues in the implementation of our method and we report on experimental results obtained during the experiments we have conducted. The approach has been implemented on a modern PC using MATLAB. The objective function parameters have been set as follows: GOP=10, GEP=0.2. We make use of BLOSUM62 for the substitution matrix score. To compute the weights W_{ij} , we used the same tree generated by CLUSTALX. In the quantum evolutionary algorithm, the tunable parameters have been set as follows: number of iteration=10000, interference angle=$\Pi/133$ and population size=1.

To assess the performance of the method, we have tested our algorithm on 14 sets data sets as shown on table 2. The sets are taken from the Balibase database: http://bess.u-strasbg.fr/BioInfo/BAliBASE2, which is widely used as alignment benchmarks. The sets are from different reference and have diverse size and identity. The results given by our algorithm are compared to those given by ClustalX. The convergence of the algorithm has been studied by monitoring the behavior of the objective function during the optimization process. In figure 5, we illustrate the values of the considered objective function corresponding to the best solution at each iteration. The figure shows the ability of the algorithm to improve the initial solution given by CLUSTALX. As a baseline comparison, we have also used two functions for performance evaluation: the WSP function as defined in equation (3) and the SPS function which measures the biological quality of an alignment. SPS measure is available on the site of BAlibase (table2). It compares our alignments with the reference alignments in BAlibase benchmarks.

Table 2. WSOP Score & SPS Score

Data set	Number of sequences	Length of sequences	Average Percent identity	WSP Clustal X	WSP QEAMSA	SPS Clustal X	SPS QEAMSA
1aboa_ref1	5	49-80	15	-406	-333	0.482	0.488
1aho_ref1	5	67-76	44	770	936	0.822	0.890
2trx_ref1	4	85-99	17	-237	-110	0.345	0.677
Gal4_ref1	5	335-395	14	-1451	-1196	0.340	0.382
Glg_ref1	5	438-486	31	4411	4747	0.762	0.782
1pgta_ref1	4	199-212	26	729	771	0.837	0.880
1ar5a_ref1	4	192-203	42	2267	2315	0.990	0.996
1aboa_ref2	16	80-89	26	1418	2365	0.751	0.760
1ubi_ref2	17	76-97	32	5979	6531	0.691	0.702
1ubi_ref3	22	63-90	20	-6828	-6081	0.374	0.370
1idy_ref3	27	49-58	19	-5522	-5074	0.526	0.530
1ar1_ref4	9	164-373	30	3952	4544	0.756	0.766
1ycc_ref4	9	105-190	36	1250	1915	0.511	0.578
1pysa_ref5	10	210-313	25	-1613	-826	0.526	0.528

In table 2, the WSP columns show the alignments scores of QEAMSA and Clustal X using the objective function mentioned in (3) while the SPS columns show the alignments scores using the Balibase function. These results show that the Clustal X solutions could be improved up to 50% using the QEAMSA.

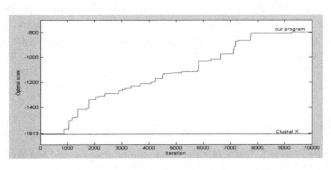

Fig. 5. The behavior of the objective function through iterations (1pysa_ref5, 10000 iterations)

Generally the use of the QEA to improve the Clustal X alignments gives good results in short time; the runtime is between 20s and 17mn depending on the length and the number of sequences. Practically, for all these test cases, we have improved both WSP score and SPS score of the Clustal results. Only in **1ubi_ref3** the SPS score does not correlate with WSP score which can be interpreted as follow: the WSP and SPS does not always correlate because there is not a mathematical cost function which gives exactly the biologically optimal solution. Another reason, the correlation between WSP and SPS depends on the settings of the alignment parameters like GOP/GEP and substitution matrix. For example, taking GEP equal to 0.5 has led to SPS score equal to 0.379 for this data set. The accuracy and the speed of the algorithm can be significantly improved, if we use a powerful machine for its implementation and reap advantage from its intrinsic parallelism. Finally in figure 6, we show the best values obtained during ten runs for QEAMSA and CLUSTALX.

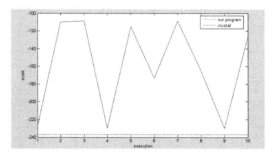

Fig. 6. The behavior of QEAMSA versus ClustalX (2trx_ref1, 10 runs)

6 Conclusion

Taking inspiration from researches on quantum computing, new ideas have been proposed in this paper to handle MSA problem. The main features of the new framework consist mainly in the quantum encoding of the MSA problem which enables to represent all potential alignments within a single representation using states superposition property. Another characteristic is the definition of quantum operations which allow better balance between the exploration and the exploitation capabilities of the optimization process. The obtained results have shown the effectiveness of the proposed approach and its ability to improve CLUSTALX solutions. The intrinsic parallelism of the algorithm can be exploited to enhance significantly its performance. Finally, the proposed framework provides an extensible platform for evaluating different objective functions. It would be an interesting attempt to study this issue as ongoing work.

References

1. T.K. Attwood and D.J. Smith, *Introduction to Bioinformatics.* Addison Wesley Longman, 1999.
2. C. Notredame, Recent progresses in MSA: a survey. *pharmacogenomic*, **3**, 1–14, 2002.

3. R.Thomsen, G.B. Fogel,. and T.A. Krink, Clustal Alignment Improver using Evolutionary Algorithms. In: Proceedings of the Fourth Congress on Evolutionary Computation (CEC-2002), vol. 1, p. 121-126, 2002.

4. C. Notredame, , L. Holm, , and D.G. Higgins, COFFEE: An objective function for multiple sequence alignments. *Bioinformatics*, **14**(5): 407-22, 1998.

5. S.B. Needlman, and C.D. Wunsch, A general method applicable to the search for similarities in the amino-acid sequence of two proteins. *Journal of Molecular Biology,* **48**, 443-453, 1970.

6. J. Kim, S. Pramanik, and M.J. Chung, Multiple sequence alignment using simulated annealing. *Computer applications in bioscience*, **10**, 419-426, 1994

7. C. Notredame and D.G. Higgins. SAGA: sequence alignment by genetic algorithm, *Nucleic Acids Research*, Vol. 24, No. 8, 1515–1524, 1996.

8. T. Riaz, , Y. Wang, and K.B. Li Multiple sequence alignment using Tabu Search. In Proc. 2nd Asia-Pacific Bioinformatics Conference *(APBC)*, **2004**, 223-232, 2004.

9. K. Chellapilla and G.B. Fogel, Multiple sequence alignment using evolutionary programming. In Proc. 1999 Congr. Evolutionary Computation, 445-452, 1999.

10. L.A. Anbarasu, P. Narayanasamy, and V. Sundararajan, Multiple molecular sequence alignment by island parallel genetic algorithm. *Current Science*, **78**, 858–863, 2000.

11. A. Narayanan, and M. Moore, Quantum-inspired genetic algorithms. Proc. IEEE Int. Conf. Evolutionary Computation, **1996**, 61–66, 1996.

12. K.H. Han, and J.H. Kim, Quantum-Inspired Evolutionary Algorithms with a New Termination Criterion, H_ε Gate, and Two-Phase Scheme. *IEEE Transactions on Evolutionary Computation*, **8**, 156–169, 2004.

13. P.W. Shor, Algorithms for quantum computation: Discrete logarithms and factoring. In *Proc. 35th Annu. Symp. Foundations Computer Science*, Sante Fe, NM, 124–134, 1994.

14. L.K. Grover, A fast quantum mechanical algorithm for database search. In Proc. 28th ACM Symp. Theory Computing, 212–219, 1996.

15. C.P. Williams, and S.H. Clearwater, *Explorations in quantum computing*. Springer Verlag, Berlin, Germany, 1998.

16. K.H. Han, and J.H. Kim, Genetic quantum algorithm and its application to combinatorial optimization problem. Proc. 2000 Congr. Evolutionary Computation, vol. 2, La Jolla, CA, 1354–1360, 2000.

Hierarchical Multi-classification with Predictive Clustering Trees in Functional Genomics

Jan Struyf[1], Sašo Džeroski[2], Hendrik Blockeel[1], and Amanda Clare[3]

[1] Katholieke Universiteit Leuven, Dept. of Computer Science,
Celestijnenlaan 200A, B-3001 Leuven, Belgium
{Jan.Struyf, Hendrik.Blockeel}@cs.kuleuven.be
[2] Jozef Stefan Institute, Dept. of Knowledge Technologies,
Jamova 39, 1000 Ljubljana, Slovenia
Saso.Dzeroski@ijs.si
[3] The University of Wales, Aberystwyth, Dept. of Computer Science,
Penglais, Aberystwyth, Ceredigion, SY23 3DB, Wales, UK
afc@aber.ac.uk

Abstract. This paper investigates how predictive clustering trees can be used to predict gene function in the genome of the yeast *Saccharomyces cerevisiae*. We consider the MIPS FunCat classification scheme, in which each gene is annotated with one or more classes selected from a given functional class hierarchy. This setting presents two important challenges to machine learning: (1) each instance is labeled with a set of classes instead of just one class, and (2) the classes are structured in a hierarchy; ideally the learning algorithm should also take this hierarchical information into account. Predictive clustering trees generalize decision trees and can be applied to a wide range of prediction tasks by plugging in a suitable distance metric. We define an appropriate distance metric for hierarchical multi-classification and present experiments evaluating this approach on a number of data sets that are available for yeast.

1 Introduction

Saccharomyces cerevisiae (baker's or brewer's yeast) is one of biology's classic model organisms, and has been the subject of intensive study for years. Its genes have annotations provided by the Munich Information Center for Protein Sequences (MIPS) under their FunCat scheme for classifying the functions of the products of genes. FunCat is a hierarchical system of functional classes. A small part of this hierarchy is shown in Fig. 1. Many yeast genes are annotated with more than one functional class.

This classification setting presents two main challenges to machine learning: (1) each instance (gene) is labeled with a set of classes instead of just one class, and (2) the classes are structured in a hierarchy; ideally the learning algorithm should also take this hierarchical information into account.

A simple approach is to ignore the hierarchy and to learn separate models for each class (indicating whether a single instance belongs to the class or not).

C. Bento, A. Cardoso, and G. Dias (Eds.): EPIA 2005, LNAI 3808, pp. 272–283, 2005.

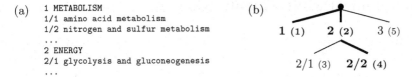

(a)
```
1 METABOLISM
1/1 amino acid metabolism
1/2 nitrogen and sulfur metabolism
...
2 ENERGY
2/1 glycolysis and gluconeogenesis
...
```

Fig. 1. (a) A part of the hierarchical FunCat classification scheme. (b) A toy hierarchy that will be used as example throughout the text. (Note that the class labels indicate the position in the hierarchy: 2/1 is a subclass of the class 2.)

In this work, we consider instead the task of learning one model for all classes. This has the advantage that the total size of the predictive theory is typically smaller, and that dependencies between different classes w.r.t. membership can be taken into account and may even be explicitated. Advantages of learning a single model for multiple related prediction tasks have been reported several times in the literature (see e.g., [6] for decision trees, [8,1] for neural networks, [15] for text classification).

Taking into account the hierarchical structure of the classes is also important while learning. The hierarchy concisely conveys relevant information about the similarity and differences between classes and also expresses the constraint that an instance belonging to a class also belongs to the parent class. The combination of multi-classification and hierarchical classification is known as hierarchical multi-classification [3].

Blockeel et al. [3] show how predictive clustering trees (PCTs) can be applied to hierarchical multi-classification. PCTs form a very general framework for prediction that can be instantiated to a particular prediction task by defining a distance metric and prototype. The distance metric used in [3] is a generic distance between sets of classes that is subsequently instantiated for hierarchical classification by plugging in the weighted shortest path distance between individual classes. The set distance has however two major disadvantages: (1) the distance between two given sets is difficult to interpret (it involves the computation of a kernel), and (2) it is not guaranteed to be positive because the kernel matrix is not positive definite. The impact of the latter is difficult to evaluate.

In this work we take an approach similar to that of [3]. We also use PCTs, but we introduce a new distance metric that is specific to hierarchical multi-classification and that does not have the disadvantages of the distance metric used in [3].

Recently, an extension to C4.5 [11] has been introduced by Clare [9] that is also capable of hierarchical multi-classification. This is accomplished by adapting the definition of entropy to take into account both the multi-class aspect and the hierarchical relationship between the classes. In the experimental evaluation included in this paper we compare our approach to the results presented in [9].

This paper is organized as follows. We first define hierarchical multi-classification more formally (Section 2). Then follows a brief description of PCTs (Section 3). Section 4 shows how PCTs can be instantiated for hierarchical multi-classification. This approach is validated experimentally in Section 5. Section 6 discusses further work, and Section 7 states the main conclusions.

2   Hierarchical Multi-classification

We represent a hierarchy on a set of classes C as a tree, defined by a set of top-level classes $T \subseteq C$ and a *parent* function that maps the children of a tree node onto the node (it is not defined for the top-level classes). A *valid set* is a set of classes that is closed with respect to the *parent* function, i.e., if $c \in S$ then $parent(c) \in S$ or $c \in T$. 2^C denotes the power set of C and $V(C) \subseteq 2^C$ denotes the set of valid sets constructed from C.

Example 1. In Fig. 1.b, $C = \{1, 2, 2/1, 2/2, 3\}$, $T = \{1, 2, 3\}$, $parent(2/2) = 2$, and $\{1, 2, 2/2\} \in V(C)$ is a valid set of classes. Note that a valid set of classes always corresponds to a subtree of the hierarchy. In the case of hierarchical single-classification, the subtree reduces to a path.

The problem of hierarchical multi-classification can now be stated as follows.
Given:
- an instance space X — a set of labeled instances $D \subseteq X \times V(C)$
- a class space C — a quality criterion Q
- a hierarchy H defined on C

Find: a function $h : X \to V(C)$ that maps an instance x onto a valid set of classes S, so that h maximizes the quality criterion Q.

The hierarchy concisely conveys relevant information about the similarity and differences between classes. Intuitively, the distance between two classes is smaller if they are closer to each other in the hierarchy. Further, the siblings of a node should be equidistant, and the distance from a node to its parent is the same for all the nodes on a given level. The distance metric that we will introduce in Section 4 fulfills these criteria.

The quality criterion Q can, but need not be based on the distance. For instance, it could be just the average precision with which all the different classes are predicted, or it could take into account the fact that predicting $\{2, 2/1\}$ is a smaller mistake for an instance that is labeled $\{2, 2/2\}$ than for an instance labeled $\{1\}$.

We finally remark that by representing the labels as subtrees of the hierarchy, the natural constraints on class membership, i.e., anything belonging to a specific class (e.g., $2/1$) automatically belongs to the more general ancestor classes (e.g., 1) are automatically honored. This would not be guaranteed if independent models were learned for all different classes.

3   Predictive Clustering Trees

A variety of algorithms for predictive modeling exists. Among the better known are algorithms that induce decision trees [7,11]. Compared to other well-known techniques such as neural networks [2], decision trees have the advantage of being more interpretable: they clearly explicitate the factors that influence the outcome most strongly.

Decision trees are most often used in the context of classification or single-target regression; i.e., they represent a model in which the value of a single variable is predicted. However, as a decision tree naturally identifies partitions of the data (course-grained at the top of the tree, fine-grained at the bottom), one can also consider a tree as a hierarchy of clusters [10]. A good cluster hierarchy is one in which individuals that are in the same cluster are also similar with respect to a number of observable properties. This leads to a simple method for building trees that allow the prediction of multiple target attributes at once. If we can define a distance measure on tuples of target variable values, we can build decision trees for multi-target prediction. Similarly, if a distance on hierarchical target values is defined, we can build decision trees for hierarchical classification. The methodology has been used successfully for a variety of applications such as conceptual clustering [5], simultaneous prediction of multiple parameters [6], and ranking tasks [13].

The algorithm for inducing these so-called predictive clustering trees (PCTs) is essentially a standard TDIDT (Top-Down Induction of Decision Trees) algorithm such as C4.5 [11]. The general idea is to recursively partition a set of data into clusters in such a way that the intra-cluster variation is minimized. (The heuristic for selecting the test to include in a node of the tree is the sum of the intra-cluster variations of the subsets induced by the test.) Intra-cluster variation is defined as the sum of squared distances between the members of the cluster and its prototype p, where the latter is defined as $p = \arg\min_q \sum_i d(x_i, q)^2$, i.e., roughly the point that is closest to all the instances in the cluster, according to the distance defined. This prototype may or may not be a valid prediction. For instance for 0-1 prediction the prototype could be the mean of all target values, e.g., 0.8, but when making a prediction for a specific instance this has to be converted into a valid prediction (0 or 1). The result of the induction process is a decision tree in which each leaf contains (a prediction derived from) the prototype of the examples covered by that leaf.

A detailed description of PCTs can be found in [5]. The main point to be made here is that the proposed method for inducing PCTs relies entirely on the definition of the distance measure, the prototypes, and the mapping of prototypes onto valid predictions. These issues are the focus of the following section.

4   PCTs for Hierarchical Multi-classification

In this section, we show how PCTs can be applied to hierarchical multi-classification. As indicated above, this comes down to defining a suitable distance metric and prototype.

4.1   Representing a Valid Set of Classes as a Vector

In the hierarchical multi-classification setting, each instance i is annotated with a valid set of classes $C_i \in V(C)$ selected from a hierarchically structured set of classes C. The distance metric and prototype that we will use are based on a vector representation of C_i. This representation is constructed as follows. The vector v_i representing C_i is a vector with $|C|$ components. Each component corresponds to a class of C. The components of v_i that correspond to classes in C_i take the value 1, the others are set to 0.

Example 2. Consider the class hierarchy shown in Fig 1.b and suppose that a given instance i is annotated with the valid set $C_i = \{1, 2, 2/2\}$. Assuming that $v_{i,k}$ corresponds to the class at position k in the preorder traversal of the hierarchy (as indicated by the numbers between parenthesis in Fig 1.b), the vector representing C_i is $v_i = [1, 1, 0, 1, 0]$.

4.2   The Distance Metric and Prototype

Because each valid set of classes is represented as a vector, we can use the Euclidean distance as distance metric and define the distance between two valid sets C_i and C_j as the Euclidean distance between their vector representations.

$$d(C_i, C_j) = d_{\text{Euclidean}}(v_i, v_j) = \sqrt{\sum_k w_k \cdot (v_{i,k} - v_{j,k})^2} \qquad (1)$$

The hierarchical relationship among the classes can be taken into account by setting the weights w_k in (1) to appropriate values. If the weight for classes deeper down the hierarchy is smaller than that of classes closer to the top, then the distance between two top-level classes will be large and the distance between sibling classes deeper down the hierarchy will be small. In the experimental evaluation, we will use weights that decrease exponentially with hierarchy depth: $w_k = w_0^{\text{depth}(c_k)}$, with w_0 a parameter, which we set ad-hoc to 0.75. It can be easily verified that this choice fulfills the criteria listed in Section 2.

Example 3. Consider two instances, the first one annotated with $C_i = \{1, 2, 2/2\}$ and the second one with $C_j = \{2\}$. The distance between C_i and C_j is $d(C_i, C_j) = d_{\text{Euclidean}}([1, 1, 0, 1, 0], [0, 1, 0, 0, 0]) = \sqrt{w_0 + w_0^2}$. Note that this distance can be interpreted as the square-root of the sum of a penalty w_0 because class 1 does not occur in C_j and a penalty w_0^2 because class 2/2 does not occur in C_j.

Consider a set of vectors V. The prototype p_V of V corresponding to the Euclidean distance is the vector mean of V, i.e., $p_V = \sum_{v_i \in V} v_i / |V|$. If D is a set of instances and V is the set of vectors representing their target values then each component of p_V represents the proportion of the instances in D that belong to the corresponding class.

Example 4. Consider the instances of Example 3. The prototype is $p_V = ([1, 1, 0, 1, 0] + [0, 1, 0, 0, 0])/2 = [0.5, 1, 0, 0.5, 0]$ and indicates that all instances belong to class 2 and 50% belong to the classes 1 and 2/2.

The intra-cluster variation of D, which is used in the heuristic when building PCTs, can now be computed as the sum of squared distances between the members of V and its prototype p_V.

Using the Euclidean distance has the advantage over other distance metrics defined on sets [12] that both the distance and the prototype can be computed efficiently. This is important in the context of PCTs because the distance and prototype are used in the computation of the heuristic and this heuristic must be evaluated for each possible split of the instances considered by the system.

4.3   Mapping a Prototype to a Prediction

The prediction associated with a leaf is the set of classes that occur in at least 50% of the training examples belonging to the leaf. Note that this set is always a valid set. It can be computed based on the prototype as the set of classes that correspond to the components that are greater or equal to 0.5.

5   Experimental Evaluation

In this section we present experiments evaluating PCTs for hierarchical multi-classification, i.e., PCTs with the prototype and distance metric discussed in the previous section plugged in. We first describe the data sets used in the evaluation, then we define the experimental setup and finally we present and discuss the obtained results.

5.1   Data Sets

We use the 12 data sets that were also used by Clare [9] (Table 1). The reason is that we will compare PCTs for hierarchical multi-classification to the hierarchical extension to C4.5 [11] presented in [9].

The data sets describe different aspects of the genes in the *Saccharomyces cerevisiae* genome (baker's or brewer's yeast). Each gene included in the data sets is annotated with one or more classes selected from the MIPS FunCat hierarchical classification scheme. The annotations and classification scheme that

Table 1. Data set properties. $|D|$ is the number of instances (genes) and $|A|$ the number of attributes.

Data set	$|D|$	$|A|$	Data set	$|D|$	$|A|$
D_1 Sequence (seq)	3932	478	D_7 DeRisi et al. (derisi)	3733	63
D_2 Phenotype (pheno)	1592	69	D_8 Eisen et al. (eisen)	2425	79
D_3 Secondary structure (struc)	3851	19628	D_9 Gash et al. (gasch1)	3773	173
D_4 Homology search (hom)	3867	47034	D_{10} Gash et al. (gasch2)	3788	52
D_5 Spellman et al. (cellcycle)	3766	77	D_{11} Chu et al. (spo)	3711	80
D_6 Roth et al. (church)	3764	27	D_{12} All microarray (expr)	3788	551

was available on 24/4/02 were used. The hierarchy has 250 classes: 17 at the first level, 102 at the second, 89 at the third, and 42 at the fourth level.

Five types of bioinformatic data for yeast are considered in the data sets: sequence statistics, phenotype, predicted secondary structure, homology, and expression. Different sources of data should highlight different aspects of gene function. Below, we describe each data set in turn. Note that the relevant references to the literature have been omitted because of space restrictions. These references are available in [9], which can be obtained together with the data sets themselves at http://www.aber.ac.uk/compsci/Research/bio/dss/yeastdata/.

(D_1, **sec**) Sequence statistics are recorded that depend on the amino acid sequence of the protein produced by the gene. These include amino acid ratios, sequence length, molecular weight and hydrophobicity. Some of the properties were calculated using Expasy's ProtParam tool, some were listed by MIPS as part of the description of the sequence such as the chromosome on which the gene was located, and some were simply calculated directly. Attributes are mostly real valued, although some (like chromosome number or strand) are discrete.

(D_2, **pheno**) Phenotype data represents the growth or lack of growth of knock-out mutants that are missing the gene in question. A gene is removed or disabled and the resulting organism is grown with a variety of media to determine what the modified organism might be sensitive or resistant to. Phenotype data was taken from EUROFAN, MIPS and TRIPLES. Attributes for this dataset are discrete, and the dataset is sparse, since not all knock-outs have been grown under all conditions.

(D_3, **seq**) The secondary structure of a protein is also known to influence the function of the protein. Secondary structure is caused by hydrogen bonding along the protein's backbone, and there are two main classes of secondary structure elements, the alpha helix and the beta sheet. Structure that can't be classified as alpha or beta is usually termed "coil". Yeast does not have known structure for all of its genes; however secondary structure can be predicted from protein sequences with reasonable precision. The program Prof was used to generate predicted secondary structure for each gene. Due to the relational nature of this type of data a preprocessing step of relational association mining was employed to generate frequent associations from the data. The discovered associations are included as binary attributes.

(D_4, **hom**) Genes are homologous when they share a common ancestor. In determining the function of a yeast gene, information about a homologous gene from another species can provide clues to the possible role of the gene. Homology is usually determined by sequence similarity. If two genes have similar sequences they are deemed homologous, and standard software exists for finding all such similar sequences in a large database. PSI-BLAST was used to compare yeast genes both with other yeast genes, and with all genes whose proteins are indexed in SwissProt version 39, a database of well-annotated genes from all species. This provided for each yeast gene, a list of homologous genes, and for each of these homologous genes various properties were extracted, such as keywords, sequence length and the names of the other databases they were known to be listed in.

This relational dataset was then mined for frequent associations in the same way as the secondary structure data, to produce binary attributes.

$(D_5, \ldots, D_{12})$ The use of microarrays to gather information on the expression of genes is currently popular in biology and bioinformatics. Microarray chips now provide the means to test the expression levels of genes across an entire genome in a single experiment. Many expression data sets exist for yeast, and several of these were used. Attributes for these datasets are real valued, representing fold changes in expression levels.

5.2   Method

Implementation. The distance metric and prototype for hierarchical multi-classification introduced in Section 4 are implemented in the CLUS system[1]. CLUS is a system for building PCTs and is essentially a propositional version of the TILDE system [4,5].

CLUS has a parameter that controls the minimum number of instances in each leaf. This parameter was set ad-hoc to 5. CLUS only considers tests that yield a significant reduction in intra-cluster variation. The significance level of this test was tuned for each experiment using a 3 fold cross-validation on the training set to maximize average class-wise precision (see further). Other parameters were set to their default values.

Obtaining Validated Predictions. As already said above, we are interested in comparing our method to the hierarchical extension of C4.5 [11] introduced by [9]. In [9], the predictions are validated on a separate validation set to obtain a higher precision at the expense of coverage. For each class predicted by a leaf of the decision tree, a significance test is performed. Suppose that the leaf covers N validation instances and that the proportion of instances belonging to the predicted class is a (the precision of the prediction). The test then computes the probability that the proportion of instances of the predicted class in a random sample of size N is greater than a (using the hypergeometric distribution). If this probability is above the significance level, then the prediction is considered insignificant and removed.

In [9], the significance level was set to 0.05 and the Bonferroni correction was used. The latter divides the significance level by the number of tests performed (in this case the sum of the predicted number of classes over all leaves of the decision tree). Such a correction is advised if the number of tests is large. We use the same significance level and perform experiments with and without the Bonferroni correction. Note that, because of the validation step, the predictions are no longer guaranteed to be valid sets.

Data Set Partition. The experiments are based on a three-way split of each data set: a training set, a validation set and a test set. The test set contains 33% of the data. The remaining 66% are split again using a 66%/33% split to

---

[1] CLUS is available from the authors upon request.

create the training and validation set. We use the same split as is used in [9]. The training set is used to induce the PCT, the validation set is used to remove predicted classes that are not significant and the test set is used to measure the predictive precision and coverage.

Note that there is a large number of classes (250) and that validated predictions are only obtained for some of them. Predictive precision is computed for each predicted class individually (class-wise precision), whereas average precision is computed over all predicted classes. Coverage is defined as the proportion of instances for which at least one class is predicted.

5.3   Results

Table 2 presents the obtained average precision and coverage for each data set. It contains results for Clus(B), the Clus system with Bonferroni correction enabled, for Clus (no Bonferroni correction) and for C4.5H, the hierarchical extension of C4.5.

The average precision obtained by Clus(B) and Clus are generally higher than those obtained with C4.5H (Clus(B) yields a higher precision on 9 data sets and Clus on 10), but this increased precision comes in most cases at the expense of a lower coverage (the coverage obtained with Clus(B) is lower than that of C4.5H in 9 data sets). Note however that domain experts prefer precise predictions over a high coverage in this domain.

By disabling the Bonferroni correction the coverage increases, but not for all data sets. There are 4 data sets where Clus yields a larger coverage than C4.5H: seq, struc, hom, and expr. For 3 of these, the precision obtained by Clus is also higher than that of C4.5H. On the other hand, on the 8 data sets where C4.5H has a higher coverage than Clus, the precision obtained with C4.5H is only higher in one case (pheno).

Table 3 lists the class-wise precision for each data set for Clus and C4.5H. In most cases, the set of classes predicted by Clus and C4.5H is similar. In 5 data sets, C4.5H predicts more classes than Clus (usually one or two extra classes are predicted). Clus usually yields higher class-wise precisions. These

Table 2. Average precision and coverage for all data sets (in percent)

| Name | Precision | | | Coverage | | | Name | Precision | | | Coverage | | |
	Clus(B)	Clus	C4.5H	Clus(B)	Clus	C4.5H		Clus(B)	Clus	C4.5H	Clus(B)	Clus	C4.5H
seq	72	61	71	8.35	80.18	14.16	derisi	75	77	61	2.90	2.90	8.39
pheno	67	67	68	3.09	3.09	3.26	eisen	84	88	48	5.73	5.73	37.63
struc	51	68	58	19.91	29.71	2.05	gasch1	89	67	38	4.20	15.77	47.24
hom	65	64	55	35.51	81.41	12.06	gasch2	96	96	60	3.09	3.09	64.06
cellcycle	79	82	54	0.86	0.86	71.34	spo	86	79	46	2.29	3.70	12.82
church	72	75	53	3.50	8.18	58.64	expr	75	77	75	7.26	27.28	5.56

Table 3. Class-wise precision. For each predicted class, the prior probability is given together with the precision obtained by CLUS and C4.5H (in percent).

pheno	Prior	CLUS	C4.5H
3/1/3	2		67
30	8	67	
30/1	6	67	69

cellcycle	Prior	CLUS	C4.5H
4	20		34
5	9	82	33
5/1	5	73	64
40	59	91	61
40/3	14	82	57

derisi	Prior	CLUS	C4.5H
2/13	2		63
5	9	76	58
5/1	5	69	54
40	59	88	
40/3	15	76	64

gasch1	Prior	CLUS	C4.5H
1	28	51	50
4	20		29
5	9	86	78
5/1	6	87	83
6/13/1	3		20
40	59	89	
40/3	15	89	43
40/10	20		25

expr	Prior	CLUS	C4.5H
3	17		44
5	9	100	87
5/1	6	93	78
40	59	72	
40/3	15	100	80

struc	Prior	CLUS	C4.5H
8/4	2		73
40	58	68	
67	8		55
67/28	1		44

church	Prior	CLUS	C4.5H
1	28		36
5	9	62	55
5/1	5	56	61
40	59	88	65
40/3	15	76	

eisen	Prior	CLUS	C4.5H
5	12	85	64
5/1	7	79	56
40	74	98	
40/3	19	88	55
40/10	27		39
40/16	12		38

gasch2	Prior	CLUS	C4.5H
2/16	1		0
5	9	95	56
5/1	6	90	100
40	59	100	64
40/3	15	98	56
40/16	9		29

spo	Prior	CLUS	C4.5H
5	9	77	56
5/1	5	72	79
40	59	88	
40/3	14	79	47
40/10	21		26

seq	Prior	CLUS	C4.5H
1	27	56	48
5	9	88	78
5/1	5	83	77
8	13	37	
29	3		81
40	57	60	
40/2	4	50	14
40/3	14	80	81
67	8	66	78

hom	Prior	CLUS	C4.5H
1	27	61	
1/5/1	7		60
4	20	73	
4/5	14	56	
4/5/1	10	41	
4/5/1/4	9	37	
5	9	84	
5/1	5	84	78
6	15	100	
6/13	4	100	
6/13/1	3	100	
8	12	86	
8/4	2	86	100
29	3	64	55
40	57	64	
40/3	14	71	35
40/7	4	100	
40/10	20	64	
40/16	9	64	
67	8	65	88

observations are consistent with the higher average precision obtained by CLUS and the larger coverage obtained with C4.5H.

The result most in favor of the CLUS system is obtained on the homology data set. Here, CLUS predicts 19 classes, including one level 4 class. C4.5H predicts 6 classes for this data set. As discussed above, both the average precision and the coverage obtained on this data set is higher for CLUS than for C4.5H. The PCT for this data set is shown in Fig. 2. The bottom-right leaf for example represents a cluster in which the genes are predicted to have two functions: 40/3 and 5/1. Note that the tests in the nodes above the leaf provide a description of the cluster. We have compared our PCT to the rules found in [9]. There are a number of similarities, but the knowledge discovered by both systems can be considered complementary.

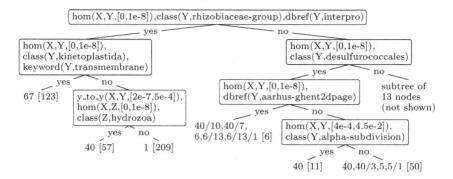

Fig. 2. Part of the PCT obtained for the homology data set. Recall that the attributes are binary relational features. Each node contains such a feature, expressed in first order logic. The variable X represents the given gene and Y and Z refer to homologous genes. Details can be found in [9]. Each leaf of the PCT shows the predicted set of classes together with the number of training examples belonging to the leaf.

6   Further Work

A first item for further work is investigating the trade-off between coverage and precision. Ideally, it should be possible to specify this trade-off by means of a parameter. This is already possible to some extent by altering the significance level used in the validation step, but also the test selection and pruning mechanism of the induction algorithm influence this trade-off. These effects should be studied further.

Ženko et al. [14] propose a system for building predictive clustering rules. By plugging in the distance metric and prototype introduced in this paper, this system will also be suitable for hierarchical multi-classification. Rules are better suited than trees in situations where a high precision is required and a coverage less than 100% can be tolerated.

It would be interesting to evaluate our approach in other domains where hierarchically structured classes occur. E.g., in ecological modeling, samples of soil or river water are collected and the species occurring in these samples are often classified using a hierarchical scheme. Our method could be used to cluster such samples.

7   Conclusions

Predictive clustering trees form a generic framework for prediction that can be instantiated to a particular task by defining the distance metric and prototype. We have introduced such a distance metric and prototype for the task of hierarchical multi-classification. This task occurs in several domains, most notably functional genomics, where each gene is annotated with a set of classes selected from a hierarchical classification scheme.

We have experimentally validated our approach (implemented in the CLUS system) on 12 data sets that are available for the yeast *Saccharomyces cerevisiae* by means of a comparison to C4.5H, a hierarchical extension to C4.5 that has recently been proposed. Our results show that CLUS generates precise predictions. In further work, we will investigate the trade-off between precision and coverage further.

References

1. B. Bakker and T. Heskes. Task clustering for learning to learn. In *Proceedings of the 13th Belgium-Netherlands Conference on Artificial Intelligence*, pages 33–40, Amsterdam, 2001.
2. C. M. Bishop. *Neural Networks for Pattern Recognition*. University Press, Oxford, 1999.
3. H. Blockeel, M. Bruynooghe, S. Džeroski, J. Ramon, and J. Struyf. Hierarchical multi-classification. In *Proceedings of the ACM SIGKDD 2002 Workshop on Multi-Relational Data Mining (MRDM 2002)*, pages 21–35, 2002.
4. H. Blockeel and L. De Raedt. Top-down induction of first order logical decision trees. *Artificial Intelligence*, 101(1-2):285–297, June 1998.
5. H. Blockeel, L. De Raedt, and J. Ramon. Top-down induction of clustering trees. In *Proceedings of the 15th International Conference on Machine Learning*, pages 55–63, 1998.
6. H. Blockeel, S. Džeroski, and J. Grbović. Simultaneous prediction of multiple chemical parameters of river water quality with tilde. In *Proceedings of the 3rd European Conference on Principles of Data Mining and Knowledge Discovery*, volume 1704 of *Lecture Notes in Artificial Intelligence*, pages 32–40. Springer, 1999.
7. L. Breiman, J.H. Friedman, R.A. Olshen, and C.J. Stone. *Classification and Regression Trees*. Wadsworth, Belmont, 1984.
8. R. Caruana. Multitask learning. *Machine Learning*, 28:41–75, 1997.
9. A. Clare. *Machine Learning and Data Mining for Yeast Functional Genomics*. PhD thesis, University of Wales, Aberystwyth, 2003.
10. P. Langley. *Elements of Machine Learning*. Morgan Kaufmann, 1996.
11. J. R. Quinlan. *C4.5: Programs for Machine Learning*. Morgan Kaufmann series in Machine Learning. Morgan Kaufmann, 1993.
12. J. Ramon and M. Bruynooghe. A polynomial time computable metric between point sets. *Acta Informatica*, 37:765–780, 2001.
13. L. Todorovski, H. Blockeel, and S. Džeroski. Ranking with predictive clustering trees. In *Proceedings of the 13th European Conference on Machine Learning*, volume 2430 of *Lecture Notes in Artificial Intelligence*, pages 444–455. Springer-Verlag, 2002.
14. B. Ženko, S. Džeroski, and J. Struyf. Learning predictive clustering rules, 2005. Submitted to the Workshop on Knowledge Discovery in Inductive Databases at the 16th European Conference on Machine Learning (ECML).
15. K. Wang, S. Zhou, and S.C. Liew. Building hierarchical classifiers using class proximity. In *VLDB'99, Proceedings of 25th International Conference on Very Large Data Bases, September 7-10, 1999, Edinburgh, Scotland, UK*, pages 363–374. Morgan Kaufmann, 1999.

Chapter 6

EKDB&W 2005: Extracting Knowledge
from Databases and Warehouses

Introduction

João Gama[1], João Moura-Pires[2], Margarida Cardoso[3],
Nuno Cavalheiro Marques[2], and Luís Cavique[4]

[1] LIACC-UP, Portugal
[2] FCT-UNL, Portugal
[3] ISCTE, Portugal
[4] ESCS-IPL, Portugal

The 2005 EKDB&W - *Extracting Knowledge from Databases and Warehouses* workshop objective was to attract contributions related to methods for non-trivial extraction of information from data. This book of proceedings includes 10 selected papers (resulting from 3 reviews). We believe that the diversity of these papers illustrates the EKDB&W objective attainment.

Unsupervised Learning (Clustering methods in particular) was addressed in 3 papers: (*i*) an extension of traditional SOM was proposed which considered specific measures of distance for categorical attributes; (*ii*) an empirical ranking of information criteria was provided for determining the number of clusters when dealing with mixed attributes in Latent Segments Models; (*iii*) CLOPE was found particularly useful to deal with binary basket data and provided the means to define web User Group Profiles. Supervised Learning was addressed in 3 papers: (*i*) multi-output nonparametric regression methods were presented comparing alternative ways to integrate co-response observations; (*ii*) Peepholing Techniques were adapted for Regression Trees, providing means to reduce the number of continuous variables and the ranges considered for nodes splitting; (*iii*) a Multi-Layer Perceptron was used to classify vector structures derived using the Law's Algorithm. Three papers address the issue of data and knowledge extraction dealing directly with databases and data warehouses: (*i*) a methodology to evaluate the quality of Meta-Data describing contents in web portals was proposed; (*ii*) a new approach to retrieve data from semi-structured text files and integrate it in a decision support system was proposed; (*iii*) an alternative approach for itemset mining over large transactional tables was presented. Finally, an alternative approach to the L* algorithm was proposed, trying to diminish the needless repetition of membership queries.

Application domains were very diverse and illustrated the practical utility of the presented methodologies. They ranged from Web services and Retail to the treatment of Sea surface data, Space Weather and Spacecraft data. Papers in these areas hopefully contributed bridge the gap between research and practice. The EKDB&W Workshop would not have been possible without the contribution of Authors, Program Committee members and EPIA 2005 Organizers. All deserve our thanks and appreciation.

C. Bento, A. Cardoso, and G. Dias (Eds.): EPIA 2005, LNAI 3808, p. 287, 2005.
© Springer-Verlag Berlin Heidelberg 2005

Multi-output Nonparametric Regression

José M. Matías

Dpto. de Estadística, Universidad de Vigo, 36310 Vigo, Spain
jmmatias@uvigo.es

Abstract. Several non-parametric regression methods with various dependent variables that are possibly related are explored. The techniques which produce the best results in the simulations are those which incorporate the observations of the other response variables in the estimator. Compared to analogous single-response techniques, this approach results in a significant reduction in the quadratic error in the response.

1 Introduction

Let the problem be the non-parametric estimation of the (vectorial) regression function $\mathbf{m}(\mathbf{x}) = \mathbb{E}(\mathbf{Y}|\mathbf{X} = \mathbf{x}) \in \mathbb{R}^c$ from n observations $\{(\mathbf{X}_i, \mathbf{Y}_i)\}_{i=1}^n$ with $\mathbf{X}_i \in \mathbb{R}^d$, $\mathbf{Y}_i \in \mathbb{R}^c$ according to the model:

$$\mathbf{Y}_i = \mathbf{m}(\mathbf{X}_i) + \varepsilon(\mathbf{X}_i),\ i = 1, ..., n \tag{1}$$

where $\varepsilon = \varepsilon(\mathbf{x})$ is random noise such that $\mathbb{E}[\varepsilon(\mathbf{x})] = \mathbf{0}_{c \times 1}$ and $\mathrm{Cov}(\varepsilon(\mathbf{x}), \varepsilon(\mathbf{x}')) = C(\mathbf{x}, \mathbf{x}')$ is the $c \times c$ matrix, which is not necessarily diagonal or symmetrical, with elements $C_{jl}(\mathbf{x}, \mathbf{x}') = \mathrm{Cov}(\varepsilon_j(\mathbf{x}), \varepsilon_l(\mathbf{x}'))$.

In what follows, the above approach may be generalized to the case in which each variable Y_j, $j \in \{1, ..., c\}$ may be observed at different points. However, for the sake of notational simplicity, we will maintain the above formulation.

The motivation for this work is the fact that, when estimating each component m_j, $j \in \{1, ..., c\}$ in $\mathbf{m}$, from a limited set of data, there are in theory no logical reasons for ignoring the information on the Y_j variable that may be held by the observations Y_{li}, $i = 1, ..., n$ of the remaining co-responses Y_l, $l \in \{1, ..., c\}$ with $l \neq j$, as is the normal practice in non-parametric regression. On the contrary, it could be claimed that, for example, in linear multivariate regression the joint estimation of the parameters produces the same results as an estimation of each response separately. Nonetheless, this property would not be necessarily true in more complex models or when using non-parametric techniques, when a limited quantity of data is available.

Despite the many areas in which multi-output non-parametric regression techniques may be useful (finance, engineering, biology, etc.), to our knowledge no formal proposals of this kind have been described in the literature, nor studies that evaluate the possible benefits of this approach.

With a view to exploring the advantages of incorporating information from all the co-responses in the estimation of each component of $\mathbf{m}$, in this work we construct different non-parametric alternatives and evaluate their behavior in simulated tests.

C. Bento, A. Cardoso, and G. Dias (Eds.): EPIA 2005, LNAI 3808, pp. 288–292, 2005.
© Springer-Verlag Berlin Heidelberg 2005

2   Non-parametric Alternatives for Multi-output Regression

Given that it supposes no restriction on our discussion, for the sake of notational simplicity we will assume just two responses ($c = 2$) denoted as $Y, Z \in \mathbb{R}$.

The multi-output non-parametric regression models which are postulated and subsequently evaluated in our simulations are described below (we shall only specify the estimator for $m_Y(\mathbf{x})$, as that for $m_Z(\mathbf{x})$ is completely analogous).

The first group of models have a **double non-parametric regression** structure in the form described as follows. Given that the regression function $m_Y(\mathbf{x})$ can be written as two expectations:

$$m_Y(\mathbf{x}) = \mathbb{E}_{Y|\mathbf{x}}(Y) = \mathbb{E}_{Z|\mathbf{x}}[\mathbb{E}_{Y|Z,\mathbf{x}}(Y)]$$

we construct the following estimator:

$$\hat{m}_Y(\mathbf{x}) = \widehat{\mathbb{E}}_{Z|\mathbf{x}}[\widehat{\mathbb{E}}_{Y|Z,\mathbf{x}}(Y)]$$

where the symbol $\widehat{\mathbb{E}}$ represents a non-parametric estimator of the corresponding expectation. In our simulations, we test the following particular cases:

1. The double Nadaraya-Watson estimator (DNW):

$$\hat{m}_Y(\mathbf{x}) = \frac{\frac{1}{n^2} \sum_{i,j=1}^{n} k_{H_1}^{(1)}(\mathbf{X}_i - \mathbf{x}) \left[k_{H_2}^{(2)}(\mathbf{V}_j - \mathbf{v}_i) Y_j \right]}{\frac{1}{n^2} \sum_{i,j=1}^{n} k_{H_1}^{(1)}(\mathbf{X}_i - \mathbf{x}) k_{H_2}^{(2)}(\mathbf{V}_j - \mathbf{v}_i)}$$

   where $\mathbf{v}_i = (\mathbf{x}^t \; z_i)^t$ and $k_{H_j}^{(j)}(\mathbf{u}) = \frac{1}{|H_j|} k^{(j)}(H_j^{-1}\mathbf{u})$, $j = 1, 2$, where $k^{(1)}$ and $k^{(2)}$ are admissible kernels.

2. The double local linear regression (DLLR), obtaining by successively resolving:

$$\min_{\alpha_{\mathbf{v}}, \beta_{\mathbf{v}}} \sum_{j=1}^{n} \left[Y_j - \alpha_{\mathbf{v}} - \beta_{\mathbf{v}}^t(\mathbf{V}_j - \mathbf{v}_i) \right]^2 k_{H_2}^{(2)}(\mathbf{V}_j - \mathbf{v}_i)$$

$$\min_{\alpha_{\mathbf{x}}, \beta_{\mathbf{x}}} \sum_{i=1}^{n} \left[\psi_i - \alpha_{\mathbf{x}} - \beta_{\mathbf{x}}^t(\mathbf{X}_i - \mathbf{x}) \right]^2 k_{H_1}^{(1)}(\mathbf{X}_i - \mathbf{x})$$

   where $\psi_i = \psi(Z_i, \mathbf{X}_i) = \widehat{\mathbb{E}}_{Y|Z_i, \mathbf{X}_i}(Y) = \hat{\alpha}_{\mathbf{v}_i}$. The final estimator is $\hat{m}_Y(\mathbf{x}) = \hat{\alpha}_{\mathbf{x}}$, the estimator of the constant term of the last regression.

3. The double empirical regression (DER), resulting from ([3], [2]) a calculation of the respective conditional expectations using the following estimators of the density functions. For the first regression $\hat{f}(\mathbf{u}) = \frac{1}{n} \sum_{i=1}^{n} f_{\mathbf{U}}(\mathbf{u}; \mathbf{U}_i)$, where:

$$f_{\mathbf{U}}(\mathbf{u}; \mathbf{U}_i) = \frac{1}{2\pi\sigma^2 |S_{\mathbf{U}}|^{1/2}} \exp\{-\frac{1}{2\sigma^2/n}(\mathbf{u} - \mathbf{U}_i)^t S_{\mathbf{U}}^{-1}(\mathbf{u} - \mathbf{U}_i)\}$$

   with $\mathbf{u} = (\mathbf{x}^t \; y \; z)^t$ and $S_{\mathbf{U}}$ as the empirical variance-covariance matrix for the variable $\mathbf{U} = (\mathbf{X}^t \; Y \; Z)^t$.

For the second regression $\hat{f}(\mathbf{v}) = \frac{1}{n}\sum_{i=1}^{n} f_{\mathbf{V}}(\mathbf{v}; \mathbf{V}_i)$, where:

$$f_{\mathbf{V}}(\mathbf{v}; \mathbf{V}_i) = \frac{1}{2\pi\sigma^2 |S_{\mathbf{V}}|^{1/2}} \exp\{-\frac{1}{2\sigma^2/n}(\mathbf{v} - \mathbf{V}_i)^t S_{\mathbf{V}}^{-1}(\mathbf{v} - \mathbf{V}_i)\}$$

with $\mathbf{v} = (\mathbf{x}^t \ \psi)^t$, $\psi = \psi(\mathbf{x}, z) = \widehat{\mathbb{E}}_{Y|z,\mathbf{x}}(Y)$ and $S_{\mathbf{V}}$ as the empirical variance-covariance matrix for the variable $\mathbf{V}$.

The resulting estimator is:

$$m_{\mathsf{Y}}(\mathbf{x}) = \frac{\frac{1}{n^2}\sum_{i,j=1}^{n}\left[\mathsf{Y}_i + S_{\mathsf{VY}}S_{\mathsf{V}}^{-1}(\mathbf{v} - \mathbf{V}_i) + S_{\mathsf{X}\psi}S_{\mathsf{X}}^{-1}(\mathbf{x} - \mathbf{X}_j)\right]w_i(\mathbf{v})w_j(\mathbf{x})}{\frac{1}{n^2}\sum_{i,j=1}^{n}w_i(\mathbf{v})w_j(\mathbf{x})}$$

where $S_{..}$ denotes the empirical cross-covariance matrix and the weights are:

$$w_i(\mathbf{v}) = \exp\{-\frac{1}{2\sigma^2/n}(\mathbf{v} - \mathbf{V}_i)^t S_{\mathbf{V}}^{-1}(\mathbf{v} - \mathbf{V}_i)\}$$

$$w_j(\mathbf{x}) = \exp\{-\frac{1}{2\sigma^2/n}(\mathbf{x} - \mathbf{X}_i)^t S_{\mathbf{X}}^{-1}(\mathbf{x} - \mathbf{X}_i)\}$$

The above estimator was used in tests with a single parameter σ^2 for each response variable. This parameterization could have been extended further, for example, by substituting the covariance matrices $S_{\mathbf{V}}$ and $S_{\mathbf{U}}$ for window matrices that can be selected during the estimation process.

A second group of techniques is based on the direct use of the co-response observations in the expression for the estimator (after homogenization of the range of the variables, for example, through standardization) as described immediately below.

An element of this group is the Nadaraya-Watson multi-output estimator (MNW):

$$m_{\mathsf{Y}}(\mathbf{x}) = \frac{\sum_{i=1}^{n}\left[k_{H_1}^{\mathsf{Y}}(\mathbf{X}_i - \mathbf{x})\mathsf{Y}_i + k_{H_2}^{\mathsf{YZ}}(\mathbf{X}_i - \mathbf{x})\mathsf{Z}_i\right]}{\sum_{i=1}^{n}\left[k_{H_1}^{\mathsf{Y}}(\mathbf{X}_i - \mathbf{x}) + k_{H_2}^{\mathsf{YZ}}(\mathbf{X}_i - \mathbf{x})\right]}$$

where k^{Y} and k^{YZ} are the kernels that reflect the influence in $\mathsf{Y}(\mathbf{x})$ of the nearby observations of Y and Z, respectively.

Likewise, the multi-output local linear regression (MLLR) estimator would be obtained by resolving:

$$\min_{\alpha_{\mathbf{x}}, \beta_{\mathbf{x}}}\left\{\sum_{i=1}^{n}\left[\mathsf{Y}_i - \alpha_{\mathbf{x}} - \beta_{\mathbf{x}}^t(\mathbf{X}_i - \mathbf{x})\right]^2 k_{H_1}^{\mathsf{Y}}(\mathbf{X}_i - \mathbf{x}) \right.$$
$$\left. + \sum_{i=1}^{n}\left[\mathsf{Z}_i - \alpha_{\mathbf{x}} - \beta_{\mathbf{x}}^t(\mathbf{X}_i - \mathbf{x})\right]^2 k_{H_2}^{\mathsf{YZ}}(\mathbf{X}_i - \mathbf{x})\right\}$$

The above estimators are philosophically related to co-kriging [1] and can be viewed as the result of applying the usual single-response non-parametric regression techniques to the extended covariables vector $\bar{\mathbf{x}} = (\theta \ \mathbf{x}^t)^t$ and to the single response $\mathsf{T}(\bar{\mathbf{x}}) = \mathsf{T}(\theta, \mathbf{x})$ where, for example, $\mathsf{T}(1, \mathbf{x}) = \mathsf{Y}(\mathbf{x})$ and $\mathsf{T}(2, \mathbf{x}) = \mathsf{Z}(\mathbf{x})$.

Table 1. Results of the simulations for the different multi-response alternatives described in the text. Shown is the sum of the squared error for prediction (ASRy) and for regression (ASRm) obtained by the best estimator of each type for the observations left out in the cross-validation process for $n = 36$, $C_0 = 0.25$, $\gamma^2 = 1$.

Estimator	m_1		m_2		Total	
	ASRy	ASRm	ASRy	ASRm	ASRy	ASRm
LLR	2.2876	2.1354	1.1206	0.9127	3.4082	3.0482
	(0.9484)	(0.9013)	(0.4442)	(0.3994)	(1.3926)	(1.3007)
MNW	**1.8361**	**1.6718**	**1.0155**	**0.8289**	**2.8516**	**2.5006**
	(0.5572)	(0.4897)	(0.2595)	(0.2171)	(0.8167)	(0.7068)
MLLR	**1.7537**	**1.5910**	**0.8263**	**0.6397**	**2.5800**	**2.2306**
	(0.5659)	(0.5290)	(0.2543)	(0.2156)	(0.8202)	(0.7446)
DNW	2.0898	1.9194	1.1037	0.9022	3.1935	2.8216
	(0.6137)	(0.5710)	(0.2859)	(0.2382)	(0.8996)	(0.8092)
DLLR	2.2797	2.1343	1.1326	0.9305	3.4123	3.0648
	(0.9169)	(0.8886)	(0.4454)	(0.4065)	(1.3622)	(1.2951)
DER	2.6355	2.4407	1.6602	1.4366	4.2957	3.8773
	(0.8601)	(0.7539)	(0.5410)	(0.4829)	(1.4011)	(1.2368)
NW_Y	3.9256	3.7917	2.8256	2.6206	6.7512	6.4123
	(1.1045)	(1.0868)	(0.8200)	(0.7307)	(1.9246)	(1.8176)
LLR_Y	4.1162	3.9744	2.7452	2.5682	6.8615	6.5426
	(1.3024)	(1.2797)	(0.6658)	(0.5973)	(1.9682)	(1.8771)

3   Results and Conclusions

The above estimators were compared with the Nadaraya-Watson (NW) and local lineal regression (LLR) estimators as usually applied separately to each response, as also with the same estimators, but adding, as an input covariable for each regression, the other response variable. This was done as an alternative means of incorporating its information in the estimation of the regression function of its companion response (we denote these estimators as NW_Y and LLR_Y, respectively).

The data were generated according to the model in (1) for $c = 2$, using as regression functions, the following additive functions:

$$m_1(\mathbf{x}) = 0.25[1.5(1 - x_1) + e^{2x_1 - 1} \sin(3\pi(x_1 - 0.6)^2)$$
$$+ e^{3(x_2 - 0.5)} \sin(4\pi(x_2 - 0.9)^2)]$$
$$m_2(\mathbf{x}) = \sin 2\pi x_1 + 4(x_2 - 0.5)^2$$

and as the isotropic covariance matrix:

$$\mathrm{Cov}(\varepsilon(\mathbf{x}), \varepsilon(\mathbf{x}')) = C(\mathbf{x}, \mathbf{x}') \equiv C(\|\mathbf{x} - \mathbf{x}'\|)$$

with elements:

$$C_{jj}(\|\mathbf{x} - \mathbf{x}'\|) = \mathrm{Cov}(\varepsilon_j(\mathbf{x}), \varepsilon_j(\mathbf{x}')) = \sigma_j^2$$

$$C_{jl}(\|\mathbf{x} - \mathbf{x}'\|) = C_{lj}(\|\mathbf{x} - \mathbf{x}'\|) = \mathrm{Cov}(\varepsilon_j(\mathbf{x}), \varepsilon_l(\mathbf{x}')) = C_0 \exp\{-\frac{1}{2\gamma^2}\|\mathbf{x} - \mathbf{x}'\|^2\}$$

for several values of σ_j^2, C_0 and γ^2.

One hundred fixed and random design samples were generated using different sample sizes n for the estimation. The data were previously standardized and the window parameters were selected using m-fold cross-validation.

Table 1 shows the average for the 100 replicas of the sum of the squared error (for prediction (ASRy) and for regression (ASRm)) obtained by the best estimator of each type for the observations left out in the cross-validation process for $n = 36$, $C_0 = 0.25$, $\gamma^2 = 1$, and with σ_j^2's such that the signal-to-noise ratio was 4 in both variables. Results were similar in the remaining cases.

As the table illustrates, the best estimators were MLLR and MNW, both of which produced highly significant reductions in the ASR – in the order of 20 % and 10% respectively – with respect to the analogous single-response estimators.

We are studying the statistical properties of these estimators, by determining the hypotheses under which these satisfactory results are achieved. However, on the face of it, the indications are that, under the usual conditions of regularity, the MLLR and MNW estimators preserve the statistical properties of the corresponding standard estimators, provided that the influence of the co-responses in the estimator for each regression tends to zero (as the sample size grows) with a speed equal or greater to that of the tendency towards zero of the window matrix of the main kernel.

References

1. Chilès, J. P., Delfiner, P.: Geostatistics. Modelling Spatial Uncertainty. (1999). John Wiley
2. Härdle, W.: Applied Nonparametric Regression. (1990). Cambridge University Press
3. Schmerling, S., Peil, J.: Improvement of the method of kernel estimation by local polynomial approximation of the empirical distribution function and its application to empirical regression. Gegenbaurs morphologisches Jahrbuch Leipzig, **132** (1986) 367–381

Adapting Peepholing to Regression Trees

Luis Torgo[1] and Joana Marques[2]

[1] LIACC-FEP, University of Porto, R. de Ceuta, 118, 6., 4050-190 Porto, Portugal
ltorgo@liacc.up.pt
http://www.liacc.up.pt/~ltorgo
[2] Aveiro Digital
jvcmarques@hotmail.com

Abstract. This paper presents an adaptation of the peepholing method to regression trees. Peepholing was described as a means to overcome the major computational bottleneck of growing classification trees by Catlett [3]. This method involves two major steps: shortlisting and blinkering. The former has the goal of eliminating some continuous variables from consideration when growing the tree, while the second tries to restrict the range of values of the remaining continuous variables that should be considered when searching for the best cut point split. Both are effective means of overcoming the most costly step of growing tree-based models: sorting the values of the continuous variables before selecting their best split. In this work we describe the adaptations that are necessary to use this method within regression trees. The major adaptations involve developing means to obtain biased estimates of the criterion used to select the best split of these models. We present some preliminary experiments that show the effectiveness of our proposal.

1 Introduction

Regression trees [5] handle multivariate regression problems obtaining models that have proven to be quite interpretable and with competitive predictive accuracy. Moreover, these models can be obtained with a computational efficiency that hardly has parallel in competitive approaches, turning these models into a good choice for a large variety of data mining problems where these features play a major role. Nevertheless, the growth rate of databases creates problems even for these efficient methods. As such, techniques for reducing the computational requirements of growing regression trees are of key importance for handling extremely large problems.

Many strategies exist to try to overcome the problems of using a certain modelling technique on very large data sets. These can be classified in two broad categories: techniques that are independent of the modelling approach; and techniques that involve the optimization of model construction. In the former we can distinguish two major approaches: reducing the number of features; and reducing the number of cases. Regards the second category, the approaches are generally model-specific and basically try to address the computational bottlenecks of the respective algorithm for obtaining the models. The work presented in this paper

C. Bento, A. Cardoso, and G. Dias (Eds.): EPIA 2005, LNAI 3808, pp. 293–303, 2005.

is of this type: we try to address the major computational bottleneck of growing regression trees.

One of the seminal works on handling large problems using tree-based models is the work by Catlett [3]. This author has thoroughly addressed the issue of the computational bottlenecks of growing classification trees, and presented several approaches to try to overcome them. One of the key contributions of Catlett's work was the identification of the major bottleneck of the process of growing a tree-based model: the selection of the best test on a continuous variable for any node of a tree. In this context, Catlett has presented a technique, *peepholing*, which specifically addresses the problem of reducing the computational complexity of this task. This technique consists of two major steps: *shortlisting* and *blinkering*. The first tries to eliminate some continuous variables from the set to be considered when searching for the best test of a node. The second tries to reduce the range of values to be considered when searching for the best cut point for a test in one of the variables not eliminated by the shortlisting step. Among these two steps, the former has the larger impact in terms of reducing the computational complexity of growing a tree according to Catlett.

Catlett has focused his work on classification trees. The peepholing method is strongly connected to the criterion used to select the best test of a node. The criteria used in classification trees are quite different from the usual criterion (least squares) used for growing regression trees. The goal of this work is to try to adapt the peepholing method to the growth of least squares regression trees. We identify the key issues that require modification and propose solutions in order to be able to use peepholing with regression trees.

The next section presents a brief overview of the theory behind the methods used to grow least squares regression trees. Section 3 describes the peepholing method presented by Catlett [3]. In Section 4 we describe our adaptation of this method to regression trees. The results of our preliminary experiments with this adaptation are shown in Section 5. Finally, the main conclusions of this work are given in Section 6.

2   Least Squares Regression Trees

Regression trees are usually obtained by using a least squares error criterion (e.g. [2]). A regression tree can be seen as a kind of additive regression model [4] of the form,

$$rt\left(x\right) = \sum_{i=1}^{l} k_i \times I\left(x \in D_i\right) \tag{1}$$

where $k_i's$ are constants; $I\left(.\right)$ is an indicator function returning 1 if its argument is true and 0 otherwise; and $D_i's$ are disjoint partitions of the training data D such that $\bigcup_{i=1}^{l} D_i = D$ and $\bigcap_{i=1}^{l} = \phi$.

These models are sometimes called piecewise constant regression models. Regression trees are constructed using a recursive partitioning (RP) algorithm (e.g. [2]). This algorithm builds a tree by recursively splitting the training sample into smaller subsets. The algorithm has three key issues:

- A way to select a split test (the splitting rule).
- A rule to determine when a tree node is terminal.
- A rule for assigning a model to each terminal node (leaf nodes).

Assuming the minimization of the least squares error it can be easily proven that if one wants to use constant models in the leaves of the trees, the constant to use in each terminal node should be the average target variable of the cases falling in each leaf. Thus the error in a tree node can be defined as,

$$Err\,(t) = \frac{1}{n_t} \sum_{D_t} (y_i - \overline{y}_t)^2 \tag{2}$$

where D_t is the set of n_t training samples falling in node t; and $\overline{y}_t$ is the average target variable (y) value of these cases. This is basically an estimate of the variance of the target variable obtained with the cases in node t.

The error of a regression tree can be defined as,

$$Err\,(T) = \sum_{l \in \widetilde{T}} P\,(l) \times Err\,(l)$$

$$= \sum_{l \in \widetilde{T}} \frac{n_l}{n} \times \frac{1}{n_l} \sum_{D_l} (y_i - \overline{y}_l)^2$$

$$= \frac{1}{n} \sum_{l \in \widetilde{T}} \sum_{D_l} (y_i - \overline{y}_l)^2 \tag{3}$$

where $\widetilde{T}$ is the set of leaves of tree T; and $P(l)$ is the probability of a case falling in leaf l.

During tree growth, a split test s, divides the cases in node t into a set of partitions. The decrease in error of the tree resulting from this split can be measured by,

$$\Delta Err\,(s,t) = Err\,(t) - \sum_i \frac{n_i}{n} \times Err\,(t_i) \tag{4}$$

where $Err\,(t_i)$ is the error on the subset of cases of branch i of the split test s.

For the usual binary regression trees, where each node has a left and a right branch, this reduces to,

$$\Delta Err\,(s,t) = Err\,(t) - \left(\frac{n_L}{n} \times Err\,(t_L) + \frac{n_R}{n} \times Err\,(t_R) \right) \tag{5}$$

For each iteration of the RP algorithm, assuming the stopping criteria are not yet met, we need to search for the best split test. This involves going through all variables of the problem and for each one finding the best test according to the criterion of Equation (5). Moreover, for each variable we have to search for the best split, which for continuous variables involves sorting all values appearing in the data and evaluating all possible intermediate cut point using again

Equation (5). Maximizing Equation (5) is equivalent to minimizing the second term, also known as pooled variance, as the first term, $Err(t)$ is constant for all candidate splits.

According to this process we can see that the computational complexity of growing regression trees is strongly dependent on the number of variables of the problem and also on the number of different values appearing on the data. Catlett has shown that continuous variables are particularly important given their large number of different values and the corresponding cost of the sorting operation. The peepholing method was designed to address these specific issues as we will see in the next section.

3   The Peepholing Method

The basic idea of the peepholing method proposed by Catlett [3] is to use a subsample (the *peephole*) to check whether some of the continuous variables, or some ranges within a continuous variable, can be removed from consideration for selecting the best split of a node without a significant loss in the overall accuracy, but with a significant gain in computation speed. Notice that, contrary to other related approaches (e.g. the sampling strategy proposed by Breiman et. al [2]), the final selection of the best test is carried out on all available data. The subsample is solely used for eliminating some candidates from this final selection process.

Peepholing is an iterative process where on each iteration we increase the size of the subsample (peephole) until certain criteria are met. For each peep size two main operations are carried out: *shortlisting* and *blinkering*.

Shortlisting consists of trying to eliminate some continuous variables from the list that will be used to select the best split of a node. The shortlist of a node starts with all continuous variables and if the estimates obtained using the current peephole size allow us to conclude that there is a very low probability that a certain variable would be a good candidate for the best split on the full sample, then that variable is eliminated from the shortlist. The variables eliminated by this process will not be considered on subsequent peepholes nor on the full sample best split selection.

Regarding blinkering it consists of maintaining a pair of numbers (the *blinkers*) for each variable in the shortlist. The interval spanned by the left and right blinkers is an estimate of the range where the best cut point for the respective variable may be contained. The process of blinkering tries to shorten this interval which brings gains in terms of computation time as we need to sort less values to find the best test of the variable.

Both steps of the peepholing process depend on obtaining reliable estimates of the gain of candidate tests using solely the data in the peepholes.

3.1   Shortlisting

The objective of shortlisting is to eliminate some of the continuous variables from the set of variables to be considered when selecting the best test for a node using all data. Catlett proposed a method based on a pair of biased estimates of the gain of a variable: the optimistic and the pessimistic estimates. These estimates are designed so that the gain assessed with the full data set is likely to lie between them. Once the estimates are obtained we can use them to eliminate all variables whose optimistic estimate falls below the greatest pessimistic estimate (GPE) of all variables in the current shortlist.

The method used for generating the biased estimates uses standard techniques from the estimation theory of statistics, namely from estimates of the mean of a population based on averages calculated with several samples with the same size.

The work of Catlett addresses classification trees grown using information gain [6] as the criterion for selecting the best split of a node. The information gain is not a function of the average of the values of examples. Instead its value is composed of several figures derived from averages, thus some adaptation of the general estimation theory was required. The basic building block of information gain is the expected information of a message. Assuming a binary class problem the expected information of the class is given by $-p \log p - n \log n$, where p is the probability of one of the classes and $n = 1 - p$. The values of p and n are obtained by estimating them with relative frequencies. These frequencies can be regarded as averages of a function $f(X) = \{1 \; if \; X = p, \; 0 \; if \; X = n\}$, over all possible messages X. The standard error of this estimate is computed using,

$$\sqrt{\frac{p(1 - p)}{N - 1}} \tag{6}$$

where N is the sample size.

By adding the standard error to the estimated frequency if p is less than 0.5, and subtracting it when it is greater, we get an optimistic estimate of p. Conversely, by subtracting the error when p is less than 0.5 and adding it when it is greater, we obtain a pessimistic estimate[1].

To calculate the information gain of a test on a variable V we need to calculate the gain resulting from its split of the examples. Assuming the standard binary splits the information content of a split is the weighed average of the information of the resulting sub-nodes entailed by the split,

$$InfGain(s, D_t) = Inf(D_t) - (p_L \times Inf(D_{t_L}) + p_R \times Inf(D_{t_R})) \tag{7}$$

where D_t is the set of examples in the node under consideration; p_L (p_R) is the probability of an example following the left (right) branch of the split test s; D_{t_L} (D_{t_R}) is the subset of D_t that fall in the left (right) branch of s; and $Inf()$ is the information content of a set of examples (given by $-p \log p - n \log n$).

The probabilities p_L and p_R are calculated using relative frequencies. Again we need to calculate optimistic and pessimistic estimates of these probabilities.

---

[1] Obviously taking into account the limit 0 and 1 for probabilities.

As the value of $Inf(D_t)$ is constant for all trial splits of the node t^2 , the best split s is the split that minimizes the weighed average of the information of the resulting branches, the estimate of the split. Catlett suggests obtaining a pessimistic estimate of the gain of a split by using the optimistic estimate of the split[3], and vice versa. In order to obtain an optimistic estimate of a split we combine the optimistic estimate of the most favorable branch with the pessimistic estimate of least favorable branch. The combination is carried out by giving more weight to the favorable branch by using the optimistic estimate of the probability of that branch, and obviously doing the inverse with the less favorable branch. The exact opposite process is done to obtain the pessimistic estimate of a split.

The above described process of shortlisting depends on obtaining optimistic and pessimistic estimates for two basic quantities: the information gain of a set of cases and the probability of a branch. These are the key issues that we need to address in order to adapt this process to regression trees.

3.2   Blinkering

The goal of blinkering is to restrict the range of values used for searching the best cut point of continuous variables. The idea is to choose an interval so that the best cut point is unlikely to fall outside of that range.

Catlett suggest the following heuristic to find the blinkers for each variable: eliminate from consideration the values whose information gain is less than half the maximum gain, or less than the average of the gains for all cut-points. These gains are calculated using the current peephole, and are updated for each new peep.

This step of peepholing requires no particular adaptation in order to use it in regression trees. Instead of the information gain of a test we use the least squares criterion of regression trees.

4   Adapting Peepholing to Regression Trees

There are two key issues that require modification in the peepholing method described in Section 3, if we want to apply it within regression trees. The most important is the adaptation of the criterion used to select the best split in a node. Catlett has described forms of obtaining pessimistic and optimistic estimates for the information gain, while in regression trees we need to provide similar facilities for the criterion used in these models (c.f. Equation (5)). The other issue is to adapt the rule for eliminating some variables. This rule needs to be adapted because while information gain is being maximized, the variance used

---

[2] This occurs because each candidate split of a node t only generates different partitionings of D_t, i.e. different values of D_{t_L} and D_{t_R}, but D_t in itself is the same set of cases.

[3] Because the largest the estimate of the split, the worse the value of the gain, according to Equation (7).

in regression trees is being minimized. This requires some adaptation in terms of what is a pessimistic (optimistic) estimate of the gain of a split.

As seen in Section 2, Equation (5), the best split is the split that minimizes the weighed average of the variance on the two sub-nodes resulting from the split (the pooled variance). Thus, provided we find means of obtaining a pessimistic and optimistic estimate of the variance of a node, we are ready to use a similar process as the one described in Section 3.1 for shortlisting. Regarding blinkering as we have mentioned before the method proposed by Catlett requires no adaptation in order to use it in regression trees.

A confidence interval for the sample variance of variable Y (S_Y^2) obtained with a sample of size N can be obtained by (e.g. [1]),

$$\left(\frac{(N-1)S_Y^2}{\chi^2_{\frac{\alpha}{2},N-1}}, \frac{(N-1)S_Y^2}{\chi^2_{1-\frac{\alpha}{2},N-1}} \right) \tag{8}$$

where $\chi^2_{\frac{\alpha}{2},N}$ is the value of the χ^2 distribution with a confidence level of α and N degrees of liberty.

Our proposal consists of using the smaller value of this interval as the optimistic estimate of the variance[4], while the largest value is used as the pessimistic estimate.

The quantity whose estimates we need to calculate to obtain the value of a test (c.f. Equations (5) and (2)) is the pooled variance,

$$var_{pool} = p_L \times var(D_{t_L}) + p_R \times var(D_{t_R}) \tag{9}$$

As soon as we have pessimistic and optimistic estimates of var_{pool} for a split s, we can calculate the respective estimates of the gain of this test as,

$$\Delta Err_{pess}(s,t) = Err(t) - var_{pool_{pess}}$$
$$\Delta Err_{opt}(s,t) = Err(t) - var_{pool_{opt}} \tag{10}$$

This is different from the method described by Catlett due to the already mentioned fact that variance is something that we want to minimize on the tree.

We now need to define how to obtain the estimates for the pooled variance. Assuming the right branch is more favorable than the left (i.e. $var(D_{t_L}) > var(D_{t_R})$), the optimistic estimate of this quantity is given by,

$$var_{pool_{opt}} = p_{L_{pess}} \times var_{opt}(D_{t_L}) + p_{R_{opt}} \times var_{opt}(D_{t_R}) \tag{11}$$

The pessimistic and optimistic estimates of the probabilities of the branches can be calculated using,

$$p_{R_{opt}} = p_R + 3 \times SE$$
$$p_{L_{pess}} = p_L - 3 \times SE \tag{12}$$

---

[4] Recall, that contrary to information gain that we try to maximize, the variance is being minimized.

where 3 corresponds roughly to a 99% confidence interval according to the normal distribution tables, and SE is the standard error of the probability estimate given by,

$$SE = \sqrt{\frac{p(1-p)}{N-1}}$$

where N is the sample size and p is the probability of the left[5] branch estimated by the relative frequency according to the current peephole.

On the other hand a pessimistic estimate of the pooled variance assuming the most favorable branch is still the right one, is given by

$$var_{pool_{pess}} = p_{L_{opt}} \times var_{pess}(D_{t_L}) + p_{R_{pess}} \times var_{pess}(D_{t_R}) \tag{13}$$

Equivalently, we could obtain similar formulas for the case where the left branch is more favorable.

Using these estimates $var_{pool_{pess}}$ and $var_{pool_{opt}}$ we can once again adapt Catlett's method, by discarding all continuous variables whose optimistic estimate is above the smallest pessimistic estimate (SPE) of all variables in the current shortlist.

5   Experimental Results

In this section we describe a series of preliminary experiments designed to assert the correctness of the adaptation we have described in Section 4. Namely, we have tried to assert the correctness of our pessimistic and optimistic estimates by checking whether they converge to the value obtained with the full training sample, as the size of the peephole increases. This is the key issue for using shortlisting to eliminate some variables from the tree growth process and thus strongly decreasing the computation time necessary to obtain these models.

Table 1. The characteristics (number of cases, number of variables) of the data sets used in our experiments

Data Set	Characteristics	Data Set	Characteristics
Abalone	4177; 9	Elevators	8752; 19
CaliforniaHousing	20460; 9	Ailerons	7154; 40
ComputerA	8192; 22	Puma32NM	4499; 33
House 16H	22784; 17	House 8L	22784; 9

We have used the data sets presented in Table 1 in our experiments.

With the goal of checking the convergence of our proposed pessimistic and optimistic estimates of the pooled variance, we have carried out the following experiment for each data set in Table 1:

---

[5] Or right, given that $p_L = 1 - p_R$.

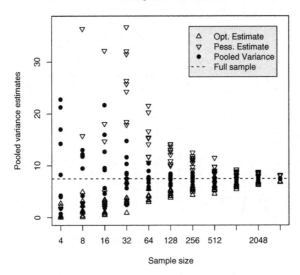

Fig. 1. The convergence of the estimates for the best root split in the Abalone data set (*Shell.Weight* < 0.16775)

1. Obtain the best split test using some regression tree program[6].
2. Divide the data set in two sub-samples according to this split.
3. Calculate the corresponding pooled variance using the full data set

$$var_{pool} = P_L \times var_L + P_R \times var_R$$

4. For increasing sizes of the peephole Do:
    – For several[7] random samples of the size under consideration Do:
        • Get a sample of the size under consideration
        • Calculate the pooled variance and its pessimistic and optimistic estimates using this sample.

Figures 1 and 2 show the results obtained for the best root splits for the data sets *Abalone* and *Ailerons*. The dashed line represents the value of the pooled variance for the best split, calculated using all training data. This is the value we want to approximate with our peephole estimates. The dots are the pooled variance estimates calculated with the peephole sample and the triangles present the respective pessimistic and optimistic estimates.

We can see in Figure 1 that for samples as small as 128 cases, which are roughly 3% of the full sample size we already obtain a quite acceptable convergence towards the pooled variance value obtained with the full sample. The same

---

[6] In our experiments we have used the function `rpart()` from the R environment [7] (http://www.r-project.org), which implements most of the ideas in the CART program [2].

[7] The graphs shown were obtained with 10 repetitions for each size.

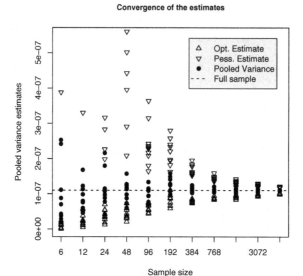

Fig. 2. The convergence of the estimates for the best root split in the Ailerons data set ($Goal < -13.5$)

occurs in Figure 2 for sample sizes around 192, which correspond to 2.6% of the full sample size. Comparable results occur for all other data sets. These results clearly indicate that it is possible to obtain reliable estimates with small peephole sizes, which provides good indications towards the possibility of discarding some of the variables from the tree growth process. In effect, provided the variables have best splits which are reasonably different in terms of decrease in error according to Equation (5), we will be able to detect the "useless" variables if we have good estimates of their best splits using solely the information on the peephole. Obviously, in domains where all continuous variables are equally good in terms of their best split, the peepholing concept will not work as we will not be able to discard variables.

6   Conclusions

In this paper we have presented an adaptation of the work of Catlett [3] concerning the peepholing method. This strategy was created with the goal of overcoming the major computational bottleneck of growing classification trees. We have described the steps necessary to adapt this method to regression trees. Namely, we have shown how to obtain pessimistic and optimistic estimates of the variance of a node that are a key step in adapting Catlett's method.

Our preliminary experiments have shown that the estimates that we have developed clearly converge to the values obtained with the full sample, thus enabling their use in the shortlisting step of the peepholing method. The other step, blinkering, is directly applicable to regression trees thus not requiring any particular adaptation. As such, we have described all means to efficiently implement the peepholing method in any regression tree algorithm. In our future work we plan to carry out this implementation task for effectively using and testing the computational gains of peepholing in regression trees.

References

1. G. Bhattacharyya and R. Johnson. *Statistical Concepts and Methods*. John Wiley & Sons, 1977.
2. L. Breiman, J. Friedman, R. Olshen, and C. Stone. *Classification and Regression Trees*. Statistics/Probability Series. Wadsworth & Brooks/Cole Advanced Books & Software, 1984.
3. J. Catlett. *Megainduction: machine learning on very large databases*. PhD thesis, Basser Department of Computer Science, University of Sidney, 1991.
4. T. Hastie and R. Tibshirani. *Generalized Additive Models*. Chapman & Hall, 1990.
5. J. Morgan and J. Sonquist. Problems in the analysis of survey data, and a proposal. *Journal of American Statistics Society*, 58:415–434, 1963.
6. J.R. Quinlan. Induction of decision trees. *Machine Learning*, 1, 1986.
7. R Development Core Team. *R: A language and environment for statistical computing*. R Foundation for Statistical Computing, Vienna, Austria, 2004. ISBN 3-900051-07-0.

An Extension of Self-organizing Maps to Categorical Data

Ning Chen[1] and Nuno C. Marques[2]

[1] Institute of Mechanics, Chinese Academy of Sciences, P.R. China
ningchen74@yahoo.com
[2] CENTRIA/Departamento de Informtica,
Faculdade de Ciencias e Tecnologia, Universidade Nova de Lisboa,
Quinta da Torre, 2829-516 Caparica, Portugal
nmm@di.fct.unl.pt

Abstract. Self-organizing maps (SOM) have been recognized as a powerful tool in data exploratoration, especially for the tasks of clustering on high dimensional data. However, clustering on categorical data is still a challenge for SOM. This paper aims to extend standard SOM to handle feature values of categorical type. A batch SOM algorithm (NCSOM) is presented concerning the dissimilarity measure and update method of map evolution for both numeric and categorical features simultaneously.

1 Introduction

Clustering is an unsupervised process to partition a set of data into homogeneous clusters. Without the supervision of classes, data segmentation in clustering is performed based on intrinsic similarity of data.

Data can be described by categorical features and numeric features [1]. Nominal features, e.g. post code, gender, transportation mode, residence choice, are typically categorical taking on values from a limited and predetermined set of categories without natural ordering. Another type of categorical feature is ordinal, e.g. education level, social status, which has particular order but unknown distance. Numeric features have numerical distance between values. Numeric features can be further categorized to discrete type with relatively few values, e.g. age, number of cars, and continuous type with a large number of values, e.g. price, salary, temperature.

Self-organizing maps (SOMs) have broad applications in pattern recognition, engineering system, medical diagnosis and image segmentation [15]. The appeal of SOM as a model exploration method in clustering is its unique advantage on data visualization and summarization. From the visualizations, the models of phenomena could be generalized and the patterns could be recognized interactively.

Generally, standard SOMs are applied to feature values of numeric type. Usually, an Euclidean function is used to calculate the distances between input vectors and reference vectors. During the learning, the update of reference vectors is performed by incremental or arithmetic operations. Unfortunately, these calculations are not practical on categorical values. Although categorical data has been discussed in some clustering algorithms (please see [4], [5] or [6]), it is not directly addressed in SOMs due to the

C. Bento, A. Cardoso, and G. Dias (Eds.): EPIA 2005, LNAI 3808, pp. 304–313, 2005.

limitation of learning laws. A traditional approach is to translate categories to numeric numbers in data preprocess and then perform standard SOMs on the transformed data [19]. Despite its feasibility on ordinal features by converting the categories into integers and preserving the natural order, an extra order is posed on nominal values. Also, this approach is not adapted to binary data as reported in [11]. In [12], an overview is made on several methods to encode categorical data for SOM, and their implications are analyzed in terms of the influence on the calculus of the best-matching unit(BMU). In this paper we work on the same direction, however the categorical mapping of our method is now done directly inside the SOM.

In order to operate categorical data, two issues should be considered: the dissimilarity measure of categorical features and the update method of map neurons. In this paper, a batch SOM algorithm is proposed based on new distance measurement and update rules in order to extend the usage of standard SOMs to categorical data. Different from the prior work [12] which mainly talks about the usage of binary-based similarity measures in SOMs, the proposed work focuses on the update method of neurons for both numeric and categorical features simultaneously.

The remaining of this paper is organized as follows. Sect. 2 presents a NCSOM learning algorithm for numeric and categorical data. Some experiments and results are shown in Sect. 3. Lastly, the contributions and future improvements are given in Sect. 4.

2   NCSOM: A Batch SOM Algorithm for Numeric and Categorical Data

Self-organizing maps (SOMs) are artificial neural networks (ANN) used to visualize and interpret high-dimensional data in a low-dimensional space. SOMs are able to reduce the amount of data and simultaneously project data nonlinearly onto a lower dimensional array. The neurons (units) are organized on a regular grid of usually one or two dimensions. Each neuron is associated with a reference vector, reflecting the strength of association to input vectors. The topological relation of neurons is described by a neighborhood kernel function. The reference vectors are initialized at the beginning and updated iteratively in the training process. As a result, the neurons become topologically ordered on the grid, where neurons close to each other in the grid space have similar features in the input space.

Batch SOM algorithms [9] update the reference vectors at the end of each iteration of whole data set. In each epoch, the data vectors are input one by one and listed under the BMUs. Then the reference vectors are calculated as the weighted mean of input vectors that are similar either to themselves or to their topological neighbors. Batch SOMs are order-insensitive, facilitate the development of parallel processing, and eliminate the influence of learning rate as a coefficient [2]. In this section, a batch SOM algorithm for numeric and categorical data will be studied based on the distance measure introduced in [6].

2.1   Dissimilarity Measure

Data projection is based on the distance or dissimilarity between input vectors and reference vectors. Due to the unknown distance between values of categorical features, a simple mismatch measurement [7] is used here. The dissimilarity between two values of single categorical feature is zero if and only if they belong to the same category, otherwise the dissimilarity is one. For a data set with mixed type features, the dissimilarity of two instances is measured on numeric and categorical features separately. Let n be the number of input vectors, m the number of map units, and d the number of features. Suppose the input vectors consist of p numeric features and $d - p$ categorical features, $\{\alpha_k^1, \alpha_k^2 \ldots \alpha_k^{n_k}\}$ is the set of variant values of the kth categorical feature. We denote $x_i = [x_{i1}, \ldots, x_{id}]$ as the ith input vector and $m_j = [m_{j1}, \ldots, m_{jd}]$ as the reference vector of the jth neuron. The dissimilarity between x_i and m_j is defined as the combination of squared Euclidean distance on numeric features and number of mismatches on categorical features [6]. To ensure all features have equal influence on distance, numeric features are usually normalized before distance calculation.

$$d(x_i, m_j) = \sum_{l=1}^{p}(x_{il}, m_{jl})^2 + \sum_{l=p+1}^{d} \delta(x_{il}, m_{jl}), \quad \delta(x_{il}, m_{jl}) = \begin{cases} 0 \ x_{il} = m_{jl} \\ 1 \ x_{il} \neq m_{jl} \end{cases} \quad (1)$$

2.2   Update Rules

In the training process, an input vector is mapped to the best-matching unit, namely, the winner with the closest reference vector. Then a Voronoi set can be generated for each unit: $V_i = \{x_k \mid d(x_k, m_i) \leq d(x_k, m_j), 1 \leq k \leq n, 1 \leq j \leq m, i \neq j\}$. As a result, the input space is divided into a number of Voronoi sets: $\{V_i, 1 \leq i \leq m\}$. At the end of each epoch, the map is updated by different strategies depending on the type of features.

The update rule of reference vectors on numeric features is same to that of standard batch SOMs [9]. Assume $m_{pk}(t)$ is the value of the pth unit on the kth numeric feature at time t. The incremental value on m_{pk} is $\Delta m_{pk}(t) = \sum_{i=1}^{n} h_{c_i p}(x_{ik} - m_{pk}(t))$, where $c_i = arg \min_j d(x_i, m_j(t))$ is the BMU of x_i and $h_{c_i j}$ is a non-increasing neighborhood function centered at the best-matching unit. At time $t + 1, m_{pk}(t + 1) = m_{pk}(t) + \frac{1}{\sum_{i=1}^{n} h_{c_i p}} \Delta m_{pk}(t)$. If $\sum_{i=1}^{n} h_{c_i p} = 0$ for some p, that means m_p is neither the winner of any input vector nor the neighbor of other winners, then $m_{pk}(t+1) = m_{pk}(t)$.

Update rule on numeric features:

$$m_{pk}(t + 1) = \frac{\sum_{i=1}^{n} h_{c_i p} x_{ik}}{\sum_{i=1}^{n} h_{c_i p}} \quad (2)$$

Due to the unknown distance between categorical values, they can not be updated incrementally as numeric values. Intuitively, the category occurring most frequently in the Voronoi sets of a neuron and its neighbors should be chosen as the new value for the next epoch. To determine the new category of a neuron, the frequency of each category is calculated as the average weight of all input vectors having the same value on this feature. For this purpose, a set of counters is used to store the frequencies of variant values for each categorical feature.

$$F(\alpha_k^r, m_{pk}(t)) = \frac{\sum_{i=1}^{n}(h_{c_ip} \mid x_{ik} = \alpha_k^r)}{\sum_{i=1}^{n} h_{c_ip}}, r = 1, 2, \ldots, n_k \tag{3}$$

For nominal features, the best category c, i.e., the value having maximal frequency, is accepted at once if its frequency is more than the total frequency of other categories or accepted randomly with a threshold θ. (The smaller value of θ implies the higher possibility to accept c. If $\theta = 0$, c is always accepted. In the experiments of section 3, θ is set as 50%.) This random acceptance strategy works profitable to avoid local minima of optimization.

Update rule on nominal features:

$$m_{pk}(t+1) = \begin{cases} c & \text{if } F(c, m_{pk}(t)) > \sum_{r=1, r \neq c}^{n_k} F(\alpha_k^r, m_{pk}(t)) \\ c & else\,if\,random(0,1) > \theta \\ m_{pk}(t) & \text{otherwise} \end{cases} \tag{4}$$

where

$$c = arg \max_r F(\alpha_k^r, m_{pk}(t))$$

For ordinal features, the category closest to the weighted sum of frequencies on all possible categories is chosen as the new value concerning about the natural ordering of values.

Update rule on ordinal features:

$$m_{pk}(t+1) = round(\sum_{r=1}^{n_k} r * F(\alpha_k^r, m_{pk}(t))) \tag{5}$$

Some neighborhood kernel functions are used for describing the topological structure of SOMs. The bubble function, $h_{r_ir_j} = \begin{cases} 1 \text{ if } \| r_i - r_j \|^2 \leq \delta(t) \\ 0 \text{ otherwise} \end{cases}$, defines a neighbor set within a neighborhood region of radius $\delta(t)$, where $\delta(t)$ monotonically decreases with regression steps in order to stabilize the effect of the input vectors on the maps. In this case, the frequency could be determined by the percent of the category occurring in the union of Voronoi sets. Gaussian function $h_{r_ir_j} = exp\left(-\frac{\|r_i-r_j\|^2}{2\delta^2(t)}\right)$ is another popular neighborhood function. Compared to bubble function, it is more effective but computationally heavier [9].

2.3 Algorithm Description

In summary, NCSOM algorithm can be described as follows.

Step 1: Initialize the reference vectors of map units.

Step 2: Input the instances one at a time. Calculate the distances between the input vector and reference vectors using Equation(1). Project the input to the best-matching unit.

Step 3: Update the reference vectors on each feature separately at the end of each epoch over the training process. The values on numeric features are the average values of all input vectors weighted by the neighborhood function values according to

Equation(2). The values on nominal features and ordinal features are updated according to Equation(4) and Equation(5) respectively. Replace old reference vectors with new ones.

Step 4: Repeat from Step 2 a few times until the solution can be regarded as steady.

3   Experiments and Discussion

The NCSOM algorithm has been implemented in an adapted version of SOM software [10], [16]. Also, the initial center selection, partitive clustering algorithms, and cluster assignment are developed. The experiments are performed on a few data sets in a machine with 256M memory and intel celeron 1.03 GHz processor running windows XP professional operating system.

3.1   Experimental Results

Empirical studies have been conducted on three pure categorical data sets: soybean, mushroom, tic-tac-toe and two mixed numeric/categorical data sets: credit approval, cleveland heart disease in UCI Machine Learning Repository [13]. All features are made to contribute to distance calculation equally, by normalizing the numeric features to unity range. Figure 1 represents the results of NCSOM on five data sets. For easy visualization, these data are shown in a 2-dimensional space through principal component projection (PCA), that is a linear transformation of high dimensional data to a low dimensional space [1].

The first well-known soybean data set consists of 47 instances with 35 nominal features. The instances are divided into four classes of 10,10,10,17 members respectively. This data set is used to classify soybean plants according to the diseases. In the bottom right of Figure 1(a), soybean data is visualized in a 2-dimensional space spanned by the eigenvectors of two maximum eigenvalues of data through PCA. Each dot represents one instance, showing in different color according to class labels. The neurons of trained map are also displayed in the same space, and adjacent neurons are connected by lines presenting the neighborhood relations between units. As it was shown, the instances of 'D0' and 'D1' form two clusters individually. It seems that the other cluster is composed of instances in 'D2' and 'D3'. On the top left graph, neurons are covered by hexagons of size proportional to hit values (the absolute number of instance histogram matching to map neurons) and marked by the hit values. Intuitively, neurons in clusters get more hits than those between clusters [21]. In fact, the four clusters are separated from each other by the zero-hit neurons. Each Voronoi set forms a subcluster of data. By looking at the top right graph, the dominating classes of subclusters are known immediately. If the members of a subcluster belong to more than one class, we can detect the constitution of subclusters from the hit values of diverse classes. In the bottom left graph, a pie chart is displayed in the place of each neuron with nonzero hit, showing the percent of classes contained in the corresponding subcluster. It can be observed that NCSOM performs on soybean data perfectly, generating a number of subclusters of individual class.

---

[1] All components are handled as numeric in data transformation.

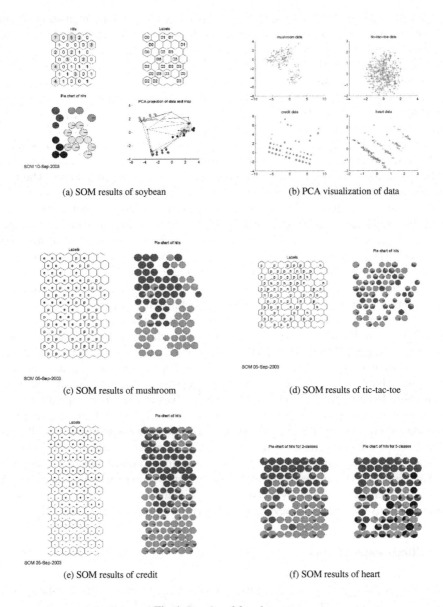

(a) SOM results of soybean

(b) PCA visualization of data

(c) SOM results of mushroom

(d) SOM results of tic-tac-toe

(e) SOM results of credit

(f) SOM results of heart

Fig. 1. Results of five data sets

The second data set under consideration is mushroom data. Although it has 8124 instances, only 500 random samples are selected as experimental data. The goal is to label the instances as 'edible' or 'poisonous' according to 21 nominally valued features. Figure 1(c) visualizes the results on mushroom data, with labels of map units on the left and pie chart of hit values on the right. Although mushroom does not present clear cluster structure (on the visualization in Figure 1(b), each of the two clusters consists of mixed instances of two classes), it still reaches exceptionally high accuracy on SOM clustering. It can be stated that mushroom is composed of a number of small and compact subclusters of instances almost coming from individual class.

Tic-tac-toe is the third data set of interest. It concerns the board configuration of games with 958 instances and 2 classes. It is described by 9 nominal features, each corresponding to one tic-tac-toe square. Also, a sample of 500 instances is randomly generated for analysis. Figure 1(d) shows the labels and hits for tic-tac-toe. As reported by other clustering algorithms [14], NCSOM also performs poorly on this data. We speculate that the poor performance could be explained by the weak cluster models in the data.

Next, we turn to mixed type data sets. Credit approval data set concerns credit card applications, consisting of 9 nominal-valued and 6 numeric-valued features. The 690 samples are classified into two classes with 307 and 483 respectively. It contains 67 missing values on both numeric and categorical features, which are ignored in distance calculation and neuron update. As given in Figure 1(e), the instances of class '+' are projected mainly to the neurons on top of map and those of class '-' to neurons on the bottom. The cluster structure can be detected from the histogram visualization. The neurons labeled by single class usually locate in the inner of clusters, while neurons labeled by multiple classes on the cluster boundary. For this data, it was observed that the neurons of pure class are surrounded by those of mixed classes.

Finally, heart data set contains the records of heart disease diagnosis for 303 patients. The data is described by 5 numeric features: age, cholesterol, max heart rate, resting blood pressure, ST depression relative to rest, and 8 categorical features: sex (male, female), chest pain type (typical angina, atypical angina, non-angina pain, asymptomatic), fasting blood sugar (< 120 or ≥ 120), resting electrocardiographic results (normal, abnormality, hypertrophy), exercise induced angina (yes or no), slope of peak exercise ST segment (up, flat, down), number of vessels colored (0,1,2,3), thalium scan (normal, fixed, reversable). Due to the natural ordering of values, these features are handled as ordinal except sex and exercise induced angina. The instances are classified to 2 classes as 'healthy' or 'sick'. The latter class can be further divided into 4 subspecies (S1, S2, S3, S4). Figure 1(f) gives the composition of subclusters on the same map labeled by 2 classes and 5 classes respectively. In comparison with the former, the pie of 'sick' class in most neurons is divided into several parts of diverse diseases in 5-classes case.

3.2 Effectiveness Studies

To test the effectiveness on categorical data, NCSOM is compared with a standard batch SOM algorithm. In the latter, the categorical values are transformed to continuous integers in random order for nominal features or in nature order for ordinal features.

Evaluation is a process to evaluate the quality of clustering algorithms. The quality of SOMs is usually measured based on quantization precision and topology preservation [18]. The former is typically estimated by the squared quantization error, namely, average distance between input vectors and corresponding best-matching units. The smaller quantization error is, the better the trained map matches to data. The latter is estimated by topology error, namely the number of inputs to which the best-matching unit and next-best-matching unit are not adjacent on the map grid. Distortion integrates quantization and topology measures, defined as the weighted average of distances between input samples and map units.

When the true clusters are known, confusion matrix and rand index are appropriate and commonly used measures for clustering evaluation. Confusion matrix detects how closely the composition of obtained clusters matches to true partition structure. Based on pairwise comparison, rand index [3] is defined as the percent of pairs of instances that locate in either the same or different clusters in both true and obtained clustering. The rand index reaches one if the obtained clusters and true clusters match to each other perfectly. Both confusion matrix and rand index are appropriate for the one-class/one-cluster case [20]. Because the neurons are much more than real clusters, a set of subclusters are obtained as the result of SOM. In such cases, the purity of subclusters is important to final clusters (the instances of a subcluster always belong to the same cluster in future summarization), so SOM clustering can be evaluated by the percent of majority vote [17]. Each unit is identified as the dominating class label (major vote) of its Voronoi set, and instances having different classes are identified as errors. Finally, the purity of subclusters is calculated as the percentage of instances clustered correctly.

In this experiment, the full data set is divided into 10 folds and only 90% data are used for map training and labeling in each run. The quality of derived map is evaluated in terms of the purity of subclusters. For the sake of minimal initialization effect, we conduct 10 trials for each subset, starting from randomly initialized map and then learning through two phases. In rough training, the map is trained for a small number of epochs with large neighborhood radius. In fine-tuning training, the map is trained for a big number of epochs with small radius. The results of different data sets are summarized in Table 1. As expected, NCSOM performs better on all data sets than standard SOM treating categorical features as numeric. Typically, NCSOM reports more than 5% improvement on credit data, which confirms the effectiveness of our methodology on categorical data. For heart data, treating some features as ordinal produces better results than pure nominal features. Compared to the accuracy of two classes, the separation of 'sick' class into four subspecies results in significant decrease of accuracy.

SOMs can be used as classifiers after labeled with classified samples. To test the performance of NCSOM on classification tasks, experiments are conducted using the same arguments as COBWEB, a well-known concept clustering algorithm for categorical data described in [20]. In each trial, the map is trained on 90% of data, then neurons are labeled by the majority vote of projected instances. Afterwards, the evaluation is only performed on the remaining data by calculating the rand index between real labels and obtained labels. Table 2 shows the performance achieved by two algorithms,

Table 1. Comparison of two approaches

data sets	#instance	#features	#classes	NCSOM	Standard SOM
soybean	47	35	4	0.9988	0.9770
mushroom	500	22	2	0.9648	0.9558
tic-tac-toe	500	9	2	0.7896	0.7732
credit	690	15	2	0.8529	0.7958
heart	303	13	2	0.8728	0.8659
heart	303	13	5	0.7152	0.7047

Table 2. Comparison of NCSOM and COBWEB

data	# instances	# attributes	NCSOM	COBWEB
soybean	47	35	0.946	0.849
tic-tac-toe	100	9	0.54	0.475
mushroom	50	22	0.619	0.667

NCSOM and COBWEB (the results of COBWEB were reported in [20]). As we observed, NCSOM outperforms COBWEB on soybean and tic-tac-toe. NCSOM behaves somewhat worse than Cobweb on mushroom, possibly due to the random effect of subset generation. A small subset of only 50 instances fails to explicitly capture the characteristic of data distribution. It was reported that NCSOM gets statistically higher accuracy to 72.4% when a subset of 200 samples was used.

4   Conclusions

SOMs have been widely used in data clustering as valuable tools due to the unique properties on data summarization and visualization. Normally, standard SOMs are applicable to numeric features through arithmetic operations on distance calculation and map evolution. In this paper, we present an approach to handle categorical data in batch SOM algorithms. The performance of proposed algorithms is demonstrated on some real data sets. In future work, we expect to deploy the proposed algorithm for data exploring on some real world problems which have been studied through previous and current funded research projects.

Acknowledgements

The authors would like to thank Dr. Robert Detrano of V.A. Medical center as the principal investigator for the collection of Cleveland clinic heart data.

References

1. Alan Agresti: Categorical data analysis. Wiley series in probability and mathematical statistics, John Wiley & Sons, New York (1990)
2. Qin Ding, Maria Canton, David Diaz, Qinghua Zou, Baojing Lu et al.: Data mining survey. http://midas.cs.ndsu.nodak.edu/~ding/
3. Arthur Flexer: On use of self-organizing maps for clustering and visualization. In J.M. Zytkow and J. Rauch (eds.), Principles of Data Mining and Knowledge Discovery, Proceedings of the 3rd European Conference (PKDD'99), Prague, Czech Republic, Lecture Notes in Artificial Intelligence 1704, Springer (1999) 80-88
4. Venkatesh Ganti, Johannes Gehrke, Raghu Ramakrishnan: CACTUS-clustering categorical data using summaries. Knowledge Discovery and Data Mining (1999) 73-83
5. Sudipto Guha, Rajeev Rastogi, Kyuseok Shim: ROCK: a robust clustering algorithm for categorical attributes. Information Systems **25(5)** (2000) 345-366

6. Zhexue Huang: Clustering large data sets with mixed numeric and categorical values. In Lu Hongjun, Motoda Hiroshi, Liu Huan (eds), Proceedings of the 1st Pacific-Asia Conference on Knowledge Discovery & Data Mining. Singapore, World Scientific (1997) 21-34

7. Zhexue Huang: Extensions to the k-means algorithms for clustering large data sets with categorical values. Data Mining and Knowledge Discovery **2** (1998) 283-304

8. Anil K. Jain, M. Narasimha Murty, Patrick J. Flynn: Data clustering: a review. ACM Computering Survey **31(3)** (1999) 264-323

9. Teuvo Kohonen: Self-organizing maps. Springer Verlag, Berlin, Second edition (1997)

10. Teuvo Kohonen, Jussi Hynninen, Jari Kangas, Jorma Laaksonen: SOM PAK: the Self-Organizing Map program package. Report A31, Helsinki University of Technology, Laboratory of Computer and Information Science (1996)

11. F. Leisch, A. Weingessel et al.: Competitive learning for binary valued data. International Conference on Artifcial Neural Networks, Skoevde, Sweeden, Springer

12. Fernando Lourenco, Victor Lobo, Fernando Bacao: Binary-based similarity measures for categorical data and their application in self-organizing maps. JOCLAD 2004 - XI Jornadas de Classificacao e Anlise de Dados, April 1-3 , Lisbon (2004)

13. Catherine L. Blake, Chris J. Merz: UCI Repository of machine learning databases. University of California, Department of Information and Computer Science UCI Machine Learning Repository (1998)

14. Robert Munro: Classification and analysis in supervised mixture-modelling. University of Sydney, technical report **536**

15. Nuno Marques and Ning Chen.Border Detection on Remote Sensing Satellite Data Using Self-Organizing Maps. EPIA'03-11th Portuguese Conference on Artificial Intelligence, 4th International Workshop on Extraction of Knowledge from Databases (EKDB'03), Fernando Moura Pires, Salvador Abreu (eds.), Springer, Beja, Portugal (2003) 294-307

16. Laboratory of computer and information sciences & Neural networks research center, Helsinki University of Technology: SOM Toolbox 2.0

17. Luis Talavera, Javier Bejar: Integrating declarative knowledge in hierarchical clustering tasks. In Proceedings of the international symposium on intelligent data anlysis. Amsterdam, Netherlands, Springer-Verlag, 211-222

18. Juha Vesanto: Data mining techniques based on the self-organizing map. M.S. Thesis (1997)

19. Juha Vesanto, J. Himberg, E. Alhoniemi, J. Parhankangas: Self-organizing map in matlab: the SOM toolbox. In Proceedings of the Matlab DSP Conference, Espoo, Finland (1999) 35-40

20. Kiri Wagstaff, Claire Cardie: Clustering with instance-level constraints. In Proceedings of the 7th International Conference on Machine Learning (2000) 1103-1110

21. Xuegong Zhang, Yanda Li: Self-organizing map as a new method for clustering and data analysis. In Proceedings of International Joint Conference on Neural Networks (IJCNN) (1993) 2448-2451

Programming Relational Databases for *Itemset* Mining over Large Transactional Tables

Ronnie Alves[*] and Orlando Belo

University of Minho, Department of Informatics, Campus de Gualtar,
4710-057 Braga, Portugal
{ronnie, obelo}@di.uminho.pt

Abstract. Most of the *itemset mining* approaches are memory-like and run outside of the database. On the other hand, when we deal with data warehouse the size of tables is extremely huge for memory copy. In addition, using a pure SQL-like approach is quite inefficient. Actually, those implementations rarely take advantages of database programming. Furthermore, RDBMS vendors offer a lot of features for taking control and management of the data. We purpose a *pattern growth mining* approach by means of *database programming* for finding *all frequent itemsets*. The main idea is to avoid *one-at-a-time record retrieval* from the database, saving both the copying and process context switching, *expensive joins*, and *table reconstruction*. The empirical evaluation of our approach shows that runs competitively with the most known *itemset mining* implementations based on SQL. Our performance evaluation was made with SQL Server 2000 (v.8) and T-SQL, throughout several synthetical datasets.

1 Introduction

The problem of finding *all frequent itemsets* [2] given a Dataset D with a minimum support threshold S is the most time consuming task on association rule mining. In order to solve this problem, two ways are likely to be chosen: one using algorithms that employed sophisticated in memory data structures, where the data is stored into and retrieved from flat files; and another using algorithms that are based on SQL statements and extensions to query and update a database. The former is very efficient when it is compared with the later. On the other hand, when we deal with data warehouse the size of tables is extremely huge for memory copy. Nevertheless, it becomes important for Relational Database Management Systems (RDBMS) to offer new analytic functionalities to support business intelligence applications.

There are a few implementations based on SQL [12, 13, 14, 15, 16], but they have performance issues concentrated in two central points: candidate-set generation and test (*Apriori-bottleneck*); and table reconstruction of conditional pattern trees (*FP-Growth-bottleneck*).

In this work we do not intend to compare the effectiveness of *itemset mining* based on database programming with the memory ones. Instead, we purpose a solution for

---

[*] Supported by a Ph.D. Scholarship from FCT-Foundation of Science and Technology, Ministry of Science of Portugal.

C. Bento, A. Cardoso, and G. Dias (Eds.): EPIA 2005, LNAI 3808, pp. 314–324, 2005.

bringing the itemset mining process to the RDBMS server side, which generates the following contributions:

1. A *procedural schema* for itemset mining, so the process can be run as a batch script on the RDBMS server side.
2. A *cascading approach* working with single tables, and also avoiding the complexity of mining frequent itemsets from several multi-tables joins.
3. A *pattern growth mining* which doesn't surfer of several tables reconstruction (of conditional pattern trees).

2   Frequent Pattern Mining

The frequent pattern mining problem can be defined as follow: Given a set of items I, a transaction database D over I, and a minimal support threshold S, find all itemsets $F(D,S)$. Indeed, we are not only interested in the set of itemsets (F), but also in the actual supports of these itemsets.

The most known implementation of frequent pattern mining algorithm is Apriori [3]. Several Apriori-based algorithms have been purposed for getting better performance and I/O costs [9, 10, 11].

Recently, an FP-tree based frequent pattern mining method, called FP-growth, developed by Han et al. [8], achieved high efficiency, when compared with the Apriori-like approaches. Basically, the FP-growth method adopts the divide-and-conquer strategy. It uses only two full I/O scans of the database, and *avoids iterative candidate generation*. In general terms, the mining process consists of making available the FP-tree data structure, and then FP-growth is applied over a FP-tree for getting frequent itemsets.

There are implementations that suggest enhancements into the frequent pattern mining in order to make the process interactive, constrained, and incremental [6, 7]. Those aspects will not be discussed in this work. Instead, we focus on the first issue, i.e., finding frequent itemsets closer to RDBMS.

The above implementations cannot be applied directly on the main problem of this work, since they need to copy tables out from the database for proper execution. Besides, after its execution, the results must be load again to the database for getting suitable analysis.

2.1   Pattern Growth Mining

Pattern Growth Mining can be viewed as first mining frequent 1-itemset and then progressively growing each such itemset by mining its conditional pattern base, which \implies first mining its frequent 1-itemset and then progressively growing each such itemset by mining its *conditional pattern base*, etc [8]. Thus, a frequent k-itemset mining problem can be transformed into a sequence of k frequent 1-itemset mining problems via a set of conditional pattern bases. The main aspects of the algorithm can be summarized as follows:

1. For each node in the *FP-tree* construct its *conditional pattern base*, which is a "sub-database" constructed with the prefix sub-path set co-occurring with the suffix pattern in the FP-tree. FP-growth traverses nodes in the FP-tree from the least frequent item in I.

2. From each conditional pattern base construct its *conditional FP-tree*.
3. Finally, if the conditional FP-tree has a single path, simply enumerate all patterns, on the contrary run *pattern growth mining recursively* over the conditional FP-tree.

2.2 SQL-Based

There are a few SQL-based implementations that can be used to mine *frequent patterns* over large transactional tables [1, 12, 13, 15, 16]. Even so, all of them are based on nature of *Apriori-like* approach. There is another approach that uses FP-Growth [14] in RDBMS. Nevertheless, the process of reconstructing conditional FP tables for large datasets may pose performance issues. Therefore, we must avoid the previous mentioned bottlenecks: *candidate set generation and test*; and *table reconstruction*. Moreover, we have designed a *procedural schema* for mining all patterns on the RDBMS server side.

We examined those assumptions, and purpose a new approach for *pattern growth mining* using database programming facilities.

By using a pattern growth approach we are able to manage the first bottleneck. However, the current SQL implementation of FP-Growth [14] cannot handle the second issue. Consequently, we need to provide a solution for pattern growth mining which must have the ability to: work in RDBMS server side, prevent multi-table joins and table reconstruction of conditional pattern trees.

3 Discovering Frequent Itemsets on Large Transactional Tables

In order to provide itemset mining over large transactional tables on the RDBMS server side, we present a *procedural schema* by means of using several database facilities such as stored procedures, SQL-cursors, and UDF functions. We also call this approach as a Pattern Growth mining with SQL-Extensions (PGS). The whole procedural schema cannot, for reasons of space, be presented here, but can be found in [4].

The whole process can be summarized into two main steps: one for generating the pattern tree and another one for mining all patterns.

Table1 shows the frequent 1-itemsets extracted from a transactional table (columns TID and Items). A new transactional table (column Freq. 1-itemsets) containing only records with frequent 1-itemsets is created, and thus its related pattern tree is also built. Finally, Table 2 presents the pattern growth method applied over the pattern

Table 1. A transaction database with a support= 3

TID	Items	Freq. 1-itemsets
1	1, 3, 5, 6, 7	3, 5, 7, 1, 6
2	2, 3, 5, 6, 7	3, 5, 7, 6
3	1, 2, 3, 4, 5	3, 5, 1
4	3, 6, 7	3, 7, 6
5	1, 4, 5, 7	5, 7, 1

Table 2. Extracting *all* patterns (R=root)

Item	SUBFP	CONFP	PATTERNS
3	*Null*	*Null*	*Null*
5	R=1, R:3=3	3:3	3%5:3
7	R:3=1, R:3:5=2, R:5=1	3:3, 5:3	3%7:3, 5%7:3
1	R:3:5=1, R:3:5:7=1, R:5:7=1	5:3	5%1:3
6	R:3:5:7=1, R:3:5:7:1=1,	3:3,7:3	3%6:3, 7%6:3,
	R:3:7=1		3%7%6:3

tree. For instance, giving that only items (column Item) are frequents, from its pattern tree, we work with only a subset (column SUBFP) for reaching its conditional pattern tree (column CONFP) and then enumerating all frequent patterns.

3.1 Step 1: Creating Pattern-Tree Table

Several tables are manipulating during the process of generating all itemsets (see Fig.1 and Fig 2). They are built just one time. In the recursive part, where pattern growth is applied, other structures are required, but they are created dynamically by using UDF functions and database cursors. In fact, they provide *SUBFP* (sub-path) tables for extracting single and not-single patterns.

We mean single patterns for those which are enumerated directly from its *conditional FP table (CONFP)* (for instance "3%5"[1]), meaning a co-occurrence of item 3 with item 5, without handling sub-path tables. A pattern such as "3%7%6" is extracted by combine those items that co-occurs added with it is respective sub-path tables [8].

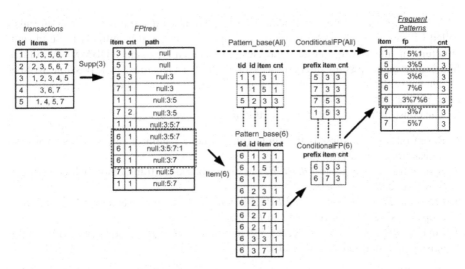

Fig. 1. An overall picture of the tables involved in the process of generating all itemsets

---

[1] The symbol % is used as a wildcard and matches any string of zero or more characters. This wildcard character can be used as either prefix or suffix for querying patterns.

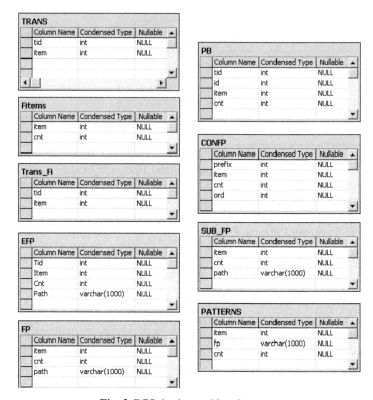

Fig. 2. PGS database table schema

As a pattern growth approach the first step requires a *pattern-tree* structure also called FP-tree. Even though FP-tree is a compact structure, it is unlikely to build such structure in memory for large databases. Consequently, using RDBMS capabilities like buffer management, query processor or SQL-Extensions, it is possible to take advantage of those mechanisms avoiding size considerations of data, in this particular case, FP (pattern-tree) tables.

The construction of *FP* table is set up on the following steps:

1. Based on a given support threshold (s), frequent 1-itemsets are selected from the transactional table *TRANS*.
2. A new transaction table *TRANSFI* is created based on transactions which contains those frequent 1-itemsets.
3. From the *TRANSFI* table, an *EFP* table which stands for Extended *FP* is built as a preprocessing step for reaching an *FP* table.
4. Finally, the *FP* table is created by means of an SQL expression, with proper aggregate function over *EFP* table.

The *EFP* table is an interesting approach for getting *FP* table, since it avoids for each frequent item to be tested if it should be or not inserted into *FP* table [14].

```
# a piece of the Pattern TREE (FP) source code #
PROCEDURE EFP
DO with (EXISTS TRANSFI)
CREATE TABLE EFP (item, cnt, path)
CREATE TABLE FP (item, cnt, path)
DECLARE
  BEGIN
    count = 1
    curpath = null
    c_transfi CURSOR for TRANSFI
    FOR each row in c_transfi
    BEGIN
      curpath = curpath + ':' + c_transfi.item
      INSERT INTO EFP
      values(c_transfi.item, count, curpath)
    END
    SELECT item, sum(cnt) as cnt, path
    INTO FP
    FROM EFP
    GROUP BY item, path
  END
```

3.2 Step 2: Mining Pattern-Tree Table

For mining *FP* table it is necessary to build two more auxiliary tables which are the *pattern base* (*PB*) and *conditional FP* table (*CONFP*). We present an approach where *CONFP* table is built based on simple SQL with proper aggregate functions over *PB* table. On the other hand, SQL-based FP-Growth [14] demands several reconstruction processes for those tables. It is almost unrealistic to create those tables several times. Therefore, we use an approach for getting *sub-paths* by means of UDF functions and database cursors with its respective support threshold over the *SUBFP* table (a SUBset of FP table).

SUBFP is a table that contains only rows from *FP* table which have itemsets enclosed in *CONFP*. By doing so, we can *reduce the search space for getting sub-paths* directly from all items in *FP* table, and also, *avoid several reconstruction* of *PB*, *FP* and *CONFP* tables. The size of *FP* is reduced significantly by using *SUBFP* mainly when dealing with low support thresholds on large datasets. The following steps are required for mining pattern tree table [4]:

1. Taking as input the same support threshold defined in 3.1, creates the related tables *PB*, *CONFP* and *SUBFP*.
2. Update the column (*pos*) in *CONF* which keeps the position of each item. This is useful for getting *sub-path* databases in such way that it preserves the order of the items on *SUBFP* table. This is important for using UDF (table-valued functions).
3. Extract *single patterns* by enumerating the *prefix-item* stored on *CONFP* table. This also creates the *PATTERNS* table.
4. Extract *not-single patterns* by applying pattern growth over *CONFP*.
5. In *Fragment Growth* step, each *prefix-item* is extracted from *SUBFP* table and verified by two UDF functions. One for generating the **sub-path** databases (function getTable_pb) and other for getting the **node support** associated to each *prefix-item*

sub-path (function getNodeSupp). Those functions coupled with the *SUBFP* table play an important role for extracting all frequent patterns, and also avoid the *reconstruction* of PB, FP and CONFP table for each *prefix-item sub-path*.

```
# a piece of the Fragment Growth source code #
   DECLARE pg_subPath CURSOR for
      SELECT *
      FROM getTable_pb(@v_prefix,@v_item) order by ord
      SELECT list_pg_item  = pg_subPath.item
      FOR each row in pg_subPath
      BEGIN
    SELECT node_path = pg_subPath.item+'%'+ c_confp.item
        SELECT node_supp =
         getNodeSupp(pg_subPath.prefix, node_path)
        SELECT pat_item = pg_subPath.item
        SELECT pat_fp = node_path+'%'+ pg_subPath.prefix
        SELECT pat_cnt =  node_supp
        SELECT exist_pat = (
                    SELECT count(*)   FROM  PATTERNS
                    WHERE item=pat_item and fp=pat_fp)
        INSERT INTO PATTERNS (item,fp,cnt)
        VALUES (pat_item, pat_fp, pat_cnt)
        SELECT list_pg_item = list_pg_item
               +'%'+ pg_subPath.item
      END

UDF FUNCTION getNodeSupp   (@item, @path)
RETURNS @node_supp ## -> node support
BEGIN
  DECLARE @supp int
  SELECT @supp = (SELECT sum(cnt)
            FROM    SUB_FP
            WHERE item=@item and
            path LIKE '%'+@path+'%')
  RETURN(@supp)
END

UDF FUNCTION getTable_pb (@prefix, @item)
RETURNS TABLE ## -> sub-path databases
AS   RETURN
        SELECT prefix,item,cnt,ord  FROM    CONFP
        WHERE   prefix=@prefix and
         item<>@item ##-> criteria for sub-path mining
```

4   PGS Evaluation on RDBMS Server Side

In order to evaluate PGS we compare our results with an Apriori (K-way join) and improved SQL-based FP-growth (EFP). Those algorithms were chosen in sense that they present the basis on the most known itemset mining implementations based on SQL [1, 12, 13, 14, 15, 16]. Both algorithms were implemented to the best of our knowledge based on the published reports on the same machine and compared in the same running environment. The former implementation uses a candidate k-table Ck, which is a slow process for *generating all joins and tables*. So, when dealing with long patterns and large datasets the K-way join seems to be not efficient. The EFP avoids candidate-set generation been more competitive in low support scenario. However, it demands *several tables reconstruction*.

Our approach takes the other way around, beyond pure SQL to SQL-Extensions. Also getting *sub-paths* databases, and restricting the search space for finding frequent itemsets by means of using an *SUBFP* table coupled with UDF functions. Consequently, we don't need to materialize *PB*, *FP* and *CONFP* tables several times.

PGS also has been used in [5] for the extraction and analysis of inter-transactional patterns. The method consists in the combination of association and sequence mining.

4.1 Datasets

We use the synthetic transaction data generation described in [3] for generating transactional tables. The nomenclature of these data sets is of the form TxxIyyDzzzK. Where xx denotes the average number of items present per transaction, yy denotes the average support of each item in the data set, and zzzK the total number of transactions in K (1000's). Table 3 summarizes those datasets.

Table 3. More information of the transactional datasets

Datasets	Dist. Items	Nof. Rows	Avg.1-it.sup	Max.1-it.sup
T5I51K (1)	775	5.112	6	41
T5I5D10K (2)	873	49.257	56	399
T25I10D10K (3)	947	245.933	259	1468
T25I20D100K (4)	981	2.478,55	2526	13.917

4.2 Comparative Study

We describe our approach PGS, comparing it with K-Way-join and EFP. Our experiments were performed with Microsoft SQL Server 2000 (v.8.0). The machine was a mobile AMD Athlon ™ 2000+ 645MHZ, 224 MB RAM. The performance measure was the execution time 'the logarithm of the execution time(log(milliseconds))' of the algorithm applied over the four datasets with different support thresholds. We took that log scale in order to get a better view of the performance comparison among all approaches, since PGS has good response time. Fig. 3 shows the total time taken by the all approaches.

From those graphs we can make the following observation: PGS can get competitive performance out of FP and K-way-join. K-way-join has low performance when dealing with large datasets. Besides, when the support decrease the length of frequent itemsets increase causing expensive joins with the transactional tables. Therefore, the other two approaches perform better than K-way-join.

The results of PGS and EFP answered our second issue. The former doesn't use table reconstruction, getting good response time. On the other hand, the latter suffers considerably by working with several table materialization processes. By those results we have accomplished our main goals.

The store procedures which deal with the construction of tables *FP* and *CONFP* are the most time-consuming tasks. They respectively took, for each dataset, 35%, 50%, 75% and 85% of the total execution time. Nevertheless, the time for the whole process was quite competitive and those tables are built only once. In order to speed up even more the whole process, we also have been applied *two clustered indexes* on tables *CONFP* and *SUBFP*.

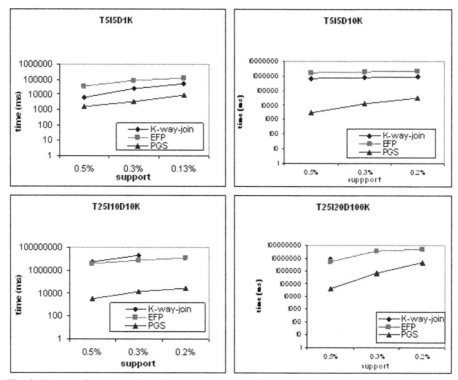

Fig. 3. Time performance of the three approaches. PGS runs competitively in sparse and dense datasets.

4.3   FoodMart Warehouse

FoodMart Warehouse is a sample database provided by Microsoft SQL Server 2000. One can use Analysis Services for applying OLAP and Data Mining techniques over data warehouses. However, only Clustering and Decision Tree methods are available.

In order to support itemset mining over FoodMart database we may use PGS. It works only in first step of association rules, which means *generating frequent itemsets*. For getting all the rules, one can program a store procedure using the pseudo-code in [2].

We choose this last example for presenting some results with a "real" database. Although we know that its size is smaller than the largest one showed in section 4.2, we also can reach interesting itemsets. Therefore we omit the performance comparison among all approaches.

It was used the *fact table* (sales_fact_1998) as the transactional table. This table has 164.558 tuples with five dimensions (product, time, customer, promotion and store). Before using PGS, we must define which dimensions in the fact table will be used as the *transaction identifier* (tid) and the *set of items*. Thus, the tid was set to the customer dimension and items to the product dimension. Furthermore, there are 1.559 distinct products distributed along 7.824 customers. The most frequent product was 277 "Great English Muffins" (143) and the less one was 1559 "CDR Apple Preserves" (43). It was executed several supports from (0.05%) to (0.01%). The most interesting itemset was "282%232" means "Best Choice Salsa Dip" and "Great Wheat Bread" in low level hierarchy. Given that the fact table was so sparse, the itemsets was selected only with very low support.

5 Conclusions

In this paper, it was purposed a *pattern growth mining* implementation which takes advantage of SQL-Extensions. Most of the commercial RDBMS vendors have implemented some features for SQL-Extensions. Integrating data mining in RDBMS is a quite promising area. Frequent pattern mining is the basic task in data mining. There are several memory-approaches to mine all patterns. However, some few efforts have been made on database perspective, in those cases, *only pure-SQL*.

Given the large size of database like data warehouse, it is interesting to take advantage of those databases capabilities in order to manage and analyze large tables. We work in this direction purposing an approach with SQL-Extensions. By doing so, we can achieve competitive results and also avoid classical bottlenecks: *candidate set generation and test* (several expensive joins), and *table reconstruction*. The Store Procedures that deals with the construction of the tables, FP and CONFP, are the most time-consuming tasks, taking 35%, 50%, 75% and 85% respectively for each *synthetic* dataset (1, 2, 3, 4) from the small one to the large one. Nevertheless, the time for the whole process was quite competitive. Moreover, it was used the FoodMart Warehouse with several supports in order to find interesting itemsets.

One issue that is controversial is code portability, in sense that PGS is tightly dependent of the database programming language with SQL-Extensions. On the other hand for huge databases, it makes more sense take all the advantages offered by the RDBMS.

As future work, we are working on enhancements for making the process more interactive, constrained and incremental. We also intend to improve the whole performance of PGS by using Table Variables (TV), which allows mimicking an array, instead of using database cursors.

References

1. Agarwal, R., Shim., R.: Developing tightly-coupled data mining application on a relational database system. In Proc.of the 2nd Int. Conf. on Knowledge Discovery in Database and Data Mining, Portland, Oregon (1996)

2. Agrawal, R., Imielinski, T., Swami, A..: Mining association rules between sets of items in large databases. In Proc. of the ACM SIGMOD Intl. Conference on Management of Data (1993) 207–216

3. Agrawal, R., Srikant., R.: Fast algorithms for mining association rules. In Proc. of the 20th Very Large Data Base Conference (1994) 487–499

4. Alves, R., Belo, O.: Integrating Pattern Growth Mining on SQL-Server RDBMS. Technical Report-003, University of Minho, Department of Informatics, May (2005) http://alfa.di.uminho.pt/~ronnie/files_files/rt/2005-RT3-Ronnie.pdf

5. Alves, R., Gabriel, P., Azevedo, P., Belo, O.: A Hybrid Method to Discover Inter-Transactional Rules. In Proceedings of the JISBD'2005, Granada (2005)

6. Cheung, W., Zaïane, O. R.: Incremental Mining of Frequent Patterns Without Candidate Generation or Support Constraint, Seventh International Database Engineering and Applications Symposium (IDEAS 2003), Hong Kong, China, July 16-18 (2003) 111-116

7. El-Hajj, M., Zaïane, O.R.: Inverted Matrix: Efficient Discovery of Frequent Items in Large Datasets in the Context of Interactive Mining, in Proc. 2003 Int'l Conf. on Knowledge Discovery and Data Mining (ACM SIGKDD), Washington, DC, USA, August 24-27 (2003) 109-118

8. Han, J., Pei, J., Yin., Y.: Mining frequent patterns without candidate generation. In Proc. of ACM SIGMOD Intl. Conference on Management of Data, (2000) 1–12

9. Hidber, C.: Online association rule mining. In A. Delis, C. Faloutsos, and S. Ghandeharizadeh, editors, Proceedings of the 1999 ACM SIGMOD International Conference on Management of Data, volume 28(2) of SIGMOD Record. ACM Press (1999) 145–156

10. Orlando, S., Palmerini, P., Perego, R.: Enhancing the apriori algorithm for frequent set counting. In Y. Kambayashi, W. Winiwarter, and M. Arikawa, editors, Proceedings of the Third International Conference on Data Warehousing and Knowledge Discovery, volume 2114 of Lecture Notes in Computer Science (2001) 71–82

11. Orlando, S., Palmerini, P., Perego, R., Silvestri, F.: Adaptive and resource-aware mining of frequent sets. In V. Kumar, S. Tsumoto, P.S. Yu, and N.Zhong, editors, Proceedings of the 2002 IEEE International Conference on Data Mining. IEEE Computer Society (2002)

12. Rantzau, R.: Processing frequent itemset discovery queries by division and set containment join operators. In DMKD03: 8th ACM SIGMOD Workshop on Research Issues in Data Mining and Knowledge Discovery (2003)

13. Sarawagi, S., Thomas, S., Agrawal, R.: Integrating mining with relational database systems: alternatives and implications. In Proc. of the ACM SIGMOD Conference on Management of data, Seattle, Washington, USA (1998)

14. Shang, X., Sattler, K., Geist, I.: Sql based frequent pattern mining without candidate generation. In SAC'04 Data Mining, Nicosia, Cyprus (2004)

15. Wang, H., Zaniolo, C.: Using SQL to build new aggregates and extenders for Object-Relational systems. In Proc. Of the 26th Int. Conf. on Very Large Databases, Cairo, Egypt (2000)

16. Yoshizawa, T., Pramudiono, I., Kitsuregawa, M.: Sql based association rule mining using commercial rdbms (ibm db2 udb eee). In In Proc. DaWaK, London, UK (2000)

Using a More Powerful Teacher to Reduce the Number of Queries of the L* Algorithm in Practical Applications

André L. Martins, H. Sofia Pinto, and Arlindo L. Oliveira

INESC-ID/IST - Av. Alves Redol, 9. 1000-029 Lisboa, Portugal
{almar, sofia}@algos.inesc-id.pt, aml@inesc-id.pt

Abstract. In this work we propose to use a more powerful teacher to effectively apply query learning algorithms to identify regular languages in practical, real-world problems. More specifically, we define a more powerful set of replies to the membership queries posed by the L* algorithm that reduces the number of such queries by several orders of magnitude in a practical application. The basic idea is to avoid the needless repetition of membership queries in cases where the reply will be negative as long as a particular condition is met by the string in the membership query. We present an example of the application of this method to a real problem, that of inferring a grammar for the structure of technical articles.

1 Introduction and Motivation

Learning using feedback from the teacher, also known as active learning, is an important area of research, with many practical applications. One of the best known approaches to apply active learning to the inference of sequential models is the L* algorithm. In this work we describe an improvement to the L* algorithm, that strongly reduces the number of queries, in a practical application in the area of ontology learning.

Ontologies provide a shared and common understanding of a domain that can be communicated between people, as well as between heterogeneous and widely spread application systems. Typically, ontologies are composed of a set of terms representing concepts (hierarchically organized) and some specification of their meaning. This specification is usually achieved by a set of constraints that restrict the way those terms can be combined. The latter set constrains the semantics of a term, since it restricts the number of possible interpretations of the term. Therefore, we can use an ontology to represent the semantic meaning of given terms.

In our case, we are interested in learning an ontology about articles. Using the semantic information, provided by the ontology, search engines can focus on the relevant parts of documents, therefore improving precision and recall.

Our starting point is a small set of 13 basic concepts: title, author(s), abstract title, abstract text, section title, simple text, formated text, subsection title,

C. Bento, A. Cardoso, and G. Dias (Eds.): EPIA 2005, LNAI 3808, pp. 325–336, 2005.

Figure caption, etc. As an intermediate step towards learning the ontology, we aim at inferring a description of an automaton that encodes the structure of articles. For that we have used query learning. However, existing algorithms for query learning use an exceedingly large number of queries for problems of reasonable size, a feature that makes them unusable in real world settings. In this work we propose a solution to the large number of queries required by the L* algorithm in this and other practical settings.

The remainder of this paper is organized as follows: first, we briefly describe the problem and related work (Sect. 2). We describe, in Sect. 3, the algorithm for query learning that is our starting point, L* . We then describe the approach we used to solve the main problem found when using the L* algorithm, the large number of membership queries that needs to be answered (Sect. 4). Our results are presented and discussed in Sect. 5. We end with conclusions (Sect. 6).

2   Related Work

This work addresses the problem of inferring a regular language using queries and counter-examples. The problem of regular language learning has been extensively studied, both from a practical and theoretical point of view.

Selecting the minimum deterministic finite automaton (DFA) consistent with a set of pre-defined, labeled, strings is known to be NP-complete [1]. Furthermore, even the problem of finding a DFA with a number of states only polynomially larger than the number of states of the minimum solution is also NP-complete [2].

Fortunately, the problem becomes easier if the algorithm is allowed to make queries or to experiment with the unknown automaton. Angluin proposed the L* algorithm [3], a method based on the approach described by Gold [4], that solves the problem in polynomial time by allowing the algorithm to ask membership queries. Schapire [5] proposes an interesting alternative approach that does not require the availability of a reset signal to take the automaton to a known state.

Our work aims at making the L* algorithm more applicable to real world problems, by using a more powerful teacher.

We have chosen a particular problem to apply the proposed approach, that of inferring a regular language that models the structure of a document (in our case, of a technical article). Such a model can later be used to label the different parts of a document, a first step towards the desired goal of semantically labeling the document.

A number of approaches have been proposed to date to the problem of inferring the structure of a document using language models. Additionally, a number of methods have been proposed to efficiently detect structures in sequences of symbols using languages (regular or context-free) as models [6, 7, 8]. However, these approaches are generally concerned with the identification of repeating structures and not, necessarily, semantic units.

We believe that the application of a grammatical inference method to the inference of semantic units in documents will only lead to interesting results if a human teacher is involved in the learning process. Automatic learning of semantic structures from (possibly labeled) sets of documents is a worthwhile goal, but is likely to require very large corpora and efficient algorithms that do not yet exist.

Other approaches that do not use languages as models for the text also exist, but are more limited in their potential scope, since they look for local features of the text, such as fonts and formats [9, 10, 11, 12, 13]. The techniques used in these approaches can also be useful, but have not yet been applied to our problem.

3   Query Learning of Regular Languages

A regular language can be defined by the set of strings that are accepted by a deterministic finite automaton (DFA), defined as follows.

Definition 1. *A DFA defined over the alphabet Σ is a tuple $D = (Q, \Sigma, q_0, F, \delta)$, where:*

Q is a finite set of states;
$q_0 \in Q$ is the initial state;
$F \subset Q$ is the set of final or accepting states;
$\delta : Q \times \Sigma \rightarrow Q$ is the transition function.

A string is accepted by a DFA if there exists a sequence of transitions, matching the symbols in the string, starting from the initial state and ending in an accepting state.

The task of learning a regular language can be seen as learning a DFA that accepts the strings belonging to the language.

Query learning is concerned with the problem of learning an unknown concept using the answers provided by a teacher or oracle. In this context, the concept will be a DFA. There are several types of queries, but here we will focus on those sufficient to learn efficiently regular languages [14], namely:

membership queries the learner presents an instance for classification as to whether or not it belongs to the unknown language;
equivalence queries the learner presents a possible concept and the teacher either acknowledges that it is equivalent to the unknown language or returns an instance that distinguishes both.

Angluin presented an efficient algorithm [3] to identify regular languages from queries, the L* algorithm. This algorithm derives the minimum canonical DFA that is consistent with the answered queries.

3.1   The L* Algorithm

In this section we briefly describe the L* algorithm, in order to be able to present the proposed changes.

The L* algorithm defines a learner, in the query learning setting, for regular languages. This learner infers DFAs from the answers to membership and equivalence queries posed to a teacher. A teacher that can answer these types of queries is referred to as a minimally adequate teacher.

The instances used in membership queries are strings defined over the alphabet Σ. The concepts in equivalence queries are DFAs defined over that alphabet.

The information obtained from membership queries is used to define a function[1] $T : ((S \cup S \cdot \Sigma) \cdot E) \to \{0, 1\}$, where S is a nonempty finite prefix-closed set[2] of strings and E is a nonempty finite suffix-closed set of strings. The set $((S \cup S \cdot \Sigma) \cdot E)$ is the set of strings for which membership queries have been asked.

The function T has a value of 1 when the answer is positive, that is, when the string belongs to the language of the target DFA, and a value of 0 otherwise. It can be viewed as an observation table, where the rows are labeled by the elements of $(S \cup S \cdot \Sigma)$ and columns are labeled by the elements of E. For example, in Table 1, $S = \{\lambda\}$, $E = \{\lambda\}$ and $S \cdot \Sigma = \{0, 1, 2\}$.

Table 1. Initial L* table at the first conjecture

		λ	} E
S {	λ	0	
	(2)	0	
$S \cdot \Sigma$	(1)	0	
	(0)	0	

To represent a valid complete DFA, the observation table must meet two properties: closure and consistency. The observation table is *closed* iff, for each t in $S \cdot \Sigma$ there exists an $s \in S$ such that $row(t) = row(s)$. The observation table is *consistent* iff for every s_1 and s_2, elements of S, such that $row(s_1) = row(s_2)$ and for all $a \in \Sigma$, it holds that $row(s_1 \cdot a) = row(s_2 \cdot a)$.

The DFA $D = (Q, q_0, F, \delta)$ that corresponds to a *closed* and *consistent* observation table is defined by:

$$Q = \{row(s) : s \in S\}$$
$$q_0 = row(\lambda)$$
$$F = \{row(s) : s \in S \wedge T(s) = 1\}$$
$$\delta(row(s), a) = row(s \cdot a)$$

For example, Fig. 1 shows the DFA corresponding to the observation table shown in Table 2. Note that when a string belongs to both S and $S \cdot \Sigma$ then it is only represented once in the observation table (at the top part). This can be seen in Table 2. To obtain the transition function value for the initial state and symbol $0 \in \Sigma$, i.e. $\delta(row(\lambda), 0)$, one must lookup $row(\lambda \cdot 0)$, namely, the line labeled by (0). This line is shown in the top part of Table 2 because $(0) \in S$.

It can be proved that any DFA consistent with the observation table, but different by more than an isomorphism, must have more states.

---

[1] Set concatenation $A \cdot B = \{ab | a \in A, b \in B\}$.

[2] A prefix-closed (suffix-closed) set is a set such that the prefix (suffix) of every set element is also a member of the set.

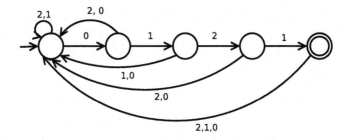

Fig. 1. Intermediate DFA

Table 2. L* table at the second conjecture

	λ	(1)	(2 1)	(1 2 1)
(0 1 2 1)	1	0	0	0
(0 1 2)	0	1	0	0
(0 1)	0	0	1	0
(0)	0	0	0	1
λ	0	0	0	0
(0 1 2 1 2)	0	0	0	0
(0 1 2 1 1)	0	0	0	0
(0 1 2 2)	0	0	0	0
(0 1 2 1 0)	0	0	0	0
(0 1 2 0)	0	0	0	0
(0 1 1)	0	0	0	0
(0 2)	0	0	0	0
(0 1 0)	0	0	0	0
(2)	0	0	0	0
(1)	0	0	0	0
(0 0)	0	0	0	0
(0 2 2 2)	0	0	0	0

Starting with the initialization of the observation table, the L* algorithm proceeds to build a DFA. The DFA is presented to the teacher as an equivalence query.

Before a DFA can be generated from the observation table, it must verify two properties: the table must be *consistent* and *closed*. Therefore, a loop must be executed until the properties are met, updating the observation table along the way.

If the observation table is not *consistent*, then there exist $s_1, s_2 \in S$, $a \in \Sigma$ and $e \in E$ such that $row(s_1) = row(s_2)$ and $T(s_1 \cdot a \cdot e) \neq T(s_2 \cdot a \cdot e)$. The set E is augmented with $a \cdot e$ and the observation table is extended using membership queries.

If the observation table is not *closed*, then there exist an $s_1 \in S$ and an $a \in \Sigma$ such that $row(s_1 \cdot a)$ is different from all $row(s)$ with $s \in S$. The set S is extended with $s_1 \cdot a$ and the observation table is extended using membership queries.

Table 3. L* execution trace

L*			L* with filter
λ ? N	(0 1 2 1 2) ? N	(0 2 2 1) ? N	λ ? N
(0) ? N	(0 1 2 1 2 1) ? N	(0 1 0 2 1) ? N	(0) ? (e (0))
(1) ? N	(0 1 2 1 1 1) ? N	(2 2 1) ? N	(1) ? (s (1))
(2) ? N	(0 1 2 2 1) ? N	(1 2 1) ? N	(2) ? (s (2))
	(0 1 2 1 0 1) ? N	(0 0 2 1) ? N	
(conjecture)	(0 1 2 0 1) ? N	(0 1 2 1 2 1 2 1) ? N	(conjecture)
	(0 1 1 1) ? N	(0 1 2 1 1 1 2 1) ? N	
(0 0) ? N	(0 2 1) ? N	(0 1 2 2 1 2 1) ? N	(0 1) ? (e (0 1))
(0 1) ? N	(0 1 0 1) ? N	(0 1 2 1 0 1 2 1) ? N	(0 2) ? (e (0 2))
(0 2) ? N	(2 1) ? N	(0 1 2 0 1 2 1) ? N	(0 1 1) ? (p ((1 1)))
(0 1 0) ? N	(1 1) ? N	(0 1 1 1 2 1) ? N	(0 1 2) ? (e (0 1 2))
(0 1 1) ? N	(0 0 1) ? N	(0 2 1 2 1) ? N	(0 1 2 1) ? Y
(0 1 2) ? N	(0 1 2 1 2 2 1) ? N	(0 1 0 1 2 1) ? N	(0 1 2 2) ? (p ((1 2) (2)))
(0 1 2 0) ? N	(0 1 2 1 1 2 1) ? N	(2 1 2 1) ? N	(0 2 1) ? (p ((0 2) (1)))
(0 1 2 1) ? Y	(0 1 2 2 2 1) ? N	(1 1 2 1) ? N	(0 1 0 1 2 1) ? (p ((0) (0)))
(0 1 2 2) ? N	(0 1 2 1 0 2 1) ? N	(0 0 1 2 1) ? N	
(0 1 2 1 0) ? N	(0 1 2 0 2 1) ? N		(conjecture)
(0 1 2 1 1) ? N	(0 1 1 2 1) ? N	(conjecture)	

Once the inner loop terminates, the DFA that corresponds to the observation table is presented to the teacher. If the teacher accepts this DFA the algorithm terminates. If the teacher returns a counter-example, then the counter-example and all of its prefixes are added to S, the table is extended using membership queries, and the algorithm continues with the first step (the loop that verifies the observation table properties).

For example, to learn the language $L = \{(0\ 1\ 2\ 1), (0\ 2\ 2\ 2)\}$, the algorithm starts a serie of queries (shown in Table 3) until it reaches a closed and consistent observation table, Table 1. It then poses the first conjecture. The first conjecture is a DFA with only one state, that accepts no strings. After receiving the string $(0\ 1\ 2\ 1)$ as (a negative) reply to the first equivalence conjecture, the algorithm poses a long sequence of membership queries (shown in Table 3) until it finally reaches a point where the observation table is again both *closed* and *consistent*, as shown in Table 2. Then the second conjecture, shown in Fig. 1, is presented to the teacher. The process could be continued until the DFA shown in Fig. 2 is reached[3] that accepts only the strings present in the target language L.

4   Learning DFAs Using a More Powerful Teacher

Query learning algorithms, such as L*, described in the previous section, produce a very large number of queries. This makes their use with human teachers impractical.

---

[3] The resulting DFA would have an additional non-accepting state, here omitted for clarity, where all the transitions that are not shown in the figure would converge.

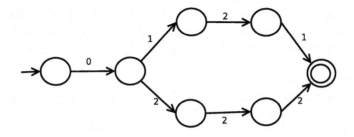

Fig. 2. Example DFA (extra state removed)

Depending on the target language, the number of queries of each type varies. Nevertheless, the number of membership queries is typically the dominant part in the total query count.

Membership queries have two possible answers, positive or negative. The negative answer is used to restrict the target language (with respect to the universal language containing all strings). As such, it is reasonable to expect that most languages will have a much larger count of negative membership queries than positive membership queries.

To deal with the large number of membership queries, that typically happens when learning non-trivial automata, we propose, in this work, to use a more powerful teacher. Should the answer to a membership query be negative, the teacher is requested to return additional information, namely, to identify a set of strings that would result also in negative answers to membership queries.

We consider three forms for the answer:

1. A string prefix – This form identifies the set of strings that start with the same prefix and that are also negative examples. Its use can be seen in Table 3, with the form *(s <string>)*.
2. A string suffix – The second form does the same as the first one, but with the string suffix. It identifies strings that end in the same manner and that are also negative examples. Its use can also be seen in Table 3, with the form *(e <string>)*.
3. A list of substrings – The third form can be used to specify a broader family of strings that are negative examples. Here one can identify strings by listing substrings that, when they are all present in a given string, in the same order, imply that the string is part of the described set and a negative example. For example, to identify the set of strings that contain two zeros, the reply would be the following list ((0)(0)), where (0) is a string with just one symbol, 0. Its use is also illustrated in Table 3, with the form *(p (<string1> ... <stringN>))*.

Note that these specifications can be viewed as non-deterministic finite automata (NFA).

Using the additional information, the learner can now find out the answer to a number of membership queries without making an explicit query, simply by matching the strings with the stored information using the NFA corresponding to the new answer form. This can clearly be seen in Table 3, right hand side column, where the same DFA is inferred with and without the proposed extension, resulting in an important reduction in the number of queries.

Although we are requiring more sophisticated answers from the teacher, this is a reasonable request when dealing with human teachers. A human teacher must have some informal definition of the target language in his mind, to use a query learning approach, and it is reasonable to expect that most negative answers could be justified using the proposed method. The use of a query learning method when an informal definition is already present in the human teacher's mind is necessary to obtain a minimal DFA with less effort than it would require to manually build one. As such, the extra required effort is a small one, since the human teacher would already have identified that justification in order to answer the original membership query. Moreover, in a graphical environment this could be easily implemented by allowing for the selection of parts of the query string using a mouse pointer (allowing for multiple-selection to indicate a list of substrings answer).

The proposed solution uses the L* algorithm as a "black box". A filter is placed between the teacher and the learner, which records the additional information returned by the teacher on negative membership query answers. This information is then used to reply, whenever possible, to the learner without consulting the teacher.

4.1   Example Results and Equivalence Queries

Table 4 shows the results obtained for the example DFA from Fig. 2. In this example, the strings used to reply (negatively) to the equivalence queries were (0 1 2 1), (0 2 2 2) and (2 2 2 2). Table 5 shows the distribution of membership query answers by type and the number of answers made by the filter using the information of each type of query answer.

Even in this simple example, the number of membership queries is substantially reduced making the method usable by human teachers (L* with filter (A) in Table 4). Further results with a real application are shown in the next section.

The extra information returned by the teacher could also be used to answer some equivalence queries, namely those containing strings that are not part of the target language and can be detected by the NFA already recorded. For example, the DFA in Fig. 1 admits strings, containing two or more 0s, that do not belong

Table 4. Query count results - simple example

	Membership Query Numbers		Equivalence Query
	Positive	Negative	Numbers
L*	2	185	4
L* with filter (A)	2	13	4
L* with filter (B)	2	13	3

(A) - Filter applied to membership queries;
(B) - Filter applied to membership and equivalence queries.

Table 5. Query counts by type - simple example

	Start with	End with	Has parts	Unjustified	Total
Teacher answers	2	4	5	2	13
Filter use counts	72	21	79	-	172

to the language. This could be detected as it was already stated in the end of Table 3 by "(p ((0) (0)))".

However, to detect these cases it would be necessary to obtain the product automaton between the recorded NFA and the DFA proposed by the learner, a process with quadratic complexity on the number of states. Note also that the number of states not only increases with the complexity of the language, but also with the number of extended answers (answers with the new proposed forms). This is a costly operation and would only remove, in general, a small fraction of the equivalence queries (L* with filter (B) in Table 4).

5 Application to the Inference of Document Structure

To demonstrate the use of the proposed solution, we applied it to the inference of a grammar that describes the structure of technical articles. This work is part of an ongoing effort to automatically derive an ontology describing the structure of technical articles.

The first step was described in [15] and resulted in the segmentation of source articles into a set of symbols. These symbols are: ConferenceTitle (0), Title (1), Author (2), AbstractTitle (3), AbstractText (4), IndexTitle (6), Index (7), SectionTitle (8), SubSectionTitle (10), SubSubSectionTitle (11), SimpleText (5), FormatedText (9), FigureCaption (12).

The next step in this effort is the inference of a DFA for technical articles, using the acquired symbols. This will later enable the inference of the ontology.

To apply the approach described in this paper, we assumed that:

- The ConferenceTitle is optional;
- There can be one or more Authors;
- The Index and IndexTitle are optional;
- A section can contain some of the text elements (SimpleText, FormatedText, FigureCaption) and lower level sections.

The equivalence queries were answered using the strings in Table 6.

Table 7 shows the number of queries resulting from the use of the L* algorithm and of the proposed solution. The resulting DFA is shown in Fig. 3. Table 8 shows the distribution of membership query answers by type and the number of answers made by the filter using the information of each type of query answer.

As the results show, the number of negative membership queries is substantially reduced. Also, at least in this example, the negative membership queries are the largest in number. This is the case for automata that have few terminal

Table 6. Strings used in equivalence queries

Q	Strings supplied to the algorithm
1	Title Author AbstractTitle AbstractText SectionTitle SimpleText
2	Title Title Author AbstractTitle AbstractText SectionTitle SimpleText
3	Title Author AbstractTitle AbstractText IndexTitle Index SectionTitle SimpleText
4	ConferenceTitle ConferenceTitle Title Author AbstractTitle AbstractText SectionTitle SimpleText
5	Title Author AbstractTitle AbstractText SectionTitle SimpleText SubSectionTitle SimpleText SubSubSectionTitle SimpleText

Table 7. Query count results

	Membership Query Numbers		Equivalence Query
	Positive	Negative	Numbers
L*	99	4118	6
L* with filter (A)	99	110	6
L* with filter (B)	99	110	5

(A) - Filter applied to membership queries;
(B) - Filter applied to membership and equivalence queries.

Table 8. Query counts by type

	Start with	End with	Has parts	Unjustified	Total
Teacher answers	11	10	88	1	110
Filter use counts	101	280	3627	-	4008

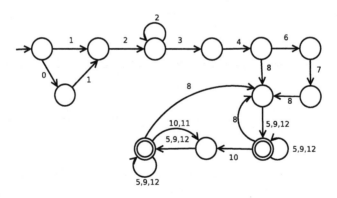

Fig. 3. DFA representing the article structure (extra state removed)

states, relatively to the total number of states, a situation that is common in real cases.

As mentioned in Sect. 4.1, the information can be used to reduce the amount of equivalence queries (L* filter (B) in Table 7), but results in only a small reduction in the number of queries.

6   Conclusion

Query learning algorithms, when used with a human teacher, suffer from the excessive number of queries that are required to learn the target concept. In this work we have presented a simple extension to the well known L* algorithm that reduces this burden considerably.

The teacher is required to provide a list of sub-strings that, when present, implies that the query string does not belong to the target language. Using this extra information, many of the subsequent queries can be answered automatically by the filter. The additional information provided represents only a small amount of selection work by the user, greatly compensating for the reduction on the number of queries.

The solution is independent of the regular language query learning algorithm used, as long as the later relies mainly on membership queries. With it's use, such algorithms become a practical possibility in dealing with human teachers.

Acknowledgements

This work was partially supported by "Fundação para a Ciência e Tecnologia" under research project PSOC/EIA/58210/2004 (OntoSeaWeb-Ontology Engineering for the Semantic Web).

References

1. Gold, E.M.: Complexity of automaton identification from given data. Information and Control **37** (1978) 302–320
2. Pitt, L., Warmuth, M.: The minimum consistent DFA problem cannot be approximated within any polynomial. Journal of ACM **40** (1993) 95–142
3. Angluin, D.: Learning regular sets from queries and counterexamples. Information and Computation **75** (1987) 86–106
4. Gold, E.M.: System identification via state characterization. Automatica **8** (1972) 621–636
5. Schapire, R.E.: The Design and Analysis of Efficient Learning Algorithms. MIT Press, Cambridge, MA (1992)
6. Nevill-Manning, C., Witten, I.H., Maulsby, D.L.: Modeling sequences using grammars and automata. In: Proceedings Canadian Machine Learning Workshop. (1994) 15–18
7. Hsu, C.N., Dung, M.T.: Generating finite-state transducers for semi-structured data extraction from the web. Information Systems **23** (1998) 521–538
8. Witten, I.H.: Adaptive text mining: inferring structure from sequences. Journal of Discrete Algorithms **2** (2004) 137–159
9. Laender, A.H.F., Ribeiro-Neto, B.A., da Silva, A.S., Teixeira, J.S.: A brief survey of web data extraction tools. SIGMOD Record **31** (2002) 84–93
10. Ribeiro-Neto, B.A., Laender, A.H.F., da Silva, A.S.: Extracting semi-structured data through examples. In: Proceedings of the 1999 ACM CIKM International Conference on Information and Knowledge Management, ACM (1999) 94–101

11. Adelberg, B.: NoDoSE - a tool for semi-automatically extracting semi-structured data from text documents. In: Proceedings ACM SIGMOD International Conference on Management of Data. (1998) 283–294
12. Califf, M.E., Mooney, R.J.: Relational learning of pattern-match rules for information extraction. In: Proceedings of the Sixteenth National Conference on Artificial Intelligence and Eleventh Conference on Innovative Applications of Artificial Intelligence. (1999) 328–334
13. Soderland, S.: Learning information extraction rules for semi-structured and free text. Machine Learning **34** (1999) 233–272
14. Angluin, D.: Queries and concept learning. Machine Learning **2** (1988) 319–342
15. Martins, A.L., Pinto, H.S., Oliveira, A.L.: Towards automatic learning of a structure ontology for technical articles. In: Semantic Web Workshop at SIGIR 2004. (2004)

User Group Profile Modeling Based on User Transactional Data for Personalized Systems

Yiling Yang and Nuno C. Marques

CENTRIA, Departamento de Informática, Faculdade Ciências e Tecnologia,
Universidade Nova Lisboa, Quinta da Torre, 2829-516 Caparica, Portugal
yiling.yang@gmx.de, nmm@di.fct.unl.pt

Abstract. In this paper, we propose a framework named UMT (User-profile Modeling based on Transactional data) for modeling user group profiles based on the transactional data. UMT is a generic framework for application systems that keep the historical transactions of their users. In UMT, user group profiles consist of three types: basic information attributes, synthetic attributes and probability distribution attributes. User profiles are constructed by clustering user transaction data and integrating cluster attributes with domain information extracted from application systems and other external data sources. The characteristic of UMT makes it suitable for personalization of transaction-based commercial application systems. A case study is presented to illustrate how to use UMT to create a personalized tourism system capable of using domain information in intelligent ways and of reacting to external events.

1 Introduction

Personalization is the process of adapting information to suit the needs of different users. The prerequisite of personalization is to acquire *user profiles* that describe user's interests, preferences and background knowledge about specified domains. Methods used for modeling user profiles include logic-based representation and inference [8], Bayesian models [6], Feature-based filtering [11], Clique-based filtering [12], and neural networks [9].

Explicit user participation is often indispensable to obtain user profiles. The most straightforward way is to ask for user preferences directly by questionnaires. Many e-commerce web sites recommend items that the user is potentially interested in based on *collaborative filtering*, which needs a user to rate items in order to make recommendation based on the ratings of similar users. For stereotype-based user profile modeling [2], however, domain experts are required to construct the initial stereotypes.

For many commercial application systems, it is easy to gather user transactional data, which are the aggregated set of items that a user browses/books/purchases in a particular time span. Transactional data can be best explained using the *market-basket* example: a transaction consists of all the items purchased together in one basket. While being a key source that reveals user's interests and needs, user transactional data hardly require any extra efforts from them.

C. Bento, A. Cardoso, and G. Dias (Eds.): EPIA 2005, LNAI 3808, pp. 337–347, 2005.

We propose a framework called UMT (User-profile Modeling based on Transactional data) for modeling user profiles based on user transactional data. UMT is a generic user profile modeling framework suitable for the transaction-based application systems. UMT can incorporate external information, either by means of an internal knowledge base or on dynamic data supplied by a specific information extraction system. User profiles in UMT are not constructed based on stereotypes but based on the results of clustering algorithms for user transactional data. As the result, UMT avoids the influence of the expert's bias. At the same time, using UMT to construct a personalized system will not bring the extra burden to end-users. A case study in an Hotel Network shows how UMT is applied to a personalized tourism system capable of reacting to external events.

The rest of this paper is organized as follows. Section 2 describes the architecture of UMT. Section 3 presents a case study of UMT in tourism domain. Finally, conclusions and future work are given.

2 UMT Framework

UMT is a generic framework of user profile modeling for personalized systems, built on top of a multi-user *application system*, through which some *relationship* between *users* and *items* are constructed. A typical example is the purchase relationship between an Internet user and a book, established through an online bookstore. Most of these application systems contain the transactional data that describes user's behaviors. UMT creates user profiles according to the results of clustering algorithms for user transactional data.

We first give the formats of a few key data elements in our framework. A *user transaction*, $t=<user\_id, \{p_1, ..., p_m\}>$, is a 2-tuple of user ID and a set of items. A *clustering* $\{C_1, ... C_k\}$ is a partition of user transactions $\{t_1, ..., t_n\}$. Each C_i is called a *cluster*. $C_1 \cup ... \cup C_k = \{t_1, ..., t_n\}$ and $C_i \neq \phi \land C_i \cap C_j = \phi$ for any $1 \leq i, j \leq k$ (i.e. we consider only disjoint non-empty clusters). A *user group profile* $UGP=<ugp\_id, \{(attr_1, val_1), (attr_2, val_2),...\}>$ is a 2-tuple with a key and a set of (attribute, value)-pairs.

Figure 1 shows the architecture of UMT. UMT consists of three modules: the data preparing module, the user modeling module, and the recommendation generating module.

Data preparing module. The data preparing module collects user transactions from the application system and specified domain information and/or other data sources. The prepared data is the input of the user modeling module. The main processing steps of this module are:

Step 1. Preprocessing. Acquire user transactions from the application systems. Standard data preprocessing techniques [7], such as data integration, data transformation, data cleaning, and data consistency checking, may be used to obtain the transactional data.

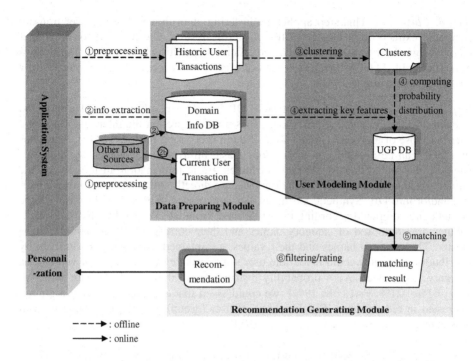

Fig. 1. The architecture of the UMT framework

Step 2. Information extraction. Acquire domain information from the application systems and/or other data sources into the domain info DB (info DB for short). The info DB has two parts: item-related data and domain-related data. For example, in a hotel reservation website, the info DB may contain data about hotels, resorts, foods, and culture events or nearby interesting places. Here hotel info belongs to item-related data; resorts, foods, and culture events belong to tourism-related data. Usually, item-related data is directly obtained from the item database of the application systems. Domain-related data can be acquired from other applications or web.

Besides the obviously highly structured information that could be inserted in a database, a huge amount of related text information is also available: specific tourist guides, bulletins and main touristic events in sport or culture are regularly issued and available on Internet. Then, web information extraction techniques (http://gate.ac.uk/) can be used to extract predefined data from web pages, such as for example postal addresses [10]. We will see that this information can be used to trigger recommendations as if it was any other user transaction (Step 2b – information extraction).

User modeling module. The user modeling module is the core of UMT. It constructs UGP (User Group Profile) DB based on the transactional data and specified domain DB. The main steps of this module are:

Step 3. Clustering. This step applies a clustering algorithm to historic user transactions and extracts item lists from the clustering results. Clustering algorithms specially designed for transactional data can efficiently partition historic user transactions into clusters [4, 11]. Each cluster is a set of transactions representing the interests of a particular user group.

Step 4. UGP generating. Construct UGP DB based on result clusters of step 3 and domain info DB of step 2. Since the profiles do not represent the interests of a single user but those of a group of users, we call them user group profiles (UGP). Attributes in a UGP can be divided into three types: basic information attributes, synthetic attributes, and probability distribution attributes. Basic information attributes, e.g. the number of items in a cluster, product names, are directly obtained from clustering result and/or info DB. Synthetic attributes, like importance degree of a cluster in all the clusters, are computed according to pre-defined formulae. Probability distribution attributes are composed of category names and their corresponding probabilities in a cluster. The category names and their values are obtained from info DB. Probability distribution attributes could reveal the user's interests degree on different values of a category, e.g. if we have a probability distribution attribute product_color = {red: 60%, blue: 21%, yellow: 19%}, we could assert that users in this cluster are more interested in red products. Similar forms of user (group) profiles have been used in personalization systems such as INTRIGUE [3].

Recommendation generating module. Recommendation generating module finds similar UGPs according to the current user transaction and generates the recommendation set according to the matching result.

Step 5. Matching. Find the most similar UGPs for current user transaction. The matching result is a set of UGPs ordered by similarities. The key problem in this step is to define the similarity measure between a UGP and the current user transaction.

Matching UGPs should also take into account external recent events, than can be inserted in the data base, e.g., by an automatically text mining engine [10]. For both approaches, we should balance the accuracy and complexity of the similarity definition. A time-consuming similarity computation will increase the latency to response the user request since this step is run in real-time.

Step 6. Filtering/rating. Generate an ordered list of recommendation items from the matching UGPs of step 5. First, the matching result in step 5 should be transformed to a list of items that occur in UGPs of the matching result. Filtering is to delete the items from the list according to user-defined filtering rules. Rating is to order the items in the list by predefined rating rules. The application systems could provide the personalized service according to the recommendation generated in this step.

The steps marked as "offline" in Figure 1 can be run regularly at background, relatively infrequent, only to refresh the user group profiles using the newest transactional data. As the result, more attention should be paid on the accuracy of user group profile. The steps marked as "online", however, run in real-time, and their response time is crucial for generating the recommendation.

3 Case Study – Pousadas Recommendation

We intend to select as a domain test bed the area of touristic information and culture. We have selected as an illustrative example for UMT, the case of domain Pousadas de Portugal - a state owned network of hotel resorts in buildings of historical interest (like Pousada Rainha Sta. Isabel, situated in a XIII century castle in the middle of Portugal) or in particularly pleasant places across Portugal (http://www.pousadas.pt). In this section, we will show how a demonstration prototype e-commerce web site providing a service of online Pousadas reservation can use UMT. A user learns basic information about each Pousada and reserves Pousadas where he/she wants to stay. The historical reservation data of each user is kept in the transaction database (we used previously studied data from [5]). We show how to add personalized Pousadas recommendation to Pousadas de Portugal using UMT.

3.1 Acquisition of Domain Info DB

Domain information about Pousadas is stored in a rational database, which we will refer to as `pousadas_DB`. It contains Pousadas name, address, telephone number, location, type, basic introduction, activities, its neighboring Pousadas, etc. In this work, the content of `pousadas_DB` was hand-fed from Pousadas web pages. There is totally information of 42 Pousadas saved to `pousadas_DB`. The data used in [6] was preprocessed to relate to `pousadas_DB`, and forms our transaction database `PT_org`. We then delete from the transaction database the single-item transactions and transactions that cover most of the Pousadas. These transactions are less useful for finding user's interests in this work. After the data preprocessing, the final transaction database, `PT_cln`, contains 6844 records that involve 1297 customers and 36 Pousadas. For the evaluation presented in section 3.6, `PT_cln` was randomly divided into two parts: 90% of the records for constructing UGPs and 10% for evaluating the accuracy rate of the recommendations.

3.2 Clustering Pousadas Transactional Data

In our work, we choose the CLOPE algorithm [13] for clustering Pousadas transactional data. CLOPE is fast, scalable, and memory saving in clustering large, sparse transactional databases with high dimensions [13].

CLOPE groups transactional data by iterative optimization of a global criterion function (Eq. 1).

$$Profit_r(\mathbf{C}) = \frac{\sum_{i=1}^{k} \dfrac{C_i.S}{(C_i.W)^r} \times C_i.N}{\sum_{i=1}^{k} C_i.N} \tag{1}$$

In Eq. 1, k is the number of clusters in the clustering result. r is a positive real number called *repulsion*, used to control the level of intra-cluster similarity. When r is large, transactions within the same cluster must share a large portion of common items. Otherwise, separating these transactions into different clusters will result in a larger profit. $C_i.W$ is the number of distinct items in C_i. $C_i.S$ is the sum of item occurrences in C_i. $C_i.N$ is the number of transactions included in C_i. When clustering transactional data, CLOPE tries to find a clustering $\mathbf{C}$ that maximizes $Profit_r(\mathbf{C})$. The final clustering is a partition of the transactions.

We apply CLOPE to PT_cln to group similar transactions based on user's reservations of Pousadas. Here we consider a Pousadas transaction as the set of all Pousadas reserved by an individual user, e.g. {Alijó, Arraiolos, Batalha, Évora, Vila Nova de Cerveira} is a Pousadas transaction. Due to the sparse nature of the transactional data, we need to adjust repulsion to avoid clusterings having a big central cluster. We choose a clustering with 246 clusters, using a repulsion of 2. From this we post-select a final subset of 22 clusters containing at least 3 transactions each.

3.3   Pousadas UGP

As we introduced in Section 2, there are three types of attributes in a UGP=<*ugp_id*, {(*attr₁*, *val₁*), (*attr₂*, *val₂*),...}>. In this case study, basic information attributes include the number of users in the cluster (*people_amount*), the number of Pousadas in the cluster (*pousadas_amount*), and the list of Pousadas in the cluster (*pousadas_list*). Synthetic attributes include *influence_factor* and *expertise*. *Influence_factor* denotes the importance of a user group profile. *Expertise* denotes the degree of familiarity about Pousadas web site of the users in this group. Their definitions are shown in Eq. 2 and 3.

$$influence\_factor = (pousadas\_amount \times people\_amount) / (total\_pousadas \times total\_people) \quad (2)$$

$$expertise = pousadas\_amount / people\_amount \quad (3)$$

Probability distribution attributes include *pousadas_type*, *interest_activities*, and *region*. The values of probability distribution features are composed of category names and their corresponding probabilities in the cluster. The category names are extracted from pousadas_DB.

Table 1 sketches the content of one UGP that covers 15 user transactions.

The users in this group are interested in 10 Pousadas that are Alvito, Gerês/Caniçada, Manteigas, Marão, Marvão, Monsanto, Óbidos, Sagres, Serpa, and Valença do Minho respectively. The influence factor is 0.0015 and the expertise of this group is 1.25. 30.43% of the Pousadas reserved by the users belong to the charm type, 58.70% for nature, 10.87% for historic, and 0% for historic_design. 39.13% of the Pousadas locates in the Norte region, 17.39% for Beiras, 13.04% for Algarve, 2.17% for Lisboa, 28.26% for Alentejo, and 0% for Azores. The probability distribution of *interest_activities* shows the user's interest on the activities around Pousadas. We just list a part of the interest_activities in Table 1.

Table 1. Representation of Pousadas UGP

Attributes	Values	Types
people_amount	8	basic
pousadas_amount	10	information
pousadas_list	Alvito, Gerês/Caniçada, Manteigas, Marão, Marvão, Monsanto, Óbidos, Sagres, Serpa, Valença do Minho	attributes
influence_factor	0.0015	synthetic
expertise	1.25	attributes
pousadas_type	charm: 0.3043, historic_design: 0, historic: 0.1087, nature: 0.5870	probability distribution
region	azores: 0.0, norte: 0.3913, beiras: 0.1739, algarve: 0.1304, lisboa: 0.0217, alentejo: 0.2826	attributes
interest_activities	swimming pool: 0.0753, family games:0.10390, horse riding:0.0571, bird watching:0.0208, canoeing:0.0208, fishing:0.0857, bicyle tours:0.0260 theme tours:0.0104 cruises:0.049351, diving:0.015584 ...... (omit)	

3.4 Similarity Measures

We need to define the similarity measure between a UGP and a user transaction in order to find the most similar UGPs. The similarity measure can be defined in different ways. In the Pousadas case, we compare two similarity definitions.

3.4.1 Maximum Profit Change
Eq. 1 is the criterion function of the CLOPE algorithm. During the clustering process, a transaction is grouped to the cluster that maximizes the profit value. Based on the notion of the profit, we compute the similarity between a UGP and a user transaction by the value change of the profit. We use cluster features S, W, and N to define profit change, shown in Eq. 4.

$$\Delta(profit) = \frac{C.S \times C.N}{(C.W)^r} - \frac{C'.S \times C'.N}{(C'.W)^r} \tag{4}$$

In Eq. 4, C is the cluster without the user transaction t added and C' is the cluster after t is added. $C.S$, $C.W$, and $C.N$ respectively refer to cluster's size, width, and transaction number. More explanations could be found in [13].

The UGP that makes a maximum profit change is the most similar one with the user transaction.

3.4.2 Euclidian Distance
If we consider UGPs and the user transaction as data points, the most commonly used metric to measure the distance between data points is the Euclidian distance. In order to compute the Euclidian distance, the user transaction is first converted to an UGP-like data structure. Table 2 shows an user transaction in the UGP form.

Table 2. User transaction in UGP data structure

Attributes	Values
pousadas_amount	5
pousadas_list	Alijó, Arraiolos, Batalha, Évora, Vila Nova de Cerveira
pousadas_type	`charme`: 0.4, `historic_design`: 0.0, `historic`: 0.4, `nature`: 0.2
region	`azores`: 0.0, `norte`: 0.4, `beiras`: 0.0, `algarve`: 0.0, `lisboa`: 0.2, `alentejo`: 0.4
interest_activities	swimming pool: 0.0769, family games: 0.0769, horse riding: 0.0615, bird watching: 0.0154, golf course: 0.0308, four-wheel driving: 0.0769, water sports: 0.0308, shooting range: 0.0462, country walks:0.0615, canoeing: 0.0308, fishing: 0.0462, ... (omit)

Each category of *pousadas_type*, *region*, and *interest_activities* in the user transaction can be taken as a vector element, e.g *type*.`charm`, *region*.`azores`. The similarity between the user transaction and UGPs is measured by the Euclidian distance between two vectors. The definition is shown in Eq. 5.

$$d(ugp,t) = \sqrt{\sum_{i=1}^{n}(ugp_i - t_i)} \qquad (5)$$

In Eq. 5, n represents the number of vector elements, and ugp_i and t_i respectively represent the vector element i in vectors ugp and t.

Table 3 lists the top five similar UGPs to the example transaction based on Euclidian distances and the profit change. We compute different Euclidian distances respectively according to pousadas_type (T), region (R), interest_activities (A), and any combination thereof.

Table 3. Top five similar UGPs based on Euclidian distances and the profit change

Similarity definition		ugp_id of top 5 similar UGPs
Euclidian distances	*pousadas_type* (T)	8, 3, 1,87,62
	region (R)	3, 8, 1, 87, 2
	interest_activities (A)	8, 3, 1, 87, 119
	TR	8, 3, 1, 87, 119
	TA	8, 3, 1, 87, 62
	RA	8, 3, 1, 87, 2
	TRA	8, 3, 1,87, 2
Profit change		87, 104, 91, 6, 85

3.5 Filtering and Rating

The final Pousadas recommendation for the current user is generated from the most similar UGPs. The principle of recommendation is to recommend the Pousadas that are included in UGP but have not been booked by the current user.

For the example transaction shown in Table 2, the recommended Pousadas based on Euclidian distances are Estremoz, Marvão, Évora, Gerês/Caniçada, and Valença do Minho. Those based on the profit change are Gerês/Caniçada, Alijó, Marão, Bragança, and Évora.

Recommendation can also be used for a first evaluation of results. We use ten 10% samples of PT_cln as held-out data to evaluate the accuracy rate of the system (for each sample, CLOPE is applied to build UGP for the remaining data). For each booked Pousada (p_i) of client transaction T_i in the test dataset, we calculate a set of recommended Pousadas. This value is based on the most similar UGP to the remaining Pousadas in transaction (i.e. $T_i - p_i$). We score a correct hit if the recommended Pousada is the same as the booked pousada (i.e. p_i).

As before, we generate the recommendation by two different similarity definitions: maximizing profit change and Euclidian distances based on pousadas_type, region, and interest_activities (abr. TRA). The accuracy rate of the recommendation is 23% (with a standard deviation of 1%) for maximizing profit change and 33% (with a standard deviation of 2%) for Euclidian distances (TRA). If we use a random selection of a Pousada as a baseline for this evaluation criteria we should have a 10% baseline (since each selected transaction has an average of 8.6 booked Pousadas, we should have a first recommendation with a ratio of 1 in 36 – 8,6 Pousadas; in average we have measured 3 recommendations available for each transaction, so we used this number for estimating baseline).

3.6 Discussion

We can discuss the acquired results based on the evaluation criteria of previous section, jointly with some analysis of acquired clusters.

On one hand, the two different similarity definitions, Euclidian distance-based TRA and profit change-based, are both significantly above the base line precision. This shows that UMT is helping to predict selected Pousadas. Although the maximization of profit only improves 10% on the random selection, we should note that our evaluation is much more demanding than a real world situation: indeed we are testing our recommendation based on real user choices, not on real user preferences. The use of more data (in TRA experiment) improves this value to 33%. This clearly shows that the inclusion of more information in the clustering process should be useful. On the other hand, the two different similarity definitions generate quite different results of top five similar UGPs. For Euclidian distance-based similarities, the results lean to the UGPs that contain as more Pousadas as possible. For profit change-based similarity, however, the result leans to those that have high support. These are a direct consequence of their respective definitions. For now, in our demo, both results are shown to end-users.

3.6.1 Matching External Nearby Events

The most natural form of storing information is text. Recently available specific domain text extraction tools (e.g. [10]) could be used to update the more static information already in domain database with up-to-date information either from the general news, from a new issue of a specific tourist guide or just from the daily inserted text menu of a Pousada restaurant.

The proposed system is capable of relating UGP clusters with this type of information. In fact it is expectable that recent events (inserted mainly by text mining) should help to trigger related UGPs. For example, let us consider that a fishing site is announcing a new sport area in north of Portugal. If this information is inserted in the database the UGP of Table 1 should be matched. Indeed it is possible to convert text extracted information by using the database (assuming there are database relations between nature - *pousadas_type-* and *interest_activities* as natural tours) to an UGP data structure.

In our example, after matching and filtering the extracted information to the most relevant UGPs (such as the one in table 2), it could then be relevant to announce the fishing article about the new sport area to all the users with transactions similar to this UGP.

4   Conclusions and Future Work

This paper presents a general user-modeling framework named UMT for personalized systems. UMT creates UGP based on the transactional data and specified domain information DB. UGPs acquired by clustering give knowledge about potential user groups. Domain information further provides additional criteria to match the current user with user profiles. All those are done without any explicit user participation. This way, UMT brings no extra burden to the end user while providing the personalized service. It is widely applicable to systems where transactional data of end users are available. As a case study, we show a prototypical application of UMT to a tourist information system. Comparing with stereotyped based profiling, UMT could reveal users actual and up-to-date interests and needs.

Our work was motivated by the need to integrate up-to-date knowledge extracted from different sources (e.x. [10]) in a personalized information system. UMT is largely inspired by Adomavicius et al [1] and INTRIGUE [3]. Here we briefly summarize the main differences. Adomavicius et al [1] use data mining methods, especially association rule discovery, to build customer profiles. The profile consists of factual data including demographic information about users, and behavioral data represented as a set of rules discovered from user transactional data. The UGPs in UMT do not include users' demographic information, which potentially involves users' privacy. We acquire the UGPs based on the clustering result on the transactional data and the information extracted from the application system. The main information of the UGP is represented as probability distribution attributes. INTRIGUE [3] is a personalized recommendation of tourist attractions. It exploits stereotypical knowledge about the typical tourist classes to construct the group-user profiles. The attractions are modeled as same properties as those in the group-user profiles. By computing the satisfaction score between the attraction and the profile to generate the recommendation set. UMT creates the UGP from the user transactional data that reveals user's real and up-to-date interests. The recommendation is generated according to the comparison between the current user transaction and the UGPs.

In future work, we will investigate the appropriate criteria for recommendation evaluation, possibly according to user's reactions to the recommended items. Factual knowledge in the database should also be included in CLOPE by adding more information (such as the TRA data used with Euclidean distance metric) in other terms of equation 1. This is also paving the way for the use of external data. Indeed, for testing this system, we plan to integrate UMT into a recommendation system capable of reacting to external events. In order to do so, an information extraction engine will use text mining techniques to insert knowledge into a turistic events portal. This information (that can be complemented by explicitly inserted information or by information extracted from RSS enabled local media) should then be related with the UGPs resulting from the clustering process here described. As a result the recommendation generated in UMT is enlarged from the internal database to any other event that could be registered at the web.

References

1. Adomavicius G., Tuzhilin A.: Using Data Mining Methods to Build Customer Profiles. IEEE Computer, vol. 34, no. 2 (2001) 74-82.
2. Aedissono L., Goy A.: Tailoring the Interaction with Users in Web Stores. In: User Modeling and User-Adapted Interaction, Vol. 10(4), Kluwer Academic Publishers (2000) 251-303
3. Ardissono L., Goy A., Petrone G., Segnan M., Torasso P.: INTRIGUE: personalized recommendation of tourist attractions for desktop and handset devices. In: Applied Artificial Intelligence, Special Issue on Artificial Intelligence for Cultural Heritage and Digital Libraries, Vol.17. Taylor & Francis (2003) 687-714
4. Guha S., Rastogi R., Shim K.: ROCK: A Robust Clustering Algorithm for Categorical Attributes. Inf. Syst. Vol. 25(5) . Elsevier (2000) 345-366
5. Cavique L., Micro-segmentação de Clientes com Base em Dados de Consumo: Modelo RM-Similis, Revista Portuguesa e Brasileira de Gestão. Pp. 72-77, volume 2, n° 3.
6. Horvitz E., Breese J., Heckerman D., Hovel D., Rommelse K.: The Lumiere Project: Bayesian User Modeling for Inferring the Goals and Needs of Software Users. In: Proceedings of the Fourteenth Conference on Uncertainty in Artificial Intelligence. Morgan Kaufmann (1998) 256-265
7. Han J., Kamber M.: Data Mining: Concepts and Techniques. Morgan Kaufmann Publishers (2001)
8. Kobsa A., Pohl W.: The BP-MS User Modeling System. In: User Modeling and User-Adapted Interaction, Vol. 4(2). Formerly Kluwer Academic Publishers (1995) 59-106
9. MacDonald R., Silver D.: Web-based User Profiling Using a Recurrent Neural Network. In: Proceedings of the IASTED International Conference on Artificial Intelligence and Soft Computing. ACTA Press (2002) 472-477
10. Marques N., Gonçalves S.. Applying a Part-of-Speech Tagger to Postal Address Detection on the Web. In Proceedings of the IV International Conference on Language Resources and Evaluation. LREC 2004. Volume I. pp. 287-290. Lisboa. Portugal.
11. Pazzani M., Muramatsu J., Billsus D.; Syskill and Webert: Identifying Interesting Web Sites. In: Proceedings of the Thirteenth National Conference on Artificial Intelligence. AAAI Press (1996) 54—61
12. Rucker J., Polanco M.: Siteseer: Personalized Navigation for the Web. In: Communication of ACM, Vol.40(3). ACM Press (1997) 73-75
13. Yang Y., Guan X., You J.: CLOPE: a fast and effective clustering algorithm for transactional data. In: KDD 2002. ACM Press (2002) 682-687

Retail Clients Latent Segments

Jaime R.S. Fonseca[1] and Margarida G.M.S. Cardoso[2]

[1] ISCSP-Instituto Superior de Ciências Sociais e Políticas,
R. Almerindo Lessa, Pólo Universitário do Alto da Ajuda,
1349-055 Lisboa, Portugal
jaimefonseca@iscsp.utl.pt
[2] ISCTE – Business School, Department of Quantitative Methods,
Av. das Forças Armadas, 1649-026 Lisboa, Portugal
margarida.cardoso@iscte.pt

Abstract. Latent Segments Models (LSM) are commonly used as an approach for market segmentation. When using LSM, several criteria are available to determine the number of segments. However, it is not established which criteria are more adequate when dealing with a specific application. Since most market segmentation problems involve the simultaneous use of categorical and continuous base variables, it is particularly useful to select the *best* criteria when dealing with LSM with mixed type base variables. We first present an empirical test, which provides the ranking of several information criteria for model selection based on ten mixed data sets. As a result, the ICL-BIC, BIC, CAIC and $\mathcal{L}$ criteria are selected as the *best* performing criteria in the estimation of mixed mixture models. We then present an application concerning a retail chain clients' segmentation. The *best* information criteria yield two segments: *Preferential Clients* and *Occasional Clients*. Keywords: Clustering, Finite Mixture Models, Information Criteria, Marketing Research

1 Introduction

Market segmentation is the division of a heterogeneous market into homogeneous sub-markets of consumers, clusters or segments, with similar behaviour within segments and different behaviour across segments. The first application of market segmentation emerged in 1956 [38].

Segmentation is an essential instrument of marketing [28], [39]. It provides a better market understanding and, consequently, means to develop more successful business strategies.

A market segmentation solution is a function of the market segmentation variables and of a specific segmentation (clustering) procedure. In what concerns base variables for segmentation, product-specific variables (see table 1) should be considered [39]. Other attributes may help profiling the segments' structures (for an overview of previous works on the use of demographics, psychographics, and other variables in segmentation studies, see [21], [28], [42].

Along with the selection of a set of potential segmentation variables, a segmentation procedure must be chosen, which delivers a segmentation solution.

In this paper we present the segmentation of clients of a retail chain which is based on product-specific variables and results from the estimation of a Latent Segments

C. Bento, A. Cardoso, and G. Dias (Eds.): EPIA 2005, LNAI 3808, pp. 348–358, 2005.

Table 1. Segmentation base variables (some examples)

General observable variables	Product-specific observable variables	General unobservable variables	Product-specific unobservable variables
Demographic	Usage frequency	Life-style	Benefits Utilities
Socio-economic	Brand loyalty	Psychographics	Preferences
Cultural	User status	Personality	Intentions
Geographic	Situations	Values	Perceptions
			Attributes

Model (LSM) [14], [42]. This approach enables the simultaneous use of categorical and continuous segmentation base variables. It is a probabilistic clustering approach which assumes that the variables' observations in a sample arise from different segments of unknown proportions. Estimation of the LSM is typically based on maximum likelihood.

2 Latent Segments Models

The aim of Latent Segments Models [14] (or Finite Mixture Models) is to identify the latent segments required to explain the associations among a set of observed variables (segmentation base variables) and to allocate observations to these segments.

The use of LSM has become increasingly popular in the marketing literature [18], [42]. This approach to segmentation offers some advantages when compared with other techniques: it identifies market segments[19]; it provides means to select the number of segments [30]; it is able to deal with diverse types of data (different measurement levels) [40]; it outperforms more traditional approaches [41].

LSM provide a clustering model based approach, a statistical model being postulated for the population from which the sample under study is coming, and assuming that the data is generated by a mixture of underlying (density) probability distributions.

Let $\underline{y}_i = (y_{ip})$ be the vector representing the scores of the ith case for the pth segmentation base variable ($i = 1,\ldots,n$; $p = 1,\ldots,P$).

Several types of segmentation variables may be considered which have a conditional (within-cluster) distribution in the exponential family (such as Bernoulli, Poisson, Multinomial or Normal distribution) [24], [25], [32], [40]. Considering S as the number of segments and $s=1,\ldots,S$, we define λ_s as mixing probability or segment size. Assuming local independence [40], the LSM may generally be presented as follows:

$$f(\underline{y}_i \mid \underline{\psi}) = \sum_{s=1}^{S} \lambda_s \prod_{p=1}^{P} f_s(y_{ip} \mid \underline{\theta}_{sp})$$ (1)

where $i = 1,\ldots,n$,

$$\sum_{s=1}^{S} \lambda_s = 1, \quad \underline{\psi} = \{\underline{\lambda}, \Theta\}, \quad \text{with} \quad \underline{\lambda} = \{\lambda_1, \cdots, \lambda_{S-1}\} \quad \text{and} \quad \Theta = \{\underline{\theta}_{1p}, \cdots, \underline{\theta}_{sp}\}.$$

When considering mixed type variables for segmentation we may additionally specify that

$$f_s(y_{ip} \mid \underline{\theta}_{sp}) \sim N(\mu_{sp}, \sigma_{sp}^2)$$

for each one of the continuous attributes, and

$$f_s(y_{ip} \mid \underline{\theta}_{sp}) \sim \text{Mult}_{C_p}(1; \theta_{sp1}, ..., \theta_{spC_p}),$$

for the categorical attributes, with C_p categories (*e.g.* see [25]).

Although continuous attributes could be categorized and also modelled by the multinomial distribution, this may result in considerable loss of information [13]. Furthermore it is difficult to establish an adequate number of categories [12]; however, discretization may be very useful in particular when continuous variables which do not belong to the exponential family are considered.

The LSM assumption of conditional independence can be relaxed by using the appropriate multivariate rather than univariate distributions for sets of locally dependent variables: multivariate normal distribution for sets of continuous variables and a set of categorical variables can be combined into a joint multinomial distribution.

The LSM estimation problem simultaneously addresses the estimation of distributional parameters and classification of cases into segments, yielding mixing probabilities.

Finally, modal allocation provides means for constituting a partition assigning each case to the segment with the highest posterior probability which is given by $\underset{s=1,...,S}{Max} \ \tau_{is}$, where

$$\tau_{is} = \hat{\lambda}_s(\underline{y}_i \mid \underline{\psi}) = \frac{\hat{\lambda}_s \prod_{p=1}^{P} f_s(\underline{y}_{ip} \mid \hat{\theta}_{sp})}{\sum_{s=1}^{S} \hat{\lambda}_s \prod_{p=1}^{P} f_s(\underline{y}_{ip} \mid \hat{\theta}_{sp})} \qquad (2)$$

Maximum likelihood estimates of the vector parameter $\underline{\psi}$ can be obtained by treating the unobserved segment labels as missing data and using the EM algorithm [22], [30], [34].

3 Model Selection Criteria

3.1 Introduction

Several criteria may be considered for the selection of Latent Segments Models (LSM). In the present work we consider theoretical information based criteria. These criteria are generally based on the likelihood function (which we want to maximize) and a measure of model complexity (which we want to minimize). Thus, all theoretical information criteria balance parsimony (fitting a model with a large number of components requires the estimation of a very large number of parameters and a potential loss of precision in these estimates [29]), and model complexity (which tends to improve the model fit to the data).

The general form of information criteria is as follows:

$$-2\log L(\hat{\psi}) + C \tag{3}$$

where the first term measures the lack of fit and the second term C includes a measure for model complexity, and a penalization factor. Some information criteria are shown on table 2.

The emphasis on information criteria begins with the pioneer work of Akaike [2]. Akaike's Information Criterion (AIC) chooses a model with S segments that minimises (3) with $C = 2n_\psi$.

Later, Bozdogan [8] suggested the modified AIC criterion (AIC3) in the context of mixture models, using 3 instead of 2 on penalizing term; so, it chooses a model with S segments that minimises (3) with $C = 3n_\psi$.

Another variant of AIC, the corrected AIC, is proposed [26], focusing on the small-sample bias adjustment (AIC may perform poorly if there are too many parameters in relation to the sample size); AICc thus selects a model with S segments that minimises (3) with $C = 2n_\psi(\frac{n}{n-n_\psi-1})$.

A new criterion is then proposed - AICu - because AICc still tends to over fit as the sample size increase [31].

With the consistent AIC criterion (CAIC), Bozdogan [9] noted that the term $n_\psi(1+\log n)$ has the effect of increasing the penalty term and, as a result, minimization of CAIC leads in general to models with fewer parameters than AIC does.

The Bayesian information criterion (BIC) was proposed by Schwarz [36], and chooses a model with S segments that minimises (3) with $C = n_\psi \log n$; in a different way, from the notion of stochastic complexity, Rissanen [35] proposed an equivalent criterion in form, the minimum descriptive length (MDL).

The CLC - Complete Likelihood Classification criterion [30] is proposed as an approximation of the classification likelihood criterion [7]. It chooses a model with S segments that minimises (3) with $C = 2EN(S)$, where the term $2EN(S)$ penalizes poorly separated segments, with

$$EN(S) = -\sum_{i=1}^{n} \sum_{s=1}^{S} \tau_{is} \log \tau_{is}$$

A particular approximation version of the integrated classification likelihood criterion (ICL) referred to as ICL-BIC by McLachlan and Peel [30], chooses a model with S segments that minimises (3) with $C = 2EN(S) + n_\psi \log n$.

Table 2. Some theoretical information criteria

Criterion	Definition	Reference
AIC	$-2LL + 2n_\psi$	[1]
AIC3	$-2LL + 3n_\psi$	[8]
AICc	$AIC + (2n_\psi(n_\psi+1))/(n-n_\psi-1)$	[26]
AICu	$AICc + n\log(n/(n-n_\psi-1))$	[31]
CAIC	$-2LL + n_\psi(1+\log n)$	[9]
BIC/MDL	$-2LL + n_\psi\log n$	[36] / [35]
CLC	$-2LL + 2EN(S)$	[4]
ICL-BIC	$BIC + 2EN(S)$	[5]
NEC	$NEC(S) = EN(S)/(L(S)-L(1))$	[6]
AWE	$-2LL_c + 2n_\psi(3/2+\log n)$	[3]
$\mathcal{L}$	$-LL + (n_\psi/2)\sum \log(n\lambda_S/12) + S/2\log(n/12) + S(n_\psi+1)/2$	[22]
S	Number of segments	
n	Number of observations	
n_ψ	Number of model parameters	
L	Likelihood function	
LL	Log Likelihood function	
LL_c	Classification Log Likelihood	
$EN(S)$	Entropy measure	

The normalised entropy criterion (NEC) was introduced by Celeux and Soromenho [11]; an improvement is due to Biernacki, Celeux, and Govaert [6]. This improved NEC chooses a model with s segments if NEC(s) ≤ 1, $(2\leq s \leq S)$ and states that NEC (1) =1; otherwise NEC declares there is no clustering structure in the data.

An approximate Bayesian solution, which is a crude approximation to twice the log Bayes factor for S segments [30], the approximate weight of evidence (AWE) proposed by Banfield and Raftery [3], uses the classification likelihood, and chooses a model with S segments that minimises (3) with $C = 2EN(S) + 2n_\psi(3/2+\log n)$.

Finally, the $\mathcal{L}$ criterion [22] depends on sample size, n, number of model parameters, n_ψ, and the mixing probabilities, λ_s, and chooses a model with S segments that minimises $-LL + (n_\psi/2)\sum \log(n\lambda_S/12) + S/2\log(n/12) + S(n_\psi+1)/2$.

3.2 Information Criteria Selection

In order to select one particular criterion for determining the number of segments in a LSM based on mixed type variables, we run some auxiliary clustering analysis. We analyse ten real data sets (table 3) with mixed variables (continuous and categorical) and known structure (the clusters in the data set are previously known) and use all the criteria presented on table 2, for the LSM estimation.

Table 3. The analyzed data sets

Data sets	source	Segmentation variables	Sample size	Data sets	source	Segmentation variables	Sample size
Bird survival	[23]	3 cont. 1 categ.	50	Imports-85	[27]	15 cont. 11 categ.	160
Methadone treatment	[23]	2 cont. 2 categ.	238	Heart	[17]	6 cont. 7 categ.	270
North Central Wisconsin	[15]	4 cont. 1 categ.	34	Cancer	[25]	8 cont. 4 categ.	471
Hepatitis	[20]	5 cont. 5 categ.	80	AIDS	[37]	3 cont. 3 categ.	944
Neolithic Tools	[16]	2 cont. 3 categ.	103	Ethylene Glycol	[33]	2 cont. 1 categ.	1028

Table 4 presents the proportion of data sets in which theoretical information criteria were able to recover the original cluster structure (in particular the true number of segments), as well as the corresponding criteria ranking.

Table 4. Information criteria performance

% of data sets where the true number of segments is identified of segments	Criteria Ranking
80	ICL-BIC
70	BIC and CAIC
60	$\mathcal{L}$
40	AIC, AICu, NEC, and AWE
30	AIC3
20	AICc
10	CLC

According to the obtained results ICL-BIC is the best performing criterion. It is able to recover the original data sets structure (it is able to detect the underlying true number of clusters or segments in the data set) in 8 of the 10 data sets (regardless the number of variables and sample size).

It is followed by CAIC and BIC (ex-aequo) and $\mathcal{L}$ (3rd place). As a consequence, we opt for the use of the ICL-BIC criterion on the retail segmentation application (we also present results for BIC, CAIC, and $\mathcal{L}$ criteria).

4 Segmentation of Retail Clients

4.1 Data Set Description

The retail data set includes attributes referring to 1504 supermarket clients. Data originates from a questionnaire responses and includes several characteristics ranging from attitudes to demographics.

Table 5. Segmentation base variables

Segmentation Base	Type	Variables' Categories
Amount spent on retail store	Continuous	-
Propotion of expenditure in retail chain	Continuous	-
Transportation	Categorical	Car, Walking, Public Transportation, Motor cycle
Usage frequency	Categorical	Every day, 2 or 3 times a week, Once a week, Once a twice a week, ..., Occasional
Visit pattern	Categorical	During the week, During the weekend, Both situation
Coming from	Categorical	Home, Job, Passing by, Other
Reasons for purchaising	Categorical	Home proximity, job proximity, Passing by, Low prices, Brand diversity, ..., Doesn't know
Travel time	Categorical	2 minutes walking (mw), 2 to 5 mw, 5 to 10 mw, more than 10 mw, ..., more than 15 m by car, 10 to 15 m by car

As already referred, product-specific base variables are preferable for segmentation purposes. In order to segment retail clients we thus select some attitudinal and behavioural variables, such as *reasons to do the purchase, purchasing habits, usage frequency, visit pattern, travel time, amount spent* and *proportion of expenditure in the retail chain* (the proportion of monthly expenditures which refers to the specific supermarket chain). These variables illustrate the relationship between consumers and retail stores. Demographics such as *gender, age, income, occupation,* and *education* are available for identifying the individuals in the segments, turning them more accessible. Table 5 presents the segmentation base variables: 2 continuous and 6 categorical.

4.2 Segment Structure

Results from the estimation of a LSM using the referred segmentation variables (see Table 2) yield a two-segments structure. The ICL-BIC values corresponding to this and alternative solutions are displayed on table 6.

Table 6. Model selection

Number of segments	Number of parameters	BIC	CAIC	$\mathcal{L}$	ICL-BIC
1	76	56227,590	56303.59	28060,284	56227,589
2	119	55358,367	55477.367	27858,108	55980,600
3	162	55224,071	54896.180	28133,315	56219,539

Number of observations: 1504

Since we found there was an interaction between some base variables we included the following in the adopted model: usage frequency and visit pattern; transportation and travel time; amount spent and proportion of expenditure in the retail chain.

As we can see the ICL-BIC criterion attains its minimum for S=2 and $\mathcal{L}$ yields the same conclusion.

Table 7. Segments and their characteristics

	Seg.1	Seg.2		Seg.1	Seg.2
Usage Frequency			*Travel time*		
Every day	41%	13%	Missing	2%	4%
2 or 3 times a week	35%	31%	2 minutes walking (mw)	21%	7%
Once a week	15%	21%	2 to 5 mw	26%	16%
Once or twice a week	2%	6%	5 to 10 mw	17%	13%
Once a month	6%	8%	More than 10 mw	7%	6%
Occasionally	1%	21%	Less or equal 5 m by car	16%	13%
Reasons for purchasing			5 to 10 m by car	5%	13%
Home proximity	75%	44%	10 to 15 m by car	4%	13%
Job proximity	3%	14%	More than 15 m by car	3%	14%
Passing by	2%	23%	*Visit pattern*		
Low prices	5%	3%	During the week	22%	40%
Brand diversity	1%	1%	During the weekend	12%	21%
Products diversity	2%	3%	Both situations	66%	38%
Habit	4%	4%	*Coming from*		
Product quality	3%	3%	Home	83%	51%
Fresh products' quality	1%	1%	Job	12%	35%
Store cleanliness	1%	1%	Passing by	3%	10%
Service promptness	1%	1%	Other	2%	4%
Service friendliness	2%	0%	*Transportation*		
Promotions	0%	1%	Car	25%	45%
Open hours	0%	1%	Walking	71%	43%
Parking conditions	0%	0%	Public transportation	4%	13%
Other reasons	0%	0%	Motorcycle	0%	0%
Doesn't know	1%	1%	-		
Proportion of expenditure in retail chain			*Amount spent on retail store*		
Mean (€)	60,66	22,03	Mean (€)	342,5	255,9

We thus select a LSM with two segments (of sizes 917 for segment 1, and 587 for segment 2, by "modal allocation"), which we characterize on table 7.

As a result from the segments' profiling we name Seg.1 as *Preferential clients* and Seg.2 as *Occasional clients*.

Preferential clients go often to the retail supermarkets; they leave nearby and walk to the super. These clients allocate 60% of their home monthly expenditures to the retail chain.

Occasional clients also include some clients that go often to the supermarket but they clearly differ from Seg.1 concerning the inclusion of occasional purchasers.

Location (Home proximity) is an important reason for purchasing for both segments; however for *Occasional clients'* job proximity is also relevant. This segment also includes more clients which go to the super by car.

These results agree, in general, with those obtained in previous segmentation based on a larger sample and on a similar inquiry conducted two years before [10]. It is thus possible to conclude that this segment structure is stable.

5 Conclusion and Future Work

In this article we discuss the use of Latent Segment Models for market segmentation. We focus on the utilization of theoretical information criteria to recover clustering structures. In particular, we discuss the use of these criteria for mixed type variables based clustering, since segmentation is typically based on attributes with diverse measurement levels. The discussion is motivated by an application: the segmentation of clients of a retail chain.

We first present the analysis of ten data sets with known clustering structure and rank several criteria according to their ability to recover the original structure, indicating the correct number of clusters. According to the obtained results we rank the best criteria as follows: ICL-BIC (1st place), BIC and CAIC (2nd place, ex-aequo) and $\mathcal{L}$ (3rd place). Using this empirical test's results we select the ICL-BIC (a criterion which was specifically designed for clustering applications) criterion as an indicator of the correct number of retail clients' latent segments.

We finally estimate a Latent Segments Model to obtain a segment structure which refers to the clients of a supermarkets retail chain. We use product specific variables as a base for segmentation (e.g. reasons for purchase). As a result (and using the ICL-BIC criterion) two segments are constituted. The Preferential clients segment and the Occasional Clients segment.

In addition to these substantive conclusions we consider that the issue concerning the selection of specific information criteria to estimate Latent Segments Models, based on mixed type data, should be further discussed. In fact, mixed type variables are commonly considered in segmentation studies and thus, the information criteria performance which is empirically observed in the present work deserves future research. In the present work empirical results provide a criteria ranking. Naturally, a larger amount of data sets with diverse characteristics (which may be obtained via simulation procedures) should be considered in order to further prove the consistency of the present conclusions.

References

1. H. Akaike, Information Theory and an Extension of Maximum Likelihood Principle, in K. T. Emanuel Parzen, Genshiro Kitagawa, ed., Selected Papers of Hirotugu Akaike, in Proceedings of the Second International Symposium on Information Theory, B.N. Petrov and F. caski, eds., Akademiai Kiado, Budapest, 1973, 267-281, Springer-Verlag New York, Inc, Texas, 1973, pp. 434.
2. H. Akaike, Maximum likelihood identification of Gaussian autorregressive moving average models, Biometrika, 60 (1973), pp. 255-265.
3. J. D. Banfield and A. E. Raftery, Model-Based Gaussian and Non-Gaussian Clustering, Biometrics, 49 (1993), pp. 803-821.
4. C. Biernacki, Choix de modéles en Classification-Ph.D. Tesis., 1997.

5. C. Biernacki, G. Celeux and G. Govaert, Assessing a Mixture model for Clustering with the integrated Completed Likelihood, IEEE Transactions on Pattern analysis and Machine Intelligence, 22 (2000), pp. 719-725.
6. C. Biernacki, G. Celeux and G. Govaert, An improvement of the NEC criterion for assessing the number of clusters in mixture model, Pattern Recognition Letters, 20 (1999), pp. 267-272.
7. C. Biernacki and G. Govaert, Using the classification likelihood to choose the number of clusters, Computing Science and Statistics, 29 (1997), pp. 451-457.
8. H. Bozdogan, Mixture-Model Cluster Analysis using Model Selection criteria and a new Informational Measure of Complexity, in H. Bozdogan, ed., Proceedings of the First US/Japan Conference on the Frontiers of Statistical Modeling: An Approach, 69-113, Kluwer Academic Publishers, 1994, pp. 69-113.
9. H. Bozdogan, Model Selection and Akaikes's Information Criterion (AIC): The General Theory and its Analytical Extensions, Psycometrika, 52 (1987), pp. 345-370.
10. M. G. M. S. Cardoso and A. B. Mendes, Segmentação de clientes de lojas de Pequena Dimensão, IX Congresso da Sociedade Portuguesa de Estatística, Ponta Delgada, 2002, pp. 157-170.
11. G. Celeux and G. Soromenho, An entropy criterion for acessing the number of clusters in a mixture model, Journal of Classification, 13 (1996), pp. 195-212.
12. J. Y. Ching, A. K. C. Wong and K. C. C. Chan, Class-Dependent Discretization for Inductive Learning from Continuous and Mixed-Mode Data, IEEE Transactions on Pattern Analysis and Machine Intelligence, 17 (1995), pp. 641-651.
13. Y.-S. Choi, B.-R. Moon and S. Y. Seo, Proceedings of the 2005 Conference on Genetic Fuzzy Discretization with Adaptive Intervals for Classification Problems, Conference on Genetic and Evolutionary Computation, ACM Press, New York, NT, USA, Washington DC, USA, 2005, pp. 2037-2043.
14. S. H. Cohen and V. Ramaswamy, Latent segmentation models, Marketing Research Magazine, Summer (1998), pp. 15-22.
15. S. L. Crawford, M. H. Degroot and J. B. Kadane, Modeling Lake-Chemistry Distributions: Approximate Bayesian Methods for Estimating a Finite-Mixture Model, Technometrics, 34 (1992), pp. 441-453.
16. P. Dellaportas, Bayesian Classification of Neolithic Tools, Appllied Statistics, 47 (1998), pp. 279-297.
17. R. Detrano, A. Janosi, W. Steinbrunn, M. Pfisterer, K. Schmid, K. Sandhu, K. Guppy, S. Lee and V. Froelicher, Rapid searches for complex patterns in biological molecules, American Journal of Cardiology, 64 (1989), pp. 304-310.
18. J. G. Dias, Finite Mixture Models; Review, Applications, and Computer-intensive Methods, Econimics, Groningen University, PhD Thesis, Groningen, 2004, pp. 199.
19. W. R. Dillon and A. Kumar, Latent structure and other mixture models in marketing: An integrative survey and overview, chapter 9 in R.P. Bagozi (ed.), Advanced methods of Marketing Research, 352-388, Cambridge: blackwell Publishers, 1994.
20. B. Efron, and Gong, G., A Leisurely at the Bootstrap, the Jackknife, and cross-Validation, The American Statistitian, 37 (1983), pp. 36-48.
21. G. Fennell, G. M. Allenby, S. Yang and Y. Edwards, The effectiveness of Demographic and Psychographic Variables for Explaining Brand and Product Category Use, Quantitative Marketing and Economics, 1 (2003), pp. 233-244.
22. M. A. T. Figueiredo and A. K. Jain, Unsupervised Learning of Finite Mixture Models, IEEE Transactions on pattern analysis and Machine Intelligence, 24 (2002), pp. 1-16.
23. D. J. Hand, F. Daly, A. D. Lunn, K. J. McConway and E. Ostrowski, Small Data Sets, Chapman & Hall, London, 1996.
24. L. Hunt and M. Jorgensen, Mixture model clustering for mixed data with missing information, Computational Statistics & Data Analysis, 41 (2003), pp. 429-440.

25. L. A. Hunt and K. E. Basford, Fitting a Mixture Model to Three-Mode Trhee-Way Data with Categorical and Continuous Variables, Journal of Classification, 16 (1999), pp. 283-296.
26. C. M. Hurvich and C.-L. Tsai, regression and Time Series Model Selection in Small Samples, Biometrika, 76 (1989), pp. 297-307.
27. D. Kibler, D. W. Aha and M. Albert, Instance-based prediction of real-valued attributes, Computational Intelligence, 5 (1989).
28. B.-D. Kim, K. Srinivasan and R. T. Wilcox, Identifying Price Sensitive Consumers: The Relative Merits of Demographic vs. Purchase Pattern Information, Journal of Retailing, 75 (1999), pp. 173-193.
29. B. G. Leroux and M. L. Puterman, Maximum-Penalized-Likelihood Estimation for Independent and Markov-Dependent Mixture Models, Biometrics, 48 (1992), pp. 545-558.
30. G. F. McLachlan and D. Peel, Finite Mixture Models, John Wiley & Sons, Inc., 2000.
31. A. McQuarrie, R. Shumway and C.-L. Tsai, The model selection criterion AICu, Statistics & Probability Letters, 34 (1997), pp. 285-292.
32. I. Moustaki and I. Papageorgiou, Latent class models for mixed variables with applications in Archaeometry, Computational Statistics & Data Analysis, In Press (2004).
33. C. J. Price, C. A. Kimmel, R. W. Tyl and M. C. Marr, The development toxicity of ethylene glycol in rats and mice, Toxicological Applications in Pharmacology, 81 (1985), pp. 113-127.
34. R. A. Redner and H. F. Walker, Mixture Densities, Maximum Likelihood and the EM Algorithm, SIAM review, 26 (1984), pp. 195-239.
35. J. Rissanen, Modeling by shortest data description, Automatica, 14 (1978), pp. 465-471.
36. G. Schwarz, Estimating the Dimenson of a Model, The Annals of Statistics, 6 (1978), pp. 461-464.
37. J.-Q. Shi and S.-Y. Lee, Latent variable models with mixed continuous and polytomous data, Journal of the Royal Statistical Society, Series A, 62 (2000).
38. W. R. Smith, Product differentiation and market segmentation as alternative marketing strategies, Journal of Marketing, 21 (1956), pp. 3-8.
39. C.-Y. Tsai and C.-C. Chiu, A purchase-based market segmentation methodology, Expert Systems with Applications, 27 (2004), pp. 265-276.
40. J. K. Vermunt and J. Magidson, Latent class cluster analysis., J.A. Hagenaars and A.L. McCutcheon (eds.), Applied Latent Class Analysis, 89-106., Cambridge University Press, 2002.
41. M. Vriens, Market Segmentation. Analytical Developments and Applications Guidlines, Technical Overview Series, Millward Brown IntelliQuest, 2001, pp. 1-42.
42. M. Wedel and W. A. Kamakura, Market Segmentation: Concepts and methodological foundations, Kluwer Academic Publishers, Boston, 1998.

Automatic Detection of Meddies Through Texture Analysis of Sea Surface Temperature Maps

Marco Castellani and Nuno C. Marques

CENTRIA, Departamento de Informática,
Faculdade Ciências e Tecnologia, Universidade Nova Lisboa,
Quinta da Torre, 2829-516 Caparica, Portugal
mcas@fct.unl.pt
nmm@di.fct.unl.pt

Abstract. A new machine learning approach is presented for automatic detection of Mediterranean water eddies from sea surface temperature maps of the Atlantic Ocean. A pre-processing step uses Laws' convolution kernels to reveal microstructural patterns of water temperature. Given a map point, a numerical vector containing information on local structural properties is generated. This vector is forwarded to a multi-layer perceptron classifier that is trained to recognise texture patterns generated by positive and negative instances of eddy structures. The proposed system achieves high recognition accuracy with fast and robust learning results over a range of different combinations of statistical measures of texture properties. Detection results are characterised by a very low rate of false positives. The latter is particularly important since meddies occupy only a small portion of SST map area.

1 Introduction

Due to its high salinity and temperature, the presence of Mediterranean water strongly influences the hydrology and the dynamics of the Atlantic Ocean [1] and transports particles, suspended material and live organisms. Mediterranean water eddies (meddies) are of crucial importance in the process of, and account for, the diffusion of Mediterranean waters over thousands of kilometers with very little mixing [2].

Meddies are mesoscale lens-like structures, in solid body cyclonic or anticyclonic rotation, with typical diameters of about 50 kilometers, periods of rotation of about 6 to 8 days and velocities of about 30 cm/s [3].

Recent studies indicate that mesoscale structures having a surface signature in temperature can be detected using satellite information. For this purpose, sea surface temperature (SST) maps created from satellite-borne infrared sensors are employed to visualise oceanic structures such as mushroom like dipoles, fronts and vortexes [4].

Despite current active research into the circulation of meddies into the Atlantic [2], [5], inspection of satellite maps still relies on visual interpretation of the images, which is labour intensive, subjective in nature and dependent on the interpreter's skill [6]. Given the large and growing body of SST data available, the development of automatic tools for analysis of such imagery is nowadays of vital importance.

C. Bento, A. Cardoso, and G. Dias (Eds.): EPIA 2005, LNAI 3808, pp. 359–370, 2005.
© Springer-Verlag Berlin Heidelberg 2005

This paper focuses on automatic detection of meddies from SST maps of the Atlantic. The study is part of a project aiming at remote identification of meddies with synergistic use of satellite thermal and colour and roughness images of the ocean (http://www.io.fc.ul.pt/fisica/research.htm - RENA project). The main problem in understanding SST maps is due to the the high structural variability of eddies that makes it difficult to express valid analytical constraints for recognition [7].

Two main approaches are customary for detection of oceanic structures. Both approaches include a pre-processing stage where high level features are extracted from the maps to highlight dynamic, structural or textural local properties.

The first approach directly matches feature information with expert knowledge that describes the target patterns [8], [9].

The second approach relies on machine learning of the decision making policy that informs the recognition system [10], [11]. This approach requires the least design effort since it is much easier for experts to identify positive instances of the desired object than it is to specify precise domain knowledge. A learning classifier is also easier to reconfigure, since other oceanic phenomena can be included in the identification algorithm simply by supplying the system with a new set of training examples.

This paper presents a new machine learning approach for automatic detection of meddies from SST maps of the North Atlantic. The chosen strategy looks at satellite images as textural patterns of water temperature and aims at revealing the structural "signature" characterising a meddy. Laws' method for texture analysis [12] is used for the purpose. Through a series of filter banks, Laws' algorithm brings to light microstructure information and generates a set of numerical features describing local textural properties. Automatic identification is performed by an artificial neural network (ANN) [13] classifier that is trained to recognise texture patterns generated by meddy phenomena. In addition to built-in learning capabilities, the ANN module ensures effective processing of large amounts of input data and a reasonable response to noisy or incomplete inputs.

Sect. 2 presents a review of the literature relevant to the subject. Sect. 3 details the problem domain. Sect. 4 presents the proposed algorithm. Sect. 5 describes implementation issues and application results of the proposed technique. Sect. 6 discusses the results and draws some comparisons with other published work. Sect. 7 concludes the paper and proposes areas for further investigation.

2 Automatic Identification of Oceanic Eddies

Mesoscale structures and in particular eddies play an important role in the dynamics of the oceans. A number of studies investigated the creation of automatic systems for detection and monitoring of such phenomena from remotely sensed SST maps.

Peckinpaugh et al. [10] used a two-step procedure, namely a pre-processing stage for image segmentation and feature extraction, and the actual identification stage performed by an ANN classifier. SST images of the Gulf Stream region were segmented into sets of overlapping "tiles". For each sub-image, the magnitude and the direction of the maximum image "energy" was calculated from analysis of the local Fourier power spectrum [14]. These magnitudes and directions were fed as inputs into the ANN. The authors reported encouraging accuracy results in the recognition of warm eddies. However, the system often failed to discriminate warm eddies from the Gulf Stream, thus generating a high rate of false positives. Moreover, the algorithm didn't target the recognition of cold eddies, which is the most difficult case.

Peckinpaugh and Holyer [15] also developed an eddy detection algorithm based on analytical description of eddy structures. An edge detection operator was used to outline the borders of oceanic phenomena. Several circle detectors were compared to locate the centre and the radius of eddies. However, the study was limited to a small sample of images and no evaluation was made on the possibility of false detections.

Alexanin and Alexanina [9] regarded SST maps as oriented texture in the temperature field and calculated the dominant orientation of radiation contrast at each point. Since dominant orientations of thermal gradient are highly correlated to sea surface velocity directions, the centre of circular motion structures can be determined from the orientation field via analytical models. The main drawbacks of this method are its computational complexity and the fact that the size of the target structures must be fixed beforehand.

Lemonnier et al. [6] used multiscale analysis of shapes to highlight areas of isotherm curvature which may contain eddy shapes. Analysis of oriented texture through phase portraits was used to classify the selected regions. The main problem reported by the authors was a high rate of false detections [8] which required further manual processing of the image.

Cantón-Garbín et al. [11] first pre-processed SST images of the Atlantic using an ANN module to mask cloudy areas. Images were then segmented using information on isothermal lines. Finally, features extracted from the segmented sub-areas were fed to a competitive layer of neuron-like processing elements for identification. A set of pre-classified examples of mesoscalar phenomena was used to train the processing elements. The authors also tested a rule-based classifier based on experts' knowledge [7]. The paper reported good accuracy results for recognition of upwellings and island wakes while the detection of warm and cold eddies was more problematic.

3 Problem Domain

The aim of this study is the automatic detection of meddies from SST data collected via the Advanced Very-High Resolution Radiometer of the National Atlantic and Atmospheric Administration satellite. Temperature readings are arranged into SST maps. Each map covers an area of the Atlantic Ocean of 700x700 kilometers between 34-41°N and 6-15°W and contains one data point per square kilometer. The resolution of temperature readings is within 0.1°C. Fig. 1 shows a sample SST map. White areas on the right part of the image correspond to land regions, namely the coastal areas of Portugal, Spain and Morocco. The white patches on the left of the image correspond to sea regions covered by clouds.

The survey of the previous section shows that automatic recognition of meddies from SST maps can be achieved following two different approaches.

The first approach usually matches thermal gradient maps with analytical descriptions of the target structures. A typical example is the work of Alexanin and Alexanina [9] which fits dominant orientation maps of thermal contrast to elliptical curve models. The main limitation of this approach is the difficulty of complying with the

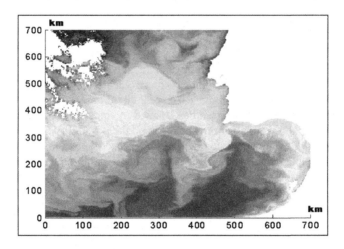

Fig. 1. SST map of the North Atlantic

high structural variability of eddies. Moreover, since temperature gradient traces in SST maps are often weak, image pre-processing is needed to enhance thermal contrast. Unfortunately, thermal contrast enhancement is likely to increase noise as well, making recognition of structural patterns harder. Identification systems tend therefore to rely on rather complex algorithms which often show a certain degree of brittleness.

The second approach uses ANNs [10], [11]. ANNs are capable of learning arbitrarily complex non-linear mappings and can handle large amounts of sensory information. The approximate nature of their pattern matching and association processes makes them particularly suitable to deal with the high variability of mesoscale phenomena. Such robustness usually makes less critical the pre-processing stage, allowing faster and simpler procedures to be used. ANN learning capabilities also remove the need for time-consuming design of the identification knowledge.

The main drawback of ANN systems is that the decision making policy is usually not transparent to the user. For this reason, expertise cannot be used to initialise the system and the learned knowledge cannot be extracted for modelling purposes.

4   Proposed Algorithm

The procedure uses Laws' method to analyse SST images with the aim of revealing those textural patterns of water temperature that characterise the presence of a meddy. For each SST map point, Laws' algorithm produces a numerical vector describing the structural properties of the surrounding region. Vectors generated by meddy formations, albeit noisy and irregular, are deemed to be separable from vectors generated by other oceanic phenomena.

The numerical vector is forwarded to an ANN classifier for meddy detection. The ANN is trained to recognise textural patterns generated by meddies on a set of positive and negative instances.

4.1 Laws' Algorithm

Laws' method for texture analysis is based on a series of convolution kernels aimed at highlighting the microstructure of texture within an image. 25 5x5 kernels are generated in a combinatorial fashion from 5 vectors of length 5, each vector associated with a basic microstructure characteristic. Fig. 2 shows the 5 primitive vectors, their 25 convolution kernels and an example of convolution kernel. All vectors except L5 are zero-sum. Each kernel is convolved with the original image to generate 25 filtered images of structural features. For example, the convolution of kernel *E5W5* with the original image generates a filtered image (likewise called *E5W5*) revealing the presence of horizontal edges and vertical waves. All images are zero-mean with the exception of L5L5, which is generally used as a normalization image and discarded.

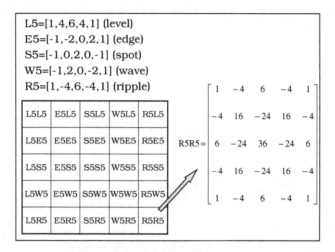

Fig. 2. Laws' primitive vectors and kernels

Images generated by symmetric filters are combined to achieve rotational invariance. For example, images E5W5 and W5E5 can be point-by-point added up to achieve the rotationally invariant E5W5R image, the latter mapping total edge and wave content. To keep all measures consistent with respect to size, images generated by homologous kernels are pointwise scaled by a factor of 2. For example, image E5E5R is obtained by multiplying by 2 all point values of the E5E5 image.

The above algorithm creates 14 images of measures of rotationally invariant texture structures. For each pixel of the 14 filtered images, Laws suggests up to 70 numerical features can be calculated, namely the amplitude mean, standard deviation, skewness, kurtosis and texture energy measure (TEM). The local TEM is generally computed as the sum of the absolute values of the pixels around a neighborhood. For example, for each point E5W5R(i,j) of image E5W5R, the local TEM E5W5RT(i,j) is calculated as follows:

$$E5W5RT(i, j) = \sum_{l=-N}^{l=N} \sum_{m=-N}^{m=N} |E5W5R(l,m)| \tag{1}$$

where NxN is the size of the neighbourhood. For each image point, the measures of feature amplitude mean, standard deviation, skewness and kurtosis are likewise calculated within the same NxN neighbourhood. A final selection step is usually necessary to identify the minimal set of most discriminant texture features.

4.2 ANN Eddy Identification

Given an SST image point, the numerical vector describing the microstructure of the neighbouring texture field is fed to a multi-layer perceptron (MLP) [13] classifier for meddy detection. The MLP is perhaps the best known and most successful type of ANN. It is a fully connected feedforward ANN [13] composed of three or four layers of processing elements. Fig. 3 shows the main features of the MLP. The input layer gathers incoming signals to the network and generally acts as a buffer. The size of the input layer is equal to the number of input signals. One or more hidden layers of neurons follow. These neurons collect the signals coming from the preceding layer and process them via a non-linear transformation function.

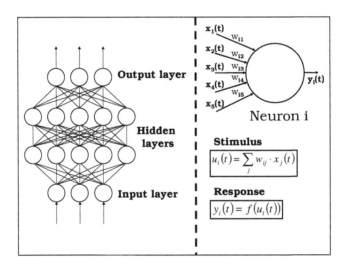

Fig. 3. Multi-layer perceptron

This is where input patterns are clustered, each layer of neurons splitting the input space into several decision regions, building onto the partition of the previous layer. The more hidden layers there are and the larger they are, the more complex the resulting decision regions. However, it can be shown that no more than two hidden layers are required to form any arbitrarily complex decision region [13].

The ouput layer collects the signals from the last hidden layer and further processes them to give the final classification result. This layer usually contains one neuron per class, the neuron with the highest output determining the identification result.

Typically, the network undergoes a training phase where the weights of the connections between neurons are adjusted. Learning modifies the system response by modifying the way the incoming signals to the neurons are scaled.

Structure optimisation is of crucial importance for the performance of the ANN. Different topologies are usually trained and their merit assessed on the learning accuracy. Once the MLP architecture is optimised and the network is trained, the classifier is ready to operate.

5   Experimental Settings and Identification Results

Tests were carried out on a set of 32 SST maps of the Atlantic Ocean taken between March and July 2001 and made available by Instituto de Oceanografia, Faculdade de Ciências, Universidade de Lisboa, Portugal, (http://www.io.fc.ul.pt). Each map is organised as a 700x700 matrix of temperature readings with pre-marked land and cloud areas.

A set of 105 instances of visible meddy structures were selected from the 32 SST images for training and testing purposes. 445 examples of other sea structures (e.g., thermal fronts, open sea, etc.) were picked from the same maps as negative instances. A total of 550 data points were thus selected, each point corresponding to the centre of a meddy or a "non-meddy" region.

5.1   Experimental Apparatus and Algorithm Implementation

Each map is pointwise pre-processed according to the algorithm described in the previous section. For each of the selected sample points, a numerical vector of 70 features is extracted according to Laws' method. Feature selection was performed retaining or discarding the whole 14 values of one of the five statistical measures, that is, TEM, amplitude mean, standard deviation, skewness and kurtosis.

To cover a larger area of the ocean, a test was also made using a set of TEM values extracted from a region surrounding the sample point. A 3x3 raster scan binary mask of 2 points step-size was used for each of the 14 images, reading the TEM value at '1' locations. A 126-dimensional feature vector of TEM measurements was in this case generated for each point.

Table 1. Experimental settings

Multi-Layer Perceptron Settings	
Input nodes	*
Output nodes	2
Hidden nodes	**
Activation function of hidden layer nodes	Hyper-tangent
Activation function of output layer nodes	Sigmoidal
Initialisation range for MLP weights	[-0.05, 0.05]
Backpropagation Rule Settings	
Learning coefficient	0.01
Momentum term	0.1
Learning iterations	**

* depending from data set
** optimised for max performance

The MLP classifier takes as input the numerical feature vector and produces a positive or negative identification response. The network is trained via the Backpropagation (BP) algorithm [13] on a set of 440 randomly selected examples representing 80% of the total positive and negative meddy instances. The remaining 110 data points are kept for validation purposes.

The above partition generates a training set containing 84 instances of meddy patterns and 356 instances of non-meddy patterns. To improve learning, the size of the two classes was balanced by duplicating instances of meddy patterns until they reached 356. Table 1 summarises the main ANN settings and BP parameters.

5.2 Experimental Results

Table 2 reports the learning results for the best combinations of statistical measures. For each case, the best performing MLP configuration was reported. For each column,

Table 2. Learning results for the best combination of statistical measures

	mean	tem-mean	tem-mean	tem-mean-std_dva	tem-mean-kurtosis	tem-mean-skewness	tem-mean-skewness
1st layer	15	15	15	20	25	20	15
2nd layer	-	-	10	-	-	-	5
Features	14	28	28	42	42	42	42
Accuracy	94.36	95.09	95.55	96.27	95.64	96.00	95.36
Std. dva	2.18	2.39	1.63	1.68	1.47	1.43	1.51
Meddies	89.05	91.43	89.05	89.05	89.05	90.48	90.00
non-Med.	95.62	95.96	97.08	97.98	97.19	97.30	96.63
iterations	22200	6000	5500	18000	20000	1100	1000

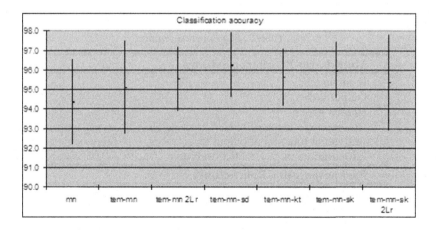

Fig. 4. Meddy identification accuracy results

accuracy results are estimated on the average of 10 independent learning trials. The recognition accuracy is reported together with the standard deviation over the 10 trials. Fig. 4 shows the average accuracy within the span of plus or minus one standard deviation.

Table 2 also breaks down the classification accuracy on each of the two classes and reports the number of BP training cycles. The latter was optimised to maximise identification accuracy.

Experimental evidence shows that the proposed algorithm is able to recognise, with high accuracy, patterns of thermal gradient direction generated by meddy phenomena. Results showed robust performances with small standard deviations over the 10 learning trials. The very high recognition accuracy on negative instances of meddy patterns is particularly important since it assures a low rate of false detections.

Fig. 4 shows that differences in learning accuracy between different tests are indistinguishable from stochastic fluctuations, since they are within the range of one or two standard deviations. However, combinations using a larger number of features seem to be more robust since they obtained the smallest standard deviations.

The size of the MLP structure also varied modestly with the size of the input vector. Larger input vectors usually required slightly larger hidden layers. There was no substantial difference in performance and learning times between structures composed of one or two hidden layers.

Table 3 reports the learning results obtained using the 3x3 raster scan mask. A first test was conducted using the 126-dimensional vector of measures of TEM. Further experiments were conducted using combinations of the 126 measures of TEM plus point values of the other statistical measures used in the previous experiments (e.g., mean, standard deviation, etc.). In addition to the results obtained using the 126-dimensional vector of TEMs, table 3 reports the results achieved using the two best performing combinations of input features. Those two combinations were obtained adding to the 126-dimensional vector of TEMs, respectively, the 14 point values of mean amplitude (140-dimensional input vector), and the 14 point values of mean amplitude plus the 14 point measures of skewness (154-dimensional input vector).

Experimental results show that sampling TEM measures in an area around a point didn't bring any improvement to the performance of the classifier. Since TEM is already an average measure of absolute intensity within a region, it is likely the benefit

Table 3. Experimental results – 3x3 mask

	TEM3x3	TEM3x3-Mean	TEM3x3-Mean-Skewness
1st layer	30	30	5
features	126	140	154
accuracy	96.27	93.82	95.73
std. dva	2.12	1.70	1.22
meddies	88.10	86.19	83.33
non-meddies	98.20	95.62	98.65
iterations	2000	700	7900

from larger neighbourhood information is outweighted by the considerable increase of complexity of the input space. In general, the second test gave slightly lower accuracy results on meddy structures and slightly higher accuracy results on non-meddy structures. This may suggest that the most distinctive information on meddy texture patterns is contained within the core of the structure. However this conjecture should be corroborated by further investigation and more statistically relevant evidence.

The final configuration for the input feature vector was chosen as the one allowing the lowest standard deviation. It comprises the sum of the 14 statistical measures of TEM, mean and skewness. Using this type of input vector, the best performing MLP classifier was obtained using an architecture containing one hidden layer of 20 units and required 1100 iterations of the BP algorithm to reach top performance.

6 Discussion

Experimental results proved that the proposed algorithm produces robust and high performing MLP solutions. These MLP solutions are able to successfully identify points in SST images that lie at the core of meddy structures. Identification is based on textural patterns of water temperature.

The proposed method can be used to scan pointwise the whole image and produce a classification result for each point. Results can be organised as a map, where each location corresponds to a positive or negative meddy detection response. Positive identifications are expected to be clustered in areas lying at the centre of meddy structures, while occasional false detections are likely to be scattered more evenly around the map. The application of a smoothing operator followed by thresholding may be sufficient to remove most of the noise from the map of detection results.

Compared to the existing literature, the proposed algorithm shares the machine learning approach of Peckinpaugh et al. [10] and Cantón-Garbín et al. [11]. Image pre-processing is the main difference between the proposed method and the one of Peckinpaugh et al. [10], while Cantón-Garbín et al. [11] also used a considerably more complex recognition system.

Regarding classification accuracy, it is difficult to draw a comparison between the proposed approach and other methods. Related work reported in this paper differs widely for geographic location, experimental settings and evaluation method. Some of the other detection algorithms also targeted other sea structures such as upwellings and island wakes [8], [11], [7] and differentiated cold eddies from warm ones [10].

As a general remark, the proposed algorithm doesn't seem to suffer from the common problem of high detection of false positives [8], [10], [11]. Unlike the system of Peckinpaugh et al. [10], the proposed algorithm is also equally able to recognise warm eddies as well as cold ones.

Recognition rates vary widely in the literature. Thonet et al. [8] report 88% accuracy on identification of well formed eddies over 100 SST images of the Bay of Biscay. Cantón-Garbín et al. [11] obtained over 80% recognition accuracy for Atlantic eddies near the Canary Islands and 66% accuracy for eddies in the Mediterranean Sea. Guindos-Rojas et al. [7] report classification accuracies varying from 80% to 95% for the recognition of island wakes, cold and warm eddies and upwellings. Conservatively, it is possible to claim that the performance of the proposed algorithm is competitive with other results in the literature.

7 Conclusions and Further Work

This paper presented a new algorithm for automatic detection of meddies from SST maps of the Atlantic Ocean. The algorithm pre-processes the imagery via simple convolution kernels aimed at revealing microstructural patterns of water temperature. For each map point, a numerical vector containing information on local structural properties is generated. This vector is forwarded to a MLP classifier for identification of meddy patterns. The network is trained on a set of pre-classified positive and negative examples of points belonging to meddy formations.

Experimental tests produced encouraging results and proved the efficacy of the proposed approach.

The proposed system achieved high accuracy with fast and robust learning results over a range of different combinations of statistical measures of texture properties. Results were also characterised by very low rates of detection of false positives. This observation is particularly important since meddies occupy only a small portion of SST map area.

Further work should focus on improvement of the image pre-processing procedure. Future investigation should aim at reduction of the number of input features, possibly discarding other statistical measures as well as rejecting unneeded measures of texture properties (i.e., some of the original 14 rotationally invariant measures).

Other image processing algorithms should be tested. Improvements should also focus on the design and training of the MLP classifier. Different classification algorithms could be investigated.

Acknowledgements

The authors would like to thank Instituto de Oceanografia, Faculdade de Ciências, Universidade de Lisboa, for their expert technical support. The presented work is part of AI-MEDEA and RENA (http://www.io.fc.ul.pt/fisica/research.htm) research projects which are sponsored by Fundação para a Ciência e Tecnologia, Ministério da Ciência e Ensino Superior, Portugal.

References

1. Reid, J.L.: On the Total Geostrophic Circulation of the North Atlantic Ocean: Flow Patterns, Tracers, and Transports. Progress in Oceanogr., Vol. 33, Pergamon, (1994) 1–92.
2. Oliveira, P.B., Serra, N., Fiúza: A.F.G., Ambar I.: A Study of Meddies Using Simultaneous in Situ and Satellite Observations. Satellites, Oceanography and Society, ed. D. Halpern, Elsevier Science B.V. (2000).
3. Armi, L. and Zenk, W.: Large Lenses of Highly Saline Mediterranean Water. J. Phys. Oceanogr., Vol. 14, (1984) 1560-1576.
4. Parisi Baradad, V.: Analysis of Mesoscale Structures though Digital Images Techniques. PhD thesis, Universitat Politècnica de Catalunya, Barcelona – Spain (2000).
5. Bower A., Armi L., Ambar, I.: Lagrangian Observations of Meddy Formation During a Mediterranean Undercurrent Seeding Experiment. J. Phys. Oceanogr., Vol. 27, No. 12, (1997) 2545-2575.

6. Lemonnier, B., Lopez, C., Duporte, E., Delmas, R.: Multiscale Analysis of Shapes Applied to Thermal Infrared Sea Surface Images. Proc. Int. Geosc. and Remote Sensing Symp. 1994 (IGARSS'94), Pasadena - CA, Vol.1, (1994) 479-481.
7. Guindos-Rojas, F. Cantón-Garbín, M., Torres-Arriaza, J.A., Peralta-Lopez, M., Piedra-Fernandez, J.A., Molina-Martinez, A.: Automatic Recognition of Ocean Structures from Satellite Images by Means of Neural Nets and Expert Systems. Proc. ESA-EUSC 2004, Madrid – Spain (2004).
8. Thonet, H., Lemonnier, B., Delmas, R.: Automatic Segmentation of Oceanic Eddies on AVHRR Thermal Infrared Sea Surface Images. Proc. OCEANS '95, San Diego - CA, Vol. 2, (1995) 1122-1127.
9. Alexanin A.I., Alexanina M.G.: Quantitative Analysis of Thermal Sea Surface Structures on Noaa Ir-Images. Proc. CREAMS'2000 Int. Symp. - Oceanogr. of the Japan Sea, Vladivostok - Rus, (2000) 158-165.
10. Peckinpaugh, S.H., Chase, J.R., Holyer R.J.: Neural Networks for Eddy Detection in Satellite Imagery. Proc. SPIE Vol. 1965, (1993) pp.151-161.
11. Cantón-Garbín, M., Torres-Arriaza, J.A., Guindos-Rojas, F., Peralta-Lopez, M.: Towards an Automatic Interpretation and Knowledge Based Search of Satellite Images in Databases. Systems Analysis Modelling Simulation, Vol. 43, No. 9, (2003) 1249–1262.
12. Laws, K.I.: Rapid texture identification. Proc. SPIE Vol. 238, (1980) 376-380
13. Lippmann, R. P.: An Introduction to Computing with Neural Nets. IEEE ASSP Magazine, (1987) 4-22.
14. Fitch, J.P., Lehmann, S.K., Dowla, F.U., Lu, S.Y., Johansson, E.M., Goodman, D.M.: Ship wake-detection procedure using conjugate gradient trained artificial neural networks. IEEE Trans. Geosc. and Remote Sensing, Vol. 29, No. 5, (1991) 718–726.
15. S.H. Peckinpaugh, R.J. Holyer: Circle Detection for Extracting Eddy Size and Position from Satellite Imagery of the Ocean. IEEE Trans. Geosc. and Remote Sensing, 1994, Vol. 32, No. 2, (1994) 267-273.

Monitoring the Quality of Meta-data in Web Portals Using Statistics, Visualization and Data Mining

Carlos Soares[1], Alípio Mário Jorge[1], and Marcos Aurélio Domingues[2]

[1] LIACC-NIAAD/Faculty of Economics, University of Porto
[2] LIACC-NIAAD, University of Porto
Rua de Ceuta, 118, 6 Andar – 4050-190 Porto, Portugal
{csoares, amjorge, marcos}@liacc.up.pt
http://www.liacc.up.pt

Abstract. We propose a methodology to monitor the quality of the meta-data used to describe content in web portals. It is based on the analysis of the meta-data using statistics, visualization and data mining tools. The methodology enables the site's editor to detect and correct problems in the description of contents, thus improving the quality of the web portal and the satisfaction of its users. We also define a general architecture for a platform to support the proposed methodology. We have implemented this platform and tested it on a Portuguese portal for management executives. The results validate the methodology proposed.

1 Introduction

The aim of many web portals is to select, organize and distribute content (information, or other services and products) in order to satisfy its users/customers. The methods to support this process are to a large extent based on meta-data (such as keywords, category, author and other descriptors) that describe content and its properties. For instance, search engines often take into account keywords that are associated with the content to compute their relevance to a query. Likewise, the accessibility of content by navigation depends on their position in the structure of the portal, which is usually defined by a specific meta-data descriptor (e.g., category).

Meta-data is usually filled in by the authors who publish content in the portal. The publishing process, which goes from the insertion of content to its actual publication on the portal is regulated by a workflow. The complexity of this workflow varies: the author may be authorized to publish content directly; alternatively content may have to be analyzed by one or more editors, who authorize its publication or not. Editors may also suggest changes to the content and to the meta-data that describe it, or make those changes themselves.

In the case where there are many different authors or the publishing process is less strict, the meta-data may describe content in a way which is not suitable for the purpose of the portal, thus decreasing the quality of the services provided.

C. Bento, A. Cardoso, and G. Dias (Eds.): EPIA 2005, LNAI 3808, pp. 371–382, 2005.

For instance, a user may fail to find relevant content using the search engine if the set of keywords assigned to it are inappropriate. Thus, it is essential to monitor the quality of meta-data describing content to ensure that the collection of content is made available in a structured, inter-related and easily accessible way to the users.

In this paper we propose a methodology to monitor and control the quality of the meta-data used to describe content in web portals. We assume that the portal is based on a Content Management System, which stores and organizes content using a database. The core of this methodology is a system of metrics, that objectively assess the quality of the meta-data and indirectly the quality of the service provided by the portal. The metrics are defined on data that is collected by the Content Management System (the meta-data) and by the portal's web servers (the access logs). We also define a general architecture for a platform to support the proposed methodology. We expect that the deployment of this methodology will support the publishing process with an increased quality of meta-data. For instance, it may be possible to publish content as soon as it is inserted. The editor can make corrections to the meta-data later on, based on the reports provided by the platform.

As part of this work, we have extended the framework for assessing the quality of Internet services, which was defined by Moorsel [1]. We have also adapted the general set of data quality dimensions proposed by Pipino et al. [2] to the particular case of content meta-data. Finally, we have successfully applied the methodology to PortalExecutivo.com, a Portuguese portal for management executives.

This paper is organized as follows. We start by presenting related work (sect. 2). In Section 3 we describe the methodology to monitor the quality of content meta-data and the general architecture to implement the new methodology. We then present a case study (sect. 4) and conclude suggesting a few of the possible lines of future work (sect. 5).

2   Related Work

Pipino et al [2] propose a set of general principles for developing metrics to assess the quality of data. The metrics are organized according to 16 dimensions, ranging from "free-of-error", representing metrics that account for incorrect values, to "value-added", representing metrics that account for the benefits brought by the data. They also describe three functional forms which are often used to develop data quality metrics, namely simple ratios, min/max and weighted averages. They ilustrate these principles with two case studies, including both subjective and objective metrics.

The evaluation of the quality of Internet services using quantitative metrics is discussed by Moorsel [1]. Three different quality levels are considered: Quality of Services (QoS), Quality of Experience (QoE) and Quality of Business (QoBiz). The author argues that the focus must be on QoE and QoBiz metrics. These attempt to quantify the quality of the service from the perspective of the user (e.g., response time of the site) and of the business (e.g., number of transactions), respectively, while QoS metrics are concerned with the platform (e.g., availability of the site). Moorsel also proposes a framework that integrates the three types of metrics, but focuses on QoBiz. This framework is then discussed in the context of three types of Internet business models.

In the Data Mining field, the emphasis has been mainly on QoE. Spiliopoulou and Pohle [3] propose a number of objective metrics to assess the usability of web sites. These metrics take into account users accesses and knowledge about the site. Visualization tools have also been used to identify difficulties in web site navigation [4], [5].

3   Methodology to Monitor the Quality of Content Meta-data

In this section, we present a methodology to monitor the quality of meta-data used to describe content in web portals.

3.1   Quality of Process in a Quality Evaluation Framework

An e-business company may have success (i.e., achieve a high Quality of Business, QoBiz) depending on whether its services can easily satisfy the needs of its users (i.e., provide a high Quality of Experience, QoE). The goal is to optimize the quality of the services provided in terms of the following criteria:

Efficiency how quickly is the answer to a need obtained? Note that we are not concerned with speed in terms of data communication. We are interested in the time required to get to a relevant content, namely in terms of how many steps must the user go through.

Completeness does the set of content items obtained for a given necessity contain all relevant information? This criterion is related to the notion of recall in information retrieval.

Relevance does the set of content items obtained for a given necessity include only relevant information? This criterion is related to the notion of precision in information retrieval.

Some of the mechanisms commonly used by web sites to provide their services are search engines and navigation in the site structure. There are many factors affecting the quality of these services: technological structure, sources of content and the processes of publishing and distributing content from the web portal.

In this work, we focus on the publishing process, which consists of the activities of the *authors* and the *editors*. Authors insert content in the web portal, control its access permissions, define the values of meta-data describing it, and integrate it into the organization of the portal (for instance, to classify content in a hierarchy of categories). The editors Editors monitor the publishing process and authorize the publication of content.

This process is very important to the success of a web site. For instance, an inadequate classification of content may make it practically invisible to the user. Nevertheless, it has been ignored in the framework for evaluation of Internet services proposed by Moorsel [1]. We extend this framework by including metrics to assess what we call the *Quality of Process* (QoP). Our goal is to assess the effect of publishing operations on the quality of the services provided by the site.

3.2   Adapted Publishing Process

In Figure 1 we describe the standard web publishing process and add two new elements (dashed lines) that are important in our methodology. The standard web publishing process includes editors/authors who insert or change content and respective meta-data. Content is made available on the portal and the user accesses are recorded in the web access logs.

We extend this process with the EdMate tool which analyses the quality of the content meta-data. Quality is assessed using a number of QoP metrics (sect. 3.3). The computation of these metrics uses the meta-data describing content, as would be expected, but it may also analyze content and data representing user behavior. The values of those metrics and their evolution in time are represented and summarized in web reports to be used by the super-editor and the editors/authors.

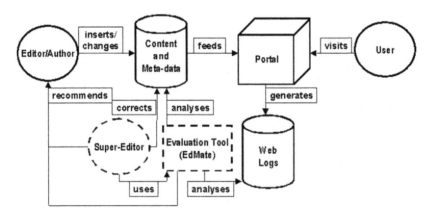

Fig. 1. Publishing process using the proposed methodology

The second new element is the *super-editor*, who processes the output of Ed-Mate and fixes problems directly or makes suggestions to authors. The possible actions for the super-editor are:

- Correction of content meta-data;
- Change of the (hierarchical) organization of the contents;
- Change of the schema of meta-database;
- Advice to the authors/editors concerning the publishing process.

3.3   Meta-data Quality Dimensions

To define a set of QoP metrics, we adapt the general approach defined by Pipino et al [2], who describes 16 dimensions along which we should assess the quality of data in general. To address the problem of assessing the quality of meta-data in a web portal, we have reinterpreted the 16 dimensions to fit our aims.[1] We have also related those dimensions to the three criteria mentioned earlier, namely speed, completeness and relevance. Furthermore, we have grouped the initial set of dimensions into three large groups, namely *error*, *adequacy* and *value*.

Error: metrics to analyse data problems related mainly with edition lapses. In this group we find, for instance, metrics that show whether a meta-data field has been filled in, and if it contains valid values. The metrics of this group can be classified in one of the following data quality dimensions:

- *Believability* - Evaluate if the meta-data describe correctly the properties of the content. An incorrect value will lead the user to irrelevant content and miss relevant ones, affecting both completeness and relevance.
- *Completeness* - Evaluate if the meta-data describe correctly all the relevant properties of the content. A relevant content may be invisible to a user if it is incompletely described. This dimension is related to the criterion with the same name.
- *Consistent Representation* - Evaluate if the meaning of values is always the same across different content. Representing the same concept with different values or associating different concepts with the same value affects both completeness and relevance.
- *Free-of-Error* - Evaluate if the meta-data are correct and reliable. Incorrect descriptions will affect completeness.

Adequacy: metrics that are related with the incorrect choice of values to describe content. These metrics can be classified in one of the following data quality dimensions:

- *Accessibility of Content* - Evaluate if the meta-data affect the visibility of content. This dimension is related to the efficiency and completeness criteria.
- *Appropriate Amount of Data* - Evaluate if the quantity of meta-data is suitable for the users and also if it enables the user to get the adequate amount of content for its needs. An insufficient amount of meta-data affects completeness while too much meta-data and content affect efficiency.
- *Concise Representation* - Evaluate if content is described by the smallest set of complete meta-data. A concise description will decrease the amount of information that the user must process, thus increasing efficiency.

---

[1] We have ignored the Security dimension, which is not relevant in the publishing process.

- *Ease of Manipulation* - Evaluate if the representation of the meta-data is simple enough for the users. Too complex a representation will affect efficiency and completeness.
- *Relevancy* - Evaluate if the meta-data are informative and useful for the activities of the users. Highly relevant values in the description of content will make the task of identifying relevant content easier, thus improving both efficiency and relevance.
- *Timeliness* - Evaluate the extent to which the meta-data enable the user to access relevant content on time. Up-to-date descriptions will increase the probability of finding relevant content and avoiding irrelevant ones. This dimension affects completeness and relevance.

Value: metrics depending on subjective choices of the author, possibly adding value to content and corresponding meta-data. In this group there are metrics that show whether particular meta-data values cause a user to become interested in other content besides the originally intended. The metrics of this group can be classified in one of the following data quality dimensions:

- *Interpretability* - Evaluate if the values used by the authors exist in the vocabulary of the users. This dimension affects both completeness and relevance.
- *Objectivity of the Author* - Evaluate if the authors describe the content independently of their background. A subjective choice of meta-data values will force the user to try to take the perspective of the author into account, which will affect all three criteria considered.
- *Reputation of the Author* - Assign a confidence degree to some value taking into account the quality of meta-data inserted previously by the same author. A more reliable author will need less attention from the super-editor. This dimension affects all three criteria considered.
- *Understandability* - Evaluate if the semantic of the values is the same for the author and the users. Different understandings affect both completeness and relevance.
- *Value-Added* - Assess the utility of the meta-data beyond the primary necessity of the user. A description that leads the user to a relevant content which, additionally, creates a new need is important. This dimension affects completeness and relevance.

3.4   Meta-data Quality Metrics

We have designed more than 60 metrics, covering all the dimensions described above. Table 1 present a few examples for illustration purposes.

Many of the data quality concepts mentioned in the previous section, are quite subjective (e.g., the adequacy of the meta-data values). Furthermore, obtaining explicit satisfaction ratings from the web user is typically difficult. This makes the objective assessment of the quality dimensions described a hard task. Thus, many of the metrics designed only assess the corresponding property indirectly. To give an example, the *believability* of a descriptor is difficult to assess objectively. However, we can determine the length of the value of a descriptor, such as a keyword. It is expected that a very long keyword is generally less adequate than a shorter one. Therefore, this metric can be used as an estimate of the believability of a descriptor (see *length of value* in Table 1). Additionally, a single metric may be used to estimate the quality of a descriptor in terms of more than one dimension. For instance, short search expressions are generally more probable than longer ones. Therefore, the *length of value* metric can also be used to assess the *ease of manipulation* dimension.

The functions used to compute metrics can be based on very simple statistics or more complex methods. For instance, The *length of value* metric is computed simply by counting the number of characters in a string. Metrics based on simple frequencies, such as the *frequency in search* (Table 1), are quite common. Alternatively, metrics can be based on probabilities. The *redundancy of descriptor* metric is based on the conditional probability of having a value x, in the description of content, given that a another value y is used(Table 1). An example of the use of a more complex method is given by association rules [6], which are used to compute the *association between values* metric (Table 1).

The computation of the metrics is always based on the meta-data. However, in some cases the portal web access log can also be used, such as in the case of the *frequency in search* metric (Table 1).

Table 1. Name, dimensions of quality affected and description of a few metrics

Name: *Length of value*
Dimensions: Believability, completeness, concise representation, acessibility and ease of manipulation
Description: Number of characters in the value of a descriptor. Extremely large or small values may indicate inadequate choice of values to represent the content.
Name: *Association between values*
Dimensions: Concise representation, relevancy, reputation
Description: The confidence level of an association rule $A \rightarrow B$ is an indicator of whether the set of values A make the set of values B redundant.The higher the value, the more redundant B is expected to be. This may indicate that the authors have developed implicit practices in the description of content.
Name: *Frequency in search*
Dimensions: Acessibility, relevancy, interpretability and value-added
Description: Frequency of the values of a descriptor in the web access logs (e.g., the frequency of a search using a given keyword). For instance, if a keyword is searched for often, this it is likely to have a high interpretability.
Name: *Redundancy of descriptor*
Dimensions: Concise representation, relevancy
Description: Conditional probability of having a value x, in the description of content, given that a another value y is used, $P(x|y)$. High values may mean that y makes x redundant. This may indicate that the authors have developed implicit practices in the description of content.

3.5   Functional Form of Meta-data Quality Metrics

Each of the data quality metrics will be computed for a large number of objects. For instance, the believability metric mentioned above will be computed for each possible keyword. This yields a huge number of values. Assessing the quality of the meta-data based on all the values computed would be inefficient. Therefore, for the process to be feasible it is necessary to use suitable forms of presentation.

For each metric a small number of *macro indicators* is computed, aggregating the corresponding individual values. The choice of functional form used to calculate a macro indicator should take into account the semantic of the metric [2]. A suitable function for the believability metric example given earlier is the minimum of the frequency values, and the corresponding macro indicator is called *minimum frequency.*

Additionally the super-editor should be able to drill-down on the macro indicators in order to obtain more detailed information concerning the values obtained with a metric. For instance, given a low value of the *minimum frequency* macro indicator the super-editor may want to find out what the corresponding meta-data descriptor is and which authors have used it. The drill-down mechanism should provide information at different aggregation levels.

Graphical representation of the values are also used to detect interesting events. For instance, it may be used to provide context information, which helps the detection of unusual values. The evolution of the values of the *minimum frequency* macro indicator may show, for instance, that, although the current value is acceptable, the values have been decreasing. This could mean that the authors are describing content less carefully.

3.6   Architecture of the EdMate Platform

The methodology proposed has been implemented as the EdMate platform (Figure 2).

The "Assessment" module periodically computes the values of more than 70 metrics and the macro indicators using data representing the activities of the authors and users. The values are then stored in the "Metrics" database. The "Presentation" module generates reports based on the values of the "Metrics" database. Note that presentation is an interative process that generates "Hyper reports". As mentioned in the previous section, the user may drill-down from the macro indicators to more detailed information.

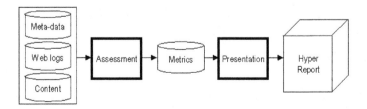

Fig. 2. Architecture of the EdMate platform

4   Case Study

In this section we describe the application of the proposed methodology to Por-
talExecutivo.com (PE), a Portuguese web portal targeted to business executives.
The business model is subscription-based, which means that only paying users
have full access to content through web login. However some content is freely
available and users can freely browse the site's structure. Content is provided
not only by PE but also by a large number of partners. The goal of PE is to
facilitate the access of its members to relevant content. Value is added to the
contributed content by structuring and interrelating them. This is achieved by
filling in a rich set of meta-data fields, including keywords, categories, relevant
companies, source, authors, among others. Therefore, the problem of meta-data
quality is essential for PE.

4.1   Results

Here we illustrate the kind of analysis that can be made using the EdMate
platform. We also demonstrate that the publishing process can be changed based
on its results so that the quality of the meta-data is improved.

Since the results of queries to the search engine are affected by the quality
of the keywords used to describe content, we focus on this meta-data field. The
meta-data used is relative to the period April/September 2004.

Concerning the quality of meta-data, Figure 3 shows that the number of
keywords which is used only once is very high. On the one hand, some of these are
caused by typographical errors, which means that this metric can be associated
with the "free-of-error" dimension. On the other, this value indicates that the
potential of keywords to interrelate content from different sources is not being
adequately exploited ("relevancy" and "value-added" dimensions).

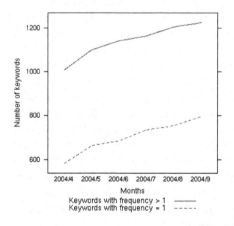
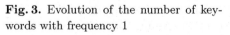
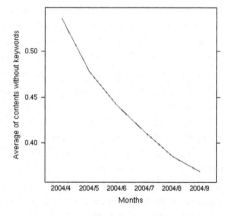

Fig. 3. Evolution of the number of keywords with frequency 1

Fig. 4. Evolution of the number of keywords not filled in

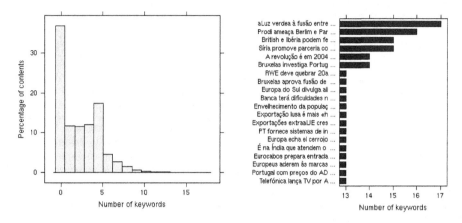

Fig. 5. Histogram of the number of key-   **Fig. 6.** Top 20 of contents with the largest
words by content   numbers of keywords

Fig. 7. Relationships between keywords obtained using association rules

The results obtained with EdMate are not only useful to detect problems with data quality but also to trigger corrective actions and monitor them. Figure 4 shows that in April more than 50% of content did not have any keywords filled-in ("completeness" dimension). This was noticed by the super-editor at that time and, consequently a semi-automatic procedure to support the process of filling-in keywords was implemented ("completeness" dimension). The same figure shows that this procedure has brought a significant improvement to the quality of metadata, with a steady decrease of this metric down to less than 40% in September.

This kind of analysis also enables the super-editor to keep an up-to-date perspective on the publishing process. Figure 5 shows that, in September, very few content items have more than 4 keywords. The super-editor may find this insufficient and, thus instruct the authors accordingly. Additionally Figure 6 shows that the maximum number of keywords associated with a content item is 17. This may look suspicious to the super-editor, who may identify the corresponding item and correct its description, if necessary.

In another metric, we have used the confidence of association rules to determine keywords more frequently used together. Additionally, we can provide a graphical representation of the associations between keywords (Figure 7). We observed that often a general keyword (e.g., fiscality - *fiscalidade*) is associated with a more specific one (e.g., international taxation - *tributação internacional*). This implicit structure of the keywords, unveiled by the discovered association rules, enables the detection of incorrect descriptions ("believability", "concise representation" and "reputation of the author" dimensions).

These results show that the methodology proposed enables:

- an assessment of the quality of the meta-data, triggering corrective action;
- monitoring of corrective procedures;
- an up-to-date perspective on the publishing process.

5   Conclusions and Future Work

Many web portals have a distributed model for the contribution of content. No matter how strict the publishing process is, low quality meta-data will sometimes be used to describe content. This decreases the quality of the services provided to the users.

In this paper we propose a methodology to monitor the quality of meta-data used to describe content in web portals. We also defined a general architecture for a platform to support the proposed methodology. We have successfully applied the methodology to a portal for business executives. Besides enabling the assessment of the quality of the meta-data, it enables the monitoring of corrective actions and it provides an up-to-date perspective of the publishing process.

As future work, we plan to formalize the quality dimensions (sect. 3.3) in order to support a more systematic process of designing new metrics. We also plan to apply other statistical and data mining techniques to improve the quality assessment process. For instance, clustering methods can be used to obtain groups of authors with similar behaviors in terms of data quality. This not only enables a different perspective on their publishing process but also different corrective actions can then be taken upon different groups.

Additionally, those techniques can be used to extend the quality assessment process with tools to support both authors and the super-editor to fill-in and correct meta-data. For instance, classification methods can be used to suggest keywords depending on the content.

Finally, to enhance the applicability of the methodology proposed, we need to integrate the Quality of Process metrics into a more general quality assessment framework, including other levels, such as Quality of Service, Quality of Experience and Quality of Business [1].

Acknowledgements

This work was partially funded by PortalExecutivo.com. The authors are grateful to PortalExecutivo.com for their support, and, in particular, to Rui Brandão and Carlos Sampaio for their collaboration.

References

[1] Moorsel, A.V.: Metrics for the internet age: Quality of experience and quality of business. In: Proceedings of the 5th Performability Workshop. (2001)

[2] Pipino, L. L.; Lee, Y.W., Wang, R.Y.: Data quality assessment. Communications of the ACM **45** (2002)

[3] Spiliopoulou, M., Pohle, C.: Data mining for measuring and improving the success of web sites. Data Mining and Knowledge Discovery **5** (2001) 85–114

[4] Berendt, B.: Using site semantics to analyze, visualize, and support navigation. Data Mining and Knowledge Discovery **6** (2002) 37–59

[5] Cadez, I., Heckerman, D., Meek, C., Smyth, P., White, S.: Model-based clustering and visualization of navigation patterns on a web site. Data Mining and Knowledge Discovery **7** (2003) 399–424

[6] Agrawal, R., Srikant, R.: Fast algorithms for mining association rules. In Bocca, J. B.; Jarke, M., Zaniolo, C., eds.: Proceedings 20th International Conference on Very Large Data Bases, VLDB. (1994) 487–499

A Real Time Data Extraction, Transformation and Loading Solution for Semi-structured Text Files

Nuno Viana[1], Ricardo Raminhos[1], and João Moura-Pires[2]

[1] UNINOVA, Quinta da Torre, 2829 -516 Caparica, Portugal
{nv,rfr}@uninova.pt
http://www.uninova.pt/ca3
[2] CENTRIA/FCT, Quinta da Torre, 2829 -516 Caparica, Portugal
jmp@di.fct.unl.pt
http://centria.di.fct.unl.pt/~jmp

Abstract. Space applications' users have been relying for the past decades on custom developed software tools capable of addressing short term necessities during critical Spacecraft control periods. Advances in computing power and storage solutions have made possible the development of innovative decision support systems. These systems are capable of providing high quality integrated data to both near real time and historical data analysis applications. This paper describes the implementation of a new approach for a distributed and loosely coupled data extraction and transformation solution capable of extracting, transforming and perform loading of relevant real-time and historical Space Weather and Spacecraft data from semi-structured text files into an integrated space-domain decision support system. The described solution takes advantage of XML and Web Service technologies and is currently working under operational environment at the European Space Agency as part of the Space Environment Information System for Mission Control Purposes (SEIS) project.

1 Introduction

The term "Space Weather" [1, 2], (S/W) represents the combination of conditions on the sun, solar wind, magnetosphere, ionosphere and thermosphere. Space Weather is not only a driver for earth's environmental changes but also plays a main role in the performance and reliability of orbiting Spacecraft (S/C) systems. Moreover, degradation of sensors and solar arrays or unpredicted changes in the on-board memories can often be associated with S/W event occurrences.

The availability of an integrated solution containing Space Weather and specific S/C onboard measurements' data, would allow performing of online and post-event analysis, thus increasing the S/C Flight Controllers' ability to react to unexpected critical situations and indirectly, to enhance the knowledge about the dynamics of the S/C itself.

Although important, this integrated data service is currently unavailable. At best some sparse data sub-sets exist on public Internet sites running on different locations and with distinct data formats. Therefore, collecting all the relevant information, transforming and interpreting it correctly, is a time consuming task for a S/C Flight Controller.

C. Bento, A. Cardoso, and G. Dias (Eds.): EPIA 2005, LNAI 3808, pp. 383 – 394, 2005.
© Springer-Verlag Berlin Heidelberg 2005

To provide such capabilities, a decision support system architecture was envisaged – the Space Environment Information System for Mission Control Purposes (SEIS) [3, 4], sponsored by the European Space Agency (ESA). The main goal of SEIS is to provide accurate real-time information about the ongoing Space Weather conditions and Spacecraft onboard measurements along with Space Weather predictions (e.g. radiation levels predictions). This platform assures the provision of distinct application services based on historical and near real-time data supported by a common database infrastructure.

This paper details the Data Processing Module – DPM, (with a special focus on the extraction and transformation component - UDET – Uniform Data Extractor and Transformer) used in SEIS, responsible for the retrieval of all source files (semistructured text files) from external data service providers, "raw" data extraction and further transformations into a usable format. Extensive research work has been also accomplished in both the conceptual Extraction, Transformation and Loading (ETL) modeling[5] and demonstrative prototypes[6, 7].

Given the number of already existing commercial[1] and open source ETL tools[2], the first approach towards solving the specific data processing problem in SEIS, was to identify which ETL tools could potentially be re-used. Unfortunately, after careful assessment, it soon became obvious that the existing solutions usually required the development of custom code in order to define the specificities of extraction, transformation and loading procedures in near real-time. Due to the high number of Provided Files (please refer to Table 1 for a list of data service providers and files) and their heterogeneity in terms of format, it was not feasible to develop custom code to address all files. In addition, gathering the entire file processing logic at implementation level would raise severe maintainability issues (any maintenance task would surely cause the modification of source code). Also, the analyzed tools did not provide cache capabilities for data that although received from different files referred to the same parameter (for these files, duplicate entries must be removed and not propagated forward as the analyzed solutions suggested). The only option was in fact to develop a custom, but generic data processing mechanism to solve the problem of processing data from remote data service providers into the target databases while also taking into account scalability and maintainability factors and possible reutilization of the resulting solution on other projects. This paper will address the design and development of the data processing solution (with a special focus on the extractor and transformer component), which fulfils the previous mentioned requisites.

The paper is organized in five sections: The first section (the current one) describes the motivation behind the data processing problem in the frame of the SEIS project as well as the paper's focus and contents. Section two highlights the SEIS architecture focusing mainly in the Data Processing Module. The third section is dedicated to the UDET component and presents a comprehensive description of how files are effec-

---

[1] IBM WebSphere DataStage (http://www.ascential.com/products/datastage.html)
  SAS Enterprise ETL Server (http://www.sas.com/technologies/dw/etl/index.html)
  Data Transformation Services (http://www.microsoft.com/sql/evaluation/features/datatran.asp)
  Informatica PowerCenter (http://www.informatica.com/products/powercenter/default.htm)
  Sunopsis ELT (http://www.sunopsis.com/corporate/us/products/sunopsis/snps_etl.htm)
[2] Enhydra Octopus (http://www.octopus.objectweb.org/)
  BEE Project (http://www.bee.insightstrategy.cz/en/index.html)
  OpenDigger (http://www.opendigger.org/)

tively processed. Section four provides the reader, an insight on the technical innovative aspects of UDET and finally, section five provides a short summary with
achieved results and guidelines for future improvements on the UDET component.

Table 1. List of available data service providers, number of provided files and parameters

Data Service Provider	Type	Provided Files	Provided Parameters
Wilcox Solar Observatory	Space Weather	1	1
Space Weather Technologies	Space Weather	1	2
SOHO Proton Monitor data (University of Maryland)	Space Weather	2	6
Solar Influences Data analysis Center	Space Weather	2	5
Lomnicky Peak's Neutron Monitor	Space Weather	1	2
National Oceanic and Atmosphere Administration/National Geophysical Data Centre	Space Weather	1	1
National Oceanic and Atmosphere Administration/Space Environment Centre	Space Weather	35	541
US Naval Research Laboratory	Space Weather	1	1
World Data Centre for Geomagnetism	Space Weather	1	1
European Space Operations Centre	Spacecraft	19	271
Multi Mission Module	Space Weather	13	118
Total		77	949

2   Data Processing in the Space Environment Information System

This section will initially provide a global view of the SEIS system and will focus
afterwards on the Data Processing Module. The Uniform Data Extractor and Transformer component will be thoroughly addressed in section 3.

2.1   SEIS System Architecture

SEIS is a multi-mission decision support system capable of providing near real-time
monitoring [8] and visualization, in addition to offline historical analysis [3] of Space
Weather and Spacecraft data, events and alarms to Flight Control Teams (FCT) responsible for Integral, Envisat and XMM satellites. Since the Integral S/C has been
selected as the reference mission, all SEIS services – offline and online – will be
available, while Envisat and XMM teams will only benefit from a fraction of all the
services available for the Integral[3] mission. The following list outlines the SEIS's core
services:
- Reliable Space Weather and Spacecraft data integration.
- Inclusion of Space Weather and Space Weather effects estimations generated by a
  widely accepted collection of physical Space Weather models.
- Plug-in functionalities for any external "black-box" data generator model (e.g.
  models based on Artificial Neural Networks - ANN).

---

[3] Following preliminary feedback after system deployment, it is expected that other missions
(XMM and Envisat) in addition to the reference one (Integral) would like to contribute with
additional data and therefore have access to the complete set of SEIS services.

- Near real-time alarm triggered events, based on rules extracted from the Flight Operations' Plan (FOP) [9] which capture users' domain knowledge.
- Near real-time visualization of ongoing Space Weather and Spacecraft conditions through the SEIS Monitoring Tool [10].
- Historical data visualization and correlation analysis (including automatic report design, generation and browsing) using state-of-art Online Analytical Processing (OLAP) client/server technology - SEIS Reporting and Analysis Tool [3].

In order to provide users with the previously mentioned set of services, the system architecture depicted in Fig. 1 was envisaged.

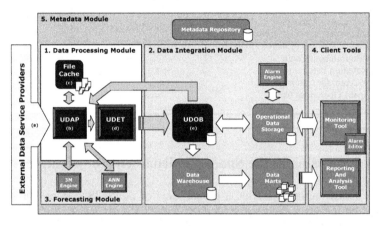

Fig. 1. SEIS system architecture modular breakdown, including the Data Processing Module which is formed by several components: (a) External Data Service Providers, (b) Uniform Data Access Proxy (UDAP), (c) File Cache, (d) Uniform Data Extractor and Transformer - UDET (the focus of this paper) and (e) Uniform Data Output Buffer (UDOB)

As clear in Fig. 1, SEIS's architecture is divided in several modules according to their specific roles.

- **Data Processing Module:** Is responsible for the file retrieval, parameter extraction and further transformations applied to all identified data, ensuring it meets the online and offline availability constraints, whilst having reusability and maintainability issues in mind (further detailed on section 2.2).
- **Data Integration Module:** Acts as the system's supporting infrastructure database, providing high quality integrated data services to the SEIS client applications, using three multi-purpose databases (Data Warehouse (DW)[11], Operational Data Storage (ODS) and Data Mart).
- **Forecasting Module:** A collection of forecast and estimation model components capable of generating Space Weather [12] and Spacecraft data estimations. Interaction with any of these models is accomplished using remote Web Services' invocation, which relies on Extended Markup Language (XML) message-passing mechanisms.

- **Metadata Module:** SEIS is a metadata driven system, incorporating a central metadata repository, that provides all SEIS applications with means of accessing shared information and configuration files.
- **Client Tools:** The SEIS system comprises two client tools, which take advantage of both the collected real time and historical data – the SEIS Monitoring Tool and the SEIS Reporting and Analysis Tool, respectively.

2.2 Data Processing Module

As previously highlighted, one of the objectives of SEIS is to provide reliable Space Weather and Spacecraft data integration. This is not a trivial task due to the numerous data formats (from "raw" text to structured tagged formats such as HTML – Hyper Text Markup Language) and to the communication protocols involved (e.g. Hyper Text Transfer Protocol – HTTP and File Transfer Protocol - FTP).

Since SEIS has near real-time data availability requirements, the whole processing mechanism should not take longer than 5 minutes to output its results into the UDOB) (i.e. the system has explicit knowledge – according to Metadata - on data refreshing time intervals for each remote Data Service Provider). Thus, several factors may interfere with this time restriction, from available network bandwidth, Round Trip Times (RTT), Internet Service Providers (ISP) availability, network status from SEIS and Data Service Provider sides, remote data service providers services' load and the number of concurrent request for processing file requests.

Since Data Service Providers are not controlled within SEIS but by external organizations according to their internal priorities, funding allocation and even scientists "good-will", server unavailability information is not accessible in advance (e.g. detection occurs only when the service actually fails and data stops being "pumped" into the data repositories). For similar reasons, text files comprising relevant parameters, contain structured data, whose arrangement may evolve. I.e. as time passes, new parameters may be added, deleted or updated into the file, thus making the format vary. Once again, notification about format change is inexistent and has to be inferred by our system and/or users. To address this issue, the DPM incorporates knowledge on the active File Format Definition (FFD) applied to a given file within a specific time-window.

2.3 UDAP, UDET and UDOB

As depicted in Fig. 1, the Data Processing Module is composed by three sub-components: UDAP, UDET and UDOB.

The UDAP component is responsible for the retrieval of all identified files from the different data service providers' locations, has the ability to handle with remote service availability failures and recover (whenever possible) lost data due access un-availability. UDAP is also in charge of dealing with both Space Weather and Space-craft data estimations outputs generated by the estimation and forecasting blocks, namely the Mission Modeling Module (3M) block and ANN models, through data files which are the results of capturing the models' outputs. Communication with these components is achieved using Web Services interfacing layers developed between UDAP's and each of the models' side.

All retrieved data is afterwards stored into a local file cache repository (to ease cached file management, a simple MS Windows Network File System (NTFS) compressed file system was used), from which is later sent for processing. By moving all data files to a local cache before performing any actual file processing, not only a virtual file access service is provided (minimizing possible problems originated by external services' failures), but also required storage space is reduced. Since all Data Processing Module components are Metadata driven, UDAP configuration and file scheduling definitions are stored in the centralized Metadata Repository.

In addition, UDAP provides a Human Machine Interface (HMI), which allows users to issue commands such as thread "start"/"stop", configuring UDET server instances (to be further discussed on the next section) and managing the request load on external data service providers and UDET engines.

Once data has been moved locally (into the UDAP's cache) preparation tasks in order to extract and transform identified parameters contained in the files may be performed. After being processed by UDET all the data will be finally loaded into the UDOB temporary storage area (implemented as relational tables) and thus made available to both the ODS and DW.

3   The Uniform Data Extraction and Transformer Component

The main goal of UDET is to process all data provided files received from UDAP. These files hold textual information structured in a human readable approach. Each provided file has associated two temporal tags; start and end dates that determine the temporal range for which the parameter values concern. These temporal tags may exist either explicitly in the file header or implicitly, being inferred from the parameter entries.

Three types of parameters are available in the input files: numerical, categorical and plain text. Most of these parameter values have a temporal tag associated, although some are time independent, containing general information only.

Provided files can also be classified as real-time or summary (both types contain a temporal sliding window of data). While real-time files (e.g. available every 5 minutes) offer near real-time / estimation data for a very limited time window, summary files (e.g. available daily) offer a summary of all measures registered during that day (discrepancies between real-time and summary files contents are possible to find). Since summary data is more accurate than real-time, whenever available, the first shall **replace** the real-time values previously received.

Fig. 2 presents the DPM processing pipeline from a high-level perspective, with special focus on the UDET component. After receiving a semi-structured text file from UDAP, UDET applies a set of ETL operations to the same file, according to definitions stored in an external file FFD, producing a set of data chunks as result. Each data chunk is characterized as a triplet, containing a global identifier for a parameter, a temporal tag and the parameter value. The size of a data chunk varies and is closely related with the nature of the data that is available in the file (e.g. Space Weather and Spacecraft data are stored in different data chunks). Depending on the UDET settings, these data chunks can be delivered to different containers (e.g. in SEIS data chunks are delivered to UDOB – a set of relational tables).

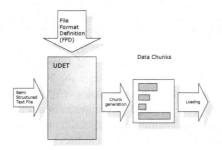

Fig. 2. UDET's processing model

The following sub-sections highlight UDET's main requirements; the model employed in SEIS and also how the ETL process is applied to the input files received from UDAP. Finally, UDET's architecture is described in detail, unfolding its main components and the existing relations between them.

3.1 Main Requirements

Since real-time files mainly hold repeated data (when compared with the previously retrieved real-time file), only the new added entries will be stored after every file processing. An output cache mechanism is then required, which is capable of improving the system's load-factor considerably on UDOB by avoiding duplicate entries in near real-time files.

In order to accomplish the SEIS near real-time requirement, data should not take more than 5 minutes to be processed (from the moment it is made available in the Data Provider until it reaches UDOB). In this sense, the performance of the DPM is fundamental to accomplish this condition and especially for the UDET component, which is responsible for most of the computational effort within the DPM. Due to the high number of simultaneous file transfers it is not feasible to sequence the file processing. Thus, a parallel architecture is required in order to process several input files simultaneously.

As previously mentioned, Data Service Providers do not provide a notification mechanism to report changes on the format of Provided Files. Thus, UDET needs the inclusion of data quality logic mechanisms, which describe the parameter data types, and possibly the definition of ranges of valid values. Furthermore, maintenance tasks for the correction of format changes must have a minimum impact in the system architecture and code, in order not to compromise maintenance.

Finally, data delivery should be configurable in a way that data resulting from the extraction and transformation process can be exported into different formats (e.g. XML, Comma-Separated Values - CVS, relational tables) although without being tied to implementation details that may restrict the solution's reusability (e.g. if a solution is based on a scheme of relational tables it should not rely directly in a specific communication protocol).

3.2 Designed Model and Developed Solution

The developed solution relies on declarative definitions that identify which operations are necessary during the ETL process, instead of implementing this logic directly at code level. These declarative definitions are stored in FFD files and their contents are directly dependent on the Provided File format, data and nature. So, it is necessary to create a dedicated FFD for each Provided File, holding the specific ETL logic necessary to process any file belonging to a Provided File class (file format detection is currently not implemented, but considered under the Future Work section). FFD are stored in XML format since this is a highly known World Wide Consortium (W3C) standard for which exists a wide range of computational efficient tools. In addition, the format is human readable, enabling an easy validation without recurring to a software translation tool to understand the content logic.

File Format Definition files holds six distinct types of information:

(1) **General Information** – Global data required to process an input file, such as: end of line character, start and end dates for which the file format is valid (for versioning purposes), decimal and thousand separator chars and any user comment.

(2) **Section Identification** – Gathers the properties responsible for composing each of the sections present in an input file (e.g. headers, user comments, data). A section can be defined according to specific properties such as absolute line delimiters (e.g. line number) or sequential and contiguous lines sharing a common property (e.g. lines that "start", "end" or "contain" a given string). In addition, it is possible to define relative sections, through other two sections, which enclose a third one ("enclosed section") using the "Start Section After Previous Section End" and "End Section Before Next Section Start" properties.

(3) **Field Identification** – Contains the definitions of all existing extractable fields, where each field parameter is associated to a given file section. Fields can be of two types: "single fields" and "table fields". The specification of single fields can be performed by defining an upper and lower char field enclosing delimiters or alternatively, through a regular expression. Additionally, several meta-information related with the field is included, such as the field name, its format, and global identifier. The specification of table fields is accomplished through the capturing of table columns using several definition types, according to the files' intrinsic format (typically, the more generic definition which best extracts the data from the columns should be chosen). Other available options include the capability of extracting columns: based on column separators (with the possibility of dealing with consecutive separator chars as a new column or not); based on fixed column positions (definition of column breaks); based on regular expression definition. Similar to single fields, meta-information about the table columns is also available, such as global identifications, column data formats, column names and missing value representations.

The use of regular expressions should be limited as much as possible to advanced users acquainted with definition of regular expressions (although its direct use usually results on considerable speed gains).

(4) **Transformation Operations** – Hold a set of sequences containing definitions of transformation operations, to be applied to single and table fields, transforming the original raw data in a suitable format. A large collection of transformation operations both valid for single and table fields (e.g. date convert, column create from field, column join, column append) is available.

(5) **Data Quality** – Contains information required for the validation of the data produced as result of the extraction and transformation process. Validation is accomplished through the association of data types, data thresholds and validation rules (e.g. 0<Measure1<50) to single and table fields, restricting the parameter values to a valid subset.

(6) **Delivering Information** – This section contains definitions on how transformed data should be formatted. The data format is dependent on the output data target's type (e.g. XML, CSV, relation database tables).

This architecture is strongly supported by the declarative assertions contained in FFD files as explained above. For each supplied input data file, and using the associated FFD, UDET performs the following sequence of operations: (*i*) section splitting; (*ii*) field extraction; (*iii*) field transformation; (*iv*) data validation; (*v*) data output formatting. The generated data chunks are then delivered to UDOB using a filtering mechanism, as will be explained later.

3.3 UDET Architecture

This section presents a detailed view of the entire UDET architecture, including internal shared library components. A detailed view of the UDET architecture can be found on the following picture (Fig. 3).

The UDET service has been implemented has a fully multi-threaded Web Service, whose core functionalities lie in data transformation and delivery libraries. When UDET receives processing requests from UDAP, under the form of pairs (input data file; FFD), the process starts by creating a new thread to handle the request (it is assumed that using multiple threads increases the number of simultaneous processed files).

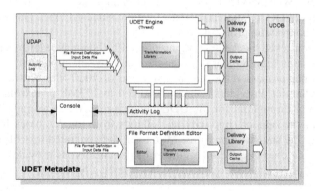

Fig. 3. UDET detailed architecture view

To process a file, the UDET engine firstly uses the transformation library to apply the extraction and transformations defined in the FFD file and afterwards, the outputs are sent into the delivery library. This library implements a global output cache mechanism, which prevents repeated records from being loaded into UDOB every time a file is processed. In addition, all UDET engine's actions are logged onto a log file with the same format as all other components (by using a common console viewer it is possible to correlate and trace all UDAP and UDET activities).

Besides the UDET engine, the architecture comprises also a FFD Editor, which provides end-users with the ability to manage FFD files via a very intuitive graphical interface. This tool takes also advantage of the same transformation and delivery libraries used by the UDET engine to allow previewing / validation of edited FFD files. This architecture allows near real-time processing of files retrieved by UDAP. To address offline file processing a separate UDET Engine/Delivery Library and respective UDOB should be installed on a supplementary machine (UDAP currently supports two separate instances).

Last but not least, it is also worth mentioning that all components of the UDET architecture interact directly with the Metadata Repository (for storage/retrieval of FFD files and other further configuration files).

4   Implementing UDET

The definition of a file to be retrieved (Provided File) is associated with a given Data Service Provider. The Provided File concept definition contains mainly info about the details of the file to be retrieved. After the file is retrieved and cached on disk, its contents are sent into UDET. UDET reads the associated File Format Definition (from the Metadata Repository) for the file and selects the corresponding format version, which correctly extracts and transforms all fields. Finally, the results are outputted into the UDOB component (the data processing pipeline's target), which is composed by a set of relational tables.

The UDET engine is a stand-alone service currently implemented as a Web Service, communicating with other system blocks in a transparent way. Besides the interfaces, which use Web Services, UDET also communicates with the UDOB component (implemented as a relational database) via the standard Open DataBase Connectivity (ODBC) connection protocol.

During system tests, the UDET engine proved to be capable of meeting the near real-time processing requirement (e.g. the current assessment points to an average of 11,83 seconds per processed file, for a daily total of 4000 files downloaded from 9 different Data Service Providers, which amounted to 113Mb of text data). The estimated processing throughput for the UDET engine reached an average of 2.3Kbytes per second. For the sake of simplicity, the outputs from the 3M block have not been included during the statistical analysis. Moreover, the generated text files formats are similar to existing ones (in size and number of parameters) as provided by the external data service providers already included in the testing procedure.

5   Conclusions and Future Work

The engineered data processing architecture fulfils the two major requirements derived from SEIS: near real-time file processing flux and offline archive processing capabilities. Tests performed after deployment (at the European Space Agency) of the SEIS infrastructure gave support to the adequacy of the proposed architecture given the SEIS expected data volumes. Nevertheless, due to the project's time and budget constrains, some future steps are advisable, to take full advantage on the DPM architecture[4].

The FFD editor shall be the main priority on future developments, since the current version of this tool has still limited functionalities. Improvements are necessary to achieve the requirement of definition of FFDs by non-programming experts, hiding from the end user the method (i.e. that XML is used to store the declarative instructions) for defining FFDs. Two valuable features have already been identified for the FFD editor:

- Automatic generation of regular expressions from the graphical specification of examples in a text file.
- FFD validation procedures for a set of text files.

The logging and notification mechanisms also need to be improved to some extent in order to detect the incorrect appliance of FFDs to input files (due to change on the input file format) and launch recovery procedures when appropriate.

Some enhancements should also be performed at the FFD's structure level, either to provide higher flexibility (e.g. specification of an undefined number of sections) or to extend language expressivity through the inclusion of further specification techniques and transformation operations.

Although all these enhancements would be useful to the end user, they should be considered as extensions to the existing UDET functionalities. The inclusion of these improvements is an added value, which would not require any change on the architecture presented in this work.

References

1. Schmieder, B., et al. *Climate and Weather of the Sun Earth System: CAWSES, SCOSTEP'S Program for 2003-2008.* in *SOLSPA: The Second Solar Cycle and Space Weather Euroconference.* 2002.
2. Daily, E. *Space Weather: A Brief Review.* in *Second Solar Cycle and Space Weather Euroconference.* 2002.
3. Pantoquilho, M., et al. *SEIS: A Decision Support System for Optimizing Spacecraft Operations Strategies.* in *IEEE Aerospace Conference.* 2005. Montana, USA.
4. Donati, A., et al. *Space Weather and Mission Control: A Roadmap to an Operational Multi-Mission Decision Support System.* in *SpaceOps 2004 - 8th International Conference on Space Operations.* 2004. Montreal, Canada.
5. Vassiliadis, P., et al., *A generic and customizable framework for the design of ETL scenarios.* Information Systems, 2005.
6. Adelberg, B. *NoDoSE—A tool for semi-automatically extracting structured and semistructured data from text documents.* in *International Conference on Management of Data (ACM SIGMOD 98).* 1998. Seattle, Washington, United States.
7. Berkeley, *Potter's Wheel A-B-C: An Interactive Tool for Data Analysis, Cleansing, and Transformation (http://control.cs.berkeley.edu/abc/).* 2000, CONTROL - Continuous Output and Navigation Technology with Refinement On-Line: Berkeley.

---

[4] All the enhancements proposed as future work are related to the UDET only, not focusing on any other DPM component.

8. Pantoquilho, M., et al. *Online and Offline Monitoring and Diagnosis of Spacecraft and Space Weather Status.* in *EUROFUSE Workshop on Data and Knowledge Engineering.* 2004. Warszawa, Poland.

9. Schmidt, M. and F.D. Marco, *INTEGRAL Flight Operation Plan.* 2003, VEGA: Darmstadt.

10. Moura-Pires, J., M. Pantoquilho, and N. Viana. *Space Environment Information System for Mission Control Purposes: Real-Time Monitoring and Inference of Space Craft Status.* in *2004 IEEE Multiconference on CCA/ISIC/CACSD.* 2004. Taipei, Taiwan.

11. Kimball, R. and M. Ross, *The Data Warehouse Toolkit: The Complete Guide To Dimensional Modelling.* 2nd Edition ed. 2002: Wiley. 436.

12. Belgian Institute for Space Aeronomy, Space Applications Services, and P.S. Institute, *SPENVIS - Space Environment Information System.* 1998.

Chapter 7

IROBOT 2005: Intelligent Robotics

Introduction

Luís Paulo Reis[1], Nuno Lau[2], Carlos Carreto[3], and Eduardo Silva[4]

[1] FEUP, Porto, Portugal
lpreis@fe.up.pt
[2] DET-UA, Aveiro, Portugal
lau@det.ua.pt
[3] ESTG-IPG, Guarda, Portugal
ccarreto@ipg.pt
[4] LSA-ISEP, Porto, Portugal
eaps@dee.isep.ipp.pt

Research in robotics has traditionally emphasized low-level sensing and control tasks, path planning and actuator design and control. In contrast, generally using robotic simulators, several Artificial Intelligence (AI) researchers are more concerned with providing real/simulated robots with higher-level cognitive functions that enable them to reason, act and perceive in an autonomous way in dynamic, inaccessible, continuous and non deterministic environments. Combining results from traditional robotics with those from AI and cognitive science will be thus essential for the future of intelligent robotics.

The purpose of the 1st International Workshop on Intelligent Robotics IRO-BOT'05 was to bring together researchers, engineers and other professionals interested in the application of Artificial Intelligence techniques in real/simulated robotics to discuss current work and future directions.

IROBOT 2005 received twenty two submissions from six countries with Portugal, México and Spain being the most contributing ones. Topics of special interest were on robot design, development and control, autonomous vehicles, distributed robotic surveillance, path planning and cooperative robotics.

Each paper was blindly reviewed by three senior program committee members. Seven high quality full papers were selected for publication in the Springer LNCS main volume of the conference proceedings, while ten papers were selected as full papers for the local UBI/IEEE proceedings. We would like to thank all the authors who submitted their work to the workshop and enabled the success of IROBOT 2005. Special thanks to all the members of the Program Committee who took upon most of the burden in reviewing the papers enabling its accurate evaluation.

The workshop besides having presentations of high quality research in the area of intelligent robotics was meant to be a forum of discussion, including two panel discussions on two very contemporary specific topics on the field of Intelligent Robotics: "Simulated vs. Real Robotics: Are the simulators really useful for Robotics?" and "Benefits and dangers of robotic competitions to promote scientific progress?". These discussions complemented the workshop enabling higher contact and experience trading between the researchers that attended the workshop.

C. Bento, A. Cardoso, and G. Dias (Eds.): EPIA 2005, LNAI 3808, p. 397, 2005.
© Springer-Verlag Berlin Heidelberg 2005

Visual Based Human Motion Analysis: Mapping Gestures Using a Puppet Model

Jörg Rett and Jorge Dias

Institute of Systems and Robotics,
University of Coimbra, Polo II, 3030-290 Coimbra, Portugal
{jrett, jorge}@isr.uc.pt

Abstract. This paper presents a novel approach to analyze the appearance of human motions with a simple model i.e. mapping the motions using a virtual marionette model. The approach is based on a robot using a monocular camera to recognize the person interacting with the robot and start tracking its head and hands. We reconstruct 3-D trajectories from 2-D image space (IS) by calibrating and fusing the camera images with data from an inertial sensor, applying general anthropometric data and restricting the motions to lie on a plane. Through a virtual marionette model we map 3-D trajectories to a feature vector in the *marionette control space (MCS)*. This implies inversely that now a certain set of 3-D motions can be performed by the (virtual) marionette system. A subset of these motions are considered to convey information (i.e. gestures). Thus, we are aiming to build up a database which keeps the vocabulary of gestures represented as signals in the *MCS*. The main contribution of this work is the computational model of the *IS-MCS-Mapping*. We introduce the guide robot "Nicole" to place our system in an embodied context. We sketch two novel approaches to represent human motion (i.e. Marionette Space and Labananalysis). We define a gesture vocabulary organized in three sets (i.e. Cohens Gesture Lexicon, Pointing Gestures and Other Gestures).

1 Introduction

Robotics field is facing the challenge to develop robots that share an environment with humans. The two basic skills social robots need to have is to interact with the people and to navigate in the world. To study possible solutions and feasible techniques we started the development of the robot guide Nicole. Nicole will guide visitors through the Institute of Systems and Robotics (ISR), talk about the research and react on gestures performed by persons recognized as "godfathers". The interaction part as well as the navigation part will strongly rely on visual cues. This paper is concerned with *robot vision for human-machine-interaction* of "Nicole".

If the perceptual system of a robot is based on vision, interaction will involve *visual human motion analysis*. The ability to recognize humans and their activities by vision is key for a machine to interact intelligently and effortlessly with

C. Bento, A. Cardoso, and G. Dias (Eds.): EPIA 2005, LNAI 3808, pp. 398–409, 2005.

a human-inhabited environment [1]. Several surveys on visual analysis of human movement have already presented a general framework to tackle this problem [2], [1], [3] and [4]. Aggarwal and Cai point out in their survey [2] that one (of three) mayor areas related to the interpretation of human motion is motion analysis of the human body structure involving human body parts. The general framework consists of: 1. feature extraction, 2. feature correspondence and 3. high level processing. The architecture we present relates to this framework in that we define: 1. Perception- , 2a. Motor/Model-, 2b. Impression- and 3. Interpretation Level. As shown in fig. 5 e.g. the body part segmentation will be found in the *Perception Level* being part of a *Human Tracking Module*.

Research on human behavior suggest, that infants could compare the sensory information from his own unseen motor behavior to a *supramodal* representation of the visually perceived gesture and construct the match required [5,6]. In imitating, infants attempt to match the organ relations they see exhibited by the adults with those they feel themselves make [5]. Infants draw information from what they see by matching it to what they do. We like to further describe this process by proposing to simulate the motion through acting on a model inside our head and interpreting the (virtual) sensor signals. We name our concept: *"The Marionette in the Head"*.

This article is about the model we use to generate human motions and the signals we extract to interpret a certain set of human gestures. To materialize the solution we contribute the mathematical concept to build a mapping between the 2-D image space (IS) of a monocular camera and the space of the signals for gesture interpretation (MCS). We introduce the guide robot "Nicole" to place our system in an embodied context. We sketch two novel approaches to represent human motion (i.e. Marionette Space and Labananalysis). We define a gesture vocabulary organized in three sets (i.e. Cohens Gesture Lexicon, Pointing Gestures and Other Gestures).

An interesting research on gesture recognition provides us with the first set of our vocabulary. In [7] Cohen et al. established a lexicon of 24 gestures which were captured by a human moving a flashlight against a black background. In our approach we are detecting and tracking the hands and the face automatically without using special device (markers). The second set of gestures was inspired by Kahn et al. [8] whose interface interprets pointing gestures. Similar to us they were using multiple cues to track the persons hand and heads. Our approach also incorporates face recognition for a personalized interaction.

Section 2, where we present our model, starts the extraction of the required 3-D data from the 2-D image and introduces entities of reference in the 3-D world. In the next part we introduce a vocabulary of gestures and relate simple commands for a mobile robot to it. In the third part we develop the puppet model and present the signals that can be extracted. Sect. 3 shows the implementation of our concept starting with a brief overview of the "Nicole" Roboticsystem, followed by the Gesture Perception system, the Visual-Inertial Sensor and the Human Tracking Module. Sect. 4 presents results on recorded gesture trajectories and Sec. 5 closes with a discussion and an outlook for future works.

2   Models

We have constrained the situation of interaction in the following way. The vision system is calibrated for a person acting at a certain distance and orientation towards the robot. In the current level of development the person needs to adopt this initial position to interact by himself. The interaction will start when the person is facing the robot and standing in a natural "at ease" position. The camera system will cover the entire "kinesphere" of the person while the person performs gestures using his Hands and Face. The position of the person's body is assumed to be static. Using our system in a situation as shown in Fig. 1 a) a motion of hands and face need to be tracked and transformed to what we will call "Marionette Space".

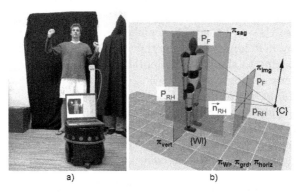

Fig. 1. a) Nicole in position to interact with Enguerran. b) Projection of 3-D point P.

2.1   Projection Space

The first step is the recovery of 3-D trajectories from 2-D images created by a projective camera. We start by defining the initial plane $\pi_{\{\mathcal{WI}\}}$ and relate it to the ground plane and the horizontal plane by $\pi_{\{\mathcal{WI}\}} = \pi_{horz} = \pi_{grd}$ (see Fig. 1 b)). We place the reference frame $\{\mathcal{WI}\}$ at the point of intersection of the vertical body plane π_{vert}, the sagittal plane π_{sag} and the ground plane π_{grd} shown in Fig. 1 b).

Any generic 3-D point $\mathbf{P} = [X\ Y\ Z]^{\top}$ and its corresponding projection $\mathbf{p} = [u\ v]^{\top}$ on an image-plane can be mathematically related using projective geometry and the concept of homogeneous coordinates through the following equation, the projective camera relation, where s represents an arbitrary scale factor [9]:

$$
\begin{bmatrix} sv \\ su \\ s \end{bmatrix} = \begin{bmatrix} a_{1,1}\ a_{1,2}\ a_{1,3}\ a_{1,4} \\ a_{2,1}\ a_{2,2}\ a_{2,3}\ a_{2,4} \\ a_{3,1}\ a_{3,2}\ a_{3,3}\ a_{3,4} \\ a_{4,1}\ a_{4,2}\ a_{4,3}\ a_{4,4} \end{bmatrix} \begin{bmatrix} X \\ Y \\ Z \\ 1 \end{bmatrix} \tag{1}
$$

Matrix $\mathbf{A}$ is called the projection matrix, and through its estimation it is possible to make the correspondence between any 3-D point and its projection in a camera's image-plane. We can likewise express the matrix $\mathbf{A}$ by using the parameters of the projective finite camera model, as stated in [10].

$$\mathbf{A} = \mathbf{C} \left[{}^{\{C\}}\mathbf{R}_{\{\mathcal{WI}\}} \quad {}^{\{C\}}\overrightarrow{\mathbf{t}}_{\{\mathcal{WI}\}} \right] \tag{2}$$

Where $\mathbf{C}$ is the camera's calibration matrix, more frequently known as the intrinsic parameters matrix, while the camera's extrinsic parameters are represented by the rotation orthogonal matrix $\mathbf{R}$ and the translation vector $\mathbf{t}$ that relates the chosen $\{\mathcal{WI}\}$ to the camera frame.

The projective camera presents us, in fact, with the solution for the intersection of planes Π_{cam1} and Π_{cam2} which, assuming $\tilde{\mathbf{P}} = [X \ Y \ Z \ 1]^\top$ (i.e. homogeneous coordinates), can be proven from its projection expression to be given by 3) (see [9]).

$$\begin{cases} (\mathbf{a}_1 - u\mathbf{a}_3)^\top \mathbf{P} + a_{1,4} - u = 0 \\ (\mathbf{a}_2 - u\mathbf{a}_3)^\top \mathbf{P} + a_{2,4} - u = 0 \end{cases} \Longleftrightarrow \begin{cases} \Pi_{cam1}\tilde{\mathbf{P}} = 0 \\ \Pi_{cam2}\tilde{\mathbf{P}} = 0 \end{cases} \tag{3}$$

This solution is called the projection or projecting line, which can be alternatively represented by equation (4) [9].

$$\overrightarrow{\mathbf{n}} = (\mathbf{a}_1 - u\mathbf{a}_3) \times (\mathbf{a}_2 - u\mathbf{a}_3) \tag{4}$$

These relations indicate that all 3-D points on the projecting line correspond to the same projection point on the image-plane, which means that the projection equation is not unique. Thus, at least one additional restriction is needed to establish an unique correspondence between the 3D point and its projection on the image-plane. One possibility being restricting the locus of 3-D points to lie on a plane.

2.2   Gestures and Labananalysis

In our search for a suitable description of human motions we found the *Labananalysis*, named after the founder R. Laban [11]. In Labananalysis the kinematic chains are observed with relation to spatial shaping possibilities and the dynamic qualities (*Effort*) accompanying them. A pioneer in the attempt to re-formulate Labanotation in computational models is Norman Badler and his early works are summarized in his book on simulating humans [12]. He suggests to not implement Labanotation directly but use it as a good set of default values for normal human movements. More recently a computational model of gesture acquisition and synthesis to learn motion qualities from live performance has been proposed in [13].

We will investigate more the qualities of a gesture while trying to add an *Impression Level* to our system. For now we only like to address the problem of space or gesture plane. An interesting spatial concept is that of *Scales*. *Scales* are movement possibilities with reference to geometric shapes and sequences. *Scales* are related to the *kinesphere* which is defined as the reach space of the body. The simplest *Scale* is called 1-D (or defense) *Scale*. It is built around

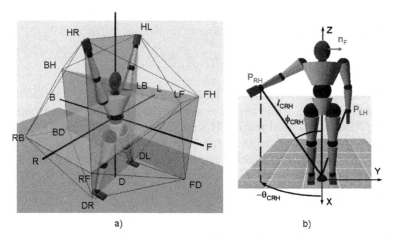

Fig. 2. Laban Scale: Icosahedron

the axes of the kinesphere (vertical, horizontal, sagittal). Figure 2 a) shows the axes and defined points (D = Deep, R = Right, L = Left, F = Front, B = Back, H = High). A 2-D *Scale* is created if the movement to six peripheral point are performed without returning to the center (e.g. a cycle around the three planes π_{vert}, π_{horz}, π_{sag}). As a suitable description for 3-D movements Laban used a Icosahedron see Fig. 2 a). The geometry of the Icosahedron can be developed from the three planes (π_{vert}, π_{horz}, π_{sag}) superimposed and their corners connected. Thus, twelve corners define maximal reach possibilities within the kinesphere. As *Scales* are ordered sequences for the most economical and expressive pathways between all the peripheral points (corners), Laban defined several different *Scales* for 3-D movements. Of particular interest is the one which goes along the outer edges of the icosahedron. Laban saw this *Scale* in many communicative gestures and dance forms, thus calling it *primary Scale*. This reflects that, although the sequences have been outlined as primarily total body movements, they are also identifiable in small movements.

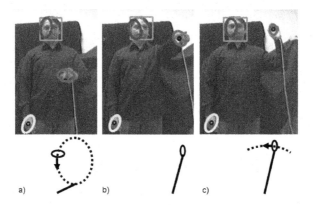

Fig. 3. a) Cohen's Gesture Lexicon. b) Pointing Gestures. c) Other Gestures.

To show the feasibility of our approach we have defined a vocabulary of gestures and recorded a group of people performing them (see fig. 3). Cohen et al. have already presented in [7] a gesture lexicon consisting of 24 planar oscillators to control an actuated mechanism. We use his lexicon as Set 1 and extend it by Pointing Gestures (Set 2) and Other Gestures (Set 3). The latter were gestures expressing information like "Speak louder!", "Be quiet!", "I am hungry!" and "Bye, bye!". We will show later in this article that Set 1 can be described by projecting the trajectory on a plane $\mathbf{\Pi}_{gest}\tilde{\mathbf{P}} = 0$ parallel to π_{vert}. Using the geometry involved in the perspective projection of the world onto the camera's image-plane and the gesture-plane's restriction, the 3D point in the scene can be uniquely related to its 2-D projection point in the image-plane of the camera using (5):

$$\left\{ \mathbf{\Pi}_{cam1}\tilde{\mathbf{P}} = 0 \quad \mathbf{\Pi}_{cam2}\tilde{\mathbf{P}} = 0 \quad \mathbf{\Pi}_{gest}\tilde{\mathbf{P}} = 0 \right\} \tag{5}$$

Our vocabulary of gestures also determines the future interaction of Nicole her "godfathers". Set 1 will be used as command primitives (e.g. turn left, move back), Set 2 to shift the focus of attention (e.g. look northwest) and Set 3 for any other form of communication (e.g. speak louder).

2.3   Marionette Space

There are some examples for the attention puppetry receives from the research community. The approaches involving marionettes are basically placed in the area of entertainment. Generally marionette figures are articulated by a set of servomotors to produce human-like motions. An early work was reported by Hoffmann [14] who used a human dancer to teach the coarse movements to the system. In [15] the marionette was used to produce gestures by superposition, inhibition and sequencing of motor primitives. The work was based on evidences for basic (innate) elementary neural motor programs from which all bodily movements are constructed [16]. The system was further developed in [17] which also gives a nice cultural summary on marionettes. Often human motion capture data is mapped to the marionette while dealing with inverse kinematics and physical constraints. In [18] the results compare the performance of two human actors and the marionette telling a story. Apart from applications in entertainment we also found comparisons of natural (human) and robot actuator systems. [19] presents a control strategy for stable movement of a marionette under a system of unidirectional muscle-like actuators. Analogies to monotonic function of the firing rate of natural muscles were drawn. The underlying question common to all contributions is: "What is the relationship between human and puppet movements?" Our answer to this questions is a model that synthesizes human movements by controlling a virtual puppet. The control vector associated to a certain gesture will be used later for gesture recognition. Our primary interest lies in the reduction of the parameters to describe the human motion i.e. to reduce the dimensionality of the parameterspace. Our secondary goal is to maintain an intuitive approach which can also be understood by non-engineers [20].

From the various types of puppets the *marionettes* have received the most scientific attention so far. We found are more promising concept in the rod puppets. The puppet hands are manipulated using (rigid) sticks see fig. 2. We will first invent a model of the puppet body considering a 3 DoF neck joint, 3 DoF shoulder joints, 1 DoF elbow joints and 3 DoF wrist joints. Next we will place three control joints at the origin of $\{\mathcal{WI}\}$ and connect them with sticks with the hand and the head. We connect the control joints by rigid control links to the wrist joints and neck joint (see fig. 2 b). The hands control joints will have two rotational and 1 translational DoF while the face control joint only has 1 rotational DoF. Thus, we have created a system with a 7-dimensional control space that is able to synthesize a certain set of movements in 3-D space. We are now able to express the relationship between the 3-D space and the control space. We establish a feature vector $\mathbf{F}$ consisting of the face normal (gaze) $\mathbf{n}_F(t)$ and the positions of the hands $\mathbf{P}_{RH}(t)$ and $\mathbf{P}_{LH}(t)$.

$$\mathbf{F}(t) = \begin{bmatrix} \mathbf{n}_F(t) \\ \mathbf{P}_{RH}(t) \\ \mathbf{P}_{LH}(t) \end{bmatrix} \tag{6}$$

We can express the components of the vector by using spherical coordinates. Omitting the dependence on (t) for the moment we get

$$\mathbf{n}_F = \begin{bmatrix} \cos\theta_{CF} \\ \sin\theta_{CF} \\ 0 \end{bmatrix} \quad \text{and} \quad \mathbf{P}_{RH} = \begin{bmatrix} l_{CRH}\ \cos\theta_{CRH}\ \sin\phi_{CRH} \\ l_{CRH}\ \sin\theta_{CRH}\ \sin\phi_{CRH} \\ l_{CRH}\ \cos\phi_{CRH} \end{bmatrix} \tag{7}$$

for $\mathbf{n}_F$ and $\mathbf{P}_{RH}$ the expression for $\mathbf{P}_{LH}$ goes accordingly. To make bimanual movements [21] more obvious we will count the azimuthal angle θ counterclockwise from the positive x-axis with $-\pi < \theta \le \pi$.

Representing the human motion in such a way is very close to proposals made by researchers from physiology. In [22] Soechting and Flanders discuss how spatial parameters may be represented by the activities of neurons. They considered different motor tasks like postural responses, orienting movements and arm movements to a spatial target. Introducing frames of reference and coordinate systems they show that in all three motor tasks, one of the coordinate axes was defined by the gravitational vertical. Another coordinate was defined by the sagittal horizontal axis. They suggest that there is a common, earth-fixed frame of reference utilized for all motor tasks. For postural responses findings in research on human (and animal) motion suggests that bipedal posture can be described using limb angles and length from the center of gravity to the base of support.

3   Implementation

3.1   Architecture

As mentioned in section 1 the whole system of the robot "Nicole" needs to deal with navigation as well as interaction. The base of Nicole is a Nomad Scout

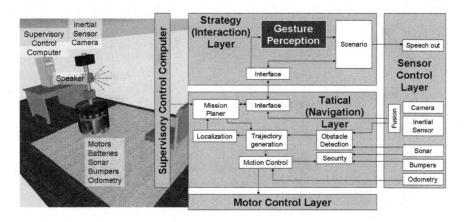

Fig. 4. a) Hardware architecture b) System Architecture

robot (see fig. 4 a)). The Motor Board Controller connects to the sonar, the bumpers and the odometry. With this data and the input from the camera and the inertial sensor the Navigation part will perform obstacle avoidance, global path planning and people tracking. The interaction part will also use the camera and the inertial sensor but additionally the loudspeaker as an output device. It will perform gesture and face recognition and use a speech synthesizer for speaking. The external hardware is supervisory control computer which is connected to the Navigation part via WLan to have the option to control Nicole and visualize her position. Fig. 4 b) shows the architecture of Nicole. In this paper we focus on the *Gesture Perception (GP)-System* which is part of the interaction layer.

3.2   The Gesture Perception (GP)-System

Fig. 5 shows the architecture of the GP-System. The system can be divided in six levels of visual perception and understanding. The Processing starts at the Perception Level with the Visual-Inertial Sensor dealing with Image Capture and Inertial Data registration. The image data is used by the Human-Tracking-Module to perform Face Detection, Face Recognition, Skin Color Detection and Object Tracking. The Projection-Module reconstructs from the 2D Image trajectory of Hands and Face the 3D trajectory. The output of the Perception Level will be used by the Motor/Model Level and Impression Level. The former transforming the trajectory to a feature vector in the *marionette control space (MCS)* the latter using the Labananlysis to create qualities related to *Effort*. The Interpretation Level will use both inputs to perform a *Emotional Tinted Gesture Recognition*. In the final step a Learning Level will refine the emotional and personal gesture vocabulary inside the database of the Knowledge level.

3.3   The Visual-Inertial Sensor

Again, we want to follow our belief that a successful perception of human motion is achieved best when the system is built in human manner. The inner ear

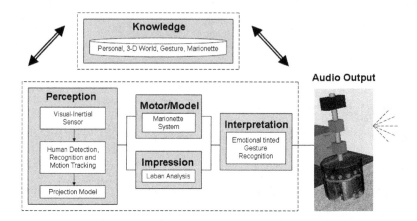

Fig. 5. Architecture of the GP-System

vestibular system in humans and in animals provides inertial sensing mainly for orientation, navigation, control of body posture and equilibrium. This sensorial system also plays a key role in several visual tasks and head stabilization, such as gaze holding and tracking visual movements [23]. Continuing the argumentation from section 2.2 about coordinate systems for human motion, Soechting and Flanders show in [22] that one of the coordinate axes was defined by the gravitational vertical. They point out the domination of gravitational force and the visual horizon and the primary role of the vestibular system as an indicator of the vertical direction.

From the practical point of view we need to establish a stable frame of reference (i.e. $\{\mathcal{WI}\}$) to infer the correct spatial trajectory. This includes also the correct initialization of the human body posture using hands and face position, anthropometric data and projective geometry. Assuming a person to start his interaction in a vertical body pose turns out to search and register the *gravity* in the image.

Recent work of Lobo and Dias present the successful integration and calibration of visual and inertial data [24] and the detection of vertical features [25]. When the system is not accelerating, gravity provides a vertical reference for the camera system frame of reference given by the sensed acceleration.

3.4   The Human Tracking Module

In brief our *Human Tracking Module* takes the images from the *Visual-Inertial Sensor* and creates three image trajectories from the head and both hands. As shown in fig. 5 the module contains of four mayor parts. The process starts with the detection if any human is present in the scene. We use a face detection module based on haar-like features as described in [26]]. In case a face is detected we try to recognize the person if belonging to the group of "godfathers" or not. This second part is based on eigen-objects and PCA as described in [27]. If the persons is identified as a "godfather". The third part will establish the communication by activating the skin color detection an the tracking of the hands. For the skin detection and segmentation we use the CAMshift algorithm presented in [28]. To deal with hands and head occlusion we predict the positions and velocities based on a Kalman-filter [29].

4   Results

Figure 6 compares the tracking results from our *Human Tracking Module* (left) with a 3D magnetic tracker (miniBird, right). In the diagrams the image coordinate system is placed next to the ZY-plane of the miniBird. The ZY-plane of the miniBird reflects a projection of the motion trajectory on the vertical plane π_{vert} (see fig. 2). It can be seen, that the trajectories from our human tracking module fits well with the ground truth data from miniBird. Furthermore the gestures of Set 1 can be well distinguished from each other and due to their repetitive character a robust recognition should be possible. Though, our diagrams show mainly the left hand trajectories they also contain the head and right hand trajectories. Using the gestures of Set 2 we have the possibility (after the projection in 3D space) to indicate the pointing direction by generating a ray from the head to the hand position. Example b) shows a difficult situation for our Human Tracking Module. The gesture "Speak louder" is represented by moving the hand to the ear. Our skin detector melts the head and the hand together interpreting it as one (bigger) head. The prediction of the hand does not cover the fact that the hand is still and predicts a trajectory above the head.

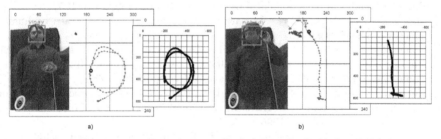

Fig. 6. Comparison of tracking results. a) Big Circle b) Speak louder.

5   Discussion and Conclusions

This article presented a framework towards a human-robot interaction based on gesture recognition. We presented the main architecture consisting of five hierarchical organized parts (i.e. Perception, Motor/Model, Impression, Interpretation and Knowledge Level). We introduced the guide robot "Nicole" to place our system in an embodied context. We sketched to novel approaches to represent human motion (i.e. Marionette Space and Labananalysis). We defined a gesture vocabulary organized in three sets (i.e. Cohens Gesture Lexicon, Pointing Gestures and Other Gestures). We presented experimental results from our

Human Tracking Module to show the feasibility of our gesture vocabulary and its representation in the vertical plane.

The future work will concerned with presenting results on 3D trajectory estimation and inertial sensor integration. To prove the benefits of a feature vector in the Marionette Control Space. Implement the Labananalysis module to produce Effort parameters.

Acknowledgements

The authors would like to thank Enguerran Boissier for his contributions to the Human Tracking Module. This work is partially supported by FCT-Fundação para a Ciência e a Tecnologia Grant #12956/2003 to J. Rett.

References

1. Gavrila, D.M.: The visual analysis of human movement: A survey. CVIU **73** (1999) pp. 82–98
2. Aggarwal, J.K., Cai, Q.: Human motion analysis: A review. CVIU **73** (1999) 428–440
3. Pentland., A.: Looking at people: Sensing for ubiquitous and wearable computing. IEEE Transactions on PAMI **22** (2000) 107–119
4. Moeslund, T.B., Granum, E.: A survey of computer vision-based human motion capture. CVIU **81** (2001) 231–268
5. Meltzoff, A.N., Moore, M.K.: Resolving the debate about early imitation. The Blackwell reader in developmental psychology, Oxford (1999) 151–155
6. Meltzoff, A.N., Moore, M.K.: Imitation of facial and manual gestures by human neonates. Science **198** (1977) 75–78
7. Cohen, C.J., Conway, L., Koditschek, D.: Dynamical system representation, generation, and recognition of basic oscillatory motion gestures. In: International Conference on Automatic Face- and Gesture-Recognition. (1996)
8. Kahn, R.E., Swain, M.J., Prokopowicz, P.N., Firby, R.J.: Gesture recognition using the perseus architecture. In: IEEE International Conference on Computer Vision and Pattern Recognition. (1996)
9. Dias, J.: Reconstrução Tridimensional Utilizando Visão Dinâmica. PhD thesis, University of Coimbra, Portugal (1994)
10. Hartley, R.I., Zisserman, A.: Multiple View Geometry in Computer Vision. Cambridge University Press (2000)
11. Bartenieff, I., Lewis, D.: Body Movement: Coping with the Environment. Gordon and Breach Science, New York (1980)
12. Badler, N.I., Phillips, C.B., Webber, B.L.: Simulating Humans: Computer Graphics, Animation, and Control. Oxford Univ. Press (1993)
13. Zhao, L., Badler, N.I.: Acquiring and validating motion qualities from live limb gestures. Graphical Models **67** (2005) 1–16
14. Hoffmann, G.: Teach-in of a robot by showing the motion. In: IEEE International Conference on Image Processing. (1996) 529–532
15. Xing, S., Chen, I.M.: Design expressive behaviors for robotic puppet. In: International Conference on Control, Automation, Robotics And Vision. Volume 1. (2002) 378–383

16. Allot, R.: Gestural equivalence (equivalents) of language. Language Origins Society UCAL Berkeley (1994)
17. Chen, I.M., Tay, R., Xing, S., Yeo, S.H.: Marionette: From traditional manipulation to robotic manipulation. In: International Symposium on History of Machines and Mechanisms. (2004)
18. Yamane, K., Hodgins, J.K., Brown, H.B.: Controlling a motorized marionette with human motion capture data. In: IEEE International Conference on Robotics and Automation. (2003)
19. Hemami, H., Dinneen, J.A.: A marionette-based strategy for stable movement. IEEE Trans. on Systems, Man, and Cybernetics **23** (1993) 502–511
20. Loeb, G.E.: Learning from the spinal cord. Journal of Physiology **533.1** (2001) 111–117
21. Shamaie, A., Sutherland, A.: A dynamic model for real-time tracking of hands in bimanual movements. In: Gesture-based Communication in Human-Computer Interaction, LNAI 2915, Springer Verlag. (2003) 172–179
22. Soechting, J.F., Flanders, M.: Moving in three-dimensional space: Frames of reference, vectors, and coordinate systems. Annual Review of Neuroscience **15** (1992) 167–191
23. Carpenter, H.: Movement of the eyes. Volume 2nd ed. London Pion Limited, London (1988)
24. Lobo, J., Dias, J.: Inertial sensed ego-motion for 3d vision. Journal of Robotic Systems **21** (2004) 3–12
25. Lobo, J., Dias, J.: Vision and inertial sensor cooperation using gravity as a vertical reference. IEEE Trans. on PAMI **25** (2003) 1597–1608
26. Jose Barreto, P.M., Dias, J.: Human-robot interaction based on haar-like features and eigenfaces. In: IEEE International Conference on Robotics and Automation. (2004)
27. Paulo Menezes, J.B., Dias, J.: Face tracking based on haar-like features and eigenfaces. In: IFAC/EURON Symposium on Intelligent Autonomous Vehicles. (2004)
28. Bradski, G.R.: Computer vision face tracking for use in a perceptual user interface. Intel Technology Journal (1998) 15
29. Kalman, R.E.: A new approach to linear filtering and prediction problems. Trans. ASME—J.Basic Eng. **82** (1960) 35–45

Acquiring Observation Models Through Reverse Plan Monitoring

Sonia Chernova, Elisabeth Crawford, and Manuela Veloso

Computer Science Department, Carnegie Mellon University,
Pittsburgh PA 15213, USA

Abstract. We present a general-purpose framework for updating a robot's observation model within the context of planning and execution. Traditional plan execution relies on monitoring plan step transitions through accurate state observations obtained from sensory data. In order to gather meaningful state data from sensors, tedious and time-consuming calibration methods are often required. To address this problem we introduce *Reverse Monitoring*, a process of learning an observation model through the use of plans composed of scripted actions. The automatically acquired observation models allow the robot to adapt to changes in the environment and robustly execute arbitrary plans. We have fully implemented the method in our AIBO robots, and our empirical results demonstrate its effectiveness.

1 Introduction

In the traditional planning and execution scenario (e.g., [7]), a plan consists of a sequence of actions defined as a set of preconditions and a set of effects. When executing a plan action, the robot first checks if the preconditions of the step are satisfied in the current state. For instance, before attempting to execute the plan action "open door A," the robot needs to be able to detect the action precondition "in front of door A." Once the action is executed the robot can then verify the effect of the action ("door A open") before deciding if the preconditions for the next action are met. These preconditions and effects are perceived through sensory data. Often the perceptions that the robot needs to make are complicated and thus the sensors must be very accurately calibrated.

In order to gather meaningful data from sensors, tedious and time-consuming calibration methods are often required. Calibration often needs to be performed for each sensor individually, and, in some cases, changes to the environment can make recalibration necessary. Traditionally, calibration processes are executed manually by a human expert until the desired behavior is achieved. We believe that many calibration tasks can be automated to a large degree, greatly reducing the level of human involvement without sacrificing the quality of the results. We propose a method to approach this problem that combines elements of calibration and plan execution.

An integrated robot planning and execution framework requires accurate state detection. However, as all actions have expected effects associated with

C. Bento, A. Cardoso, and G. Dias (Eds.): EPIA 2005, LNAI 3808, pp. 410–421, 2005.

them, we can also consider blindly executing a sequence of plan steps and then letting the robot associate the perceived state with the expected state. In this paper, we contribute a novel way of approaching plan execution - we *reverse* the perception role. Instead of expecting the robot to be able to accurately perceive the preconditions of actions, our approach, Reverse Monitoring, assumes that the robot knows the effects of the actions, can detect triggers of actions at a reduced level of detail, and can then associate its full perceived state with the effect of the actions. As we show in this paper, the robot is capable of refining its perception models to a higher level of detail through the execution of scripted plans. In this way, robots can autonomously acquire the accurate models they need to execute plans that require detailed sensing.

We demonstrate the effectiveness of our approach using the vision calibration system developed for the Sony AIBO robot. A typical vision calibration sequence on an AIBO robot requires a human to place the robot at various points in the domain to collect images of landmarks for calibration. The user must then hand-label each of the pixels in the images to classify it into one of the discrete color classes. Our proposed method allows the robot to collect and classify images with very little human assistance. This is accomplished by providing the robot with a plan that allows it to navigate by relying on sensing data in a reduced dimensionality space. As the robot proceeds with the plan and gathers information, its observation model is enriched, allowing the robot to sense in higher dimensions. When the execution of the plan is completed, the robot's sensors have been fully calibrated and it is then able to execute plans that require more detailed sensing.

We are not aware of any previous work combining the elements of plan execution and observation model refinement in a formal framework. Planning literature dealing with robots in the real world generally assumes a working sensor model and focuses mainly on issues of noisy sensors and partially observed states [4,5,7]. A large body of work relating to autonomous sensor calibration also exists, however these methods tend to focus on domain-specific or sensor-specific solutions [6,9,11,12,14]. We propose a general-purpose framework for updating a robot's observation model in the context of planning that is independent of the particular system or domain being used. The following sections present our approach in greater detail and present results demonstrating its effectiveness when applied to an existing robotic system.

2   Observation Models from Reverse Monitoring

2.1   Monitoring

A plan is a series of actions to be carried out in sequence. In classical planning actions have no duration; their effects are instantaneous and therefore the termination point of each action is clear. More realistic planning domains require the use of actions with durations. Durative actions typically represent a period of time where certain conditions are true at the beginning and at the end of the action execution. The action terminates when the execution time runs out, so the termination point is easy to detect.

In the real world, the execution of a plan is dependent upon the ability to observe the state and detect state changes. Although action duration can be defined in terms of a specific time interval, most complex actions require some form of state monitoring in order to determine when the action is completed. Termination conditions are thus defined in terms of specific state features, such that the current state features must match the state features that symbolize the end of the action. We will refer to the process of tracking action transitions through the detection of state features as *Monitoring*.

One of the difficulties of this approach is that it relies heavily on accurate state detection, which can be very challenging when dealing with real-world domains. Robots acting in the real world must accurately detect a large number of states through a complex set of features. Common approaches to feature detection include thresholding, classification, and a number of other methods. Regardless of the feature detection method used, if a robot encounters a new situation or the environment changes causing the feature detection to fail in a previously known state, the robot must update its observation model in order to detect states correctly. For example, a robot that recognizes a particular door by the feature "Door is GREEN" will be unable to find the door if it is repainted in a different color. The robot's observation model must be updated to use the new color for the state detection to work accurately.

Observation models of robots acting in real world domains frequently need to be updated since features of the environment often change without the robot's knowledge. Corrections of the robot's model are frequently done through manual calibration, which is often a tedious and repetitive task. To address this problem we introduce *Reverse Monitoring*, a process of learning an observation model through the use of plans composed of scripted actions.

2.2   Reverse Monitoring

We defined Monitoring as the process in plan execution of detecting state changes in order to determine whether the current action has been completed. Monitoring requires the robot to have a rich observation model in order to accurately detect the state. Reverse Monitoring is the process of updating the observation model through the execution of a plan consisting only of basic actions, which we refer to as *scripted actions*.

Scripted actions are actions with termination conditions that depend only on the state of the robot and that are independent of the state of the rest of the world. Examples are actions whose termination conditions are defined in terms of parameters such as time, number of steps, or the press of a button. These conditions do not require the robot to sense anything in the environment.

In Reverse Monitoring, a robot is provided with a plan and a specified state, which is true upon the termination of that plan. The process begins by executing a plan composed of a sequence of scripted actions. Upon termination, the robot observes its state. Unlike normal Monitoring where the robot uses its observation model to detect various features and classify the state, in Reverse Monitoring the robot extracts new features from the environment and updates its observation model. For example, the previously mentioned robot that was looking for a green door, would execute a plan to navigate to the door and then observe the state, updating its model of the door to the new color.

People often rely on a process similar to the one described above to navigate in unfamiliar environments. One example is the task of navigating from a hotel to an unfamiliar conference building. The person may not be able to find the conference building because he would have no association between the building's name and any descriptive features. However, a basic set of directions can be used to navigate to the appropriate place and then learn what the building looks like. An example set of directions is: "Travel south for 2 blocks and then turn left. Travel another block. Stop. The conference center is on your left." Upon completing the specified actions blindly, the person arrives at the destination and creates an association between the surroundings and the target location.

The person may use some previous knowledge during the association task. For instance if the person has visited other conference centers, he may be able to use certain features to determine specifically which building he wants by distinguishing it from neighboring residential buildings. Once the association is made, the person is able to use the conference center as a feature in future plans.

An important detail of this approach is the issue of feature extraction. So far we have glossed over the topic by stating that the robot will extract various features from the environment in order to update its model. Specifically, we expect the robot is able to sense its surroundings, although at a reduced level of detail. For example, the person looking for a conference center knows that he is looking for a building and can see the various buildings around him, without yet knowing the names of the buildings. Similarly we will assume that part of the robot's plan includes a description of the types of features it should be looking for. This information is used to make a correct association between the state and the model object of interest.

Of course, there exists the possibility that the robot will become lost. Odometry errors and uncertainty in the environment can sometimes make it challenging for a robot to execute even a simple plan accurately. In some cases it may be possible for the robot to determine that it is lost if the features in the environment do not match the expected features specified in the plan. In other situations wrong associations between location and features will be made. Detailed analysis and discussion of what to do in such cases, is beyond the scope of this paper, but provides an interesting direction for further research.

2.3   Combining Monitoring and Reverse Monitoring

The use of regular Monitoring alone in planning allows for complex behaviors but makes the algorithm very sensitive to errors in state detection. The use of Reverse Monitoring alone supports only basic behaviors but allows the robot to update the observation model. We propose to combine the two approaches, resulting in an algorithm that alternates between the two methods as needed. In cases where state detection is accurate and reliable, regular Monitoring is used to execute arbitrary plans as usual. When state detection breaks down, Reverse Monitoring is applied to update the model. The updated model is then used to make action termination decisions in more complex plans that use regular Monitoring.

An important issue to consider is where the scripted action plans come from for Reverse Monitoring. The presence of these plans implies that an expert of some sort is needed in order to guide the robot. Even in the human example, help is needed in order to acquire the directions to the destination. In this paper we assume that an expert is available and can provide a scripted action plan for getting from some known point to the destination. Another assumption we make here is that the robot's designer selects when to transition between Monitoring and Reverse Monitoring.

Although these assumption may seem strong at first, they are quite practical in most cases when a robot is acting in the real world. In most cases the robot's user knows when changes to the environment occur and the features of any new locations the robot needs to learn. User involvement required to produce these plans is usually trivial compared to the amount of input required for the alternative manual model update method, and plans can be reused an arbitrary number of times. However, it remains an important problem to develop methods in which these functions may be performed autonomously. Detecting when to switch between the two algorithms is a particularly compelling problem several aspects of which are already being studied in other areas [1,10].

The following sections present our experimental results, which demonstrate how the combination of these two methods can lead to greater autonomy and reliability in a robotic system.

3   Experimental Domain

3.1   Problem Overview

We chose to demonstrate the effectiveness of the proposed approach using the Sony AIBO ERS7 robots (Figure 1(a)). The robot's set task is navigation in the robot soccer domain using the on-board camera for sensory input. The robot's vision system recognizes objects by their color and shape. Since an object's color changes with the lighting in the environment, it often becomes necessary for the robot to update its model of what each particular color looks like. It is this task of vision color calibration that we will be focusing on for our experiment. Our aim is to show that by applying the Reverse Monitoring method, the robot is able to autonomously update its model and then return to regular plan execution using Monitoring, bypassing a tedious manual calibration process.

3.2   Robotic Platform and Domain

We used the commercially available Sony AIBO ERS-7 quadruped robot as the robotic platform. The robot is a complete autonomous system, with a 576 Mhz MIPS processor, wireless communication and variety of on-board sensors. The

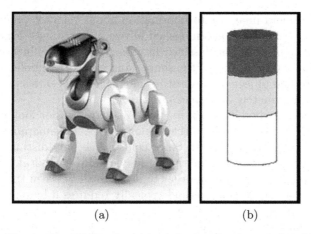

(a)   (b)

Fig. 1. The ERS7 robot (a), and a localization marker (b)

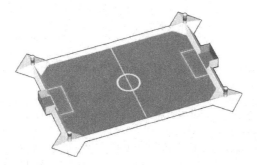

Fig. 2. The robot's environment

main sensor, and the one we will be focusing on, is a color camera located in the head of the robot.

The robot's environment is the standard robot soccer field designed according to the rules of The RoboCup Federation [13]. The field is comprised of a green carpeted area surrounded by a white 10cm high wall, see Figure 2. Two goals are located on opposite sides of the field, and four uniquely colored markers are located at the corners. Each marker is 30cm tall with two 10cm-wide bands of color at the top, see Figure 1(b). Three colors are used to identify the markers and the goals - yellow, cyan and pink. The color combinations of the marker bands make it possible to uniquely identify each of the markers. The robot performs all navigation tasks by using the camera images to determine the relative location of the corner markers and triangulate its position on the field.

3.3   The Vision System

We will give a brief overview of the robot's vision system, which allows the robot to sense the environment. The vision system is responsible for converting the raw YUV camera images into information about relevant objects that the robot sees [2,3]. This task is accomplished in two major stages. First each pixel in the 208x160 color image is classified into one of the predefined color classes using a color lookup table. Then, the shapes and sizes of symbolic color regions are examined to find objects of interest in the image. This entire process runs in real-time at approximately 30 frames per second.

For the vision method to work, it is vital to have a color lookup table that will map raw YUV pixel values to their color classes. This mapping is the final product of the calibration method. Since color is the only distinguishing characteristic between different landmarks in this domain, it is vital that the color threshold mapping be accurate in order to distinguish between them.

The traditional calibration method typically requires a human to place the robot at various points in the domain to collect images of landmarks for calibration. The user must then hand-label each of the pixels in the images to classify it into one of the discrete color classes. This tedious process results in the robot being able to recognize certain colors and then use that information in combination with object shape to recognize objects. In the following section we will describe how we have applied the Reverse Monitoring method to automate this process.

4   Reverse Monitoring for Landmark Modeling

Our goal in this domain is for the robot to navigate in the environment using the markers as features in order to determine its location. When the observation model is available and the robot is able to accurately map pixel values in the image to their appropriate color label, the navigation task can easily be accomplished through regular Monitoring. However, if the lighting conditions are changed and the color mapping is no longer accurate, the robot's ability to navigate deteriorates until in the worst case it has no color information at all.

Using the Reverse Monitoring method, the robot's color model can be updated to use the new color values. Given a scripted action plan, the robot is able to blindly navigate to the defined points on the field, record the state at that point, and use the features of that state, i.e. pixel color values, to update the observation model. This method allows the robot to collect and analyze the images with very little human assistance. Once this is complete, the robot is able to execute arbitrary plans in the domain.

4.1   Scripted Plan Execution

The key steps of the scripted plan are outlined in Table 1. The robot is directed on a path that visits each of the landmarks to be modeled. Once the images for a particular landmark are obtained, they are analyzed to extract the object's features, mainly the pixel colors of the marker bands. Once the full plan has been executed, the robot has a complete observation model, which allows it to execute arbitrary navigation plans in the domain.

As discussed earlier, the scripted plan includes a description of the key features the robot should focus on. In this particular case, the robot is told the

Table 1. Scripted Plan for Landmark Model Acquisition

---

1. Robot is at start point, P_0.
   The robot is placed at the preset start position.
2. For $i = 1 to N$, for N landmarks that the robot will model:
   (a) Execute scripted step S_i by walking to point P_i using a series of scripted actions
       The robot walks using odometry (and not sensory data) to traverse the preset distance.
   (b) At point P_i, collect image data for landmark L_i
       The robot automatically perturbs its position and angle to get images from several vantage points.
   (c) Learn observation models from acquired image data.

---

physical size and shape of the marker. This information is not sufficient for accurate navigation in the robot environment since the only distinguishing characteristic of the landmarks in our domain is color. However, it is enough to locate the marker and the bands in the image (see the next section for more details). Since the plan specifies exactly which marker the robot is near, the colors can be appropriately assigned to the marker bands.

4.2 Image Analysis

Several standard vision algorithms were applied to extract the marker features from the images. This process replaces the method traditionally used in this system of a human labeling the marker regions by hand. Figure 3 shows an example of an image at various stages in the image processing pipeline. The Sobel edge filter is first applied to the raw image, resulting in the edge image seen in the second stage in Figure 3. This step reduces the dimensionality of the observations from a multiple color image to a binary edge image containing only color transition information. A Hough transform [8] is then used to locate the two colored bands of the marker (see image 3 of Figure3). The bands of the marker are then labeled with the appropriate colors, while the rest of the image is marked in black to symbolize the background, or non-marker, region

Fig. 3. The image analysis pipeline: original YUV image; edge image, the marker detected; the coloring of the detected marker; the original image color segmented with the updated thresholds

(see image 4 of Figure3). The achieved color mapping is then used to generate an updated lookup table, mapping pixel color values in the raw image into the symbolic color space. The final image in Fig. 3 shows the original image after it has been color segmented using the newly learned mapping.

5   Experimental Results

To test the performance of the algorithm, we evaluate the accuracy of the robot's model and its ability to navigate in the environment. The robot's performance is compared to its normal performance under the traditional system, where the observation model is manually calibrated by the user. The following sections describe the results for model and navigation accuracy.

5.1   Model Accuracy

The robot's observation model was tested by evaluating the accuracies of the color class mapping and the marker detection. Specifically, we analyzed:

- the percent of pixels accurately labeled by the marker detection as marker regions;
- the percent of pixels accurately mapped by the model to their correct color class;
- the accuracy of the marker distance estimates generated by the model.

The accuracy of the marker detection during the image analysis step is very important to the success of the algorithm. The more pixels that are labeled with their correct color class during training, the more accurate the model will be at detecting markers in new images. Incorrectly labeled pixels will lead to poor performance. As a result, our marker detection algorithm is designed to be conservative, preferring not to label anything in the image if it is not sure of the marker's location instead of labeling the wrong part of the image. The labeling also avoids the edges of the marker in order to avoid classifying parts of the background as marker colors. Overall, the automatic classification did not label markers in 17% of the images due to low confidence about their location. In the remaining 83% of the images the algorithm labeled an average of 9% fewer pixels than a human. Figure 4 shows several sample images in the marker detection stage.

The color lookup table generated from the automatically labeled images was compared to a lookup table generated from a human labeling of the same images. Both color lookup tables were applied to a set of previously unlabeled test images. On average, automatic calibration accurately labeled 89% if the marker pixels, while manual calibration resulted in 98% accuracy compared to a manual labeling of the test images. Figure 5 shows a sample image of a marker classified using the two lookup tables.

Finally, we evaluated the effect of the decreased number of labeled pixels on the marker distance estimates. After classifying the images, each one was used to

(a)   (b)

Fig. 4. Marker identification in robot camera images. Green boxes mark the boundaries of regions classified as marker bands. Yellow boxes mark boundaries of candidate regions in images where no marker was found.

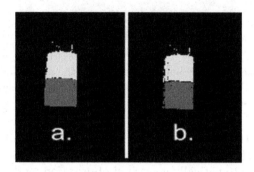

Fig. 5. Image of a marker after it has been color segmented using manual (a) and automatic (b) calibrations

calculate the location of the displayed marker relative to the robot. We found that the 9% decrease in the number of labeled pixels did not have a significant impact on the distance estimates, causing an average of 3mm difference in the distance measurements (0.6% of the actual marker distance). We therefore conclude that the model generated though automatic labeling is comparable to the manually generated model.

5.2 Navigation Accuracy

The robot's navigation abilities were tested to determine the effects of the generated model on task execution. The robot was presented with a task of navigating to and stopping at seven set points on the field. The only information given to the robot was the sequence of points that it should visit. The only input used by the robot were the marker observations.

The robot's performance was evaluated based on the accuracy with which it was able to reach the set points, as well as the directness of the path from point to point. Figure 6 shows the trajectories the robot took when executing the task using the automatically generated (red) and manually generated (yellow) models. The target points are marked in the image with a white 'X'. The robot performed equally well using both models, stopping an average of 8.7cm off target using manual calibration and 6.3cm off target with the automatic calibration. The path taken between the points was direct for both trials with a few exceptions.

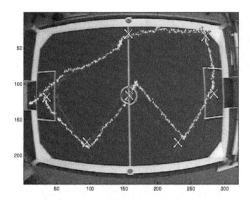

Fig. 6. The path taken by the robot while executing the navigation task as seen from an overhead camera. Trial of the robot using manual calibration shown in yellow, trial of automatic calibration shown in red.

We consider both results to be good, and the difference in trajectories not significant due to the unavoidable noise of the environment. This experiment indicates that the automatically generated observation model results in performance that is comparable to that of manual calibration methods.

6   Conclusion

In this paper we present a general-purpose framework for updating a robot's observation model in the context of planning. By applying this framework, which we call Reverse Monitoring, a robot is able to update its model through the execution of a simple scripted plan. This allows the robot to adapt to changes in the environment and results in a more robust planning system. This method replaces the manual sensor calibration stage that, although not part of traditional planning, is a fundamental part of any robotic system that planning may be implemented on. We demonstrated the effectiveness of this approach by replacing one of the key calibration stages in an existing robotic system without experiencing any degradation in performance.

References

1. M. Basseville and I. Nikiforov. Detection of Abrupt Change - Theory and Application PrenticeHall, Englewood Cliffs, N.J., 1993.
2. J. Bruce, T. Balch, and M. Veloso, CMVision (http://www.coral.cs.cmu.edu/cmvision).
3. J. Bruce, T. Balch, and M. Veloso, "Fast and inexpensive color image segmentation for interactive robots", In the Proceedings of IROS-2000, 2000.
4. Fernadez, J. and Simmons, R., "Robust Execution Monitoring for Navigation Plans", Proceedings of the Conference on Intelligent Robots and Systems, 1998.

5. Fichtner, M., Gromann, A., and Thielscher, M., "Intelligent execution monitoring in dynamic environments", Fundamenta Informaticae, Volume 57, pp. 371-392, 2003.
6. Graefe, V., "Object- and Behavior-oriented Stereo Vision for Robust and Adaptive Robot Control", In the Proceedings of the International Symposium on Microsystems, Intelligent Materials, and Robots, Sendai, 1995.
7. K. Z. Haigh and M. Veloso, "Planning, Execution and Learning in a Robotic Agent", In the Proceedings of the Fourth International Conference on Artificial Intelligence Planning Systems, 1998.
8. P.V.C. Hough, "Machine Analysis of Bubble Chamber Pictures", In the Proceedings of the International Conference on High Energy Accelerators and Instrumentation, CERN, 1959.
9. Jüngel, M., Hoffmann, J. and Lözsch, M., "A Real-Time Auto-Adjusting Vision System for Robotic Soccer", In the Proceedings of the 7th International Workshop on RoboCup 2003.
10. S. Lenser, "On-line Robot Adaptation to Environmental Change", PhD thesis CMU-CS-05-165, Carnegie Mellon University, 2005.
11. Livyatan, H., Yaniv, Z., Joskowicz, L., "Robust Automatic C-Arm Calibration for Fluoroscopy-Based Navigation: A Practical Approach", Lecture Notes in Computer Science, Volume 2489, pp. 60-68, 2002.
12. Mayer, G., Utz, H., and Kraetzschmar, G., "Towards Autonomous Vision Self-Calibration for Soccer Robots", In the Proceedings of the IEEE/RSJ International Conference on Intelligent Robots and Systems, 2002.
13. RoboCup Four-Legged Robot League Rules (http://www.tzi.de/4legged/bin/view/Website/WebHome).
14. Zrimec, T., and Wyatt, A., "Learning to Recognize Objects - Toward Automatic Calibration of Colour Vision for Sony Robots", In the Proceedings of the Machine Learning in Computer Vision Workshop, ICML 2002.

Applying Biological Paradigms to Emerge Behaviour in RoboCup Rescue Team

Francisco Reinaldo[1,2], Joao Certo[1], Nuno Cordeiro[1], Luis P. Reis[1], Rui Camacho[1], and Nuno Lau[3]

[1] LIACC-NIAD&R, Faculty of Engineering, University of Porto,
R. Dr. Roberto Frias, 4200-465 Porto, Portugal
reinaldo.opus@gmail.com, nuno_cordeiro@hotmail.com,
{joao.certo, lpreis, rcamacho}@fe.up.pt
[2] GIC, Dept. of Computer Science, UnilesteMG,
Av. Pres. Tancredo Neves, n°3500, 35170-056 Cel. Fabriciano - MG, Brasil
[3] IEETA/DET, University of Aveiro, 3810-193 Aveiro, Portugal
lau@det.ua.pt

Abstract. This paper presents a hybrid behaviour process for performing collaborative tasks and coordination capabilities in a rescue team. RoboCup Rescue simulator and its associated international competition are used as the testbed for our proposal. Unlike other published work in this field one of our main concerns is having good results on RoboCup Rescue championships by emerging behaviour in agents using a biological paradigm. The benefit comes from the hierarchic and parallel organisation of the mammalian brain. In our behaviour process, Artificial Neural Networks are used in order to make agents capable of learning information from the environment. This allows agents to improve several algorithms like their Path Finding Algorithm to find the shortest path between two points. Also, we aim to filter the most important messages that arise from the environment, to make the right choice on the best path planning among many alternatives, in a short time. A policy action was implemented using Kohonen's network, Dijkstra's and D* algorithm. This policy has achieved good results in our tests, getting our team classified for RoboCup Rescue Simulation League 2005.

1 Introduction

Search and rescue of victims in large-scale disaster are serious and very difficult tasks presenting several challenges from a scientific point of view. Unprepared cities can suffer tremendous consequences in a natural catastrophe as was reported in Kobe's earthquake [8]. Every city needs an emergency plan, to reduce the loss of human life in a natural disaster. In recent years, staggering technological breakthroughs brought some science fiction dreams closer to us. The innovations in robotics and artificial intelligence have opened doors and allowed for a complete new use of rescue agents and emergency plans.

RoboCup Rescue international project was started in 1999 to solve disaster and rescue problems by integration of disaster information, prediction, planning and

C. Bento, A. Cardoso, and G. Dias (Eds.): EPIA 2005, LNAI 3808, pp. 422–434, 2005.

training for rescue actions. Built upon the success of RoboCup Soccer project, it aims to offer a comprehensive urban disaster simulator, forums of technical discussions and competitive evaluation for researchers and practitioners.

This paper presents our team and its decision system to support planning/control of tasks. The system uses learning modules and path finding algorithms. The use of Kohonen's network [10], Feedforward network, Dijkstra's algorithm [4] and the D* (Dynamic A*) algorithm [14] are discussed, to provide an understanding of how they are applied in agents. Consequently, collaborative actions are emerged and optimal strategies are achieved with high performance for path-finding and other related tasks.

The rest of the paper is as follow. Section 2 presents an overview of RoboCup Rescue Simulation System. Section 3 shows rescue teams and rescue behaviours. Section 4 provides an overview of Artificial Neural Networks, showing the similarity between rescue team and human brain to validate the choice of Kohonen's network for emergent reasoning and Feedforward for producing simple behaviours. Section 5 introduces our team, giving contributions in: functionalities, structure and layer learning building. In Section 6 we present some results and conclude the paper.

2 RoboCup Rescue Simulation System

RoboCup Rescue Simulation League is a rescue project that simulates an urban disaster, heterogeneous team agents and human behaviours [24]. Proposed by Kitano et al. [7], it looks after autonomous agents, complex high-level plans and adjustment of heterogeneous behaviours to save citizens in disasters and to preserve the town (Figure 1). Every year a competition is organized where researchers meet, compare approaches and exchange ideas.

Some emergent methodologies and/or behaviour architectures try to offer suitable solutions for providing emergency decision support. But an unconcern with the requirements of disaster simulation or the topologic structure of the system can suggest an arduous policy of solution elaboration process in the simulation phase.

Challenges and requirements are the guidelines of the rescue simulation system and competition. The challenges are: limited time for rescuing injured citizens; simulation of rescue behaviours, centre agents and team agents; best route planning for moving vehicles allowing detours around blocked ways; distribution of water to extinguish burning buildings; and others. In order to solve this, it is necessary to develop useful reasoning/reactive modules to deliberate/perform secure actions. These modules offer strategies for saving lives and preserving buildings. In addition, Takahashi [24] has presented and categorized, according to their usage, three main classes of requirements in a disaster simulation:

- **Before disasters:** Prevention plans for disasters and how to supply provisions to refuges. This phase is considered in some way as the agents may have a set of adjustable parameters according to the map of the City in which they act.
- **During disasters:** Rescue operations at the field are done to save lives, prevent the destruction of households and so on. These operations are estimated to last for the 72 hours immediately after the disaster.
- **After disasters:** Disasters in urban cities may have effects for a long time.

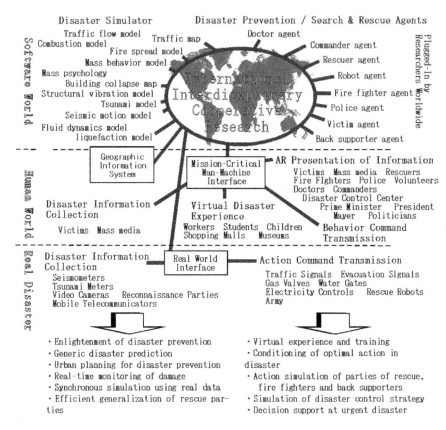

Fig. 1. Concept of the RoboCup Rescue simulation project, extracted from [23]

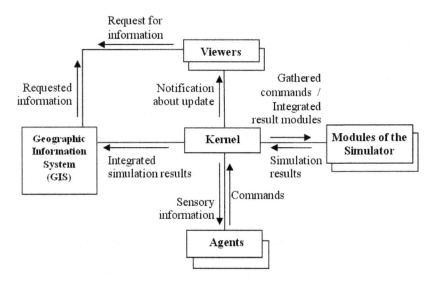

Fig. 2. RoboCup Rescue Simulation System

The RoboCup Rescue Simulator is a framework that is divided by modules that can run in several computers. These modules are independent to run particular characteristics of the world, as can be seen in figure 2. The modules also represent simulation domains as earthquake, buildings on fire or collapsing, spreading of fire to neighbouring buildings, blocked ways and health status of citizens.

The main components that comprise the simulator are [3]:

- **Geographic Information System (GIS):** the GIS module holds the state of the simulated world;
- **Kernel:** this module is connected to all the other modules. The kernel updates the objects in the GIS and sends the world update for every connected module.
- **Sub-simulators:** Fire-simulator, Collapse-simulator, Traffic-simulator etc. are modules connected in the kernel, each one simulating a particular disaster feature – fire, collapses, traffic, etc.
- **Agents:** agent modules are connected to the kernel and represent intelligent entities in the real word, such as civilians, polices agents, fire agents etc.
- **Viewers:** their task is to get the state of the world, communicating with the kernel module, and graphically displaying it, allowing the user to easily follow the simulation process.

The simulator presents a world model with fire brigades, ambulances, police cars, civilians, roads, buildings and fire, as can be seen on figure 3.

Time: 20   Score: 108,283911

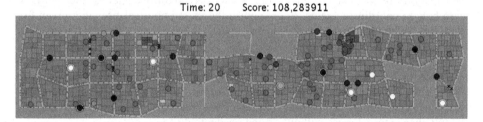

Fig. 3. Rescue Scenario

The RoboCup Rescue domain [2,3] includes approximately 40 agents in six different types to preserve the town and citizens´ life: Fire Brigade agents, Police Force agents, Ambulance agents and three different Control Centres. Centre agents coordinate platoons with collaborative tasks, which are based on information from the external world, received by mobile agents. These centre agents send/receive several messages of world state to/from its mobile agents. The updated messages are sent to the rescue agents. Platoons have the autonomy to learn and to decide on the best course of action on unexpected states. Police agents have the responsibility to clear important blocked ways for extreme traffic and to report to base the detection of a citizen crying for help. Ambulance agents search for buried citizens, rescuing and transporting them to refuges. Fire Brigade agents extinguish buildings on fire. Each centre is responsible for its team. All tasks performed by mobile agents are centred on saving lives.

3 Related Work

RoboCup Rescue intends to promote research and development to this socially significant domain at various levels, involving multi-agent team work coordination, development of physical robotic agents for search and rescue, development of information infrastructures, personal digital assistants, and standard rescue simulators [13]. The promotion of an annual rescue challenge becomes a way to get together some different teams for searching the best planned actions to minimize the damage and to test them in a virtual city. The methodical laying of practical strategy and tactics is the key to victory.

There are several teams developing agents, with advanced learning and coordination capabilities, for RoboCup Rescue Simulation. Paquet et al. [15] presented a very good survey concerning the use of coordination methodologies in RoboCup Rescue. Several other teams present very interesting work on applying coordination methodologies to Rescue [1, 5, 9, 15].

DAMAS Rescue team [15] concentrates its work on improving the agent's ability to extinguish buildings on fire. The ability consists in classifying the best fire to extinguish by perception learning method. Agents are using a global view and a specific view decision making process to choose the best fire zone to attack. Global view focuses on the various burning areas. Specific view makes use of more detailed information to choose which specific building to extinguish in the chosen fire zone. The correlation between utility, and expected reward, can be seen as an estimate of the capability to extinguish a given fire. Using perception techniques, the aim is to learn how to coordinate agents, to extinguish the most important fires in a given fire zone. In the development of the agents' plan, DAMAS Rescue team used Jack Intelligent Agent programming language [6], decision tree algorithms and reinforcement learning. During the simulation, the agents use the tree, created offline, to decide the best fire zone and, inside the fire zone, the best building to extinguish. This has the effect of reducing the state space of the reinforcement learning algorithm and, thus, facilitating the learning process. Other interesting point is that fireman doesn't change target areas without a good reason to do so.

ResQ Freiburg [9] deals with a sequence of planning methods. The objective is to build hierarchic commands that mean hierarchic behaviours. The goal of limiting damage to people and buildings is achieved by successfully coordinating teammates by deliberative high-level decisions of the centre agents. The decision about the execution of actions is decomposed in a reactive level by the platoon agents and a deliberative level by the centre agents. Agents have prediction methods instead of classical planning research. This prediction method is an evaluation function for possible targets with respect to the current state of the environment. This function is extended to use hierarchical reinforcement learning. Centre agents decide task execution in the long term by allocating groups of platoon agents to particular tasks. Their decision making is based on a module for state prediction and abstraction, which generates the input for a novel multi-agent planner.

Caspian [5] uses a three phase model approach to develop their agents: World Model, Dynamic Path Finding and Decision Making. The first phase is the development of a World Model. The importance of this phase is crucial as the better the model is, and better the update of that model, the better the decision will be.

The model for the world is the best for the available sensory information, as every agent knows everything that is sensed by other agents. As the number of messages each agent can listen is limited, this is achieved by centre agents who collect every humanoid agent messages, and other centre agent messages, and send a new one with all the new (based on timestamp) information. Decision Making is only done in humanoid Agents, each of them as a priority assigning algorithm witch chooses the most important (homogeneous) job. Each Police Force agent is assigned a zone to work on. Ambulance Teams always work collectively when rescuing. Their task and coordination is handled by a *leader*. If there are no civilians to rescue in the world model, each ambulance agent is assigned a zone to search. Fire Brigade behaviour is similar to the one on Ambulance Teams, with the exception that, some times, they get separated into two or more groups.

SOS team [20] develops a general-purpose rescue agent for implementing high-level strategies and learning algorithms. The SOS agent has a state-based architecture with an explicit state-selection and state switching policy. It uses two path-finding modules that are D* and Dijkstra's algorithm. The search for fire sources and buried civilians is done by clustering the search function space into regions of equal size. Using the idea of Kohonen's network, a Voronoi diagram is constructed from those clusters. Agents are assigned regions extracted from the diagram. Tasks are prioritized according to their importance. The Fire Brigade agents use a two level priority scheme for increasing the locality of successive tasks, and reducing the amount of time wasted on move actions. After defining a Fiery Region as a connected group of burning buildings, firstly the agents are assigned to a region and secondly to a building on fire. A method of Reinforcement Learning based on Q-Learning is used by Fire Brigade agents, which suffer awards or penalties according to their efficiency in performing tasks. Police agents perform actions by use of centralized and decentralized decision-making rules. After the simulation is started, the Police Office assigns some Police Forces to clear the blocked ways that are around a discovered fire focus. These routes will be used to facilitate the free movement of agents around these critical spots. When no jobs are received from the Police Office, agents scout for fire and buried civilians. In order to decide the best ways to clean, SOS uses a concept of *cell temperature* that reflects the importance for the overall performance of the team: the higher the *temperature* the more important and obstructed is that piece of terrain, therefore the agents try to lower the *temperature* of the *hottest cell* to an acceptable level. The ambulance teams use an algorithm to estimate the remaining *lifetime* of injured civilians. This estimation is achieved through the use of a 3-layer Back-Propagation Neural Network. In this case, only injured citizens are rescued.

4   Artificial Neural Network and Biologic Plausibility

Some algorithmic methods do not give a suitable solution to multiagent problems because the agents´ actions are largely intricate. The problem must be treated by dividing the problematic phases in specialized modules in order to reduce their complexity. So we turn to Nature, studying Brainstem and Forebrain, to demonstrate why we have used Kohonen's network in centre agents, as can be seen in figure 4.

An Artificial Neural Network (ANN) is a data processing paradigm that is inspired by biological neural networks of the brain. An ANN has the ability to learn by examples which gives it a lot of power and flexibility. It is composed of several interconnected neurons that perform excitatory and inhibitory connections to adjust their synaptic weights between neurons to solve a problem and to produce the correct output. The massive parallelism of neurons in an ANN structure can offer data compression, because information can be stored in the weights of the connections. Depending on the network type and its topology, an ANN has the capacity to obtain meaning from complex or imprecise inputs and adjust them to any situations or even to model a complex decision system.

Inside mammalian brain, we can find the Brainstem, that is able to create a far simpler sensory world, and Forebrain, that is thought to coordinate advanced cognitive functions, such as thinking, planning and language [11]. Brainstem is divided in Hindbrain and Midbrain. Hindbrain and Midbrain are, essentially, extensions of the Spinal Cord that receive signals from the environment as well. Hindbrain coordinates and supports movements of walking, and Midbrain orients the body to stimuli. This orientation to stimuli requires both sensory input and motor output. Forebrain is divided in Neocortex, Basal Ganglia, Limbic system and Thalamus. All sensory information reaches the Forebrain through the Thalamus in Diencephalon. The Neocortex creates a perceptual world and regulates the mental activities such as perception and complex planning. The Limbic Cortex is thought to play a role in controlling motivational states, and regulating emotions and behaviours that require memory. The Basal Ganglia and Cerebellum modify movements through inhibitory output and excitatory output, respectively, because the motor cortex sends information to both, and both structures send information right back to the cortex via the Thalamus.

In rescue simulation, the agent's orientation is in response to the world state. Teammates use their sensory input to design a far and simpler sensory world. Massive amounts of data are received from the environment and processed to produce oriented behaviours by rescue agents. Data input is sent to centre agents that will produce, actualize and share a perceptual world. In order to produce it, the sensory systems share some sort of common map of the external world. Moreover, centre agents deliberate cognitive functions to coordinate teammates by overlapping their behaviours. The cognitive functions are responsible for the emergence of reasoning, planning, and memorizing/updating messages to soften the communication. These characteristics of deliberation depend of sensory input of teammates. Each register in the world state is associated with a time stamp, so that the most recent information is always the one recorded. Success and punishment of an agent is regulated by activation/inhibition between the units using their connections, as well as processes for modifying the connections. In the whole rescue simulation system, success and punishment allow for smooth and coordinated movement.

This analogy between mammalian brain and rescue simulation demonstrates that the whole rescue simulation system can be manipulated as a biologic system. We can see in figure 4 that the two systems have a similar production of behaviours. This shows that Kohonen's network can be used as a Neocortex in the centre agents because it reaches complex cooperative deductions with learning ability. In this topology, Kohonen's network allows the creation of a self-organized map based on input data. This ANN has a massive parallelism in the manner that the neurons are interconnected. Our rescue architecture permits overlapping behaviours in teammates as a hierarchy. These qualities make it a motivating addition to agents as they can progressively adjust themselves to provide a more challenging experience for the FC Portugal Rescue Team simulation.

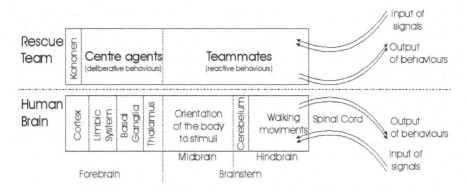

Fig. 4. An analogy between Rescue Team and Human Brain

5   FC Portugal Rescue Team

The search and rescue of citizens, in difficult conditions, on a hostile environment, is a very serious social issue, involving a large number of heterogeneous agents, working together as a team. FC Portugal Rescue Team has elaborated its own learning process to improve the exploration of the world by rescue agents. Agents have the ability to acquire a variety of symbols from the environment and manipulate them in order to emerge knowledge. Using a connectionist approach and path finding algorithms, the agents learn about the surrounding environment and consequently decide on new actions to perform.

5.1   Agent Learning Capabilities

The learning process of decision making is composed of modules. Those are disposed in a hierarchic and hybrid structure. In accordance with Reinaldo [16], the knowledge is hierarchical from simple to complex. Simple knowledge types used in the rescue domain include the position of burning buildings, blocked roads and buildings with buried people. Complex knowledge may include team formation and communication methods.

This disposition of modules reaches fast negotiation and coordination of behaviours to centre agents and reactivity to team agents. Cooperative behaviours are emerged in deliberative level and can offer a class of predefined behaviours aspects. Predefined behaviours can be formulation of routes, anticipation and modification of plans accordingly to the ability of sharing an inner world mental map. Centre agents with cognitive capabilities can perform better tasks than reactive behaviours in this domain.

An ANN is robust enough to model a complex collaborative decision, by searching new ways to solve an unknown but similar problem. This quality is devoted to deal with large quantities of data with high performance. Experimental tests involving Kohonen's networks make it clear that the knowledge improves performance and decreases communication among centre and team agents. On the other hand, in a dynamic environment with unknown states and priority of actions, we are using Feedforward. In the routing module, the information provided to an agent includes the positions and neighbours of each building and road in the environment. The combination of D* path-finding algorithm and Dijkstra's algorithm provides us a hybrid module for finding the best path from origin to destination. In this module there is a limit on the depth of the search tree, for safety.

Dijkstra's algorithm is one of the most efficient algorithms to calculate the minimum cost of the path between vertexes. This algorithm chooses a vertex as root of search and calculates the minimum cost of this vertex for all sequent vertices. It has an acceptable performance but does not offer guaranties of the exact solution if there are negative arcs. This algorithm stipulates an initial approximation to minimum cost and incrementally adjusts this value.

We are using D* algorithm because it plans optimal traverses by repairing paths to the agent's state as new information is discovered in dynamic environments. In accordance with Stentz [22], the algorithm computes an initial path from the goal state to start state and then efficiently modifies this path during the traverse. Stentz had shown, in his research, that this algorithm produces an optimal traverse, meaning that an optimal path to the goal is followed at every state in the traverse, assuming all known information at each step is correct.

5.2 Functionality and Coordination Methodologies

We are interested in the research of new methodologies that promote the development of effective, efficient and practical solutions for fast and stable agents. In order to work with lower-level rescue behaviour the details are important, in order to feed the learning methods and instantaneous decisions modules. In addition, higher-level rescue behaviour is responsible for emerging actions by use of coordination modules.

First we are mainly interested in researching new coordination and learning methodologies. In order to abstract from lower-level rescue simulation details, and be able to run efficiently most of our planned algorithms, we need a more efficient language. Thus, we moved to C/C++ code using, as a reference, Michael Bowling Agent Development Kit [2] and SOS 2003 source code [21]. However since most of our other RoboCup teams [12, 19] are implemented using C++, it is a lot easier to adapt our code to a Rescue team implemented also in C++.

Our agents' low-level strategy is mainly the following: at the beginning of the search and rescue operation, **Police agents** try to free strategic routes, in order to enable ambulance agents and fire brigade agents to move freely between important locations. These points include not only fire spots and civilian refuges, but also map strategic crossings. **Ambulance strategy** is fairly simple and is based on taking close, severely injured, civilian agents to refuges, following known free paths. The D* algorithm is used in order to find the fastest free known paths for ambulance navigation in the map. **Fire brigades** try to combat the fire using pre-defined collective plans for: attacking directly a fire, minimizing fire spread, or containing the fire. Fire combat strategy is more elaborate and is based on defining attack perimeters for known fires. If fire is contained, fire brigades are used to search for buried civilians, in order to maximize team global scoring. **Centre agents** are responsible for message routing and global tactical reasoning for each type of agent.

Our main focus is a high-level methodology that uses complex behaviours, in order to emerge cooperative actions in a coordinated fashion. These coordination methodologies include:

- **Concept of Global Situation.** A situation is a high-level analysis of the search field that must be simple to perform by all agents, resulting in common global knowledge for all [20], like avoiding fire spreading, attacking fire and other.
- **Situation Based Strategic Positioning.** This coordination mechanism [12, 17, 20]enables a team of agents to move in a coordinated way in a spatial domain, based on common a-priori tactical knowledge and simple environment knowledge [20].
- **Definition of a Team Strategy for a Competition.** This strategy is composed by tactics with activation rules. Tactics include several high-level parameters like group mentality, level of risk taken and also the formation to be used in fire attack, sustaining fire in a line, etc. [17, 20]
- **COACH UNILANG.** Coach Unilang [6][18] was the first high-level standard language introduced in RoboCup for RoboSoccer Team. In a search and rescue scenario, it enables the improvement of team coordination, by allowing a supervisor agent to define the team strategy, before the competition and perform the tactical changes in the team during the execution of a cooperative task by a group of agents. This strategy will be followed by the Centre Agents in order to coordinate the moving agents. Our coach for RoboCup Rescue performs off-line analysis of logfiles showing the team behaviour, and decides the strategy for each rescue operation before the start of the competition.
- **ADVCOM.** Intelligent Communication is the mechanism to evaluate the low-bandwidth available at these competitions in a communicated world state. The communication is based on agent's deciding the relevance of communicating a given piece of information, by comparing their own world states with a world state constructed using only communication. Based on the differences between these two world states, agents decide which pieces of information to communicate [12, 17].

6 Preliminary Results

Although there is much work to be done, and our team is only starting to implement some of the proposed ideas, a few changes have already been made to our source code which resulted in some mild improvements as can be seen in the following graph.

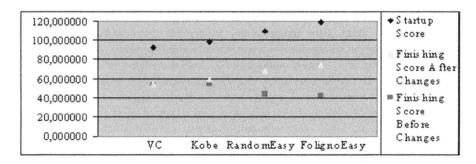

Fig. 5. Score evolution due to improvements in the code

7   Conclusions and Future Work

This paper has presented the development of a rescue team using a biological approach, path finding algorithms, and new coordination methodologies aimed at accomplishing a good performance at the rescue championship. We have addressed coordination methodologies with Configurable Flexible Team Strategy and our Situation Based Strategic Positioning to focus on the RoboCup Rescue problem. We are using Kohonen's network and Feedforward network to increase the adaptation in unfamiliar environments by agents and to save the most possible injured citizens. The use of both hierarchic and parallel organisation of behaviours can enable agents to learn information from the environment and subsume behaviours, from centre agents to teammates. Moreover, we have satisfactory results for making the right choice to the best path planning among many alternatives in a short time, using Dijkstra's and D* algorithm. Finally, our code has been fully used by students to promote the advance of freely open source code and speed up of rescue technologies, to minimize the consequences of disasters.

Acknowledgements

This project is a collaboration between the Univesities of Aveiro and Porto. The authors wish to thank UnilesteMG/BR and FCT/PT for the fellowship granted. This research was supported by FCT under grant # POSI/EIA/63240/2004. Any opinions, findings and conclusions or recommendations expressed in this material are those of the author(s) and do not necessarily reflect those of the sponsor.

References

1. Amraii, S. A., Behsaz, B., Gheibi, H., Izadi, M., Janzadeh, H., Molazem, F., Rahimi, A., Ghinani, M. T., and Vosoughpour, H., "S.O.S. 2004: an attempt towards a multi-agent rescue team", Amirkabir Univ. of Tecnology, Tehran, Iran 2004.
2. Bowling, M., "Robocup Rescue: Agent Development Kit", Dept. of Comp. Science, Univ. of Alberta, Alberta, PDF Doc. Avaliabe at http://www-2.cs.cmu.edu/~mhb/research/rescue/.

3. d'Agostino, F., Farinelli, A., Grisetti, G., Iocchi, L., and Nardi, D., "Monitoring and information fusion for search and rescue operations in large-scale disasters", in Proceedings of Int. Conf. Information Fusion, AnnaPolis, July 2002, pp. 672-679.
4. Dijkstra, E. W., "A note on two problems in connection with graphs", in Numerische Mathematik 1. Amsterdam, The Netherlands: Mathematisch Centrum, 1959, pp. 269--271.
5. Hamraz, S. H., Feyzabadi, S. S., and Motlagh, A. K., "Caspian RoboCup Rescue Simulation Agent: Team Description", 2005.
6. Howden, N. and Rnnquist, R., "Jack Intelligent Agents - Summary of an agent infrastructure", in Proceedings of 5th Int. Conf. on Autonomous Agents, Montral, Canada, 2001.
7. Kitano, H., Asada, M., Kuniyoshi, Y., Noda, I., Osawa, E., and Matsubara, H., "RoboCup: A Challenge Problem for AI and Robotics", AI Magazine, vol. 18, no. 1, 1997, pp. 73-85.
8. Kitano, H., Hahn, W., Hunter, L., Oka, R., Wah, B., and Yokoi, T., "Grand challenge AI applications", in Proceedings of 13th Int. Conf. on Artificial Intelligence, Chambery, Fr, 1993, pp. 1677-1683.
9. Kleiner, A. and Brenner, M., "ResQ Freiburg: Deliberative Limitation of Damage", Univ. of Freiburg, Freiburg im Breisgau, Germany, PDF Doc. Avaliable at http://www.informatik.uni-freiburg.de/~rescue 2004.
10. Kohonen, T., Self-Organizing Maps, Berlin, Springer, 2001.
11. Kolb, B. and Whishaw, I. Q., An Introduction to Brain and Behavior, 2nd ed., New York, Worth Publishers Inc, 2005.
12. Lau, N. and Reis, L. P., "FC Portugal Homepage", University of Porto, Online at http://www.ieeta.pt/robocup Visited in Oct, 5, 2004.
13. Lau, N., Reis, L. P., and Reinaldo, F., "FC Portugal 2005 Rescue Team Description: Adapting Simulated Soccer Coordination Methodologies to the Search and Rescue Domain", Univ. of Porto, Porto, PDF Doc. Avaliable at http://paginas.fe.up.pt/~lpreis/fcportugal/rescue 2005.
14. Likhachev, M., Ferguson, D., Gordon, G., Stentz, A., and Thrun, S., "Anytime Dynamic A*: An Anytime, Replanning Algorithm", in Proceedings of Int. Conf. on Automated Planning and Scheduling (ICAPS), June 2005, pp. 10.
15. Paquet, S., Bernier, N., and Chaib-draa, B., "DAMAS-Rescue Description Paper", in Proceedings of RoboCup-2004: Robot Soccer World Cup VIII, Springer Verlag, Berlin, 2004, pp. 12.
16. Reinaldo, F. A. F., Projecting a framework and programming a system for development of modular and heterogeneous artificial neural networks, Dept. of Computer Science, Federal Univ. of Santa Catarina, Florianópolis, MSc Thesis, 2003.
17. Reis, L. P. and Lau, N., "FC Portugal Team Description: RoboCup 2000 Simulation League Champion", in Proceedings of RoboCup-2000: Robot Soccer World Cup IV, Berlin, 2001, pp. 29-40.
18. Reis, L. P. and Lau, N., "COACH UNILANG - A Standard Language for Coaching a (Robo)Soccer Team", in Proceedings of RoboCup-2001: Robot Soccer World Cup V, Berlin, 2002, pp. 183-192.
19. Reis, L. P., Lau, N., Costa, P., Nabais, A., Rentes, M., Baixinho, L., Oliveira, E., and Moreira, A. P., "FC Portugal: New Coordination Methodologies in RoboCup Legged League", Univ. of Porto, Porto, Team Description Paper 2005.
20. Reis, L. P., Lau, N., and Oliveira, E., "Situation Based Strategic Positioning for Coordinating a Simulated RoboSoccer Team", in Proceedings of Balancing Reactive and Social Deliberation in MAS, Berlin, 2001, pp. 175-197.

21. SOS, "Official SOS Home Page", Amirkabir University of Technology, Online at http://ce.aut.ac.ir/~sos/ Visited in Feb 23, 2005.

22. Stentz, A., "The Focussed D* Algorithm for Real-Time Replanning", in Proceedings of Int. Conf. on Artificial Intelligence, Montreal, Canada, Aug. 20-25 1995, pp. 1652-1659.

23. Tadokoro, S., Kitano, H., Takahashi, T., Noda, I., Matsubara, H., Shinjoh, A., Koto, T., Takeuchi, I., Takahashi, H., Matsuno, F., Hatayama, M., Nobe, J., and Shimada, S., "RoboCup-Rescue: An international cooperative research project of robotics and AI for the disaster mitigation problem", in Proceedings of Unmanned Ground Vehicle Technology II, Orlando, FL, USA, 2000, pp. 303-312.

24. Takahashi, T. and Nobe, J., "Evaluation methods for rescue activities by agents and a disaster prevention plan", in Proceedings of 41st SICE, 2002, pp. 858-859.

Survival Kit: A Constraint-Based Behavioural Architecture for Robot Navigation

Pedro Santana[1] and Luís Correia[2]

[1] IntRoSys S.A., Quinta da Torre, Campus FCT-UNL,
2829-516 - Portugal
[2] University of Lisbon,
Campo Grande, 1749-016 - Portugal

Abstract. This article presents a constraint-based behavioural architecture for low-level safe navigation, the Survival Kit. Instead of approaching the problem by customising a generic Behaviour-Based architecture, the Survival Kit embodies a dedicated semantics for safe navigation, which augments its expressiveness for the task. An instantiation of the architecture for goal-oriented obstacle avoidance in unstructured indoor environments is proposed. Special attention is given to an environmental feature, the gap, which allows to optimise paths based on immediate ranging data. Experimental results in simulation confirm the capabilities of the approach.

1 Introduction

The motivation for this work is the development of control systems for disposable robots to be applied in hazardous tasks. In those tasks, global localisation and communication mechanisms are reduced or even absent; in addition, robots may get lost or damaged. Another driving force towards the development of simple robot control architectures is the increasing interest on micro and nano-robots. In this sense, the main set of requirements for this work is: the control system should rely as little as possible on localisation mechanisms, complex sensory apparatus, and it should target implementations for simple computational units (e.g. micro-controllers).

Previous work on Behaviour-Based architectures, such as those based on priority (e.g. [2,3]) and action-selection coordination (e.g. [6]) mechanisms either are extremely complex or fail to produce smooth and optimised trajectories. Since only a single behaviour is active at a time, either it includes other skills increasing complexity and reducing modularity, or it will not be goal-oriented (e.g. avoiding obstacles without considering which direction would also benefit a goal seeking behaviour). In voting- (e.g. [8]) and fusion-based (e.g. [1]) Behaviour-Based architectures, the produced action may not satisfy all constituent behaviours, which may reduce the robustness of the system, in case those behaviours are responsible for maintaining robot's safety. In addition, (tedious) tuning of each behaviour contribution to the overall behaviour is usually required, which often compels to choose between robustness and path smoothing.

C. Bento, A. Cardoso, and G. Dias (Eds.): EPIA 2005, LNAI 3808, pp. 435–446, 2005.

Typically, Behaviour-Based architectures are tackled in a holistic perspective, where the same semantics is used in all parts of the control system, such as safety keeping and task-achieving parts. This paper approaches the problem differently, it assumes that different semantics are required at each level. In this sense, this work introduces an architecture, the Survival Kit (SK) architecture, whose semantics is specially designed for safe navigation, delegating task-achieving requirements to upper-layers, which can be implemented by any other architecture (not necessarily a Behaviour-Based one). The coordination mechanism implemented in the SK architecture is based on constraints, which are added by several reflexes running in parallel, according to their skills. This type of *cooperation by negation* guarantees that the resulting action does not disagree with any of the reflexes. Although this feature is essential for safe navigation, it may be restrictive for task-achieving behaviours.

As it will be shown, the semantics of the SK will allow the implementation of a simple yet robust goal-oriented obstacle avoidance method, which taking into consideration the target implementation, i.e. disposable robots, is capable of competing with the most popular methods, such as *Dynamic Window Approach* [4], *Curvature Velocity Method* [9], *VFH+* [11], *Nearness Diagram* [7], and *Potential Fields* based approaches [1]. Since the obstacle avoidance method herein proposed is supported by a behavioural architectural framework, it is potentially more generalisable and modular than the previously referred algorithmic based approaches.

2   The Survival Kit Architecture

The SK architecture intends to be used as the bottom layer of a robot control system, providing it with safe navigation capabilities. Thus, everything required

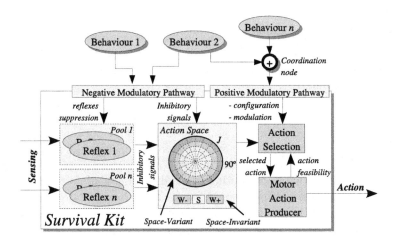

Fig. 1. The Survival Kit Architecture. Behaviours are exemplifying a task-achieving upper-layer.

to maintain the survival (in terms of immediate reactions) of the robot should be implemented within the SK architecture. The constrained application of this architecture to safe navigation allows the definition of a well adapted semantics to the problem at hand, avoiding to lose time customising a generic architecture. Relying on the SK to guarantee safe navigation, upper decision/control layers are relieved of handling real-time events.

On the other hand, a too restrictive SK architecture would fail in its applicability; therefore, in order to introduce some plasticity to the SK, upper-layers are allowed to modulate the SK activity. In addition, the SK architecture has been designed to disturb as less as possible the task-achievement of upper-layers.

Figure 1 illustrates the main components of the SK architecture. Briefly, a set of reflexes **inhibits** some of the available action features according to sensory information. Then, according to a given criteria, the best action is selected and sent to the actuators. Upper layers can **modulate** the SK by inhibiting action features, as reflexes do, and by defining which motor action pattern is preferred (e.g. *desired heading* and *desired linear velocity*).

2.1   The Action Feature Space

The core of the architecture is the *action feature space*, which describes indirectly all available actions to the robot. An example of an action feature is v_{max}, which stands for *the maximum linear velocity allowed for a given sector of the environment*. The *action feature space* is composed of two sub-spaces: the *space-variant* and the *space-invariant*.

Space-Variant Action Feature Sub-space. The *space-variant action feature sub-space* is sectorial (see figure 1). Each sector $j \in J$ with an angular size ϕ, where J is the set of all possible sectors, corresponds to a region in the environment with the same shape. This design is motivated by the fact that most sensory information is radial; thus, a similar representation facilitates further processing. A set of *space-variant action feature descriptors* F_{sv} must be defined every time the SK architecture is instantiated. In each sector, associated to each feature descriptor $f_{sv} \in F_{sv}$, there are two slots, one for a constraint c on the respective action feature, and another one for its temporal validity τ.

Setting a constraint c (e.g. to $1\,\mathrm{ms}^{-1}$) and its corresponding τ (e.g. to $100\,\mathrm{ms}$) associated to a feature descriptor f_{sv} (e.g. v_{max}), in a given sector j (e.g. 2), will affect the set of available actions for that sector. Thus, a constraint added by a reflex on a *space-variant action feature* has the following format: $cons(j, f_{sv}, c, \tau)$ (e.g. $cons(2, v_{max}, 1\,\mathrm{ms}^{-1}, 100\,\mathrm{ms})$).

A set of conditions must be met when accepting a new constraint. If a new constraint reduces the possible set of actions (e.g. if the feature is v_{max} with a current value of $1\,\mathrm{ms}^{-1}$ and the new constraint intends to reduce the value to $0.5\,\mathrm{ms}^{-1}$), then it is immediately accepted. If the new constraint validity is greater than the current one, then the constraint validity is updated with the newer value.

The constraint validity can be used for three purposes: to reduce the system sensitivity to noisy sensors, to specify Fixed Action Patterns, and to create a myopic local environment representation in terms of *space-variant action features*. The representation is myopic due to the absence of self-localisation mechanisms, which, in general, hinders spatial transformations, specially translations. However, if heading information exists, the *space-variant action feature sub-space* can be geo-referenced. In such case, if the robot is pointing north and a constraint is set to sector $j = 0$, while still valid, that constraint will always refer to the sector pointing north independently of robot's subsequent headings.

Space-Invariant Action Feature Sub-space. A second action feature sub-space, the space-invariant action feature sub-space, allows reflexes to constrain certain dynamics of the robot, such as angular velocities, independently of any spatial relationship. Setting a constraint in this sub-space is in everything similar to the previous case, except that a feature $f_{si} \in F_{si}$ is considered, and any spatial relationship discarded. Thus, a constraint is defined by $cons(f_{si}, c, \tau)$. Notice that $F_{sv} \bigcap F_{si} = \emptyset$.

2.2   Reflex Pools

Two loops can be found in the SK architecture. A set of reflexes perceives the world, acts upon the *action feature space* (i.e. produce a set of constraints), an action is selected which will change the world, and in turn the world affects robot's perception. This is the first loop. The second loop is internal, where reflexes are able to sense actions produced by other reflexes, a sort of *internal stigmergy*. There is also some resemblance with the concept of *black board*.

To implement the second loop, reflexes are split into several pools, which are iterated in sequence. The system designer can allocate reflexes to pools as required. In general, reflexes of pool n will support their actions on information set by reflexes of pools $m < n$, described in terms of constraints.

To better understand this concept, let us assume the existence of two reflex pools. So, reflexes of the first pool act according to the current state of the internal (i.e. *action feature space*) and external (i.e. sensory information) environments. Reflexes of the second pool act in the same manner; however, since the *action feature space* already considers constraints set by reflexes of the first pool, reflexes of the second one can act accordingly.

2.3   Descendent Pathways

Upper-layers are allowed to modulate the SK, via two descendent pathways, one inhibitory and other excitatory. Via the inhibitory pathway, upper-layers can constrain the *action feature space* as if they were reflexes. The SK requests those behaviours for their contribution (i.e. constraints), before any other reflex pool. To increase plasticity, the inhibitory pathway also allows upper-layers to suppress reflexes' output; otherwise, some high-level behaviours would be impossible to achieve (e.g. obstacle avoidance would impair a docking behaviour).

In opposition to the inhibitory pathway, the excitatory one is exclusive; hence, in order to guarantee that only one behaviour can send a message to the SK through this channel, a coordination mechanism must be provided. The excitatory modulation signal allows to select, configure, and request the action selection mechanism for a certain motor action pattern (e.g. *desired heading*, and *desired linear velocity*). The SK architecture could include a coordination node allowing several behaviours to send excitatory signals, which would require to commit to a coordination philosophy. Since the goal of the SK architecture is confined to provide safe navigation, such decision is left to upper-layers.

2.4 Action Selection

The SK can aggregate as many *action selection* mechanisms as desired; still, only one can be active at a time, which is selected and configured via the descendent pathway. Constrained by the available action features, and modulated by the excitatory signal, the *action selection* module selects the best action according to a given criteria.

The *motor actions producer* module is responsible for converting the best action into robot's actuators outputs, and to cooperate with the *action selection* mechanism so to guarantee that a certain action is both feasible in terms of actuators, and respects both *action feature sub-spaces* constraints. For instance, the *space-variant sub-space* may allow the robot to move in sectors on the right of the robot, whereas the *space-invariant* one inhibits positive angular velocities (i.e. turning right). This apparent contradiction is only relevant in some locomotion methods, such as differential ones, and not in others, such as those present in omni-directional robots.

We define the concept of *main axis of motion*, which may not coincide with the robot's front. This concept allows to handle different types of locomotion within the same framework. The *main axis of motion* is displaced by an angle $\hat{a}$ from robot's front, and represents the side of the robot that should match the *desired heading* (provided in the excitatory signal). In other words, this feature allows to set the *desired posture* of the robot.

3 A Survival Kit Instance

In order to demonstrate the SK architecture, an instance for a simulated indoor differential robot with a rectangular shape is herein presented. The robot carries a 5 m full-sonar ring, composed of 32 evenly separated elements, a set of bumpers, and a compass.

3.1 Action Feature Space

The *space-variant action feature* set is $F_{sv} = \{v_{max}, d_{max}, enable\}$, which represents for a given sector, the maximum linear velocity allowed, the maximum distance free of obstacles, and a flag indicating if movement in that sector is allowed at all, respectively. When a feature is constrained, a limit value will be established. Constraints associated to action features v_{max} and d_{max} are real, whereas those associated to *enable* are boolean. This action feature sub-space is *geo-referenced*. Notice that constraints in the following text are described in *ego-referenced* coordinates; an internal process is responsible for making them *geo-referenced*.

The *space-invariant action feature* set is $F_{si} = \{\omega^+, \omega^-, stop\}$. These features, when constrained, disable positive angular velocities, negative angular velocities, and the possibility of stopping the robot, respectively. Thus, in this sub-space, constraints are boolean.

3.2   Reflexes

Five reflexes have been implemented: *range-based reflex, touch reflex, shape constraints reflex, linear velocity constraint reflex*, and *dynamic constraints reflex*. The first three are contained in the first reflex pool, the fourth reflex in the second reflex pool, whereas the last reflex is located in the third pool.

Range-Based Reflex. In the experiments performed for this work, the robot uses a full-sonar-ring of 32 elements, which are displaced by $\alpha = \frac{2 \cdot \pi}{32}$ radians. An obstacle i has the following format, (β_i, r_i), where β_i is the angle between the front of the robot and the obstacle's direction, and r_i is the distance to the obstacle.

In the following text, the term obstacle will be used to something that is perceived by a sonar, and not necessarily to a complete object in the environment (see figure 2.a); that is to say that there is an obstacle per each sonar that detects something. This approach avoids the computational burden of creating elaborate representations of obstacle shapes as they are in the environment. The d_{max} feature of each sector containing an obstacle i, is constrained by the range data r_i.

It is necessary to enlarge the obstacle so a sector not containing it is in fact navigable; i.e. obstacles have to be considered in the configuration space (c-space). This work simplifies this problem by exploiting the fact that obstacles' angular size is equal to the sonar's field of view (i.e. it is fixed). Hence, taking into account the ratio between obstacle's diameter, roughly defined as $d_i = r_i \cdot \sin \alpha$, and robot's diameter w, it is possible to determine, in the c-space, all sectors affected by obstacle i; namely, $j_{obs_i} \in [\Omega(\Delta_i - \beta_i), \Omega(\Delta_i + \beta_i)]$, where $\Omega(.)$ returns the sector of a given angle, and $\Delta_i = \frac{1}{2} \cdot \alpha \cdot \left(\frac{w}{r_i \cdot \sin \alpha} + 1 \right)$.

Further, as previously referred, the d_{max} feature of each sector affected by the enlarged version of the obstacle must be constrained. This is performed by adding, for each sector j_{obs_i}, a constraint $cons(j_{obs_i}, d_{max}, r_i, 100 \, ms)$. The constraint validity has been set empirically. The process is repeated for all detected obstacles.

Touch Reflex. This reflex intends to handle situations where the robot collides with obstacles, which by their nature, e.g. small height, are not detectable

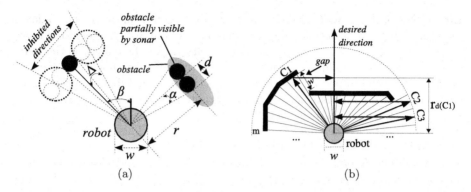

Fig. 2. The c-space transformation in a). The gaps mechanism in b), where obstacles are in c-space and a *corridor* is represented by C_i. On the sake of simplicity, only corridor C_1 has its range projected over the desired direction. It will be the chosen one because $r_d(C_1)$ is the largest of all $r_d(C_i)$.

by the sonar ring. When a bumper is triggered, this reflex reports the obstacle by adding a constraint $cons(j_{touch}, d_{max}, 0, 4000\,\text{ms})$ per each $j_{touch} \in [\Omega(-\frac{\pi}{2}), \Omega(\frac{\pi}{2})]$. To avoid the robot to rotate as it moves away from the obstacle, constraints $cons(\omega^+, false, 2000\,\text{ms})$ and $cons(\omega^-, false, 2000\,\text{ms})$ are also set. Finally, to guarantee that the robot actually moves, i.e. it does not choose to stop, the constraint $cons(stop, false, 2000\,\text{ms})$ is added. The way the robot moves away from the obstacle will be a function of the constraints and excitatory modulation signal. Briefly, after the collision, the robot moves straight backwards for two seconds. Afterwards, it turns away from the detected obstacle bearing towards best direction; progressively the robot gains velocity. Meanwhile the d_{max} constraint validity expires and the robot moves as that obstacle is not there anymore. Thus, this reflex triggers a Fixed Action Pattern described in terms of validity constraints that helps the robot to contour an obstacle invisible to the range sensors.

Shape Constraints Reflex. To consider robot shapes different from the circular one, it is regularly necessary to take into account that, when the robot turns, even around its centre, it may hit an obstacle. Instead of considering robot's shape explicitly in a model-based decision making process, a reflexive method is proposed. Let us assume a situation where a rectangular robot, which due to the current *desired heading* and absence of obstacles on the right side of the robot, decides to turn right. However, a small obstacle hits the back left side of the robot as soon as it turns. To avoid that situation, every time an obstacle is detected in that area, a constraint $cons(\omega^+, false, 500\,\text{ms})$ is added.

Defining constraints to other similar situations endows the controller with the ability to negotiate cluttered environments with non-circular robots, without explicitly modelling them. A careful choice of sensors localisation may discard the need of a full-sonar-ring set for this reflex.

Linear Velocity Constraint Reflex. The maximum linear velocity allowed for each sector j, considering a linear trajectory and uniformly accelerated movement, is $v_{allowed}(j) = \sqrt{2 \cdot a_{max} \cdot \max(0, r_j - d_{safety})}$, where a_{max} is the maximum deceleration capability of the robot, r_j is the minimum linear distance free of obstacles in the respective sector, d_{safety} is the minimum distance the robot is allowed to be from an obstacle, and max guarantees that $r_j - d_{safety}$ is never negative. Thus, the maximum velocity allowed is such that guarantees the robot does not hit any obstacle when decelerating as much as it can. This acceleration can be set for other purposes in addition to dynamical constraints; for instance, to guarantee that robot's payload does not suffer accelerations and vibrations greater than certain values. Then, a constraint $cons(j, v_{max}, v_{min}, 100\,\text{ms})$ is added per each sector, where v_{min} is the minimum velocity of all $v_{allowed}$ calculated in the sectors between the *main axis of motion* and j.

Since this reflex is in the second pool, it can measure the free distance to obstacles by perceiving the d_{max} action feature of the corresponding sector (i.e. to make $r_j = d_{max_j}$), which has been set by reflexes of the first pool, and already considers the c-space. Consequently, this reflex takes into account information set by all previous reflexes. The constraint validity has been set empirically.

Dynamic Constraints Reflex. Considering the robot's dynamical constraints, this reflex disables those sectors that would require unfeasible actions. In particular, a constraint $cons(j_{dyn}, enable, false, 1\,iteration)$ is added per each sector j_{dyn}; j_{dyn} is a sector whose v_{max} is smaller than the robot's minimum velocity achievable until the next iteration (i.e. taking into consideration a_{max}).

3.3 Action Selection Mechanism

The implementation of the action selection mechanism is based on the environmental feature *gap*. It represents a discontinuity greater than the width, w, of the robot in the d_{max} feature between two adjacent sectors. From the two sectors involved in the discontinuity, the one with greater d_{max} is considered to be a *corridor*. Since a *corridor* is defined in the c-space (by means of d_{max}), the robot is kept safe of collisions as it moves in it (see figure 2.b). Every sector in which the d_{max} feature is greater or equal to m (a value provided in the excitatory signal) is also considered to be a *corridor*. Reducing m allows the robot to move towards obstacles and consequently approaching a goal set between itself and the obstacle. Finally, $d_{max_i} = \min(m, d_{max_i})$.

The best action of the current iteration n is composed of a *selected corridor* and a *selected linear velocity*. If the maximum linear velocity allowed in the *selected corridor* is smaller or equal than the desired linear velocity, provided in the excitatory signal, then it is selected; otherwise, the desired linear velocity is the one selected. After discarding all *corridors* that have been either inhibited or rejected by the *motor actions producer* (see below), the *selected corridor*, s_c, is chosen by maximising an objective function:

$$s_c[n] = \max_l (\lambda_1 \cdot r_d(corridor_l) + \lambda_2[n] \cdot dist_\angle(corridor_l, s_c[n-1]))$$

where, the first term (r_d) provides goal-oriented behaviour, the second term ($dist_\angle$) allows to *commit* to the previously selected *corridor* in order to reduce oscillatory behaviour (similar to the definition provided in [11]), and weights λ_1 and $\lambda_2[n]$ enable a proper integration of both components, all normalised between $[0, 1]$.

$r_d(corridor_l)$ refers to the d_{max} value of *corridor_l* projected on the desired direction axis (see figure 2.b). $dist_\angle$ grows with the angular distance between $geo_\angle(corridor_l)$ and $geo_{\angle [n-1]}(s_c[n-1])$, where $geo_\angle(\cdot)$ transforms the bisector angle of a given sector to geo-referenced coordinates, whereas $geo_{\angle [n-1]}$ does the same for iteration $n-1$. This mechanism is simple to tune due to the little number of parameters, which only exist to reduce possible oscillations.

In order to remove heading static errors, λ_2 is made dynamic. Briefly, if the robot's heading is nearby the desired heading, and the selected action does not change significantly between consecutive iterations (i.e. $\{(heading\,error < \frac{\pi}{8}) \wedge (\angle(geo_\angle(s_c[n]), geo_{\angle [n-1]}(s_c[n-1])) < \phi)\}$, where $\angle$ returns the angular distance between two given angles), then λ_2 is decreased at rate τ_{λ_2}; otherwise, λ_2 is set to its maximum value, α. As a result, in the presence of heading static error the $dist_\angle$ component is reduced and the robot becomes more goal-oriented. If instead a sudden change of heading is required (e.g. due to the presence of an obstacle) the former weights trade-off is restored.

If no action is possible, then the *action selection* mechanism switches the *main axis of motion* to other possible value and tries again. Since the robot is differential, it is only reasonable to assume that the *main axis of motion* is either 0 or π; i.e., that the robot will either try to move forward or backwards, respectively. This is in fact what happens in the *Touch Reflex*, where no motion is possible if moving forward, which forces to try moving backwards.

As aforementioned, the robot's locomotion method is differential, i.e. an action is composed of a *linear velocity* and an *angular velocity*; so, it is non-holonomic. The linear velocity is set by the *action selection* mechanism as previously described, and the angular velocity is proportional to the angle between the *selected corridor* and the robot's front. This process is implemented within the *motor action producer*, which also confirms the feasibility of an action, taking into consideration the differential locomotion method.

4   Experimental Results

The experiments herein presented were carried out in the Player/Stage simulator [5][1]. Acceleration ramps have been implemented between the simulator and the control system, to emulate the robot's dynamical constraints (i.e. a_{max}).

Figure 3 illustrates two experiments of the SK instance presented in the previous section. In both experiments, the SK is modulated to move towards north (top of the figure) at a speed of $2\,ms^{-1}$. λ_1, α, a_{max}, m, d_{safety}, and τ_{λ_2} have been set to 1.0, 0.75, $0.5\,ms^{-2}$, 5 m, 0.5 m, and 1 s respectively. The

---

[1] http://playerstage.sourceforge.net/

space-variant action feature sub-space is split into 128 sectors. The *gap* feature allows detection of the dead-end in run 1, which is not present in the second run, allowing the robot to follow the shorter path. In run 1 the touch reflex is triggered forcing the robot to move backwards (situation A). Notice that, the robot moves backwards while rotating towards the best direction (i.e. left), which demonstrates the cooperative nature of the method. In the beginning of the second run, the robot can not move towards north due to the presence of an obstacle, which triggers the shape reflex. In some situations, such as situations B and C, the *concave* nature of the environment is responsible for the emergence of *fake gaps*. In situation B, the robot temporarily turns right towards the *corridor* containing the *fake gap*, whereas in situation C, the robot is insensitive to the *fake gap* due to the effect of the myopic local environment representation, which allows the robot passing by the situation before it realises the existence of the *fake gap*.

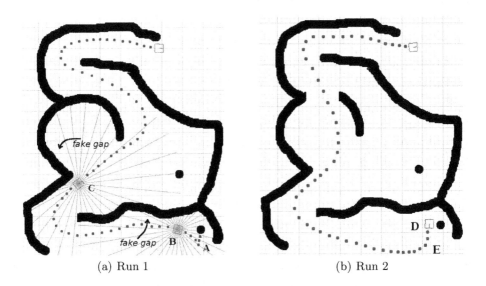

(a) Run 1   (b) Run 2

Fig. 3. Set of experiments using Player/Stage simulator

5   Discussion

Although the SK instance herein presented does not explicitly accommodate arc trajectories, it guarantees collision free navigation. Nevertheless, the main advantage of this approach is its simplicity as it discards complex geometric reasoning while keeping robust navigation; thus, the requirements for disposable robots have been attained. In fact, it is questionable the need of handling, in a refined way, kinematics and dynamical constraints for simple and small robots. Still, if arc trajectories have to be considered in a more sophisticated way, then a w_{min} action feature could be added. Such feature would be set to the widest arc trajectory, represented by the tuple (v_{max}, w_{min}), that would lead the robot to the sector in question without crossing by any obstacle. Then, angular velocity dynamical constraints could be considered in the same way linear velocities already are. In the limit of the aforementioned extension, only one arc would have to be computed by *corridor*, whereas in the *Dynamic Window Approach* [4] and *Curvature Velocity Method* [9] more than a single arc has to be considered per *obstacle*. Hence, even with this improvement, the SK architecture would remain simpler. In addition, the SK instance herein proposed does not suffer from local minima as *Potential Fields* based methods (e.g. [1]) in general do, and it deals with dynamical constraints in opposition to the *Nearness Diagram* method [7].

Since r_d already embodies information on the distance to obstacles, heading error, and speed, the objective function is simpler and more predictable than the ones used in the *Dynamic Window Approach, VFH+* [11], and *Curvature Velocity Method*, where all those features have to be considered explicitly.

Previous work used the *gap* feature, but none in the same way as introduced in this work. In the *Gap Navigation Trees* [10], the *gap* environmental feature is used as a mean of producing a topological map; however, a reactive obstacle avoidance method is still required. The SK architecture merges, to some extent, optimised navigation and reactive obstacle avoidance instead. The concept of *gap* was also used in the *Nearness Diagram* method, but not as a direct target of motion; instead, it is exploited differently in five separable situations, which requires additional computational load.

6   Conclusions

First experimental results in simulation suggest that the SK architecture, via cooperation by negation (i.e. constraints) and modulatory signalling, is a good option for safe navigation, while locally optimising robot's trajectory; in other words, it merges the benefits of both cooperative and competitive-based Behaviour-Based architectures. The *gap* feature is a promising approach to optimise trajectories and avoid dead ends based on immediate ranging data; moreover, it allows the application of a simpler objective function than those found in previous work. Dynamical constraints are also considered in a simplistic but robust fashion. Finally, the resulting behaviour is predictable, local-minima and oscillations free, and it does not require upper-layers supervision, just modulation. The low-computational load that this method requires is of special interest for disposable robots, which can only afford simple computational units, such as micro-controllers. In fact, it is the trade-off between performance and low computational load that makes this approach original and interesting.

Acknowledgements

The authors wish to thank Pedro Mariano and Ana Belchior by their valuable comments.

References

1. Arkin, R.C.: Motor schema-based mobile robot navigation. International Journal of Robotics Research **8**(4) (1989) 92–112
2. Brooks, R.: A robust layered control system for a mobile robot. IEEE Journal of Robotics and Automation **2**(1) (1986) 14–23
3. Correia, L., Garção, A. S.: Behavior Based Architecture with Distributed Selection. In NATO Advanced Study Institute – The Biology and Technology of Intelligent Autonomous Systems **144** (1995) 377–389
4. Fox, D., Burgard, W., Thrun, S.: The dynamic window approach to collision avoidance. IEEE Robotics & Automation Magazine **4**(1) (1997) 23–33
5. Girkey, B.P., Vaughan, R.T., Howard, A.: The Player/Stage Project: tools for multi-robot and distributed sensor systems. In Proceedings of the International Conference on Advanced Robotics (ICAR) (July 2003)
6. Maes, P.: How to do the right thing. Connection Science Journal **1**(3) (1989) (291–323)
7. Minguez, J., Montano, L.: Nearness diagram navigation (ND): collision avoidance in troublesome scenarios. IEEE Transactions on Robotics and Automation (2004) **20**(1) (2004) 45–59
8. Rosenblatt, J.K.: DAMN: a distributed architecture for mobile navigation. In Proceedings of the AAAI Spring Symp. on Lessons Learned from Implemented Software Architectures for Physical Agents (1995)
9. Simmons, R.: The curvature velocity method for local obstacle avoidance. In Proceedings of the IEEE International Conference on Robotics and Automation (1996)
10. Tovar, B., Guilamo, L., LaValle, S.M.: Gap navigation trees: a minimal representation for visibility-based tasks. In Proceedings of the Workshop on Algorithmic Foundations of Robotics (2004) 11–26
11. Ulrich, I., Borenstein, J.: VFH+: reliable obstacle avoidance for fast mobile robots. In Proceedings of the International Conference on Robotics & Automation (1998)

Heuristic Algorithm for Robot Path Planning Based on a Growing Elastic Net*

José Alí Moreno[1] and Miguel Castro[2]

[1] Universidad Central de Venezuela, Laboratorio de Computación Emergente,
Facultades de Ciencias e Ingeniería
`jose@neurona.ciens.ucv.ve`
[2] Universidad Simón Bolívar, Grupo de Inteligencia Artificial,
Departamento de Computación y T.I.
`mcastro@gia.usb.ve`

Abstract. A simple effective method for path planning based on a growing self-organizing elastic neural network, enhanced with a heuristic for the exploration of local directions is presented. The general problem is to find a collision-free path for moving objects among a set of obstacles. A path is represented by an interconnected set of processing units in the elastic self organizing network. The algorithm is initiated with a straight path defined by a small number of processing units between the start and goal positions. The two units at the extremes of the network are static and are located at the start and goal positions, the remaining units are adaptive. Using a local sampling strategy of the points around each processing unit, a Kohonen type learning and a simple processing units growing rule the initial straight path evolves into a collision free path. The proposed algorithm was experimentally tested for 2 DOF and 3 DOF robots on a workspace cluttered with random and non random distributed obstacles. It is shown that with very little computational effort a satisfactory free collision path is calculated.

1 Introduction

For several decades motion planning has been a very fertile field of research. Work in this area has not only impacted robotics, but also other non-robotics fields like graphics animation, surgical planning or computational biology, see [11] for a review. In any case, research in robot motion planning remains as one of the important fields of study in the task of building autonomous or semi-autonomous robot systems. In the last decade, path planning has received considerable attention from the robotic community since this fundamental operation poses the solution of a variety of challenging theoretical and practical problems. In consequence a broad class of algorithms for path planning designed over different technologies and general approaches have resulted. In general the path planning

---

* This research was supported by the Fondo Nacional de Ciencia, Tecnologia e Innovacion (Fonacit) under project S1-2001000814.

C. Bento, A. Cardoso, and G. Dias (Eds.): EPIA 2005, LNAI 3808, pp. 447–454, 2005.

problem is PSPACE-hard and all known complete planning algorithms take exponential time in the number of degrees of freedom of the robot. That is, the curse of these algorithms is their high complexity which hinders useful real time applications. In the present work an algorithm that deals with this complexity issue in a very simple way is presented.

The path planning problem involves searching the system configuration space for a collision-free path that connects a given start and goal configurations, while satisfying constraints imposed by a complicated obstacle distribution. This definition of the problem simplifies some of the aspects of robot motion planning. The dynamic properties of the robot are ignored and the problem is transformed to a purely geometrical path planning problem. In this way we concentrate on the most basic version of the path planning problem, that of moving a robot in a static environment. Efficient solutions of that simplified problem contribute to improvements in the solution of problems with additional constraints. According to [10] there are three general approaches to path planning: potential field, road map and cell decomposition. In the randomized potential field methods [5] the robot is represented as a particle moving under the influence of an artificial potential field produced by the sum of a repulsive potential, generated by the obstacles, and an attractive potential, generated by the goal configuration. The path is obtained by a descent along the negative gradient of the total potential. The algorithms based on roadmaps [1][9] construct a network of one-dimensional curves, called the roadmap, lying in the free space of the workspace. The final path result from the concatenation of a subpath connecting the initial configuration to the roadmap, a subpath belonging to the roadmap and a subpath from the roadmap to the goal configuration. The approach based on cell decomposition consists on a partition of the free space into a set of exact cells, [4], or approximate cells [2]. The path is a sequence of cells with the following properties: (1) The first cells contains the initial configuration. (2) The final cell contains the goal positions. (3) Neighbouring cells in the sequence are cells in free space with a common boundary. In most current robot systems developed to date the motion planning is, at its lowest level, based on a heuristic or potential field method and many extend this upward to the level of path navigation [3].

In this contribution we present a path planning algorithm based on an enhanced elastic net algorithm [6] with a growing structure [7]. The network consists of a line of processing units (PUs) with an attractive interaction between the PUs [8] over which a unsupervised learning scheme is applied. A path is represented by a interconnected set of line segments, the successive connectivities of the processing units in the elastic network. Initially the network contains a small number of PUs, as time advances the PUs are updated in response to stimuli from randomly selected points in the configuration space and successively new PUs are inserted. The stimuli to the PUs are attractive if the stimulating point belongs to free space otherwise they are repulsive. This adaptation process is enhanced with a local heuristic that encourage the PUs to move to free space. The self organizing process induces a local topologically ordered network in free space representing a collision free path.

The organization of the paper is as follows: In the next section a brief introduction to the configuration space formalism is presented. In section three the elastic net algorithm, the sampling scheme for the configuration space, the insertion and adaptation dynamics and the algorithm initialization and parametrization are described. In the fourth section some experimental results are presented.

2   The Configuration Space

The robot moves in an Euclidean space called the workspace containing a finite number of obstacles 0_i. For a robot with size and shape, its location in the Cartesian worspace $W = \mathbb{R}^N$, ($N = 2$ or 3) can be uniquely determined by the position vector $\mathbf{r}$ of its centroid and the orientation (polar) angles θ, ϕ with respect to fixed axis in W. Thus, the state of the robot in W, also called robot configuration, is uniquely defined by the point $(\mathbf{r}, \theta, \phi)$. The configuration space C is defined as the space of all possible configurations of the robot in workspace. Robot path planning can generally be considered a search in configuration space [10,12]. The configuration space is defined as $C = C_{free} \cup C_{forb}$ where C_{forb} is that part of space covered by the obstacles. Thus an acceptable path of the robot must be composed of line segments, connecting the start and goal configurations, completely contained in C_{free}.

3   The Algorithm

The proposed algorithm consists of a growing linear elastic net with an adaptation and growing dynamics induced by stimuli coming from randomly selected points in configuration space. The algorithm is initiated with a straight path defined by a network composed of a small number N_{init} of PUs uniformly spaced between the start and goal positions. The two units at the extremes of the network are static and are located at the start and goal positions, the remaining units are adaptive. The algorithm finds the winning PU (best matching unit BMU) with weight vector nearest to the current stimulating point $\mathbf{x} \in C$. The weights of the BMU and those of its direct neighbours are updated. The weight update moves the positions of the BMU and of its neighbouring PUs a fraction in or against the direction of the stimulating point. Every fixed number of iterations the algorithm finds the largest distance between two consecutive PUs and inserts a new PU in the midpoint of the segment. This growing dynamics is iterated until the number of PUs reaches a maximum value N_{max} and the algorithm completes a maximum number t_{max} of iterations.

3.1   Sampling Strategy

A smooth adaptation of the network during the learning phase can only be obtained if the stimulating points belong to a certain neighbourhood of the PUs. This is achieved sampling the points in configuration space in a region within a radius $r(t)$ around each PU. This radius $r(t)$ is initially set to a high value in order to include points in a large extension of the workspace and it is decreased in time to accentuate the locality of the stimuli. The variation of the sampling radius goes according to:

$$r(t) = r_i(r_f/r_i)^{t/t_{max}} \tag{1}$$

with r_i the initial radius and r_f its final value. The generation of a random stimuli proceeds in two steps: First a PU is selected at random from the elastic net, and second a point $\mathbf{x}$ is randomly chosen within a radius $r(t)$ of the PU.

In this strategy points belonging to C_{free} or to C_{forb} can equally be sampled. The stimuli belonging to C_{free} are assumed to be attractive whereas those from points in C_{forb} are considered repulsive. This is taken into account by defining the following attraction-repulsion function:

$$F(\mathbf{x}) = \begin{cases} +1 \ if \ \mathbf{x} \in C_{free} \\ -1 \ if \ \mathbf{x} \in C_{forb} \end{cases} \tag{2}$$

3.2   Adaptation and PU Insertion Dynamics

The update of the PU weights proceed in a way similar to that proposed by Durbin and Willshaw [6]. Given an stimuli $\mathbf{x}$ the BMU, say PU_j, and its two neighbouring PUs are selected for adaptation. The appropriate update to be applied depends on the values of $F(\mathbf{w}_j)$ and $F(\mathbf{x})$. The reason is that with the available local information the update must be in the sense of encouriging the PUs to move to C_{free}. Updates in the wrong direction could lead to dead-lock situations. In the following the PUs adaptation relations for the four possibilities of the $F(\mathbf{w}_j)$ and $F(\mathbf{x})$ values are presented.

1. $F(\mathbf{w}_j) = 1$, $F(\mathbf{x}) = \pm 1$ or $F(\mathbf{w}_j) = -1$, $F(\mathbf{x}) = 1$: In these common cases

$$\Delta\mathbf{w}_j = \eta(\mathbf{x} - \mathbf{w}_j)F(\mathbf{x}) + \beta(\mathbf{w}_{j+1} - 2\mathbf{w}_j + \mathbf{w}_{j-1}) \tag{3}$$

   The first term corresponds to a Kohonen like adaptation dynamics where the stimulating point $\mathbf{x}$ attracts or repels the weight vector according to the value of function $F(\mathbf{x})$ [7]. The second term $\beta(\mathbf{w}_{j+1} - 2\mathbf{w}_j + \mathbf{w}_{j-1})$ only considers the mutual attraction between nearest neighbour PUs in order to maintain them equidistant [6].

2. $F(\mathbf{x}) = F(\mathbf{w}_j) = -1$: In this case a random update of the PU_j corresponding to a perturbation in the perpendicular direction of $(\mathbf{w}_{j+1} - \mathbf{w}_{j-1})$ is proposed:

$$\Delta\mathbf{w}_j = \alpha\frac{(\mathbf{w}_{j+1} - \mathbf{w}_{j-1})_\perp}{|\mathbf{w}_{j+1} - \mathbf{w}_{j-1}|} \tag{4}$$

   where α is a randomly selected value between $[-\beta, \beta]$. The intention of this stochastic type of weight update is to drive $\mathbf{w}_j$ into a region belonging to any of the three above cases.

3. In all cases the weight vectors of the BMU nearest neighbours are updated according to:

$$\varDelta \mathbf{w}_{j\pm1} = \eta_{neighb}(\mathbf{x} - \mathbf{w}_{j\pm1}) \tag{5}$$

The insertion of new PUs is carried out every fixed number of iterations, given by the Growing Rate Parameter λ. The mechanism is the following: the two consecutive PUs with greater weight vector difference ($\mathbf{w}_{k+1} - \mathbf{w}_k$) are found, they are used to define a new PU with weight vector

$$\mathbf{w}_{new} = (\mathbf{w}_{k+1} + \mathbf{w}_k)/2 \tag{6}$$

This process is repeated until a maximum number of PUs N_{max} is reached.

The described PU adaptation and insertion dynamics is iterated until a maximum number of repetitions is achieved. The resulting organization of the linear network of PUs is such that all the weight vectors are driven by the adaptation dynamics to C_{free} defining a collision free path.

3.3   Initialization and Parametrization of the Algorithm

The network is initialized as a line conecting initial $\mathbf{q}_{init}$ and goal $\mathbf{q}_{goal}$ points in configuration space. It is composed of N_{init} PUs (typically 10) with uniformly distributed weights. The PUs at the extremes of the net are not adaptive and have weights set to $\mathbf{w_1} = \mathbf{q}_{init}$ and $\mathbf{w_{N_{init}}} = \mathbf{q}_{goal}$.

In the algorithm only a small number of parameters are involved: Growing_Rate_Parameter λ, number of PUs to be grown N_{max}, learning rate of the BMU η, the learning rate of the neighbours η_{neighb} and the elastic force constant β. In addition two parameters initial and final radius r_i and r_f are needed for the sampling strategy in configuration space. The adequate values for these parameters can be found after a small round of trial and error experimentation. It is experimentally found that of the seven parameters only three of them (η, β and r_i) are important in overall performance and must be more or less carefully fine tuned. The values used in all the experiments were:

- Growing_Rate_Parameter between 200 and 1000, we used 400 for all experiments.
- Learning rate of the BMU $\eta = 0.05$.
- Learning rate of the neighboring PUs $\eta_{neighb} = 0.01$.
- Elastic force constant $\beta = 0.0025$.
- The number of PUs to be grown $N_{max} = 30$.
- Initial and final sampling radius $r_i = 200$ $r_f = 70$.

4   Experiments

For experimentation purposes the proposed algorithm has been implemented in C++ on a 2.4 GHz Pentium IV based machine. In order to evaluate the algorithm's path generation capability a number of simulations, for 2 and 3 DOF

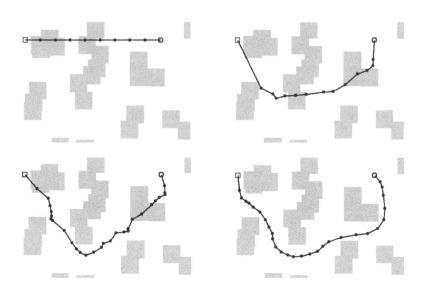

Fig. 1. Four instances of the path planning algorithm for a point robot 2 DOF. (Top Left) $PUs = 10$ at $t = 0$. (Top Right) $PUs = 15$ at $t = 4000$. (Bottom Left) $PUs = 30$ at $t = 16000$. (Bottom Right) $PUs = 30$ at $t = 40000$.

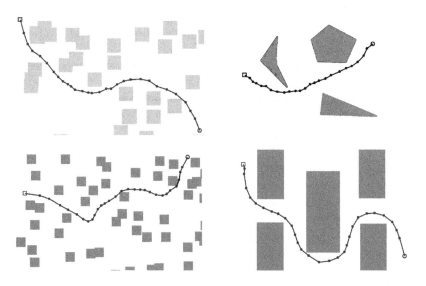

Fig. 2. Some resulting paths for a 2 DOF robot on workspaces with different obstacle distributions

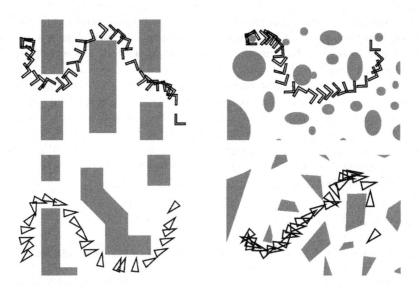

Fig. 3. Some examples of resulting paths for a L and a triangular shaped free-flying robot

robots on several 2D workspaces with distinct obstacle distributions, have been conducted. The images used to depict the 2D workspace had a size of 800x500 pixels and the rotation angle in $[0, 2\pi]$ for the 3 DOF robots was discretized in steps of one degree. In each iteration of the algorithm one point of C is sampled, that is one pixel of the workspace image and one rotation angle. Since the maximum number of iterations t_{max} was 40000 the path generation requires in general the sampling of less than 10 percent of configuration space.

In Figure 1, different instances of the path generation process for a 2 DOF point robot are depicted. It can be noted that in a small number of iterations the adaptation dynamics drives the PUs to C_{free}. In the last stages the elastic net attains a self organized configuration that represents a reasonable good collision free path. The execution time for the 40000 iterations was of 360 msec. Figure 2, depicts the resulting collision free paths for a point robot on several 2D workspaces cluttered with obstacles. It can be seen that the algorithm produces, in all cases, reasonable good path solutions. The execution times for these experiments are of the order the 300 msec. Finally Figure 3, shows the path planning results for an L shaped and a triangular 3 DOF robots on several 2D workspaces. As before in all cases the algorithm generates good collision free paths in execution times of the order of the 600 msec.

5   Conclusion

A heuristic adaptive approach for solving the robot path planning problem that yields very efficient experimental performance on simulated scenarios is proposed. The algorithm, based on the self organizing procedure of elastic nets, is computationally very simple and efficient with very short execution times. It dos not requiere the aplication of complex procedures like special search methods, the optimization of global functions or any tessalation of the workspace. The adaptation dynamic of the path planner is driven by a local sampling strategy that uses only a small portion of configuration space ($\leq 10\%$). The algorithm was experimentally tested for a nonholonomic 2 DOF robot and free flying L and triangular shaped 3 DOF robots on different random generated workspace configurations. In all cases the observed performances were very good. The algorithm can be easily extended to more complicated situations like robots with higher degrees of freedom or articulated robotic arms in 3 dimensional workspaces. These are themes for future work.

References

1. N. Amato and Y. Wu: A Randomized Roadmap for Path Manipulation Planning. IEEE, International Conference on Robotics and Automation. (1996) 113-120
2. M. Bracho and J.A. Moreno: Heuristic Algorithm for Robot Path Planning based on Real Space Renormalization. Lecture Notes in Artificial Intelligence 1952. Springer, Berlin (2000) 379-388
3. J. Bruce and M. Veloso: Real-time randomized path planning for robot navigation. Proceedings of the 2002 IEEE/RSJ International Conference on Intelligent Robots and Systems (IROS '02). (2002)
4. C. Behring, M. Bracho, M. Castro and J.A. Moreno: An Algorithm for Robot Path Planning with Cellular Automata. Theoretical and Practical Issues on Cellular Automata. Springer, Berlin (2000) 11-19
5. S. Caselli, M. Reggiani and R. Rocchi: Heuristic methods for randomized path planning in potential fields. IEEE International Symposium on Computational Intelligence in Robotics and Automation. (2001) 426 - 431
6. R. Durbin and D. Willshaw: An analogue approach to the travelling salesman problem using an elastic net method. Nature, Vol. 326. (1987) 689-691
7. B. Fritzke: Wachsende zellstrukturen - Ein selbstorganisierendes neuronales netzwerk. Arbeits bericht des IMMD Universitaet Erlangen - Nuernberg. (1992)
8. J. Hertz, A. Krogh and R.G.Palmer: Introduction to the theory of neural computation. Addison-Wesley, Redwood City, CA (1991)
9. L.E. Kavraki and J.C. Latombe: Randomized Preprocessing of Configurations Space for Path Planning. IEEE, International Conference on Robotics and Automation. (1994) 2138-2139
10. J.C. Latombe: Robot Motion Planning. Kluwer Academic Publisher, Boston, MA. (1991)
11. J.C. Latombe: Motion Planning: A Journey of Robots, Molecules, Digital Actors and Other Artifacts. Journal of Robotics Research, Especial Issue on Robotics at the Millenium - Part I, Vol. 18. (1999) 1119-1128
12. Lozano Pérez: Spatial planning: A Configuration Space Approach. IEEE Transactions on Computers. Vol. C-32(2). (1983) 108-120

Robust Artificial Landmark Recognition Using Polar Histograms

Pablo Suau

Departamento de Ciencia de la Computación e Inteligencia Artificial,
Universidad de Alicante, Ap. de correos 99, 03080 Alicante, Spain
pablo@dccia.ua.es

Abstract. New results on our artificial landmark recognition approach
are presented, as well as new experiments in order to demonstrate the
robustness of our method. The objective of our work is the localization
and recognition of artificial landmarks to help in the navigation of a mobile robot. Recognition is based on interpretation of histograms obtained
from polar coordinates of the landmark symbol. Experiments prove that
our approach is fast and robust even if the database has an high number
of landmarks to compare with.

1 Introduction

Robot navigation is a research field where a great variety of different mechanisms are being studied in order to achieve an interesting goal: having a physical
autonomous agent capable of navigating without any human interaction, just interpreting the surrounding environment. Information exchange with this environment leans on several types of sensors, like sonar, laser range sensors, and so on.

Vision based navigation systems can achieve a high degree of flexibility, allowing the robot to take complex decisions. Some of these systems are based on
landmark recognition; however, papers explaining this kind of systems (like, for
example, [1]) focus more on the system description or on the use of environmental characteristics as landmarks (natural landmarks) rather than explaining the
recognition process. Our research deals with the landmark recognition process
from another point of view. We present our landmark localization and recognition approach itself, without considering a concrete robot system where this
process could be included, so it could be included in other kind of systems.

The use of landmarks with roadsign symbols has been chosen so in a future
this method could be applied to the problem of the recognition of this kind of
signals. It is possible to find several papers talking about the roadsign recognition
problem ([2],[3],[4]), but they explain more complex techniques that the one we
present here. The objective has been to find an efficient and robust recognition
method. Although the papers about roadsign detection mentioned before show
us some ways of solving this problem, our method is simpler and give us better
results.

This paper is divided in the following sections: in section 2 we define polar
histograms, in section 3 we explain how to compare different polar histograms,

C. Bento, A. Cardoso, and G. Dias (Eds.): EPIA 2005, LNAI 3808, pp. 455–461, 2005.

in section 4 the complete approach to localize and recognize artificial landmarks is shown, and finally, in section 5, some experimental results are shown.

2   Polar Histograms

Polar histograms are introduced as a way of comparing symbols, without being affected by little changes in shape, orientation and displacement (scale variations are solved in the localization part of our system, which is explained above). These polar histograms are created from polar coordinates of symbols. Some works have proven that using polar coordinates allows an efficient and low computational cost two dimensional irregular shape comparison, invariant to displacement and rotation (on the plane of the image, no 3D rotations) [5].

The first step to build a polar histogram from a symbol is to have a binary image containing that symbol. This image is represented by means of cartesian coordinates, and it must be transformed into a polar coordinates image, using the gravitational center of the symbol as pole and a polar axis which origin is this pole (some examples are shown in Figure 1). Using the equations (1) and (2) we can know which cartesian pair (x, y) corresponds to each polar pair (ρ, θ). This translation can be done in two ways: calculating the polar coordinates for each cartesian pair in the original image, or calculating the cartesian coordinates corresponding to each polar pair in the destination image. This second method is more efficient and faster, avoiding gaps to be present in the resulting polar image.

$$x = \rho \cdot cos(\theta) \tag{1}$$
$$y = \rho \cdot sin(\theta) \tag{2}$$

Finally, from the polar image, we can obtain a histogram that represents the original symbol. In the polar image, the distance ρ increases with each column; so, all the pixels in the same column are at the same distance from the symbol's gravitational center in the original image. If we add all the pixels with value 1 in each column in the polar image, we generate a histogram that indicates us for all the distances from the gravitational center of the symbol, how many pixels

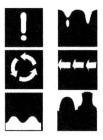

Fig. 1. Some examples of symbols represented in cartesian coordinates (left) and the same symbols represented in polar coordinates (right), using the gravitational center as a pole

have value 1 (an example is shown in figure 2). This histogram is rotation invariant (because we use polar coordinates and the camera is always straight) and displacement invariant (because we use the gravitational center of the symbol as polar center). We call this structure *polar histogram*.

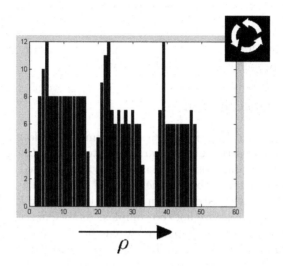

Fig. 2. An example of polar histogram created from a landmark symbol

We will use polar histograms to recognize symbols extracted from a landmark localized in an image, comparing its polar histograms with polar histograms created from symbols stored in a database.

3   Comparing Polar Histograms

If we have a symbol database, and we have created a polar histogram for each of those symbols, the recognition task is as easy as to build a polar histogram for the symbol we want to recognize and then try to find the one in the database whose polar histogram is more similar. In order to test this similarity, several histogram comparison methods, like Kolmogorov-Smirnov test or Chi-Square Distance could be used.

As can be seen in the experimental results section, we have test some different histogram comparison methods, like L1 norm, L2 norm ([6]), Prefix Sum ([7]) and Chi-Square distance (Kolmogorov-Smirnov was not suitable to our problem). We had better results with Chi-Square Distance, so this is the distance we use in our system in order to compare polar histograms.

The Chi-Square distance, applied to two histograms, can give us a weighted average of the difference between all the positions of these histograms, so it tells us which of the histograms in the database is more similar to the histogram of the symbol we want to recognize. We can calculate this distance χ^2 between two histograms i and j using equations (3) and (4).

$$\chi_{ij}^2 = \sum_k^n \frac{(H_i(k) - \hat{H}(k))^2}{\hat{H}(k)} \tag{3}$$

$$\hat{H}(k) = \frac{H_i(k) + H_j(k)}{2} \tag{4}$$

Although the Chi-Square disttribution is not symmetric, the Chi-Square distance has this property, so it can fit our purposes.

4   System Description

The system aim is to locate the nearest landmark inside a digital image containing one or more artificial landmarks, and to extract the symbol inside it to recognize it, after a comparison with a set of symbols stored in a database. Such a digital image is obtained by a camera placed on a mobile robot.

Since this work is focused more on recognition than on localization or image segmentation, landmarks are not too complex. As we can see in examples in Figure 3, a landmark is square shaped, with blue border and a black symbol inside the border. Symbols inside the landmarks have been taken from real roadsigns.

Fig. 3. Landmark examples

Our approach for landmark localization and recognition was based on [2], with some changes. Figure 4 shows the complete process from the moment the image is obtained from the camera on the robot to the moment the symbol inside the landmark is recognized. This process can be summarized with the following steps:

- Colour segmentation: After transforming the input image to a HSV color model, a color quantization is applied to it, reducing it to eight basic colours ([2]). A binary image is created containing the pixels of the original image which have the same colour than the landmark borders (one of these eight basic colours).
- Landmark localization: from the binary image corresponding to the landmark borders, we try to localize the nearest one, by means of horizontal and vertical projections. We don't use stereo vision (we have only a camera on top of the robot) so we don't have depth information. Therefore we consider that the nearest landmark is the biggest one, the landmark with the greatest number of pixels. The localization is explained in [2], but instead of creating projections as the total sum of blue pixels in each row and column, we

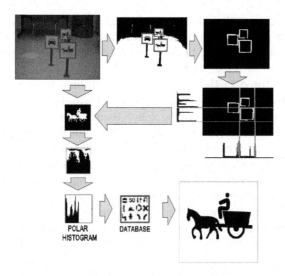

Fig. 4. The complete localization and recognition process

have verified that using the maximum sum of consecutive blue pixels give us better results in the case we have several landmarks very close each other.

- Landmark's symbol extraction: once the nearest landmark has been detected, and after checking it is approximately square-shaped, we apply the k-means algorithm only to the part of the original image where the nearest landmark is placed, splitting pixels in two groups: pixels having a high V value and pixels having a low V value. As a consequence, we create a binary image with the same size than the images stored in the database, containing only one symbol.
- Recognition: a polar histogram is created from the extracted symbol, and it is compared with the histograms created from symbols stored at the database. At the end, recognized landmark is shown on screen.

At the landmark's symbol extraction step there is an interesting issue we must discuss. If we follow [2], we should use the black colour plane to recognize the symbol inside the nearest landmark. However, using this method has proven to be not very robust with varying light conditions. That's why we use k-means algorithm.

5   Experimental Results

Finally we show some experimental results. The images caught by the camera on the robot had a size of 320x240 pixels, and the images stored in the landmark database had a size of 96x96 pixels (so, the nearest landmark extracted from the image would be scaled to a size of 96x96). Not all the landmarks inside the images caught by the robot had an orthofrontal position, so these results include

the recognition of several slightly out of plane rotated landmarks. However, if
the nearest landmark is too rotated from robot point of view, we can consider
that landmark not interesting, because the robot must only interpret landmarks
in front of it.

The symbols stored in the database were obtained from SEÑALECTICA[1],
a vectorial image repository of real roadsigns. A group of test sets with several
images caught by the camera on the robot (containing from 89 to 380 images)
were create to estimate the recognition error rate. The first one had 10 landmarks
stored in the database, the second one 20 landmarks, the third one 30 landmarks,
and so on. The last one had 100 landmarks. All the landmarks from the database
appeared in at least 3 images in the corresponding test set. In these images
appeared from 1 to 3 landmarks, at different distances.

Localization error rate was allways between 1-3%. To calculate recognition
error rates we ignore the images were nearest landmark is not localized correctly.

First we could see the effect of changing the size of the polar images from
where we calculate the polar histograms. Figure 5(a) shows the recognition error
rate when we have 100 landmarks in the database for different polar image
resolutions (and, in consequence, different number of polar histogram elements).
As we can see, with a low number of polar histogram elements there is not enough
information in order to achieve an adequate recognition. From the moment we
use 100 elements, error rate converges, so we use histograms with 100 elements
in the rest of experiments.

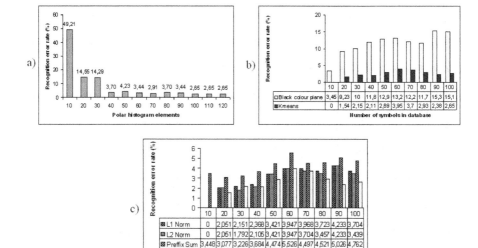

Fig. 5. Experimental results

Figure 5(b) shows that is better to use k-means algorithm to extract the symbol inside the nearest landmark instead of using black colour plane, like in [2]. The recognition error rate is calculated for each of the test cases described before.

Finally, Figure 5(c) shows the recognition error rate of our approach for each of the test cases, using different distance metrics for comparing polar histograms.

As we can see, the mixture of polar histograms for image characterization and Chi-Square distance for image recognition results in a low recognition error rate. Our approach is very fast and has a recognition error low enough to allow a correct robot navigation guided by artificial landmarks.

6   Conclusions and Future Work

New results for our fast and robust method to recognize symbols inside artificial landmarks to help in robot navigation have been presented. The method is based on the comparison of polar histograms, using the Chi-Square distance. An high number of right guesses is achieved when the number of symbols in the database is high enough.

Actually we are working on improving landmark localization, so our approach could be used with images containing complex environments. Our final goal is to use this method with a real robot platform and see how it works.

References

[1] Todt, E., Torras, C., Detection of Natural Landmarks Through Multiscale Opponent Features, *15th International Conference on Pattern Recognition (ICPR00)*, Barcelona, Spain, 2000, Vol. 3, pp. 3988-3991.
[2] Hsien, J.C., Chen, S.Y., Road Sign Detection and Recognition Using Markov Model, *14th Workshop on Object-Orient Technology and Applications (OOTA 2003)*, Taiwan, 2003, pp. 529-536.
[3] Piccioli, G., De Micheli, E., Parodi, P., Campani, M., A Robust method for road sign detection and recognition, *Image and Vision Computing*, Vol. 14, 1996, pp. 209-223.
[4] Zadeh, M.M., Kasvand, T. Suen, C.Y., Localization and Recognition of Traffic Signs for Automated Vehicle Control Systems, *Conf. on Intelligent Transportation Systems, part of SPIE's Intelligent Systems and Automated Manufacturing*, Pittsburgh, USA, 1997. pp. 272-282.
[5] Bernier, T., Landry, J.A., A New Method for Representationg and Matching Shapes of Natural Objects, *Pattern Recognition*, Vol. 36(8), 2003, pp. 1711-1723.
[6] Fekete, S. P., Simplicity and Hardness of the Maximum Traveling Salesman Problem under Geometric Distances, *Proc. Tenth ACM-SIAM Symposium on Discard Algorithms (SODA 99)*, Maryland, USA, pp. 337-345.
[7] Cha, S. H., Srihari, S. N., Distance Between Histograms of Angular Measurements and its Application to Handwritten Character Similarity, *15th International Conference on Pattern Recognition (ICPR 2000)* , Barcelona, Spain, 2000, pp. 21-24.

An Architecture of Sensor Fusion for Spatial Location of Objects in Mobile Robotics

Luciano Oliveira[1], Augusto Costa[1], Leizer Schnitman[1], and J. Felippe Souza[2]

[1] Universidade Federal da Bahia, Brasil,
Programme of Post-graduation in Mechatronics
{lrebouca, augusto.loureiro, leizer}@ufba.br
[2] Universidade da Beira Interior, Portugal
felippe@ubi.pt

Abstract. Each part of a mobile robot has particular aspects of its own, which must be integrated in order to successfully conclude a specific task. Among these parts, sensing enables to construct a representation of landmarks of the surroundings with the goal of supplying relevant information for the robot's navigation. The present work describes the architecture of a perception system based on data fusion from a CMOS camera and distance sensors. The aim of the proposed architecture is the spatial location of objects on a soccer field. An SVM is used for both recognition and object location and the process of fusion is made by means of a fuzzy system, using a TSK model.

1 Introduction

The field of mobile robotics has evidenced an enormous potential for research and real experiments. Mobile robots with intelligent behavior are constructed in various parts which by themselves show potential for study [1].

In particular, the sensing is responsible for supplying the robot with the necessary information for the construction of a representation of its surroundings, where the robot is placed, thereby allowing a dynamic description of the obstacles and useful landmarks for the orientation of the robot. Such a task must be made by computational methods whose objective is to reduce the inaccurate nature of the sensors. In order to do this, sensor fusion techniques have been applied successfully, providing a more suitable description of the surroundings due to both redundancy and complementation of data.

To evaluate a perception system and its architecture, it must be submitted to some specific task. For the proposed system, robot soccer is chosen and the Robocup rules for small size robots (F-180 league) are used for the local vision system constraints. For a team of robots to participate in a soccer match, various technologies must be present: principles of autonomous agent design, multi-agent collaboration, robotic and sensor fusion, among others. The main objective of the application of the mobile robot in a soccer environment is, therefore, the analysis of multiple areas of knowledge which serves to support socially significant problems as well as industry.

C. Bento, A. Cardoso, and G. Dias (Eds.): EPIA 2005, LNAI 3808, pp. 462–473, 2005.

For the perception system proposed in this work, a CMOS camera and infrared distance sensors are used. An SVM (Support Vector Machine) is applied for the classification of objects by a single color, without any image processing. Another SVM is used for obtaining the polar coordinates of the objects, by regression, from the image; for the sensor fusion, a fuzzy system using the TSK (Tagaki-Sugeno-Kang) zero order model integrates the information of angles of the objects with the data from the distance sensors, in order to refine the information obtained.

In Section 2, aspects of the classifier used are shown. Section 3 describes some architectures for sensor fusion. Section 4 describes the communication between the vision system and the robot. The architecture proposed, as well as its model, are presented in Section 5, while Section 6 presents general results obtained at each stage. To finish, Section 7 presents some conclusions.

2   Support Vector Machine

SVM is a hybrid technique of statistical and deterministic approaches. This means that to find the best space for classification hypothesis, a probability distribution is determined from the input space. The technique originated from the work of Vapnik on the Principle of Risk Minimization, in the area of Statistical Learning [2].

The technique is applied in the following way: in the case of linear space, determine the hyperplanes of separation by an optimization problem; in the case of non-linear space, a kernel function is applied and the new space obtained is denominated the feature space – now linearly separable, of a dimension greater than the original.

Fig. 1 illustrates the application of a kernel in the input space. In the feature space, a hyperplanes is obtained for separation.

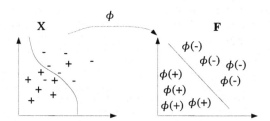

Fig. 1. Mapping of an input space non-linearly separable for a feature space

Another important aspect is the relationship between dimension VC (Vapnik-Chervonenkis), number of support vectors and generalization of the classification. To determine the dimension VC of a space, it is necessary to also determine the number of support vectors; in this case to find the oriented hyperplanes, within the smaller space of hypothesis defined by the function of risk estimation, which determines the limit of classified data. These ratios are determined by the probability of classification error of test data, after finding the support vectors through Eq. (1):

$$E_\ell[P(error)] \leq \frac{E[\text{nVS}]}{\ell} \tag{1}$$

where E_ℓ denotes the expectation for the input data set size ℓ and nVS is the number of support vectors of the SVM. In this way, the fewer the number of SVM support vectors, the greater will be its degree of generalization, obviously respecting a minimum limit, which will be determined empirically.

3   Sensor Fusion Architectures

Sensor data fusion represents the process of combining data or information from multiple sensors for the estimation or prediction of states of entities (objects for measurement) [3]. Some objectives for diverse scenarios for application of sensor fusion can be cited: detection of the presence of an object or environmental condition, object recognition, tracking of objects or monitoring of a continuous event, the combining of information to make intelligent decisions, among others.

In the area of sensor fusion, the principal organization for regulating terminology is the Joint Directors of Laboratories (JDL) Data Fusion Workgroup. This organization defines a model of processes for data fusion, by levels of information, besides a dictionary of terms related to this area [3]. The JDL determined three levels for sensor fusion: data, features and decision.

An interesting work in the area of sensor fusion is presented in [4]. The work is dedicated to the question of temporal sensor fusion and four types are suggested: centralized, decentralized, sequential and statistical. Centralized fusion is suitable when the system has only one active sensor. When more than one sensor is present in the system, decentralized fusion (pure, sequential or statistical) is better applied through a timeline.

Another important work on a flexible architecture for sensor fusion is proposed in [5]. The author proposes six categories based on three levels of JDL, yet used as processing input/output modes.

4   Communication with the Mobile Robot

The architecture of the agent used to control the mobile robot is illustrated in Fig. 2 and proposed in [6]. The processes which comprise the agent utilize an onboard multi-threaded program.

The Cognitive Level consists of a system based on symbolic knowledge which manipulates both the information received at the Instinctive Level as well as asynchronous messages received from other agents, generating the symbolic information for updating of the knowledge base at the Cognitive Level and implemented at an instinctive levels.

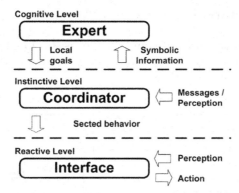

Fig. 2. Agent architecture used to controle the mobile robot. Proposed by [6].

As the Reactive Level is responsible for processing of messages of perception from the mobile robot, this becomes a point of communication between the agent and the artificial vision system proposed. The Reactive Level is composed of fuzzy controllers, input filter, output filter and mailbox. The process responsible for the control of these elements, in Reactive Level, is called the Interface.

All messages sent by the perception system are stored in the mailbox. The input filter extracts the value of the linguistic variables from the fuzzy visual information used by the fuzzy controllers, while the output filter checks the fuzzy controller outputs and combines them to define the action for the actuators.

The communication between the autonomous agent and the perception system is made by a frame sent by the last one to the agent mailbox, as presented in Fig. 3.

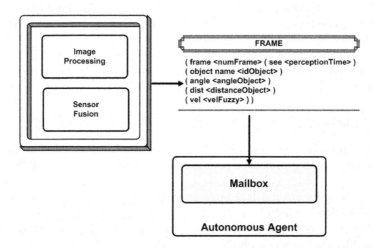

Fig. 3. Communication between the autonomous agent that control the mobile robot and the perception system

5   System Architecture

The system architecture, illustrated in Fig. 4, consists of four principle modules: data acquisition, feature extraction/classification, sensor data fusion and internal representation of object recognition.

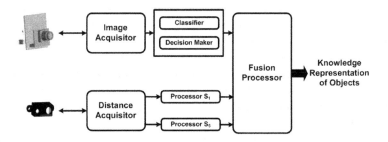

Fig. 4. Architecture of the perception system

The goal of the system is to recognize and locate both the robots and the ball, by theis colors. The Aquisitor modules are responsible for the acquisition of data from the camera and distance sensors. Once an image frame is obtained, this is classified by an SVM. The centroid of each extracted object is calculated and sent to the Decision Maker to obtain information such as angle (θ) relative to the robot and estimated distance (d) of each object. At the same time, the acquired data of all the distance sensors is separated and sent to each Processor S_i, where $i \in [1, 5]$, and a function of interpolation is applied with the objective of finding the distance from the decimalized value of each of these. Finally, all extracted information is sent to the Fusion Processor in order to generate knowledge representation of each object in the scene. The location of objects recognized in the image is given by its polar coordinates relative to the center of the robot (θ, d).

The processors S_i, as well as, the Classifier and Decision Maker are implemented in two distinct threads and synchronized in the Fusion Processor, once the fusion is made from the active sensors.

5.1   Acquisition

The camera used is the CMUCam2 designed by the Carnegie-Mellon University and comprises a microprocessor SX52 made by Ubicom and a CMOS OV6620 detector.

In order to reduce as much as possible the acquisition time of a camera frame, without reduction in quality of recognition, the obtained image is re-dimensioned to 44x36 pixels. The acquisition time for this frame is 245 ms on average and is determined by the camera's hardware.

The distance sensors used are GP2D02 made by Sharp and use infrared technology and the time for acquisition of a distance value is 75 ms.

5.2   Object Recognition

The Classifier module for image pattern and Decision Making is responsible for processing of the output of the image Aquisitor module. The image pattern classification has the objective of identifying moving objects on the soccer field. These objects could be: own team robots, opponent's robots and the ball.

The CMUCam2 offers a color tracking function. The technique used is straightforward thresholding and consists of tracking determined pixels whose colors belong to the interval R_{min}, G_{min}, B_{min} and R_{max}, G_{max}, B_{max}, in the RGB space. The disadvantage of this function is the high sensitivity to variation in luminosity of the environment. Because of this, an SVM is used with the objective of building a classifier which is more robust to variations in luminosity.

5.3   Object Location

From the features extracted from the image (area of the object, height, width, centroid) the location of objects is determined through its polar coordinates (θ, d), where θ represents the angle and d the distance relative to the center of the robot. To achieve this, two SVM responsible for effecting regression are used: one to determine the angle of the object and map each pixel to its corresponding angle; the other for distance and to map the height of each object in the image and its distance to the robot.

To obtain the pixel-angle function, rays and parallel lines are defined on a blank sheet of paper. The ball is put at the intersection between each ray and line, where the origin of the rays is the center of the robot. Fig. 5 illustrates this situation. A set of pairs (pixel, angle) is then obtained from the centroid of each object and the respective location of the angle relative to the center of the robot is determined.

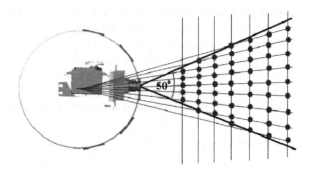

Fig. 5. Determination of the relationship between pixel and angle

The artificial vision head proposed is controlled by two servo-motors and, therefore, has two planes of movement (panoramic movement by rotation on the y axis in the camera system of coordinates and tilt movement by rotation through axis z). In order to reduce the effect of radial distortion of images, occurring when the artificial vision head is at different angles in relation to the z, a value of the vertical axis of the head is added to the pair (pixel, angle) previously obtained. Fig. 6 illustrates the angles used. For each angle (20°, 35°, 50° and 65⁰) a set of pairs (pixel, angle) is determined and the tuple (pixel, angle, angle of head) is submitted to the classifier.

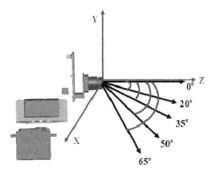

Fig. 6. Angles of the moving head used to determine the pixel–angle mapping function

The distance information extracted from the image is only used as a rough estimate, in case an object is in the shade of the distance sensors. In fact the estimate of distance only functions as a reference for the location of the robot in relation to moveable obstacles. When the robot moves, it can refine the distance information, rotating its body for example, to obtain a more reliable measurement.

5.4   Distance Sensor Processor

The distance sensor processor is responsible for separating the data obtained by the thread of data acquisition of the sensors and determination of the distance corresponding to the values decimalized from each sensor.

Once the sensor data is obtained, this is then submitted to a polynomial function of interpolation. The useful range of operation of these sensors is 10 to 80 cm. For an interpolation of greater precision, two polynomials are defined in two ranges: one for a range of 10 to 35cm and another for the range 35 to 80cm.

5.5   Fusion Processor

Once the values for decision for each sensor (camera and distance sensors) are selected, these are submitted to the Fusion Processor. The sensor data fusion is made by way of two distinct stages: angle and distance selection from the image, and fusion between these values of decision and the values obtained by the distance sensors. As the vision sensor is the slowest of the sensors used and having greater density of space-temporal data by acquisition, this is used as a synchronizer of fusion process.

The timeline of the classes of sensors used is illustrated in Fig. 7. The acquisition time of a distance value and conversion to centimeters is approximately 75 ms. This corresponds to approximately four readings of distance in the processing of an image and selection of variables of decision in the image (300 ms). In view of this the three first readings of the distance sensors are discarded and only the last represents the distances of the objects recognized. This is illustrated by the dotted lines in Fig. 7.

$$\underbrace{\hspace{4cm}}_{245 + 55}\ \text{Camera}$$

$$\underset{73+2}{\vdash \text{-- --} \vert}\underset{73+2}{\vdash \text{-- --} \vert}\underset{73+2}{\vdash \text{-- --} \vert}\underset{73+2}{\vdash \text{------} \vdash}\ \text{Distance sensors}$$

Fig. 7. Timeline of sensors involved in the fusion process (acquisition and processing)

The temporal alignment of the sensors information is necessary, as the sensors used are of the active type. After making this alignment, the values of decision are used for the sensor fusion. In order to do this, the fuzzy sets are determined from the physical disposition of the distance sensors, as per Fig. 8.

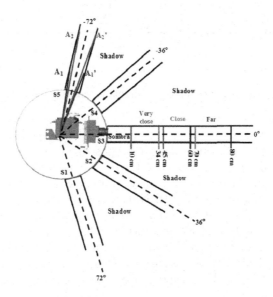

Fig. 8. Determination of fuzzy sets from distance sensors

In Fig. 8, the three sensors (S3) are used as an illustrative reference of the fuzzy set, used for the fusion processing through the linguistic variable distance in all the sensors. The final distance and angle are determined by a fuzzy system using the TSK zero order model. The reason for this choice is determined by the performance of this system for processing data samplese.

Once the angle is determined by the camera its value can be refined by the distance sensors. The disposal of the distance sensors is known, and for reasons of simplicity, the angles are supplied from the imaginary line (dotted line in Fig. 8) which comes from the origin of the robot and passes through each central point of the distance sensors. It can be seen in Fig. 8, that the further the object is from the distance sensor, the more precise its angle is determined. This is verified in the following way: the spread of each distance sensor is made by way of a cylinder 3 cm wide (space between receptor and emitter) an object between A_1 and A_1' will have an angle less precise than an object between A_2 and A_2'.

Therefore, from the geometry of the sensors, the fuzzy sets are obtained illustrated in Fig. 9.

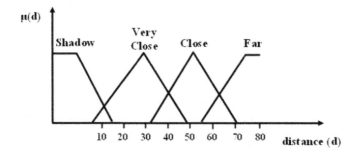

Fig. 9. Fuzzy sets for the linguistic variable distance

From these fuzzy sets, eight rules are proposed:
R_1: IF distance = SHADOW THEN distance = d(camera)
R_2: IF distance = SHADOW THEN angle = a(camera)
R_3: IF distance = VERYCLOSE THEN distance = d(S_i)
R_4: IF distance = VERYCLOSE THEN angle = a(camera)
R_5: IF distance = CLOSE THEN distance = d(S_i)
R_6: IF distance = CLOSE THEN angle = a(camera)*0,5 + a(S_i)*0,5
R_7: IF distance = FAR THEN distance = d(S_i)
R_8: IF distance = FAR THEN angle = a(S_i)

The functions $a(.)$ e $d(.)$ represent respectively the angle and distance obtained by the camera and distance sensors. The real values of distances and angles, after evaluation of the rules, are determined through Eq. (2).

$$S = \frac{\sum \psi_i z_i}{\sum \psi_i} \qquad (2)$$

where ψ_i is the T-norm of each antecedent and z_i is the result of function $f(x,y)$, responsible for describing the relationship between the fuzzy sets of the antecedent.

At the end of the fusion process, each object identified and located is represented internally by the following structure. For each image frame $\langle$numFrame$\rangle$, all objects located identified with an $\langle$idObject$\rangle$ and with three characteristics supplied: angle relative to the center of the base of the robot $\langle$angleObject$\rangle$, distance of object to the front of the robot $\langle$distanceObject$\rangle$ and fuzzy velocity of each object $\langle$fuzzyVel$\rangle$.

(**frame** $\langle$numFrame$\rangle$ (**see** $\langle$timePerception$\rangle$))
(**object_name** $\langle$idObject$\rangle$)
(**angle** $\langle$angleObject$\rangle$)
(**dist** $\langle$distanceObject$\rangle$)
(**vel** $\langle$fuzzyVel$\rangle$))

The fuzzy velocity $\langle$fuzzyVel$\rangle$ is determined by Eq. (3). Fig. 10 shows the fuzzy sets used.

$$\langle fuzzyVel \rangle = [\mu_l(difP), \mu_m(difP), \mu_h(difP)] \tag{3}$$

where $\mu_i(difP)$ are membership functions, and i represents each of fuzzy sets of linguistic variable velocity (low, medium and high). $difP$ is the difference between centroid location of an object in relation of frames n and $n-1$.

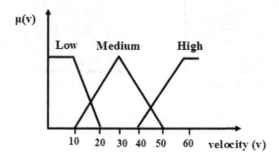

Fig. 10. Fuzzy sets for linguistic variable velocity

6   Results Analysis

Three parameters are analyzed with the objective of evaluating the general performance of the system: for object recognition, the application of the classifier in different ranges of lights; for the location of objects recognized, the square error and standard deviation of angles found.

For evaluation of the classifier, Table 1 illustrates the rate of precision for different luminosities. The range of luminosity tested was between 570 and 980 lux and is in accordance with the Robocup rules for small robots competition

(F-180 league), which define an illumination of between 700 and 1000 lux, for each tournament.

Table 1. Results for different ranges of light

Illumination (lux)	Precision
570	87.75%
660	84.08%
780	84.87%
800	86.36%
920	87.72%
980	90.00%

Figs. 11(a) and 11(b) illustrate the results of classification of robots and ball image.

(a) Image obtained   (b) Objects classified

Fig. 11. Classification results

Table 2. Standard deviation

Head angle	Standard deviation
20	2,34
35	2,15
50	2,00
65	2,18

For evaluation of determination method of angle measurement of an object relative to the robot, the standard deviation between the measured and real angle for each position chosen for the vision head is calculated. The values for standard deviation of sixteen random measures (determined and real) are illustrated in Table 2.

The parameters analyzed previously point, therefore, to a robustness of recognition of an object and efficiency in their location. Through the fusion process, the values obtained can be refined at each instance of robot actuation.

7 Conclusions

A perception system based on sensor fusion and applied in a mobile robot is here presented. An SVM is applied to either recognize patterns and to extract the decision attributes from objects in the image. For the sensor fusion, a TSK model is used. A critical point of the system is the acquisition time of an image frame and it must be evaluated and changed through the use of dedicated circuits and a faster image processor.

The contributions of this work are: a system with a modular architecture, making easier to repeatedly use modules in the system and also their inclusion; robust pattern recognition with luminosity variation and just one training sample; an efficient time classification through an SVM applied to the color space YCrCb; an adaptive system of information from sensors using Fuzzy Logic applied in the Fusion Processor. Another particular contribution of the system is that the symbolic information sent to the mobile robot allows it to build a model of the environment, which will be used in the decision process.

References

1. Kortenkamp, D., Bonasso, R., Murphy, R.: Artificial Intelligence and Mobile Robots, Menlo Park (1998)
2. Vapnik, V.: The Nature of Statistical Learning Theory. Springer Verlag (1995)
3. Hall, D., Llinas, J.: Handbook of multisensor data fusion. (2001)
4. Bruder, S., Faronq, M., Bayoumi, M.: Robotic heterogenous multi-sensor fusion with spatial and temporal alignment. In: Proceedings of the 30th IEEE Conference on Decision and Controle, IEEE (1991) 506–511
5. Dasarathy, B.: Sensor fusion potential exploitation – innovative and illustrative applications. In: Proceedings of the IEEE Special Issue on Sensor Fusion. Volume 85., IEEE (1997) 24–38
6. Costa, A., Bittencourt, G.: From a concurrent architecture to a concurrent autonomous agentarchitecture. In: IJCAI'99, Third International Workshop in RoboCup. (1999) 85–90 Springer, Lecture Notes in Artificial Inteligence.

CATRAPILAS – A Simple Robotic Platform

Nuno Cerqueira

FEUP - Faculdade de Engenharia da Universidade do Porto,
Rua Roberto Frias, s/n, 4200-465 Porto, Portugal
cerqueira@fe.up.pt

Abstract. This paper describes Catrapilas, a small robotic platform, designed to be capable of solving some well known robot problems. Among these are some of the most popular robotic contests, like Micro Mouse, Fire Fighting and Autonomous Driving. It describes the major decisions and details of the physical architecture of the robot, but emphasizes on the high level approach used to control the robotic agent. This approach is based on the creation of a 2D map of the agent's environment, which should contain all the information needed in order to solve the current problem. There is also a description of the implementation used for the Autonomous Driving Competition, from the 2005 Portuguese National Robotics Festival, and the results that were obtained. There is a focus on the robot's ability to accomplish the objectives of the contest, and how this proved that the concept and ideas behind Catrapilas are correct.

1 Introduction

The major goal of robotic contests has always been to promote the growth and advance of all the sciences involved in the construction of inteligent robots for many tasks that until now were only performed by humans. Despite the controversial question of whether the competition side of these events brings more benefit than not, it is undeniable that many advances were achieved due to the sharing of ideas and the imitation of some ot the most useful features of the other robots. Among these contests are Micro Mouse [2] [3], Fire Fighting [4] [5] and Autonomous Driving [6].

But this sharing has some setbacks. In the early ages of small robot competitions the only possible approach was based on a completely custom made solution. Now, as then, the most natural approach to some parts is still based on a custom made solution. This is particularly true in mechanic components (motors, wheels...) and in hardware (sensor configuration mostly), since these are the physical components that could make a difference between equally "smart" robots.

The common practice in some of these contests is to use simple microcontrollers on the control part of the hardware. Maybe because the study area of the majority of the contestants is electronics, there is a normal tendency to use this kind of technology. However, computer technology has suffered so many breakthroughs that it's possible to fit one PDA or PC, with a processing power several

C. Bento, A. Cardoso, and G. Dias (Eds.): EPIA 2005, LNAI 3808, pp. 474–484, 2005.

dozen times bigger, in the space occupied by one of these simple microcontrollers. Processing power alone is a good justification for choosing this kind of technologies, allowing the use of Computer Vision and more complex techniques and algorithms. But this is not the only advantage. Computer technologies also simplify a great deal of tasks like using a camera or any other standard connection device (using USB, IEEE1394[1]). It's also very probable that some parts of the system (image processing libraries [7], data structures, etc...) were already been done by somebody else and might even be free to use. And in the future it will be possible to buy a new, cheaper and more powerful PC and easily use the same software previously implemented (maybe with minor changes).

All these advantages assert this approach as a good one. This idea is also shared by Sony, the company that is investing more in robotics for personal use worldwide, with its Aibo.

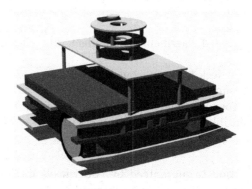

Fig. 1. Catrapilas 3D design

2   Catrapilas Architecture

2.1   Mechanics

Chassis. The robot chassis is made of expanded PVC plastic, due to it's extremely low weight, good structural resistance and easy crafting. It is composed by several decks that support all the electronics and mechanics needed and that also provide a good weight distribution and an increase in the structural resistance. This structure can be seen in Fig. 2.

All the robot's design was made keeping in mind the final weight of the whole. The weight is very important for a mobile robot, because if the robot is heavy its motors must be more powerful. More powerful motors are not only more costly but are also heavier, and require more powerful batteries that are also heavier. These heavier components make the need for a more resistant chassis structure, which must also be heavier. This is a vicious cycle, that only stops on a much

---

[1] Commonly FireWire.

Fig. 2. Catrapilas' lower deck structure and sensor rotating tower

higher weight than needed, sacrificing the budget, the efficiency and the agility of the robot.

Our robot's upper deck is made from a thinner kind of PVC because of the low weight it has to support (just a few switches, servo motors and sensors). It contains a rotating tower in which different kinds of sensors can be installed, providing a more flexible perception of the environment. This rotating turret can also be seen in Fig. 2.

Traction. The traction is guaranteed by two wheels in the front part of the robot. They are made of the same material used in the chassis and are covered by two rubber o-rings each. These "tires" ensure good traction in carpet floors (tipically used in robotic competitions) and in most smooth surfaces (concrete, tiled and wood surfaces,...).

There is also a third wheel which serves as a caster. This wheel is omnidireccional, offering almost no resistance to frontal and lateral movement, introducing negligible distortion in the robot's motion.

Specific Changes for the Autonomous Driving Application. No changes were made to the original mechanics.

2.2   Hardware

Personal Computer. All the control is centralized in a small PC light enough to be carried inside the robot. The PC used is the Asus S5200N, with an Intel Centrino 1,6GHz processor and 512MB of RAM. The bigger side of the PC has about 28 centimeters, which is smaller than the common dimension limit of some of the Portuguese robotic contests (a bounding box of 30 centimeters). The great advantage of this option is that all the programming needed can be made using the x86 platform, undoubtedly one of the most popular, flexible and powerful platforms of its kind. Other advantages that the Centrino architecture provides are: very low weight (less than 2 kg in this case) and long battery duration (up to 7 hours).

It features an 802.11b wireless interface, which provides valuable help in the test and debug process. There are 3 USB 2.0 ports which allow an easy connection of several input / output devices (very common nowadays). There is also an IEEE1394 port (less common than USB). Both these technologies supply their devices with power and allow the connection to hubs that increase the number of simultaneously used devices.

Sensors. The only sensor in the current configuration of the robot is a webcam. However a camera is a very powerful sensor because it is really composed of thousands of very precise and rich sensors. The data provided by the camera is also of very intuitive analysis and use. The selected webcam is the Creative NX Pro, with 320 by 240 RGB[2] pixels and USB 1.1 interface.

Actuators. All the actuators used in this configuration are of the same kind: servo motors [8]. Two regular servo motors are used to control the pan and tilt of the webcam. Two quarter scale servo motors (bigger and with more torque than regular servo motors) were hacked for continuous rotation [9] and are used to implement the robot's differential drive.

All these servos are controlled using PWM[3] signals sent by a servo control board [10] which is connected to the PC via USB.

Power. The PC has it's own power source (it's battery), and provides the power to the webcam and the servo control board via USB. The rest of the robot's electronics is powered by regular rechargeable NiMH AA batteries.

Specific Changes for the Autonomous Driving Application. Some lamps were inserted to light the tunnel, as can be seen in Fig. 3.

2.3   Software

Architecture. The robot's software is based on layers, as can be seen in Fig. 4, on a call and return architectural style. This style's major advantage is that changes inside a specific layer do not imply changes in other layers. This feature allows solving problems in the most adequate layer on a way that is invisible for the other layers. OOP[4] paradigm is used in order to simplify code reuse. There are 3 major layers in the software agent: World State, Meditator and Actuator.

World State receives data from the sensors and stores their current state as well as the actuators'. It also stores some higher level information, created from sensorial fusion, that can be of great use for the robot.

---

[2] Red, Green, Blue.
[3] Pulse Width Modulated.
[4] Object Oriented Programming.

Fig. 3. Catrapilas being placed inside the tunnel for light testing

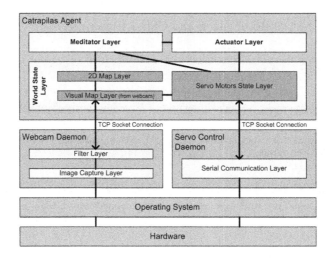

Fig. 4. Catrapilas Architecture

Meditator uses the information provided by the World State to select the best action[5] to perform. This action is then sent to the Actuator that ensures it's execution and corresponding change in the World State.

Image Processing. Most of the processing of the aquired image takes place in the Filter Layer (Webcam daemon). This allows the Visual Map Layer (World State Layer) to ignore this process as it receives an almost "perfect" image. The Filter Layer can offer different filters that can be changed by an explicit order via the socket.

---

[5] An action can be composed of many actuators' orders, as long as they aren't conflicting.

Neighbourhood Map Drawing. The agent bases its actions entirely on its current believed location and on a 2D map of the neighbourhood of the robot. This map is maintained in the World State's 2D Map Layer and it is created by the Visual Map Layer, using the Servo Layer (which provides the camera direction) and the filtered image got from the webcam. The map drawn this way could then be used to calculate the actions that are to be executed.

The image received is in fact a 3D perspective of the world, which does not provide an easy to use information. The process to make this information useful, in a 2D map, bases itself on a warping transformation of the image: a new image is created, in which all the pixels (corresponding to the 2D coordinates) are filled with the contents of the related pixels in the 3D perspective image. Obviously this relation depends on the pan and tilt of the camera, which are obtained from the values of the respective servo motors, available from the Servo Layer. An example of this warping process is depicted in Fig. 5, being the first the 3D filtered perspective image, and the second the 2D warped image.

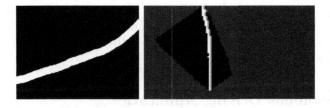

Fig. 5. Filtered 3D perspective image and 2D warped map

There are several possible methods to calculate the related coordinates on both images. The currently used method is based on a previous calibration. In this calibration some snapshots of a big pattern are taken, in different angles. This pattern contains stripes of a certain width, that allow the program to determine the coordinates of all the pixels of the image. Examples of this calibration can be seen in Fig. 6.

Fig. 6. Horizontal and vertical coordinate calibration images, for 2 different tilt values

Environment and Programming Languages Used. The system is implemented in Microsoft Windows XP due to some still limiting issues in hardware interface of the Linux operating system (like wireless lan).

The agent and daemons are programmed in C++ because it supports OOP, it is very eficient and it is very widely used. Java is also used on the viewer which connects to the daemons using TCP sockets.

Specific Changes for the Autonomous Driving Application. This was obviously the part that needed more changes. Firstly, there were used 2 filters in the Filter Layer: a Track Filter and a Signal Filter. The Track Filter allows to clearly "see" the limits of the track, the crossing, and the elements of the working zone. It uses binarization as well as eroding for "cleaning" the image. The Signal Filter emphasizes the color and form of the signal that the robot has to identify and obey to. It also uses binarization as well as some simple pattern recognition techniques. These filters allow the higher level to solve an easier problem, since a part of the original one was already taken care of.

The higher level, after translating this image into a 2D map, can use it to: calculate the distance and direction of the side line that limits the track, determine if the crossing is in front of the robot and align with the crossing, among others. The results of the refered calculations can then be used to decide which are the best actions to take.

3   Autonomous Driving Application

3.1   Introduction

In order to test the platform constructed, it was developed an agent for the Autonomous Driving Competition [6], from the 2005 Portuguese National Robotics Festival. This choice might seem weird, since from all the three major Portuguese robotic competitions, this is the less oriented to small robots and where PCs are used profusely (in oposition to the problem stated in 2.2). However it was chosen, due to the short amount of time available to implement the solution, and to the fact that it is the easiest to solve using only the camera as a sensor.

3.2   Contest Description

The Autonomous Driving Competition is a contest where robots must be capable of driving correctly through a eight-shaped track like the one that can be seen in Fig. 7. The contest is composed of three rounds:

First Round. The robot starts from the oposite side of the parking lot, just before the crossing line. It has to accomplish 2 complete laps (passing over the crossing line 4 times). When it is completing the second lap, it must stop over the crossing line. This is a speed run and no other rules apply. The score is based only on the elapsed time.

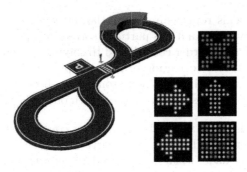

Fig. 7. Track layout and signals used during the contest

Second Round. The basic structure of the round is very similar to the first one. However there are introduced some new rules: after stoping at the crossing line, the robot must follow the orders imposed by the signals depicted in Fig. 7; and at the end of the round the robot must park in the according zone. Failure to accomplish these rules imply a time penalty that is added to the time score.

Third Round. The basic structure of the round is the same as the previous round. There are also introduced some new obstacles: a tunnel where visual guidance is not possible under normal conditions; and an optional working zone. This zone is a detour from the original track and is delimited by small yellow cylindrical landmarks. Scoring is similar to the last round, with a penalty to the robots that decide not to run with the working zone setup.

Final Score. The final score is the sum of the scores of all the three rounds. The winner is the robot with the smaller score.

3.3   Results

This is a short description of Catrapilas' participation in the competition.

First Round. This round was the first real test to Catrapilas as an autonomous driving robot. Despite the easiness of the round, the robot was only able to complete one lap, going off the track on the second pass through the crossing. This was due to a hardware bug that ocurred when the batteries were weaker, causing the robot to oversteer when cruising at low speeds (in the approach to the crossing) and was only found during the real contest, since it was the first time it was tested for a longer period of time. It's worth mentioning that the track is very hard to reproduce because of it's size, and the first full track test was only a few hours before. Fortunately all the ideas that could not be tested before, were proven right in these tests. Catrapilas scored 520 points and was ranked 10th out of 17 robots in this round.

Second Round. This round surely was the most successful of all. The bug observed in the previous round was partially solved by a program around: it was verified if the robot's last order contributed to solving the current sub-goal, and if this case wasn't true a correcting order was applied. The robot was able to recognize correctly all the signals despite some bugs discovered in the test stage. Catrapilas scored 380 points and was ranked 11th out of 17 robots in this round.

Final Round. This round was a disappointment compared to the previous one. The lamps used were found too weak to correctly light the tunnel. So another program around was made: when Catrapilas detected the tunnel (when captured images became very dark) it would apply a fixed value to the motors. This value was calculated by many tests and trials, and was proven very acceptable during the tests. However it failed during the round and because of this the robot was unable to even complete a single lap. The choice was made to go into this run without the working zone of the track, because although a strategy for the working zone was fully implemented, it was not very tested at the time. Catrapilas scored 528 points and was ranked 8th out of 17 robots in this round.

End of Contest. Catrapilas ended the contest with 1428 points and ranked 12th out of 17 robots. However this result is promising since this robot's top speed was not even closer to the majority of the other contestants. However, there were two slower robots that were better ranked than Catrapilas, due to the fact that their performances were more regular.

From the point of view of the robot's concept this participation was a success, since it proved that the basic idea of operation is correct. A good example of that is the fact that the winner robot followed a very similar strategy, only more tuned and with a better hardware.

For academic and personal purposes it was also a success since there was a lot of idea sharing and an introduction to the competition environment.

Just one more fact worth of notice: Catrapilas was the favorite robot of the competition. Not only to the crowd, that cheered when the successful run was accomplished and also when the robot camera moved (this was the robot that more clearly showed what and how it was "thinking"); but also to the organization, that described the robot as the "visually more well achieved robot".

4   Future Work

4.1   Hardware

Camera. There were detected some faults in the camera used. Although having a good frame rate the camera introduces a lag in image capture. This lag is around 500 ms to 1000 ms and has no relevance at its intended use (webcam). However, this lag is very bad for robotic applications were several decisions must be made each second. Another problem was discovered in images where there are fast color changes. The autoregulation of the camera blends these colors and makes impossible to detect the flashing checkered signal, for instance. So, a replacement must be found.

Encoders. The implementation of wheel encoders is already underway, and will allow better positioning, adding the capability of merging with older maps. An encoder is a mechanism that allows the robot to know how much it has moved since the beggining of its execution. The encoders that are being implemented are quadrature encoders [11] and give more information than regular ones.

Sensors. Inclusion and connection of new kinds of sensors is being planned. Some examples are: IR[6] distance, IR ground color, IR beacon detector and UV[7] flame detector. These sensors will allow more precise information gathering, and will also help in the reduction of the global uncertainty factor.

Portable Remote Access. Debugging, controling and testing the robot is very difficult without another machine with GUI[8] capabilities. The use of a PDA with wireless connection will simplify the entire process.

4.2   Software

Image Filters. The used image filters were a bit slow in their operation. The implementation of faster filters can improve the performance of the robot. Investigation will be made in order to determine if there is an already implemented visual library (like CMVision [7]) that offer all the needed features and others that could increase the robot's capabilities.

Other Applications. Implementations of the robotic agent are intended for the Micro Mouse contest [2] and the Firefighting [4] contest.

5   Conclusions

We can say that the project and the competition have had a very positive outcome. The major accomplishment was to prove that the concept of the high level approach based on a 2D map to solve a specific problem was not only correct, since the robot was clearly able to accomplish the goals it was programmed for; but also that it is very easy to implement.

We can see that the needed changes in the entire platform were of little difficulty and in very low quantity. The changes that are planned in order to solve other kinds of problems are also of this degree of difficulty.

The participation in the contest also reinforced the idea that robotic competitions of this kind are very useful events, since it is a very inspirational and motivating environment that promotes the sharing of ideas and approaches.

---

[6] Infra Red.
[7] Ultra Violet.
[8] Graphical User Interface.

References

1. Reis, Luis Paulo et al.: *Proceedings of the Scientific Meeting of the Portuguese Robotics Open*, FEUP Edicoes, Coleccao Colectaneas, Vol. 14, ISBN 972-752-066-9, April 23-24, 2004

2. *Micro Mouse Contest*, University of Aveiro, [online] available at http://microrato. ua.pt [consulted on May 2005]

3. *Micromouse UK*, University of London, [online] available at http://micromouse.cs. rhul.ac.uk/ [consulted on April 2005]

4. *Fireman Robot Contest*, Informatics Department, E.S.T.G, I.P. Guarda, [online] available at http://www.ipg.pt/estg/robobombeiro/ [consulted on April 2005]

5. *Fire Fighting Home Robot Contest*, Trinity College, [online] available at http://www. trincoll.edu/events/robot/ [consulted on April 2005]

6. *Competition, Autonomous Driving class - Rules and technical specifications*, National Robotics Festival 2004, [online] available at http://www.robotica2004.org/ regulamentos/competicao_ca_040124.pdf [consulted on June 2004]

7. *CMVision*, CORAL Group's Color Machine Vision Project, [online] available at http://www-2.cs.cmu.edu/~jbruce/cmvision/ [consulted on June 2005]

8. *What's a Servo?*, Seattle Robotics Society, [online] available at http://www. seattlerobotics.org/guide/servos.html [consulted on April 2005]

9. *Hacking a Servo*, Seattle Robotics Society, [online] available at http://www. seattlerobotics.org/guide/servohack.html [consulted on April 2005]

10. *USB 16-Servo Controller*, Pololu, [online] available at http://www.pololu.com/ products/pololu/0390/ [consulted on February 2005]

11. McManis, Chuck: *Quadrature Encoder*, Pololu, [online] available at http:// www.mcmanis.com/chuck/robotics/projects/encoders/enc_quad.htm   [consulted on June 2005]

Chapter 8

MASTA 2005: Multi-agent Systems: Theory and Applications

Introduction

João Balsa[1], Luís Moniz[1], and Luís Paulo Reis[2]

[1] University of Lisbon, Portugal
{jbalsa, hal}@di.fc.ul.pt
[2] University of Porto, Portugal
lpreis@fe.up.pt

Multi-Agent Systems (MAS) is now one of the most relevant and attractive research areas in the field of computer science. Since 1993 the area of Multi-Agent Systems/Distributed Artificial Intelligence has been present in the EPIA conferences, both as individual tracks in the main conference and as autonomous workshops.

The *3rd Workshop on Multi-Agent Systems: Theory and Applications* (MASTA 2005) took place in the University of Beira Interior, Covilhã, Portugal, December 6-8, 2005, as part of EPIA 2005 – 12th Portuguese Conference on Artificial Intelligence. Focusing on a fundamental area of research in Artificial Intelligence, the 3rd MASTA workshop was the forum for presenting and discussing the most recent and innovative work in the areas of multi-agent systems and autonomous agents.

MASTA 2005 received 36 submissions from 11 countries with Portugal, Brazil and The Netherlands being the most contributing countries. Although submissions covered almost all areas in the agents and multi-agent research field, some topics of special interest were on: agent architectures, agent-based applications, agent-oriented software engineering, formal methods for modelling agent based systems, negotiation in MAS, coordination and MAS learning.

Each paper was blindly reviewed by three senior program committee members. From the 36 submitted, 9 high quality full papers were selected for publication in the Springer LNCS main volume of the conference proceedings, while 10 papers were selected for the local UBI/IEEE proceedings, 6 as full papers and 4 as posters. We would like to thank all the authors who submitted their work to the workshop and enabled the success of MASTA 2005. We would also like to give a special thanks to all the members of the Program Committee who took upon most of the burden in reviewing the papers enabling its accurate evaluation.

C. Bento, A. Cardoso, and G. Dias (Eds.): EPIA 2005, LNAI 3808, p. 487, 2005.
© Springer-Verlag Berlin Heidelberg 2005

A Model of Pedagogical Negotiation

Cecilia D. Flores[1], Louise J. Seixas[2], João C. Gluz[1,3], and Rosa M. Vicari[1]

[1] Federal University of Rio Grande do Sul, Informatics Institute,
P.O. Box 15064, 91501-970, Porto Alegre-RS, Brazil
[2] Federal University of Rio Grande do Sul, Post-graduate Course on Computer Education,
P.O. Box 15064, 91501-970, Porto Alegre-RS, Brazil
[3] Digital Systems Engineering, State University of Rio Grande do Sul, Guaíba-RS, Brazil
{dflores, jcgluz, rosa}@inf.ufrgs.br,
seixas@farmacia.ufrgs.br

Abstract. This paper presents a model of pedagogical negotiation developed for the AMPLIA, an Intelligent Probabilistic Multi-agent Learning Environment. Three intelligent software agents: Domain Agent, Learner Agent and Mediator Agent were developed using Bayesian Networks and Influence Diagrams. The goal of the negotiation model is to increase, as much as possible: (a) the performance of the model the students build; (b) the confidence that teachers and tutors have in the students' ability to diagnose cases; and the students' confidence on their own ability to diagnose cases; and (c) the students' confidence on their own ability to diagnose diseases.

1 Introduction

The paper discusses the pedagogical negotiation process and the model involved in the implementation of a real environment – AMPLIA [1].

Discussions about the use of negotiation mechanisms in learning environments are not recent. According to Self [2], there are two major motivations for the use of negotiation in ITS: i) they make possible to foster discussions about how to proceed, which strategy to follow, which example to look for, etc. in an attempt to decrease the control that is typical of ITS, and ii) they give room for discussions that yield different viewpoints (different beliefs), provided that the agent (tutor) is not infallible.

The approach of pedagogic negotiation can be applied to areas of knowledge that share some characteristics such as incomplete knowledge and different points of view or even domains where there is no "knowledge" – considered in its classical definition, in which knowledge is always something true – but a set of justified beliefs about what one can argue and debate. These characteristics foresee the transformation of viewpoints, both from the system and student, into beliefs instead of knowledge. This implies a special type of teaching dialogue, provided that an interactive change of justified beliefs is a simplified definition of argumentation [3]. This is a complex process because it involves the student's autonomy, the symmetry of relations among teacher and students or among agents, and the levels of flexibility, which involve the agents' level of freedom to perform their actions [4]. We do not see the presence of 'conflict' (either openly declared or acknowledged or not) as essential in the definition of negotiation. The basic requirement is that the interaction among agents

C. Bento, A. Cardoso, and G. Dias (Eds.): EPIA 2005, LNAI 3808, pp. 488–499, 2005.
© Springer-Verlag Berlin Heidelberg 2005

shares a common goal so that an agreement is reached with respect to the negotiation object. Usually, different dimensions of the negotiation object will be negotiated simultaneously. The initial state for a negotiation to take place is the absence of an agreement, which can include a conflict or not. In the case of a teaching and learning process, a point of conflict is the relation of self-confidence and mutual confidence between teachers and students, besides their own beliefs about the knowledge domain. A process of teaching and learning is a way of reducing the asymmetry between the teacher's and the student's confidence on the topic studied.

AMPLIA was designed as an extra resource for the education of medical students [5][6]. It supports the development of diagnostic reasoning and modeling of diagnostic hypotheses. The learner activities comprise representing a clinical case in a Bayesian Network (BN) model; such a process is supported by software agents. BN have been widely employed in the modeling of uncertain knowledge domains [7]. Uncertainty is represented by the probability and the basic inference of the probabilistic reasoning, that is, the calculus of the probability of a variable or more, according to the evidence available. This evidence is represented by a set of variables with known values.

The main goal of a pedagogic negotiation is to provide and establish a high degree of confidence[1] among the participants of the process. We are not talking about a generic confidence, but about a very specific and objective one, associated with the abilities the student demonstrates when dealing with the learning domain. The degree of belief on an autonomous action is an important component of confidence that will take place in a given teaching and learning process, that is, how much the student's actions are guided by trials or hypotheses. This variable corresponds to the system's *credibility* on the student's actions and is inferred by the Learner Agent. *Self-confidence* (the confidence the student has on his BN model) is another variable used in the pedagogic negotiation, once the student must be confident on his hypothesis, or at least trust them more and more, as he builds his knowledge. The *quality of the BN model* is the third element considered in the negotiation process, as the student must be able to formulate a diagnosis that will probable be compliant with the case, as the diagnosis proposed by an expert would be. Quality is evaluated by the Domain Agent. The Mediator Agent uses these three elements presented above as parameters for the selection of pedagogic strategies and tactics, as well as to define the way how they will be displayed to the student.

The negotiation is characterized by: i) the negotiation object (belief on a knowledge domain), ii) the negotiation initial state (absence of an agreement, which is characterized by an unbalance between credibility, confidence, and a low BN model quality); iii) the final state (highest level of balance between credibility and confidence, and good BN model quality); and iv) the negotiation processes (from state ii to state iii). This is the base of the negotiation model developed in AMPLIA.

---

[1] The notion of confidence we adopted is turned towards an expectation with the future actions of an agent, which is similar to the notion of confidence by Fischer & Ghidini [12]. They base it on a modal logic of beliefs and abilities, which intuitively is according to the idea of considering someone reliable because we know how this person is going to behave in given situations [13].

The paper is organized as follows: Section 2 describes the object of the negotiation that takes place in AMPLIA. Section 3 describes the initial and final states of this negotiation. Section 4 shows the process involved in negotiation and discusses the roles played by each software agent. Section 5 brings some discussions, examples and results about the process of pedagogic negotiation and, finally, in section 6, we draw some final considerations and discuss future work.

2   The Object of Negotiation in AMPLIA

The object of negotiation in AMPLIA is the belief on a diagnostic hypothesis outlined for a clinical case. The student's diagnosis model is built through an editor of BN. From the pedagogic point of view, BN is a tool that students use to represent their knowledge by means of probabilistic models. They can build and observe their study object and formulate and test their hypotheses through those BN model. As AMPLIA is a computational resource, the process is supported by intelligent software agents that aid the student build his BN model for the present case.

The teacher's beliefs are also modeled through BN, named expert's model and stored in the environment database. As these beliefs are concerned to an uncertain domain, the expert's BN model can be incomplete, the reason why a base of real cases, which is continuously updated, is used to validate the expert's beliefs. A belief expresses how much one believes x, or how much x is considered right. Under this viewpoint, the students' and teacher's confidence are two parameters comprised in negotiation. The participants of a negotiation process use the resource of argumentation to persuade the other participants to change their beliefs (or viewpoints). In AMPLIA, the argumentation resources are represented by the teacher's actions, translated into the selection of a strategy that is considered more adequate to convince the student. The student's argumentation is represented by the modifications (or not) of his BN and by the level of confidence he is asked to declare.

Provided that the object of the negotiation is a BN model, it is probable that it has problems both in its topologic structure and in the tables of conditional probabilities. The problems identified in the student's BN model are classified as Table 1 shows. The student's BN model classification is the third parameter used by the negotiation process.

Table 1. Student's BN model classification

Not feasible	It is not a BN, there are cycles or disconnected nodes
Incorrect	Absence of diagnostic node or diagnostic node represented as father node of symptoms, presence of excluding node with incorrect representation of probabilities
Potential	It has at least one trigger node or one of the essential or additional nodes; presence of unnecessary nodes
Satisfying	The majority of nodes are essential and additional; some relations are missing
Complete	It has a good performance as compared to the expert's model and to the database of real cases

3   Initial and Final States of the Pedagogical Negotiation

The pedagogical negotiation in AMPLIA can be seen as a way of reducing the initial asymmetry in the confidence relation between teacher/student in what concerns the topic studied. Such a negotiation is intended to maximize the confidence of all. The following schema shows an example:

— Initial state of the pedagogical negotiation process:
   Teacher:
    (IP.1)   High level of confidence in his own knowledge.
    (IP.2)   Low level of confidence in the student's knowledge.
   Student:
    (IA.1)   Low level of confidence in his own knowledge.
    (IA.2)   High level of confidence in the teacher's knowledge.
— Final (expected) state of the pedagogical negotiation process:
   Teacher:
    (FP.1)   High level of confidence in his own knowledge.
    (FP.2)   High level of confidence in the student's knowledge.
   Student:
    (FA.1)   High level of confidence in his own knowledge.
    (FA.2)   High level of confidence in the teacher's knowledg.

Conditions **(IP.1)** and **(FP.1)**, as well as **(IA.2)** and **(FA.2)** should not change, being only bases for an adequate beginning, development and end of the process. The result of the process would be the increase in the level of confidence that the teacher has on the student: **(IP.2)** for **(FP.2)**, and of the student on himself/herself: **(IA.1)** for **(FA.1)**.

4   The Negotiation Processes

The participants of a pedagogic negotiation are the student and the teacher. In AMPLIA the student is represented by the Learner Agent and the teacher tasks are performed by three software agents: (A) Learner Agent, which besides representing the student, infers the credibility level, as a teacher that only observes the student's actions but does not interfere using the parameters required in the pedagogic negotiation process; (B) Domain Agent, which evaluates the quality of the student's BN model and checks the performance both of the student's and teacher's BN model against a database of real cases, and (C) Mediator Agent, which selects the pedagogic strategies.

Figure 1 shows the main elements of the negotiation model: initial state, final state, the negotiation object, and negotiation process. The negotiation object is represented by circles and indicates the status of the student's BN model. Status is labeled as Main Problem, which is identified by the Mediator Agent. The initial state is defined in terms of specific elements, student's and system's individual and mutual goals and beliefs. The only element required is the mutual goal of agreeing on some negotiation object. The final state will be reached when a symmetry between the student's (*Self-confidence*) and the system's (*Credibility*) confidence is reached, and when the student's BN model reaches the status *Satisfying* or *Complete*, with a similar or even better performance than the expert's BN model. The negotiation process has the purpose of achieving the final state from the initial state. The inverted triangle in Figure 1 is meant to indicate convergence towards this final state.

The pedagogic strategy is selected with basis on the *Main Problem* (MP) of the student's BN model and his *Self-confidence*. *Credibility* represents the "fine tune" and determines which tactics will be applied to the student, the tactics is meant to be the way how the strategy will be displayed.

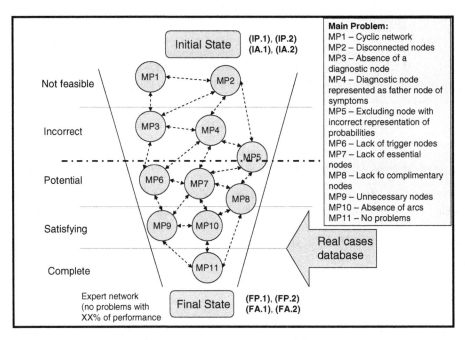

Fig. 1. Negotiation process in AMPLIA

In the initial state, the object of negotiation – the student's BN model – is not built yet; therefore, there is no negotiation. The pedagogic strategy used in this case will be to guide the student: the tactics can be to present a problem or suggest that the student check his BN model again and look for conceptual problems. In the following level, in which there is a mistake in the representation of the object, the Mediator Agent disagrees with the student's BN model. In these first levels, the focus of the Mediator Agent is on a concrete object (the BN model) and does not include the student's confidence on his BN model. In the following levels, the negotiation process starts: the objective of the Mediator Agent is now to make the student reflect and enhance his diagnostic hypothesis represented by the BN model by including lacking nodes and indicating the relationship among them. When the student's BN model starts to enter the satisfactory level (as compared to the expert's), the Mediator Agent starts to warn the student that some adjustments in the *a priori* and conditional probabilities of the BN model are required. At the same time, the student's BN model is submitted to the database of real cases for the evaluation of performance. The expert's BN model is also submitted to this base. The database is continuously updated, so that the Mediator Agent is able to accept BN models built by students that are better than BN models built by experts. It is worth saying that the conditions **(FP.1)** and **(FA.2)** are the basis for this process to take place.

Even if the student's BN model is classified as complete but the Learner Agent detected low credibility, or if the student declared a low confidence, the Mediator Agent will use different strategies, such as demos or discussions, in order to enhance the model, these actions correspond to the **(FP.2)** and **(FA.1)**. While this status is not reached, the Mediator Agent does not consider that negotiation has come to an end.

4.1 The Role of the Learner Agent in the Pedagogical Negotiation

When the student builds his BN model, his actions are registered in a log. Thus, node by node, arc by arc, the way how the student selects the variables, makes relationships, builds his hypotheses, asks for help or employs the strategies offered by AMPLIA are analyzed by the Learner Agent. The Learner Agent is able to assess if the student has a hypothesis to guide his actions or if he is making combinatory trials that can occasionally hit a diagnosis. The Learner Agent uses the student's log to mathematically manage the variables it observes. These variables are conditional nodes of the BN (see Figure 2), and the outcomes of the *Credibility* node are the probabilities that the Learner Agent informs to the Mediator Agent.

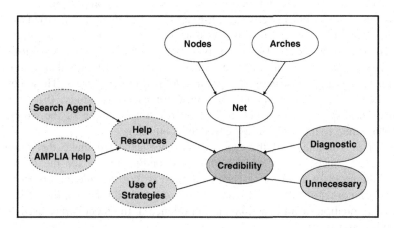

Fig. 2. Learner Agent BN. Empty nodes represent variables inferred from the student's actions log and mathematically calculated. Grey-filled nodes represent observed variables. Dotted nodes will be implemented.

The *Diagnostic* and *Unnecessary* variables refer to the types of nodes that can compose the student's BN model, and, therefore may present two states: "Absent" or "Present", which are defined after direct observation of the log. The *Nodes* and *Arcs* variables can present "A few changes", "Some changes" or "Many changes", defined through mathematical expressions calculated from elements present in the BN model and from the set of actions the student employed to accomplish his BN model. The empirical justification for such modeling is directly based on a qualitative analysis that a human agent (teacher) could make by observing students presentially or reading their logs. Data collected in a pilot experience show quite an agreement between the professor's inferences and the logs of five students in their process of BN model construction. We observe that the fewer the number of alterations are during the addition of nodes, the higher will be credibility, understood here as the student's autonomy [8].

4.2 The Role of the Domain Agent in the Pedagogical Negotiation

The Domain Agent analyses the student's BN model and sends the result to the Mediator Agent. The analysis is not only a simple comparison between the student's and the expert's knowledge, as it happens with the most traditional models (overlay, differential and perturbation), which are strongly based on the expert's knowledge and where the student's knowledge is either a subset of the first or it is compared against a set of errors, foreseen by the expert. Besides following the BN model construction, the Domain Agent will also assess the performance of the student's and the expert's BN model, comparing them against a database of real cases.

The student's BN model is assessed as for feasibility, correctness and completeness by the Domain Agent, which makes a qualitative evaluation (the network topology) and a quantitative evaluation (the conditional probabilities tables).

Qualitative analysis is based on a process of BN model comparison, equivalent to the problem of isomorphism between sub-graphs. This problem is classified as an NP-complete problem [9], therefore it is necessary to use heuristic information, based on the BN semantics, to reduce the search space (the set of comparison possibilities) and thus make the comparison algorithm efficient. So, some constraints that do not affect the teaching-learning constructivist dynamics defined in the process. These heuristics are (a) the use of a list of variables, specific for each case study, (b) the type of inference one expects the student makes and (c) simplification of the expert's BN model, according to the study case the student is building.

The list of variables and the type of inference expected make the comparison process easier, once they provide starting and ending points for the comparison, avoiding the need for confronting each node (and arc) of the student's model against all nodes (and arcs) of the expert's model. In order to build the list, the node's name and its classification as for function and importance in the model were used. Table 2 shows this classification.

A BN makes possible to make different types of inferences, such as causal (starting from causes, considered as available evidence, and reaching the effects), diagnosis (from the effects, i.e. evidence, to the causes), intercausal (differentiates among causes of common effect) and mixed (combination of two or more of the types described above). As AMPLIA is primarily developed for the medical education area, the diagnostic inference was given priority, because it is what professionals of this domain use.

Table 2. Nodes classification

Diagnostic	Must be always present
Trigger	When it is present, it selects the diagnosis as potential solution
Essential	It must be present to assure the diagnosis identification
Complementary	Its presence increases the diagnosis probability
Excluding	Its presence decreases the probability of diagnosis confirmation
Unnecessary	It is not needed for the diagnosis confirmation

The definition of the type of inference expected has the effect of reducing the search space as well, because it works as an "arrival point" that can be used to make comparison easier.

Each case study has specific diagnosis that can be part of the expert's BN model. The Domain Agent simplifies this network, excluding the diagnostic nodes that do not apply to the case and consequently all the nodes related only to these diagnoses, generating a simplified expert's network.

The Domain Agent analyses the distribution of conditional probabilities among the variables (the quantitative evaluation) when there is not evident progress in the student's BN model. In the quantitative evaluation, the student's BN model is submitted to a database of real cases. The goal is to check if the BN model can provide a correct diagnosis with the nodes chosen. At the end of the process, the Domain Agent provides a list of the problems found in the student's BN model, which will be managed by the Mediator Agent.

4.3   The Role of the Mediator Agent in the Pedagogical Negotiation

The role of this agent in AMPLIA is to mediate the interactions between the student (represented by the Learner Agent) and the Domain Agent (which represents the expert) at each cycle of the BN model construction.

In AMPLIA, an Influence Diagram is proposed to select the tactics that will present the best utility in different moments of the interaction. The parameters used are the results of the BN model evaluation, the level of the student's declared confidence, and the credibility. Thus, the Mediator Agent aims at making possible to represent the dependence relations among these parameters and assimilates the need of incorporating the constant changes that take place in the learning process. Figure 3 presents the influence diagram of the Mediator Agent.

The value of the *Credibility* node corresponds to *High*, *Medium* and *Low* states, according to the information received from the Learner Agent. The node *Main Problem* may present one of the states shown in Figure 1. This node is used to classify the student's BN model. Its initial probabilities represent the teacher's initial belief on the student's capacity to formulate a diagnostic hypothesis. The *Learner Network* node represents a possible classification for the student's BN model, according to major problems, as shown in Figure 1. The deterministic node *Confidence* presents *Low*, *Medium* and *High* states which are selected according to what the student informs. The *a priori* probabilities of this node are related to the classification of the BN model and were inspired in the works of Petr [10] and Lo [11]. The low confidence was higher than high confidence, because AMPLIA is a learning environment, and we consider that students do no feel totally skilled in the contents presented. The node *Tactics* is responsible for the presentation of pedagogic tactics, such as correction, experimentation, search, reflection, example, discussion, and hypothesis. Such tactics are selected from a function of utility (node *Utility*).

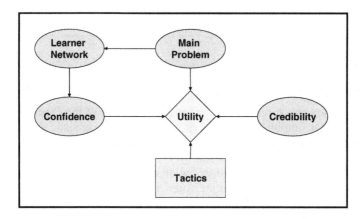

Fig. 3. Influence diagram for tactics selection

5   Discussion and Results

The results of the agents' implementation and of the AMPLIA environment are under observation in a seminar offered to medical professors at the Hospital de Clínicas de Porto Alegre. The seminar is divided in two phases: discussion of pedagogic resources and of theoretical concepts about uncertain domains, probabilistic networks, and knowledge representation. After that, the medical specialists will build expert's BN models on their domain areas, which will be used by the Domain Agent. A group of students will then use AMPLIA and we expect to observe and collect data for further analysis.

Figure 4 shows graphic with a student's performance (A) in AMPLIA. This graphic is generated on the fly by the Mediator Agent, making possible to visualize the student's BN model construction. In each cycle of the interaction, defined by the BN model submission, the left column indicates the student'*Self-confidence*, and the right column indicates the inferred *Credibility*. The horizontal line represents the BN model classification, from the lowest (*Not feasible*) to the highest point (*Complete*).

In the first cycle *Self-confidence* is *low*, *Credibility* is *medium* (Médio), and the network is *not feasible* (Inv). The tactic is to ask the student to identify the problem – presence of cycles or disconnected nodes. The student makes some changes, has no difficulties (high credibility) and declares high confidence, but the problem persists as the following cycle shows. The tactic suggests that the student checks the BN model again. Up to this point there are no negotiations, only different orientations, once there is not a BN. In the third cycle, the student reaches a satisfactory BN model and his self-confidence decreases. Negotiation starts at this point: the tactic selected is to raise hypothesis providing extra material, which can increase the student's self-confidence, as it happens in the fourth cycle (high *Self-confidence* and high *Credibility*, satisfying network). The Mediator Agent then insists on a new discussion displaying more material in order to enhance the BN model quality until it is *Complete*, this means it matches the study case proposed, and the student has high *Self-confidence* and autonomy. The negotiation process is then finished. The student's BN model does not need to be exactly the same as the expert's, it may be even better, once the final process will be to compare both networks against the real cases database.

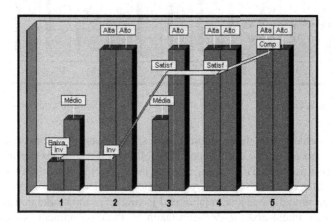

Fig. 4. Graphic showing a student's network (A) construction process

The graphic in Figure 5 shows the construction process of another student (B). In this example, the student (B) starts to build his BN model with low *Self-confidence* and *Credibility*, and errors. The Mediator Agent suggests the student test his BN model. In the second cycle, the student corrects his BN model with no major difficulties (potential network and high credibility) and medium confidence level. The Mediator Agent starts the negotiation, and confirms that there are some nodes lacking in the network so it provides material for further discussion. The student tries to improve the BN model, but is not very sure, as we can see for his trials in the third cycle. The tactic at this point is to give an example, so that the student can check what is missing in his BN model. The fourth cycle shows high confidence and satisfactory network. The new tactic is to ask the student which changes are still to be done in network and/or probability tables (fifth and sixth cycle). By observing the seventh cycle, we see that the network has its quality decreased and *Credibility* is low. We infer that during the several trials the student made he removed important nodes. The Mediator Agent changes its tactic and displays a list of nodes so that the student can check what is missing. This tactics is effective: the network becomes satisfactory again and the student has his confidence increased (eighth cycle). The negotiation has two more cycles, in which we see that the student has more autonomous actions (high *Credibility*). However, in the final of the tenth interaction cycle, the student leaves the process because his BN model satisfies the study case, even though the performance is worst than the expert's model.

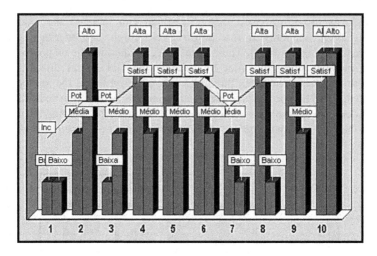

Fig. 5. Graphic II, showing a student's network (B) construction process

The results obtained in these preliminary tests have shown a convergence with the observations carried out by the teacher who followed the students during the process of network construction. This means that the teacher probably would use tactics and strategies similar to those selected by the system, to mediate the process. Summing up, the student model the teacher elaborated is similar to the model constructed in the AMPLIA environment and the decision taken by the environment is compliant with the teacher pedagogical position.

6   Final Considerations

During AMPLIA development we have been studying if the use of BNs as a pedagogical resource would be feasible, if they would enable the student to model his knowledge, follow the student's actions during the learning process, make inferences through a probabilistic agent, and select pedagogical actions that have the maximum utility for each student at each moment of his knowledge construction process. All these applications are assumed to be probabilistic, as they involve all the complexity and dynamics of a human agent learning process, but with the possibility of being followed by artificial agents.

The set of ideas described in this paper shows our perspective on how to analyze, interpret and model the complex phenomena that occurs in the teaching-learning process, through modeling the student and the process of pedagogical negotiation. The validation of these ideas and their generalization can only happen over time and within the real world application and testing.

The experimental seminars will take place, at first, in a LAN environment, allowing the fine-tuning of AMPLIA. As future work we intend to make it available over the Web and finish the development of a collaborative editor, so that a number of students will be able to work in the same case. The student self confidence declaration will also be the focus of future work, where the student's emotions, which are not being investigated here, will be taken into account.

Acknowledgements

The authors gratefully acknowledge the Brazilian funding agencies CAPES and CNPq for partial support to this research project, and M.A. Viviane Possamai, for translating this article from Portuguese into English.

References

1. Vicari, R.M., Flores, C.D., Seixas, L., Silvestre, A., Ladeira, M., Coelho, H.: A Multi-Agent Intelligent Environment for Medical Knowledge. In: Journal of Artificial Intelligence in Medicine, Vol.27. Elsevier Science, Amsterdam, (2003) 335-366.
2. Self, J. (1992). Computational Viewpoints. In Moyse & Elsom-Cook, pp. 21-40
3. Schwarz, B.B.; Neuman, Y.; Gil, J.; Ilya, M. (2001). Effects of argumentative activities on collective and individual arguments. European Conference on Computer-Supported Collaborative Learning – Euro-CSCL 2001, Maastricht, 22 - 24 March 2001.
4. Baker, M.J. (1994). A model for negotiation in teaching-learning dialogues Journal of Artificial Intelligence in Education, 5 (2), 199-254.
5. Flores, C.; Ladeira, M.; Viccari, R.; Höher, C. (2001) Una experiencia en el uso de redes probabilísticas en el diagnóstico médico. Informática Médica, Argentina, n.8, p. 25-29, 2001.
6. Flores, C., Seixas, L., Gluz, J.C., Patrício, D., Giacomel, F., Gonçalves, L., Vicari, R.M. (2004) AMPLIA Learning Environment Architecture. In: Workshop on Architectures and Methodologies for Building Agent-based Learning Environments. Sociedade Brasileira de Computação, São Luis, Maranhão, Brazil.
7. Heckerman, D.; Mamdani, A.; Wellman, M. (1995) Real-world Applications of Bayesian Networks: Introduction. Communications of the ACM, Vol. 38, n. 3. ACM, New York.
8. Seixas, L.; Flores, C.; Gluz, J.; Vicari, R. (2004) Acompanhamento do processo de construção do conhecimento por meio de um agente probabilístico. In: Procedings of XV Simpósio Brasileiro de Informática na Educação. Manaus - AM: EDUA, 2004.v.1, p.31-40.
9. Lewis, H.R., Papadimitriou, C.H. (1998) Elements of the Theory of Computation, 2nd edn. Prentice-Hall, New Jersey.
10. Petr, D.W. (2001) Measuring (and enhancing?) Student Confidence with Confidence Scores. In: Procedings of 30th ASEE/IEEE Frontiers in Education Conference. Kansas City, MO, USA, T4B-1.
11. Lo, J.-J., Wang, H.-M., Yeh, S.-W. (2004) Effects of Confidence Scores and Remedial Instruction on Prepositions Learning in Adaptive Hypermedia. Computers & Education, Vol. 42. Elsevier Science, Amsterdam, p:45-63.
12. Fischer, M., Ghidini, C., 2002. The ABC of Rational Agent Modelling. In: AAMAS 2002, Bologna, Italy, 849-856, 2002.
13. Flores, C.D., Gluz, J.C., Seixas, L., Viccari, R.M. (2004) Amplia Learning Environment: A Proposal for Pedagogical Negotiation. In: Proceedings of 6th International Conference on Enterprise Information Systems. Porto, Portugal, INSTICC, Vol. IV, p:279-286.

Towards a Market Mechanism for Airport Traffic Control*

Geert Jonker, John-Jules Meyer, and Frank Dignum

Institute of Information and Computing Sciences,
Utrecht University

Abstract. We present a multiagent decision mechanism for the airport traffic control domain. It enables airlines to jointly decide on proposals for plan conflict solutions. The mechanism uses weighted voting for maximizing global utility and Clarke Tax to discourage manipulation. We introduce accounts to ensure that all agents are treated fairly, to some extent. The mechanism allows an airport to determine the pay-off between optimality and fairness of schedules. Also, it compensates for agents that happen to be in practically unfavourable positions.

1 Introduction

Airports nowadays are more and more faced with air traffic congestions as a result of increased capacity demands. Much effort has been put into the development of software tools to assist the air traffic controllers in their decision-making process. These tools typically try to optimize a part of the planning on an airport, like the arrival and departure sequence and the gate assignment. Usually a strict hierarchy between planners exists to facilitate compliance to the several safety constraints. On the delay of an incoming aircraft, the arrival manager will typically replan its schedule first, to which the gate planner will adjust its schedule, after which the departure manager will adjust its planning.

A current trend in air traffic control (ATC) automation is that of distributed planning. An example is the Free Flight program [1,2], which enables aircraft to plan their own path of flight while communicating with aircraft around them to avoid collision. In the context of *collaborative decision-making*, a lot of work is done on information sharing between parties to increase quality of planning [3,4].

This article focuses on distributed airport traffic planning (ATP), i.e., the planning of the arrival, gate and departure process. We will look at the most important aspects of this planning and present a coordination mechanism by which aircraft can jointly decide on and enforce plan changes.

---

* This research is supported by the Technology Foundation STW, applied science division of NWO and the technology programme of the Ministry of Economic Affairs. Project DIT5780: Distributed Model Based Diagnosis and Repair.

C. Bento, A. Cardoso, and G. Dias (Eds.): EPIA 2005, LNAI 3808, pp. 500–511, 2005.

2   Airport Traffic Planning

The planning of airport traffic starts months before it is executed. Based on the flight requests of airlines, provisional arrival and departure schedules are made. As time progresses and more information becomes available, these schedules become more and more detailed. On the day before execution the optimal gate assignment is determined and 'frozen', i.e., no more flight requests can be added. On the day of execution all flights are assigned *time slots*, 15 minute time periods in which they have to depart or arrive[1]. If a flight 'misses' its slot it has to request a new slot which is often not immediately available.

There are many reasons why things don't always go as planned. An aircraft might arrive at an airport later than planned, it might not be able to land on arrival because of congestions, a runway might be closed, etc. It might not be able to occupy its gate on time because the previous aircraft hasn't left yet. The *turn-around process* of an aircraft, the time that it is at the gate and is cleaned, refuelled, boarded, etc., might take longer than planned. It might not be able to depart on time because of congestion on the runway. And so on. It is up to the air traffic controllers to deal with these disruptions as efficiently as possible. This last phase of planning just before execution is called *tactical planning*. In general the main aim for ATC is to minimize the total amount of delay while complying with the safety constraints. The most important safety constraints are the separation constraints that indicate the minimal distance aircraft should maintain in different situations. Other constraints follow from taxi distances, ground services (catering, refuelling, cleaning, etc.), transfer passengers, etc. Of course flights should be kept within their timeslots if possible.

An important criterion for ATC to observe in the tactical planning phase is *fairness*. In case global plan changes have to be made because of disrupting circumstances, the different airlines should each bear an equal share of the burden. On a smaller scale, if at one occasion a flight from airline X has to be delayed in order to resolve a planning problem, the next time a flight has to be delayed it should be one from another airline than X. A factor that usually gets very little attention is the preferences of airlines themselves. It can very well be that an airline (or a group of airlines) prefers situation X over Y, while ATC has decided Y but wouldn't object to X. This might be because ATC doesn't have the time to research Y, or that it lacks information on the airlines' preferences.

In general, it is hard for ATC to assess plan change costs for airlines and thus to involve airlines' preferences. On the one hand ATC doesn't know exactly the state of affairs of an airline, its schedule details and dependencies needed to correctly assess plan change costs. Also, it is hard for ATC to compare for instance the costs of changing gates to changing runways. On the other hand, airlines can not and are not willing to give all the information ATC would need. They can not because this would result in a communication overload for ATC. They also don't want to give all their information because this can be disadvantageous to

---

[1] The fair allocation of slots to airlines is a challenging problem on its own, see for instance [5].

them, see for instance [4]. It would be beneficial if the private information of agents can be involved in the decision making process without revealing it.

From the multiagent point of view, ATP can be seen as a coordination problem between self-interested agents that have different preferences and private utility functions. These actors need to agree on an efficient and fair planning to be executed collectively, under continuously changing circumstances. The general challenge is to transform the current ATP situation of centralized planning, authority and responsibility to a decentralized one, utilizing distributed knowledge.

3   Coordination in Multiagent Systems

In the context of multiagent research, coordination is usually seen as a process between two or more autonomous agents that try to achieve their individual goals, but cannot do so without adapting their behaviour to each other. For instance when agents have plannings that involve shared resources or task interdependencies, they must coordinate their plannings. A framework developed for this kind of cooperation is *generalized partial global planning* (GPGP) by Lesser and others [6]. When some agents are specialized in certain tasks it can be useful to delegate tasks. This gives the problem of *task allocation*, for which the multiagent auction protocol *Contract Net* is developed [7].

In the above-mentioned systems, as in most multiagent systems, the coordination is based on the concept of *mutual benefit gain*; agents engage in a deal or contract when it is beneficial for all of them. In terms of Contract Net, agents engage in a contract if it is *individually rational* for them to do so. In terms of GPGP, an agent accepts a proposal if its marginally utility gain is greater than its marginally utility cost. The same concept is also called *principled negotiation*, for instance in [8] where it is applied to runway slot allocation.

Generally, if mutual benefit gain is used, agents will eventually arrive at a *Pareto optimal* point, i.e., an outcome that cannot be improved without an agent decreasing its utility. A negotiation protocol that arrives at a Pareto optimal solution is called *Pareto efficient*. There are usually many Pareto efficient solutions for a given problem, together forming the *Pareto front*. An important question is which one of these points we want our mechanism to reach. A possible solution is to maximize the product of the utilities of the different agents, generally known as the Nash point [9]. In case the Pareto front is convex, this corresponds to the intuition that a good solution is one that is pareto optimal and gives agents approximately equal utilities. There are however many other ways to choose a best outcome. One could maximize a weighted sum of the utilities, maximize the minimum utility of the agents, minimize the differences in utilities, etc. Two important underlying motivations play a role here: *optimality* and *fairness*. Maximizing the sum of the utilities is a method ensuring optimality, while minimizing the differences in utility is aimed at fairness.

Using mutual benefit gain is not always desired in multiagent coordination. Take for instance the case where Anne and Ben have inherited a painting and want to decide how to distribute it between the two of them. There are three options: either Anne gets it, Ben gets it or they both get half of it. Obviously, half a painting is of little worth to them, but assume that they prefer half a painting above nothing. The three options can be denoted as tuples of the respective utilities: $(10, 0)$, $(0, 10)$ and $(1, 1)$. All three options are Pareto efficient. Maximizing the product of the utilities or any other decision function aimed at fairness would have the third option as outcome. Suppose that Anne and Ben settle for this option. The problem arises when Anne and Ben inherit another painting. If they use the same mechanism again, they would end up both with half a painting again. But now they are unhappy. Although the solution of the two negotiations together are fair, they are not Pareto efficient. Both of them would have preferred to get one painting each.

If we look at the two negotiations together it is easy to find a good solution. In this case the solution of one painting each is both optimal and perfectly fair. If we look only at the first negotiation however and we are not sure which other negotiations will 'come up', we need different motivations to choose to give the painting to one or the other. This choice can be justified only if we expect more negotiations to follow and we expect to maximize optimality by benefiting one agent now and the other next time. Thus, we have to relax the fairness constraint temporarily but remember the exact utilities of the enforced decisions, to arrive at more optimal and fair solutions in the long run. We will do this more formally in section 6.

4   Mechanism Design

Mechanism design is concerned with the design of procedures in which several parties participate to reach a certain outcome, where the procedure has to meet a number of criteria. The previous section has already stressed two important criteria a negotiation mechanism should meet: optimality and fairness. In this section we will list these and a number of other important criteria. For more information on mechanism design we refer the reader to [10] and [11].

Optimality - The outcome of a mechanism should be optimal with respect to the utilities the agents ascribe to the outcome. The most common requirement is that the outcome is Pareto optimal. When the sum of the utilities is maximized, we speak of maximizing *social welfare.*

Individual rationality - It should be attractive for a user to participate in the process, i.e., it may only gain utility by participating.

Nonmanipulability - A mechanism should motivate agents to behave in the manner that leads to the desired outcome. Usually this means that an agents dominant strategy should be to be truthful. This is also called *stability* and *incentive compatibility.* We will go more deeply into this subject in section 5.

Fairness - Although usually not explicitly named as a criterion in mechanism design, the ATP case shows that fairness is of crucial importance in airline negotiations. An airline will simply not accept to be delayed repeatedly while others are not. A mechanism should thus to a certain extend provide for an even distribution of utility gain or loss among the agents.

5   The Clarke Tax Mechanism

A way to enable a group of agents to decide on which option to choose from a set of options is by *voting*. An well known method to reach an optimal decision is *sealed bidding*, in which every agent specifies an amount of money (positive or negative) for each alternative. The bids are added up and the option with the highest accumulated preference wins.

A problem with this and many other kinds of voting is the fact that an agent might be tempted to vote *strategically*. This happens when they vote not in accordance to their own preferences in an attempt to manipulate the outcome. In the example where the agents submit their costs for each option so that the option with the lowest total costs will be chosen, an agent has an incentive to underbid. If it assumes that a certain outcome will be achieved even without the full force of its vote, he can submit a lower cost, pay less and still get his most preferred outcome. In the literature of economics this is known as the *free rider problem*.

A mechanism is called *nonmanipulable, stable* or *incentive compatible* when it yields the optimal social outcome when agents use their dominant strategy. In such protocols participants are best off when they are truthful. An example of a single-object nonmanipulable auction is the *Vickrey auction* [12], where every agents submits its bid for the single object on sale, and the object it sold to the highest bidder at the price of the second highest bid. Vickrey showed that a bidder's dominant strategy is to bid his true valuation [12].

An example of a nonmanipulable decision protocol using cardinal preferences is the *Clarke Tax Mechanism*[13,14]. In this mechanism agents need to decide on which solution from a set of solutions to choose, and do this by giving their valuations to each of the alternatives. The agents however run a risk of having to pay a tax, which happens if their vote made a difference to the outcome. The tax is equal to the total value of the outcome minus the value of the outcome that would have happened if it hadn't voted, and not less than zero. This tax discourages an agent to overbid on an alternative it likes; if overbidding means changing the outcome, the amount of tax it has to pay might be higher than difference in valuation between this and its next best alternative. At the same time, the tax doesn't encourage them to underbid; if underbidding changes the outcome, the saved tax will never compensate for the loss of utility. Therefore, revealing true preferences is the optimal strategy in the Clarke Tax mechanism. For a formal proof see [13] and [15].

The Clarke Tax mechanism (CTm) can be used in subsequent negotiations, such as occur in our domain. An example of this is the nonmanipulable meeting scheduling system of Ephrati et al [16]. In this mechanism agents decide on the best time for a meeting, using credits to express their preferences over alternatives. Clarke Tax encourages the agents to be truthful. However, the article doesn't address the issue of fairness, which is important in our domain. Neither does it identify a phenomenon we will deal with later called *enriching*.

6   A Voting Mechanism for ATP

The problem we are facing is the following: given a group of agents with different preferences and a set of proposals, which nonmanipulable decision mechanism allows them to find the most preferred proposal while fairness is maintained? In this section we will introduce such a decision mechanism. We use *weighted voting* with *Clarke tax* as the main principle to determine the most preferred solution among the voters, and *accounts* to ensure fairness.

We will describe the problem more formally now. When a planning conflict occurs, ATC generates a set of plan repair proposals $Q = \{q_1, q_2, \ldots, q_n\}$. We have k airlines, and each airline a has a utility function u_a describing a monetary valuation of a plan change. Such a utility will typically be a negative number, since plan changes often involve delays and gate or runway changes. As an example, $u_a(p, q) = -1000$ is to be read as "if the current planning is p, it would cost airline a 1000 euro to switch to planning q" or "airline a is indifferent between changing the current plan p to q or sticking with p and paying 1000 euro." It is of course possible that an airline has a positive utility for a plan change, for instance when an airline had a flight delayed against its will and the new proposal cancels this delay.

Each airline gives it utility as a weighted vote for every proposal. Clarke tax is in effect to prevent manipulation. If we add up all the valuations of the airlines for a single proposal, we get the group utility of this proposal:

$$U_G(p, q) = \sum_{a=1}^{k} u_a(p, q)$$

We will need the average utility per agent later on:

$$\overline{u}(p, q) = \frac{U_G(p, q)}{k}$$

To measure the (group) fairness of a proposal, we could add up the amounts to which each agents utility differs from the average utility of this proposal. This would give us an *unfairness* measure:

$$\mathtt{unf}_G(p, q) = \sum_{a=1}^{k} |u_a(p, q) - \overline{u}(p, q)|$$

However, we want to involve the agents' histories in the calculation of fairness. If an agent was previously burdened with a lower-than-average utility, it would be fair to compensate this with a higher-than-average utility the next time. Therefore we ascribe *accounts* to the agents on which the monetary utilities of the enforced decisions in the past are stored. They idea is that if an agent is involved in a planning conflict repair that has utility x to him, he earns the inverted utility, $-x$, on its account. So if an agent has an account of 20000 euro, it means that its contributions to conflict repairs in the past have cost

him 20000 euro. When calculating the unfairness of a proposal, we now involve
these accounts to get an *contextual unfairness*, i.e., the fairness of a proposal
in the context of previous decisions. Given the current balances of the agents
$B = \{ b_1, b_2, \ldots, b_n \}$, the current planning p and a proposal q, the contextual
unfairness is calculated as follows:

$$\mathrm{unf}_C(B, p, q) = \sum_{a=1}^{k} |(b_a - u_a(p, q)) - \overline{u_C}(B, p, q)|$$

where

$$\overline{u_C}(B, p, q) = \frac{\sum b_a - u_a(p, q)}{k}$$

Thus, instead of comparing utilities of single decisions, we take for each agent
the sum of its balance and the inverted utility for the proposal in question and
compare those.

This gives us for each proposal in Q both an unfairness measure and a optimality measure. Figure 1 illustrates the difference between a fair but suboptimal
solution and an optimal but not so fair solution. The bars denote for nine agents
the balances plus the inverted utilities or *costs*. At the top the current balances
of the agents are depicted; each agent has already contributed some costs to plan
repairs in the past. There are two proposals to choose between. At the left the
inverted utilities for the first proposal are added to the balances, resulting in the
new balances if this proposal would be chosen. This shows a relatively evenly
distribution of the new balances. On the right, the second proposal is depicted
that is more optimal, i.e., has a lower group cost / higher utility, but leads to
a less fair distribution of the balances. Thus, each proposal has its fairness and
optimality value. For a whole set of proposals, we could depict these values in a
diagram. Figure 2 shows such a diagram for an example proposal set. The point
on the far right for instance corresponds to a proposal that has a global cost
of only 1000 euro, but is not so fair since agents utilities differ on average 1600
euros from the average utility. The point on the far left top corresponds with a
very fair but very suboptimal solution.

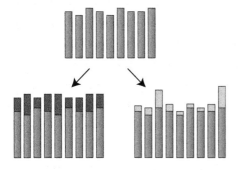

Fig. 1. Fair versus optimal

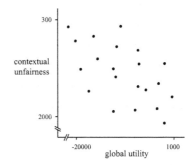

Fig. 2. An example proposal set

Out of these proposals one has to be chosen. It requires a weighing between optimality and fairness to decide on the winner. This weighing resembles the weighing of agents utilities we described in section 3. This time however fairness is explicitly weighed against optimality. This calls for other weighing functions - fairness and optimality are different concepts than individual utilities. Depending on the airport, the mechanism designer might choose to ensure a minimum level of fairness and then maximize optimality, or vice versa. It could also maximize a weighted sum of the two or choose the point closest to an ideal point. For the remainder of this article we will assume that the mechanism uses a weighted sum of optimality and fairness as its decision function.

7   Nonmanipulability

An important question is whether the introduction of accounts affects the non-manipulability of CTm. First note that CTm stimulates the agents to reveal their true preference relation over the proposals, but that this doesn't guarantee that they bid their *exact* valuations. An agent might just as well bid too high values for all of the proposals by adding a constant value c to its utilities, thus bidding $u_a(p,q)+c$ for every proposal q. CTm makes agents reveal their *relative* utilities, but not their *absolute* utilities. Adding a constant value to its bids doesn't influence the tax the agent might have to pay nor does it make one proposal more optimal compared to another. It can however influence the relative fairness of proposals in this way. Furthermore, if the agent uses a negative constant value, it will make him acquire a higher balance on its account than if it didn't.

A remedy for this kind of manipulation is to fix some of the agents bids. If for a set of proposals, every agent finds at least one of his bids been set for him already, it will have to make its other bids relative to this one. Of course, if these fixed utilities are different than the real utilities of the agents, things are not fair. It is however possible to correctly fix the utilities for some of the proposals, namely the proposals in which an agent doesn't participate. It is realistic to say that a plan repair proposal in which an airline doesn't have to do anything has a utility of zero for this airline. So if we make sure that for every agent there is at least one proposal in the proposal set in which he doesn't participate, and the bids for these proposals are fixed to zero, we make it unattractive to overbid or underbid.

Nevertheless, because of the introduction of accounts the mechanism isn't strictly nonmanipulable any more. In the original CTm the agent could never gain more than it would lose by lying. In our mechanism however, the extra credits earned by lying might in some cases be preferable above the extra tax the agent has to pay, especially when the amount of tax he has to pay is less than the amount he lied about.

8   Richness

In the mechanism described so far agents jointly vote over which proposal to enforce, are best off by being honest and can trust that they will not be very unfairly treated. An understandable worry that one might have is the question whether some agents aren't worse off than others still. In a credit based decision mechanism, an agent can be *rich*, i.e., it has a high balance on its account. Being rich means having a lot of negotiation power, since the mechanism favours agents with a lot of credits. Wouldn't it be reasonable to assume that some agents are in a *better economic position* than others, for instance because they are often able to help others, thus earning a lot of credits and becoming rich en mighty? Indeed these differences will surely exist. Some airlines might have their gates close together, making it easier for them to swap, other airlines might have flights from or to busy destinations, making it harder to change landing and take-off times. In other words, some agents will be in *practically preferable positions* compared to others. Fortunately, in the mechanism we described these practical differences don't lead to better economic positions. In fact, the mechanism smooths out practical advantages and disadvantages agents might have. Take for instance two airlines that can both solve the same problem. The first happens to be in such a situation that it is easy for him to solve it, for the second it is harder. The first is in this respect in a practically preferable position compared to the other and will bid a higher utility, the second agent will bid a lower utility. The first few times the problem occurs the first agent will be elected to solve the problem. When his expenditures are so high that it would no longer be fair that he is chosen again, the other agent is chosen. In this way agents in practically preferable positions are more often involved in plan repairs than others. Similarly, agents in practically unpreferable positions are compensated for this by having to contribute less to plan repairs.

There are other reasons however why richness can be undesirable. Note that richness can lead to locally suboptimal and unfair solutions. For instance, if A is a rich agent and $(a\ b\ c)$ is a solution that costs a credits to A, b credits to B and c credits to C, then the solution $(0\ 3\ 3)$ might be preferred above $(1\ 1\ 1)$, while the latter is clearly locally more optimal and fair. This is because the algorithm tries to spare rich agents and $(0\ 3\ 3)$ is a solution that spares agent A. In other words, richness means power.

From a global perspective, there is nothing wrong with a rich agent being favoured in decisions. This agent has already contributed a lot to the system, so it is only just if he is spared in future decisions. But from the perspective of an air traffic controller, this might not always be acceptable. It might very well be that in the example above a human air traffic controller would object against the fairer solution $(0\ 3\ 3)$ simply because it would in such a situation always choose $(1\ 1\ 1)$, no matter what happened in the past. Thus, *local fairness* or *fairness per decision* plays a role in human decisions. If we want our mechanism to have the same behaviour, we could do this by putting a maximum on the fairness per decision $U_G(p, q)$ or integrate it more subtly into the decision function.

There is however a more pressing reason why agents shouldn't become too rich. Privileges that are earned by helping others don't last forever. If for instance at a certain moment an aircraft from Air France is delayed and one from British Airways is not, and later that day it is exactly the other way around, both parties would agree. But if these two events are one month apart, British Airways would certainly not accept the first event as a justification for its delay. Apparently, earned privileges wear off. This means that in our mechanism, earned credits shouldn't last forever. The simplest way to achieve this is to impose a tax on the agents' accounts such that it reduces the differences in richness between agents. The tax function and frequency should be chosen such that it corresponds to reality; richness should be suppressed over time while fairness should still hold in short term. For instance, it could be chosen such that an earned amount of credits is halved after three days.

9   Exploitation

One pitfall that we haven't dealt with yet occurs in the following situation. Suppose we use the mechanism described as the decision making mechanism with taxes in effect. Suppose that in a very tightly packed schedule a conflict occurs that can most easily be solved by one aircraft being delayed for a short time. The conflict can also be solved in other ways, but these involve many more actions and are much more expensive. The single agent that is involved in the easy solution knows all of this, or has at least a very strong suspicion that the simple solution is much cheaper than all the other solutions. For the simple proposal, it can now submit a price higher than its actual costs, thereby earning more credits. For the proposals in which it isn't involved its valuation is fixed by the ATC-agent at zero. This doesn't however keep him from overbidding; he can make a good estimation of how far he can overbid without changing the outcome and having to pay a Clarke Tax. In this way he earns more credits than he is entitled to. We will call this principle *exploitation*, since the agent finds himself in an advantageous position and can exploit this.

Unfortunately, it is not easy to counteract exploitation. Just as in real life, people in key positions have more power than others. One drastic measure against exploitation would be the fixing of an initial solution by the ATC-agent. This initial solution is the solution the ATC-agent thinks is the most optimal. The airline agents can then negotiate over alternatives to this initial solution, using the CTm. All costs to the agents are now relative to the initial solution. The effect of exploitation is now greatly reduced, because if the conflict is such that it obviously needs the cooperation of a certain party to be solved, the initial solution will already entail this cooperation and the party involved looses its advantage. A clear deficit of this method is that it is not very fair. Agents are not compensated for the costs that are involved in executing the initial solution, not even if they decide on another solution. A workaround would be to let the ATC-agent estimate the costs of the initial solution to all the agents involved. Thus, when voting over alternatives, the valuations of the initial proposal are fixed for all agents. This will bring some fairness back into the mechanism, although a lot depends on the estimation capabilities of the ATC-agent of course. This method is also guaranteed to raise discussions. If the ATC-agent comes up with an initial solution where an aircraft X is delayed by 10 minutes and if it estimates its costs to be 200 euro, this aircraft might respond with: "No, no! There are transfer passengers on this plane who will miss their connection flight, the cost of this solution is 5000 euro!". Thus, the estimation capabilities of the ATC-agent are crucial. It would be most interesting to see how this mechanism might be augmented with argumentation, by which agent could found their submitted costs. This is however out of the scope of this article.

10   Related Work

The mechanism described here resembles the nonmanipulable meeting scheduler of Ephrati et al. [16], in which the CTm is used in repeated decisions. The issues of richness and exploitation we have identified in this paper apply to this mechanisms as well. Therefore, our work adds to the already many insights into the workings and application of the CTm [14].

11   Conclusion and Further Research

Decentralization is a trend that is gaining ground in air traffic control systems nowadays. In this context we have looked at automating the tactical planning and plan repair phase of airport traffic planning. We adopted a multiagent point of view, viewing ATP as a coordination problem between autonomous, competitive agents using private information whose plannings are highly dependent on each other. We introduced a weighted voting mechanism for distributed decision making with Clark Tax to discourage manipulation. To ensure a certain degree of fairness, we've introduced accounts on which an agent's contributions are stored. These accounts ensure that disadvantages resulting from different planning disruptions are fairly distributed over airlines. We have shown that the mechanism designer can determine the pay-off between optimality and fairness. In reality, some agents will be in better practical positions than others. We have shown how the mechanism compensates for this.

We've identified a number of pitfalls in the mechanism and how to avoid them. In order to keep agents from overbidding, a central agent should fix for every agent at least one valuation of a proposal, preferably a proposal in which it doesn't participate. If an agent still has an incentive to overbid because of exploiting, the central agent should estimate the costs of an initial solution. To prevent agents from becoming rich and thereby gaining too much power, either local fairness or taxes can be enforced.

We would like to look more closer to the matter of nonmanipulability. Questions we like to investigate are whether the extent to which an agent can manipulate can be formaly captured and whether we can contruct reasonable assumptions under which the *expected* utility of manipulation is negative.

We intend to test our mechanism in simulations of the ATP problem with real-world data. We expect this to give us an insight into a number of issues described above: the efficiency of the mechanism, the ideal pay-off between optimality and fairness, to what extent richness will occur, the effect of taxes and voting rules to name a few.

References

1. Radio Technical Commission for Aeronautics: Final report of RTCA task force 3: Free flight implementation. Technical report, Washington DC (1995)
2. Schultz, R., Daner, D., Zhao, Y.: Free-flight concept. Technical Report AIAA-97-3677, AIAA (2000)
3. European Organisation for the Safety or Air Navigation: Airport CDM applications guide (2003)
4. Chen, C., Ball, M.O., Hoffman, R., Vossen, T.: Collaborative decision making in air traffic management: Current and future research directions. Technical report (2000)
5. Brough, W., Clarke, E., Tideman, N.: Airport congestion and noise: Interplay of allocation and distribution. Transportation Research Record **1450** (1995) 3–7
6. Lesser, V., Decker, K., Wagner, T., Carver, N., Garvey, A., Horling, B., Neiman, D., Podorozhny, R., NagendraPrasad, M., Raja, A., Vincent, R., Xuan, P., Zhang, X.: Evolution of the GPGP/TAEMS Domain-Independent Coordination Framework. Autonomous Agents and Multi-Agent Systems **9** (2004) 87–143
7. Smith, R.: The contract net protocol: High-level communication and control in a distributed problem solver. In: IEEE Transaction on Computers. Number 12 in C-29 (1980) 1104–1113
8. Wangermann, J., Stengel, R.: Optimization and coordination of multiagent systems using principled negotiation. Journal of Guidance, Control and Dynamics **22** (1999) 43–50
9. Raiffa, H.: Lectures on Negotiation Analysis. Program on Negotiation at Harvard Law School, Harvard Law School, Camebridge (1996)
10. Sandholm, T.W.: Distributed rational decision making. In Weiss, G., ed.: Multiagent Systems: A Modern Approach to Distributed Artificial Intelligence. The MIT Press, Cambridge, MA, USA (1999) 201–258
11. Parkes, D.C.: Iterative Combinatorial Auctions: Achieving Economic and Computational Efficiency. PhD thesis, Department of Computer and Information Science, University of Pennsylvania (2001)
12. Vickrey, W.: Counterspeculation, Auctions and Competitive Sealed Tenders. Journal of Finance (1961) 8–37
13. Clarke, E.H.: Multipart pricing of public goods. Public Choice **18** (1971) 19–33
14. Ephrati, E., Rosenschein, J.S.: Deriving consensus in multi-agent systems. Journal of Artificial Intelligence **87** (1996) 21–74
15. Groves, T.: Incentive in teams. Econometrica **41** (1973) 617–631
16. Ephrati, E., Zlotkin, G., Rosenschein, R.: A non–manipulable meeting scheduling system. In: Proceedings of the 13th International Workshop on Distributed Artificial Intelligence, Seatle, WA (1994)

Intentions and Strategies in Game-Like Scenarios

Wojciech Jamroga[1], Wiebe van der Hoek[2], and Michael Wooldridge[2]

[1] Institute of Computer Science, Clausthal University of Technology, Germany
wjamroga@in.tu-clausthal.de
[2] Department of Computer Science, University of Liverpool, UK
{wiebe, mjw}@csc.liv.ac.uk

Abstract. In this paper, we investigate the link between logics of games and "mentalistic" logics of rational agency, in which agents are characterized in terms of attitudes such as belief, desire and intention. In particular, we investigate the possibility of extending the logics of games with the notion of agents' intentions (in the sense of Cohen and Levesque's BDI theory). We propose a new operator $(\mathbf{str}_a\sigma)$ that can be used to formalize reasoning about outcomes of strategies in game-like scenarios. We briefly discuss the relationship between intentions and goals in this new framework, and show how to capture dynamic logic-like constructs. Finally, we demonstrate how game-theoretical concepts like Nash equilibrium can be expressed to reason about rational intentions and their consequences.

Keywords: Multi-agent systems, strategic reasoning, common sense reasoning.

1 Introduction

In this paper, we investigate the link between logics of games (in particular, ATL – the temporal logic of coalitional strategic ability) and "mentalistic" logics of rational agency, in which agents are characterized in terms of attitudes such as belief, desire and intention. It is our contention that successful knowledge representation formalisms for multi-agent systems would ideally embrace both traditions. Specifically, we propose to extend ATL with agents' intentions (in the sense of Cohen and Levesque's BDI theory) in order to reason about agents' intended actions and their consequences.

This is especially interesting in game-like situations, where agents can consider hypothetical strategies of other agents, and come up with a better analysis of the game. We define a counterfactual operator $(\mathbf{str}_a\sigma)$ to reason about outcomes of strategy σ; in consequence, one can reason explicitly about *how* agents can achieve their goals, besides reasoning about *when* does it happen and *who* can do it, inherited from temporal logic and logic of strategic ability. We discuss the notion of intending *to do* an action, as opposed to of intending *to be* in a state that satisfies a particular property; we analyze the relationship between action- and state-oriented intentions, and point out that our framework allows for a natural interpretation of *collective* intentions and goals. We show how a dynamic-like logic of strategies can be defined on top of the resulting language, and argue that propositional dynamic logic can be embedded in it in a natural way. We present a model checking algorithm that runs in time linear in the size of the model and length of the formula. Finally, we suggest that this operator sits very well in game-like reasoning about rational agents, and show examples of such reasoning. Most concepts that we present here have been discussed only briefly due to space limitations.

C. Bento, A. Cardoso, and G. Dias (Eds.): EPIA 2005, LNAI 3808, pp. 512–523, 2005.

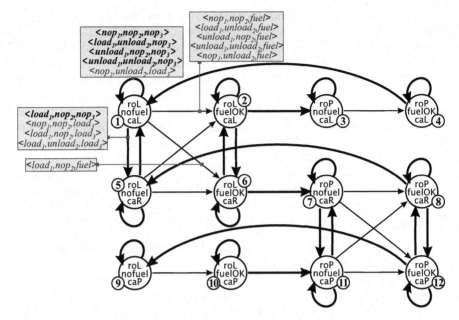

Fig. 1. Simple Rocket Domain. The "bold" transitions are the ones in which agent 3 intends to always choose nop_3.

2   What Agents Can Achieve?

Alternating-time Temporal Logic (ATL) [1] is a generalization of the branching time temporal logic CTL [8], in which path quantifiers are replaced by *cooperation modalities*. Formula $\langle\!\langle A \rangle\!\rangle \varphi$, where A is a coalition of agents (i.e., a subset of the "grand" set of agents Agt), expresses that there exists a collective plan for A such that, by following this plan, A can enforce φ. ATL formulae include temporal operators: "$\bigcirc$" ("in the next state"), $\square$ ("always") and $\mathcal{U}$ ("until").[1] Every occurrence of a temporal operator is preceded by exactly one cooperation modality in ATL (which is sometimes called "vanilla" ATL). The broader language of ATL*, in which no such restriction is imposed, is not discussed here. It is worth pointing out that the extension of ATL, proposed in this paper, makes use of terms that describe strategies, and in this sense is very different from ATL, in which strategies appear only in the semantics and are *not* referred to in the object language. We will introduce the semantic concepts behind ATL formally in Section 3. For now, we give a flavor of it with the following example.

Example 1. Consider a modified version of the Simple Rocket Domain from [3]. There is a rocket that can be moved between London (roL) and Paris (roP), and piece of cargo that can lie in London (caL), Paris (caP), or inside the rocket (caR). Three agents are involved: 1 who can load the cargo, unload it, or move the rocket; 2 who can unload the cargo or move the rocket, and 3 who can load the cargo or supply the rocket with

---

[1] An additional operator $\Diamond$ ("now or sometime in the future") can be defined as , $\Diamond\varphi \equiv \top \mathcal{U} \varphi$.

fuel. Every agent can also stay idle at a particular moment (the *nop* – "no-operation" actions). The "moving" action has the highest priority. "Loading" is effected when the rocket does not move and more agents try to load than to unload; "unloading" works in a similar way (in a sense, the agents "vote" whether the cargo should be loaded or unloaded). Finally, "fueling" can be accomplished only when the rocket tank is empty (alone or in parallel with loading or unloading). The rocket can move only if it has some fuel (fuelOK), and the fuel must be refilled after each flight. A model for the domain is shown in Figure 1 (we will refer to this model as M_1). All the transitions for state 1 (the cargo and the rocket are in London, no fuel in the rocket) are labeled; output of agents' choices for other states is analogous.

Example ATL formulae that hold in $M_1, 1$ are: $\neg\langle\langle 1\rangle\rangle\Diamond$caP (agent 1 cannot deliver the cargo to Paris on his own), $\langle\langle 1, 3\rangle\rangle\Diamond$caP (1 and 3 can deliver the cargo if they cooperate), and $\langle\langle 2, 3\rangle\rangle\Box$(roL $\wedge \langle\langle 2, 3\rangle\rangle\Diamond$roP) (2 and 3 can keep the rocket in London forever, and still they retain the ability to change their strategy and move the rocket to Paris). ■

Players' strategies and players' preferences are key concepts in game theory. Preference Game Logic (PGL) [20] has been an attempt to import the concept of preferences into the framework of ATL via formulae $[A : p]\varphi$, meaning that "*if agents A prefer outcome p then φ holds*". We would like to follow the basic idea behind PGL in this paper; however, it models agents' behavior in a rather arbitrary way. Roughly, the idea behind $[A : p]\varphi$ is that, if A prefer outcome p, they will only perform certain strategies, and they all lead to φ. In this paper, we disconnect these two notions, one giving the agents recommended strategies (given their preferences), the other calculating the effects of certain strategies being chosen. Our primary focus is on reasoning about outcomes of strategies, regardless of where the strategies come from (and whether they are rational or not). We formalize this kind of reasoning in section 3. However, having a device for reasoning about outcomes of *all* strategies, and a criterion of rationality, we can combine the two to reason about outcomes of strategies that *rational* agents may or should follow. This issue is discussed in more detail in Section 4.

3   ATL **with Intentions**

The language of ATL+I (with respect to a set of agents Agt, atomic propositions Π, and sets of primitive strategic terms $\Upsilon_{a_1}, ..., \Upsilon_{a_k}$ for agents $a_1, ..., a_k$ from Agt) can be formally defined as the following extension of ATL:

$$\varphi ::= p \mid \neg\varphi \mid \varphi \wedge \varphi \mid \langle\langle A\rangle\rangle\bigcirc\varphi \mid \langle\langle A\rangle\rangle\Box\varphi \mid \langle\langle A\rangle\rangle\varphi\mathcal{U}\varphi \mid (\mathbf{str}_a\sigma_a)\varphi$$

where $p \in \Pi$ is a proposition, $a \in$ Agt is an agent, $A \subseteq$ Agt is a group of agents, and $\sigma_a \in \Upsilon_a \cup \{$ any $\}$ is a strategic term for a. Models for ATL+I extend *concurrent game structures* from [1] with intention-accessibility relations, strategic terms and their denotation, and can be defined as:

$$M = \langle\text{Agt}, Q, \Pi, \pi, Act, d, o, \mathcal{I}_{a_1}, ..., \mathcal{I}_{a_k}, \Upsilon_{a_1}, ..., \Upsilon_{a_k}, [\![]\!]_{a_1}, ..., [\![]\!]_{a_k}\rangle.$$

Agt $= \{a_1, ..., a_k\}$ is the set of all agents (the "grand coalition"), Q is the set of states of the system, Π the set of atomic propositions, $\pi : \Pi \to \mathcal{P}(Q)$ a valuation of propositions, and Act the set of (atomic) actions; function $d :$ Agt $\times Q \to \mathcal{P}(Act)$ defines actions available to an agent in a state, and o is the (deterministic) transition function that assigns the outcome state $q' = o(q, \alpha_1, \ldots, \alpha_k)$ to every state q and tuple of actions $\langle \alpha_1, \ldots, \alpha_k \rangle$ that can be executed by the grand coalition in q.

$\mathcal{I}_a \subseteq Q \times Act$ is the intention-accessibility relation of agent a ($q\mathcal{I}_a\alpha$ meaning that a possibly intends to do action α when in q). A *strategy* of agent a is a conditional plan that specifies what a is going to do in every possible situation (state). We represent a's strategies as functions of type $s_a : Q \rightarrow \mathcal{P}(Act)$ such that, for every $q \in Q$: (1) $s_a(q)$ is non-empty, and (2) $s_a(q) \subseteq d_a(q)$. Thus, strategies can be non-deterministic – we only require that they specify choices of agents, and at least one choice per state. Strategic terms $\sigma \in \Upsilon_a$ are interpreted as strategies according to function $[\![\ ]\!]_a : \Upsilon_a \rightarrow (Q \rightarrow \mathcal{P}(Act))$ such that $[\![\sigma]\!]_a$ is a valid strategy for a. We also define $[\![\,\text{any}\,]\!]_a$ as the strategy that collects all valid actions of a, i.e. $[\![\,\text{any}\,]\!]_a(q) = d_a(q)$ for every q. A *collective strategy* for a group of agents $A = \{a_1, \ldots, a_r\}$ is simply a tuple of strategies $S_A = \langle s_{a_1}, \ldots, s_{a_r} \rangle$, one per agent from A. A *path* $\Lambda = q_0 q_1 q_2 \ldots$ in M is an infinite sequence of states that can be effected by subsequent transitions, and refers to a possible course of action (or a possible computation) that may occur in the system. We define $\Lambda[i]$ to be the ith state in path Λ.

In ATL, agents can choose any legal action at each state. Having added intentions to ATL models, we assume that *agents only do what they intend.* We say that strategy s_a is *consistent with a's intentions* if the choices specified by s_a are never ones that a does *not* intend, i.e. $q\mathcal{I}_a\alpha$ for every q and $\alpha \in s_a(q)$. A collective strategy S_A is consistent with A's intentions if s_a are consistent with a's intentions for all $a \in A$. The set of outcome paths of a (collective) strategy S_A from state q, denoted by $out(q, S_A)$, is defined as the set of paths in M, starting from q, that can result from A executing S_A. Unlike in ATL, we are going to consider only courses of action that are consistent with intentions of all agents:

$$out(q, S_A) = \{\Lambda = q_0 q_1 \ldots \mid q_0 = q \text{ and for every } i = 1, 2, \ldots \text{ there exists a tuple}$$
of all agents' actions $\langle \alpha_{a_1}^{i-1}, \ldots, \alpha_{a_k}^{i-1} \rangle$ such that $\alpha_a^{i-1} \in s_a(q_{i-1})$ for $a \in A$, and $q_{i-1}\mathcal{I}_a\alpha_a^{i-1}$ for $a \in \text{Agt} \setminus A$, and $o(q_{i-1}, \alpha_{a_1}^{i-1}, \ldots, \alpha_{a_k}^{i-1}) = q_i\}.$

Semantics of ATL+I can be given via the following clauses:

$M, q \vDash p$ iff $q \in \pi(p)$, for an atomic proposition p;

$M, q \vDash \neg\varphi$ iff $M, q \nvDash \varphi$;

$M, q \vDash \varphi \wedge \psi$ iff $M, q \vDash \varphi$ and $M, q \vDash \psi$;

$M, q \vDash \langle\!\langle A \rangle\!\rangle \bigcirc \varphi$ iff there is a collective strategy S_A consistent with A's intentions, such that for every $\Lambda \in out(q, S_A)$, we have that $M, \Lambda[1] \vDash \varphi$;

$M, q \vDash \langle\!\langle A \rangle\!\rangle \Box \varphi$ iff there is S_A consistent with A's intentions, such that for every $\Lambda \in out(q, S_A)$ and $i = 0, 1, 2, \ldots$, we have $M, \Lambda[i] \vDash \varphi$;

$M, q \vDash \langle\!\langle A \rangle\!\rangle \varphi \mathcal{U} \psi$ iff there is S_A consistent with A's intentions, such that for every $\Lambda \in out(q, S_A)$ there is $i \geq 0$ such that $M, \Lambda[i] \vDash \psi$ and for all j such that $0 \leq j < i$, we have $M, \Lambda[j] \vDash \varphi$;

$M, q \vDash (\mathbf{str}_a\sigma)\varphi$ iff $revise(M, a, [\![\sigma]\!]_a), q \vDash \varphi$.

The function $revise(M, a, s)$ updates model M by setting a's intention-accessibility relation $\mathcal{I}_a = \{\langle q, \alpha \rangle \mid \alpha \in s(q)\}$, so that s and $\mathcal{I}_a$ represent the same mapping in the resulting model. In a way, *revise* implements agents' intention revision (or strategy change) in game structures with intentions.

Example 2. Let us go back to the rocket agents from Example 1. If we have no information about agents' intended actions and strategies, we can model the game with model M_1' which augments M_1 with the least restrictive intention-accessibility relations, so that $q\mathcal{I}_a\alpha$ for every $q \in Q$, $a \in \mathbb{A}\text{gt}$ and $\alpha \in d_a(q)$. Let *nop* denote the "lazy" strategy for agent 3, i.e. $[\![nop]\!]_3(q) = nop_3$ for every q. Model $M_2 = revise(M_1', 3, [\![nop]\!]_3)$ depicts the situation where 3 intends to play *nop* and the other players have no specific intentions. Transitions, consistent with the intention-accessibility relations, are indicated with bold face font and thick arrows in Figure 1. Note that, for example, $M_2, 1 \models \langle\!\langle 2 \rangle\!\rangle \Box \neg \text{caR}$ (agent 2 can keep the cargo outside the rocket), and $M_2, 1 \models \langle\!\langle \rangle\!\rangle \Box \text{nofuel}$ (the rocket tank is always empty for all courses of action).[2] Thus, also $M_1', 1 \models (\text{str}_3 nop)\langle\!\langle 2 \rangle\!\rangle \Box \neg \text{caR}$ and $M_1', 1 \models (\text{str}_3 nop)\langle\!\langle \rangle\!\rangle \Box \text{nofuel}$.   ∎

In ATL+I, agents' current strategies are added to typical ATL models via modal relations $\mathcal{I}_a$. This resembles to some extent the semantics of epistemic temporal strategic logic from [19], where ATL-like formulae are interpreted over models *and* strategies. However, the strategies in [19] are used mostly as a technical device to define the semantics of cooperation modalities: they cannot be referred to in the object language of ETSL, and they change only in a very limited way on the semantic side.

The counterfactual intention operator $(\text{str}_a\sigma)$, on the other hand, is very similar to the commitment operator from [17]. However, committing to a strategy is modeled in [17] through an update operator that *removes* the unintended choices from the system, and hence it refers to *irrevocable* commitments. Here, intended strategies can be freely revised or revoked, which makes our proposal close to Stalnaker's work on hypothetical reasoning about strategies [15], cf. Section 3.3 for more discussion.

Remark 1. Our semantics of cooperation modalities deviates from the original semantics of ATL [1] in two respects. First, we employ "memoryless" strategies in this paper, while in [1] strategies assign agents' choices to *sequences* of states (which suggests that agents can recall the whole history of the game). It should be pointed out that both types of strategies yield equivalent semantics for "vanilla" ATL, although the choice of one or another notion of strategy affects the semantics (and complexity) of the full ATL* and most ATL variants for games with incomplete information. Thus, we use memoryless strategies to increase the simplicity and extendability of our approach.

Second, we allow for non-deterministic strategies here, while only deterministic strategies are used in [1]. One reason is that we need the "all actions possible" strategic term *any* to express some important properties. Additionally, we consider nondeterministic strategies vital for modeling situations in which some agents may play at random (inherent nondeterminism)[3] or we have only partial information about agents' intentions (underspecification). Note that, if agents A have a non-deterministic strategy

---

[2] The "empty set" cooperation modality $\langle\!\langle \rangle\!\rangle$ is equivalent to the CTL's "for every path" quantifier A. Similarly, $\langle\!\langle \mathbb{A}\text{gt} \rangle\!\rangle$ is equivalent to the CTL's "there is a path" quantifier E.

[3] This interpretation makes nondeterministic strategies similar to *mixed strategies* from game theory. However, we do not assume any probability distribution for the agents' choices here.

S_A to guarantee φ *for all computations that may result from playing* S_A, then every deterministic sub-strategy of S_A guarantees φ as well. In consequence, non-deterministic strategies do not change the semantics of cooperation modalities (even for ATL*).   ∎

It might be convenient to add collective strategies to the language of ATL+I. For $A = \{a_1, ..., a_r\}$, we define:

$$(\mathbf{str}_A \langle \sigma_{a_1}, ..., \sigma_{a_r} \rangle) \varphi \equiv (\mathbf{str}_{a_1} \sigma_{a_1}) ... (\mathbf{str}_{a_r} \sigma_{a_r}) \varphi.$$

In what follows, we will sometimes overload the symbol any to denote a tuple of strategies $\langle$ any , ..., any $\rangle$.

Remark 2. ATL+I semantically subsumes the original "pure" ATL from [1], as ATL models can be treated as a special case of ATL+I models, in which every available choice is possibly intended by agents at each state.   ∎

Remark 3. ATL+I syntactically subsumes ATL, as the ATL formulae $\langle\!\langle A \rangle\!\rangle \bigcirc \varphi$, $\langle\!\langle A \rangle\!\rangle \Box \varphi$, and $\langle\!\langle A \rangle\!\rangle \varphi \mathcal{U} \psi$ are equivalent to ATL+I formulae $(\mathbf{str}_{\mathrm{Agt}}$ any $) \langle\!\langle A \rangle\!\rangle \bigcirc \varphi$, $(\mathbf{str}_{\mathrm{Agt}}$ any $) \langle\!\langle A \rangle\!\rangle \Box \varphi$, and $(\mathbf{str}_{\mathrm{Agt}}$ any $) \langle\!\langle A \rangle\!\rangle \varphi \mathcal{U} \psi$ respectively.   ∎

3.1   Intentions *to Do* vs. Intentions *to Be*

In this paper – among other issues – we consider a particular notion of *intentions*. Most models from the classical literature on intentions [6,14] suggest that intentions refer to properties of *situations*, i.e. agents intend to *be* in a state that satisfies a particular property. However, another notion of "intending" seems to be equally common in everyday language (and even in papers that refer to agents from a more practical perspective, e.g. [13]): namely, an agent may intend to *do* a particular action or execute a plan. In fact, "intending to do" was already considered in [7]; however, in that work, intentions were treated as a secondary notion that had to be derived from primitive concepts like beliefs or desires. We propose to model these "dynamically-oriented" intentions as first-class entities instead. Having the intentions "to do" in the models, we can also enable reasoning about them in the object language via another modal operator Int_a with the following semantics:

$$M, q \models \mathsf{Int}_a \sigma \;\textit{iff}\;\textit{for each}\; \alpha \in Act\; \textit{we have}\; q \mathcal{I}_a \alpha \Leftrightarrow \alpha \in [\![\sigma]\!]_a(q).$$

Note that $\mathsf{Int}_a \sigma$ formalizes a *local* notion of intention, i.e. intention to do an *action* in a particular state, while the counterfactual operator $(\mathbf{str}_a \sigma)$ is global in its scope. Collective intentions can be defined as:

$$\mathsf{Int}_{\{a_1, ..., a_r\}} \langle \sigma_{a_1}, ..., \sigma_{a_r} \rangle \equiv \mathsf{Int}_{a_1} \sigma_{a_1} \wedge ... \wedge \mathsf{Int}_{a_r} \sigma_{a_r}.$$

Furthermore, intentions "to be" can be defined as follows. Let us assume that nondeterministic strategies model *genuine non-determinism* of agents, i.e. that, if $q \mathcal{I}_a \{\alpha_1, \alpha_2, ...\}$ then agent a does not know himself whether he is going to execute α_1 or α_2 or ... etc. in state q. Under this interpretation, we propose the following definition of coalition A's intentions "to be" (we call such intentions *goals* after Cohen and Levesque):

$$\mathsf{Goal}_A \varphi \equiv (\mathbf{str}_{\mathrm{Agt} \setminus A} \text{ any }) \langle\!\langle \rangle\!\rangle \varphi \wedge \neg (\mathbf{str}_{\mathrm{Agt}} \text{ any }) \langle\!\langle \rangle\!\rangle \varphi.$$

That is, A intend to bring about goal φ iff φ is an inevitable consequence of A's intended strategy, regardless of what other agents do – but φ is not *"physically"* inevitable (i.e. inevitable for all possible intentions, cf. Section 3.3). The definition is somewhat preliminary, since it does not fully address e.g. unwelcome but inevitable consequences of one's intended course of action; we hope to discuss such issues further in future work. Note that, in the above definition, φ is a property of paths (courses of action) rather than states. Thus, Goal_a says which courses of action a intends to take part in (or bring about), rather than which states he intends to be in. This approach allows us to express subtle differences between various types of an agent's intentions "to be": the agent may intend to be in a state that satisfies φ right in the *next* moment ($\mathsf{Goal}_a \bigcirc \varphi$), or he may intend to *eventually* bring about such a state ($\mathsf{Goal}_a \Diamond \varphi$), or be in "safe" states all the time ($\mathsf{Goal}_a \square \mathsf{safe}$) etc. For instance, the "lazy" strategy of agent 3 in model M_2 (Example 2) implies that the rocket will never get out from London if 1 is the initial state – regardless of what 1 and 2 do. Thus, $M_2, 1 \vDash \mathsf{Goal}_3 \square \mathsf{roL}$.

3.2 A Dynamic Logic of Strategies

It should be easy to see from previous examples how we can reason about outcomes of agents' strategies with ATL+I. We point out that our $(\mathbf{str}_a \sigma)$ operator can be used to facilitate reasoning about strategies in the style of dynamic logic [10]. In particular, formulae $[A/\sigma]\varphi$ meaning that *"every execution of strategy σ by agents A guarantees property φ"*, or, more precisely, *"for every execution of strategy σ by A, φ inevitably holds (regardless of what other agents do)"* can be defined as:

$$[A/\sigma]\varphi \equiv (\mathbf{str}_A \sigma)(\mathbf{str}_{\mathrm{Agt} \setminus A} \text{ any })\langle\!\langle \rangle\!\rangle \varphi.$$

Note that, in that case, φ should be a temporal formula (path formula), as execution of a strategy is a process that happens over time.

Moreover, we observe that strategies in ATL are very similar to the way in which *programs* (or *actions*) are modeled in dynamic logic. In fact, our strategic terms and their denotations can refer to both strategies and actions. The difference lies not in the semantic representation of actions vs. strategies, but in the way their execution is understood: actions are one-step activities, while a strategy is executed indefinitely (or until it is replaced with another strategy). A fragment of propositional dynamic logic can be embedded in ATL+I with the following definitions, where σ is a program executed by the grand coalition of agents (i.e. by the whole *system*):

$$[\sigma]\varphi \equiv [\mathrm{Agt}/\sigma] \bigcirc \varphi, \text{ and consequently}$$
$$<\sigma> \varphi \equiv \neg [\mathrm{Agt}/\sigma] \bigcirc \neg \varphi.$$

A richer language of strategic terms is needed to embed the full syntax of PDL in ATL+I.

3.3 Properties of Intention Revision in ATL+I

Proposition 1. *Let φ be a formula of ATL+I, and let $\mathbf{Ph} \equiv (\mathbf{str}_{\mathrm{Agt}} \text{ any })$ be a shorthand for the counterfactual operator that yields the bare, "physical" system without any specific intentions assumed (i.e. the system with all actions "marked" as possibly intended by respective agents). The following formulae are tautologies of ATL+I:*

1. $(\mathbf{str}_a\sigma_1)(\mathbf{str}_a\sigma_2)\varphi \leftrightarrow (\mathbf{str}_a\sigma_2)\varphi$: *a new intention cancels the former intention.*

2. $(\mathbf{Ph}\langle\!\langle\rangle\!\rangle\bigcirc\varphi) \rightarrow (\mathbf{str}_a\sigma)\langle\!\langle\rangle\!\rangle\bigcirc(\mathbf{Ph}\varphi)$, $(\mathbf{Ph}\langle\!\langle\rangle\!\rangle\square\varphi) \rightarrow (\mathbf{str}_a\sigma)\langle\!\langle\rangle\!\rangle\square(\mathbf{Ph}\varphi)$,
and $(\mathbf{Ph}\langle\!\langle\rangle\!\rangle\varphi\,\mathcal{U}\psi) \rightarrow (\mathbf{str}_a\sigma)\langle\!\langle\rangle\!\rangle(\mathbf{Ph}\varphi)\,\mathcal{U}(\mathbf{Ph}\psi)$.

3. $(\mathbf{str}_a\sigma)\langle\!\langle\mathbb{A}\mathrm{gt}\rangle\!\rangle\bigcirc(\mathbf{Ph}\varphi) \rightarrow (\mathbf{Ph}\langle\!\langle\mathbb{A}\mathrm{gt}\rangle\!\rangle\bigcirc\varphi)$, *and similarly for* $\square\varphi$ *and* $\varphi\mathcal{U}\psi$.

The counterfactual operator $(\mathbf{str}_A\sigma)$ is based on model update, which makes it similar to the preference operator from [20] and the commitment operator from [17]. Unlike in those approaches, however, model updates in ATL+I are *not* cumulative (cf. Proposition 1.1). This is because the choices we assume unintended by a via $(\mathbf{str}_a\sigma)$ are not removed from the model, they are only left "unmarked" by the new intention-accessibility relation $\mathcal{I}_a$. The update specified by $(\mathbf{str}_a\sigma)$ does not change the "hard", temporal structure of the system, it may only change the "soft" modal relations that encode agents' mental attitudes. In a way, it makes it possible to distinguish between the "physical" abilities of agents, and their intentional stance. Two important properties of such non-cumulative model updates are addressed by Propositions 1.2 and 1.3: first, a property that holds in the next moment for all *physical* paths of a system, is also *physically* true in the next moment for the paths consistent with agents' intentions; second, if there is an intentionally possible path along which ϕ holds physically in the next moment, then such a path exists in the system physically as well. Similar results hold for other temporal operators. We note that properties 1.2 and 1.3 are analogues of Lemma 1 from [18] and Proposition 2 from [17], but it is not necessary to restrict their scope to universal (resp. existential) formulae in ATL+I.

An interesting kind of property that can be expressed in ATL+I is: $(\mathbf{str}_A\sigma)\langle\!\langle\rangle\!\rangle\square(\varphi\wedge(\mathbf{str}_A\text{ any})\langle\!\langle A\rangle\!\rangle\Diamond\neg\varphi)$: agents A can use strategy σ to enforce that always φ, and at the same time retain *physical* ability to falsify φ. For instance, for our rocket agents, we have that $M_2, 1 \models (\mathbf{str}_{2,3}\langle nop_2, nop_3\rangle)\langle\!\langle\rangle\!\rangle\square(\mathsf{roL}\wedge(\mathbf{str}_{2,3}\text{ any})\langle\!\langle 2,3\rangle\!\rangle\Diamond\mathsf{roP})$. Note that this kind of property is not even *satisfiable* in logics with models updated by removing transitions, e.g. for the "ATL+commitment" logic introduced in [18].

ATL+I makes it also possible to discuss the dynamics of intentions: we can consider what happens if some agents change their strategies after some time. For example, formula $(\mathbf{str}_b\sigma_1)\langle\!\langle\rangle\!\rangle\Diamond(\mathbf{str}_b\sigma_2)\langle\!\langle\rangle\!\rangle\Diamond\varphi$, says that φ must be eventually achieved if agent b starts with playing strategy σ_1, but after some time switches to σ_2. Another formula, $(\mathbf{str}_b\sigma_1)\langle\!\langle a\rangle\!\rangle\Diamond((\mathbf{str}_b\text{ any})\langle\!\langle a\rangle\!\rangle\square\varphi)$, states that, if b plays σ_1 initially, then a can secure φ afterwards, even if b changes his strategy. (Example: if b refrains from selling his assets of company a for some time, then a can keep away from bankruptcy, regardless of what b decides to do when a's recovery plan has been executed.)

3.4 Model Checking ATL+I

The *model checking problem* for ATL+I is the problem of determining, for any given ATL+I formula φ, model M, and state q in M, whether or not $M, q \models \varphi$. There are three reasons for the importance of model checking. First, in many real-life situations, it is relatively easy to come up with a "natural" model of the reality. Next, checking if a property holds in a given model is computationally less expensive than checking if it holds in *all* models. Finally, the idea of "planning as model checking" [9] gives it a practical flavor: model checking algorithms can be adapted for generating plans in various domains.

The following algorithm extends the ATL model checking algorithm from [1] to compute the set of states Q_φ in which φ holds in M.

- Cases $\varphi \equiv p$, $\neg\psi$, $\psi_1 \wedge \psi_2$: tackle in the standard way.
- Case $\varphi \equiv (\mathbf{str}_a \sigma)\psi$: compute $M' = revise(M, a, [\![\sigma]\!]_a)$, and check ψ in M'.
- Case $\varphi \equiv \langle\!\langle A \rangle\!\rangle \bigcirc \psi$: compute Q_ψ for the *original* model M, then go through M deleting transitions where any agent a performs an action not dictated by $\mathcal{I}_a$. Finally, use the ATL model checking algorithm for formula $\langle\!\langle A \rangle\!\rangle \bigcirc Q_\psi$ and the resulting ("trimmed") model.
- Cases $\varphi \equiv \langle\!\langle A \rangle\!\rangle \Box \psi$, $\langle\!\langle A \rangle\!\rangle \psi_1 \mathcal{U} \psi_2$: analogous.

Let us observe that given M, a, and σ, computing $revise(M, a, s_a)$ and the "trimming" procedure can be done in time $O(m)$, where m is the number of transitions in M. As ATL model checking enjoys complexity of $O(ml)$, it gives us the following result.

Proposition 2. *Model checking an* ATL+I *formula* φ *in model* M *can be done in time* $O(ml)$, *where* m *is the number of transitions in* M, *and* l *is the length of* φ.

4   Reasoning About Rational Intentions

Using the counterfactual operator $(\mathbf{str}_A \sigma)$, we do not assume anything about payoffs and/or preferences of players, about their rationality, optimality of their strategies etc. – we simply assume that A intend to play σ (for whatever reasons), and ask what are the consequences. Reasoning about *rational* agents can be done on top of this: we should define what it means for an intention to be rational and then reason about outcomes of such intentions with $(\mathbf{str}_A \sigma)$.

There is a growing literature on using temporal [5], dynamic [11,16], and ATL-style logics [17,4] for reasoning about solution concepts.[4] We note that ATL operators $\langle\!\langle A \rangle\!\rangle$ can be seen as a formalization of reasoning about strategic game forms [17], or, even more naturally, *extensive game forms* – since concurrent game structures generalize[5] game trees with perfect information, except for agents' utilities. In order to "emulate" utilities, we follow the approach of [2]. Let U denote the set of all possible utility values in the game; U will be fixed and finite for any given game. For each value $v \in U$ and agent $a \in \mathrm{Agt}$, we introduce a proposition $(u_a \geq v)$ into our set Π of primitive propositions, and fix the valuation function π so that $(u_a \geq v)$ is satisfied in state q iff a gets at least v in q. The correspondence between a traditional game tree Γ and a concurrent game structure M can be captured as follows. Let $\Gamma = \langle \Sigma, \mathcal{A}, H, ow, u \rangle$, where Σ is a finite set of players, $\mathcal{A}$ a finite set of actions, H a

---

[4] Among these, we come perhaps closest to [11] with our approach in this section. In [11], however, the notion of Nash equilibrium is captured via propositional *dynamic* logic, which restricts the discussion to traditional games on finite trees (since only properties of strategies whose execution *terminates* can be addressed). Another consequence of using PDL is that outcomes of strategies are classically defined in terms of properties achieved *eventually* in terminal states, while we propose a more general approach (i.e. temporal properties of *runs*).

[5] Concurrent game structures may include cycles and simultaneous moves of players, which are absent in game trees.

finite set of (finite) action sequences (i.e. legal game histories), and $ow(h)$ defines which player "owns" the next move after history h. We define the set of actions available at h as $\mathcal{A}(h) = \{\alpha \mid h\alpha \in H\}$, and the set of terminal situations as $Term = \{h \mid \mathcal{A}(h) = \varnothing\}$. Function $u : \Sigma \times Term \rightarrow U$ assigns agents' utilities to every final position of the game [12]. We say that $M = \langle \text{Agt}, Q, \Pi, \pi, Act, d, o \rangle$ corresponds to Γ iff: (1) $\text{Agt} = \Sigma$, (2) $Q = H$, (3) Π and π include propositions $(u_a \geq v)$ to emulate utilities for terminal states in the way described above, (4) $Act = \mathcal{A} \cup \{nop\}$, (5) $d_a(q) = \mathcal{A}(q)$ if $a = ow(q)$ and $\{nop\}$ otherwise, (6) $o(q, nop, ..., \alpha, ..., nop) = q\alpha$, and (7) $o(q, nop, nop, ..., nop) = q$ for $q \in Term$. Additionally, for an ATL+I model M' that adds intentions and strategic terms to M, we define that Γ corresponds to M' iff Γ corresponds to M and $q\mathcal{I}_a\alpha$ for every $q \in Q, a \in \text{Agt}, \alpha \in d_a(q)$ (all choices are possibly intended). Note that for every extensive form game Γ, there is a corresponding concurrent game structure, but the reverse is not true.

Now we can show how Nash equilibrium can be specified in ATL+I, and how one can reason about outcomes of agents whose rationality is defined in terms of Nash equilibrium. As games specified by concurrent game structures are usually infinite, there are no terminal positions in these games in general. Therefore it seems reasonable to define outcomes of strategies via properties of resulting paths (courses of action) rather than single states.[6] For example, we may be satisfied if a utility value v is achieved eventually: $\Diamond(u_a \geq v)$, preserved until a property p holds: $(u_a \geq v)\mathcal{U}$p etc. To capture such subtleties, we propose the notion of T-Nash equilibrium, parametrized with a unary temporal operator $T = \bigcirc, \square, \Diamond, \_\mathcal{U}\psi, \psi\mathcal{U}\_$. Thus, we have a family of equilibria now: $\bigcirc$-Nash equilibrium, $\square$-Nash equilibrium etc. Let σ describe a collective strategy for the grand coalition Agt, and let $\sigma[a]$ be the strategic term for a's strategy in σ. Similarly, $\sigma[A]$ is the part of σ that refers to the strategy of A. We write $BR_a^T(\sigma)$ to denote the fact that strategy $\sigma[a]$ is a_i's best response to $\text{Agt} \setminus \{a\}$ playing $\sigma[\text{Agt} \setminus \{a\}]$. For example, $BR_a^\square(\sigma)$ means that a cannot increase his minimal guaranteed payoff by deviating from $\sigma[a]$ unilaterally. Likewise, $BR_a^\Diamond(\sigma)$ says that a cannot increase his maximal guaranteed payoff (i.e. the payoff that can be obtained *eventually* along *every* possible course of action) by a unilateral deviation from $\sigma[a]$. We write $NE^T(\sigma)$ to denote the fact that σ is a T-Nash equilibrium.

$$BR_a^T(\sigma) \equiv (\mathbf{str}_{\text{Agt}\setminus\{a\}}\sigma[\text{Agt} \setminus \{a\}])(\bigwedge_{v\in U} (\langle\langle a \rangle\rangle T(u_a \geq v)) \rightarrow (\mathbf{str}_a\sigma[a])\langle\langle\rangle\rangle T(u_a \geq v))$$

$$NE^T(\sigma) \equiv \bigwedge_{a\in\text{Agt}} BR_a^T(\sigma).$$

Proposition 3. *Let Γ be a game, and M a concurrent game structure with intentions, corresponding to Γ. Then $M, \varnothing \vDash NE^\Diamond(\sigma)$ iff σ denotes a Nash equilibrium in Γ.*

Thus, Nash equilibrium in traditional games is the special case of our temporal Nash equilibrium, in which we ask about utilities one must get eventually at the end of the game. NE^T extends this notion by focusing on temporal patterns rather than single utility values. Moreover, as concurrent game structures specify interactions that are usually infinite and may include simultaneous moves of players (as well as cycles of transitions), the concept of Nash equilibrium naturally extends to such generalized games in our definition.

---

[6] The idea of assigning utilities to *runs* rather than states is not entirely new, cf. [21].

1	x, 1, 0	7	x, −3, −1
2	x, 1, 2	8	x, −3, 1
3	x, 1, 0	9	1, −3, 0
4	x, 1, 2	10	1, −3, 2
5	x, 1, −1	11	1, −3, 0
6	x, 1, 1	12	1, −3, 2

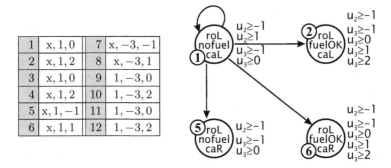

Fig. 2. The rocket game: Utility table and a fragment of the game structure

Example 3. Let us consider an infinite game played by the "rocket agents" from previous examples. Figure 2 shows the table of utilities for the game, as well as a fragment of system M_3, that augments M_1' with propositions encoding agents' utilities. Note that, unlike for game structures corresponding to traditional game trees, there are no final states in the model, and utility values are defined for most states.

Let *carry* denote the strategy for agent 1, in which the agent loads the cargo in states $1, 2, 5$, moves the rocket in states $4, 6$, unloads the cargo in $7, 8$ and does nothing in $3, 9, 10, 11, 12$. Moreover, *fuel* denotes the strategy in which 3 executes $fuel_3$ in $1, 3, 5, 7, 9, 11$, and nop_3 elsewhere. Now, $M_3, 1 \vDash NE^\Diamond(\langle carry, nop, fuel \rangle)$ because $BR_1^\Diamond(\langle carry, nop, fuel \rangle)$ and $BR_2^\Diamond(\langle carry, nop, fuel \rangle)$ and $BR_3^\Diamond(\langle carry, nop, fuel \rangle)$. Also, $M_3, 6 \vDash NE^\Box(\langle nop, nop, nop \rangle)$: 2 and 3 are satisfied at state 6, and 1 cannot achieve $\Box$caP anyway. Thus, the system is in $\Diamond$-Nash equilibrium in state 1, and in $\Box$-Nash equilibrium in state 6. ∎

Properties of rational strategies can be now verified through formulae of form $NE^T(\sigma) \wedge (\mathbf{str}_{\mathrm{Agt}}\sigma)\varphi$, where φ is the property we would like to check. For example, we have that $M_3, 6 \vDash NE^\Box(\langle nop, nop, nop \rangle) \wedge (\mathbf{str}_{\mathrm{Agt}}\langle nop, nop, nop \rangle)\langle\langle\rangle\rangle\Box$caR.

Remark 4. Building upon the concept of Nash equilibrium, we may like to express rationality of strategies as: *"rational$_A^T(\sigma_A)$ iff there is $\sigma'_{\mathrm{Agt} \setminus A}$ such that $NE^T(\sigma_A, \sigma'_{\mathrm{Agt} \setminus A})$"*. In a similar way, it seems natural to reason about behavior of rational agents with sentences like *"suppose that A intend to play any strategy σ_A such that rational$_A^T(\sigma_A)$, then φ holds"*, Note that reasoning of this kind is beyond the scope of ATL+I, as the logic does not include explicit quantification over strategies yet. ∎

5 Conclusions

What ATL offers, is in fact an abstraction of strategies. ATL modalities quantify over strategies in game theory-like fashion, but the strategies are hidden in the semantics: we can only specify *who* can do *what* and *when* in the object language of ATL, but we cannot tell *how* it can be done. In this paper, we propose to extend ATL with a notion of agents' intentions, and with an operator that enables addressing agents' strategies explicitly. The resulting logic, ATL+I, provides a formal language to express (and reason about) facts concerning strategies of agents in multiagent settings. We believe that the logic offers more than just a sum of its parts: counterfactual reasoning in game-like situations, dynamic logic of strategies, intention revision, rationality criteria, reasoning about rational intentions as well as relationship between intentions and goals are example issues that can be formalized and investigated with ATL+I. Thus, most of all, we see ATL+I as a potent framework for modeling and specifying systems that include multiple agents, and for discussing and verifying their properties.

We thank Peter Novak and the anonymous reviewers for their helpful remarks.

References

1. R. Alur, T. A. Henzinger, and O. Kupferman. Alternating-time Temporal Logic. *Journal of the ACM*, 49:672–713, 2002.
2. A. Baltag. A logic for suspicious players. *Bulletin of Economic Research*, 54(1):1–46, 2002.
3. A. L. Blum and M. L. Furst. Fast planning through graph analysis. *Artificial Intelligence*, 90:281–300, 1997.
4. G. Bonanno. Modal logic and game theory: Two alternative approaches. *Risk Decision and Policy*, 7:309–324, 2002.
5. G. Bonanno. A characterization of von Neumann games in terms of memory. *Synthese*, 139(2):237–256, 2004.
6. M.E. Bratman. *Intentions, Plans, and Practical Reason*. Harvard University Press, 1987.
7. P.R. Cohen and H.J. Levesque. Intention is choice with commitment. *Artificial Intelligence*, 42:213–261, 1990.
8. E. A. Emerson. Temporal and modal logic. In J. van Leeuwen, editor, *Handbook of Theoretical Computer Science*, volume B, pages 995–1072. Elsevier Science Publishers, 1990.
9. F. Giunchiglia and P. Traverso. Planning as model checking. In *ECP*, pages 1–20, 1999.
10. D. Harel, D. Kozen, and J. Tiuryn. *Dynamic Logic*. MIT Press, 2000.
11. B.P. Harrenstein, W. van der Hoek, J.-J. Meyer, and C. Witteveen. A modal characterization of Nash equilibrium. *Fundamenta Informaticae*, 57(2–4):281–321, 2003.
12. M. Osborne and A. Rubinstein. *A Course in Game Theory*. MIT Press, 1994.
13. M. Pollack. The uses of plans. *Artificial Intelligence*, 57(1):43–68, 1992.
14. A.S. Rao and M.P. Georgeff. Modeling rational agents within a BDI-architecture. In *Proceedings of KR-91*, pages 473–484, 1991.
15. R. Stalnaker. Knowledge, belief and counterfactual reasoning in games. *Economics and Philosophy*, 12:133–163, 1996.
16. J. van Benthem. Games in dynamic epistemic logic. *Bulletin of Economic Research*, 53(4):219–248, 2001. Proceedings of LOFT-4.
17. W. van der Hoek, W. Jamroga, and M. Wooldridge. A logic for strategic reasoning. In *Proceedings of AAMAS'05*. 2005.
18. W. van der Hoek, M. Roberts, and M. Wooldridge. Social laws in alternating time: Effectiveness, feasibility and synthesis. *Synthese*, 2005.
19. S. van Otterloo and G. Jonker. On Epistemic Temporal Strategic Logic. In *Proceedings of LCMAS*, pages 35–45, 2004.
20. S. van Otterloo, W. van der Hoek, and M. Wooldridge. Preferences in game logics. In *Proceedings of AAMAS-04*, 2004.
21. M. Wooldridge. *An Introduction to Multi Agent Systems*. John Wiley & Sons, 2002.

Semantics and Pragmatics for Agent Communication

Rodrigo Agerri and Eduardo Alonso

Dept. of Computing, City University,
EC1V 0HB London, UK
{rag, eduardo}@soi.city.ac.uk

Abstract. For the successful management of interactions in open multi-agent systems, a social framework is needed to complement a standard semantics and interaction protocols for agent communication. In this paper a rights-based framework in which interaction protocols and conversation policies acquire their meaning is presented. Rights improve interaction and facilitate social action in multi-agent domains. Rights allow agents enough freedom, and at the same time constrain them (prohibiting specific actions). A general framework for agent communication languages (ACLs) is proposed, defining a set of performatives (semantics) and showing why a set of conversation policies to guide agent's interactions (pragmatics) is needed. Finally, we show how it is possible to model interaction protocols within a rights-based normative open MAS.

1 Introduction

One of the distinguishing properties of Multi-Agent Systems (MAS) is the ability of their members to interact with one other. Communication is a kind of interaction that should not affect the autonomy or heterogeneity of the agents, in the sense that agents are not forced to send or receive messages; in theory, agents are free to reject requests or not to answer any received messages. This is particularly true in open environments, such as the electronic commerce applications based on the Internet, where agents are designed by different constructors and work for their individual interests. The adoption of a standard Agent Communication Language (ACL) is crucial for artificial agents to interact in open environments.

Following the main tradition in this research area, the specification of a standard ACL is based on speech act theory [18]. Organizations like FIPA (Foundation for Intelligent Physical Agents [9]), define an ACL from a *mentalistic* point of view: The meaning of the performatives are defined in terms of the mental states of the agents, namely, beliefs, intentions and desires. It has been argued that the mentalistic approach can be useful for *cooperative* agents. However, in open environments, in which agents are heterogeneous and competitive, it is not sensible for agents to trust their opponents in a negotiation process, or to make assumptions about their current beliefs or intentions ([19,10]). We believe that these criticisms are partially motivated by not distinguishing between the

C. Bento, A. Cardoso, and G. Dias (Eds.): EPIA 2005, LNAI 3808, pp. 524–535, 2005.

semantics and the pragmatics of the ACLs. Traditionally, the pragmatic level consist only of the definition of Interaction Protocols (IPs) to be applied in particular scenarios (e.g., auctions). These protocols merely dictate the order in which performatives are to be used, but they do not take into account the social consequences that the use of a particular performative may cause.

We understand agent communication as an activity in which agents' actions entail social consequences. However, unlike other social approaches ([19,10]) in which the semantics of the communicative actions are defined in terms of commitments, we understand that the social aspect of agent communication is a constituent of the pragmatics of the language. In our approach, the social consequences of sending a message are regulated by conversation policies (CPs) which help agents to both interpret and send an appropriate answer upon the reception of a message. For example, CPs may give the right to an agent to send a query, or obliging it to refuse a particular proposal.

It is argued here that the concept of commitment is not sufficient to express all the social aspects involved in communicative interaction, but a more general framework of coordination is needed. Unlike other approaches based on the idea of institution ([11]), our right-based approach, while maintaining agents' autonomy, can establish a mechanism of sanction. Besides, given its social nature, a rights-based ACL is public, so it is possible to determine whether an agent is acting according to the pragmatics of the language (conversation policies).

In this paper we provide a set of normative notions such as right, permission, obligation, which are used to model agents' social and communicative interactions within a normative framework. This enable us to define interaction protocols based on a meaningful set of messages. ACLs based on a semantics approach take only into account the isolated action of the utterance. They do not consider the sequences of interactions which are established in a conversation.

Interaction protocols represent the conventions adopted by agents when exchanging messages. In particular, these conventions represent the *legal* sequence of messages that agents have to follow. It has been argued ([19]) that focusing only on the specification of protocols (e.g.,[12,4]) limit agents' autonomy. It also transforms communication in a meaningless exchange of ordered tokens since agent's behaviour is reduced to follow a predetermined conversational template. Conversely, we believe that interaction protocols should rely on a standard set of communicative actions which guarantees that the communication is meaningful. Besides, it should be possible to determine whether agents are behaving according to the specified protocol. Other approaches [8] take into account the meaning of the performatives, but they are not based on a standard ACL but on a set of *ad hoc* defined messages. In our approach, interaction protocols are defined on the basis of a previously defined set of communicative actions.

The remainder of the paper is structured as follows: In the next section, we define the main components needed to define a complete standard ACL. In Section 3, a set of communicative actions (semantics) and their STRIPS-based semantics are provided. Section 4 formally specifies, using CTL with deontic operators, the normative notions (rights) needed to define a set of conversation policies (pragmatics). Besides, it shows, upon the social and communicative framework previously defined, how conversation policies and interaction protocols regulate the use of the semantics. Section 5 discusses other related work, and some conclusions are drawn.

2   ACL Framework

Agent Communication consists of agents exchanging messages which are well-formed formulae of a communication language $\mathcal{L}_c$. By sending messages, agents perform speech acts or communicative actions. An *illocution* is the central component of a communicative action and it corresponds to what the action is intended to achieve. This goal should be distinguished from the effect that the communicative action is meant to produce on the receiver (*perlocution*), as well as from how the actual communication is physically carried out (*locution*). The perlocutionary effects of the communicative actions are difficult to specify. Since we deal with autonomous agents, it is not possible to guarantee the satisfaction of the perlocutionary action. ACL performatives can be classified in terms of their illocutionary point [18].

A well defined semantics is a central component of the ACL specification. However, most of the ACLs proposed so far lack of a pragmatic level in which properly regulate the use of the semantics. Traditionally, ACL specifications would just consist of a set of communicative actions, and several interactions protocols would then separately define conversational templates for specific scenarios (e.g., auctions). The commitment-based protocols include the social component in order to facilitate verification [22], but they fail to capture the general intuition about communication, namely, that agents perform speech acts in order to achieve a certain goal(s). Conversely, our approach places the social aspect of communication at the pragmatic level, maintaining the illocutionary aspect as a central feature of the semantics (communicative actions). The pragmatics of an ACL can be represented by conversation policies, which take into account the social effects of performing a communicative action and thereby facilitate the achievement of perlocutionary effects. In other words, CPs guide and constrain the use of the performatives. The concept of right plays a central role in the definition of CPs, allowing us to express the social consequences of performing a particular communicative action. Other approaches (notably [17]), simply consider the perlocutionary component of communication which is embedded in the semantics of the language (they do not consider a separate pragmatic component). We believe that this consequentialist approach does not allow to decide whether or not the satisfaction of the perlocutionary action is intentional, which means that it is not possible to assign responsibility, sanctions, etc., in a normative system.

In our view, an ACL should include both social and mental aspects of communication. Thus, a complete ACL will be composed by the set of communicative actions, that is, the language $\mathcal{L}_c$ expressing the semantic meaning of the primitives; a set CPs restricting its use, $\mathcal{L}_r$, and the semantic languages $\mathcal{L}_s$ and $\mathcal{L}_p$

for $\mathcal{L}_c$ and $\mathcal{L}_r$ respectively (our framework builds on [22]). Note that IPs would also be defined using $\mathcal{L}_r$. In short, the set of communicative actions defined by $\mathcal{L}_c$ represent the semantics of the ACL, whereas the set of policies defined by $\mathcal{L}_r$ represent the pragmatics. The semantics encode the illocutionary character of communication between autonomous agents. The pragmatic level takes into account the use of the semantics and the social consequences its use entail. Thus, an ACL is the tuple:

$$\mathcal{ACL} = \langle \mathcal{L}_c, \mathcal{L}_s, \mathcal{L}_r, \mathcal{L}_p \rangle$$

The communication language $\mathcal{L}_c$ is based on a STRIPS-like language with preconditions and effects. The preconditions establish the conditions to be true for the agent to send a message (including the goal the sender intends to achieve by sending that message). On the other hand, the effects state the sender wants to cause by performing the communicative action. As it has been already discussed, autonomous agents, by definition, cannot be forced to guarantee the effects. The semantics of $\mathcal{L}_c$ are given by a function

$$[\![-]\!]_c : \mathit{wff}(\mathcal{L}_c) \rightarrow \mathit{wff}(\mathcal{L}_s)$$

The language $\mathcal{L}_s$ is based on Computation Tree Logic (CTL) extended with operators for Beliefs, Goals and Intentions. Using a type of temporal logic would facilitate to relate the language $\mathcal{L}_s$ to a computational model and, as a consequence, its verification [22]. The aim of this paper is not to discuss the specifics of the computational model, although it could be based on the work by Manna and Pnueli [14]. Besides, by introducing operators to express mental states it is possible to capture the goal-based character of communication. Mental states are not understood in this paper as private mental states of the agents; as in theory of planning, goals represent states of the world which are desirable for the agents. Regarding intentions, when an agent expresses the intention to execute an action, it is expressing publicly its willingness to perform such an action. Intentions refer to the actions that the agent is committed to perform in order to achieve one or more goals. Besides, holding an intention to execute an action presupposes the ability to perform it. This approach differs from others (e.g. Cohen and Levesque [3]) that use both concepts interchangeably.

CTL extended with deontic operators for Rights and Obligations is used to define the language $\mathcal{L}_p$. Using CTL as the core of both semantic languages will facilitate the verification of the ACL. The semantics of the pragmatic language $\mathcal{L}_r$ are given by a function:

$$[\![-]\!]_r : \mathit{wff}(\mathcal{L}_r) \rightarrow \mathit{wff}(\mathcal{L}_p)$$

The definition of a pragmatic language is beyond the scope of this paper, but we believe that the role can be filled by a declarative language like prolog. An interesting lead would be to investigate whether these CPs could be imported as reasoning rules in an programming environment for cognitive agents like 3APL [5]. In the following section we will present the logic that will be used to specify the communicative actions of the ACL.

3   Communicative Actions

CTL is a type of branching temporal logic which describes properties of a computation tree [7]. Temporal model checking using CTL is one of the most used techniques for verifying properties of state-transition systems. Although it is not the purpose of this paper to develop a verification method for ACLs, by using an extension of CTL to define the semantics of the ACL we are indirectly choosing the computational model for the verification. The language presented here, $\mathcal{L}_s$, extends CTL by adding modal operators for beliefs, goals and intentions. The main difference with other extensions (e.g. [16] [19]) is the use of a Goal operator which cannot conflict with beliefs, that is, we distinguish between goals and desires. Besides, we consider that the objects of goals are states (ϕ) whereas the objects of intentions are actions (α).

Definition 1. (Syntax)
Language $\mathcal{L}$ consists of two classes, state and path formulae. Consider n agents.

C1 If ϕ is an atomic proposition of AP then ϕ is a state formula.
C2 If ϕ and ψ are state formulae, then so are $\neg\phi$ and $\phi \wedge \psi$.
C3 If φ is a path formula and then $E\varphi$ and $A\varphi$ are state formulae.
C4 If ϕ is a state formula then $B_i(\phi), G_i(\phi), I_i(\phi)$ are also state formulae.
P0 If ϕ and ψ are state formulae, then $X\phi$ and $\phi U\psi$ are path formulae.

The boolean operators are standard; E and A are quantifiers over paths, meaning "there exists an execution" and "for all executions" respectively; $\phi\,U\psi$ means that ψ does eventually hold and that ϕ will hold everywhere until ψ holds. The rest of the formulae can be introduced as abbreviations: $EF\phi$ for $E\ true\ U\phi$; $AF\phi$ for $A\ true\ U\phi$; $EG\phi$ for $\neg(A\ true\ U\neg\phi)$; finally, $AG\phi$ abbreviates for $\neg(E\ true\ U\neg\phi)$. Beliefs are represented by a $KD45$ axiomatization relative to each agent. For goals and intentions, we assume a minimal KD axiomatization to ensure consistency.

Definition 2. (Kripke Structure)
A structure is a tuple $M = \langle S, R, L, T, A, \mathcal{B}, \mathcal{G}, \mathcal{I}, \rangle$ where

- *S is a set of states,*
- *R is a total binary relation $\subseteq S \times S, \forall s \in S s.t.(s, t,) \in R$,*
- *$L : S \rightarrow PowerSet(\Phi)$ is an interpretation $L : S \rightarrow 2^{\Phi}$ where Φ is a set of atomic propositions,*
- *$T : S \rightarrow P$ gives the real path conveyed by a state, where P is the set of paths derived from L; PP gives the powerset of P.*
- *A is a set of agents,*
- *$\mathcal{B} : S \times A \rightarrow S$ gives the accessibility relation for beliefs,*
- *and $\mathcal{G} : S \times A \rightarrow PP$ and $\mathcal{I} : S \times A \rightarrow PP$ an interpretation for goals and intentions respectively.*

For a Kripke structure M and a state s_0, we write $M, s_0 \models \phi$, for a state formula ϕ. For a structure M and a full path χ, we say that $M, \chi \models \phi$ for a path formula ϕ.

Definition 3. (Semantics)

C1 $M, s_0 \models \phi$ iff $\phi \in L(s_0)$, for $\phi \in AP$

C2 $M, s_0 \models \phi \wedge \psi$ iff $M, s_0 \models \phi$ and $M, s_0 \models \psi$

$\quad M, s_0 \models \neg\phi$ iff it is not the case that $M, s_0 \models \phi$

C3 $M, s_0 \models E\phi$ iff $\exists$ a full path $\chi = (s_0, s_1, s_2, \ldots)$ in M and $M, \chi \models \phi$

$\quad M, s_0 \models A\phi$ iff $\forall$ full paths $\chi = (s_0, s_1, s_2, \ldots)$ in M, and $M, \chi \models \phi$

C4 $M, s_0 \models B_i(\phi)$ iff $\forall s_1 : s_1 \in \mathcal{B}(i, s_0) \Rightarrow M, s_1 \models \phi$

$\quad M, s_0 \models G_i(\phi)$ iff $\forall \chi : \chi \in \mathcal{G}(i, s_0) \Rightarrow M, \chi \models \phi$

$\quad M, s_0 \models I_i(\phi)$ iff $\forall \chi : \chi \in \mathcal{I}(i, s_0) \Rightarrow M, \chi \models \phi$

P0 $M, \chi \models \phi U \psi$ iff $\exists i, M, s_i \models \psi$ and $\forall j < i, M, s_j \models \phi$

$\quad M, \chi \models X\phi$ iff $M, s_1 \models \phi$

We can use now the semantic language $\mathcal{L}_s$ to express the meaning of the relevant classes of communicative actions. Following Searle's taxonomy [18], we classify actions into assertives, commissives, directives, declarations and expressives. The last category is not relevant for the purposes of this paper, so it will not be included. The syntax of $\mathcal{L}_c$ is based on the FIPA ACL. Table 1 presents a performative for each of the remaining four types of categories, plus two more (agree and refuse) which will be used later to characterized the request interaction protocol. The two performatives at the top, inform and request, represent the assertives and directives respectively. Agree and refuse are included as possible exchanges after the reception of a request. Declare is an action of the declarative class and promise is a commissive.

Table 1. A complete set of performatives

$\langle i, inform(j, \phi)\rangle$	$\langle i, request(j, \alpha)\rangle$
$FP : B_i(\phi) \wedge G_i(B_j(\phi))$	$FP : G_i(I_j(F\alpha))$
$RE : B_j\phi$	$RE : EF\alpha$
$\langle i, agree(j, \alpha)\rangle$	$\langle i, refuse(j, \alpha)\rangle$
$\langle i, inform(j, I_iF\alpha)\rangle$	$\langle i, inform(j, \neg I_iF\alpha)\rangle$
$FP : I_iF\alpha$	$FP : \neg I_iF\alpha$
$RE : B_j(I_iF\alpha)$	$RE : B_j(\neg I_iF\alpha)$
$\langle i, promise(j, \alpha)\rangle$	$\langle i, declare(j, \phi)\rangle$
$FP : I_iF\alpha$	$FP : G_i(\phi)$
$RE : F\alpha$	$RE : \phi$

When sending an inform message, the sender expresses its belief that some proposition is true. The first part of the FPs requires the sender to believe ϕ which means that we want the sender to be sincere. This is a good assumption by default, but if we want agents to be able to negotiate in competitive scenarios they may need to deceive. We believe that a feasible solution is to specify another speech act *convince* that could be used when an agent *just* aims that other agent believes a proposition ϕ, irrespective of the beliefs of the sender.

The are two classes of directives: Questions and requests. Both types share the basic feature of the sender holding a goal which can be achieved by the receiver performing a specific action. The goal of questions is to elicit some proposition from the receiver, which involves the receiver performing an answer. Requests have the goal of getting the receiver to perform some action.

If the receiver accepts the request, it will expresses the intention to execute the action requested. Having the intention of executing an action means that the agent will execute that action in order to achieve a specific goal. Note that by agreeing, the agent actually informs the receiver that it intends to perform a requested action. Conversely, if the receiver rejects the request, it will inform about its intention not to comply with it. The use of precommitments [10] to analyze requests fails, in our view, to express that the sender explicitly states its interest of having the receiver executing a particular action.

Commissives commit the sender to perform the action uttered by the message. That is, once sent, the sender states its intention to perform the action.

Declarations have immediate effects in an extra-linguistic institution. Declaratives are the original *performative* verbs [2]. Declarations are particularly useful for institutional actions. For example, performatives to start or terminate an interaction are declaratives. In that kind of situations, it is necessary to identify which agents are *allowed* to perform a specific declaration. Usually, agents has a right or a permission to perform a communicative action depending on its role in the particular scenario. In an auction, for instance, the auctioneer has the right to exercise an action: declaring the beginning of an auction. An agent wishing to participate should be given the permission (by the auctioneer) to do so. An agent may perform an action for which it has not the right to.

In the next section, we introduce the language $\mathcal{L}_p$ which define the notions of rights and permissions in which the conversation policies (pragmatics) are based.

4 Pragmatics

Interaction protocols (IPs) define the sequences in which communicative actions can be performed, so agents can engage in a meaningful conversation. We believe that IPs can be modelled as the right agents have to use a performative based on the previous speech acts performed. Thus, IPs provide the set of performatives that can be used at a given time. IPs are in turn constrained by the pragmatics of the language specified as a set of CPs.

In open environments, agents work on behalf of the particular interest of their designers. Because agents are designed by different vendors, they present different internal structures. Therefore, to guarantee that interactions between agents are successful, agents need to behave according to their role within a normative system. This does not mean that we adopt an institutional approach in which agents must follow the rules imposed by a set of norms defined by the institution.

In general, if an agent has the right to execute a set of actions, then: (i) it is permitted to perform it (under certain obligations); (ii) the rest of the agents are not allowed to perform any action that inhibits the right-holder's action, and (iii), the rest of agents, the group, has the obligation to prevent or sanction any inhibitory action. The function of rights for agent communication is to stabilize social interactions, by making the behaviour of agents predictable to the other agents of the system. Permissions are usually defined as the dual of obligation, meaning that an agent that is not obliged not to do α is permitted to do α. Rights are not simply the absence of obligations. For an agent to have the right to execute α, is must be given permission to do so. Not being obliged not do to α it does not mean that the agent has the right to do α.

The formal specification of the normative language, $\mathcal{L}_p$, which defines rights, obligations and permissions, is based on the semantic language $\mathcal{L}_s$ presented in the previous section. Thus, for the language $\mathcal{L}_p$, we extend CTL using normative notions, and we add a deontic accessibility relation. The syntax is given the following BNF expression:

$$\varphi := \phi|\neg\varphi|\varphi_1 \wedge \varphi_2|G_i\varphi|O_i\varphi|E\varphi|A\varphi|X\varphi|\varphi_1 U\varphi_2$$

Where $O_i\phi$ means that agent i has the obligation to bring about ϕ. The rest of the notions, such as permissions, are defined as abbreviations. The axiomatization of obligation is given by the system KD. We add a deontic accessibility relation $\mathcal{O}$, $\mathcal{O} : 2^A \to 2^{S \times S}$. Thus, the semantics of $\mathcal{L}_p$ are inherited from $\mathcal{L}_s$ except $C4$ which is substituted by:

$$M, s_0 \models O_i\phi \text{ iff } \forall s_1 \text{ such that } s_0\mathcal{O}s_1 \text{ we have } M, s_1 \models \phi$$

In order to define the notion of right, we need to introduce first the concept of violation. Rights are considered here exceptions of obligations [20], that is, rights are different from permissions. An agent has right to do α under some condition ϕ if, when the agent that gives the right believes that ϕ holds, it has the goal not to believe α as a violation $(\neg V(\alpha))$. From each literal built from a variable α, $V \in N$, $V(\alpha)$ means that agent N determines that α is a violation.

Definition 4. (Right)
Let NS be a set of norms $\{n_1, \ldots, n_m\}$, and let the variables of agent N contain a set of violation variables $V = \{V(\alpha)$ such that $\alpha \in AP\}$ Agent i believes that it has the right given by agent N to do α, under situation ϕ, $\phi \in S$ iff for some $n \in NS$

1. $\phi \wedge \alpha \to \neg V(\alpha) \in G_N$

IPs aim to constrain the interaction to facilitate the desired outcomes; for example, that the highest bidder is found in an auction. Besides, CPs make coordination easier since they assign permissions and obligations on the participants, and specify which communicative actions are appropriate at certain states. The agent playing the role of auctioneer establishes the rights and permissions of the participants. The conformity of the participants to the protocol is based on the meaning of the performatives used.

The language $\mathcal{L}_p$ provides the set of normative notions needed to specify CPs for agent communication ($\mathcal{L}_r$). Using a declarative language to express the CPs is inspired by work related to 3APL [5], and within the Semantic Web framework [13]. A policy consists of the following components: communicative actions, domain actions, normative rules and facilitator actions. The first component is given by $\mathcal{L}_c$ and the second is defined by $\mathcal{L}_p$; the kind of domain actions agents can perform will depend on the abilities agents have; like the communicative actions, domain actions are expressed in terms of goals, preconditions and effects.

$$action(Agent, Goal, Precondition, Effect)$$

Facilitator actions depend on the platform in which agents run. That is, facilitator actions are defined by the programming language in which agents are built. For example, in Java built platform like JADE, sending messages is simply a case of creating an ACLMessage, setting the parameters (sender, receiver, reply-to, performative, etc.) and then sending it using the send() method in the agent object.

Normative rules consist of a deontic operator (obligations, rights) and a condition that has to be true so the rule is applicable:

$$right(X, request(X, Y, Condition)$$

Agents hold the right to do α as long as α does not constitute a violation. An obligation rule states that an agent must perform an action before its applicability condition becomes false; a permission rule establishes that the agent can perform an action α if its condition(s) is true. We can now use the language $\mathcal{L}_r$ whose semantics are specified by $\mathcal{L}_p$ to model IPs of FIPA ACL in terms of the rights of the agents to use the performatives.

In the request interaction protocol, an agent X request agent Y to perform an action A. The receiver has the right to either agree or refuse the request. In the case that agent Y agrees, then it has obligation to send a notification which can be: (i) a failure message, i.e., the action A could not be executed, (ii) an inform stating that the action has been performed, and (iii) informing of the result of executing A.

```
right(X, request(X, Y, A), _).

right(Y, agree(Y, X, A));
right(Y, refuse(Y,X,A)) :-
    receive(request(X,Y,A).

obligation(Y, inform (Y, X, A));
obligation(Y, failure(Y, X, A)) :-
    send(agree(Y, X, A), _).
```

Policies can then be defined to constrain the agents' use of the performatives in virtue of their content. For example, agent Y, acting on behalf of a airline company serving flights to European countries, could have a CP that state that it should agree to every request regarding flight tickets to Europe (i.e., searching a suitable ticket and providing the best offer for a potential buyer) and another one specifying that it has the obligation to refuse every request about flights to non European countries.

```
obligation(Y, agree(Y, X, A) :-
    receive(request(X, Y, A)), europeanFlight(A)).

obligation(Y, refuse(Y, X, A) :-
    receive(request(X, Y, A), nonEuropeanFlight(A)).
```

Other CPs can be defined to state that an agent can deceive, or that it has the right to do so in particular circumstances. It can be specified that an agent X will always answer to every message it receives, for example. There are two interesting leads of our proposal: first, we need to work on its application in a development platform for cognitive agents such as 3APL [6]. In this programming environment, prolog programs can be part of the belief base, which contain general rules to be applied for some problem domain. The second lead is to extend our current formalism with other organizational concepts such as roles and group, and a formal definition of sanction. Agents playing roles in specific scenarios will allow the specification of more accurate CPs, since the role an agent is playing will add further conditions to its behaviour. Thus, the previous example can be enriched by adding that agent Y is seller and X is a customer.

5   Concluding Remarks

Our proposal presents two semantic languages based on CTL that give the semantics for the communicative actions and conversational policies of the ACL. We believe that using a temporal logic traditionally used for model-checking verification would facilitate the compliance testing of our ACL.

Although trying to overcome some of its problems, the ACL specification proposed here intends to be as close as possible to the FIPA ACL specification. Thus, we propose new communicative actions with the aim of improving the current FIPA Communicative Actions Library (CAL). With this purpose, we provide definitions for the actions absent in the FIPA CAL: commissives and declaratives. We understand that, in the FIPA CAL some of the definitions are unnecessarily complex. This is partially due to the multimodal language used as semantic language. Besides, it is not a language that can be grounded in a computational model as CTL does.

Besides, our approach analyzes agent communication in terms of the social consequences of executing an action. In this sense, our ACL is public, since it is possible to establish whether an agent is acting according to the pragmatics of the language. The idea of using rights to constrain agent's communicative behaviour is inspired by [15] and [1]. Our proposal is also related to [13], but here we present a complete semantics for the deontic operators.

We have shown with an example, how our proposal can be used to define IPs using a declarative language. In so doing, the right-based ACL is not confined to a meaningless sequential exchange of tokens. Future work will involve extending such protocol to cover other patterns of conversations, which include concurrent interactions. Moreover, we want to consider sanctions mechanisms to punish violations. We believe that van der Torre et al's approach [21] provides an interesting lead for this purpose.

References

1. Alonso, E.: Rights and argumentation in open multi-agent systems. Artificial Intelligence Review **21** (2004) 3–24
2. Austin, J.L.: How to do Things with Words. Oxford University Press, Oxford (1962)
3. Cohen, P., Levesque, H.: Intention is Choice with Commitment. Artificial Intelligence **42** (1990) 213–261
4. Cost, R.S., Chen, Y., Finin, T., Labrou, Y., Peng, Y.: Modeling agent conversations with colored petri nets. In: Workshop on Specifying and Implementing Conversation Policies, Third International Conference on Autonomous Agents (Agents '99), Seattle (1999)
5. Dastani, M., van der Ham, J., Dignum, F.: Communication for goal directed agents. In Huget, M.P., ed.: Communication in Multiagent Systems - Agent Communication Languages and Conversation Policies. Springer-Verlag (LNCS 2003) 239–252
6. Dastani, M., Riemsdijk, M., Dignum, F., Meyer, J.J.: A programming language for cognitive agents: Goal-directed 3apl. In Dastani, M., Dix, J., Fallah-Seghrouchni, A.E., eds.: Programming Multi-Agent Systems (LNAI 3037). Springer-Verlag, Berlin (2004) 111–130
7. Emerson, E.A.: Temporal and modal logic. In van Leeuwen, J., ed.: Handbook of Theoretical Computer Science, volume B. North Holland, Amsterdam (1990) 995–1072
8. Esteva, M., Rodriguez, J.A., Sierra, C., Garcia, P., Arcos, J.L.: On the formal specification of electronic institutions. In Dignum, F., Sierra, C., eds.: Agent-mediated Electronic Commerce (The European AgentLink Perspective). Volume volume 1191 of LNAI. Springer, Berlin (2001) 126–147
9. FIPA ACL: FIPA Communicative Act Library Specification (2002) http://www.fipa.org/repository/aclspecs.html.
10. Fornara, N., Colombetti, M.: A commitment-based approach to agent communication. Applied Artificial Intelligence **18** (2004) 853–866
11. Fornara, N., Vigano, F., Colombetti, M.: Agent communication and institutional reality. In: AAMAS 2004 Workshop on Agent Communication (AC2004), New York (2004)
12. Greaves, M., Holmback, H., Bradshaw, J.: What is a Conversation Policy? In Dignum, F., Greaves, M., eds.: Issues in Agent Communication. Heidelberg, Germany: Springer-Verlag (2000) 118–131
13. Kagal, L., Finin, T., Joshi, A.: A policy language for a pervasive computing environment. In: IEEE 4th International Workshop on Policies for Distributed Systems and Networks. (2003)

14. Manna, Z., Pnueli, A.: The Temporal Logic of Reactive and Concurrent Systems. Springer-Verlag, Berlin, Germany (1995)
15. Norman, T.J., Sierra, C., Jennings, N.R.: Rights and commitment in multi-agent agreements. In: Proceedings of the Third International Conference on Multi-Agent Systems. (1998) 222–229
16. Rao, A., Georgeff, M.: Modeling rational agents within a BDI-architecture. In Allen, J., Fikes, R., Sandewall, E., eds.: 2nd International Conference on Principles of Knowledge Representation and Reasoning (KR'91), Morgan Kaufmann Publishers (1991) 473–484
17. Rovatsos, M., Nickles M., Weiss G.: Interaction is Meaning: A new Model for Communication in Open Systems. In Proceedings of the Second International Joint Conference on Autonomous Agents and Multi-Agent Systems (AAMAS-03), Melbourne, Australia, (2003)
18. Searle, J.R.: Speech Acts. An Essay in the Philosophy of Language. Cambridge: Cambridge University Press (1969)
19. Singh, M.P.: A social semantics for agent communication languages. In: Issues in Agent Communication, volume 1916 of LNAI. Berlin: Springer-Verlag (2000)
20. van der Torre, L.: Contextual deontic logic: Normative agents, violations and independence. Ann. Math. Artif. Intell. 37 (2003) 33–63
21. van der Torre, L., Hulstijn, J., Dastani, M., Broersen, J.: Specifying multiagent organizations. In: Proceedings of the Seventh Workshop on Deontic Logic in Computer Science (Deon'2004), LNAI 3065. Springer (2004) 243–257
22. Wooldridge, M.: Semantic issues in the verification of agent communication languages. Journal of Autonomous Agents and Multi-Agent Systems 3 (2000) 9–31

Logical Implementation of Uncertain Agents

Nivea de C. Ferreira, Michael Fisher, and Wiebe van der Hoek

Department of Computer Science, University of Liverpool, UK
{niveacf, michael, wiebe}@csc.liv.ac.uk

Abstract. We consider the representation and execution of agents specified using *temporal logics*. Previous work in this area has provided a basis for the direct execution of agent specifications, and has been extended to allow the handling of agent beliefs, deliberation and multi-agent groups. However, the key problem of *uncertainty* has not been tackled. Given that agents work in unknown environments, and interact with other agents that may, in turn, be unpredictable, then it is essential for any formal agent description to incorporate some mechanism for capturing this aspect. Within the framework of executable specifications, formal descriptions involving uncertainty must also be executable. The contribution of this paper is to extend executable temporal logic in order to allow the representation and execution of uncertain statements within agents. In particular, we extend the basis of the METATEM temporal framework with a *probabilistic belief* dimension captured by the recently introduced $P_F K D45$ logic. We provide a description of the extended logic, the translation procedure for formulae in this extended logic to an executable normal form, and the execution algorithm for such formulae. We also outline technical results concerning the correctness of the translation to the normal form and the completeness of the execution mechanism.

1 Introduction

The logical characterisation of agent-based systems is now a well established area [6,19,21]. Such a characterisation can not only provide an unambiguous semantics for agents but can also allow key techniques such as formal specification to be used in the analysis of agent-based systems. An important aspect is the direct execution of these formal agent specifications. Here, a model satisfying the agent specification is extracted, with the process of extracting such a model corresponding to an execution. This is analogous to the use of Prolog in classical logic whereby the system searches for a model satisfying the specification. Such direct execution also provides a strong link between the semantics of an agent and its implementation, something that is often lacking in contemporary agent programming frameworks [5].

Given that agents essentially work in unpredictable environments, and interact with other agents that may, in turn, be unpredictable, it is vital for any formal description of an agent to incorporate some mechanism for capturing uncertainty [14] on a level that is more fine-grained than assuming the agent has just knowledge, or even beliefs. In dealing with uncertainty one can choose among many existing approaches, often categorised as either numerical or symbolic. We here opt for a framework incorporating *Probability Theory* as, at least semantically, this allows us to remain close to the *possible worlds paradigm*. This possible-worlds view is by far the most popular way (see also [20]) to model the varieties of agent we require (cf. [19]).

C. Bento, A. Cardoso, and G. Dias (Eds.): EPIA 2005, LNAI 3808, pp. 536–547, 2005.

In our work, we choose to extend a standard temporal logic, to which execution has previously been applied, with an added element of uncertainty. Thus, we produce a new logic from the combination of standard temporal logic with a novel logic of *probabilistic belief*, $P_F K D45$ [8]. This provides a simple, and intuitive, basis for specifying agents uncertain about their environment and their choices.

Once we have the temporal specification of an uncertain agent, an implementation can be developed in a number of ways, for example by refinement to a standard programming language or the automatic synthesis of an automaton [17,16]. Such a synthesis approach is necessarily complex, generating an implementation that is guaranteed to satisfy the specification in all environments. However, the route we choose is to directly execute the temporal specification in order to provide an implementation. Note that this just involves searching for *one* acceptable execution, which is generally less complex (and often much quicker) than attempting full synthesis [2]. Our approach to direct execution extends the METATEM programming language [3], which executes purely temporal statements, and can be utilised to animate agent specifications.

The contribution of this paper is to devise a logical framework for uncertainty in agents that (1) is conceptually clear and simple, (2) can be used in modal (intensional) logical specifications of agents, and (3) can be added on top of METATEM to give a rich but still executable temporal/doxastic logic. The executable framework we develop is called PROTEM.

The rest of this paper is organised in the following way. Section 2 presents a brief overview of the METATEM Framework and the $P_F K D45$ logic. We then describe how these systems can be combined forming the basis for uncertain agent implementation, with the associated normal form and execution mechanism being subsequently described in Sections 3 and 4, respectively. Finally, in Section 5, comments on related work, potential applications, and future research, together with concluding remarks, are provided.

2   A Temporal Doxastic Logic

2.1   Temporal Basis of METATEM

In previous work on the METATEM framework, the representation of simple dynamic agents using temporal logic [12], the representation of deliberation within these agents, and an extension to agents that have beliefs [10] were considered. In the work presented in this paper we provide an extension of this framework, using an appropriate logical formalism to incorporate uncertainty.

In METATEM, logical formulae represent an agent's specification. The framework allows the animation of an agent's specification by direct execution of these formulae, essentially providing an implementation of the agent's behaviour. This approach follows the *imperative future* paradigm [4], and applies an iterative *forward-chaining* process to a set of temporal formulae in a specific normal form in order to (attempt to) construct a model for the specification.

Temporal logic is an extension of classical logic in which temporal order is important. Thus, statements are not just true or false, but are true or false dependent upon the moment in time at which they are evaluated. Typical operators of the temporal logic used are '$\bigcirc$' ("in the next moment in time"), '$\diamondsuit$' ("at some point in the future"), '$\square$' ("always in the future"), '$\mathcal{U}$' ("until") and **'start'** ("at the start"), e.g.'$\diamondsuit happy$'.

Since the underlying temporal model is a linear, discrete sequence of states, and since forward chaining is applied, model construction in this way mimics execution in more standard programming languages [12]. This approach is captured in the METATEM programming language [3], where execution involves forward chaining via temporal formulae from initial conditions, while constraining the execution in an attempt to satisfy eventualities. The underlying mechanism here is relatively straightforward, forward chaining through formulae of the form

$$antecedent\ (present)\ \Rightarrow\ consequent\ (future)$$

attempting to construct a model. If a disjunction, such as *red* $\vee$ *blue* is executed, a choice must be made. If this choice leads to a contradictory situation, then backtracking occurs and an alternative choice is made.

The main complication comes from execution of $\diamondsuit$-formulae (or 'eventualities'). When a formula, such as $\diamondsuit\varphi$, is executed, the system must attempt to ensure that φ *eventually* becomes true. As such eventualities might not be able to be satisfied immediately, a record of the outstanding eventualities must be kept, so that they can be re-tried as execution proceeds. The standard heuristic used is to attempt to satisfy as many eventualities as possible, starting with the *oldest outstanding eventuality* [4]. This helps ensure fairness and completeness of the execution mechanism.

Remark 1. Although we will not consider it here, it is important to note that, just as in Logic Programming, the backtracking nature of individual agents must be modified when situated in a multi-agent environment. Typically, agents are allowed to backtrack, but *not* past the point where the agent affects its environment. Sending a message, for example to other agents, effectively acts as a "cut" operation on the search space. Thus, agents are often programmed to have phases of "thinking" (using backtracking) interspersed with phases of communication.

2.2   Probabilistic Doxastic Logic

While temporal logic is used to capture the dynamic behaviour of an agent, *modal logics* can be used to extend this basic framework with beliefs, abilities, etc. $P_F KD45$ [8][1] is a complete, compact and conceptually simple modal formalism for probabilistic reasoning. In particular, it is useful for representing and reasoning about (static) uncertainty within computational agents. The language of $P_F KD45$ consists of a countable set of propositional symbols, the logical connectives $\neg$ and $\vee$ (with standard definitions for $\perp, \top, \wedge, \Rightarrow, \Leftrightarrow$), and parentheses. Its basic modal operator is $P_x^>$ (where x is a rational number within the interval $[0, 1]$), and the intended meaning of $P_x^> \varphi$ is:

φ is believed to have a probability strictly greater than x

---

[1] Interested readers will find in this paper a more detailed comparison between $P_F KD45$ and other Probabilistic Logics.

The operators $P_x^\geq$, $P_x^<$, $P_x^\leq$ and $P_x^=$ can all be defined in terms of the basic one (having self-explanatory meanings). In addition, $P_1^\geq$ can be identified with the classical (KD45) modal belief operator B. An important feature of $P_F KD45$ is that, although its syntax allows for an operator $P_x^\geq$ for every rational number x in the interval $[0, 1]$, in the semantics it is assumed that probabilities are only taken from a finite base $F = \{r_0, r_1, ..., r_n\} \subseteq [0, 1] \cap \mathbb{Q}$ thus allowing representation of probabilities in terms of this simple set.

This restriction first of all restores *compactness* of the logic (without the finiteness constraint on F, note that $\Gamma = \{P_\alpha^\geq q \mid \alpha \in [0, 1)\}$ *semantically entails* that $P_1^= q$, but no finite subset of Γ can *prove* $P_1^= q$). Related to this, when searching for models for formulae of $P_F KD45$, the constraint on F implies that we only have to consider finitely many different models. In addition, it appears that the restriction to a finite base, F, still allows us to model realistic problems: agents in general do not need an infinite granularity to express their uncertainty. For example, if the probabilistic belief in some fact is under a certain threshold, the agent might either assume the probability is 0, or, in case the certainty about φ has become too low to act upon, it might want to carry out a sensing operation to increase its confidence in φ.

In short, $P_F KD45$ builds upon the natural framework of Kripke models (the basis of modal logics), while extending it to a probability structure. Formulae are interpreted on what are called *Probabilistic Kripke Models over F* (or $\mathcal{P}_F\mathcal{K}D45$ models). That is, $P_x^\geq \varphi$ is true at a world w if, and only if, the probability values in F that are assigned to the possible worlds which verify φ, sum up to a value greater than x. Note that these probabilities are assigned globally, and do not depend on the world w of evaluation. Properties of $P_F KD45$ include soundness, completeness and finite modelling for consistent formulae [8]. Another property is that *nested* belief formulae can be removed, i.e. any nested belief formula is equivalent to one without nesting. In [8] we described a decision procedure for $P_F KD45$, which we will call $P_F KD45$ DEC PROC$(\cdot)$ in this paper. This decision procedure aims at finding a finite model for an agent specification (φ), if such a model exists. Roughly, $P_F KD45$ DEC PROC$(\cdot)$ first transforms φ into a normal form, without nesting of probabilistic operators, and then translates, for instance $P_{0.8}^\geq p \wedge P_{0.7}^\geq q$, formulae into a system of linear inequalities[2]:

$$p0q0 + p0q1 + p1q0 + p1q1 = 1$$
$$p1q0 + p1q1 \qquad\qquad \geq 0.8$$
$$p0q1 + p1q1 \qquad\qquad \geq 0.7$$

Inequalities, together with the constraints $piqj \in F$, are fed to a constraint solver, which generates a possible solution, P_F, if this exists. Note that we can conceive of every combination, $piqj$, as a set of possible worlds, or, if p and q are the only propositional atoms, as possible worlds[3].

2.3 Combining Time and Probabilistic Belief

We now combine the METATEM and $P_F KD45$ approaches to derive PROTEM. By a *fusion* of the two logics we guarantee [15] that several key properties of both of these

---

[2] Disjunctions of (sets of) formulae are attempted one at a time, as explained in Section 4.1.

[3] In such a case, $p0q1$ for instance indicates the assigned probability to the set of worlds satisfying $\neg p \wedge q$.

logics are preserved in PROTEM. The language of PROTEM is obtained by the union of the two underlying languages, where we assume the basic operators to be **start**, $\bigcirc$, and $\mathcal{U}$ for the temporal component, and $P_x^>$ for the probabilistic component. Other operators, such as $\square, \Diamond, \mathcal{W}$ (weak until) and $P_x^\sim$ (where $\sim$ is in $\{\geq, =, \leq, <\}$) can be defined in terms of the basic ones.

A model for PROTEM, M, can be conceived of as having countably many timelines $\ell, \ell', \ell'', \ldots$, each being a copy of $\mathbb{N}$. A world in M is a pair (ℓ, i) with $i \in \mathbb{N}$. We assume there is a probability function P_i for every i, such that $P_i(\{(\ell, j) \mid j = i\}) = 1$, and for every ℓ, $P_i(\ell, i) \in F$, the finite based set for the probabilities. Below we only give the main clauses for the truth definition.

$$M, (\ell, i) \models \textbf{start} \text{ iff } i = 0$$

$$M, (\ell, i) \models \bigcirc \varphi \text{ iff } M, (\ell, i+1) \models \varphi$$

$$M, (\ell, i) \models \varphi \mathcal{U} \psi \text{ iff } \exists j \ [(j > i) \ \& \ M, (\ell, j) \models \psi$$
$$\& \forall k \ (i \leq k < j \Rightarrow M, (\ell, k) \models \varphi)]$$

$$M, (\ell, i) \models P_x^> \varphi \text{ iff } P_i(\{(\ell', i) \mid M, (\ell', i) \models \varphi\}) > x$$

Note that the truth valuation of $P_x^> \varphi$-formulae does not depend on the specific timeline ℓ: $M, (\ell, i) \models P_x^> \varphi$ iff $M, (\ell', i) \models P_x^> \varphi$.

Axioms of the language, as shown in Fig. 1, reflect basic properties of probability theory, together with the peculiarity of having this base set F (axiom $A10$). Those axioms can also be found in [8], together with some meta-theorems about $P_F KD45$.

Since the two underlying logics are well behaved [3,8] and fusion, in general, preserves good behaviour [15] we obtain the following.

Theorem 1. *The logic of PROTEM:*
* *is sound and complete with respect to the above semantics;*
* *is decidable; and*
* *has the finite model property.*

$A1$	All propositional tautologies	$A2$	$\bigcirc \neg \varphi \Leftrightarrow \neg \bigcirc \varphi$
$A3$	$\bigcirc (\varphi \Rightarrow \psi) \Rightarrow (\bigcirc \varphi \Rightarrow \bigcirc \psi)$	$A4$	$\varphi \mathcal{U} \psi \Leftrightarrow (\psi \vee (\varphi \wedge \bigcirc (\varphi \mathcal{U} \psi)))$
$A5$	$P_1^\geq (\varphi \Rightarrow \psi) \Rightarrow [(P_x^\sim \varphi \Rightarrow P_x^\sim \psi)$	$A5'$	$P_1^\geq (\varphi \Rightarrow \psi) \Rightarrow [(P_x^> \varphi \Rightarrow P_x^\geq \psi)$
$A6$	$P_1^\geq (\varphi \Rightarrow \psi) \Rightarrow (P_x^\geq \varphi \Rightarrow P_z^> \psi)$	$A7$	$P_0^\geq \varphi$
$A8$	$P_{x+y}^> (\varphi \vee \psi) \Rightarrow (P_x^> \varphi \vee P_y^> \psi)$ $\Rightarrow ((P_x^\geq \varphi \wedge P_y^\geq \psi) \Rightarrow P_{x+y}^\geq (\varphi \vee \psi))$	$A9$	$P_1^\geq \neg (\varphi \wedge \psi)$
$A10$	$P_{r_i}^\geq \varphi \Rightarrow P_{r_{i+1}}^\geq \varphi$	$A11$	$(P_0^> P_x^\geq \varphi \Rightarrow P_x^\geq \varphi) \wedge (P_0^> P_x^\leq \varphi \Rightarrow P_x^\leq \varphi)$
$A12$	$(P_x^\geq \varphi \Rightarrow P_1^\geq P_x^\geq \varphi) \wedge (P_x^\leq \varphi \Rightarrow P_1^\geq P_x^\leq \varphi)$	$A13$	$\square (\varphi \Rightarrow \bigcirc \varphi) \Rightarrow (\varphi \Rightarrow \square \varphi)$
$R1$	$\vdash \varphi, \vdash \varphi \Rightarrow \psi \ \rightarrow \vdash \psi$		
$R2$	$\vdash \varphi \ \rightarrow \vdash \bigcirc \varphi$	$R3$	$\vdash \varphi \ \rightarrow \vdash P_1^\geq \varphi$

Fig. 1. Axioms of PROTEM. Everywhere, $x, y, z, x + y \in [0, 1] \cap \mathbb{Q}$, and $z < x$. In $A10$, the numbers r_i and r_{i+1} are both in F. In $A5$, $\sim \in \{>, \geq\}$.

3   Normal Form for PROTEM

We will now describe a transformation, τ, that takes an arbitrary formula from PROTEM and returns a formula of the form $\Box^* \bigwedge F_i$ where each F_i is a formula in one of the following four forms.

$$
\begin{aligned}
\textbf{start} &\Rightarrow \bigvee l_b \\
\bigwedge k_a &\Rightarrow \bigcirc \bigvee l_b \\
\bigwedge k_a &\Rightarrow \Diamond l \\
\bigwedge k_a &\Rightarrow \bigvee P_x^{\sim} l_b
\end{aligned}
\tag{1}
$$

Here k_a, l_b and l are classical literals, $\sim$ is in $\{\geq, =, \leq, <\}$ and $\Box^*$ represents the universal modality. This normal form is an extension of that (called SNF) developed both for temporal logics and their modal extensions [13].

In this way, we split the satisfiability problem into a part relating to the beginning of time (**start**), a part that relates to the next state, a part that collects the eventualities, and a part that deals with the probabilistic beliefs (at the current time).

The transformation τ works as follows, on a given PROTEM formula φ. First of all, it yields (where f is a new atom) **start** $\Rightarrow f, f \Leftrightarrow \varphi$. Next, complex subformulae are renamed, for example $\Diamond(\psi \wedge \varphi)$ becomes $\Diamond g$, $g \Leftrightarrow (\psi \wedge \varphi)$, where g is a new atom. For any $h \Leftrightarrow \psi$ that is generated (h an atom, ψ not already in normal form), τ replaces $h \Leftrightarrow \psi$ by $h \Rightarrow \psi$, $\neg h \Rightarrow \neg \psi$. In the temporal case, more complex operators such as '$\Box$' are reduced to their fixpoint definitions in terms of '$\bigcirc$' and '$\Diamond$'. The reader might compare this with [13,11], to which the '$\Leftrightarrow$' cases were added.

For the treatment of $P_x^{\sim}$ formulae, we carry out the following. First of all, we know that such formulae can all be rewritten using only $P_y^{>}$ operators. Secondly, by [8–Theorem 2], we may assume that φ is without any direct nesting of operators $P_x^{>}$. That is, nested probabilistic operators collapse to a single non-nested one. So, if any $P_x^{>}$ occurs in the scope of a $P_y^{>}$, there must be a temporal operator that separates them. For τ, we do the following: replace all occurrences of $h \Rightarrow D \vee P_x^{>} \psi$ (where D is a disjunction and ψ is not a literal) by $h \Rightarrow D \vee P_x^{>} g, g \Leftrightarrow \psi$ (where g is a fresh atom). Similarly, occurrences of $h \Rightarrow D \vee \neg P_x^{>} \psi$ are rewritten to $h \Rightarrow D \vee \neg P_x^{>} g, g \Leftrightarrow \psi$.

Theorem 2. *If a PROTEM formula, φ, is satisfiable, then so is $\tau(\varphi)$.*

Since τ introduces new atoms, we are not *a priori* guaranteed, when building a model for $\tau(\varphi)$, to have a model for φ. However, using '$\Leftrightarrow$' to define new atoms in τ takes care of this:

Theorem 3. *If $\tau(\varphi)$ is satisfied in M, then so is φ.*

As presented in [13], the use of '$\Leftrightarrow$' in the renaming transformation of formulae implies a potential exponential increase in terms of the size of the set of formulae. This is due to the fact that, in the worst case, all the subformulae of the initial formulae would have to be replaced by new propositional symbols. However, it is important to notice that in practise the complexity of this renaming tends to be much smaller.

4   Execution Mechanism

Now we consider execution of the formulae within the above normal form. The semantics for the temporal component is based on models that are discrete linear orders. From [8], we know that models for the probabilistic part of our language can be conceived of as structures $\langle W, w, P_F \rangle$, where W is a set of valuations, w is a designated world and $P_F : W \to F$ is a probability function, yielding a probability value from F to every valuation. These models are the probabilistic version of '$KD45$-balloons': every balloon represents valuations (or possible w). If w is not doxasticly possible, it receives a probability of 0. Otherwise, it receives a positive probability value. For simplicity, we will refer to such $P_F KD45$ models as 'balloons'. An easy calculation gives an upper bound on the number of possible different models for a formula $P_F KD45$-formula φ:

Lemma 1. *Suppose φ has $n = |\varphi|$ atoms. Then φ is $P_F KD45$ satisfiable if, and only if, φ has a model $\langle W, w, P_F \rangle$ with $|W \cup \{w\}| \leq 2^n$. Moreover, if F consists of $|F|$ different numbers, there are at most $|F|^{2^n}$ different models for a formula in n atoms.*

Note that the number of different models for φ is given by a rough upper bound: it considers *all* possible assignments of probabilistic values from F to conjunctions of objective literals, whereas in practise many of them will not be real probability assignments (with the property that the sum of any two partitions of such conjunctions must be 1, for example).

Adding this result on the upper bound for models for the temporal component, we obtain[4]:

Theorem 4. *Let $n = |\varphi|$. Then φ is satisfiable in PROTEM if, and only if, it is satisfiable in a model with at most $2^{5 \cdot n}$ balloon models (in the temporal dimension). Moreover, we only need to consider at most $|F|^{2^n}$ different balloon models (in the probabilistic dimension).*

Remark 2. It is important to note that it is generally only in the case of unsatisfiable specifications that *all* these possibilities must be explored. Typically, the search for an execution does not consider all these models.

The key idea underlying METATEM is to directly execute a temporal formula by attempting to build a model (as a sequence of states) for the agent description (a single logical statement has both declarative and procedural readings). When including beliefs, instead of generating a set of choices based upon temporal rules, both temporal and belief rules must be considered. That is, the execution now uses temporal formulae in the normal form to build a temporal sequence of *balloons*. When no temporal rules are fired, we have to 'fill a balloon' and explore the beliefs that currently should be satisfied. For this, we use the decision procedure of [8], which, in turn, heavily relies on a constraint solver for linear inequalities (generated by the probabilistic formulae). Of course, if the solver finds a solution, it means that in the newly generated balloons

---

[4] The simulation of temporal states is, by definition, infinite. However, as we will explain in Section 4.2, there is an upper bound for the number of unsatisfiable temporal states generated in our execution. And this leads us to the result in Theorem 4.

we may have some atoms that give rise to new potential timelines in the belief context (see Fig. 2, keeping in mind that every bullet '•' represents a balloon $\langle W, w, P_F \rangle$). The execution mechanism is organised in such a way that this exploration of beliefs will not continue forever.

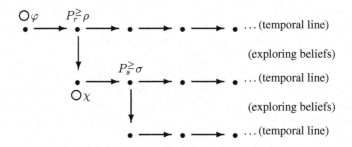

Fig. 2. Sample PROTEM Model Construction

We claim that this is a complete algorithm that can, if necessary, be used as a decision procedure for the combined logic. We know that the extended METATEM + $P_F K D45$ framework, PROTEM, inherits the finite modelling properties that both systems have. We further show that the execution algorithm is effective in searching for a specification's model: it either finds a model for the specification or ends the execution failing to produce one (having exhaustively explored all the possible execution paths). In the case of failure, we know that the specification is unsatisfiable.

4.1   The Algorithm

In this section we describe an execution algorithm that constructs a model for a formula φ in the normal form. We will refer to the implications as displayed in (1) as the set of rules, R, of φ, and attempt to build a model for R, if one exists. The model construction (hence, execution) algorithm basically comprises two mutually recursive procedures, TEMPEXPAND and PROBEXPAND.

The function TEMPEXPAND(R, s, Ev) attempts to build a temporal model from the (belief) state, s. It follows the previous METATEM algorithm presented in [4] and so we only give an informal outline here. At any given state, the algorithm checks which rules (within R) are relevant and collects together the constraints on future temporal execution. These constraints are represented as a disjunction, together with a number of eventualities yet to be satisfied. During execution, a disjunct is chosen and as many eventualities are satisfied as possible. The disjunct, together with the satisfied eventualities, generate a new temporal state which will be used in a recursive call of TEMPEXPAND; similarly, unsatisfied eventualities are passed on to this recursive call. In this way, a temporal sequence is constructed. If backtracking occurs, then an alternative disjunct is chosen. If no unexplored alternative exists, then the rules R represent an unsatisfiable formula.

At each state, s, being constructed using TEMPEXPAND, the relevant *probabilistic* constraints are examined using PROBEXPAND, which carries out probabilistic belief exploration. Given the current state s, it looks for all disjunctions of probabilistic literals that need to be satisfied in s. If there are no such disjunctions, we successfully terminate and return **true**. Otherwise, to make all disjunctions true in s, we have to satisfy at least one combination of disjuncts d_i, one for each $D_i = d_{1_i} \vee \ldots \vee d_{n_i}$. We collect all those possible combinations as conjunctions in Unexplored Options (UnexplOpt). Now, PROBEXPAND(R, s) should return **true** if, and only if, UnexplOpt is satisfiable.

For each such combination C in UnexplOpt, we call the decision procedure for $P_F K D45$. If C is satisfiable, this procedure generates a set of possible $P_F K D45$ models, which we call "Balloons" in the procedure. Each of these Balloons, t, is then exposed to TEMPEXPAND, which tries to solve the temporal constraints for t. If it succeeds, we are done. Otherwise we choose another Balloon t'. If none yields a successful temporal expansion, we try another possibilistic combination C' from UnexplOpt. If all possibilities fail, then there are no satisfiable possibilities at this point and backtracking occurs.

PROBEXPAND (P, R, s)
1   ProbDis $\leftarrow \{\vee P_x^\sim g \mid h \Rightarrow \vee P_x^\sim F \in R$ and $s \models h\}$
2   **if** ProbDis $= \emptyset$ **then**
3   **return true**
4   **endif**
5   UnexplOpt $\leftarrow \emptyset$
6   **for** $D_i \leftarrow D_1 = \vee P_x^\sim g, D_2, \ldots, D_n \in$ ProbDis **do**
7   select exactly one disjunct d_i from D_i
8   UnexplOpt $\leftarrow$ UnexplOpt $\cup \{d_1 \wedge \ldots \wedge d_n\}$
9   **endfor**
10   **while** UnexplOpt $\neq \emptyset$ **do**
11   Select C from UnpexplOpt
12   Balloons $= \{\langle W, w, P_F \rangle\} \leftarrow P_F K D45$ DEC PROC(C)
13   **while** Balloons $\neq \emptyset$ **do**
14   select $t = \langle W, w, P_F \rangle$ from Balloons
15   **if** TEMPEXPAND$(R, t, \emptyset)$ succeeds **then**
16   **return true**
17   **endif**
18   Balloons $\leftarrow$ Balloons $\setminus \{t\}$
19   **endwhile**
20   UnexplOpt $\leftarrow$ UnexplOpt $\setminus \{C\}$
21   **endwhile**
22   **return false**

Fig. 3. Procedure PROBEXPAND

4.2   Correctness of Execution Algorithm

As to the correctness of METATEM, [4] states that a set of formulae, R, is satisfiable, if, and only if, the METATEM interpreter generates a model for R (here, we will only require a boolean if the model exists). The 'oldest eventualities' are attempted first at each step; when the number of attempts to satisfy any eventuality reaches $2^{5|R|}$, backtracking is forced and another choice is attempted.

The proof for the whole extended system follows by showing that the execution with probabilistic beliefs (potentially) explores all the linear sequences of states. In detail, the execution algorithm implements a search in the space of possible models for the given beliefs, together with a simulation of temporal aspects associated with them. Thus, the search explores models in two dimensions: a doxastic and a temporal one. In terms of beliefs, we know that the search represents a simple verification of a probability assignment that satisfies the given formulae. By the finite model property of the language, we know that every consistent set of formulae has a finite model. And the $P_F K D45$ decision procedure is used to obtain a model for the set of formulae, or return an empty set of probability assignments if the set is unsatisfiable. The second dimension is the temporal line to be simulated. This is done by using a construction of temporal states similar to the basic algorithm for the METATEM framework.

Lemma 2. *Given a set of formulae, R, and a state, s,* PROBEXPAND *returns* **false** *iff R has no model.*

As a proof outline, recalling how the computation tree is built, we know that the algorithm starts by exploring one of the disjuncts of the given formula. We also know that PROBEXPAND has a finite number of potential ways to recurse. Recall that PROB-EXPAND invokes the $P_F K D45$ decision procedure in order to verify the existence of a model for the given set of formulae. So, if in a node the given formulae are unsatisfiable, no model is going to be generated. If all branches express unsatisfiable formulae, all the possible disjunctions would be unsatisfiable and the algorithm would fail to produce a model for the graded beliefs.

Theorem 5. *A set of rules, R, is satisfiable if, and only if, the extended framework algorithm returns* **true**.

Remark 3. Note that part of the exploration of probabilistic beliefs involves also a simulation of temporal aspects, by calling TEMPEXPAND. This part of the algorithm is similar to the basic METATEM one. Moreover, one can extend the two procedures in such a way that they generate the required model, rather than returning **true**, if it exists.

5   Conclusion

In previous research on executable agent specifications, the problem of handling uncertainty has rarely been tackled, an exception being extensions of Logic Programming providing *probabilistic logic programs* [9]. In contrast, our approach uses non-classical logics as the basis for agent specification and forward chaining as the basis for agent execution.

Simple and expressive formalisms that deal with the combination of uncertainty and time have many interesting and non-trivial applications. For instance, *Probabilistic Planning* [7] is a field where both probabilistic beliefs and temporal aspects are crucial.

In Computer Science, reasoning about probabilistic properties of concurrent systems is increasingly important [1]. Also, recently, reasoning about agents in game-like scenario has received considerable attention from the Logic community [2]. Typically, reasoning about strategies in such games has a temporal aspect and, moreover, games with *incomplete information* are only recently put fully on the logical agenda. Moreover, for certain games, it is well-known that only if we allow agents to play *mixed strategies*, which means that they play each (*pure*) strategy with a certain probability, solutions like that of Nash Equilibrium are guaranteed (c.f. [18]). In these, and other, areas we believe that PROTEM offers an appropriate framework in which to allow agents to reason about uncertain information.

There are many directions to further our framework. First of all, PROTEM represents the simplest way to combine two logics, i.e. via a fusion. When adding additional assumptions on the relation between the temporal and the doxastic dimensions, it is not clear whether we can adjust our algorithm easily. And, if so, will we retain important results? The extension to *multi-agent* systems seems less problematic, from this point of view, since the most straightforward way to extend PROTEM to the multi-agent case still is a fusion of several logics. It becomes more intricate when adding even the simplest dependencies, however, such as the property that what is believed by a given agent A, is also believed by another agent B.

Acknowledgement

The first author gratefully acknowledges support by the Brazilian Government under CAPES-scholarship.

References

1. P. Abdulla, C. Baier, P. Iyer, and B. Jonsson. Reasoning about Probabilistic Lossy Channel Systems *LNCS*, 1877, 2000.
2. R. Alur, T. A. Henzinger, and O. Kupferman. Alternating-time temporal logic. *J. ACM*, **49**(5): 672 – 713, 2002.
3. H. Barringer, M. Fisher, D. Gabbay, G. Gough, and R. Owens. METATEM: An Introduction. *Formal Aspects of Computing*, **7**(5): 533 – 549, 1995.
4. H. Barringer, M. Fisher, D. Gabbay, R. Owens, and M. Reynolds, editors. *The Imperative Future: Principles of Executable Temporal Logics*. Research Studies Press, Chichester, UK, 1996.
5. J. Bradshaw, M. Greaves, H. Holmback, T. Karygiannis, B. Silverman, N. Suri, and A. Wong. Agents for the Masses? *IEEE Intelligent Systems*, **14**(2), 1999.
6. P. R. Cohen and H. J. Levesque. Intention Is Choice with Commitment. *Artificial Intelligence*, **42**(2-3): 213 – 261, March 1990.
7. International Planning Competition: Probabilistic Planning Track., 2004. http://www.cs.rutgers.edu/~mlittman/topics/ipc04-pt.
8. N. de Carvalho Ferreira, M. Fisher, and W. van der Hoek. Practical Reasoning for Uncertain Agents. In *Proc. Ninth European Conf. on Logics in Artificial Intelligence (JELIA)*, pp. 82 – 94, 2004.
9. J. Dix, S. Kraus, and V. S. Subrahmanian. Heterogenous Temporal Probabilistic Agents. *ACM Transactions on Computational Logic*, **5**(3), 2004.

10. M. Fisher and C. Ghidini. Programming Resource-Bounded Deliberative Agents. In *Proc. International Joint Conf. on Artificial Intelligence (IJCAI)*. Morgan Kaufmann, 1999.

11. M. Fisher, C. Dixon, and M. Peim. Clausal Temporal Resolution. *ACM Transactions on Computational Logic*, **2**(1): 12 – 56, January 2001.

12. M. Fisher. Representing and Executing Agent-Based Systems. In M. Wooldridge and N. R. Jennings, editors, *Intelligent Agents*. Springer-Verlag, 1995.

13. M. Fisher. A Normal Form for Temporal Logic and its Application in Theorem-Proving and Execution. *J. Logic and Computation*, **7**(4): 429 – 456, 1997.

14. J. Y. Halpern. *Reasoning About Uncertainty*. MIT Press, 2003.

15. M. Kracht and F. Wolter. Properties of Independently Axiomatizable Bimodal Logics. *Journal of Symbolic Logic*, 56(4):1469 – 1485, 1991.

16. P. Madhusudan and P.S.Thiagarajan. Branching-time Controllers for Discrete Event Systems. *Theoretical Computer Science*, **274**: 117 – 149, 2002.

17. Z. Manna and P. Wolper. Synthesis of Communication Processes for Temporal Logic Specifications. *ACM Transactions on Programming Languages and Systems*, **6**: 68 – 93, 1984.

18. M. J. Osborne and A. Rubinstein. *A Course in Game Theory*. MIT Press, 1994.

19. A. S. Rao and M. Georgeff. BDI Agents: from Theory to Practice. In *Proc. First International Conf. on Multi-Agent Systems (ICMAS)*, pp. 312 – 319, 1995.

20. W. van der Hoek and M.J. Wooldridge. Towards a Logic of Rational Agency. *Logic Journal of the IGPL*, **11**(2): 135 – 160, 2003.

21. M. Wooldridge. *Reasoning about Rational Agents*. MIT Press, 2000.

Subgoal Semantics in Agent Programming

M. Birna van Riemsdijk, Mehdi Dastani, and John-Jules Ch. Meyer

ICS, Utrecht University, The Netherlands
{birna, mehdi, jj}@cs.uu.nl

Abstract. This paper investigates the notion of subgoals as used in plans in cognitive agent programming languages. These subgoals form an abstract representation of more concrete courses of action or plans. Subgoals can have a procedural interpretation (directly linked to a concrete plan) or a declarative one (the state to be reached as represented by the subgoal is taken into account). We propose a formal semantics for subgoals that interprets these declaratively, and study the relation between this semantics and the procedural subgoal semantics of the cognitive agent programming language 3APL. We prove that subgoals of 3APL can be programmed to behave declaratively, although the semantics is defined procedurally.

1 Introduction

This paper presents an *observation* about the cognitive agent programming language 3APL [8]. The observation is related to the notion of a *goal*. This is an important concept in cognitive agent programming languages. Goals are introduced to specify an agent's proactive behavior. Many languages and platforms have been proposed to implement (represent and process) an agent's goals [11,8,15,4,16,3,14,2]. The way in which goals are dealt with varies from language to language. In some programming languages goals are interpreted in a *procedural* way as processes that need to be executed. In others goals are interpreted in a *declarative* way as states to be reached. Yet other languages combine both aspects. Procedural goals are also often called *plans*, which is a terminology we will also use in this paper.

While the procedural interpretation might arguably be considered more standard, the declarative interpretation of goals also has several advantages. Most importantly in this context, is the fact that declarative goals provide for the possibility to decouple plan execution (i.e., the execution of a procedural goal) and goal achievement (i.e., the achievement of a declarative goal) [16]. If a plan fails, the goal that was to be achieved by the plan remains a goal of the agent. The agent can then for example select a different plan or wait for the circumstances to change for the better.[1]

A common usage of goals, and the one we are concerned with in this paper, is that of *subgoals* as occurring in the plans of the agent.[2] These plans are often

---

[1] See e.g. [13] for a more elaborate discussion on the advantages of declarative goals.

[2] A usage of the term subgoal that we do not consider in this paper is usage in the logical sense, where for example p is considered to be a subgoal of the goal $p \wedge q$ [13].

C. Bento, A. Cardoso, and G. Dias (Eds.): EPIA 2005, LNAI 3808, pp. 548–559, 2005.

built from basic actions which can be executed directly, and subgoals which can be viewed as representing a course of action in a more abstract way. An agent can for example have the plan to go to the bus stop, to take the bus into town,[3] and then to achieve the goal of buying a birthday cake. This goal of buying a birthday cake will have to be fulfilled by selecting a more concrete plan of for example which shop to go to, etc.

Just as goals in general, subgoals of plans can also be categorized as either procedural or declarative. In the procedural interpretation, subgoals are linked directly to plans. Their only role is the abstract representation of a more concrete plan. In the declarative interpretation, the fact of whether the state that is represented by the subgoal is achieved (for example through the execution of a corresponding concrete plan), is somehow taken into account. In the birthday cake example, this means that it is important whether the execution of the concrete plan of which shop to go to etc., has resulted in a state in which the birthday cake is actually bought. If it turns out that the goal of buying the cake is not reached after having gone to the specific shop, the agent could select another plan to try a different shop. A declarative interpretation of subgoals could yield more flexible agent behavior, because of the decoupling between plan execution and goal achievement.

We thus argue that it is important to be able to express a declarative notion of subgoals in a cognitive agent programming language. This paper aims to investigate whether these declarative subgoals can be expressed in the language 3APL. In order to do this, we first make precise what we mean exactly by declarative subgoals, by defining a simple formal semantics for subgoals that interprets these in a declarative way (sections 2 and 3). We then compare this semantics with the semantics of 3APL (section 4). We show that 3APL has a notion of subgoal, but it is a procedural kind of subgoal. It turns out, however, that although subgoals of 3APL are defined to have a procedural semantics, a 3APL agent can nevertheless be *programmed* to have these subgoals behave *declaratively*. This observation (and a formal proof that it is correct) is the main contribution of this paper.

The 3APL language family [8,15,4] is an example of a set of languages in which subgoals are interpreted procedurally. Languages and platforms from the AgentSpeak family [9,5,11,1,6] also have a procedural view on subgoals, although the mechanism differs from that of 3APL. We conjecture that a similar result for an implementation of declarative subgoals can be obtained for AgentSpeak, although this is left for future research. An example of a declarative view on subgoals is the high-level language of Winikoff et al. [16]. The declarative semantics we propose in section 3 is comparable with that of [16], although [16] has a much more elaborate plan language. An elaborate plan language is however not needed for the purpose of comparison with the procedural subgoals of 3APL. Establishing a formal relation with the work of Winikoff et al. is left for

---

[3] Assuming that both going to the bus stop and taking the bus into town are actions that can be executed directly.

future research. The Jadex platform [2] incorporates declarative and procedural interpretations, although the platform does not have a formal semantics.

2 Syntax

In this section and the next, we present the syntax and semantics of a simple programming language with plans containing subgoals that have a declarative interpretation. Throughout this paper, we assume a language of propositional logic $\mathcal{L}$ with negation and conjunction and based on a set of atoms Atom. The symbol $\models$ will be used to denote the standard entailment relation for $\mathcal{L}$. Below, we define the language of plans. A plan is a sequence of basic actions and statements of the form $achieve(p)$ (subgoals), where $p \in$ Atom. Informally, basic actions can change the beliefs of an agent if executed, and a statement of the form $achieve(p)$ means that p should be achieved, before the agent can continue the execution of the rest of the plan.

Definition 1 *(plans).* Let BasicAction with typical element a be the set of basic actions and let $p \in$ Atom. The set of plans Plan with typical element π is then defined as follows.

$$\pi ::= a \mid achieve(p) \mid \pi_1; \pi_2$$

We use ϵ to denote the empty plan and identify $\epsilon; \pi$ and $\pi; \epsilon$ with π.

We use a simple plan language, focused on subgoals. The language could however be extended to include, e.g., test and non-deterministic choice. Also, the subgoals could be extended to arbitrary formulas, rather than just atoms. For atomic subgoals however, a correspondence with the procedural goals of 3APL can be established. For arbitrary subgoals this cannot be done in the general case, as we conjecture.

In order to define the plans that can be used for achieving the subgoals, we use so-called plan generation rules. Informally, a plan generation rule $p \Rightarrow \pi$ specifies that the plan π can be selected to try to achieve the subgoal p. One could add a condition on the beliefs of the agent to the rule, specifying that the rule can only be applied if the agent has a certain belief. We however leave this out for reasons of simplicity.

Definition 2 *(plan generation rule).* The set of plan generation rules $\mathcal{R}_{\mathsf{PG}}$ is defined as follows: $\mathcal{R}_{\mathsf{PG}} = \{p \Rightarrow \pi \mid p \in \mathsf{Atom}, \pi \in \mathsf{Plan}\}$.

An agent in this paper is a tuple, consisting of an initial belief base (a consistent set of formulas from $\mathcal{L}$ representing what the agent believes about the world), an initial plan, a set of plan generation rules and a belief update function $\mathcal{T}$. This function $\mathcal{T}$, taking a basic action and a belief base and yielding a new belief base, is used to define how belief bases are updated if a basic action is executed. The function is undefined for a basic action and belief base, if the basic action cannot be executed on this belief base. This function is used for technical convenience and is not further specified, as it is not needed for the purpose of this paper.

Definition 3 *(subgoal achievement agent).*   Let $\Sigma = \{\sigma \mid \sigma \subseteq \mathcal{L}, \sigma \not\models \perp\}$ be the set of belief bases. A subgoal achievement agent, typically denoted by $\mathcal{A}$, is a tuple $\langle \sigma, \pi, \mathsf{PG}, \mathcal{T} \rangle$ where $\sigma \in \Sigma$ is the belief base, $\pi \in \mathsf{Plan}$ is the initial plan, and $\mathsf{PG} \subseteq \mathcal{R}_{\mathsf{PG}}$ is a set of plan generation rules. $\mathcal{T}$ is a partial function of type $(\mathsf{BasicAction} \times \Sigma) \rightarrow \Sigma$.

When defining the semantics of plan execution, we use the notion of a configuration. A configuration consists of a belief base and a plan, which are the elements of an agent that can change during its execution.

Definition 4 *(configuration).*   A configuration is a pair $\langle \sigma, \pi \rangle$ where $\sigma \in \Sigma$ and $\pi \in \mathsf{Plan}$.

3   Semantics

In this section, we provide a semantics for the execution of plans containing subgoals, that interprets these declaratively. We define the semantics using a transition system [10]. A transition system for a programming language consists of a set of axioms and derivation rules for deriving transitions for this language. A transition is a transformation of one configuration into another and it corresponds to a single computation step. Let $\mathcal{A} = \langle \sigma, \pi, \mathsf{PG}, \mathcal{T} \rangle$ be a subgoal achievement agent. The transition system $\mathsf{Trans}_{\mathcal{A}}$ for this agent is then given by the definitions below.

A basic action at the head of a plan can be executed in a configuration if the function $\mathcal{T}$ is defined for this action and the belief base in the configuration. The execution results in a change of belief base as specified through $\mathcal{T}$, and the action is removed from the plan.

Definition 5 *(action execution).*   Let $a \in \mathsf{BasicAction}$.

$$\frac{\mathcal{T}(a, \sigma) = \sigma'}{\langle \sigma, a; \pi \rangle \rightarrow \langle \sigma', \pi \rangle}$$

The following two definitions specify the possible transitions in case a statement of the form $achieve(p)$ is the first "action" of the plan. Both transitions rely upon a declarative interpretation of p, as it is checked whether p is believed to be reached. Definition 6 gives the transition in case p is achieved. The statement $achieve(p)$ is then removed from the plan.

Definition 6 *(subgoal achievement).*

$$\frac{\sigma \models p}{\langle \sigma, achieve(p); \pi \rangle \rightarrow \langle \sigma, \pi \rangle}$$

The next transition rule specifies the transition for an $achieve(p)$ statement in case p is not achieved. In this case, a plan should be generated in order to achieve p. This can be done if there is a plan generation rule of the form $p \Rightarrow \pi'$ in the rule base of the agent. The transition that can then be derived, specifies that the plan π' is placed at the head of the plan.

Definition 7 *(plan generation)*. Let $p \Rightarrow \pi' \in \mathsf{PG}$.

$$\frac{\sigma \not\models p}{\langle \sigma, achieve(p); \pi \rangle \rightarrow \langle \sigma, \pi'; achieve(p); \pi \rangle}$$

It is important to note that the statement $achieve(p)$ is not removed from the plan if a plan generation rule is applied. If π' is executed and p is still not derivable from the agent's beliefs (p is not reached), a different rule with p as the head could be applied (if it exists), to achieve p by other means. In any case, a statement $achieve(p)$ will not be removed from the plan if p is not reached.

Given the transition system $\mathsf{Trans}_{\mathcal{A}}$ for subgoal achievement agent $\mathcal{A}$ as specified above, one can construct computation runs for $\mathcal{A}$. A computation run is a sequence of configurations, such that each consecutive configuration can be obtained from the previous through the application of a transition rule. The initial configuration of the computation run is formed by the initial belief base and plan of $\mathcal{A}$. A successful computation run is a run of which the final configuration has an empty plan. The semantics of $\mathcal{A}$ is then defined as the set of successful computation runs of $\mathcal{A}$.

Definition 8 *(semantics   of   a   subgoal   achievement   agent)*.   Let $\mathcal{A} = \langle \sigma_0, \pi_0, \mathsf{PG}, \mathcal{T} \rangle$ be a subgoal achievement agent. Let a computation run be a sequence of configurations. A successful computation run of agent $\mathcal{A}$ is a computation run $\langle \sigma_0, \pi_0 \rangle, \ldots, \langle \sigma_n, \epsilon \rangle$, such that $\forall_{1 \leq i \leq n} : \langle \sigma_{i-1}, \pi_{i-1} \rangle \rightarrow \langle \sigma_i, \pi_i \rangle$ is a transition that can be derived in $\mathsf{Trans}_{\mathcal{A}}$. The semantics of $\mathcal{A}$ is the set $\{\theta \mid \theta$ is a successful computation run of $\mathcal{A}\}$.

A property of the semantics that reflects that subgoals are interpreted declaratively, is the following: if a plan of the form $achieve(p)$ is the initial plan of the agent, then it holds for any successful computation run of this agent ending in some belief base σ_n, that p follows from σ_n.

Proposition 1.   Let $\mathcal{A} = \langle \sigma_0, \pi_0, \mathsf{PG}, \mathcal{T} \rangle$ be a subgoal achievement agent, and let $\theta = \langle \sigma_0, \pi_0 \rangle, \ldots, \langle \sigma_n, \epsilon \rangle$ be a successful computation run of $\mathcal{A}$. If π_0 is of the form $achieve(p)$, we have that $\sigma_n \models p$.

At this point we remark that the semantics of our *achieve* statement is closely related to the "bringing it about" operator as introduced by Segerberg [12] in the area of philosophical logic. His operator δ satisfies the property $[\delta p]p$ (expressed in a kind of dynamic logic), which would in our notation be the property $[achieve(p)]p$, stating that p always holds after the "execution" of $achieve(p)$. This is a reformulation of the above proposition in dynamic logic. A formal study of the relation of our work with that of Segerberg is left for future research.

4   Comparison with 3APL

4.1   Syntax and Semantics

In this section, we present a propositional and otherwise slightly simplified version of 3APL [8]. We introduce these simplification for reasons of clarity and simplicity, but they are not fundamental. 3APL is similar to the language as presented in section 2. A 3APL agent has a belief base (set of formulas from $\mathcal{L}$), a plan, a set of so-called plan revision rules for manipulating its plan, and a belief update function $\mathcal{T}$.

The language of plans of 3APL agents is similar to the plan language of definition 1. A 3APL plan however does not contain *achieve* statements. The 3APL counterpart of these subgoals is called an *achievement goal* [8], and was dubbed *abstract plan* in later papers [15,4]. An abstract plan is basically a string, just as a basic action is a string (but as we will see, abstract plans have a different semantics). For the comparison with subgoal achievement agents however, we take the set of abstract plans as consisting not of an arbitrary set of strings, but of exactly the atoms of $\mathcal{L}$. Further, we add the possibility to test whether an atom follows from the belief base or not, and we add non-deterministic choice.

Definition 9 *(3APL plans).* Let BasicAction with typical element a be the set of basic actions and let AbstractPlan with typical element p be the set of abstract plans, such that AbstractPlan = Atom and AbstractPlan $\cap$ BasicAction = $\emptyset$. The set of 3APL plans Plan$'$ with typical element π is then defined as follows.

$$\pi ::= a \mid p \mid p? \mid \neg p? \mid \pi_1; \pi_2 \mid \pi_1 + \pi_2$$

We use ϵ to denote the empty plan and identify $\epsilon; \pi$ and $\pi; \epsilon$ with π.

Abstract plans obtain their meaning through the plan revision rules of the 3APL agent. These rules have a plan as the head and as the body. During execution of a plan, a plan revision rule can be used to replace a prefix of the plan, which is identical to the head of the rule, by the plan in the body. If the agent for example executes a plan $a; b; c$ and has a plan revision rule $a; b \Rightarrow d$, it can apply this rule, yielding the plan $d; c$. Here we do not use the general plan revision rules that can have a composed plan as the head. We only use rules with an abstract plan as the head and a plan as the body.

Definition 10 *(plan revision rule).* The set of plan revision rules $\mathcal{R}_{\mathsf{PR}}$ is defined as follows: $\mathcal{R}_{\mathsf{PR}} = \{p \Rightarrow \pi \mid p \in \mathsf{AbstractPlan}, \pi \in \mathsf{Plan}'\}$.

Plan revision rules thus very much resemble the plan generation rules of definition 2 (syntactically, that is), but the body is a 3APL plan, i.e., a plan from Plan$'$. As we will explain shortly, the *semantics* of plan revision rules however differs from that of plan generation rules in important ways.

The semantics of 3APL agents is defined by means of a transition system, as given below. The first transition rule is used to derive a transition for action execution, and is similar to the transition rule of this kind for subgoal achievement agents (definition 5). The second transition specifies the application of a plan revision rule of the form $p \Rightarrow \pi'$ to a plan of the form $p; \pi$. If the rule is applied, the abstract plan p is replaced by the body of the rule, yielding the plan $\pi'; \pi$. It is important to note that it is *not* tested whether p holds, and further that p is *replaced* by π', rather than yielding the plan $\pi'; p; \pi$.

The transition rules for test and non-deterministic choice are fairly standard. Note however that a test for $\neg p$ succeeds if it is *not* the case that p follows from the belief base, rather than having this test succeed if $\neg p$ *does* follow. The reason for this choice should become clear in the sequel. Further, some transitions are labelled with i, which we will also need in the sequel.

Definition 11 *(3APL transition system).*   A 3APL agent $\mathcal{A}'$ is a tuple $\langle \sigma, \pi, \mathsf{PR}, \mathcal{T} \rangle$, where $\sigma \in \Sigma$, $\pi \in \mathsf{Plan}'$, $\mathsf{PR} \subseteq \mathcal{R}_{\mathsf{PR}}$ and $\mathcal{T}$ as in definition 3. The transition system $\mathsf{Trans}_{\mathcal{A}'}$ for this 3APL agent is then defined as follows, where $a \in \mathsf{BasicAction}$ and $p \Rightarrow \pi' \in \mathsf{PR}$.

$$1) \quad \frac{\mathcal{T}(a, \sigma) = \sigma'}{\langle \sigma, a; \pi \rangle \to \langle \sigma', \pi \rangle} \qquad\qquad 2) \quad \frac{}{\langle \sigma, p; \pi \rangle \to_i \langle \sigma, \pi'; \pi \rangle}$$

$$3) \quad \frac{\sigma \models p}{\langle \sigma, p?; \pi \rangle \to_i \langle \sigma, \pi \rangle} \qquad\qquad 4) \quad \frac{\sigma \not\models p}{\langle \sigma, \neg p?; \pi \rangle \to_i \langle \sigma, \pi \rangle}$$

$$5) \quad \frac{\langle \sigma, \pi_1 \rangle \to \langle \sigma', \pi_1' \rangle}{\langle \sigma, (\pi_1 + \pi_2); \pi \rangle \to \langle \sigma', \pi_1'; \pi \rangle} \qquad 6) \quad \frac{\langle \sigma, \pi_2 \rangle \to \langle \sigma', \pi_2' \rangle}{\langle \sigma, (\pi_1 + \pi_2); \pi \rangle \to \langle \sigma', \pi_2'; \pi \rangle}$$

Before we move on to formally investigating the relation between 3APL and subgoal achievement agents, we elaborate on the notion of an abstract plan or achievement goal as used in 3APL. Hindriks et al. [8] remark the following with respect to achievement goals:

> *Achievement goals are atomic propositions from the logical language $\mathcal{L}$. The use of atoms as achievement goals, however, is very different from the use of atoms as beliefs. Whereas in the latter case atoms are used to represent and therefore are of a declarative nature, in the former case they serve as an abstraction mechanism like procedures in imperative programming and have a procedural meaning.*

Hindriks et al. thus take the set of achievement goals/abstract plans to be the atoms from $\mathcal{L}$ (a first order language in their case). Then they remark that although achievement goals are atoms, they do *not* have a declarative interpretation. The fact that an achievement goal is an atom and could thus in principle be tested for example against the belief base, is not used in defining its semantics. The language of achievement goals could thus have been any language of strings (which is in fact the approach of later papers [15,4]). Hindriks et al. [8] however do remark the following with respect to a possible assertional reading of achievement goals:[4]

---

[4] As a first order language is used in [8], the original text states $p(\vec{t}\,)$ instead of p. This is a predicate name parameterized with a sequence of terms.

Apart from the procedural reading of these goals, however, an assertional reading is also possible. An achievement goal p would then be interpreted as specifying a goal to achieve a state of affairs such that p. We think such a reading is valid in case the plans for achieving an achievement goal p actually do establish p.

The *"plans for achieving an achievement goal p"* are the plans as specified through the plan revision rules, i.e., a plan revision rule $p \Rightarrow \pi$ specifies that π is a plan for achieving p. According to Hindriks et al., this assertional or declarative reading of achievement goals is thus *only* valid under the strong requirement that π actually reaches p. This is thus in contrast with the semantics for subgoals as we have introduced, as these subgoals are by definition interpreted in a declarative manner.

4.2   3APL and Subgoals

We will show in this section that, although the semantics of plan generation rules and plan revision rules differ in important ways, it *is* possible to define a mapping from an arbitrary subgoal achievement agent to a 3APL agent, such that the 3APL agent "simulates" the behavior of the subgoal achievement agent. In the sequel, the plan π_s denotes π in which all occurrences of statement of the form $achieve(p)$ are replaced with p.

We first remark that the naive translation, in which a plan generation rule $p \Rightarrow \pi$ is translated to a plan revision rule $p \Rightarrow \pi_s$, does not do the trick. The reason that this translation does not work, is precisely the difference of interpretation between *achieve* statements and abstract plans, i.e., declarative versus procedural. If an abstract plan p occurs at the head of a plan $p; \pi$, the plan revision rule $p \Rightarrow \pi'$ can be applied, yielding $\pi'; \pi$. After the execution of π', the plan π will be executed, *regardless* of whether p is actually achieved at that point. In the case of a plan $achieve(p); \pi$ of a subgoal achievement agent, the plan generation rule can be applied (if p is not believed), yielding the plan $\pi'; achieve(p); \pi$. After the execution of π', the agent will test whether p is achieved. If it is achieved, it will continue with the execution of π. If however p is *not* achieved, it will apply a rule once more to generate a plan to achieve p. It is nevertheless important to mention that *if* it is the case that π' actually establishes p (and this holds for all plan generation rules), it *can* be proven that the 3APL agent as obtained through this naive translation, simulates the subgoal achievement agent. For reasons of space, we however omit this proof.

Translation. We now turn to the translation of a subgoal achievement agent into a 3APL agent, for which it holds that the 3APL agent as obtained in this way, simulates the subgoal achievement agent. As would be expected, the important part of the translation is the mapping of plan generation rules onto plan revision rules.

Definition 12 *(transformation of subgoal achievement agent into 3APL agent).*
Let $s : \mathsf{Plan} \to \mathsf{Plan}'$ be a function that takes a plan π of a subgoal achievement

agent (definition 1), and yields this plan in which all statements of the form $achieve(p)$ are replaced by p, thus yielding a plan in Plan' (definition 9). We will in the sequel use the notation π_s for $s(\pi)$.

The function $t : \mathcal{R}_{\mathsf{PG}} \to \mathcal{R}_{\mathsf{PR}}$, taking a plan generation rule and yielding a corresponding plan revision rule, is then defined as follows.

$$t(p \Rightarrow \pi) = p \Rightarrow ((\neg p?; \pi_s; p) + p?)$$

The function t is lifted to sets of plan generation rules in the obvious way.

Let $\mathcal{A} = \langle \sigma, \pi, \mathsf{PG}, \mathcal{T} \rangle$ be a subgoal achievement agent. The 3APL agent corresponding with $\mathcal{A}$ is then $\langle \sigma, \pi_s, t(\mathsf{PG}), \mathcal{T} \rangle$. Finally, we define a function τ that takes a configuration from the transition system of $\mathcal{A}$ of the form $\langle \sigma, \pi \rangle$, and yields the configuration $\langle \sigma, \pi_s \rangle$.

Informally, this mapping can be used to obtain a 3APL agent that simulates a subgoal achievement agent, because of the following. Consider a 3APL agent with the plan $p; \pi$, and the plan revision rule $p \Rightarrow ((\neg p?; \pi'_s; p) + p?)$ as obtained from the plan generation rule $p \Rightarrow \pi'$. This plan revision rule can then be applied to this plan (regardless of whether p is believed or not), yielding the plan $((\neg p?; \pi'_s; p) + p?); \pi$.

Now assume that p is believed. In that case, the test $p?$ succeeds and $\neg p?$ fails, which means that the plan in the next configuration will have to be π. This thus implements that p is skipped if believed to be achieved, which corresponds with the semantics of the statement $achieve(p)$.

Now assume that p is not believed. In that case, the plan in the next configuration will have to be $\pi'_s; p; \pi$. This corresponds with the semantics of $achieve(p)$ in case p is not believed: the plan π' is placed at the head of the plan, not replacing the $achieve(p)$ statement. After the execution of π'_s, we are left with the plan $p; \pi$. The plan revision rule $p \Rightarrow ((\neg p?; \pi'_s; p) + p?)$ (or a different rule with p as the head) will then be applied again. If p is achieved, the agent will continue with the execution of π as explained. If p is not achieved, the mechanism as just described will be set in motion. All this thus corresponds with the behavior of $achieve$ statements in the subgoal achievement agent.

Bisimulation Theorem. We now move on to formally establishing this correspondence. For this, we introduce the notion of a translation bisimulation as used in [7–Chapter 8] (slightly adapted). Informally, a translation bisimulation translates an agent from a so-called source language to an agent from the target language that "can do the same things". In our case, we translate subgoal achievement agents to 3APL agents.

We have to show that for each transition in the transition system for a subgoal achievement agent $\mathcal{A}$, there is a corresponding transition in the transition system for the corresponding 3APL agent $\mathcal{A}'$. This "transition" in $\mathsf{Trans}_{\mathcal{A}'}$, actually does not have to be a single transition, but may consist of a number of so-called idle transitions, and one non-idle transition. The idle transitions in $\mathsf{Trans}_{\mathcal{A}'}$ are those labelled with i. Intuitively, these idle transitions form implementation details of

$\mathcal{A}'$, and do not have to be matched by a transition of $\mathcal{A}$.[5] In the sequel, the transition relations of $\mathcal{A}$ and $\mathcal{A}'$ will respectively be denoted by $\rightarrow^{\mathcal{A}}$ and $\rightarrow^{\mathcal{A}'}$, and $\rightarrow_i^{\mathcal{A}'}$ denotes the restriction of $\mathcal{A}'$ to idle transitions.

The new transition relation that abstracts from idle steps is denoted by $\rightarrow_*^{\mathcal{A}'}$. It only exists for $\mathsf{Trans}_{\mathcal{A}'}$, as $\mathsf{Trans}_{\mathcal{A}}$ does not contain idle steps. It is defined as follows, where d_j with $1 \leq j \leq n$ are configurations derivable in $\mathsf{Trans}_{\mathcal{A}'}$: $d_1 \rightarrow_*^{\mathcal{A}'} d_n$ iff there is a (possibly empty) series of idle transitions $d_1 \rightarrow_i^{\mathcal{A}'} d_2 \rightarrow_i^{\mathcal{A}'} \ldots \rightarrow_i^{\mathcal{A}'} d_{n-1}$ and a single non-idle transition $d_{n-1} \rightarrow^{\mathcal{A}'} d_n$.

If we can show that for each transition in the transition system for a subgoal achievement agent $\mathcal{A}$, there is a corresponding transition in the transition system for the corresponding 3APL agent $\mathcal{A}'$, we will have established that $\mathcal{A}'$ generates *at least* the behavior of $\mathcal{A}$. In order to establish that $\mathcal{A}'$ does not generate any (alternative) behavior not having a counterpart in $\mathcal{A}$, we also have to show that any non-idle transition of $\mathcal{A}'$ corresponds with a transition of $\mathcal{A}$. A transition $c_1 \rightarrow^{\mathcal{A}} c_2$ corresponds with a transition $d_1 \rightarrow^{\mathcal{A}'} d_2$ or $d_1 \rightarrow^* d_2$ iff $d_1 = \tau(c_1)$ and $d_2 = \tau(c_2)$.

The result can only be proven if we assume that at least one plan generation rule of the form $p \Rightarrow \pi$ exists for every $p \in \mathsf{Atom}$. If this would not be the case, there would be a mismatch: a statement $achieve(p)$ could be removed from a plan if p holds (without there being a plan generation rule for p), but an abstract plan p can only be "removed" if first a plan revision rule is applied.

Theorem 1 *(translation bisimulation).* Let $\mathcal{A} = \langle \sigma, \pi, \mathsf{PG}, \mathcal{T} \rangle$ be a subgoal achievement agent such that for each $p \in \mathsf{Atom}$ there is at least one rule of the form $p \Rightarrow \pi$ in PG, and let $\mathcal{A}' = \langle \sigma, \pi_s, t(\mathsf{PG}), \mathcal{T} \rangle$ be the corresponding 3APL agent. We then have that for every configuration c_1 of $\mathcal{A}$, $d_1 = \tau(c_1)$ implies the following:

1. If $c_1 \rightarrow^{\mathcal{A}} c_2$, then $d_1 \rightarrow_*^{\mathcal{A}'} d_2$, such that $d_2 = \tau(c_2)$.
2. If $d_1 \rightarrow^{\mathcal{A}'} d_2$, then for some c_2, $c_1 \rightarrow^{\mathcal{A}} c_2$, such that $d_2 = \tau(c_2)$.

Proof: 1. We have to show that for every transition $c_1 \rightarrow^{\mathcal{A}} c_2$ in $\mathsf{Trans}_{\mathcal{A}}$, there is a corresponding (sequence of) transition(s) $d_1 \rightarrow_*^{\mathcal{A}'} d_2$ in $\mathsf{Trans}_{\mathcal{A}'}$ such that $d_2 = \tau(c_2)$.

Let $\langle \sigma, a; \pi \rangle \rightarrow^{\mathcal{A}} \langle \sigma', \pi \rangle$ be a transition as derived through the transition rule of definition 5. We then have that the transition $\langle \sigma, a; \pi_s \rangle \rightarrow^{\mathcal{A}'} \langle \sigma', \pi_s \rangle$ can be derived in $\mathsf{Trans}_{\mathcal{A}'}$, by means of the first transition rule. We also have that $\langle \sigma', \pi_s \rangle = \tau(\langle \sigma', \pi \rangle)$, yielding the desired result for action execution transitions.

Let $\langle \sigma, achieve(p); \pi \rangle \rightarrow^{\mathcal{A}} \langle \sigma, \pi \rangle$ be a transition as derived through the transition rule of definition 6, which means that $\sigma \models p$ has to hold. Let $p \Rightarrow \pi'$ be a

---

[5] The choice of idle transitions for 3APL might seem strange, as the application of a plan revision rule is an idle transition, whereas the non-deterministic choice is not, although the latter might seem an implementation detail, rather than the former. The reason is, that the application of a plan revision rule cannot be matched directly with a transition of a goal achievement agent, whereas the particular usage of non-deterministic choice, as specified through the translation, *can*.

plan generation rule of $\mathcal{A}$ (a rule of this form has to exist by assumption). We then have, because $t(p \Rightarrow \pi')$ is a plan revision rule of $\mathcal{A}'$, that the transitions

$$\langle \sigma, p; \pi_s \rangle \rightarrow_i^{\mathcal{A}'} \langle \sigma, ((\neg p?; \pi_s'; p) + p?); \pi_s) \rangle \rightarrow^{\mathcal{A}'} \langle \sigma, \pi_s \rangle$$

can be derived in $\mathsf{Trans}_{\mathcal{A}'}$, by means of the transition rule for plan revision and those for test and non-deterministic choice. We also have that $\langle \sigma, \pi_s \rangle = \tau(\langle \sigma, \pi \rangle)$, yielding the desired result for subgoal achievement transitions.

Let $\langle \sigma, achieve(p); \pi \rangle \rightarrow^{\mathcal{A}} \langle \sigma, \pi'; achieve(p); \pi \rangle$ be a transition as derived through the transition rule of definition 7, which means that $\sigma \not\models p$ has to hold, and $p \Rightarrow \pi'$ has to be a plan generation rule in PG. We then have that the transitions

$$\langle \sigma, p; \pi_s \rangle \rightarrow_i^{\mathcal{A}'} \langle \sigma, ((\neg p?; \pi_s'; p) + p?); \pi_s) \rangle \rightarrow^{\mathcal{A}'} \langle \sigma, \pi_s'; p; \pi_s \rangle$$

can be derived in $\mathsf{Trans}_{\mathcal{A}'}$, by means of the transition rule for plan revision and those for test and non-deterministic choice. We also have that $\langle \sigma, \pi_s'; p; \pi_s \rangle = \tau(\langle \sigma, \pi'; achieve(p); \pi \rangle)$, yielding the desired result for plan generation transitions. We have shown the desired result for every transition $c_1 \rightarrow^{\mathcal{A}} c_2$, thereby proving 1. For reasons of space, we omit the proof of 2. $\square$

5   Conclusion

In this paper, we have studied the relation between declarative and procedural interpretations of subgoals as occurring in the plans of cognitive agents. In particular, we have compared our definition of declaratively interpreted subgoals with the semantics of the procedurally interpreted achievement goals in the language 3APL. As we have shown, it is possible to obtain a 3APL agent that simulates the behavior of the subgoal achievement agent, by translating plan generation rules to plan revision rules in a specific way.

Future research will address the relation between our subgoal achievement agents and AgentSpeak(L), and with the work of Winikoff et al. [16]. Also, we will investigate other semantics for subgoals, e.g., semantics making use of a goal base.

To the best of our knowledge, this is the first time that a correspondence between declarative and procedural subgoals is investigated and established. We believe that the investigations as described in this paper shed some light on the expressiveness of languages with procedural goals, and that this is an important piece of the puzzle of the incorporation of declarative goals in cognitive agent programming languages.

References

1. R. H. Bordini and A. F. Moreira.   Proving the asymmetry thesis principles for a BDI agent-oriented programming language. *Electronic Notes in Theoretical Computer Science*, 70(5), 2002. http://www.elsevier.nl/gej-ng/31/29/23/125/23/29/70.5.008.pdf.

2. L. Braubach, A. Pokahr, D. Moldt, and W. Lamersdorf. Goal representation for BDI agent systems. In *Programming multiagent systems, second international workshop (ProMAS'04)*, volume 3346 of *LNAI*, pages 44–65. Springer, Berlin, 2005.
3. M. Dastani and L. van der Torre. Programming BOID-Plan agents: deliberating about conflicts among defeasible mental attitudes and plans. In *Proceedings of the Third Conference on Autonomous Agents and Multi-agent Systems (AAMAS'04)*, pages 706–713, New York, USA, 2004.
4. M. Dastani, M. B. van Riemsdijk, F. Dignum, and J.-J. Ch. Meyer. A programming language for cognitive agents: goal directed 3APL. In *Programming multiagent systems, first international workshop (ProMAS'03)*, volume 3067 of *LNAI*, pages 111–130. Springer, Berlin, 2004.
5. M. d'Inverno, D. Kinny, M. Luck, and M. Wooldridge. A formal specification of dmars. In *ATAL '97: Proceedings of the 4th International Workshop on Intelligent Agents IV, Agent Theories, Architectures, and Languages*, pages 155–176, London, UK, 1998. Springer-Verlag.
6. R. Evertsz, M. Fletcher, R. Jones, J. Jarvis, J. Brusey, and S. Dance. Implementing industrial multi-agent systems using JACK™. In *Proceedings of the first international workshop on programming multiagent systems (ProMAS'03)*, volume 3067 of *LNAI*, pages 18–49. Springer, Berlin, 2004.
7. K. V. Hindriks. *Agent programming languages - programming with mental models.* PhD thesis, 2001.
8. K. V. Hindriks, F. S. de Boer, W. van der Hoek, and J.-J. Ch. Meyer. Agent programming in 3APL. *Int. J. of Autonomous Agents and Multi-Agent Systems*, 2(4):357–401, 1999.
9. F. F. Ingrand, M. P. Georgeff, and A. S. Rao. An architecture for real-time reasoning and system control. *IEEE Expert: Intelligent Systems and Their Applications*, 7(6):34–44, 1992.
10. G. D. Plotkin. A Structural Approach to Operational Semantics. Technical Report DAIMI FN-19, University of Aarhus, 1981.
11. A. S. Rao. AgentSpeak(L): BDI agents speak out in a logical computable language. In W. van der Velde and J. Perram, editors, *Agents Breaking Away (LNAI 1038)*, pages 42–55. Springer-Verlag, 1996.
12. K. Segerberg. Bringing it about. *Journal of Philosophical Logic*, 18:327–347, 1989.
13. M. B. van Riemsdijk, M. Dastani, F. Dignum, and J.-J. Ch. Meyer. Dynamics of declarative goals in agent programming. In J. A. Leite, A. Omicini, P. Torroni, and P. Yolum, editors, *Proceedings of the second international workshop on Declarative agent languages and technologies (DALT'04)*, pages 17–32, 2004.
14. M. B. van Riemsdijk, M. Dastani, and J.-J. Ch. Meyer. Semantics of declarative goals in agent programming. In *Proceedings of the fourth international joint conference on autonomous agents and multiagent systems (AAMAS'05)*, Utrecht, 2005. To appear.
15. M. B. van Riemsdijk, W. van der Hoek, and J.-J. Ch. Meyer. Agent programming in Dribble: from beliefs to goals using plans. In *Proceedings of the second international joint conference on autonomous agents and multiagent systems (AAMAS'03)*, pages 393–400, Melbourne, 2003.
16. M. Winikoff, L. Padgham, J. Harland, and J. Thangarajah. Declarative and procedural goals in intelligent agent systems. In *Proceedings of the eighth international conference on principles of knowledge respresentation and reasoning (KR2002)*, Toulouse, 2002.

The Multi-team Formation Precursor of Teamwork

Paulo Trigo[1] and Helder Coelho[2]

[1] Instituto Superior de Engenharia de Lisboa, Departamento da Engenharia da Electrónica e Telecom. e de Computadores, R. Conselheiro Emídio Navarro, 1, 1949-014 Lisboa, Portugal
ptrigo@isel.ipl.pt
[2] Faculdade de Ciências da Universidade de Lisboa, Departamento de Informática, Bloco C5, Piso 1, Campo Grande, 1749-016 Lisboa, Portugal
hcoelho@di.fc.ul.pt

Abstract. We formulate the multi-team formation (M-TF) domain-independent problem and describe a generic solution for the problem. We illustrate the M-TF preference relation component in the domain of a large-scale disaster response simulation environment. The M-TF problem is the precursor of teamwork that explicitly addresses the achievement of several short time period goals, where the work to achieve the complete set of goals overwhelms the working capacity of the team formation space (all teams formed from the finite set of available agents). Decisions regarding team formation are made by the agents considering their own probabilistic beliefs and utility preferences about the whole (known) set of goals to achieve. The RoboCupRescue simulated large-scale disaster domain is used to illustrate the design of the preference relation domain-specific M-TF component.

1 Introduction

Teamwork has emerged as the dominating coordination paradigm for multiple agents aiming to achieve goals within dynamic, uncertain and hostile environments [1]. The key precursor of teamwork is team formation, which is the process of how best to organize the agents into a collaborating team in order to achieve a specific goal [2].

The team formation process is usually triggered by a goal that overwhelms the individual (single agent) capability. Therefore, when faced with several overwhelming goals, the immediate response is to repetitively apply the team formation solution to each goal. As the number (and difficulty) of goals increase, also new sets of available agents are required to form new teams.

The continued demand for new teams, although theoretically admissible, becomes operationally infeasible within a resource-bounded environment. The mitigation of a large-scale disaster, caused either by a natural or a technological phenomenon (e.g. an earthquake or a terrorist incident), is such a resource-bounded environment where teamwork is the critical response to the disaster; several simultaneous goals call for the immediate response of multiple specialized teams.

There are no standards on how many resources are sufficient to mitigate a large-scale disaster and the general rule is to use as many resources as possible to reduce damages; more resources being required to rescue larger areas and harder

C. Bento, A. Cardoso, and G. Dias (Eds.): EPIA 2005, LNAI 3808, pp. 560–571, 2005.
© Springer-Verlag Berlin Heidelberg 2005

disasters. This general rule cannot be used in earthquakes because fires occur simultaneously throughout cities and resources (fire brigades) are finite [3]. In order to use finite resources effectively, it is necessary to evaluate the multiple and simultaneous damages and the resources' ability to mitigate those damages.

The operational perspective of teamwork is that agents and goals are resource-bounded elements. The *agent availability* is the first boundary; the agent set is finite and each agent only belongs to a single team. The *time to goal* achievement is the second boundary; goals are to be achieved within pressing deadlines.

The resource-bounded perspective of teamwork is best understood while trying to mitigate a large-scale simulated disaster. The RoboCupRescue [4] is a simulation environment of large-scale disasters. It is a resource-bounded simulated context that brings forth a semi-optimal behavior planning problem with extremely complex constraints and having time-varying multiple goals [5].

The work described in this paper is highly impelled by the concrete difficulties we came across during the participation at the RoboCupRescue 2004 International Championship (with the 5Rings team [6]). Our agents were qualified for the competition semi-finals but, at the end, their competitiveness revealed insufficient to achieve an high ranked classification. It became clear that the weakness of our agents followed from a team formation lacuna. We lacked a situation evaluation under uncertainty mechanism and a decision making technique that accounted for several simultaneous achievement goals given a finite set of agents.

The resource-bounded perspective of teamwork, materialized through the experienced difficulties of RoboCupRescue, shaped our formulation of the multi-team formation (M-TF) problem.

We conceive the M-TF problem as the most general precursor of teamwork. The M-TF is defined as a domain-independent problem that explicitly accounts for both a global and a local rationality for teamwork (respectively, the preference relation, $\Psi\gamma$, component and the derogation function, X_G, component) and also explicitly considers the impact of simple futuristic causal relations (the expected achievement goal set, Λ_G, component) on the teamwork performance. In this paper we illustrate the design of the preference relation, $\Psi\gamma$, component in the RoboCupRescue domain.

The solution of the M-TF problem is a team formation decision. The major quest for the M-TF solution is to determine "which goal should an agent commit to". We formulate two basic strategies. Both strategies depart from the definition of a total order importance relation among goals; agents commit to goals as to minimize the cost of team formation and reformation. One strategy searches for the minimal global cost of commitments. The other strategy considers that higher importance goals "choose agents first"; it searches for several locally minimal cost commitments.

The M-TF problem formulation represents our initial contribution towards an agency (collective) enforcement of teamwork.

This paper is organized as follows. In Section 2, we define the M-TF problem and in Section 3 the general solution of the M-TF problem is described. The Section 4 characterizes a simulated domain (taken from RoboCupRescue) and in Section 5 that domain is used to illustrate the design of the M-TF preference relation component. The Section 6 summarizes our proposals and outlines the future work.

2   The Multi-team Formation (M-TF) Problem

In this paper we present an intuitive and simplified description of the multi-team formation (M-TF) problem. We refer to [7] for the formal and comprehensive presentation of the M-TF problem.

Intuitively we see the multi-team formation as the problem to decide, at each time instant, the most important goals to achieve and the most effective agents to establish a joint commitment to achieve each goal, taking into account expected (future) goals and the team reformation (reorganization) required to counteract possible deviations from a desirable behavioral performance.

Given, at a time t, a finite set of agents, α, motivated to perform some joint task, a finite set of achievement goals, γ, and a finite set of teams, τ, we intend to build new teams committed to achieve the goals at γ that, at time t, are unattended.

The M-TF problem is represented as a 5-tuple, $< t, \Psi\gamma, \{\Lambda_G\}, \{X_G\}, \{T_G\} >$, for all $G \in \gamma$, where $\Psi\gamma$ is a preference relation over γ, Λ_G is the set of the expected achievement goals given that G is an achievement goal, X_G is the derogation function concerning G, and T_G is a team of agents that is "favorably disposed" to establish a commitment to achieve G.

The "favorably disposed" concept, formally described in [7], essentially reflects an operational teamwork perspective; team activity is to initiate as soon as possible. This perspective emerges from the *time to goal* resource-bounded revisited interpretation of the *joint intentions* [8] theoretical foundation of teamwork. The revisited interpretation states that team formation occurs even in the presence of individual disbelief regarding the goal to achieve, which relaxes the original *mutual belief* [8] assumption.

The preference relation, $\Psi\gamma$, over the set of all achievement goals is a total order relation, $\Psi: \gamma \to \Re$. This relation materializes the global rationality for teamwork and it is a central component of the M-TF problem.

The global rationality for teamwork gives higher priority to achieving those goals that, given the current knowledge, are expected to maximize a global performance measure. Such rationality operates under uncertainty as the agent's perceptions are incomplete and the relations in the domain are of a non-deterministic type. We assume that each team is selfless as its own interests do not overtake others' (e.g. teams do not dispute the most important goals). Thus we expect each agent to believe $\Psi\gamma$ at the individual level; that is, we expect each team member to want exactly what is best for the multitude of teams as a whole.

The expected achievement goal set, Λ_G, is a concept that captures the necessity of a teamwork rationality that accounts for expectations regarding futuristic causal relations in the domain. We adopt a relaxed approach to futuristic causality, such as to separately consider each achievement goal as the main cause for future effects. The reduced problem is stated as "given that G is an achievement goal, what are the propositions that I believe will turn false in a near future world?".

The derogation function, X_G, represents the local rationality for the team committed to achieve G, throughout the time period of such commitment. Intuitively the derogation function represents the justification for a team to keep committed working to achieve a specific goal; or, the other way around, it expresses the penalization for total agents' inaction regarding that goal. A selfless and rational team member accepts that, the least its team is penalized regarding its own goal, the least the multitude of teams gets penalized as a whole.

The design of each $\Psi\gamma$, Λ_G and X_G component is a domain-specific task to be attained by the agent's designer with the hopeful assistance of a domain specialist.

3   The Multi-team Formation (M-TF) Solution

Each M-TF solution is an instance of the 5-tuple, $< t, \Psi\gamma, \{\Lambda_G\}, \{X_G\}, \{T_G\} >$, general M-TF problem's characterization.

We consider that an M-TF solution construction is a two step process. The first step's input is the $\Psi\gamma$, Λ_G and X_G domain-dependent specifications while the output is the instance of $\Psi\gamma$, Λ_G and X_G, given the available perceptions (evidences) at the t time instant. The second step takes the previous step's output and builds the instance of the T_G component.

The T_G instance depends on $\Psi\gamma$, Λ_G and X_G instances; the Fig. 1 "Prolog like" syntax (with boldface output parameters), shows the directives of the predicate used to build the $\{T_G\}$ instance.

```
m-tf( Time, τ, γ, α, Ψγ, {Xₐ}, {Tₐ} ):-
    achievedGoals( Time, τ, γ, AG ),
    impossibleToAchieveGoals( Time, γ, {Xₐ}, IAG ),
    agentsNotCommitted( Time, τ, α, AG, IAG, αₒ ),
    bestMultiTeamFormation( Time, Ψγ, αₒ, {Tₐ} ).
```

Fig. 1. The Multi Team Formation Predicate

Each output parameter (boldface at Fig. 1) is defined as follows:

- AG $\equiv$ the difference between the set of goals for which there is a team (in τ) and γ; any goal that is not already in γ is assumed to have been achieved,
- IAG $\equiv$ the set of G goals such $X_G(\text{Time}) > \varepsilon$, where ε is the maximum penalization that any team is willing to accept, while committed to achieving G,
- $\alpha_0 \equiv$ the difference between α and the set of committed agents, which are those that belong to a team (in τ) whose goal does not belong to AG neither to IAG,
- $T_G \equiv$ a team of agents with the lowest team formation cost to achieve G, subject to the following guidelines i) for any two goals, $g_1 \in \gamma$ and $g_2 \in \gamma$, such that $\Psi(g_1) > \Psi(g_2)$, then the team formation of Tg_1 is to be achieved before the team formation of Tg_2 (informally we say that the priority of Tg_1 is higher then that of Tg_2), and ii) the only teams under consideration are those with sufficient number of agents to achieve the goal.

To formally express the above T_G guidelines, we introduce the α_i and $|s|$ symbols. We write α_i ($i \geq 1$) to represent the set of agents committed to achieve the G_i goal, which is the ith goal (as defined by $\Psi\gamma$); we recall that α_0 symbolizes the set of agents not committed to any goal (at a certain time instant). We write $|s|$ to represent the cardinality of the s set. We have $|\alpha_i|=0$ ($i \geq 1$) whenever the set of available agents is not sufficient to achieve the G_i goal. Also, during team formation, the construction order of each α_i follows the $\Psi\gamma$ prescribed (highest lo lowest) order.

Our team formation guidelines are formulated as follows:

- $\alpha_1 \subseteq \alpha_0$, and $\alpha_{i+1} \subseteq \alpha_{i-1} - \alpha_i$
- subject to, $\Psi(G_i) > \Psi(G_{i+1})$, for i=1..n−1 (where n = $|\gamma|$)
- such that, $|\alpha_i| \neq 0 \Leftrightarrow |\alpha_i|$ = "sufficient team cardinality to achieve G_i".

The "sufficient team cardinality to achieve a goal" is a function to be designed in the context of each specific domain; it depends on the domain and also on the available perception of the environment.

In order to define the lowest team formation cost to achieve a goal, G_i, we specify the cost function as follows:

$$\text{cost}(\alpha_i, G_i) = \text{cost}_{\text{formation}}(\alpha_i, G_i) + \kappa \times \Sigma_{r=1..m} \, \text{cost}_{\text{reformation}}(T_r), \qquad (1)$$

where, T_r is a team in τ with agents in α_i (a team to suffer reformation)
$\kappa \geq 0$, and m = number of team reformations to build α_i.

The $\text{cost}_{\text{formation}}(\alpha_i, G_i)$ is a domain dependent metric that represents the effort of α_i agents to start working to achieve G_i; e.g. the total (or maximum) amount of time spent, to physically move all α_i agents to the geographical location of G_i.

The $\text{cost}_{\text{reformation}}(T_r)$ is a domain dependent metric that represents the reformation effort of T_r team; e.g. the derogation value of the team at that time instant.

We now use equation (1) to specify two basic strategies to build the $\{T_G\}$. Both strategies comply with the team formation guidelines (previously described).

The first strategy, described at equation (2), is to build the globally best agent to goal commitment.

$$\text{argmin}_{< \alpha_1, \alpha_2, ..., \alpha_n >} \Sigma_{i=1..n} \, \text{cost}(\alpha_i, G_i), \text{ where n = } |\gamma| \qquad (2)$$

The second strategy, described at equation (3), is to build each goal's locally best agent to goal commitment. With this strategy we give a higher priority goal the privilege to first choose the best agents to achieve that goal.

$$\text{argmin}_{\alpha_i} \, \text{cost}(\alpha_i, G_i), \text{ for i=1..n, where n = } |\gamma| \qquad (3)$$

A third strategy is to apply equation (3) for some first goals and equation (2) for the remaining goals. Such strategy is to be applied whenever a big gap (over a certain threshold) exists between some first $\Psi\gamma$ values and the remaining values.

4 The M-TF Problem Illustration

For concreteness and to illustrate the design of the M-TF domain-dependent components we materialize the $\Psi\gamma$ component in the context of a simulated domain.

To characterize the illustrative domain we used the RoboCupRescue simulation system and devised a disaster scenario that evolves at the Nagata ward in Kobe, Japan (one of the official city maps used at RoboCupRescue 2004 competition).

Two buildings, B_1 and B_2, not too far from each other (about 90 meters) catch a fire. The B_1 building is located near Kobe's harbor within a low density neighborhood. The B_2 building is completely surrounded by other buildings and it is farther from the harbor than B_1. As time passes, the fires' intensity increases and each neighbor building is also liable to catch a fire.

The Fig. 2 depicts the Kobe's map section of the disaster scenario. Each opaque rectangle represents a building and a small circle is positioned over B_1 and B_2. The two larger filmy squares define the neighborhood border of B_1 and B_2 within a d distance (measured in meters); we set $d = 25m$, thus a ground area of $2,500m^2$ per neighborhood. The set of neighborhood buildings is denoted as neighborhood(B_i, d).

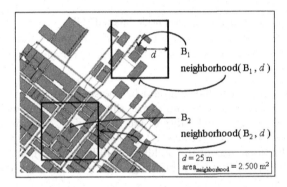

Fig. 2. The buildings, B_1 and B_2, and each neighborhood (at $d = 25m$ distance)

To simplify our illustrative scenario we assume that: i) all buildings being considered use the same construction method (wooden), ii) there are neither offices nor industries inside the buildings being considered (only residential buildings), and iii) there are no civilians, caught by fires, within the buildings. A further simplifying assumption is that agents get informed about B_1 and B_2 fires the moment each fire starts and we are not concerned on how (through which communication channel) the agent gets the fire information.

We now carry on with the design of the $\Psi\gamma$ component, in the context of this illustrative domain.

5   The Design of the Preference Relation $\Psi\gamma$

The preference relation, $\Psi\gamma$, is central to our perspective of a globally rational teamwork (cf. Section 2). We take the decision-theoretic notion of rationality to describe and predict the importance of goals. The consequences of each decision are unknown so our aim is to choose the decision alternative (achievement goal) that minimizes the eventual disadvantageous consequences of such decision.

The influence diagram [9] (ID) is a decision-theoretic framework that combines uncertain beliefs about the world and the expected gain (utility) of decisions. Within the ID framework, rationality is a matter of choosing such a decision alternative that will lead to the highest expected gain (utility), given the evidence of all available information.

An ID may be viewed as an extension to a Bayesian or belief network [10], with additional node types for decisions and utilities. An ID has three types of nodes (chance, decision and utility) and two types of arcs (influences and informational). Just as in belief networks, chance nodes represent random variables or features, i.e. the agent's uncertain beliefs about the world. A decision node holds the available choices, i.e. the possible goals to achieve. An utility node represents the agent's preferences. The links between the nodes summarize their dependence relationships.

We propose the following guidelines, to structure the $\Psi\gamma$ decision problem, using the ID framework:

- for each $G \in \gamma$, we define a decision node labeled "G",
- for each "G" node, we set its domain to "yes" and "no" values, which represent respectively the decision to achieve the G goal (G=yes) and the decision to disregard the G goal (G=no).

The Fig. 3 shows an ID with the "extinguish" decision node where the chance nodes represent all world features that influence this decision making process. For a particular building, the expected utility of the "extinguish" decision if influenced by: i) the intensity of the fire ("fireIntensity"), ii) the building's neighborhood density ("density"), iii) the total area of the building ("allFloorsArea"), and iv) the expected destruction ("destruction") of the building, which in turn is influenced by the "extinguish" decision.

The "U1" utility node represents the preferences of extinguishing a fire, considering the building's expected final destruction. For example, a low intensity fire is expected to cause a lower destruction then a high intensity fire (considering equivalent total areas and neighborhood density) thus, higher utility values are ascribed to initial low intensity fires.

The U2 utility node represents the preferences regarding the fire intensity and the neighborhood density; e.g. the highest utility is ascribed to a high intensity fire within a high density neighborhood.

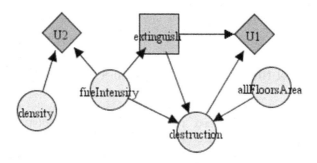

Fig. 3. Influence Diagram (ID) for the "extinguish" achievement goal

The intelligibility of Fig. 3 also evidences that, from the design perspective, the ID is particularly useful in showing the structure of the decision problem.

The Fig. 4 shows the ID evaluation of each decision's utility for all possible evidences regarding the chance nodes of "density" (low, normal and high values), "fireIntensity" (1, 2 and 3 values) and "allFloorsArea" (low, normal and high values). For clearness, we denote an evidence as a <density, allFloorsArea, fireIntensity> valued 3-tuple. For example, the B_2 tagged circle represents a <normal, normal, 1> evidence and the B_1 tagged circle represents a <low, low, 1> evidence. We also use the term "situation" to refer to such 3-tuple evidence.

The density represents the ratio between the total neighborhood ground area $(2.500m^2)$ and the ground area occupied by all buildings contained within that neighborhood. The Table 1 shows the B_1 and B_2 ratio and density values (each density value is ascribed to a ratio interval), assuming the Fig. 2 Kobe's map section.

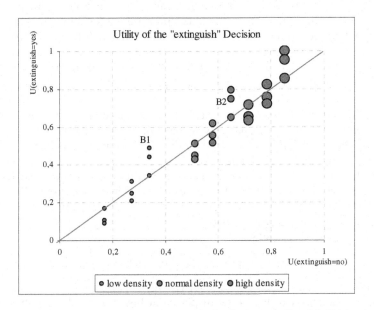

Fig. 4. "Extinguish" given evidence on "density", "fireIntensity" and "allFloorsArea"

Table 1. The area and density of B_1 and B_2 neighborhood

	area		ratio	**density**
	Σ groundArea	neighborhood	ratio	**density**
B_1	399.08 m^2	2,500 m^2	0.16	low
B_2	1,385.79 m^2	2,500 m^2	0.55	normal

Each plotted circle represents the normalized utility of the "yes", U(G=yes), and "no", U(G=no), values of the "extinguish" decision node. The radius of each plotted circle enlarges as the "density" value gets higher.

The ID construction assumes three *generic fire attack strategies*, acquired after the experimentation with RoboCupRescue:

- the earlier a fire is attacked, the easier it is to extinguish the fire,
- the smaller the building, the less time it takes to extinguish the fire,
- the higher the neighborhood density, the higher the necessity to extinguish the fire.

The Fig. 4 exhibits our generic fire attack strategies. It shows a linear growth of "yes" and "no" utilities as the "density" increases and evidences a pattern, within each density value, that shows the relative importance of the fire intensity and the building total area. For each density value, we see a pattern of equal radius circles organized in three vertical lines (similar U(G=no) value). Each of such vertical line represents a fire intensity value (the higher the intensity, the higher the U(G=no) value); within a single line, the higher U(G=yes) corresponds to the lowest area buildings.

The Fig. 4 shows the utilities of each decision within a particular situation (3-tuple evidence), but at the same time instant, several different situations may occur. This implies the definition of an order relation between each two different situations.

Given, at a specific time instant, the evidence regarding the agent's beliefs, we define a preference relation, $\Psi\gamma$, that considers the utility of the decision to achieve each G goal, U(G=yes), weighted by the "importance", $m_{U(G=yes)}$, ascribed to that decision.

According to Corrêa and Coelho [11], the "importance" is a criterion related to a valuation in terms of benefits and costs an agent has of a mental state situation. Here, the mental state situation is represented by the agent's uncertain beliefs (ID's chance nodes) and desires (ID's decision nodes).

We materialize the "importance" criterion as the difference between the benefit and the cost to achieve G goal (benefit$_{G=yes}$ − cost$_{G=yes}$). The G achievement's benefit is given by its utility and the cost is given by the difference between the utilities of disregarding and achieving the G goal.

Thus, we define $\Psi\gamma$ as follows:

$$\Psi\gamma = U(G=yes) \times m_{U(G=yes)}, \text{ for each } G \in \gamma, \tag{4}$$

where, $m_{U(G=yes)}$=benefit$_{G=yes}$ − cost$_{G=yes}$ = U(G=yes) − [U(G=no) − U(G=yes)].

The same situations of Fig. 4 are displayed at Fig. 5 as small gray diamonds. At Fig. 5 a line goes through each gray diamond in a course that links each two adjacent priority situations. The darker line segment highlights the path from B_2 to B_1.

The Fig. 5 shows that the highest priority corresponds to the <high, low, 1> situation; an early fire (fireIntensity=1) in a small building at a high density neighborhood. The lowest priority is the <low, high, 3> situation; a most intense fire in a large building at a low density neighborhood. To better analyze this $\Psi\gamma$ relation the Table 2 presents each situation from B_2 to B_1.

From Table 2 it is interesting to note that, the three early fires (fireIntensity=1) are interleaved with situations of higher intensity fires located in increasing density neighborhoods or decreasing area buildings. Such interleaving represents the trade-off, obtained from equation (4), among our three *generic fire attack strategies*.

For example, the 4th row is located in a high density neighborhood but the 5th row is an early fire; given two fires in buildings with similar areas we better extinguish first the one located in a higher density neighborhood even though it is not an early fire.

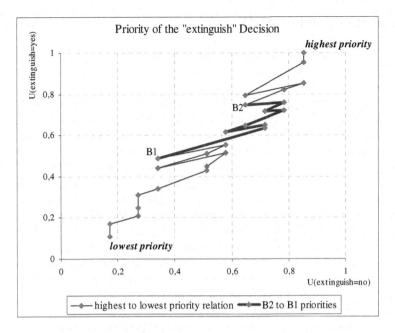

Fig. 5. The priority relation, $\Psi\gamma$, for the "extinguish" decision

Table 2. Ordered normalized priorities (from B_2 to B_1)

	density	allFloorsArea	fireIntensity	$\Psi\gamma$ / max($\Psi\gamma$)
B_2	normal	normal	1	0.55
	high	normal	2	0.48
	high	low	3	0.44
	high	high	2	0.41
⋮	normal	high	1	0.36
	normal	low	2	0.35
	high	normal	3	0.33
	high	high	3	0.30
B_1	low	low	1	0.27

As another example, the 5th's row represents an early fire but 6th row is a smaller building; given similar density neighborhoods we better extinguish an early fire even if it is a larger building.

The Table 2 ordering clearly reflects our three *generic fire attack strategies* (described above). The rationality of those strategic guidelines may be disputed by a domain specialist for their verisimilitude with the real-world fire brigade strategies. Such dispute is a relevant contribution to better adjust and mature the design of the ID as a way to find the globally rational teamwork. Despite its relevance, the evolution of the design of the ID is not a central discussion in this paper.

6 Summary and Future Work

This work addresses a major shortcoming of the current work in team formation for dynamic real-time domains: the formation of multiple teams in response to the occurrence of several simultaneous achievement goals.

The shortcoming is most relevant within RoboCupRescue-like complex environments; hostile, uncertain and dynamically changing environments where each achievement goal overwhelms the personal capability and the complete set of achievement goals overwhelms the total teamwork capability.

The shortcoming was addressed by the formulation of the M-TF problem. The M-TF problem formulation assumes a set of achievement goals and a set of existing teams and constructs the team formations required by those achievement goals.

The illustrative design of the $\Psi\gamma$ component uses the RoboCupRescue environment and follows the decision-theoretic notion of rationality to describe and predict the importance of each achievement goal. We used the influence diagram (ID) framework to design both the uncertainty of beliefs and the expected gain with regard to the decision of whether to achieve or not each goal. The general criterion of "importance" established a total order among goals that is consistent with our initial design (domain expert) strategies.

We consider the multi-team formation an important teamwork issue within complex domains (e.g. the RoboCupRescue) and we intend to further exploit the formation of teams equipped with the multitude of capabilities that are expected to be required in the near future. We are currently exploring the usage of simulations to learn the value of team activity (perception to action transitions), given that agents acquire too much sensory raw data and that their perceptual limitations is likely to hide environmental crucial features.

References

[1] N. Schurr, S. Okamoto, R. Maheswaran, P. Scerri, and M. Tambe, *Cognition and Multi-Agent Interaction: From Cognitive Modeling to Social Simulation*, chapter entitled *Evolution of a Teamwork Model*, Cambridge University Press, 2004.

[2] R. Nair, M. Tambe, and S. Marsella, "Team formation for reformation in multi-agent domains like RoboCupRescue," in G. Kaminka, P. Lima and R. Rojas (eds.), *RoboCup 2002: Robot Soccer World Cup VI. Lecture Notes in Computer Science #2752*, Springer 2003, pp. 150-161.

[3] T. Takahashi, Y. Kaneda, and N. Ito, "Preliminary Study – using RoboCupRescue Simulations for Disasters Prevention," *in Proceedings of the Second International Workshop on Synthetic Simulation and Robotics to Mitigate Earthquake Disaster (SRMED 2004)*, Lisbon, Portugal , June 28th and July 3rd, 2004.

[4] H. Kitano, S. Tadokoro, I. Noda, H. Matsubara, T. Takahashi, A. Shinjou and S. Shimada, "RoboCupRescue: Search and Rescue in Large-Scale Disasters as a Domain for Autonomous Agents Research," *In Proceedings of IEEE International Conference on Man, System and Cybernetics (MSC-99)*, vol. VI, pp. 739-743, Tokyo, Japan October 12-15, 1999.

[5] S. Tadokoro, H. Kitano, T. Takahashi, I. Noda, H. Matsubara, A. Shinjoh, T. Koto, I. Takeuchi, H. Takahashi, F. Matsuno, M. Hatayama, J. Nobe and S. Shimada, "The RoboCup-Rescue Project: A Robotic Approach to the Disaster Mitigation Problem," *In Proceedings of the IEEE International Conference on Robotics and Automation (ICRA00)*, pp. 4090-4095, April 23-28, San Francisco, USA, 2000.

[6] P. Trigo, P. Araújo, A. Remédios, C. Lopes, B. Basílio, T. Loureiro, L. Moniz and H. Coelho, "The 5Rings Team Description Paper," *In Proceedings of the RoboCup2004 Symposium, Team Description Papers*, July 4-5, Lisbon, Portugal, 2004.

[7] P. Trigo, H. Coelho, M. Ladeira, "A Preliminary Discussion on Multi-Team Formation," submitted to the *Autonomous Agents and Multi-Agent Systems* Journal, 2005.

[8] P. Cohen and H. Levesque, "Teamwork," *Special. Issue on Cognitive Science and Artificial Intelligence, Noûs*, vol. 25(4), pp. 487–512, 1991.

[9] R. Howard and J. Matheson, "Influence diagrams," *In Readings on the Principles and Applications of Decision Analysis*, vol. 2, pp. 721-762, 1981.

[10] J. Pearl, *Probabilistic Reasoning in Intelligent Systems: Networks of Plausible Inference*, Morgan Kauffman, San Mateo, CA, 1988.

[11] M. Corrêa and H. Coelho, "Collective Mental States in Extended Mental States Framework," *In Proceedings of the International Conference on Collective Intentionality IV*, Siena, Certosa di Pontignano, Italy, October 13-15, 2004.

Seeking Multiobjective Optimization in Uncertain, Dynamic Games

Eduardo Camponogara[1,*] and Haoyu Zhou[2]

[1] Universidade Federal de Santa Catarina, Florianópolis, SC 88040-900, Brasil
[2] University of Pittsburgh, Pittsburgh, PA 15260, USA

Abstract. If the decisions of agents arise from the solution of general unconstrained problems, altruistic agents can implement effective problem transformations to promote convergence to attractors and draw these fixed points toward Pareto optimal points. In the literature, algorithms have been developed to compute optimal parameters for problem transformations in the seemingly more restrictive scenario of uncertain, quadratic games in which an agent's response is induced by one of a set of potential problems. This paper reviews these developments briefly and proposes a convergent algorithm that enables altruistic agents to relocate the attractor at a point at which all agents are better off, rather than optimizing a weighted function of the agents' objectives.

1 Introduction

Initially confined to mathematical modeling of decision making and economic players, game theory has drawn the attention of researchers and practitioners from a wide range of fields, including robotics, artificial intelligence, and control theory. The interest arises in part from the ever increasing complexity of systems composed of distributed, autonomous agents that may collaborate and compete for the resources in operating these systems. But also because the game-theoretic framework neatly generalizes problems in these domains, offering standard concepts of stability (*Nash equilibria*) and global optimality (*Pareto efficiency*).

In robotics, game theory has laid the foundation to generalize path planning problems to motion planning strategies [10,9]. While the former concerns the computation of a collision-free path from an initial configuration to a goal state, the latter explicitly considers dynamic environments [12], uncertainty in sensor data and motion, and constraints, among others. Within the game-theoretic framework, the motion planning strategy problem can be formulated to account for these complications in a unified way, whereby the uncertainties and decisions from other entities are viewed as competitive players from the part of the robot.

In multiagent systems, game theory has been the cornerstone of the extension of the single agent learning problem to optimal decision making in stochastic games [2]. In these generalized contexts, the optimal decision policy of one agent is dependent upon the policies of the others which creates policy dynamics as the

---

* Partially supported by CNPq, Brazil, under grant number 306398/2003-6.

C. Bento, A. Cardoso, and G. Dias (Eds.): EPIA 2005, LNAI 3808, pp. 572–583, 2005.

agents pursue their own interests. Here the concept of Nash equilibrium comes into play to formalize the concept of optimality: the agents' policies can be optimal only if each agent has no incentive to deviate from its policy, which can be attained only at Nash equilibria. The existence of and convergence to Nash equilibria are recurring themes in the literature. These issues have been addressed recently in more practical, but complicated scenarios in which the agents have limited abilities and not necessarily make optimal decisions [4]. Further, promising policy-learning algorithms that promote convergence to Nash equilibria of stochastic games have also been the focus of research [3].

In control theory, the game-theoretic framework has been applied to model the operation of large, dynamic systems with networks of distributed control agents [11]. The distributed game can arise from (i) imperfections in a decomposition of the dynamic optimization problem of operating the system into a set of distributed, dynamic optimization sub-problems, one for each agent, or (ii) from a distributed specification of the agents' sub-problems that consider only the local state and local goals in operating the system. Here the policies are not given explicitly as in multiagent systems, nor focused on a single agent as in the robotics case, but rather specified as the solution of optimization problems. The top-down approach whereby the overall problem is decomposed, also known as distributed model predictive control, is somewhat mature [5,7] with conditions for perfect decomposition of constrained problems, convergence of distributed iterative processes to fixed points, and convergence to Pareto efficient solutions. On the other hand, the bottom-up approach, in which the distributed problems are not given by a central agency, is much less mature. Preceding research has produced means for altruistic agents, those that are interested in the overall performance and that can be programmed, to promote convergence to Nash equilibria and draw their location toward the Pareto optimal set [6]. The means are simple, yet effective problem transformations induced by factors referred to as *altruistic factors* for convergence and attractor location. In this paper, we extend these developments by proposing an algorithm that enables altruistic agents to move the attractor to locations that optimize not a combination, but rather optimize simultaneously an arbitrary subset of the agents' objectives in quadratic games. Besides being interesting in their own right, quadratic games can appear in decompositions of distributed model predictive control applied to linear systems and also locally approximate more general games.

2 Preliminaries

Definition 1. $\mathcal{P}_m = \{P_m^1, \ldots, P_m^{\kappa_m}\}$ *is the family of problems being solved by agent m which are given by:*

$$P_m^k : \underset{x_m}{\text{Minimize}} \; f_m^k(x_m, y_m)$$

where: $x_m \in \mathbb{R}^{n_m}$ is the agent's decision vector; y_m contains the decisions of the remaining agents; f_m^k is a smooth objective function; and κ_m is the cardinality of the agent's problem set.

Definition 2. $\mathcal{F}_m = \{f_m^1, \ldots, f_m^{\kappa_m}\}$ *denotes the set of objective functions of agent* m.

Definition 3. $P_m(t) \in \mathcal{P}_m$ *is a random variable with the problem that agent* m *solves during time window* t *whose distribution is* Pr_m[1].

Definition 4. $P(t)$ *is the random variable obtained by aggregating the elements of* $\{P_m(t)\}$, *that is,* $P(t) = (P_1(t), \ldots, P_M(t)) \in \mathcal{P}$, *where* $\mathcal{P} = \mathcal{P}_1 \times \ldots \times \mathcal{P}_M$.

Assumption 1. The reaction set $R_m(t, y_m)$ of agent m to the exogenous decisions, for the extent of time window t, consists of solutions to $P_m(t)$ that satisfy the first-order optimality conditions, i.e. $R_m(t, y_m) = \{x_m : \nabla f_m(t, x_m, y_m) = 0\}$. Additionally, the agent's reaction function $G_m(t)$ results from choosing one element from $R_m(t)$, which leads to the iterative process $x_m(t, k+1) = G_m(t, y_m(t, k))$, where $x_m(t, k)$ is the kth iterate of x_m (during time window t) and $G_m(t)$ is a function such that $G_m(t, y_m) \in R_m(t, y_m)$.

Definition 5. $G(t) = (G_1(t), \ldots, G_M(t))$ *is the parallel, iteration function induced by the reactions of* M *agents, within time window* t. *The parallel iterative process is therefore* $x(t, k+1) = G(t, x(t, k))$ *where* $x(t, k)$ *denotes the* k^{th} *iterate of the decisions of the agents.*

Because the agents are pursuing the best for themselves, stability of decisions is reached only at Nash equilibria. At a Nash equilibrium point $x^*(t)$, no rational agent has any incentive to deviate from its decision $x_m^*(t)$ as long as the others sustain their decisions since, otherwise, the agent would incur losses to itself. Algebraically, any fixed point $x^*(t)$ to the iterative process $G(t)$ induces a Nash equilibrium, that is, $x^*(t) = G(t, x^*(t))$. It becomes then relevant, for the sake of stability of a system, to have the decisions of the agents converge to Nash equilibria and, for the sake of overall operating quality, to have these equilibria located near the Pareto optimal set. Because convergence and attractor location depend as much on the agents' problems as on the iterative processes they use, agents concerned with the overall performance can alter their behavior to improve the system's operating quality. Simple problem transformations have been developed in the literature [6] to influence convergence and location of attractors. The factors that render these transformations are referred to as *altruistic factors* and the agents that implement them, *altruistic agents*.

2.1   Affecting Convergence

By tweaking their behavior with altruistic factors, agents can increase convergence speed to Nash equilibria and render convergent an otherwise divergent iterative process.

---

[1] $Pr_m(P_m(t) = P_m^k)$ is the probability that agent m's behavior is dictated by the solution of P_m^k for the duration of interval t. Correspondingly, $f_m(t) \in \mathcal{F}_m$ is a random variable with the objective function of $P_m(t)$.

Definition 6. *A vector $\alpha_m \in \mathbb{R}^{n_m}$, $\alpha_m > 0$, is the altruistic factor for convergence of agent m. The agent remains competitive if $\alpha_m = 1$.*

Definition 7. *$\alpha = (\alpha_1, \ldots, \alpha_M)$ is the vector of convergence factors of all the agents.*

Proposition 1. *Let agent m replace its objective function $f_m(t) \in \mathcal{F}_m$ by $\tilde{f}_m(t)$ $= f_m(t, D(\alpha_m)^{-1} x_m, y_m)$ during time window t, where $D(\alpha_m)$ is a diagonal matrix of dimension $n_m \times n_m$ whose diagonal corresponds to the entries of α_m. Then, the agent's iterative process becomes $x_m^{t,k+1} = D(\alpha_m) G_m^t(y_m^{t,k})$.*

Definition 8. *$G_m^t(\alpha_m, y_m) = D(\alpha_m) G_m^t(y_m)$ is agent m's iteration function under altruism.*

Proposition 2. *Let $\alpha = (\alpha_1, \ldots, \alpha_M)$ be a vector with the altruistic factors. If the agents modify their problems according to Proposition 1, G^t is Lipschitz continuous, and $\|\alpha\|_\infty < 1$, then the iterative process effective within window t, $x^{t,k+1} = D(\alpha) G^t(x^{t,k})$, becomes more contractive by a factor of at least $\|\alpha\|_\infty$.*

In view of the developments above, the altruistic agent m can promote convergence and increase the rate of convergence by choosing a suitable factor α_m.

2.2   Affecting Attractor Location

Akin to the factors for convergence, altruistic agents can relocate the attractor by changing their behavior according to altruistic factors. A brief overview of these factors follows.

Definition 9. *A vector $\beta_m \in \mathbb{R}^{n_m}$ is referred to as agent m's altruistic factor for attractor location. The agent behaves competitively if $\beta_m = 0$.*

Definition 10. *$\beta = (\beta_1, \ldots, \beta_M)$ is the vector with the factors for attractor location of all the agents.*

Proposition 3. *If the mth agent uses the altruistic factor β_m to replace its objective function $f_m(t)$ by $\tilde{f}_m(t) = f_m(t, x_m - \beta_m, y_m)$, then its iterative process becomes $x_m^{t,k+1} = G_m^t(y_m^{t,k}) + \beta_m$.*

Definition 11. *Under altruism for attractor location, the iteration function of agent m becomes $G_m^t(\beta_m, y_m) = G_m^t(y_m) + \beta_m$.*

Proposition 4. *Let $\beta^t = (\beta_1^t, \ldots, \beta_M^t)$ be a vector with the altruistic factors for attractor-location within time window t. If the agents modify their problems as delineated in Proposition 3, then the resulting iterative process inherits the same contraction properties of the original process while, on the other hand, the attractor is relocated at the point $x^*(t, \beta)$ that solves $x = G^t(x) + \beta^t$.*

In view of this proposition, the convergence properties of the iterative process are invariant to the influence of the altruistic factors for location. It empowers agent m to improve the location of the attractor by searching for a suitable β_m without interfering with the convergence property.

2.3   Quadratic Games

Quadratic games are more structured games in which the objectives are quadratic functions, rather than general nonlinear functions. They are interesting in their own right, but can also serve as local approximations to general games and provide an algorithmic framework for computing agents' reactions in more general scenarios. Below we survey the basics of quadratic games, discuss issues of convergence, and address means to predict attractor location under the influence of altruistic factors. In the domain of uncertain, quadratic games, each element of $\mathcal{P}_m$ takes on the form:

$$P_m^k : \underset{x_m}{\text{Minimize}} \; f_m^k = \tfrac{1}{2} x^T A_m^k x + b_m^{k\,T} x + c_m^k \tag{1}$$

where: x_m is the vector with agent m's decision variables; $x = (x_1, \ldots, x_M)$ is the vector with the decisions of all the agents; A_m^k is a symmetric and positive definite matrix; b_m^k is a vector; and c_m^k is a scalar. By breaking A_m^k into submatrices and b_m^k into subvectors, (1) can be recast as:

$$P_m^k : \underset{x_m}{\text{Minimize}} \; \tfrac{1}{2} \sum_{i=1}^{M} \sum_{j=1}^{M} x_i^T A_{m,i,j}^k x_j + \sum_{i=1}^{M} b_{m,i}^{k\,T} x_i + c_m^k$$

The random variable $P_m(t)$ will be equivalently represented by the triple $(A_m(t), b_m(t), c_m(t))$ for the sake of convenience. Using this terminology, the iterative process of an agent m within a time window t can be put in the form:

$$
\begin{aligned}
x_m^{t,k+1} &= G_m^t(y_m^{t,k}) \\
&= -A_{m,m,m}^t{}^{-1} [\sum_{j \neq m} A_{m,m,j}^t x_j^{t,k} + b_{m,m}^t]
\end{aligned} \tag{2}
$$

The end result of coalescing the iterative processes of all the agents is the overall iterative process, G^t, which is obtained by solving the system of linear equations:

$$A(t) x^{t,k+1} = -B(t) x^{t,k} - b(t) \tag{3}$$

where:

$$
A(t) = \begin{bmatrix}
A_{1,1,1}(t) & 0 & 0 \ldots & 0 \\
0 & A_{2,2,2}(t) & 0 \ldots & 0 \\
\vdots & 0 & \vdots \ddots & 0 \\
0 & & \ldots & 0 \; 0 \; A_{M,M,M}(t)
\end{bmatrix}
$$

$$
B(t) = \begin{bmatrix}
0 & A_{1,1,2}^t & A_{1,1,3}^t & \cdots & A_{1,1,M}^t \\
A_{2,2,1}^t & 0 & A_{2,2,3}^t & \cdots & A_{2,2,M}^t \\
\vdots & \vdots & \vdots & \ddots & \vdots \\
A_{M,M,1}^t & A_{M,M,2}^t & \cdots & A_{M,M,-1}^t & 0
\end{bmatrix}
$$

$$b(t) = \begin{bmatrix} b_{1,1}(t) & b_{2,2}(t) & \ldots & b_{M,M}(t) \end{bmatrix}^T$$

Solving (3) leads to the iterative process:

$$x^{t,k+1} = G^t(x^{t,k}) = -A(t)^{-1} [B(t) x^{t,k} + b(t)] \tag{4}$$

Inducing Convergence. By becoming altruistic with respect to convergence, agent m's problem assumes the form:

$$\text{Minimize } \frac{1}{2} \sum_{i=1}^{M} \sum_{j=1}^{M} x_i{}^T D(\alpha_{m,i})^{-T} A_{m,i,j}(t) D(\alpha_{m,j})^{-1} x_j$$
$$x_m \qquad + \sum_{i=1}^{M} b_{m,i}(t)^T D(\alpha_{m,i})^{-1} x_i + c_m(t)$$

where $\alpha_{m,m} = \alpha_m$ is the vector with agent m's altruistic factor and $\alpha_{m,j} = 1$ for all $j \neq m$. The solution to this problem renders agent m's iterative process:

$$x_m^{t,k+1} = G_m^t(\alpha_m, y_m^{t,k})$$
$$= -D(\alpha_m) A_{m,m,m}^t{}^{-1} [\sum_{j \neq m} A_{m,m,j}^t x_j^{t,k} + b_{m,m}^t]$$

As in the preceding developments, the solution to the equation $A(t)[D(\alpha)^{-1} x^{t,k+1}] = -B(t) x^{t,k} - b(t)$ leads to the overall iterative process $G^t(\alpha)$ induced by the altruistic agents where the competitive agent m sets $\alpha_m = 1$. More precisely, the iterative process is:

$$x^{t,k+1} = G^t(\alpha, x^{t,k}) \qquad (5)$$
$$= -D(\alpha) A(t)^{-1} [B(t) x^{t,k} - b(t)]$$

Proposition 5. *If $H = D(\alpha) A(t)^{-1} B(t)$ has $|||H||| < 1$, for a matrix norm $||| \cdot |||$ induced by some vector norm $\| \cdot \|$, then the iterative process (5) induces a contraction mapping that converges linearly to an attractor $x^*(t, \alpha)$.*

For the sake of stability, the agents can behave altruistically by forcing $G^t(\alpha)$ to be contractive, regardless of the prevailing problems within time window t. It suffices to implement α_m with $\|\alpha_m\|_\infty$ sufficiently high.

Relocating Attractors. Here we deal with the issue of moving the attractor of a convergent, quadratic game towards its Pareto solutions, giving the specifics of altruistic factors and their use in quadratic games. The next section elaborates on the prediction of the attractor's location as a function of these factors.

An agent m that implements altruism for attractor location will solve the following variant of its original problem:

$$\text{Minimize } \frac{1}{2} \sum_{i=1}^{M} \sum_{j=1}^{M} [x_i - \beta_{m,i}]^T A_{m,i,j}(t) [x_j - \beta_{m,j}]$$
$$x_m \qquad + \sum_{i=1}^{M} b_{m,i}(t)^T [x_i - \beta_{m,i}] + c_m(t) \qquad (6)$$

where $\beta_{m,m} = \beta_m$ is the vector with agent m's altruistic factor and $\beta_{m,j} = 0$ for all $j \neq m$, while the other variables and parameters are as in $P_m(t)$. The iterative solution of problem $P_m(t, \beta_m)$ gives rise to the agent's iterative process:

$$x_m^{t,k+1} = G_m^t(\beta_m, y_m^{t,k})$$
$$= -A_{m,m,m}^t{}^{-1} [\sum_{j \neq m} A_{m,m,j}^t x_j^{t,k} + b_{m,m}^t] + \beta_m \qquad (7)$$

As in the previous section, the full iterative process $G^t(\beta)$, which spells out the way the altruistic agents behave assuming that any competitive agent m holds $\beta_m = 0$, is obtained by solving $A(t)[x^{t,k+1} - \beta] = -B(t)x^{t,k} - b(t)$, where $A(t)$, $B(t)$, and $b(t)$ are as above, and $\beta = (\beta_1, \ldots, \beta_M)$. The iterative process is:

$$
\begin{aligned}
x^{t,k+1} &= G^t(\beta, x^{t,k}) \\
&= -A(t)^{-1}[B(t)x^{t,k} + b(t)] + \beta.
\end{aligned}
\tag{8}
$$

Assumption 2. For every $P(t) \in \mathcal{P}$, the corresponding $A(t)$ and $B(t)$ satisfy $|||A(t)^{-1}B(t)||| < 1$, for some matrix norm $||| \cdot |||$ induced by some vector norm $\|\cdot\|$, thereby ensuring that G^t as well as $G^t(\beta)$ are contraction mappings.

Predicting Attractor Location. By manipulating (8), the location of the attractor $x^*(t, \beta)$ can be expressed as a liner function of its original location (when $\beta = 0$) and the elements of $\{\beta_m : m = 1, \ldots, M\}$, namely:

$$
\begin{aligned}
x^*(t, \beta) &= -[I + A(t)^{-1}B(t)]^{-1}[A(t)^{-1}b(t) - \beta] \\
&= x^*(t, 0) + Z(t)\beta \\
&= x^*(t, 0) + Z_1(t)\beta_1 + \ldots + Z_M(t)\beta_M.
\end{aligned}
\tag{9}
$$

Remark 1. $[I + A(t)^{-1}B(t)]$ admits an inverse because $|||A(t)^{-1}B(t)||| < 1$.

Henceforth, $\Psi \subseteq \{1, \ldots, M\}$ will denote the subset containing the ids of the agents that behave altruistically. These agents can organize themselves to learn their individual influence on the attractor's location: for each $m \in \Psi$, agent m can systematically perturb the value of each entry of β_m, measure the resulting attractor $x^*(t, \beta)$, and then compute Z_m^t. The procedure below elaborates on these steps. We remark that the altruistic agents can obtain (9) without having knowledge about the prevailing problems of the other agents. (Agent m needs only to sense the current attractor; its influence on the location of the attractor, quantified by $Z_m(t)$, can be obtained from agent m's problem and the attractor's location.)

Procedure 1. Computing the elements of $\{Z_m(t) : m \in \Psi\}$

- The altruistic agents coordinate to set $\beta_m = 0$ for each $m \in \Psi$.
- The altruistic agents schedule themselves to run one at a time, so that for each $m \in \Psi$, agent m executes the steps below.
  - For $k = 1$ to $n(m)$ do
    - Set $(\beta_m)_k = 1$.
    - Allow the agents to iterate until they reach the attractor $x^*(t, \beta)$.
    - According to (9), the kth column of $Z_m(t)$ is the vector $x^*(t, \beta) - x^*(t, 0)$.
    - Set $(\beta_m)_k = 0$.
  - At the end of the for-loop, $Z_m(t)$ is known.

---

3   Simultaneous Optimization

An alternative to minimizing the expected, weighted sum of the agents' objective functions proposed in [6] is to carry out the minimization over all the objectives. According to this, the altruistic agents would solve a multicriteria problem:

$$\hat{P}(t) : \underset{\beta^t}{\text{Minimize}} \quad \{f(x^*(t, \beta^t)) : f \in \mathcal{F}_C\}$$

$$\text{Subject to: } f(x^*(t, \beta^t)) \leq f(x^*(t, 0)), \ \forall f \in \mathcal{F}_C$$

(10)

where $\mathcal{F}_C \subseteq \cup_{m=1}^{M} \mathcal{F}_m$ is the subset of the agents' objective functions to be optimized simultaneously, while not exceeding the values attained at the initial attractor, $x^*(t, 0)$.

To solve $\hat{P}(t)$, the altruistic agents proceed by coordinating among themselves to, first, develop predictors for the attractor's location as a function of their altruistic factors (refer to Procedure 1) and, second, iteratively draw the attractor towards Pareto solutions.

3.1   Sliding the Attractor

Once the agents have obtained predictors for the attractor, they schedule their iterations serially whereby agent m solves approximately a reduced form of $\hat{P}(t)$ that is restricted to the influence of its altruistic factor, β_m^t. After expanding (10) and substituting the predictor (9) in the objective and constraints of $\hat{P}(t)$, the problem becomes:

$$\hat{P}(t) : \underset{\beta^t}{\text{Minimize}} \quad \{\hat{h}_f(t, \beta^t) : f \in \mathcal{F}_C\}$$

$$\text{Subject to: } \hat{h}_f(t, \beta^t) \leq \hat{c}_f(t), \ \forall f \in \mathcal{F}_C$$

where: $\hat{h}_f(t, \beta^t) = \frac{1}{2}\beta^{t^T}\hat{A}_f(t)\beta^t + \hat{b}_f(t)^T \beta^t + \hat{c}_f(t)$; $\hat{A}_f(t)$ is a suitable matrix; $\hat{b}_f(t)$ is a vector; and $\hat{c}_f(t) = f(x^*(t, 0))$ is a scalar, all of which can be obtained by expanding $f(x^*(t, 0) + Z(t)\beta^t)$ to obtain $\hat{h}_f(t, \beta^t)$.

Remark 2. $\hat{A}_f(t)$ is symmetric and positive definite for every $f \in \mathcal{F}_C$.

Herein, the difficulty lies in the relative hardness of solving $\hat{P}(t)$ in comparison to the elements $P_m(t)$ of $P(t)$, which are unconstrained quadratic problems. To keep the computation to a minimum, we propose a procedure similar to the preceding one, only this time the mth agent does not solve its subproblem, but rather find an approximate solution along a direction that is descent for all the objectives of $\hat{P}(t)$, this way guaranteeing that the constraints hold throughout. In essence, the suggested approach extends the method of multicriteria optimization proposed by Fliege and Svaiter [8] to dynamic games. Agent m's reduced form of $\hat{P}(t)$ is:

$$\hat{P}_m(t, \beta^t) : \underset{\beta_m^t}{\text{Minimize}} \quad \{\hat{h}_f(t, \beta^t) : f \in \mathcal{F}_C\}$$

$$\text{Subject to : } \beta_k^t \text{ is held constant, } \forall k, k \neq m$$

$$\hat{h}_f(t, \beta^t) \leq \hat{c}_f(t), \ \forall f \in \mathcal{F}_C$$

(11)

Let $\beta^{t,k}$ be the tentative solution to $\hat{P}(t)$ at the kth iteration. To produce an improving direction, agent m will solve:

$$\hat{H}_m(t, \beta^{t,k}) : \underset{\delta, d}{\text{Minimize}} \quad \delta$$
$$\text{Subject to} : \quad \nabla_{\beta_m^t} \hat{h}_f(t, \beta^{t,k})^T d \leq \delta, \ \forall f \in \mathcal{F}_C \tag{12}$$
$$\|d\|_\infty \leq 1$$

where $\delta \in \mathbb{R}$ and $d \in \mathbb{R}^{n_m}$. Notice that $\hat{H}_m(t, \beta^{t,k})$ can be recast as a linear programming problem. The procedure followed by the agents to solve $\hat{P}(t)$ is detailed below. Though convergence to an optimal solution to $\hat{P}(t)$ cannot be guaranteed, we will show that the sequence $\{\beta^{t,k}\}$ converges to a solution that cannot be improved by any altruistic agent.

Procedure 2. Solving $\hat{P}(t)$

- The altruistic agents follow Procedure 1 to obtain $\{Z_m^t\}$.
- They compute $\hat{A}_f^t$, $\hat{b}_f^t$, $\hat{c}_f^t$, $\forall f \in \mathcal{F}_C$ to assemble $\hat{P}(t)$.
- Let the iteration index be $k = 0$ and set $\beta^{t,k} = 0$.
- The agents take turns, in any order, each time performing the steps below.
  - Let $m \in \Psi$ correspond to the agent of the turn.
  - Agent m solves $\hat{H}_m(t, \beta^{t,k})$ with a linear-programming algorithm.
  - If $\delta = 0$ then $\beta^{t,k+1} \leftarrow \beta^{t,k}$, $k \leftarrow k+1$, and agent m transfers the turn to the next (agent m could not produce a descent direction about $\beta^{t,k}$).
  - Otherwise, if $\delta < 0$, then agent m performs the backtrack procedure delineated in [8] to find a step-length $\tau \in (0, 1]$, and thereby a solution $(\beta_m^{t,k} + \tau d)$ to $\hat{P}_m(t, \beta^t)$, that satisfies a generalization of the Armijo rule [1] for some $\sigma \in (0, 1)$; more formally, τ is the maximum of the set:

$$T = \{\lambda = 1/2^j : j \in \{0, 1, \ldots\} \text{ and}$$
$$\hat{h}_f(t, \beta^{t,k} + [0, \ldots, 0, \beta_m^{t,k} + \lambda d, 0, \ldots, 0])$$
$$\leq \hat{h}_f(t, \beta^{t,k}) + \sigma\lambda\nabla_{\beta_m^t}\hat{h}_f(t, \beta^{t,k})^T d, \ \forall f \in \mathcal{F}_C\}$$

Agent m obtains $\beta^{t,k+1}$ by replacing $\beta_m^{t,k}$ in $\beta^{t,k}$ with $(\beta_m^{t,k} + \tau d)$; agent m implements the revised factor $\beta_m^{t,k+1}$ in its iterative process, allowing the attractor to reach the improved location; it increments k and transfers the turn to the next agent.

Proposition 6. *Let $\{\beta^{t,k}\}$ be the series of iterates produced by the altruistic agents as they follow Procedure 2, but constrained to the iterates that yield a reduction to the value of $\hat{h}_f(t, \beta^t)$ for each $f \in \mathcal{F}_C$. If the iteration function G^t is contractive, then $\{\beta^{t,k}\}$ converges to a solution $\beta^*(t)$ that cannot be improved by any altruistic agent m.*

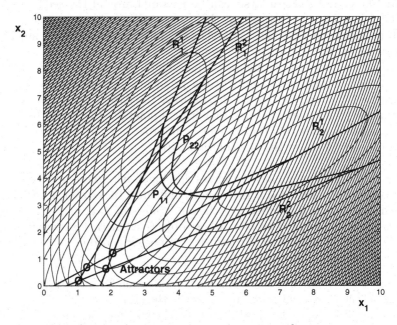

Fig. 1. The objective landscape of a quadratic game between two agents

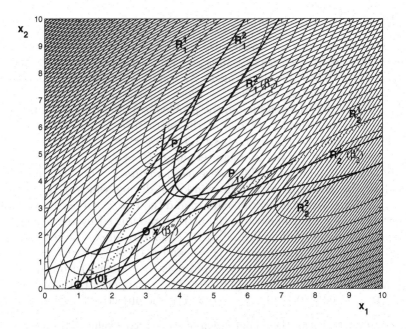

Fig. 2. Illustration of the simultaneous minimization over all the agents' objectives

Proof: The convergence analysis can be centered around the sequence $\{\beta^{t,k}\}$ since G^t is contractive. Notice that the constraints on the values of the objectives that appear in $\hat{P}(t)$ and $\hat{P}_m(t)$ can be omitted—Procedure 2 implements a descent algorithm whose starting point is $\beta^{t,0} = 0$, thereby ensuring that the constraints are satisfied throughout. This allows Procedure 2 to regard these problems as unconstrained, multicriteria problems. Because each update that produces $\beta^{t,k+1}$, from the iterate $\beta^{t,k}$, satisfies the Armijo rule as stated in [8], the sequence $\{\beta^{t,k}\}$ must converge to a critical point for $\hat{P}(t)$ (refer to Theorem 1 of [8]) or reach a solution that cannot be improved by any altruistic agent. In either case, $\{\beta^{t,k}\}$ converges to a solution $\beta^*(t)$. ∎

The method for localizing attractors developed heretofore and those developed in [6] can be integrated without much difficulty. To see that, let $\bar{P}(t)$ be the problem that results by embedding the constraints of $\hat{P}(t)$ in $\tilde{P}(t)$, where the latter is the unconstrained problem whose objective function is a weighted function of the agents' objectives[2]. Procedure 2 can be extended in a straightforward manner to tackle $\bar{P}(t)$, namely:

(i) vector d is computed so as to be a descent direction for the objective function and for the constraints that are active at the current iterate $\beta^{t,k}$;
(ii) by using the results from [8], it can be shown that the sequence $\{\beta^{t,k}\}$ of iterates produced by this procedure is convergent to a solution $\beta^*(t)$ which cannot be improved by any altruistic agent.

3.2   Illustrative Example

The illustrative scenario has two agents. Agent 1's family of problems $\mathcal{F}_1$ has two elements: $f_1^1 = 44.5x_1{}^2 - 28x_1x_2 + 10x_2{}^2 - 150x_1 - 20x_2$; $f_1^2 = 35x_1{}^2 - 35x_1x_2 + 12.5x_2{}^2 - 65x_1 - 25x_2$. Similarly, agent 2's family of problems $\mathcal{F}_2$ is composed of: $f_2^1 = 19x_1{}^2 - 34x_1x_2 + 25.5x_2{}^2 - 120x_1 + 10x_2$; $f_2^2 = 15x_1{}^2 - 30x_1x_2 + 30x_2{}^2 - 150x_1 + 20x_2$. Depending on the problem configuration $P(t)$, the agents' iterative processes converge to one of the attractors: $x_{11}^* = (2.0546, 1.1737)$; $x_{12}^* = (1.8756, 0.6044)$; $x_{21}^* = (1.2458, 0.6345)$; or $x_{22}^* = (1.0159, 0.1746)$ where $x_{k_1 k_2}^*$ is the attractor for the problem setting $f_m(t) = f_m^{k_m}$.

The agents' families of problems are as in Figure 1. The contour lines correspond to the problems of a time window t during which $f_1(t) = f_1^2$ and $f_2(t) = f_2^2$, along with the reaction curves, and the Pareto curves of two problem configurations. Figure 2 illustrates the attractors induced by the agents' altruistic behavior, as they follow Procedure 2. The figure shows the reaction curves induced by the altruistic factors $\beta_1^*(t) = 1$ and $\beta_2^*(t) = 1$, which were produced by the altruistic behavior of agents 1 and 2 as they followed Procedure 2. The resulting attractor $x^*(t, \beta^*(t)) = (3.0159, 2.1746)$ is superior to the initial attractor $x^*(t, 0) = (1.0154, 0.1740)$. At $x^*(t, \beta^*(t))$, the objective function values are:

---

[2] That is, $\bar{P}(t)$ stands for the minimization of the expected value of the agents' objective functions, but restricted to not increasing the value that any objective function $f \in \mathcal{F}_C$ attains at the initial attractor.

$f_1^1 = -227.4679$; $f_1^2 = -102.4849$; $f_2^1 = -269.7406$; and $f_2^2 = -327.3394$. While, at $x^*(t,0)$, the objective function values are: $f_1^1 = -114.5563$; $f_1^2 = -40.0725$; $f_2^1 = -105.7556$; and $f_2^2 = -137.7588$.

4   Final Remarks

Based upon the recapitulation of the notions of altruistic factors for convergence and location of attractors in dynamic games, the paper proposed the simultaneous optimization by altruistic agents of the objectives of an arbitrary subset of the agents' objectives. The paper delivered a convergent algorithm to compute problem-transformation parameters for the case of quadratic games. Despite being simple, quadratic games can approximate general games locally and also serve as models of distributed model predictive control of linear systems. Recently, we have designed a trust-region based algorithm for general, unconstrained games. Future research will address constrained problems via transformation to a series of unconstrained sub-problems.

References

1. Bertsekas, D. P.: Nonlinear Programming. Athena Scientific (1995)
2. Bowling, M., Jensen, R., Veloso, M.: A formalization of equilibria for multiagent planning. In Proc. AAAI Workshop on Planning with and for Multiagent Systems (2002)
3. Bowling, M., Veloso, M.: Scalable learning in stochastic games. In Proc. AAAI Workshop on Game Theoretic and Decision Theoretic Agents (2002)
4. Bowling, M., Veloso, M.: Existence of multiagent equilibria with limited agents. Journal of Artificial Intelligence Research (2004)
5. Camponogara, E., Jia, D., Krogh, B. H., Talukdar, S. N.: Distributed model predictive control. IEEE Control Systems Magazine **22 (1)** (2002) 44–52
6. Camponogara, E.: On the convergence to and location of attractors of uncertain, dynamic games. In Advances in Artificial Intelligence, LNAI **3171** (2004) 484–493
7. Camponogara, E., Talukdar, S. N.: Designing communication networks to decompose network control problems. INFORMS Journal on Computing **17 (2)** (2005)
8. Fliege, J., Svaiter, B. F.: Steepest descent methods for multicriteria optimization. Mathematical Methods of Operations Research **51 (3)** (2000) 479–494
9. LaValle, S.: Planning Algorithms. From http://msl.cs.uiuc.edu/~lavalle/ (2005)
10. LaValle, S. M.: Robot motion planning: a game-theoretic foundation. Algorithmica **26** (2000) 430–465
11. Talukdar, S. N., Camponogara, E.: Network control as a distributed, dynamic game. In Proc. 34th Hawaii International Conference on System Sciences (2001)
12. Zheng, T., Liu, D. K., Wang, P.: Priority based dynamic multiple robot path planning. In Proc. 2nd Int. Conf. on Autonomous Robots and Agents (2004)

Learning to Select Negotiation Strategies in Multi-agent Meeting Scheduling

Elisabeth Crawford and Manuela Veloso*

Computer Science Department, Carnegie Mellon University,
Pittsburgh PA 15213, USA
{ehc, mmv}@cs.cmu.edu

Abstract. In this paper, we look at the Multi-Agent Meeting Scheduling problem where distributed agents negotiate meeting times on behalf of their users. While many negotiation approaches have been proposed for scheduling meetings, it is not well understood how agents can negotiate strategically in order to maximize their users' utility. To negotiate strategically, agents need to learn to pick good strategies for negotiating with other agents. We show how the *playbook* approach, introduced by [1] for team plan selection in small-size robot soccer, can be used to select strategies. Selecting strategies in this way gives some theoretical guarantees about regret. We also show experimental results demonstrating the effectiveness of the approach.

1 Introduction

Personalized software agents for meeting scheduling have the potential to reduce the daily cognitive load on computer users. Scheduling meetings can be a time consuming process requiring many email messages to be exchanged, and often existing meetings need to be moved to make room for new ones. Potentially, software agents can remove this burden entirely by communicating with each other to schedule meetings. Since user's have ownership of their own calendars, and private preferences about meeting scheduling, it makes sense to approach this problem in a distributed manner. Automated negotiation has been proposed as a method for multiple agents to reach agreement on meeting times. Negotiation approaches have many advantages over the open calendar approach taken by Microsoft Outlook (see [2] for a discussion).

Typically negotiation protocols feature a meeting initiator that proposes meeting times and collects the proposals of other participants. Consider, for instance, the following simplified protocol:

- while there is no intersection in proposals
  - the initiator proposes some times to the other agents
  - each agent proposes some times to the initiator

---

* Thanks to the reviewers and Michael Bowling for helpful comments and suggestions. This material is based upon work supported by the Defense Advanced Research Projects Agency (DARPA) under Contract No. NBCHD030010. Any opinions, findings and conclusions or recommendations expressed in this material are those of the author(s) and do not necessarily reflect the views of the Defense Advanced Research Projects Agency (DARPA), or the Department of Interior-National Business Center (DOI-NBC).

C. Bento, A. Cardoso, and G. Dias (Eds.): EPIA 2005, LNAI 3808, pp. 584–595, 2005.

In this context, a negotiation strategy is a set of rules for deciding what times to propose at each point in the process. The space of possible negotiation strategies is extremely large. Even if we restrict the space in some way, e.g. to strategies that offer a fixed number, x, of new times per negotiation round, there are still a huge number of options. In particular, there is a different strategy for each possible value of x, and then there are all the ways of combining these values of x with rules for deciding what particular times to offer. In developing software agents for meeting scheduling, we are faced with the problem of: (i) deciding which negotiation strategies agents should consider, and (ii) designing methods that agents can use to choose between these strategies when negotiating a particular meeting.

In order to most effectively satisfy user preferences, we would like our agents to adapt their behavior to each of the agents they negotiate with. There is a wide range of important ways in which agents can differ. For instance, agents can represent users of different importance and busyness, use very different negotiation strategies, and can have users with very different preferences. Clearly a strategy that works well for negotiating with one agent may work very poorly with another. Poor strategy choice can lead to meetings being scheduled at times the user does not like, or to the negotiation process taking a very long time. In general, we would like an agent to trade-off satisfying its user's preferences, with minimizing the length of the negotiations, in a way that maximizes its user's utility.

One method for deciding what strategy to use when negotiating with a particular agent is to use a model based approach that tries to construct a model of the agent and then based on this model select a strategy. There are a number of reasons why this approach would be difficult to use in practice. Firstly, obtaining an accurate enough model of another agent is a very difficult learning problem, since the only interaction agents have is through the exchange of times when they negotiate meetings. From this information, it is hard to make accurate conclusions about what times an agent prefers, how busy the agent is, what negotiation strategy it is employing etc. Secondly, to build a model of another agent, many training examples are required. It would be preferable if an agent was able to learn to negotiate, while actually negotiating.

In this paper, we show how an agent can learn online which strategies to use by observing its own rewards, as opposed to trying to model the other agents. Our approach is based on the idea of *plays* introduced by Bowling, Browning and Veloso [1]. Bowling *et al.* focus on the domain of robot soccer (small-size league) where they equip a team with a series of multi-agent plans called a *playbook*. The team plan to use at a given point in time is selected according to a no-regret learning algorithm. We show how we can apply these ideas to the problem of learning how to negotiate with different agents. Our experimental results demonstrate that this approach allows a learning agent to converge to sensible strategies for negotiation with different fixed strategy agents. We also show that an agent learning online using this approach can perform well in comparison to the best (in hindsight) fixed strategy.

2   Related Work

A variety of methods for reaching agreements on meeting times have been proposed in the last ten years, including negotiation based approaches, e.g. [3,4], Distributed

Constraint Reasoning (DCR) approaches [5], and market based approaches [6]. In this section, we describe work on the first two methods, looking in particular at how user preferences are dealt with.

Sen and Durfee [4] conducted a probabilistic and simulation based analysis of negotiation strategies. The basic framework they considered was:

1. Host announces meeting
2. Host offers some times
3. Agents send host some availability information
4. Repeat 2 and 3 until an intersection is found.

Similar protocols have been looked at by other researchers, for example, [3], and [7], while [8] looked at a more complex protocol. These negotiation approaches have handled user preferences for meeting times in quite different ways. Shintani *et al.* [8] propose a persuasion based approach. The persuasion mechanism involves compromising agents adjusting their preferences so that their most preferred times are the persuading agent's most preferred times. This method relies strongly on the agents complying with the protocol.

Garrido and Sycara [7] and Jennings and Jackson [3] take the approach of allowing agents to not only propose meeting times, but also to quantify their preferences for proposals. The agent that is collecting the proposals, then makes decisions based on the reported utilities of all the meeting participants. This style of approach involves a lot of trust, since for the procedure to work well all the agents must report their preferences truthfully.

While the approaches outlined are all concerned with user preferences they differ from the work described here in that we are interested in *how an agent can negotiate strategically in order to satisfy its user's preferences.*

Distributed Constraint Reasoning (DCR) approaches have also been applied to multi-agent meeting scheduling. For example Modi and Veloso [5] model the meeting scheduling problem according to the DCR paradigm and evaluate strategies for making *bumping decisions.* The way in which agent's decide when to *bump* (i.e., move an existing meeting to accommodate a new meeting) can have implications for the efficiency of the meeting scheduling process. Intuitively, if the agents want the scheduling process to finish quickly, they should try to bump meetings that will be easy to reschedule. Similarly to the negotiation approaches, the work on DCR has not focused on how agents can act strategically, rather the agents have been assumed to be cooperative.

3   Plays for Meeting Negotiation

In the context of small-size robot soccer (where an overhead camera and an off-board computer allow for coordinated team planning) Bowling *et al.* [1] introduce the notion of a play as a team plan. Each play must assign a role to each of the robots, e.g. one robot is instructed to shoot, another to guard the team's own goal, and so forth. Each play also has an applicability condition that determines in which scenarios it applies, and a termination condition that is used to decide when the play finished and a new one needs to be selected. An offensive play, for example, might be applicable whenever the ball is in the opponent's half of the field, and terminate either when a goal is scored, or the applicability condition is violated.

The *playbook*, captures all the plays that are available to the team. Bowling *et al.* provide a simple language that a human expert can use to add new plays. During the course of a game, plays are weighted according to their level of success or failure, and the play to use at each decision point is selected based on these weights. The weights on plays are adapted in such away that regret (difference between how well the team did and how well it could have done had it used the best, in hindsight, fixed play) about play selection goes to zero in the limit.

The meeting negotiation problem has a number of important features in common with small-size robot soccer. In both domains, the space of available strategies is huge. It is not possible for agents to adapt online if they must consider the entire space. Furthermore, the environment in both domains is dynamic, the models of the 'opponents' are unknown, and online learning is required for good performance. In this section, we will discuss how we adapt the plays formulation to the problem of learning how to negotiate with different agents.

We can map the plays terminology, from robot soccer, to the meeting scheduling problem. The plays correspond to complete negotiation strategies, the opponent corresponds to the agent the learning agent is negotiating with, and the playbook is simply the set of negotiation strategies available to the learning agent. Unlike in robot soccer, in the meeting scheduling problem, we are playing with multiple 'opponent' agents at the same time. As such, the learning agent must adapt strategy selection for each of the different agents it negotiates with simultaneously.

We let a negotiation strategy consist of 4 elements: (i) an applicability condition, (ii) a rule for deciding at each negotiation round what times (if any) to offer independent of the exact proposals received, (iii) a rule for deciding which times (if any) to offer based on the proposals received, and (iv) a rule for deciding when to give up[1]. Fig. 1. shows an example strategy, Offer-k-b, that offers k new available times each round, and after b rounds starts taking into account the proposals it has received. If necessary, Offer-k-b will offer times that would require an already scheduled meeting to be bumped. Depending on the values of k and b this strategy can be very selfish and cause the negotiation to take a long time. As such, if the 'opponent' agent is very important, the strategy is only applicable if the value of k is large and the value of b is small.

Each time a new meeting needs to be scheduled, if the learning agent is an attendee, it selects which strategy to use according to the adapted playbook for the initiator agent. If the learning agent is initiating the meeting, it selects a possibly different negotiation strategy for communicating with each attendee according to the adapted playbook for that attendee. The learning agent considers the execution of a strategy to be complete when (i) the meeting it was selected to schedule has been added to the agent's calendar and (ii) any meetings that the learning agent is involved in that have been bumped have been rescheduled for new times. A strategy is also considered to have been completely executed, if the learning agent has given up on scheduling the new meeting, or on rescheduling a bumped meeting. Each time a strategy terminates, the playbook weights are updated according to the success of the strategy.

---

[1] The distinction between (ii) and (iii) is unnecessary. It is made to assist the exposition.

1. **APPLICABILITY**: if the other agent is very-important and ($k < 20$ and $b > 5$) return false; else return true.
2. **INDEPENDENT OFFER**: in any negotiation round offer my k most preferred, available, un-offered times.
3. **DEPENDENT OFFER**: if negotiation round $> b$. Apply the simple compromiser sub-strategy which works as follows:
   - If I am an attendee of the meeting, search for any times proposed by the initiator that I have free but have not offered. If one or more such times exist offer my most preferred time. Else, offer the time proposed by the initiator that contains the meeting with the fewest participants.
   - If I am the initiator rank all the times proposed by other agents according to the number of agents that have proposed that time. Out of all the times with the highest number of proposals if any of these times are available, offer my most preferred such time, otherwise offer the unavailable time containing the meeting with the fewest participants.
4. **ABANDON**: if negotiation round > 50 return true.

Fig. 1. Offer-k-b negotiator

4   Adapting Weights and Selecting Strategies for Negotiating with Different Agents

For each 'opponent' agent, the learning agent must learn which strategies to select. The learning algorithm has the following key components, (i) a rule for updating the weights on strategies in the playbook and (ii) a rule for selecting the strategy to apply based on these weights. Bowling *et al.* [1] used results in the literature on *experts* problems (also commonly referred to as *k-armed bandits* problems) to derive the rules required. We are able to use these rules for adapting weights on negotiation strategies. In this section, we briefly describe the approach and its basis in the experts literature. For a more complete treatment we refer to the reader to [1].

In the experts problem, an agent choses actions or options repeatedly based on the instructions it receives from a set of *experts*. Each time the agent needs to make a choice it selects which expert to listen to. In the traditional formulation, once the action or option has been selected, the agent receives a pay-off from that action. In addition, the pay-offs it would have received had it followed the advice of each of the other experts are revealed. The performance of the agent is measured by the notion of regret. Let the reward received from following the advice of expert i at choice point p be r_i^p. The regret of the agent after k choices have been made is given by the following formula:

$$regret_k = \max_{over\ experts\ i} \sum_{p=0}^{k} r_i^p - \sum_{p=0}^{k} r_{x_p}^p$$

where x_p denotes the expert the agent chose at choice point p. Regret is simply the award achievable by always asking the best expert minus the reward actually achieved. A desirable property of an experts algorithm is that average regret goes to zero as the number of choices approaches infinity. There exist algorithms for various formulations of the problem that achieve no-regret in the limit e.g. [9,10].

Bowling *et al.* [1] show how algorithms for selecting experts with no regret can be used to select plays. In the context of plays (and in the context of selecting strategies for negotiation), we need to use a different formulation of regret that takes into account the fact that not all plays (or strategies) are applicable at each choice point. This can be done by using the notion of *Sleeping Experts* developed by Freund et. al [11]. We say an expert is awake when it is applicable at a particular choice point, and asleep otherwise. Following the notation used in [1], we let $a_i^p = 1$ if expert i is awake at choice point p, and $a_i^p = 0$ otherwise. Then if $\Delta(n)$ is the set of probability distributions over all n experts, we get the following formula for sleeping regret (SR) after k choices:

$$SR_k = \left(\max_{x \in \Delta(n)} \sum_{p=1}^{k} \sum_{i=1}^{n} a_i^p \left(\frac{x(i)}{\sum_{j=1}^{n} x(j) a_j^p} \right) r_i^p \right) - \sum_{p=0}^{k} r_{x_p}^p$$

The first half of the formula simply quantifies the reward the agent could have received if the best possible distribution over awake experts had been selected at each choice point.

In the context of plays, and negotiation strategies, there is one final difficulty. Unlike in the traditional experts problem, agents only find out the reward of the action they actually take. In order to account for this, Bowling *et al.* [1] combine elements of the Exp3 algorithm proposed by Auer et al [10] (which handles the problem of unknown rewards) with the sleeping regret approach of [11]. We describe their approach here, and use it to adapt playbook weights for each 'opponent' agent, and select the strategy to use according to these weights.

Let $R_i^k = \sum_{p=0}^{k} \hat{r}_i^p$. Where $\hat{r}_i^p = 0$ if i not selected at point p and $\frac{r_i^p}{Pr(x_p=i)}$ otherwise. We call the weight for strategy i at decision point p, w_i^p, and we let $w_i^p = e^{R_i^p}$. The value $e^{r_i^p}$ is denoted as m_i^p, and we refer to this value as the multiplier and use it to adjust the weights according to the reward received from carrying out the negotiation strategy (or play). The probability that the strategy chosen at point p, denoted x_p, is strategy i is given by the following equation:

$$Pr(x_p = i) = \frac{a_i^p w_i^p}{\sum_j a_j^p w_j^p}$$

Once strategy x_p has been executed, and the reward $r_{x_p}^p$ received, we update the weights as follows:

$$w_i^t = \hat{w}_i^p . N_i^p$$

where $\hat{w}_i^p = w_i^{p-1}$ for i not selected, but for i selected:

$$\hat{w}_i^p = w_i^{p-1} (m_i^p)^{\frac{1}{Pr(x_p=i)}}$$

The N_i^p term is used to ensure that sleeping does not affect a strategy's probability of being chosen. $N_i^p = 1$ if $a_i^p = 0$ and otherwise:

$$N_i^p = \frac{\sum_j a_j^p w_j^{p-1}}{\sum_j a_j^p \hat{w}_j^p}$$

To apply the approach to negotiation we need to decide how we are going to set the multipliers. The multipliers specify the degree to which the success or failure of a strategy affects the weight. We base the multipliers on a model of user utility. We let the utility a user derives from a negotiation strategy take into account three elements:

1. the user's preference for the time-of-day (tod) the new meeting is scheduled for – $val(tod)$.
2. the increase (or decrease) in utility from moving other meetings, i.e., for all meetings that were moved, the agent's utility is increased by $\sum_{moved} val(tod_{new}) - \sum_{moved} val(tod_{old})$.
3. the number of negotiation rounds r required to schedule the new meeting and move any old meetings.

The user's utility function is parametrized by two constants α and β which specify the relative importance of time-of-day valuations and negotiation cost. Formally a user's utility for the outcome of a negotiation strategy is modeled as:

$$U(i) = \alpha(val(tod) + \sum_{moved} val(tod_{new}) - \sum_{moved} val(tod_{old})) - \beta r$$

We use the user's utility function and highest time-of-day value to estimate the maximum possible utility a negotiation strategy can achieve. We then set the multiplier according to how the reward actually achieved relates to this maximum. The multiplier is set according to the first row of Table 1 that applies. Also note that if the negotiation strategy fails to schedule the new meeting, or to reschedule any bumped meetings, a failure has occurred. Currently we use a multiplier of 0.25 for this case.

The bounds on regret obtained by using the plays approach are strongest if the 'opponent' agent is using a fixed strategy and we assume that changes to the environment (i.e., the calendars) are not affecting the rewards. If the other agent is also learning, then in the terminology of [10], we are dealing with a *non-oblivious* adversary. As such, since the playbook approach builds on Exp3, the theoretical bounds on regret are weaker.

Table 1. The multiplier is given by the first row for which the left hand entry evaluates to true

$U(i) > 0.75 * maxU$	1.75
$U(i) > 0.5 * maxU$	1.5
$U(i) > 0.25 * maxU$	1.25
$U(i) > 0$	1
$U(i) > 0 - 0.25 * maxU$	0.75
$U(i) > 0 - 0.5 * maxU$	0.5
$U(i) > 0 - 0.75 * maxU$	0.25

5   Evaluation

In this section, we describe how we have evaluated the effectiveness of using a plays approach to selecting negotiation strategies.

1. **APPLICABILITY**: if importance(other-agent) $>=$ moderately-important return true.
2. **INDEPENDENT OFFER**: in the first round offer all available times for the current week, in second round offer all available times for the following week and so on until all available times up until the last possible time for the meeting have been offered.
3. **DEPENDENT OFFER**: if negotiation round > 5, apply the simple compromiser sub-strategy described in Fig. 1.
4. **ABANDON**: if negotiation round > 50 return true.

Fig. 2. Availability Declaring Negotiator

5.1 Communication Protocol

We have created a simulation environment consisting of a set of agents equipped with a common protocol for communicating about meetings. The protocol has three basic stages: a negotiation phase, in which agents exchange proposals, a pending stage, in which a time proposed by all the agents is agreed upon, and a confirmation stage, after which the meeting is entered into the agents' calendars. Support is also provided for *bumping* (canceling and rescheduling) meetings. There are a number of different types of messages that the agents exchange:

- meeting time proposals
- requests to bump meetings
- cancellation notices for meetings
- pending requests for times – when a meeting initiator finds an intersection in proposals, it sends a pending request for one of the times in the intersection to each of the participants.
- pending responses – when an attendee receives a pending request it responds with either:
  - a pending acceptance and marks the meeting as pending, or
  - a pending rejection (if the time is pending for another meeting, we require that the agent rejects the request).
- confirmation notices – sent out by the initiator when all attendees reply to a pending request with a pending acceptance.

5.2 Negotiation Strategies

We have implemented a number of negotiation strategies that comply with the protocol outlined. We use two of these strategies in our experiments in this paper. The first strategy – Offer-k-b was previously described (see Fig. 1.). This strategy is parametrized, and hence it covers a large number of distinct strategies. The second strategy we use is called Availability-Declarer (Fig. 2.). This strategy can be very useful in practice, particularly in situations where the agents are very busy. The key feature of this strategy is that it offers all the available times in the first week straight away. In subsequent negotiation rounds it does the same for later weeks.

5.3 Preferences

We use a simple model of time-of-day preferences. Each agent has a preference ordering over morning times, middle of the day times and afternoon times. For example, if an agent prefers the morning, then the middle of the day, and then the afternoon, times in the morning are assigned a value of 3, times in the middle of the day a value of 2 and times in the afternoon, a value of 1.

5.4 Experiments and Results

We have empirically evaluated the effectiveness of using a plays approach to select negotiation strategies. The experiments we describe consist of one learning agent, which we are evaluating, and three fixed strategy agents of varying preferences and busyness. We also look at the effect of adding another learning agent into the mix. The learning agents have three strategies in their playbooks – Availability-Declarer, Offer-10-5 and Offer-3-5. In the experiments discussed, these strategies are always applicable.

Convergence. In each experiment, the agents schedule approximately 80 new two person meetings (we restrict our attention to two-person meetings to simplify the discussion). The learning agent is an attendee (not an initiator) of each of these 80 meetings. We show how the learning agent's playbook weights converge to sensible strategies for each of the fixed strategy agents.

In our first experiment the learning agent's time preference is morning, then midday and then afternoon. The α and β values of the learning agent's utility function are 4 and 0.1 respectively. The agent's calendar is approximately 25% full when the experiment is started. Unlike the meetings we schedule in the testing phase, the initial meetings in the calendar can involve any number of the agents.

Fig. 3. shows how the learning agent's playbook weights adapt for Agent2. Agent2 starts out with a similar number of initial meetings to the learning agent, uses the Availability-Declarer strategy, and has the same time preferences as the learning agent. Fig. 3. shows how the playbook weights quickly converge to towards the Availability-Declarer strategy. While the other two strategies are also likely to work well in this instance, the Availability Declarer strategy offers the possibility resolving the negotiation faster. Since the learning agent and Agent2 have the same preferences, there is no strategic advantage to the learning agent only releasing its availability slowly.

Fig. 4. shows the weight adaptation for Agent3. Agent3 uses the Availability-Declarer strategy and starts out with a similar calendar density to the learning agent, but with opposite preferences. Agent3 most prefers afternoons, then the middle of the day, and then the morning. Fig. 4. shows that the learning agent quickly establishes that the Availability-Declarer strategy is less useful for negotiating with Agent3 than the Offer-10-5 and Offer-3-5 strategies. After about 25 meetings have been scheduled the weights converge on the the Offer-3-5 strategy. Note that the Availability-Declarer strategy is a poor choice for use with Agent3. When both agents negotiate with this strategy, the initiator (always Agent3 in these experiments) is likely to quickly find a large intersection of available times. The initiator can choose its most preferred time in this intersection and since Agent3's and the learning agent's preferences clash, the time chosen will

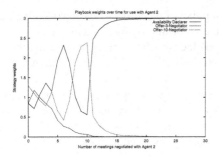 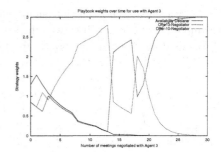

Fig. 3. Weights adaptation for Agent2   **Fig. 4.** Weight adaptation for Agent3

likely be bad for the learning agent. The learning agent has a clear strategic incentive to declare its available times more slowly and in order of preference. Since the learning agent's utility function rates achieving good times-of-day much higher than minimizing the number of negotiation rounds, it converges on the Offer-3-5 strategy rather than the Offer-10-5. This is despite the learning agent's calendar being quite full (93%), and hence mutually available slots fairly rare, by the time the experiment concludes.

Fig. 5. shows the weight adaptation for Agent4. Agent4 has similar preferences (midday, morning, then afternoon) to the learning agent. Agent4 uses the Offer-10-5 negotiator and starts with a dense calendar (about 80% full). Fig. 5. shows that the learning Agent quickly determines that the Offer-3-5 strategy is not very effective when dealing with a very busy agent that has similar preferences. After approximately 15 meetings have been scheduled, the learning agent converges on the Availability-Declarer strategy.

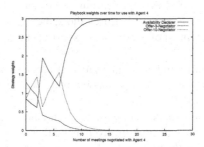

Fig. 5. Weight adaptation for Agent4

We ran the same experiment described above but with a different utility function for the learning agent and different initial calendars. The utility function had α as 4, and β as 1. This change caused the weights to converge on Availability-Declarer for each of the agents, since the negative effect of negotiation length was greatly increased.

Performance. No regret algorithms bound the average difference between the performance of the learning algorithm, and the best fixed strategy in the limit. However, since a learning agent does not schedule an infinite number of meetings with each other agent, it is important to examine how well the learning algorithm performs in practice.

We used the 4 agents previously described (the play learning agent and the three fixed agents) and ran 10 trials. In each trial the agents' calendars were randomly initialized with 160 meetings. 200 new meetings were scheduled in each trial, but the calendars were cleared to their initial state after every 20 meetings were scheduled. This reflects the common scenario where people have a set of meetings that occur weekly and new meetings that arise over time. Fig. 6. shows the learning algorithm achieving higher utility than playing a random strategy or using any fixed strategy.

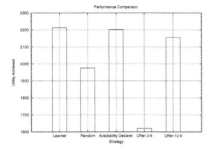 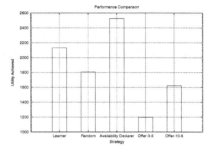

Fig. 6. Performance against only fixed agents   **Fig. 7.** Performance when another learning agent is added

The learning algorithm used gives the strongest regret guarantees when the other agents are fixed. Fig. 7. shows that the learning algorithm also performs reasonably well when we add a learning agent (that uses the same algorithm), to the three fixed agents. These results are typical of a variety of experimental configurations.

Discussion. Using a small number of alternative strategies and agents, we were able to show that the learning converged in a sensible way. We were also able to show that when the other agents used fixed strategies, the learning algorithm performed better than using the best fixed strategy. It is important to remember that the theoretical results only bound the regret between the pay-off from using the learning algorithm, versus the best fixed strategy that is *in the playbook*. This means that the strategies that appear in the playbook must be carefully selected by a human expert. It is also worth noting that a large playbook would make learning impractical. As such, it might be worthwhile, in practice, to use a hierarchy of playbooks. For instance, initially a very diverse playbook might be used to decide which was the best class of strategies. A playbook containing different strategies from that class could then be used to tune parameters. This seems a promising avenue for future research.

Another avenue for future research is improving the performance results for the case where more than one agent is learning. In the future, we would like to experiment with a variety of no-regret style algorithms that are more specifically designed for this case.

6   Conclusions

We introduced the idea of using a *playbook* approach for learning to select the best strategies for negotiating with different agents. The space of negotiation strategies is huge, and thus it is not possible for an agent to learn how to negotiate in the complete space. The plays-based approach cuts the strategy space down to a set of strategies that are effective in different situations, allowing an agent to learn which of these strategies work best with different fixed-strategy agents. This approach provides some theoretical bounds on the regret the learning agent can experience. We have demonstrated experimentally that using a plays-based approach leads to good performance.

References

1. Bowling, M., Browning, B., Veloso, M.: Plays as effective multiagent plans enabling opponent-adaptive play selection. In: Proceedings of International Conference on Automated Planning and Scheduling (ICAPS'04). (2004)
2. Crawford, E., Veloso, M.: Opportunities for learning in multi-agent meeting scheduling. In: Proceedings of the AAAI Symposium on Artificial Multiagent Learning. (2004)
3. Jennings, N.R., Jackson, A.J.: Agent based meeting scheduling: A design and implementation. IEE Electronics Letters **31** (1995) 350–352
4. Sen, S., Durfee, E.: A formal study of distributed meeting scheduling. Group Decision and Negotiation **7** (1998) 265–289
5. Modi, P.J., Veloso, M.: Bumping strategies for the private incremental multiagent agreement problem. In: AAAI Spring Symposium on Persistant Agents. (2005)
6. Ephrati, E., Zlotkin, G., Rosenschein, J.: A non–manipulable meeting scheduling system. In: Proc. International Workshop on Distributed Artificial Intelligence, Seatle, WA (1994)
7. Garrido, L., Sycara, K.: Multi-agent meeting scheduling: Preliminary experimental results. In: Proceedings of the First International Conference on Multi-Agent Systems. (1995)
8. Shintani, T., Ito, T., Sycara, K.: Multiple negotiations among agents for a distributed meeting scheduler. In: Proceedings of the Fourth International Conference on MultiAgent Systems. (2000) 435 – 436
9. Littlestone, N., Warmuth, M.: The weighted majority algorithm. In: IEEE Symposium on Foundations of Computer Science. (1989) 256–261
10. Auer, P., Cesa-Bianchi, N., Freund, Y., Schapire, R.: Gambling in a rigged casino: the adversarial multi-armed bandit problem. In: Proceedings of the 36th Annual FOCS. (1995)
11. Freund, Y., Schapire, R., Singer, Y., Warmuth, M.: Using and combining predictors that specialize. In: STOC. (1997)

Chapter 9

TEMA 2005: Text Mining and

Applications

Introduction

Gabriel Pereira Lopes[1], Joaquim Ferreira da Silva[1],
Victor Rocio[2], and Paulo Quaresma[3]

[1] New University of Lisbon, Portugal
{gpl, jfs}@di.fct.unl.pt
[2] Open University, Portugal
vjr@univ-ab.pt
[3] University of Évora, Portugal
pq@di.uevora.pt

This chapter contains papers presented in the workshop on Text Mining and Applications (TeMA 2005), organized in the framework of the Portuguese Association for Artificial Intelligence conference (EPIA). This workshop is aimed at attracting quality papers and enhancing the knowledge in this area.

27 papers were submitted. From these, 9 papers were selected for publication in this Springer volume. These numbers show current importance of this field in AI and suggest that the organization of equivalent events in future EPIA editions should be pursued.

First paper works on bilingual lexical acquisition from non parallel corpora, applicable in Machine Translation. Second paper describes work on Text Summarization. Third uses Transformation Based learning for NP Identification applied to Portuguese. Fourth uses linguistic knowledge for passage retrieval and question answering. Fifth describes the use of weakly supervised learning for extraction of semantic patterns. Sixth paper proposes a method for semantic indexing and evaluates it on traditional Information Retrieval tasks. Seventh works on unsupervised language independent extraction of multi-word terms, applicable in multiple domains and evaluates their results for Slovene and English. Eighth paper presents a variant of a known method for Anaphora resolution, adapted to Portuguese. Last paper proposes a stemmer for Brazilian Portuguese.

C. Bento, A. Cardoso, and G. Dias (Eds.): EPIA 2005, LNAI 3808, p. 599, 2005.
© Springer-Verlag Berlin Heidelberg 2005

An Approach to Acquire Word Translations from Non-parallel Texts*

Pablo Gamallo Otero[1] and José Ramom Pichel Campos[2]

[1] Departamento de Língua Espanhola, Faculdade de Filologia,
Universidade de Santiago de Compostela, Galiza, Spain
pablogam@usc.es
[2] Departamento de Tecnologia Linguística da Imaxin, Software,
Santiago de Compostela, Galiza
jramompichel@imaxin.com

Abstract. Few approaches to extract word translations from non-parallel texts have been proposed so far. Researchers have not been encouraged to work on this topic because extracting information from non-parallel corpora is a difficult task producing poor results. Whereas for parallel texts, word translation extraction can reach about 99%, the accuracy for non-parallel texts has been around 72% up to now. The current approach, which relies on the previous extraction of bilingual pairs of lexico-syntactic templates from parallel corpora, makes a significant improvement to about 89% of words translations identified correctly.

1 Introduction

In the last decade, many works have been carried out to automatically extract word and/or multi-word translations from bilingual parallel corpora [15, 1, 20, 13]. These works share a common strategy: they perform first the alignment of segments and then, on the basis of such an alignment, they compute word correspondences in each pair of segments. In some of these experiences, word-level translation accuracy achieved very high scores: about 99%. Unfortunately, the amount of available bilingual parallel texts is still small, specially in specific, academic or technological domains. Given a particular knowledge domain, the number of parallel texts is much lower than that of monolingual texts. This type of texts are known as comparable, *non-parallel* corpora. Nowadays, in the World Wide Web, comparable non-parallel corpora are more prevalent than parallel corpora. However, the highest rate to date in word-level translation from non-parallel corpora is relatively small, 72% [18], in comparison to the accuracy rate achieved from parallel corpora.

In this paper, we present a method to extract word translations, which takes advantage from the positive aspects of both parallel (high accuracy) and non-parallel corpora (high coverage). The strategy we propose is the following.

---

* This work has been supported by Ministerio de Educacin y Ciencia of Spain, within the project GARI-COTERM, ref: HUM2004-05658-D02-02.

C. Bento, A. Cardoso, and G. Dias (Eds.): EPIA 2005, LNAI 3808, pp. 600–610, 2005.

We first extract, from small parallel texts, a representative set of bilingual correspondences between unambiguous lexico-syntactic templates. Then, these pairs of bilingual templates are used as *local contexts* to extract word translations from comparable, non-parallel corpora. A word $w1$ in the source language can be the translation of a word $w2$ in the target language if $w1$ tends to occur in local contexts that are translations of the local contexts $w2$ occurs in. Using this method, we achieved 89% accuracy, which is close to the scores reached by the extraction approaches from aligned, parallel texts. In the following sections, we first recall previous approaches to word translations from non-parallel text, then we describe our own method, and finally, we provide and discuss two different experimental results.

2   Related Work

There are few approaches to extract bilingual lexicons from non-parallel corpora in comparison to those using a strategy based on aligned, parallel texts. The most efficient method to extract word translations from comparable, non-parallel corpora is described in [6, 7, 18]. The starting point of this strategy is as follows: word w_1 is a possible translation of w_2 if the words with which w_1 co-occurs within a particular window are translations of the words with which w_2 co-occurs within the same window. This strategy relies on a list of bilingual word pairs (*seed words*) provided by an electronic bilingual dictionary. w_1 is a candidate translation of w_2 if they tend to co-occur with the same seed words. There are three drawbacks to this method. First, it is not a knowledge-poor approach since it needs external lexical resources such as a bilingual dictionary. Second, not all the words of the dictionary seem to be reliable seed words. Polysemic words should be removed from the list of seed words since they may introduce semantic noise. And third, according to the Harris's hypothesis [12], counting co-occurrences within a window of size N is less precise than counting co-occurrences within local syntactic contexts. In the most efficient approaches to thesaurus generation [11, 14], word similarity is computed using co-occurrences between words and specific syntactic contexts. Syntactic contexts are less ambiguous and more sense-discriminative than contexts defined as windows of size N. In order to overcome these drawbacks, we will use as seed expressions, not word entries from an external bilingual dictionary, but pairs of bilingual lexico-syntactic templates which were extracted from a small parallel corpus. As the lexico-syntactic templates represent unambiguous local contexts of words, they are discriminative and confident seed expressions to extract word translations from non-parallel texts.

There exist other approaches to bilingual lexicon extraction which do not use external bilingual dictionaries [5, 17, 4]. Yet, [5] failed to reach an acceptable accuracy rate for actual use, [17] had strong computational limitations, and [4] was applied only to non-parallel texts in the same language. On the other hand, [3] describes a particular strategy based on a multilingual thesaurus instead of a external bilingual dictionary.

Finally, some researchers have focused on a different issue: disambiguation of candidate translation. According to [16], the process of building bilingual lexicons from non-parallel corpora is a too difficult and ambitious objective. He preferred to work on a less ambitious task: to choose between several translation alternatives previously selected from a bilingual dictionary.

In this paper, the objective of our extraction method is to build bilingual lexicons from comparable non-parallel corpora, with the help of some lexico-syntactic information extracted from small parallel corpora. No external lexical ressource will be used.

3　The Approach

Our method can be divided into the following steps:

- text processing,
- extraction of bilingual lexico-syntactic templates from parallel corpora,
- extraction of word translations from non-parallel texts.

3.1　Text Processing

Parallel and non parallel corpora are tokenized, lemmatized, and tagged. English texts are tagged using TreeTagger [19], while the Spanish part is tagged with Freeling [2]. As no manual correction is made, the extraction of word translations will inherit errors and problems introduced by the tagger. Finally, we identify binary dependencies in order to extract lexico-syntactic templates. From each binary dependency, we extract two complementary lexico-syntactic templates. Table 1 shows some representative examples. A lexico-syntactic template represents the local context of a set of syntactically related words. Given the binary dependency:

of (import, sugar)

template < import of [NOUN] > represents the set of nouns that can appear after "import of", for instance, "sugar", "goods", "oil", etc. On the other hand, < [NOUN] of sugar > represents the set of nouns appearing before "of sugar": "import", "export", "sell", etc. We follow the notion of *co-requirement* introduced in [9].

Table 1. Binary dependencies and their corresponding templates

Binary Dependencies	Templates	
of (import, sugar)	< import of [NOUN] >	< [NOUN] of sugar >
robj (approve, law)	< approve [NOUN] >	< [VERB] law >
lobj (approve, president)	< president, [VERB] >	< [NOUN] approve >
modAdj(legal, document)	< legal [NOUN] >	< [ADJ] document >
modN(area, protection)	< protection [NOUN] >	< [NOUN] area >

Note that *lobj* represents the relationship between a verb and the noun immediately appearing at its left; *robj* is the relationship between a verb and the noun
appearing at its right. On the other hand, *modAdj* is the relationship between
a noun and its adjective modifier and *modN* is the relation between two nouns:
the head and its modifier.

3.2   Extracting Bilingual Templates from Parallel Corpora

Once the lexico-syntactic templates have been identified, we aim at extracting
bilingual correspondences between templates from aligned, small parallel corpora. For this purpose, we use a standard learning method, already described
and evaluated in [8]. The pairwise correlation between two lexico-syntactic templates is computed by taking into account their occurrence in each aligned segment. We use the Dice coefficient to compute similarity between templates. Each
template of the source language is linked to the most similar template of the target language provided that the Dice coefficient is higher than an empirically set

Table 2. Bilingual correlations between templates derived from dependencies "noun-
adjective" (excerpt of a list extracted from the Proceedings of the European Parliament
- EuroParl)

English	Spanish	Dice
< active [NOUN] >	< [NOUN] activo >	0,65
< african[NOUN] >	< [NOUN] africano >	0,65
< agricultural [NOUN] >	< [NOUN] agrícola >	0,63
< alarming [NOUN] >	< [NOUN] alarmante >	0,45
< albanian [NOUN] >	< [NOUN] albanés >	0,61
< alcoholoic[NOUN] >	< [NOUN] alcohólico >	0,48
< alternative[NOUN] >	< [NOUN] alternativa >	0,75
< ambitious [NOUN] >	< [NOUN] ambicioso >	0,44
< american [NOUN] >	< [NOUN] americano >	0,48
< annual [NOUN] >	< [NOUN] anual >	0,77

Table 3. Bilingual correlations between templates derived from nominal dependencies
with preposition (excerpt of a list extracted from EuroParl)

English	Spanish	Dice
< [NOUN] after year>	< [NOUN] tras año>	0,41
< crime against [NOUN] >	< crimen contra [NOUN] >	0,66
< fight against [NOUN] >	< lucha contra [NOUN] >	0,43
< violence against [NOUN] >	< violencia contra [NOUN] >	0,81
< [NOUN] against discrimination >	< [NOUN] contra discriminación >	0,50
< [NOUN] against fraude >	< [NOUN] contra fraude >	0,48
< [NOUN] against humanity >	< [NOUN] contra humanidad >	1.00
< [NOUN] against poverty >	< [NOUN] contra pobreza >	0,60
< [NOUN] against racialism >	< [NOUN] contra racismo >	0,68
< [NOUN] against woman >	< [NOUN] contra mujer >	0,79

Table 4. Bilingual correlations between templates derived from noun-verb dependencies, i.e. from left-objects (excerpt of a list extracted from EuroParl)

English	Spanish	Dice
< africa [VERB] >	< frica [VERB] >	0,66
< agreement [VERB] >	< acuerdo [VERB] >	0,45
< agriculture [VERB] >	< agricultura [VERB] >	0,50
< aid [VERB] >	< ayuda [VERB] >	0,57
< alcohol [VERB] >	< alcohol [VERB] >	0,76
< ambition [VERB] >	< ambición [VERB] >	0,58
< amsterdam [VERB] >	< amsterdam [VERB] >	0,63
< angola [VERB] >	< angola [VERB] >	0,70
< animal [VERB] >	< animal [VERB] >	0,44
< article [VERB] >	< artículo [VERB] >	0,50
< assistant [VERB] >	< asistente [VERB] >	0,66

threshold. Tables 2, 3, and 4, depict some bilingual correlations extracted from an English-Spanish parallel corpus.

Bilingual links between lexico-syntactic templates will be used as *seed* local contexts in the following step. Such templates will serve as the textual anchor points in non-parallel corpora.

3.3   Extracting a Bilingual Lexicon from Non-parallel Corpora

We propose the following algorithm for finding word translation pairs from non-parallel corpora:

```
Given a bilingual list of lexico-syntactic templates
(i.e., seed contexts):
```

- for every word w_{i} in the source language, find the number of times it instantiates each template of the bilingual list in order to build a vector with this information;
  AND
- for every word w_{j} in the target language, find the number of times it instantiates each template of the bilingual list in order to build a vector with this information:

> Compute Weighted Jaccard similarity: $WJ(w_{i}, w_{j})$;
> if w_{j} is the most similar word to w_{i}, then both words define a translation pair.

Let's take an example. Table 5 shows some positions in the feature vector that defines word "president". Each feature corresponds to a lexico-syntactic template extracted from the parallel corpus. The value of the feature is the number of times the word instantiates that template in the non-parallel corpus, i.e., the co-occurrence frequency between the word and the linguistic context

Table 5. Excerpt of the vector associated to "president"

president

00034	<conference of [NOUN]>	323
00176	<[NOUN] of council>	218
00182	<[NOUN] of court>	69
00234	<[NOUN] of republic>	35
00701	<former [NOUN]>	69
00776	<new [NOUN]>	63
01324	<[NOUN] declare>	52
01543	<congratulate [NOUN]>	13

associated to the template. Every template in the vector must have a Spanish correlation. The first column of Table 5 represents the position of a feature in the vector.

Table 6 depicts the corresponding vector positions associated to the Spanish noun "presidente". The features appearing in these positions are then the translations of those depicted in Table 5.

Table 6. Excerpt of the vector associated to the Spanish word "presidente"

presidente

00034	<conferencia de [NOUN]>	509
00176	<[NOUN] de consejo>	1013
00182	<[NOUN] of tribunal>	54
00234	<[NOUN] of república>	134
00701	<antiguo [NOUN]>	36
00776	<nuevo [NOUN]>	86
01324	<[NOUN] declarar>	90
01543	<felicitar a [NOUN]>	31

As tables 5 and 6 shows, the Spanish noun "presidente" occurs in templates that are translations of English templates also instantiated by "president". To compute the degree of similarity between these two words, we use a weighted version of Jaccard coefficient. This measure was proposed by [11] and [10] to generate clusters of semantically related words from monolingual corpora. As in our work, these authors perform a shallow syntactical analysis before constructing the co-occurrence vectors.

Jaccard measure calculates the similarity value between two words by comparing the templates they share and do not share. The weighted Jaccard coefficient considers a global and a local weight for each template . The global weight gw takes into account how many different words are associated with a given template. It is computed by the following formula:

$$gw(template_j) = 1 + \frac{\sum_i p_{ij} \log_2(p_{ij})}{Ndeps}$$

where

$$p_{ij} = \frac{frequency\,of\,template_j\,with\,word_i}{total\,number\,of\,templates\,of\,word_i}$$

and $Ndeps$ is the total number of binary dependencies extracted from the non-parallel corpus. The local weight lw is the number of times a word instantiates a template:

$$lw(word_i, template_j) = \log_2(frequency\,of\,template_j\,with\,word_i)$$

The whole weight w of a template given a word is the multiplication of both the global and the local weights. So, the weighted Jaccard similarity WJ between two words m and n is computed by:

$$WJ(word_m, word_n) = \frac{\sum_j \min(w(word_m, template_j), w(word_n, template_j))}{\sum_j \max(w(word_m, template_j), w(word_n, template_j))}$$

Each bilingual pair of words is compared by computing WJ similarity. The most similar Spanish words to a given English word are considered as their possible translations.

4   Experiments and Evaluation

4.1   Text Corpora

In our experiments, we used two small English-Spanish parallel corpora: one that was selected from the proceedings of the European Parliament (*EuroPal*); each part contains about 1 million words. The other corpus is constituted by the English and Spanish version of the European Constitution (*EuroConst*). Each part contains about 150,000 words. These two parallel corpora allowed us to extract translation correspondences between lexico-syntactic templates. We learned 2,551 translation pairs from EuroPal, and 1,667 from EuroConst. The reunion of the two sets gives rise to 3,830 different translation pairs.

Word translations were learnt from a larger English-Spanish non-parallel corpus selected from the proceedings of EuroPal. The English part consists of 14 million words while the size of the Spanish part is about 17 million words. The two parts were selected in such a way that no English subparts were translations of Spanish subparts. The bilingual templates we have extracted from the parallel corpus are used here as local contexts of words.

4.2   Results

By selecting only those translation pairs whose Jaccard coefficient is higher than a given threshold ($>= 0.1$), we generated a lexicon of 11,701 word entries. These entries are lemmas belonging to three syntactic categories: nouns, verbs, and adjectives.

Table 7. Results for 40 out of 100 test words

English test nouns	Top 5 candidate translations				
coherence	credibilidad	**coherencia**	claridad	rigor	visibilidad
cohesion	**cohesión**	integración	solidaridad	estabilidad	igualdad
colleague	**colega**	diputado	amigo	ministro	pueblo
comment	**comentario**	observación	pregunta	reflexión	palabra
commissioner	**comisario**	presidente	colega	diputado	gobierno
commitment	**compromiso**	obligación	respuesta	responsabilidad	criterio
committee	grupo	consejo	parlamento	**comité**	comisión
communication	**comunicación**	información	documento	diálogo	iniciativa
community	unión	**comunidad**	estado	política	país
company	**empresa**	industria	mercado	economía	sector
competition	**competencia**	igualdad	inversión	cooperación	democracia
compromise	consenso	planteamiento	**compromiso**	solución	discusión
concept	**concepto**	idea	planteamiento	enfoque	exigencia
concern	**preocupación**	interés	responsabilidad	exigencia	consideración
conclusion	**conclusión**	resultado	declaración	idea	punto
condition	**condición**	criterio	norma	regla	aspecto
conference	**conferencia**	reunión	cumbre	convención	declaración
confidence	**confianza**	consenso	solidaridad	credibilidad	respaldo
conflict	**conflicto**	crisis	tensión	guerra	diálogo
connection	vínculo	**conexión**	contacto	consulta	vinculación
consequence	**consecuencia**	efecto	repercusión	resultado	impacto
consideration	**consideración**	aspecto	razón	criterio	dimensión
consumer	**consumidor**	población	ciudadano	democracia	empresa
content	**contenido**	alcance	elemento	calidad	orientación
context	**contexto**	marco	vista	plano	término
contribution	**contribución**	aportación	respuesta	papel	apoyo
control	**control**	gestión	responsabilidad	competencia	información
convention	**convenio**	tratado	**convención**	protocolo	carta
cooperation	**cooperación**	relación	colaboración	diálogo	acuerdo
coordination	**coordinación**	colaboración	diálogo	cooperación	equilibrio
cost	**coste**	gasto	necesidad	efecto	consecuencia
country	**país**	estado	región	europa	unión
course	**curso**	año	resultado	plazo	enfoque
court	**tribunal**	ley	autoridad	comité	gobierno
creation	**creación**	integración	existencia	establecimiento	crecimiento
crime	delito	**crimen**	terrorismo	violencia	enfermedad
crisis	**crisis**	conflicto	catástrofe	dificultad	situación
criterion	**criterio**	regla	requisito	condición	exigencia
criticism	**crítica**	comentario	mensaje	petición	observación
culture	**cultura**	sociedad	dimensión	democracia	agricultura
currency	democracia	**moneda**	economía	mercado	sociedad

4.3   Evaluation 1: Accuracy

The first evaluation test was inspired from the protocol defined in [18]. 100 test nouns with a frequency of 100 or higher were randomly selected from the English corpus[1]. Using the similarity coefficient, the test nouns was compared to all nouns occurring in the Spanish corpus. Table 7 shows the results for 40 out of

---

[1] In [18], the 100 test words were not randomly selected. They belong to a list of stimulus words used in [21] for an association experiment.

the 100 English test nouns. For each English test word, the top five translations are listed. The word considered to be the most expected, salient, and appropriate translation is in bold. As in [18], only one word is selected as the most appropriate translation, except in those cases where the test word can be translated by several nouns considered as synonyms in almost all contexts: for instance, "convention" is correctly translated by both "convenio" and "convención". If we look at Table 7, we see that in most cases our system predicts the most appropriate translation, with other semantically related nouns immediately following. Note that in some cases, behind the most appropriate translation, the other 4 candidates can also be possible translations of the test word: see for instance the candidate translations for "comment", "conference", or "consequence". Even if the first candidate suggested by the system is clearly the most expected translation ("comentario", "conferencia", "consecuencia"), the rest of candidates can be considered as synonyms in certain linguistic contexts.

To measure the accuracy of the system, we counted the number of times where a correct translation of the source word is ranked first. This was true for 89 out of 100 test words (89% accuracy). For comparison, [18] reports an accuracy of 72% and [6] of 30%, when only the top candidate is counted. In another test, we checked whether a correct translation appeared among the top 5 of the ranked list. This was true in 96 cases, while in [18], it was true in 89. This evaluation shows that our system makes a significant improvement in comparison to the two most similar approaches to identification of word translations from non-parallel texts.

4.4   Evaluation 2: Precision and Recall

The previous evaluation does not allow to check the completeness of the translations (recall and precision) since it does not observe the behaviour of word tokens in real text. For this purpose, we selected at random a test corpus containing 150 English word tokens, tagged as nouns, verbs, and adjectives. Each selected word was extracted with its immediate context in order to allow evaluators to make appropriate decisions. Word tokens can belong to word types with a frequency of 1 or higher than 1. Given a word token of the test corpus, the evaluators had to decide if there is a correct Spanish translation between the top 10 most similar words. The results are summarized in Table 8. In general terms, we call *Precision* the number of correct translations proposed by the system divided by the number of all translations which have been suggested. *Recall* is the number

Table 8. Results concerning precision and recall

$Prec_1$	$Prec_{10}$	$Recall_1$	$Recall_{10}$	Number of bilingual templates
.72	.88	.63	.77	2,551
.74	.92	.66	.81	3,830

of correct translations proposed by the system divided by the number of all test instances. Concerning $precision_1$ and $recall_1$ the correct translation is the first word proposed by the system. As regards $precision_{10}$ and $recall_{10}$, the correct translation is within the top 10 candidate translations proposed by the system. In addition, we made two different experiences: in the first experiment, we use as seed contexts the 2,551 bilingual templates extracted from only one parallel corpus: EuroPal. However, in the second experiment, we put together the 3,830 templates extracted from both EuroPal and EuroConst. As Table 8 shows, the higher the number of bilingual templates taken as seed contexts, the better the scores associated to precision and recall. It means that we could improve the learning method if the experiences are made using a larger set of discriminative template pairs. The results of this evaluation cannot be compared to other approaches, since as far as we know this type of experience has not been made yet in related work.

5   Conclusion and Discussion

Few approaches to extract word translations from non-parallel texts have been proposed so far. This is a difficult task. Whereas for parallel texts, word translation extraction reaches in some studies about 90%, the accuracy for non-parallel texts has been around 72% up to now. The main contribution of the approach proposed in this paper is to use bilingual pairs of lexico-syntactic templates as seed expressions. This makes a significant improvement to about 89% of words translations identified correctly.

The ability to identify word translations from non-parallel corpora could be seen as an indicator in favor of the idea that machines, like humans, are able to acquire new linguistic knowledge without being directly exposed to that knowledge.

References

1. Lars Ahrenberg, Mikael Andersson, and Magnus Merkel. A simple hybrid aligner for generating lexical correspondences in parallel texts. In *36th Annual Meeting of the Association for Computational Linguistics and 17th International Conference on Computational Linguistics (COLING-ACL'98)*, pages 29–35, Montreal, 1998.
2. X. Carreras, I. Chao, L. Padró, and M. Padró. An open-source suite of language analyzers. In *4th International Conference on Language Resources and Evaluation (LREC'04)*, Lisbon, Portugal, 2004.
3. H. Dejean, E. Gaussier, and F. Sadat. Bilingual terminology extraction: an approach based on a multilingual thesaurus applicable to comparable corpora. In *COLING 2002*, Tapei, Taiwan, 2002.
4. Mona Diab and Steve Finch. A statistical word-level translation model for comparable corpora. In *Proceedings of the Conference on Content-Based Multimedia Information Access (RIAO)*, 2001.
5. Pascale Fung. Compiling bilingual lexicon entries from a non-parallel english-chinese corpus. In *14th Annual Meeting of Very Large Corpora*, pages 173–183, Boston, Massachusettes, 1995.

6. Pascale Fung and Kathleen McKeown. Finding terminology translation frmo non-parallel corpora. In *5th Annual Workshop on Very Large Corpora*, pages 192–202, Hong Kong, 1997.

7. Pascale Fung and Lo Yuen Yee. An ir approach for translating new words from nonparallel, comparable texts. In *Coling'98*, pages 414–420, Montreal, Canada, 1998.

8. Pablo Gamallo. Extraction of translation equivalents from parallel corpora using sense-sensitive contexts. In *10th Conference of the European Association on Machine Translation (EAMT'05)*, pages 97–102, Budapest, Hungary, 2005.

9. Pablo Gamallo, Alexandre Agustini, and Gabriel Lopes. Clustering syntactic positions with similar syntactic requirements. *Computational Linguistics*, 31(1), 2005.

10. Pablo Gamallo, Caroline Gasperin, Alexandre Agustini, and Gabriel P. Lopes. Syntactic-based methods for measuring word similarity. In V. Mautner, R. Moucek, and K. Moucek, editors, *Text, Speech, and Discourse (TSD-2001)*, pages 116–125. Berlin:Springer Verlag, 2001.

11. Gregory Grefenstette. *Explorations in Automatic Thesaurus Discovery*. Kluwer Academic Publishers, USA, 1994.

12. Z. Harris. Distributional structure. In J.J. Katz, editor, *The Philosophy of Linguistics*, pages 26–47. New York: Oxford University Press, 1985.

13. Oi Yee Kwong, Benjamin K. Tsou, and Tom B. Lai. Alignment and extraction of bilingual legal terminology from context profiles. *Terminology*, 10(1):81–99, 2004.

14. Dekang Lin. Automatic retrieval and clustering of similar words. In *COLING-ACL'98*, Montreal, 1998.

15. Dan Melamed. A word-to-word model of translational equivalence. In *35th Conference of the Association of Computational Linguistics (ACL'97)*, Madrid, Spain, 1997.

16. Hiroshi Nakagawa. Disambiguation of single noun translations extracted from bilingual comparable corpora. *Terminology*, 7(1):63–83, 2001.

17. Reinhard Rapp. Identifying word translations in non-parallel texts. In *33rd Conference of the ACL'95*, pages 320–322, 1995.

18. Reinhard Rapp. Automatic identification of word translations from unrelated english and german corpora. In *ACL'99*, pages 519–526, 1999.

19. Helmut Schimd. Treetagger. In *A language independent part-of-speech tagger*, http://www.ims.uni-stuttgart.de/projekte/corplex/TreeTagger/DecisionTreeTagger.html, 2002.

20. Jorg Tiedemann. Extraction of translation equivalents from parallel corpora. In *11th Nordic Conference of Computational Linguistics*, Copenhagen, Denmark, 1998.

21. Manfred Wettler and Reinhard Rapp. Computation of word associations based on the co-occurrences of words in large corpora. In *1st Workshop on Very Large Corpora*, pages 84–93, Columbus, Ohio, 1993.

Experiments on Statistical and Pattern-Based Biographical Summarization

Horacio Saggion and Robert Gaizauskas

Department of Computer Science,
University of Sheffield,
Sheffield - S1 4DP - United Kingdom
Tel: +44-114-222-1947
Fax: +44-114-222-1810
{saggion, robertg}@dcs.shef.ac.uk

Abstract. We describe experiments on content selection for producing biographical summaries from multiple documents. The method relies on a set of patterns to identify descriptive phrases, an available co-reference resolution algorithm, and a greedy, corpus-based sentence deletion procedure for document compression. We show that in an automatic evaluation of content using ROUGE, the proposed method obtains very good performance.

1 Introduction

Extracting relevant information from massive amounts of free text about people in order to construct profiles or biographies is a challenging problem not only because it is very difficult to elicit in a precise way what type of information about a person is relevant for a biography, but also because even if some types of information were known to be relevant (e.g. birthdate or profession), there are many ways of expressing that information in natural language texts. As free text is by far the main repository of human knowledge, solutions to the problem of extracting information about people have many applications in areas of knowledge management and intelligence:

- In intelligence analysis activities: there is a need for access to personal information in order to create briefings for meetings; and for tracking activities of individuals in time and space;
- In journalism: there is a need to find relevant information for writing backgrounds or profiles for the main actors of a breaking news story;
- In publishing: the need is to update/create entries about famous people in Encyclopedias and dictionaries;
- In knowledge engineering: ontologies and other knowledge repositories need to be populated with instances such as persons and their attributes extracted from text.

C. Bento, A. Cardoso, and G. Dias (Eds.): EPIA 2005, LNAI 3808, pp. 611–621, 2005.
© Springer-Verlag Berlin Heidelberg 2005

Recent natural language processing challenges such as the Document Understanding Conferences (DUC) and the Text Retrieval Conferences (TREC) Question Answering (QA) evaluations have focused on this particular problem and are creating useful language resources to study the problem and measure technical advances. For example, in task 5 in the recent DUC 2004 system participants had to create summaries from sets of documents answering the question "Who is X?", and from 2003 onwards, the TREC/QA evaluations have a specific task which consists of finding relevant information about a person in a massive text repository.

In this paper, we concentrate on the problem of creating a profile or biography for a particular person given a set of documents referring to that person as defined in the DUC 2004 evaluation. This is an instance of the more general summarization problem (see [1] for an overview of the field).

A multidocument summarization system takes as input a set of documents (or *cluster*) related by some "topic" and produces a summary of the whole set. If the cluster of documents refers to a given event instance (e.g. a particular earthquake), it is likely that sentences from different documents in the cluster will report the same information (e.g. damages, victims). Therefore, multi-document summarization algorithms can take advantage of the *redundancy* of information in order to measure relevance. However, when the collection of documents refers to a particular person other techniques seem to perform better than redundancy alone. For example, one of the best performing systems in the recent DUC 2004 evaluation (task 5) used syntactic criteria alone to select sentences in order to create a biographical summary [2]. Only two types of construction were used in that work: *appositive* and *copula* constructions both of which rely on syntactic analysis.

In the experiments to be reported in this paper, we focus on the problem of *extracting* the necessary information to create the person's profile; the problem of synthesis – the production of a coherent and cohesive biography – will not be discussed in this work. We take as a point of departure the ideas used in [2], however we follow a shallow pattern-based approach to the identification of profile information combined with a greedy search algorithm informed by corpus statistics. We will show that, unlike other methods, the proposed solution is ranked consistently high on the DUC 2004 Task 5 data. The rest of the paper is organized as follows: in the next section we describe the natural language processing tools and in Section 3 the process of content selection. Section 4 gives details of the process of document reduction. In Section 5 experiments using DUC 2004 data and results are presented. In Section 6 we report on past work and Section 7 closes with our conclusions and future work.

2   The System

We have developed a sentence selection mechanism which, given a target person and a cluster of documents referring to the target, extracts relevant content from the cluster and produces a summary such as the one presented in Figure 1.

It is a summary about "Stephen Hawkings" produced from a cluster of ten documents. It contains relevant information such as Hawkings' profession (e.g., "professor", "scientist") , age ("56"), and life events (e.g. "suffers from Lou Gehrig's Disease"). Note that because of the shallow approach taken, the third sentence in the summary of Figure 1 is not appropriate.

The summary is created with sentence fragments from the documents, which have been analysed by a number of natural language processing components. The main steps in the process are:

- First, a pool of candidate relevant sentences is identified in the input documents using a pattern-matching algorithm;
- Second, redundancy removal is carried out to eliminate from the pool sentences containing repeated information.
- Finally, the set of candidate sentences is reduced to match the required compression rate by a greedy sentence rejection mechanism;

As will be shown two components are crucial in the process: a coreference resolution algorithm which identifies all mentions of the same person in full and reduced form (e.g. pronoun) and a pattern matching mechanism which targets specific contexts in which a person is mentioned.

Hawking, 56, is the Lucasian Professor of Mathematics at Cambridge, a post once held by Sir Isaac Newton. Stephen Hawking, the Cambridge theoretical physicist who wrote "A Brief History of Time," said Thursday that women and scientists are the most important people of the 20th century. Hawking, a unified theory may not have a solution that is applicable all the time. Hawking, 56, suffers from Lou Gehrig's Disease, which affects his motor skills, and speaks by touching a computer screen that translates his words through an electronic synthesizers.

Fig. 1. Multi-document summary answering the question "Who is Stephen Hawking?"

2.1   Pre-processing

The system for text analysis uses tools for text structure identification, tokenization, sentence boundary detection, named entity recognition, and coreference resolution adapted from the GATE library [3] and from a generic system for text summarization [4]. Some functionalities of the summarization system rely on an implementation of the vector space model in which text spans are represented as vectors of weighted terms. Terms are weighted using the well-known *term frequency * inverse document frequency* weighting (see, e.g. [5]). Vectors of terms are produced for each sentence in the input documents as well as for full documents. The *cosine* measure in the vector space model is used to compute proximity values between different text units. In order to support redundancy detection, the system also computes n-grams for all the input documents. A *centroid* of the cluster of related documents is created in the vector space model (a vector of terms which is in the centre of the document vectors in the cluster) which is used during content selection (see [6]).

In addition to minor modifications to the ANNIE[1] sentence identification module, we have adapted the ANNIE named entity recogniser in the following way: because ANNIE relies on gazetteer lists and contextual rules to carry out name entity recognition, we create, on-the-fly, additional lists needed to identify the target entity in the text. These lists contain the full name of the target person and his/her last name. We also provide gender information to the named entity recogniser by identifying the gender of the target in the input set. Using the distribution of male and female pronouns in the person cluster, the system guesses the gender of the target entity (the most frequent gender). This information is very valuable during coreference resolution. During testing, this method identified the correct gender in 94% of the cases, assigned the "neutral" gender in 4% of the cases and made a mistake in 2% of the cases. This information is key for the coreference algorithm which uses information provided by the named entity recogniser to decide upon coreferent pronouns with the target.

A process of part-of-speech tagging and noun phrase chunking [7] is also applied, but no syntactic or semantic analysis is required in our system. These tools are also available in the GATE library.

2.2   Coreference Resolution

Coreference resolution, the identification of the referent of anaphoric expressions such as pronouns or definite expressions, is of major importance for natural language applications. It is particularly important in order to identify information about people as well as other types of entities. Because one cannot safely assume that sentences referring to a particular target will contain explicit mentions of the target ("Stephen Hawkings was born in..." vs "He was born in..."), a process of coreference resolution becomes essential. We rely on two processes for the identification of coreference in text: an orthographical name matcher and a pronominal coreferencer algorithm. The orthographical name matcher associates *names* in text based on a set of rules, typically the full name of a person is associated with a condensed version of the same name (e.g., "R. Rubin" and "Robert Rubin"). The pronominal coreferencer used in this work uses simple heuristic rules identified from the analysis of a corpus of newspaper articles and broadcast news [8], and so it is well adapted for our task. The method assigns salience values to potential antecedents within a three sentence window based on the heuristic rules and then chooses as antecedent of an anaphoric expression the candidate with the best value. The reported accuracy of the algorithm is an f-measure of 78.2 for third person personal pronouns. A post-hoc step identifies a coreference chain – the sequence of expressions within a single text referring to the same entity – for the target entity and marks each member of the chain with special feature values so that a pattern matching mechanism can be applied.

---

[1] The Information Extraction System provided as part of GATE.

3   Content Selection

In order to select sentence candidates to create an extract we rely on a number of patterns that have been proposed in the past to identify *descriptive phrases* in text collections [9]. The complete set of patterns used in the experiments described here are shown in Table 1 together with an example of text fragment matching the pattern. In the patterns, *dp* is a *descriptive phrase* that in [9] is taken as a noun phrase.

Our implementation of the patterns make use of coreference information so that *target* is *any* expression in text which is coreferent with sought person. The patterns in our system are implemented in JAPE (Java Annotation Pattern Engine), a pattern-matching engine provided with GATE, to identify and annotate regular expressions over annotations. In order to implement the *dp* element in the patterns we use the information provided by the noun phrase chunker [7].

Table 1. Set of patterns for identifying profile information

Patterns	Example
target (is | was |...) (a | an | the) dp	Gen. Clark is a superv commandant...
target, (who | whose | ...)	Glass, who has written...
target, (a | the | one ...) dp	Sonia Ghandi, the Italian-born widow...
target, dp	Hawkings, 56...
target's	Darforth's law offices...
target and other	Reno and other federal officials...

The process of content selection is simple: a sentence is considered a candidate for the extract if it matches a pattern. We perform sentence compression by removing from each candidate sentence the longest suffix which does not match a pattern. The selected sentences are sorted according to their similarity to the centroid of the input cluster of documents referring to the target person. In order to filter out redundant information, we use an n-gram similarity detection metric. Our approach is shallow in that we use a metric for identifying similar content that relies on n-gram overlap between text units. The n-gram based similarity metric between two text fragments T_1 and T_2 is computed as follows:

$$\sum_{k=1}^{n} w_k * \frac{|grams(T_1,k) \cap grams(T_2,k)|}{|grams(T_1,k) \cup grams(T_2,k)|}$$

where n means that all n-grams 1, 2, ... n are to be considered, $grams(T,k)$ is the set of k-grams of fragment T, and w_k is the weight associated with the k-gram similarity of two sets.

A pattern-matched sentence is included in a list of candidate sentences if it is *different* from all other candidates in the list. In order to implement such a procedure, a threshold for our n-gram similarity metric has to be established so that one can decide whether two sentences contain different information. Such a threshold can be obtained if one has a corpus annotated with sentences known to be different. As such a corpus is not available to us, we make the hypothesis that in a given document all sentences will report different information, therefore we can use the n-gram similarity values between them to help estimate a similarity threshold. We computed pairwise n-gram similarity values between sentences in documents and have estimated a threshold for dissimilarity as the average of the pairwise similarity values. The redundancy removal algorithm is given in Algorithm 1. It takes as input the list of candidate sentences and the similarity threshold and returns a reduced list of sentences which are further reduced until the required compression is reached (see Section 4).

Algorithm 1. Creating the candidate list of sentences

Given: L1: list of pattern-based sentences sorted by similarity to the cluster centroid; THR: a similarity threshold
begin
candidates ← []
for all sentence$_i$ ∈ L1 **do**
    similar ← false
    for all sentence$_j$ ∈ candidates **do**
        if ngram_similarity(sentence$_i$,sentence$_j$) > THR **then**
            similar ← true
        end if
    end for
    if not similar **then**
        candidates ← candidates ∪ sentence$_i$
    end if
end for
return candidates
end

4   Greedy Sentence Removal

Most sentence extraction algorithms work in a constructive way: given a document and a sentence scoring mechanism, the algorithm ranks sentences by score, and then chooses sentences from the ranked list until a compression rate is reached. We take a different approach which consists in removing sentences from a pool of candidate sentences until the desired compression is achieved. The question is, given that an exhaustive search in implausible, how to reduce the given candidate set so that the content is optimal. The algorithm used can be seen in Algorithm 2. It follows a similar approach to Marcu's algorithm [10] for the creation of extracts from pairs of $< document, abstracts >$. In his approach clauses from the document are greedily deleted in order to obtain an extract which is maximally similar to the abstract. In our case, as we do not have an oracle that gives us the ideal abstract we want to construct, we assume that the candidate list of sentences which refers to the person target is the ideal content to include in the final summary.

Given a set of sentences C which covers "essential" information about a person, the algorithm creates an extract which is "close" in content to C but which is reduced in form. The measure of proximity between documents is

---

Algorithm 2. reduce algorithm

Given:
(a) profile_vector (a vector of terms)
(b) extract (a document extract)
(c) compression (an integer)
begin
if size of extract $\leq$ compression **or** extract has only one sentence **then**
   return extract
else
   /* VAL is an array of reals */
   for all sentence$_i$ $\in$ extract **do**
      DOC $\leftarrow$ extract \ sentence$_i$
      VEC $\leftarrow$ create_vector(DOC)
      VAL[i] $\leftarrow$ cosine(VEC,profile_vector)
   end for
   /* get the index which makes the pseudo document more similar to the sought profile */
   k $\leftarrow$ argmax(VAL)
   return reduce(profile_vector, (extract \ sentence$_k$),compresion);
end if
end

---

taken to be the cosine between two term vectors representing the documents (as in an information retrieval context). At each step, the algorithm greedily rejects a sentence from the extract. The rejected sentence is one which if removed from the extract produces a pseudo-document which is maximally close to C among all other possible pseudo-documents. The algorithm is first called with a vector of terms created from the candidate list of sentences obtained using Algorithm 1, and a given compression rate. Note that summarisation by sentence rejection has a long history in text summarisation: it has been used in the ADAM system [11] to reject sentences based on a cue-word list, and also in the British Library Automatic Abstracting Project (BLAB) in order to exclude sentences with dangling anaphora which cannot be resolved in context [12].

5   Experiments

The data used in the experiments reported here is the DUC 2004 Task 5 data which consists of 50 "Who is X?" questions and 50 document clusters (one per question): each cluster contained around 10 documents from news agencies. For each of the clusters in the data set, human analysts have created ideal or referent summaries against which the peer (system) summaries are compared. In order to take advantage of the document markups, we have transformed the original documents into XML in such a way that the processing components can concentrate on the textual information of the document alone. Given the question target and the document cluster we have created 665-byte long summaries following the method described in this paper. We have followed the method used in DUC 2004 to evaluate the content of the automatic summaries and have compared our system against other algorithms.

5.1   Evaluation Metrics

Since human evaluation requires human judgements and these are expensive to obtain, automatic evaluation metrics for summary quality have been the focus of research in recent years [13]. In particular, the Document Understanding Conferences have adopted ROUGE [14], a statistical method for automatic evaluation of summaries. ROUGE allows for the computation of recall-based metrics using n-gram matching between a *candidate summary* and a *reference set of summaries*.

The official DUC 2004 evaluation is based on six metrics ROUGE-N (N=1,2,3,4) based on n-gram matches, ROUGE-L, a recall metric based on the longest common subsequence match between peer and ideal summary, and ROUGE-W which is a weighted longest common subsequence that takes into account distances when applying the longest common subsequence. When multiple references are available in an evaluation, the ROUGE statistic is defined as the best score obtained by the summary when compared to each reference. Recent experiments have shown that some ROUGE scores correlate with rankings produced by humans [14]. In Tables 2 and 3 we show the ROUGE scores obtained by our system: **GBS**. Other systems are: 17 (CL Research), 24 (Laris Laboratory), 43 (Fudan University), 49 (Columbia University), 62 (Concordia University), 71 (NSA), 72 (NSA), and 109 (Language Computer Corporation).

5.2   Results and Discussion

According to ROUGE scores, our pattern-based summarizer consistently obtains the highest scores for all ROUGE metrics. The other algorithms are generally less consistent in ranking. System 49 is also rather consistent obtaining the second score for all metrics but ROUGE-4. In spite of these encouraging results, automatic methods are still far short of human performance in this task.

The patterns used in our system are rather simplistic and do not implement all the ways in which relevant information is expressed in text. For example, and unlike [15], our method ignores any sentences referring to important life events ("Desmond Tutu *won* the Nobel Prize..."). One method we are working on consists of inducing cue-word lists from newswire profiles as a means to identify such relevant information.

Table 2. ROUGE-1, ROUGE-2 and ROUGE-3 scores for the top four systems

System	ROUGE-1	System	ROUGE-2	System	ROUGE-3
GBS	0.34148	GBS	0.08322	GBS	0.03270
49	0.33790	49	0.08130	49	0.03119
71	0.33234	71	0.07959	109	0.03033
72	0.33161	72	0.07843	62	0.02953

Table 3. ROUGE-4, ROUGE-L, and ROUGE-W scores for the top four systems

System	ROUGE-4	System	ROUGE-L	System	ROUGE-W
GBS	0.01657	GBS	0.31150	GBS	0.13866
62	0.01507	49	0.30423	49	0.13595
109	0.01480	43	0.29458	43	0.13082
17	0.01449	24	0.29248	24	0.13049

6   Related Work

SUMMONS [16] was one of the first multi-document summarization systems in which summaries were produced not from text but from a set of templates instantiated by information extraction systems in the terrorism domain. One of the key components of that system which is relevant to the work presented here, is a knowledge base of person profiles which supports the summarizer in a process of generation of descriptions during summary generation. The database is populated from on-line sources by identifying descriptions using a set of linguistic patterns which represent pre-modifiers or appositions. Schiffman *et al.* [15] use corpus statistics together with linguistic knowledge to identify and weight descriptions of people to be included in a biography. Syntactic information is used to identify appositives describing people as well as sentences where the target person is the subject of the sentence. The mutual information statistic computed between verbs and subjects in a corpus is used to score and rank descriptions of the sought entity. Zhou *et al* [17] use similar content reduction techniques to our greedy rejection algorithm, however the initial content of the summary is identified by a sentence classifier trained over a corpus of annotated biographies. The classifier identifies sentences referring to different aspects of a person's life.

7   Conclusions and Future Work

In a context such as the Internet where any relevant event will be reported in multiple sources, summarization tools are of paramount importance. We have developed and evaluated an approach to multidocument summarization for generating biographical summaries based on a combination of symbolic and statistical techniques – this is an instance of the more general multidocument summarization problem. Our work uses available techniques for text analysis and generic (e.g. statistics) as well as specific (e.g. patterns) summarization components. The few patterns used in the experiments seem to work well, however they are far too simple and their coverage of relevant information is rather low when compared with that of humans in the same task. We have presented experiments in content selection using DUC 2004 data and demonstrated that our method ranks consistently higher than other methods in an automatic evaluation of content. Our future work concentrates on the study of techniques to improve the content of the summaries by incorporating non-stereotypical material through the exploitation of a cue-based feature which is being induced from a corpus of profiles from news wires.

Acknowledgements

We would like to thank three anonymous reviewers for their comments which helped us improve the final version of this paper. We are also grateful to Diana Maynard for proofreading the paper. We gratefully acknowledge the support of the UK Engineering and Physical Sciences Research Council, under research grant: R91465.

References

1. Mani, I.: Automatic Text Summarization. John Benjamins Publishing Company (2001)
2. Lacatusu, F., Hick, L., Harabagiu, S., Nezd, L.: Lite-GISTexter at DUC2004. In: Proceedings of DUC 2004, NIST (2004)
3. Cunningham, H., Maynard, D., Bontcheva, K., Tablan, V.: GATE: A framework and graphical development environment for robust NLP tools and applications. In: ACL 2002. (2002)
4. Saggion, H. and Bontcheva, K. and Cunningham, H.: Generic and Query-based Summarization. In: European Conference of the Association for Computational Linguistics (EACL) Research Notes and Demos, Budapest, Hungary, EACL (2003)
5. Baeza-Yates, R., Ribiero-Neto, B.: Modern Information Retrieval. ACM Press Books (1999)
6. Saggion, H., Gaizauskas, R.: Multi-document summarization by cluster/profile relevance and redundancy removal. In: Proceedings of the Document Understanding Conference 2004, NIST (2004)
7. Ramshaw, L., Marcus, M.: Text chunking using transformation-based learning. In Yarovsky, D., Church, K., eds.: Proceedings of the Third Workshop on Very Large Corpora, Somerset, New Jersey, Association for Computational Linguistics (1995) 82–94
8. Dimitrov, M., Bontcheva, K., Cunningham, H., Maynard, D.: A Light-weight Approach to Coreference Resolution for Named Entities in Text. In A. Branco, T.M., Mitkov, R., eds.: Anaphora Processing: Linguistic, Cognitive and Computational Modelling. John Benjamins Publishing Company (2004)
9. Joho, H., Sanderson, M.: Retrieving Descriptive Phrases from Large Amounts of Free Text. In: Proceedings of Conference on Information and Knoweldge Management (CIKM), ACM (2000) 180–186
10. Marcu, D.: The automatic construction of large-scale corpora for summarization research. In Hearst, M., F., G., Tong, R., eds.: Proceedings of SIGIR'99. 22nd International Conference on Research and Development in Information Retrieval, University of California, Beekely (1999) 137–144
11. Pollock, J., Zamora, A.: Automatic abstracting research at Chemical Abstracts Service. Journal of Chemical Information and Computer Sciences (1975) 226–233
12. Johnson, F.C., Paice, C.D., Black, W.J., Neal, A.: The application of linguistic processing to automatic abstract generation. Journal of Document & Text Management **1** (1993) 215–241

13. Saggion, H., Radev, D., Teufel, S., Lam, W.: Meta-evaluation of Summaries in a Cross-lingual Environment using Content-based Metrics. In: Proceedings of COLING 2002, Taipei, taiwan (2002) 849–855
14. Lin.C.-Y.: ROUGE: A Package for Automatic Evaluation of Summaries. In: Proceedings of the Workshop on Text Summarization, Barcelona, ACL (2004)
15. Schiffman, B., Mani, I., Concepcion, K.: Producing Biographical Summaries: Combining Linguistic Knowlkedge with Corpus Statistics. In: Proceedings of EACL-ACL. (2001)
16. Radev, D.R., McKeown, K.R.: Generating natural language summaries from multiple on-line sources. Computational Linguistics **24** (1998) 469–500
17. Zhou, L., Ticrea, M., Hovy, E.: Multi-document Biography Summarization. In: Proceedings of Empirical Methods in Natural Language Processing. (2004)

Constrained Atomic Term: Widening the Reach of Rule Templates in Transformation Based Learning

Cícero Nogueira dos Santos[1] and Claudia Oliveira[2]

[1] Departamento de Informática,
Pontifícia Universidade Católica, Rio de Janeiro, Brazil
`nogueira@inf.puc-rio.br`
[2] Departamento de Engenharia de Sistemas,
Instituto Militar de Engenharia, Rio de Janeiro, Brazil
`cmaria@de9.ime.eb.br`

Abstract. Within the framework of Transformation Based Learning (TBL), the rule template is one of the most important elements in the learning process. This paper presents a new model for TBL templates, in which the basic unit, denominated here as an atomic term (AT), encodes a variable sized window and a test that precedes the capture of a feature's value. A case study of Portuguese NP identification is described and the experimental results obtained are presented.

1 Introduction

During the last decade Machine Learning (ML) has proven to be a very powerful tool to enable linguistic tasks which would otherwise require an unfeasible amount of time and human resources. ML has been applied to central Natural Language Processing (NLP) problems such as: part-of-speech tagging, word-sense disambiguation, shallow parsing and prepositional phrase attachment ambiguity resolution. The most used ML techniques for these types of learning tasks are Hidden Markov Models, Maximum Entropy Models, Support Vector Machines, Memory Based Learning and Transformation Based Learning (TBL).

Within the TBL framework, the rule template is one of the most important elements in the learning process. This paper presents a new model for TBL templates, in which the basic unit, denominated here as an atomic term (AT), encodes a variable sized window and a test that precedes the capture of a feature's value. The use of this type of AT assumes that an item's feature X should only be captured if another feature Y of the same item complies with a certain test condition.

The research work was initiated as an attempt to build a noun phrase (NP) chunker using TBL for Portuguese. In the initial stages, the framework set up by Ramshaw and Marcus in [1] was used, including the concept of base NP and the rule templates. The results obtained were considerably inferior, which lead

C. Bento, A. Cardoso, and G. Dias (Eds.): EPIA 2005, LNAI 3808, pp. 622–633, 2005.

to the investigation of the classification errors produced: a large proportion of them were preposition-related mis-taggings.

Indeed, NP identification in Portuguese involves prepositional phrase attachment as a major sub-task, which in turn requires greater flexibility in the manipulation of the context being observed during the learning process. The idea behind the extension in the TBL template model is to provide such flexibility, by enabling long distance dependencies to be learned.

The remainder of this paper is organized as follows: in Sect. 2 we present a brief overview of TBL; in Sect. 3 the concept of constrained atomic term is introduced; in Sect. 4 some details of the implementation of this new type of template component are shown; and Sect. 5 presents a case study of Portuguese NP identification, describing the experiments that were carried out and the results obtained.

2 Transformation Based Learning

Transformation Based error-driven Learning (TBL) is a very successful symbolic machine learning method, introduced by Eric Brill in 1992. It has since been used for several important linguistic tasks, such as part-of-speech (POS) tagging [2], parsing, prepositional phrase attachment [3] and phrase chunking [1,4,5], having achieved state-of-the-art performance in many of them.

The central idea of the TBL algorithm is to generate an ordered list of rules, which will correct tagging mistakes in the corpus, which have been produced by an initial guess. The application determines which linguistic feature will be learned, and this feature will be represented by a tag-set (in the case of POS, for instance, the POS tags). The requirements of the algorithm are:

- two instances of a corpus, one that has been correctly annotated with the feature's tag-set, and another that remains un-annotated;
- an initial tagger, the baseline system, which will tag the un-annotated corpus by trying to guess the correct classification of each token, based on the annotated corpus's statistics; and
- a set of rule templates, which are meant to capture the relevant feature combinations, in the neighbourhood of a token, which would determine the tag of that token. Concrete rules are acquired by instantiation of this predefined set of template rules.

The learning algorithm is a mistake-driven greedy procedure that iteratively acquires a set of transformation rules. Figure 1 shows the rule generation process in TBL.

Learning starts with the initial guess classification of the un-annotated training corpus by the baseline system. The resulting classification is compared with the correct one and, whenever a classification error is found, all the rules that can correct it are generated by instantiating the templates with the current token's context. Normally, a new rule will correct tagging errors, but will also generate some other errors by changing correctly tagged tokens. Therefore, after computing the rules' scores (errors repaired − errors created) the best scoring rule will be selected and stored in order of generation. This rule is applied to the corpus, and the rule generation process will re-start until it fails to produce a rule with a score above an arbitrary threshold. For practical purposes, this minimum score can be tuned to reduce learning time and to avoid overfitting to the training data. The resulting sequence of rules is to be applied in order of generation when annotating a new text.

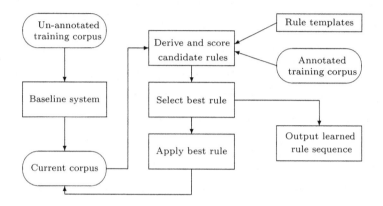

Fig. 1. Transformation based error-driven learning

The most attractive property of TBL is that the learned rules are interpretable by humans. Furthermore, the lists of rules tend to be more economical than the output of a stochastic tagger. As Brill [2] points out, 200 TBL rules trained on 64,000 words resulted in comparable tagging accuracy to a set of 10,000 contextual probabilities emitted by a stochastic tagger.

TBL's disadvantages are mostly time-performance related. The learning algorithm can be unfeasible time consuming for certain tasks, but it can be improved in a number of ways (see [6]) including rule indexing [7], which we used to implement our chunker. Similarly, the application of the learned rules can be improved, as shown in [8,9].

3   Constrained Atomic Term

Context rules generated by TBL have the following general format:

$$\langle p_1 \rangle = val_1 \ \ \langle p_2 \rangle = val_2 \ \ ... \ \ \langle p_n \rangle = val_n \ \rightarrow \ \langle ftr \rangle = val$$

To the left of the arrow a conditional expression is understood as the conjunction of pairs $\langle p_i \rangle = val_i$ where p_i is an AT and val_i is a valid value for it. To the right of the arrow, the value val is being associated with the feature $\langle ftr \rangle$. A rule is applicable to an item s in the corpus (target item) if $ftr \neq val$ for s and the conditional expression is true, which is verified by substituting feature values of items in the vicinity of the target item for the terms $\langle p_i \rangle$. If a rule is applicable, then the association $\langle ftr \rangle = val$ can be made.

The TBL method generates rules based on templates that determine the possible types of conditional expressions. In the pairs $(AT, value)$, AT defines the item and the corresponding feature that during the learning process will be captured in $value$ to compose the rule. Therefore, a template is simply a sequence of ATs $\langle p_1 \rangle$ $\langle p_2 \rangle$ $\langle p_3 \rangle$ ... $\langle p_n \rangle$.

In the TBL applications that have been reported in the literature, the ATs for context rules[1] are, in general, of type (a) and (b) as follows:

(a) **ftr_index**: captures the feature ftr of an item, the position of which is $index$ items to the left or to the right of the target item. Examples of such patterns are: $word\_0$, representing feature $word$ of the target item; $tpos\_-1$ and $tpos\_2$ representing $tpos$ (part-of-speech tag) of items "one to the left" and "two to the right" of the target item, respectively.

(b) **ftr [$begin\_index$; end_index]**: captures the feature ftr in an interval of items positioned between $begin\_index$ and end_index, in relation to the target item. An example of an AT for such a pattern is $word[1; 3]$, which captures a determined lexical unit within items in positions $+1$, $+2$ and $+3$ in relation to the target item.

The following template is formed using such AT patterns, where tnp is a feature indicating the Ramshaw and Marcus's [1] IOB tagset:

$$tnp\_ - 1 \quad tnp\_0 \quad word[1; 3]$$

Such a template may be instantiated so as to form the following rule:

$$tnp\_ - 1 = I \quad tnp\_0 = O \quad word[1; 3] = of \quad \rightarrow \quad tnp = I$$

that should be read as, "**If** $tnp\_ - 1 = I$ **and** $tnp\_0 = O$ **and** $word[1; 3] = of$ **Then** $tnp\_0 = O$" (**If** the value of the previous item's feature tnp is I **and** the value of the target item's feature tnp is O **and** the feature $word$ of one of the three items to the right of the target item is "of" **Then** change the value of target item's feature tnp to I.

The types of TA (a) and (b) are suitable when the width of the context window – where the information leading to the right classification is to be found – is well delimited and relatively narrow. Empirically, this window is seven items wide, including the target item, three items to the left and three to the right of the target. This type of template is not adequate for certain NLP problems where the classification depends on items with varying distances between them.

The identification of NPs that include prepositions is such a problem. More complex than *NP chunking*, it involves prepositional phrase attachment, which is a question of distinguishing whether the preposition is introducing the complement of a verb and should be classified as out of the complementing NP,

---

[1] Morphological rules in part of speech tagging may present variations to the types described.

or whether it is introducing the complement of a noun and should be included within the corresponding NP with the preceding noun. The followin example illustrates this point. The verb "pedimos" subcategorizes the preposition "para" in Brazilian Portuguese. Thus, the phrase "a chave da porta da cozinha para o Beto" is precluded as a chunk. This is a case when the seven items wide context window is insufficient.

a)   Pedimos $_{NP}$[a chave da porta da cozinha]$_{NP}$ para $_{NP}$[o Beto]$_{NP}$
b) * Pedimos $_{NP}$[a chave da porta da cozinha   para   o Beto]$_{NP}$
     We asked   the kitchen door key   to   Beto.

The most prominent idea that arises from this description of the NP identification problem is to enable the verification of a possible dependency between the preposition to be classified and the preceding verb. In order to do this, the following obstacles related to ATs (a) and (b) have to be overcome:

(1) While conditional expressions are being generated with ATs (a) and (b), the value of the feature is captured regardless of any pre-condition over the corresponding item, except its distance from the target item. The format of these templates is inadequate for defining an AT that captures the indicated value only if a certain condition is met by the item. For instance, it is not possible to define an AT that captures the lexical unit of an item (feature *word*) enforcing the condition that it is a preposition (feature $tpos = PREP$); and otherwise prevents the rule from being created.

(2) Since the exact distance between the preposition and the preceding verb is not known it is not possible to use an AT of type (a) to try to link them. Assuming that the preceding verb is found inside an arbitrary sized window, using an AT of type (b) would entail the production of many unnecessary rules, which would be a waste of memory and time resources during the learning phase. The wider the window, the larger the number of undesirable rules that will be created. If the verb is outside the reach of the interval, then the relationship between preposition and verb will not be established.

In order to overcome such difficulties, we propose a new type of AT, the constrained AT, introducing a variable sized window and a test that precedes the capture of the feature's value. The use of this type of AT assumes that an item's feature X should only be captured if another feature Y of the same item complies with a certain test condition. In principle, this test is the equality between the feature and a pre-defined value. The proposed format for this AT is as follows:

$$ftrX\ [begin\_index; end\_index](ftrY = valY)$$

An example of AT with this pattern is:

$$word[-2; -8](tpos = V)$$

It should be interpreted as "Capture feature *word* of the item nearest to the target item, within the closed interval of -2 and -8, for which the feature *tpos* equals V".

With this type of AT it is straightforward to construct a template that generates conditional expressions to link a preposition and its preceding verb, as in (T1).

$$word[0; 0](tpos = PREP) \quad word[-2; -10](tpos = V) \qquad \text{(T1)}$$

Consider the following sentence:

O/ART/I aluno/N/I esqueceu/V/O o/ART/I caderno/N/I de/PREP/I caligrafia/N/I amarelo/ADJ/O em/PREP/I casa/N/I

translated word for word as "The student left the notebook of calligraphy yellow at home". The annotation contains two errors: "amarelo" should be tagged as "I" (in the NP "o caderno de caligrafia amarelo"); and "em" should be tagged as "O" (outside that NP). The application of template (T1) to the sentence would generate only the following rule:

$$word[0; 0](tpos = PREP) =\text{em} \quad word[-2; -10](tpos = V) =\text{esqueceu} \quad \rightarrow \quad tnp=O$$

The rule is to be read as: "**If** for the target item (index 0) the features $tpos$=PREP **and** $word$=em, **and** $word$=esqueceu, for the first item in the closed interval [-2;-10] complying with the test $tpos$=V, **Then** change the value of feature tnp to O for the target item".

The proposed type of AT increases the specification power of the rule templates considerably. As shown by the above example, it is possible to specify rules having application restricted to specific items and also generate rules that, even when considering a very wide context, take into consideration only those elements that are important to the problem at hand. An example of the application of constrained ATs to the identification of NPs in Portuguese is described in section 5. More details about constrained ATs can be found in [10].

4   Implementation of Constrained AT

In order to implement the TBL tool proposed in this work, the version of the TBL algorithm presented by Ngai and Florian [7], the *FastTBL* algorithm, was chosen. The choice was motivated by the fact that fastTBL is much faster than the original TBL algorithm, while maintaining the same efficacy in results.

In implementing the constrained ATs, the principal difference is in the procedure for capturing the features indicated by the rule template ATs, in the generation as well as in the application of the rules. No alterations were made in relation to the algorithm presented in [7], given that it does not fully indicate the way in which the rules should be generated or applied.

The act of observing an item in the corpus and obtaining the value of a given feature of that item shall be designated as *feature capture*. This procedure is necessary in two separate instants during the computation: during the generation of each rule, for instantiating the template in the creation of the rule's conditional expression; and during the application of a rule, for capturing the values of the features in the items inside the context specified by the rule and thus verifying whether the context complies with the conditional expression.

When an AT is used without testing, as in $word_- - 2$ for instance, capturing the feature is carried out directly, that is, it is only necessary to access the item in the context with the specified distance of -2 and then capturing the value of $word$, if it exists. In the case of an AT without constraint of the type $word[-1, -3]$, it is necessary to scan the whole interval and to generate an instance for each item found therein.

However, when the feature indicated by a constrained AT needs to be captured as in:

$$featureX[begin\_index;end\_index](featureY{=}valY),$$

then it is not sufficient to compute the distance and directly capture the feature of the item. It is also necessary to ensure that the item complies with the test, that is, make sure that the value of $featureY$ is equal to $valY$.

Function get_feature(w: array, i: integer, $ATerm$: Atomic Term) {

Let w be a sentence represented by a vector with n positions, each position containing an item of the sentence;

Let i be the index in w of the current target item;

Let $featureX$ be the feature to be captured and let $featureY$ be the feature to be tested with value $valY$ pre-defined in $ATerm$;

Let ini and fin be integers representing the interval range to be looked into;

Let $desloc$ be an integer representing the distance from the target item i;

$desloc = ini + i$;

While ($desloc > 0$ **and** $desloc < n + 1$ **and** $absolute(ini) < absolute(fin)$)

    If the value of $featureY == valY$ for the item of w

    with position $desloc$ **Then**

        Return value of $featureX$ for the item of w

        with position $desloc$;

    $desloc = \pm 1$;

    $ini = \pm 1$;

If ($absolute(ini) < absolute(fin)$) **Then**

    Return "ZZZ";

Return $null$;

}

Fig. 2. Algorithm for capturing the feature indicated by a constrained AT

The function $get\_feature$, shown in Figure 2, implements the procedure that captures $featureX$ of a constrained AT. The function takes as input: an array w that represents a sentence in the corpus; an integer i that indicates the index of the target item in the sentence; and the AT to be used. This algorithm scans all items in the sentence w belonging to the interval defined in the AT, checking whether $featureY$ of the item being scanned complies with the test (*featureY=valY*). The value of *featureX* of the first item that tests positively will be captured and returned by the function. During the scan, upon reaching one of the limits of the sentence, the value "*ZZZ*" is returned. If the interval is fully scanned and no item satisfying the test is found, a *null* value is returned and the AT will not be instantiated. This function may be used to capture the features of constrained ATs, both in the creation and in the application of a rule.

5 Case Study: Application of Constrained ATs in the Identification of Portuguese NP

5.1 Portuguese NPs vs. English Base NPs

The task of identifying English NPs using machine learning techniques has been normally associated with the concept of *base NP*, defined by Ramshaw and Marcus in [1] as a non-recursive NP, including determiners but not including post-modifying prepositional phrases or clauses.

In Portuguese this notion provides a very poor set of NPs. Let us consider the following example of base NP and its Portuguese translation.

$_{NP}$[the first Government drug manufacturing plant]$_{NP}$
$_{NP}$[a primeira planta de $_{NP}$[fabricação de $_{NP}$[remédios do $_{NP}$[governo]]]]

The translation has necessarily four nested NPs and it is a very common construction that has to be extracted as such. Thus, for the Portuguese language, it is necessary to consider nested (recursive) NPs as opposed to base NPs. For this reason the task has been re-defined as the extraction of NPs with post-modifying prepositional phrases and adjectives but excluding post-modifiers containing subordinate clauses. Thus, according to this model, the previous example in Portuguese would comprise a single NP, as follows:

$_{NP}$[a primeira planta de fabricação de remédios do governo]$_{NP}$

As a result, the classification task becomes more difficult than the identification of base NPs since it includes the problem of prepositional phrase attachment. The usual seven items context window is not sufficient anymore.

5.2 Encoding Choices

We used the same NP tagset as Ramshaw and Marcus [1]: I, for in NP; O, for out of NP; B for the leftmost word of an NP beginning immediately after another NP. Henceforth, we will refer to these as NP tags.

5.3 Training and Test Data

The training and test corpora used in this study were derived from the Mac-Morpho corpus [11], containing 1.1 million words taken from one year of publication (1994) of the Brazilian newspaper Folha de São Paulo, which can be obtained on the Web at http://www.nilc.icmc.usp.br/lacioweb/, as of October 2004. The corpus is annotated with POS tags in the Lacio-Web (LW) Tagset. The corpus was chosen because it consists of Brazilian Portuguese texts of sufficient quantity for the training task, and because the LW tagset was developed to provide a simplified tagset that guarantees such requirements as recoverability, consistency and adaptability to automated learning of POS tagging.

Fig. 3 shows the format of the Mac-Morpho files. In total, there are 109 files, all with line breaks between each word and POS tags indicated by an underscore.

```
O_ART time_NPROP está_V quase_ADV rebaixado_PCP para_PREP a_ART
segunda_ADJ divisão_N ._.
```

Fig. 3. Mac-Morpho file sample

For the derivation of the corpora we used the parser PALAVRAS [12], to obtain the parsing of the whole Mac-Morpho corpus and from there we developed an interpreter to identify, from the parser's output, the NPs boundaries. Note that NPs containing subordinate clauses or commas were not included.

We created a training corpus, with 200K token, containing all the news sections in the newspaper included in Mac-Morpho. The test corpus has approximately 50K tokens. Fig. 4 shows a sample of the resulting training corpus.

```
O_ART_I time_NPROP_I está_V_O quase_ADV_O rebaixado_PCP_O para_PREP_O
a_ART_I segunda_ADJ_I divisão_N_I ._._O
```

Fig. 4. Training corpus sample

Another interesting point is that all verbs present in the corpus were rewritten in the infinitive form.

5.4   Baseline System

The baseline system provides an initial class assignment. In our case, this means a baseline assignment of NP tags to the words in the corpus. We have used a baseline system to assign to each word the NP tag that was most frequently associated with the part-of-speech of the word. The only exception was the initial classification of the prepositions, which was done on an individual basis: each preposition had its frequency individually measured and the NP tag was assigned accordingly, in a lexicalized method. This procedure generates fewer errors and reduces the training time.

5.5   Rule Templates

For the task of identifying English base NPs with TBL, Ramshaw & Marcus [1] used a set of rule templates with 100 patterns formed by ATs that make reference to combinations of NP tags with lexical units and combinations of NP tags with POS tags. The rules that are generated by such a set of templates have a context window of at most seven items.

The experiments were carried out in order to compare the performance of the constrained ATs in relation to other types of ATs. To cover the case of NP identification in Portuguese, including the prepositional phrase attachment problem, we trained a TBL tool using the following three separate sets of templates:

(C1) the Ramshaw & Marcus's templates set described previously;

(C2) an extended version of C1, where all ATs having an interval [-1,-3] and [1,3], were widened to [-1,-6] e [1,6], respectively, with the addition of a further 18 templates that make reference to the features *tnp* and *tpos* in a local context, and to the feature *word* in a context of up to 8 items to the right and to the left;

(C3) a set consisting of the 80 templates from Ramshaw & Marcus that do not contain ATs of the type *ftr*[*begin_index*; *end_index*], together with 6 other models specifically designed to classify prepositions, as shown in Figure 5. Those 6 templates were modeled to check some items in the context that might contribute with information to the resolution of prepositional phrase attachments, linking the preposition to the preceding verb or to the first preceding lexical unit that is outside a NP ("O" tag); and

(C4) a set consisting of the same 86 templates of C3, where the 6 templates containing constrained ATs were changed to contain only traditional ATs as shown in Figure 6.

1.	tnp_-1 tpos[0;0](tpos=PREP) word[-1;-20](tnp=O)
2.	tnp_-1 word[0;0](tpos=PREP) word[-1;-20](tnp=O)
3.	tnp_-1 tnp_1 tpos[0;0](tpos=PREP) word[-1;-20](tpos=V)
4.	tnp_-1 tnp_1 word[0;0](tpos=PREP) word[-1;-20](tpos=V)
5.	tnp_-1 tnp_1 tnp_0 tpos[0;0](tpos=PREP) word[-2;-20](tpos=V)
6.	tnp_-1 tnp_1 tnp_0 word[0;0](tpos=PREP) word[-2;-20](tpos=V)

Fig. 5. Templates, with constrained ATs, used for preposition tagging

1.	tnp_-1 tpos_0 word[-1;-20]
2.	tnp_-1 word_0 word[-1;-20]
3.	tnp_-1 tnp_1 tpos_0 word[-1;-20]
4.	tnp_-1 tnp_1 word_0 word[-1;-20]
5.	tnp_-1 tnp_1 tnp_0 tpos_0 word[-2;-20]
6.	tnp_-1 tnp_1 tnp_0 word_0 word[-2;-20]

Fig. 6. Templates, without constrained ATs, used for preposition tagging

5.6 Experimental Results

A summary of the results of the experiments with the Portuguese corpus are shown in this section, in terms of token-by-token accuracy (# of correctly tagged tokens/# of tokens), NP precision (# of correctly identified NPs/# of identified NPs), NP recall (# of correctly identified NPs/# of NPs in the corpus) and NP F-measure ($F_{\beta=1} = (\beta^2 + 1) * Precision * Recall/\beta^2 * Precision + Recall$).

The results of the application to the test corpus of the rules generated during the training phase, using the training corpus and the sets of templates C1, C2, C3 and C4, are shown in the Table 1. In these tables, the fifth row indicates the number of prepositions that were wrongly tagged in the test corpus.

Table 1. NPs identification results using the four different template sets

Measure	Template set C1	Template set C2	Template set C3	Template set C4
Accuracy	96.85%	96.93%	**97.17%**	96.85%
Recall	82.9%	83.3%	**84.6%**	83.1%
Precision	83.0%	83.4%	**85.2%**	82.7%
$F_{\beta=1}$	83.0%	83.4%	**84.9%**	82.9%
NEP[1]	703	716	**591**	716

[1]NEP: Number of errors in prepositions

Comparing the columns of Table 1, it can be seen that the best results were obtained using the set of templates containing constrained ATs (template set C3). There was an improvement of nearly 2% of $F_{\beta=1}$ over the experiments using template sets C1 and C4, and an improvement of 1.5% over the experiments using template set C2.

In terms of preposition tagging error reduction, the results show that the greater expressive power of the rules containing constrained ATs has indeed helped to significantly decrease this specific type of error. The deciding factor was that the 6 templates containing constrained ATs were focused on prepositions only, using a widened context but limiting the collection of information to that relevant to the problem of prepositional phrase attachment. Using template set C3, the reduction on preposition tagging errors was 16%, 17.5% and 17,5% over template sets C1, C2 and C4, respectively.

Another advantages of constrained ATs were observed in the experiments using template sets C3 and C4. Using template set C3, the training time was 7 times faster than using the set C4, and the rule set created from templates with constrained ATs was very small than the one created from templates without constrained ATs. These results validate our affirmation about difficulties in the use of traditional ATs to construct rules involving variable sized and wider context, and shows that constrained ATs can help to overcome these difficulties.

6   Concluding Remarks

The constrained ATs have shown to be a suitable mechanism to deal with NLP classification problems requiring variable sized, or simply wider, contexts. They can also be used to generate rules that correct specific errors. The templates containing constrained ATs have been more efficient then the templates containing only the customary types of ATs with respect to accuracy, precision, recall and training time. The experiments of Portuguese NP identification reported here involve prepositional phrase attachment, which is an essential part of NP identification in Romance languages.

We believe that further tests with other combinations of templates specifically for the correction of preposition tagging errors should result in greater improvements, considering the number of error is still high.

References

1. Ramshaw, L., Marcus, M.: Text chunking using transformation-based learning. In Yarovsky, D., Church, K., eds.: Proceedings of the Third Workshop on Very Large Corpora, New Jersey, USA, ACL (1995) 82–94
2. Brill, E.: Transformation-based error-driven learning and natural language processing: A case study in part-of-speech tagging. Computational Linguistics **21** (1995) 543–565
3. Brill, E., Resnik, P.: A rule-based approach to prepositional phrase attachment disambiguation. In: Proceedings of COLING'94, Kyoto, Japan (1994)
4. Florian, R., Henderson, J., Ngai, G.: Coaxing confidence from an old friend: Probabilistic classifications from transformation rule lists. In: Proceedings of Joint Sigdat Conference on EMNLP/VLC, Hong Kong (2000)
5. Megyesi, B.: Shallow parsing with pos taggers and linguistic features. Journal of Machine Learning Research **2** (2002) 639–668
6. Hepple, M.: Independence and commitment:assumptions for rapid training and execution of rule-based pos taggers. In: Proceedings of the 38th Annual Meeting of the ACL, Hong Kong, Association for Computational Linguistics (2000) 278–285
7. Ngai, G., Florian, R.: Transformation-based learning in the fast lane. In: Proceedings of North American Chapter of the ACL. (2001) 40–47
8. Satta, G., Brill, E.: Efficient transformation-based parsing. In: Proceedings of the 34th conference on Association for Computational Linguistics, California, USA, Association for Computational Linguistics (1996) 255–262
9. Roche, E., Schabes, Y.: Deterministic part-of-speech tagging with finite-state transducers. Computational Linguistics **21** (1995) 227–253
10. Santos, C.N.: Aprendizado de máquina na identificação de sintagmas nominais: o caso do português brasileiro. Master's thesis, IME, Rio de Janeiro - RJ (2005)
11. Marchi, A.R.: Projeto lacio-web: Desafios na construção de um corpus de 1,1 milhão de palavras de textos jornalísticos em português do brasil. In: 51° Seminário do Grupo de Estudos Lingüísticos do Estado de São Paulo, São Paulo, Brasil (2003)
12. Bick, E.: The Parsing System Palavras: Automatic Grammatical Analysis of Portuguese in a Constraint Grammar Framework. PhD thesis, Aarhus University (2000)

Improving Passage Retrieval in Question Answering Using NLP

Jörg Tiedemann

Alfa Informatica, University of Groningen,
Groningen, The Netherlands
j.tiedemann@rug.nl
http://www.let.rug.nl/~tiedeman

Abstract. This paper describes an approach for the integration of linguistic information in passage retrieval in an open-source question answering system for Dutch. Annotation produced by the wide-coverage dependency parser Alpino is stored in multiple index layers to be matched with natural language question that have been analyzed by the same parser. We present a genetic algorithm to select features to be included in retrieval queries and for optimizing keyword weights. The system is trained on questions annotated with their answers from the competition on Dutch question answering within the Cross-Language Evaluation Forum (CLEF). The optimization yielded a significant improvement of about 19% in mean reciprocal rank scores on unseen evaluation data compared to the base-line using traditional information retrieval with plain text keywords.

1 Introduction

Question Answering (QA) systems aim at locating answers to natural language questions in large document collections. This is usually achieved using a combination of Information Extraction (IE) and Information Retrieval (IR) components. Natural Language Processing (NLP) and linguistic resources are frequently used in QA systems, see e.g. [1,2], although not very often for the retrieval component (some exceptions are [3,4,5]). Using NLP in information retrieval has been the goal for many researchers. However, it has been argued that NLP tools are still to brittle and inefficient to be used in information retrieval [4]. Several experiments using NLP techniques have been reported in the literature, e.g. lemmatization and compound splitting [6,7,8,9,10], query term selection and weighting [11,12], extraction of noun phrases and other linguistically motivated units [13,14,3]. However, most of the studies using deep linguistic analyses resulted in only little success or even decreasing performance, see, e.g., [15,16]. Simple techniques such as stemming and stop word removal seem to be much more effective than more sophisticated techniques at least for languages with relatively poor morphological variation. However, in [4], the authors show that syntactic analyses can be very useful for retrieval performance in QA when selected carefully. They argue that NLP technology should only be used in cases where we know that

C. Bento, A. Cardoso, and G. Dias (Eds.): EPIA 2005, LNAI 3808, pp. 634–646, 2005.
© Springer-Verlag Berlin Heidelberg 2005

they are helpful without abandoning simpler techniques. Along these lines we like to use deep syntactic analyses in the retrieval component of our QA system in such a way that we select features and feature combinations that have shown to improve the performance. In contrast to [4], we do not investigate selected linguistic phenomena but a whole spectrum of natural language questions as defined by the Cross-Language Evaluation Forum (CLEF) in their question answering track. This paper describes an iterative learning approach for feature selection and query optimization.

The next section includes a brief description of our retrieval component in our question answering system. Thereafter the query optimization algorithm is described followed by experimental results using questions from the CLEF competitions on Dutch QA.

2   Question Answering with Dependency Relations

In our investigations we focus on open-domain question answering for Dutch. The system we are building, [17], consists of two streams: a table look-up strategy using off-line information extraction and an on-line strategy using passage retrieval and on-the-fly answer extraction. In both strategies we use syntactic information produced by a wide-coverage dependency parser for Dutch, Alpino [18]. In the off-line strategy we use syntactic patterns to extract information from unrestricted text to be stored in fact tables [19]. For the on-line strategy, we assume that there is a certain overlap between syntactic relations in the question and in passages containing the answers. Hence, the entire document collection has to be parsed to apply syntactic patterns for off-line information extraction and to match questions to possible answers. The corpus provided by CLEF contains about 1.1 million paragraphs that include altogether about 4 million sentences. They have been parsed by Alpino and stored in XML tree structures (about 0.35% of the sentences could not be analyzed because of parsing timeouts). Incoming questions are parsed in the same way. The system uses the analyzed questions to determine the question type and to formulate a query to the information retrieval component.[1] The parse tree and the question type are then used to locate possible answers in passages retrieved by IR. Information retrieval is used to reduce the search space for the answer extraction components to make it feasible to run on-line QA. Hence, the system relies on the passages retrieved by this component and fails if IR does not provide relevant documents containing answers.

Traditional IR uses a bag-of-word approach using plain text keywords to be matched with word-vectors describing documents. The result is a ranked list of documents. This approach will be our base-line (including Dutch stemming and stop word removal). In our system, we integrated an interface to several off-the-shelf IR engines. Here, we will use Lucene from the Apache Jakarta project [20].

---

[1] The table look-up strategy is used if the question type matches a table in the fact databases extracted off-line. Information retrieval and the on-line strategy is used if table look-up fails.

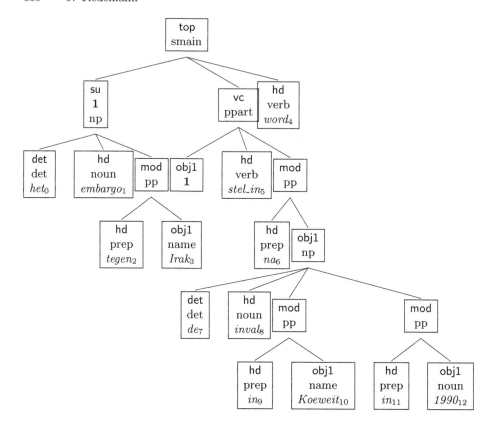

Fig. 1. A dependency tree produced by Alpino. (*Het embargo tegen Irak werd ingesteld na de inval in Koeweit in 1990.* (The embargo against Iraq has been declared after the invasion of Kuwait in 1990.))

The goal is now to incorporate linguistic information produced by the syntactic analyzer. Figure 1 shows a dependency tree produced for one of the sentences in the CLEF corpus. The first row in each box contains the relation name (e.g. 'su' for subjects, 'mod' for modifiers, 'obj1' for direct objects and 'hd' for the heads of dependency relations). The second row contains either the word class for leafs in the tree or syntactic phrase types for other nodes.

Lucene supports multiple index fields that can be filled with different kinds of data. This is a useful feature to store various kinds of information derived from parse trees in different fields in the index. The parser also produces part-of-speech (POS) tags, named-entity labels and linguistic roots (e.g. first person singular forms of verbs) besides of the dependency relations. It also recognizes compositional compounds and particle verbs. We like to include various combinations of linguistic features in the index to make it possible to check their impact on retrieval performance. Index fields can be seen as different *layers* of information describing passages in the corpus. We distinguish *token layers* containing certain features for each token in the passage, *type layers* containing certain word types

Table 1. Index layers

token layers		type layers	
text	plain text tokens	compound	compounds
root	root forms	ne	named entities
RootPOS	root form + POS tag	neLOC	location names
RootHead	root form + head	nePER	person names
RootRel	root form + relation name	neORG	organization names
RootRelHead	root form + relation + head		

occurring in the passage, and *annotation layers* containing labels included in the analysis of the passage. Table 1 lists token and type layers defined in our index.

The *text* layer is used for the base-line approach. It includes plain text keywords (stop words removed) stemmed with a Dutch stemmer. Combined features in token layers are simple concatenated using special delimiter symbols. For example, the *RootHead* layer contains concatenated dependent-head bigrams taken from the dependency relations in the tree. Compositional words (such as particle verbs and compounds) in the *root* layer have been split whereas the compound field contains compounds in a compositional form (this applies also to particle verbs and multi-word names). Type layers containing named entities include both, multi-word units in compositional and in split form. The only annotation layer in our index contains labels of named entities (ORG, PER, LOC) and special units such as temporal expressions (TMP, YEAR), measure units (MEASURE), and scores (SCORE). Table 2 shows an example of the contents of each index layer for one sentence from the corpus, namely the one from figure 1.[2]

3   Formulating Multi-layer Queries

Questions are also parsed with Alpino to get similar annotation as sentences in documents. An example parse tree for a question is shown in figure 2. Now we can extract appropriate units from analyzed questions to be matched with the various layers in the extended index. We can, e.g., extract root-head word pairs to query the RootHead layer. Furthermore, we can also use linguistic labels to restrict our query terms in several ways. For example, we can use part-of-speech labels to exclude keywords of a certain word class. We can also use the syntactic relation name to define query constraints. Each token layer can be restricted in this way (even if the feature used for restriction is not part of the layer). For example, we can limit our set of root keywords to *nouns* only even though part-of-speech labels are not part of the root layer. We can also combine constraints, for example, RootPOS keywords can be restricted to *nouns* that are in an *object* relation within the question.

---

[2] Note that stemming and stop word removal in the *text* layer is handled internally by Lucene. The table shows the input before sending it to the Lucene indexer, i.e. without stemming and including stop words.

Table 2. Example items in the multi-layer index

layer	contents
text	Het embargo tegen Irak werd ingesteld na de inval in Koeweit in 1990
root	het embargo tegen Irak word stel in na de inval in Koeweit in 1990
RootPOS	het/det embargo/noun tegen/prep Irak/name word/verb stel_in/verb na/prep de/det inval/noun in/prep Koeweit/name in/prep 1990/noun
RootHead	het/embargo embargo/word tegen/embargo Irak/tegen word/ stel_in/word na/stel_in de/inval inval/na in/inval Koeweit/in in/inval 1990/in
RootRel	het/det embargo/su tegen/mod Irak/obj1 word/ stel_in/vc na/mod de/det inval/obj1 in/mod Koeweit/obj1 in/mod 1990/obj1
RootRelHead	het/det/embargo embargo/su/word tegen/mod/embargo Irak/obj1/tegen word// stel_in/vc/word na/mod/stel_in de/det/inval inval/obj1/na in/mod/inval Koeweit/obj1/in in/mod/inval 1990/obj1/in
compound	stel_in
ne	Irak Koeweit
neLOC	Irak Koeweit
nePER	
neORG	
neTypes	LOC

Lucene also supports keyword weighting using so-called "boost factors". These factors can be any positive floating number and 1 is the default value. In other words, the importance of keywords can be reduced using values below 1 and increased using values above 1. Keywords can also be marked as "required" in Lucene's query language. Boost factors and required markers can be used with all kinds of keywords we have described so far.

The following list summarizes possible keyword types in our passage retrieval component:

basic: a keyword in one of the index layers

restricted: *token-layer* keywords can be restricted to a certain word class and/or a certain relation type. We use only the following word class restrictions: *noun, name, adjective, verb*; and the following relation type restrictions: *direct object, modifier, apposition* and *subject*

weighted: keywords can be weighted using a *boost factor*

required: keywords can be marked as required

Query keywords from all types can be combined into a single query. We simply connect them in a disjunctive way which is the default operation in Lucene. The query engine provides ranked query results and, therefore, each disjunction may contribute to the ranking of the retrieved documents but does not harm the query if it does not produce any matching results. We may, for example, form a query with the following elements: (1) all plain *text* tokens; (2) Named entities (*ne*) boosted with factor 2; (3) *RootHead* bigrams where the root is in an object

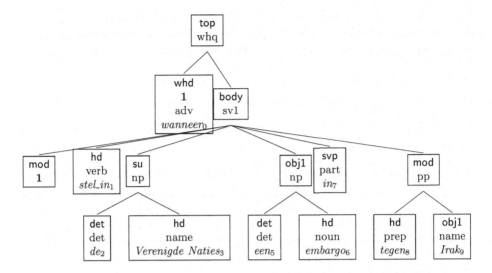

Fig. 2. A dependency tree for a question. (*Wanneer stelde de Verenigde Naties een embargo in tegen Irak ?* (When did the United Nations declare the embargo against Iraq?))

relation; (4) *RootRel* keywords for all nouns. Applying these parameters to the question in figure 2 we get the following query:[3]

```
text:(stelde Verenigde Naties embargo Irak)
ne:(Verenigde_Naties^2 Verenigde^2 Naties^2 Irak^2)
RootHead:(Irak/tegen embargo/stel_in) RootRel:(embargo/obj1)
```

Now, query terms from various keyword types may refer to the same index layer. For example, we may use weighted plain text keywords restricted to nouns together with unrestricted plain text keywords. To combine them we use a preference mechanism to keep queries simple and to avoid disjunctions with conflicting keyword parameters: (a) Restricted keyword types are more specific than basic keywords; (b) Keywords restricted in relation type *and* POS are more specific than keywords with only one restriction; (c) Relation type restrictions are more specific than POS label restrictions. Using these rules we define that weights of more specific keywords overwrite weights of less specific ones. Furthermore, we define that the "required-marker" ('+') overwrites keyword weights. Using these definitions we would get the following query if we add two elements to the query from above: (5) plain text keywords in an object relation with boost factor 3 and (6) plain text keywords labeled as names marked as required.

```
text:(stelde +Verenigde +Naties embargo^3 Irak^3)
ne:(Verenigde_Naties^2 Verenigde^2 Naties^2 Irak^2)
RootHead:(Irak/tegen embargo/stel_in) RootRel:(embargo/obj1)
```

---

[3] Note that stop words have been removed.

Finally, we can also use the question type determined by question analysis in the retrieval component. The question type corresponds to the expected answer type, i.e. we expect an entity of that type in the relevant text passages. In some cases, the question type can be mapped to one of the named entity labels assigned by the parser, e.g. a *name question* is looking for names of persons (ne = PER), a question for a *capital* is looking for a location (ne = LOC) and a question for organizations is looking for the name of an organization (ne = ORG). Hence, we can add another keyword type, the expected answer type to be matched with named entity labels in the *neTypes* layer.

There are many possible combinations of restrictions even with the small set of POS labels and relation types listed above. However, many of them are useless because they cannot be instantiated. For example, an adjective cannot appear in subject relation to its head. For simplicity we limit ourselves to the following eight combined restrictions (POS + relation type): names + {direct object, modifier, apposition, subject} and nouns + {direct object, modifier, apposition, subject}. These can be applied to all token layers in the same way as the other restrictions using single constraints.

Altogether we have 109 different keyword types using the layers and the restrictions defined above. Now the question is to select appropriate keyword types among them with the optimal parameters (weights) to maximize retrieval performance. The following section describes the optimization procedure used to adjust query parameters.

4   Query Optimization

In the previous sections we have seen the internal structure of the multi-layer index and the queries we use in our passage retrieval component. Now we have to address the question of selecting layers and keyword restrictions to optimize the performance of the system according to the QA task. For this we like to employ an automatic optimization procedure that learns appropriate parameter settings from example data. We use annotated training material from the CLEF competition on Dutch QA from the years 2003 and 2004. They contain natural language questions annotated with their answers found in the CLEF corpus (answer strings and IDs of documents in which the answer was found). Altogether there are 570 questions with 821 answers.[4]

For evaluation we used the mean reciprocal rank (MRR) of relevant paragraphs retrieved by IR:

$$MRR = \frac{1}{x} \sum_x \frac{1}{rank(first\_doc\_with\_answer)}$$

---

[4] Each question may have multiple possible answers. We also added some obvious answers which were not in the original test set when encountering them in the corpus. For example, names and numbers can be spelled differently (*Saoedi-Arabië* vs. *Saudi-Arabië*, *bijna vijftig jaar* vs. *bijna 50 jaar*).

We used the provided answer string rather than the document ID to judge if a retrieved paragraph was relevant or not. In this way, the IR engine may provide passages with correct answers from other documents than the ones marked in the test set. We do simple string matching between answer strings and words in the retrieved paragraphs. Obviously, this introduces errors where the matching string does not correspond to a valid answer in the context. However, we believe that this does not influence the global evaluation figure significantly and therefore we use this approach as a reasonable compromise when doing automatic evaluation.

4.1   A Genetic Algorithm for Parameter Optimization

As discussed earlier, there is a large variety of possible keyword types that can be combined to query the multi-layer index. Furthermore, we have a number of parameters to be set when formulating a query, e.g. the keyword weights. Selecting the appropriate keywords and parameters is not straightforward. We like to carry out a systematic search for optimizing parameters rather than using intuition. Here, we use the information retrieval engine as a black box with certain input parameters. We do not know how the ranking is done internally and how the output is influenced by parameter changes. However, we can inspect and evaluate the output of the system. Hence, we need an iterative approach for testing several settings to optimize query parameters. The output for each setting has to be evaluated according to a certain objective function. For this, we can use the MRR measure described above and the annotated CLEF question. Part of the annotated material is then used for training and another disjoint set is used for evaluation.

We decided to use a simplified genetic algorithm to optimize query parameters. This algorithm is implemented as an iterative "trial-and-error beam search" through possible parameter settings. The optimization loop works as follows:

1. Run initial queries (one keyword type per IR run) with default weights.
2. Produce a number of new settings by combining two previous ones (= *crossover*). For this, select two settings from an N-best list from the previous IR runs. Apply *mutation* operations (see next step) until the new settings are unique (among all settings we have tried so far).
3. Change some of the new settings at random (= *mutation*) using pre-defined mutation operations.
4. Run the queries using the new settings and evaluate the retrieval output (determine *fitness*).
5. Continue with 2 until some stop condition is satisfied.

This optimization algorithm is very simple but requires some additional parameters. First of all, we have to decide the size of the *population*, i.e. the number of IR runs (*individuals*) to be kept for the next iteration. We decided to keep the population small with only 25 individuals. *Natural selection* is simplified to a top-N search (using the MRR measure to determine fitness) without giving individuals with lower fitness values a chance to survive. This also means that we can update the population directly when a new IR run is finished without waiting for an entire new generation. We also have to set a maximum number of new settings to be created at a time. In our experiments we limit the process to a maximum of 50 settings that may be tried out simultaneously. A new setting is created as soon as there is a spot available.

An important part of the algorithm is the combination of parameters *crossover*. We simply merge the settings of two previous runs (*parents*) to produce a new setting (a *child*). That means that all keyword types (with their restrictions) from both parents are included in the child's setting. Parents are selected at random without any preference mechanism. We also use a very simple strategy in cases where both parents contain the same keyword type. In these cases we compute the arithmetic mean of the weight assigned to this type in the parents' settings (default weight is one). Furthermore, if the keyword type is marked as required in one of the parents, it will also be marked as required in the child's setting (discarding weights set to this keyword type in the other parent).

Another important principle in genetic optimization is *mutation*. It refers to a randomized modification of settings when new individuals are created. First, we apply mutation operations where new settings are not unique.[5] Secondly, mutation operations are applied with fixed probabilities to new settings.

In most genetic algorithms, settings are converted to genes consisting of bit strings. A common mutation operation is then defined as flipping the value of one randomly chosen bit. In our approach, we do not use bit strings but define several mutation operations to modify parameters directly. The following operations have been defined:

- a new keyword type is added to new settings with a chance of 0.2
- a keyword type is removed from the settings with a chance of 0.1
- a keyword weight is modified by a random value between -5 and 5 with a chance of 0.2 (but only if the weight remains a positive value)
- a keyword type is marked as required with a chance of 0.01

All these parameters are arbitrary and their influence on the optimization procedure should be investigated further in future work. We assigned rather high probabilities to the mutation operations to reduce the risk of local maximum traps. Note also that there is no obvious condition for termination. In randomized approaches like this one the development of the fitness score is most likely not monotonic and therefore, it is hard to predict when we should stop the optimization process. However, we expect the scores to converge at some point and we may stop if a certain number of new settings does not improve the scores anymore.

---

[5] We require unique settings in our implementation because we want to avoid recomputation of fitness values for settings that have been tried already. "Good" settings survive anyway using our top-N selection approach.

5   Experimental Results

From the CLEF data we selected a random set of 150 questions for evaluation and used the remaining 420 questions for training. The genetic algorithm described above was run in parallel on several Linux workstations in our local network. Figure 3 shows a plot of the development of the fitness scores on training and on evaluation data.

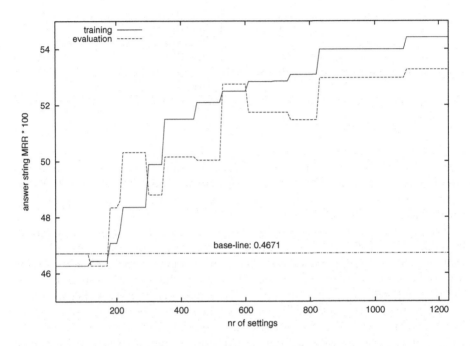

Fig. 3. Parameter optimization

The base-line of 0.4671 refers to the retrieval result on evaluation data when using traditional IR with plain text keywords only (i.e. using the text layer). The base-line performance on training data is similar with 0.4627 MRR. After 1150 settings the MRR scores increased to 0.5442 MRR for training data and 0.5327 for evaluation data which is a relative improvement of about 14%.

Figure 3 also illustrates the relation between training and evaluation scores in the optimization process. The development of the MRR scores on evaluation data is not monotonic but shows a similar tendency as the training curve. After about 800 settings the optimization procedure starts to level out. Further iterations do not produce significant improvements anymore.

Table 3 shows the selected keyword types and their weights after running 1150 settings. The largest weights were assigned to the unrestricted text layer keywords (which are also the best performing keywords when only one keyword

Table 3. Optimized query parameters after 1150 settings

layer	restrictions POS	relation	weight/ required
text			14.82
text	noun		7.97
text	verb		4.65
text	name	mod	2.16
root			+
root	adj		2.95
root		obj1	2.98
root	noun	app	+
root	name	app	5.25
root	noun	obj1	1.80
ne			1
compound			1
Q-type			11.39

layer	restrictions POS	relation	weight/ required
RootPOS			3.43
RootPOS	noun		+
RootHead	verb		1
RootHead	name		0.54
RootHead		obj1	2.97
RootHead	noun	su	5.92
RootHead	name	app	3.91
RootRel			1
RootRel		su	9.05
RootRel	noun	su	7.60
RootRel	noun	mod	4.85
RootRelHead	adj		1

type is used) and the question type keywords. Root form keywords are marked as required as well as RootPOS keywords for nouns. Many keywords are restricted to nouns and names. Furthermore, keywords in a subject relation are weighted with a high boost factor.

Finally, we used the optimized setting for running the entire QA system in its on-line mode (off-line has been disabled) to see if the improvements in IR also lead to increased QA performance. Again, we compared the optimized setting with the base-line of plain text keyword retrieval within our QA system. For this, the IR component was set to retrieve a maximum of 20 passages per question. The performance was measured in terms of mean reciprocal rank scores using the first 5 answers provided by the QA system. Here, the base-line approach yielded a score of 0.342 on the evaluation data. Using the optimized IR settings the score was improved to 0.406 which is statistically significant (with 99% confidence) according to the Wilcoxon matched-pairs signed-ranks test. The improvement amounts to about 19% over the base-line.

6 Summary and Conclusions

In this paper we have shown that linguistic information derived from deep syntactic analyses can successfully be integrated in passage retrieval for question answering. In our approach, various features and feature combinations derived from dependency relations are stored in multiple index layers. Questions are analyzed in the same way in order to extract appropriate keywords for querying the extended index. We also demonstrate how linguistic annotation can be used to select different sets of keywords to be combined in complex queries. We describe a genetic algorithm for query optimization in terms of feature selection and keyword weighting. Our retrieval component was trained on questions from the

CLEF competition on open-domain question answering for Dutch which are annotated with corresponding answers in the corpus. For evaluation we compared the performance of our QA system using the optimized retrieval component with the performance of the base-line approach using plain text keywords in passage retrieval. In our experiments we yielded a statistically significant improvement of about 19% in mean reciprocal rank scores when using the optimized query parameters compared to the base-line.

References

1. Bernardi, R., Jijkoun, V., Mishne, G., de Rijke, M.: Selectively using linguistic resources throughout the question answering pipeline. In: Proceedings of the 2nd CoLogNET-ElsNET Symposium. (2003)
2. Moldovan, D., Harabagiu, S., Girju, R., Morarescu, P., Lacatusu, F., Novischi, A., Badulescu, A., Bolohan, O.: LCC tools for question answering. In: Proceedings of TREC-11. (2002)
3. Strzalkowski, T., Guthrie, L., Karlgren, J., Leistensnider, J., Lin, F., Pérez-Carballo, J., Straszheim, T., Wang, J., Wilding, J.: Natural language information retrieval: TREC-5 report (1996)
4. Katz, B., Lin, J.: Selectively using relations to improve precision in question answering. In: Proceedings of the EACL-2003 Workshop on Natural Language Processing for Question Answering. (2003)
5. Neumann, G., Sacaleanu, B.: Experiments on robust NL question interpretation and multi-layered document annotation for a cross-language question/answering system. In: Proceedings of the CLEF 2004 working notes of the QA@CLEF, Bath (2004)
6. Krovetz, R.: Viewing morphology as an inference process,. In: Proceedings of the Sixteenth Annual International ACM SIGIR Conference on Research and Development in Information Retrieval. (1993) 191–203
7. Hollink, V., Kamps, J., Monz, C., de Rijke, M.: Monolingual document retrieval for European languages. Information Retrieval (2003)
8. Vilares, J., Alonso, M.A., Vilare, M.: Morphological and syntactic processing for text retrieval. In Galindo, F., Takizawa, M., Traunmüller, R., eds.: Database and Expert Systems Applications. Volume 3180 of Lecture Notes in Computer Science. Springer-Verlag, Berlin-Heidelberg-New York (2004) 371–380
9. Méndez, E., Vilares, J., Cabrero, D.: Cole at CLEF 2004: Rapid prototyping of a QA system for Spanish. In Peters, C., Borri, F., eds.: Results of the CLEF 2004 Cross-Language System Evaluation Campaign, Working Notes for the CLEF 2004 Workshop, 15-17 September, Bath, UK. (2004) 413–418
10. Kraaij, W., Pohlmann, R.: Comparing the effect of syntactic vs. statistical phrase indexing strategies for Dutch. In Nicolaou, C., Stephanidis, C., eds.: Research and Advanced Technology for Digital Libraries. Volume 1513 of Lecture Notes in Computer Science. Springer-Verlag, Berlin/Heidelberg/New York (1998) 605–614
11. Monz, C.: From Document Retrieval to Question Answering. PhD thesis, University of Amsterdam (2003)
12. Pasca, M.: High-Performance Open-Domain Question Answering from Large Text Collections. PhD thesis, Southern Methodist University (2001)
13. Zhai, C.: Fast statistical parsing of noun phrases for document indexing. In: Proceedings of the fifth conference on Applied natural language processing, San Francisco, CA, USA, Morgan Kaufmann Publishers Inc. (1997) 312–319

14. Fagan, J.L.: Automatic phrase indexing for document retrieval. In: SIGIR '87: Proceedings of the 10th annual international ACM SIGIR conference on Research and development in information retrieval, New York, NY, USA, ACM Press (1987) 91–101

15. Alonso, M.A., Vilares, J., Darriba, V.M.: On the usefulness of extracting syntactic dependencies for text indexing. In O'Neill, M., Sutcliffe, R.F.E., Ryan, C., Eaton, M., Griffith, N.J.L., eds.: Artificial Intelligence and Cognitive Science. Volume 2464 of Lecture Notes in Artificial Intelligence. Springer-Verlag, Berlin-Heidelberg-New York (2002) 3–11

16. Mittendorfer, M., Winiwarter, W.: Exploiting syntactic analysis of queries for information retrieval. Data & Knowledge Engineering. **42** (2002) 315–325

17. Bouma, G., Mur, J., van Noord, G.: Reasoning over dependency relations for QA. In: Knowledge and Reasoning for Answering Questions (KRAQ'05). IJCAI Workshop, Edinburgh, Scotland (2005)

18. Bouma, G., van Noord, G., Malouf, R.: Alpino: Wide coverage computational analysis of Dutch. In: Computational Linguistics in the Netherlands CLIN, 2000, Rodopi (2001)

19. Jijkoun, V., Mur, J., de Rijke, M.: Information extraction for question answering: Improving recall through syntactic patterns. In: Proceedings of COLING-2004. (2004)

20. Jakarta, A.: Apache Lucene - a high-performance, full-featured text search engine library. http://lucene.apache.org/java/docs/index.html (2004)

Mining the Semantics of Text Via Counter-Training

Roman Yangarber

Department of Computer Science, University of Helsinki, Finland

Abstract. We report on a set of experiments in text mining, specifically, finding semantic patterns given only a few keywords. The experiments employ the Counter-training framework for discovery of semantic knowledge from raw text in a weakly supervised fashion. The experiments indicate that the framework is suitable for efficient acquisition of semantic word classes and collocation patterns, which may be used for Information Extraction.

1 Introduction

In this paper we describe experiments with automatic, minimally supervised acquisition of semantic knowledge for Information Extraction (IE). In particular, our experiments employ the Counter-training framework for automatic acquisition of semantic patterns, and introduce variations on the framework in an attempt to broaden its applicability.

Counter-training has been successfully deployed previously for acquisition of semantic resources. For example, [1] shows how it can be used to acquire classes of related terms in various domains, starting with a very small set of "seed" terms. [2] presents acquisition of semantic collocation patterns, which are then used for building IE systems, again starting with a small seed. Semantic term classes and patterns are essential components in a (pattern-based) IE system, and both types of resource are notoriously difficult to develop manually. As a parallel development, a variety of supervised methods have been investigated for acquisition of semantic resources. Supervised training requires an investment in the manual labor of tagging training corpora, which can be substantial. Our goal is to reduce the amount of supervision necessary for building semantic resources, even if we trade off some of the precision of the resulting resources for a reduction in the amount of supervision required. The rationale is twofold: first, it has been shown (e.g., in [3]) that the time needed to verify the resulting resources is usually shorter than the time necessary for tagging corpora for supervised training. Second, an unsupervised, as opposed to supervised, method will allow us to leverage a much larger training corpus to improve recall.

In our experiments we used a general corpus of news articles, and smaller subsets of documents extracted from the general corpus by means of a simple keyword-based IR query. We have then processed our corpus with tools designed to acquire word co-occurrence patterns and word classes from text. These resources are then used for proposing candidate IE templates, along with example members of the word classes for filling slots in these templates. The patterns describe of the major events/facts, and were found to cover (i.e., match) a substantial portion (50–60%) of the documents retrieved by the queries—so that they may be considered representative of the retrieved collections.

C. Bento, A. Cardoso, and G. Dias (Eds.): EPIA 2005, LNAI 3808, pp. 647–657, 2005.
© Springer-Verlag Berlin Heidelberg 2005

The following sections describe the data used in the experiments (2), the methods (3), and the results (4).

2   Data

The base corpus consists of a collection of about 35,000 English-language articles, from the Associated Press (AP), from 1989 and 2000.

In each experiment, a keyword-based query was issued against this corpus, and the top 1000 documents returned were used as a "reference" corpus.[1] In preparation for the experiments the corpus was further pre-processed, as described below. The goal of these experiments was to apply unsupervised learning to cover a representative portion of the reference corpus. We describe an experiment in which a simple query consisted of the names of four African countries: Nigeria, Kenya, Ethiopia and Uganda.

The key idea we are exploring is summarized as follows: ideally, in IR, one hopes that the sub-collection retrieved in response to a query somehow constitute a unified "semantic whole." It should be possible to demonstrate this, by capturing the semantics in concise form, namely, as a set of patterns which describe the semantics (and further, which enable us to build an IE system to extract events from text). To use the weakly supervised pattern discovery methods mentioned above, one must provide seed patterns; however, to provide the seed patterns one must have some prior knowledge of the domain(s) in the retrieved sub-collection(s). We'd like to help obtain this knowledge automatically.

3   Methods

Several methods have been proposed for learning patterns relevant to a specific scenario.[2] This includes supervised learning algorithms (e.g., [4,5]), and weakly supervised algorithms ([6,3]), which start from a small set of seed patterns, and iteratively bootstrap a larger set of relevant patterns.

The intent of the present work is to investigate what happens when *no* specific scenario is given *a priori*. Rather the input to the learning algorithm is the retrieved reference corpus—a set of documents, which likely cover multiple, different topics. We would like to induce the topics themselves automatically, without reading through any portion of the 1000-document corpus, which may be time-consuming, and may not yield a clear result.

We planned to experiment with the ExDisco algorithm, [6], in this setting, but found that it is not well suited for two reasons. First, the target scenarios are not known in advance. Second, even when a scenario is given manually, ExDisco tends to overgeneralize after a few dozen initial iterations: the learner begins to acquire patterns that are too general (with respect to the target scenario). At that point, ExDisco also acquires documents which do not belong to the scenario and the entire learning process diverges.

---

[1] In section 4, we discuss some of the problems encountered during data preparation, which reduced the number of usable documents below 1000.

[2] The term *scenario* is used in its traditional IE sense: the topic of interest in which events are to be extracted, e.g., "company mergers and acquisitions," or "terrorist attacks."

The ideas underlying [6] can be seen as related to work on "pseudo-relevance feedback" from IR, [7].

Recent work, on Counter-training, [2], went beyond [6] to address this divergence problem, and thus seemed more appropriate to use here. We now briefly review the Counter-training learning framework.

The Counter-Training method builds upon previously described approaches to iterative unsupervised pattern acquisition. One characteristic of prior approaches is that the output of the algorithm is a continuous stream of patterns, with gradually degrading precision, (cf., e.g., [8]).

To deal with the divergence problem, Counter-Training introduces competition among several scenarios simultaneously. This allows the competing scenarios to provide negative evidence for each other, which focuses the learning process, and prevents the divergence observed with the earlier techniques.

We next introduce the basic algorithm for pattern acquisition, similar to [6], and then place it in the framework of Counter-training in section 3.3.[3]

3.1   Pre-processing

Before learning, the training corpus goes through several pre-processing stages. The algorithm is based on the fundamental redundancy in natural language, and this pre-processing reduces factors which may mask redundancy in text.

0.a Name Factorization: We use a regular-expression-based, general-purpose proper name/expression classifier to classify noun phrases (NPs) as person, location, organization, unidentified name, date/time, monetary and numeric expressions; we replace each such NP with a special token indicating its type.

The name tagger has about 92% accuracy. Factoring names from the corpus helps in the following step, syntactic parsing, by reducing parser errors on domain-specific phenomena—which can in many cases be described by simple regular-expression rules. However, the main contribution of name factorization to the discovery process is that it helps to maximize redundancy in text.

0.b Parsing and syntactic regularization: We apply a general dependency parser, [9], to the name-tagged corpus. We then further reduce syntactic variation by transforming the subtree under each verb into a "standard" representation, similarly to the transformations of, e.g., [10]: we convert passive, relative, various subordinate subtrees, etc., into active trees. The parser produces at least one tree for over 80% of the sentences.[4]

0.c Pattern creation: Each regularized subtree induces a single subject–verb–object tuple. The tuple consists of three literals [s,v,o], which are the head of the verb phrase, and the heads of the subject and object phrases. For example, the text "Chase Corp. was bought by the highest bidder" induces the tuple [bidder, buy, Company][5]; "the army was planning to attack the city [in the morning]" produces two trees for two verbs: [army, plan, attack] and [army, attack, city]. These tuples serve as a kind of index for the document collection.

---

[3] This description is similar to that in the referenced paper; please see [2] for details.

[4] No tree is produced if the sentence contains no verb, or if the parser fails.

[5] The company name was replaced by the token *Company*.

3.2 Minimally Supervised Learner (Single-Scenario)

We now summarize the basic learning algorithm, and the formulas used in it.

1. Input: a set of seed patterns (tuples), relevant to the target scenario, S.

2. Relevance: Assign relevance weights to all documents in the corpus. A document d is *relevant*—has weight 1—if a seed pattern matches some clause in d, and non-relevant otherwise, with weight 0. On later iterations, documents are assigned weights between 0 and 1.

3. Pattern Ranking: Assign a score to each candidate pattern—each pattern in some relevant document (non-zero weight) is a *candidate* pattern. The score depends on how accurately the candidate predicts the relevance of a document, with respect to the current distribution of relevance weights, and on how much *support* it has—the total weight of the relevant documents it matches in the corpus (in Equation 2). We pick the highest-scoring candidate p_i (on iteration i), as the pattern most closely correlated with the documents that have high relevance. Add p_i to the expanding set of accepted patterns, $\{p_i\}$.

4. Update Relevance: For each document d covered by any of the accepted patterns in $\{p_i\}$, recompute $Rel^S(d)$, the relevance of d to the target scenario S. Relevance of d is based on the cumulative accuracy of patterns from $\{p_i\}$ which match d—i.e., how confident we are on iteration i that d belongs to S.

5. Repeat: from *Pattern ranking* in step 3, as long as learning is possible.

Scoring of the candidate patterns, in step 3, is similar to that in [3,11]:

$$Score(p) = \frac{Sup(p)}{|H|} \cdot \log Sup(p) \tag{1}$$

where $H = H(p)$ is the set of documents where the pattern p matched, and the support $Sup(p)$ is computed as the sum of their relevance:

$$Sup(p) = \sum_{d \in H(p)} Rel(d) \tag{2}$$

The relevance of a document d is given by the formula

$$Rel(d) = 1 - \prod_{p \in K(d)} \left(1 - Prec(p)\right) \tag{3}$$

where $K(d)$ is the set of *accepted* patterns that match the document d; this is a rough estimate of the likelihood of relevance of d, based on the *accuracy* of the patterns accepted so far. The accuracy, or precision, of the pattern p is the average relevance of the documents matched by p:

$$Prec(p) = \frac{1}{|H|} \sum_{d \in H(p)} Rel(d) = \frac{Sup(p)}{|H|} \tag{4}$$

Therefore, Equation 1 can be re-written more simply as:

$$Score(p) = Prec(p) \cdot \log Sup(p) \tag{5}$$

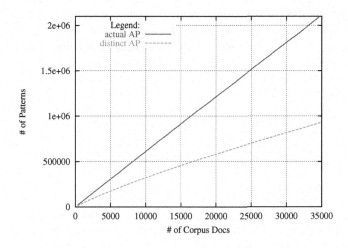

Fig. 1. Pattern Distribution in AP Corpus

3.3 Counter-Training

The two terms in Equation 5 capture the trade-off between precision and recall. As mentioned before, the simple learner will eventually acquire patterns that are too general for the scenario, which will then assign positive relevance to non-relevant documents, and the entire procedure will diverge.

To correct this problem, we train n learners, for n different scenarios $\{\mathcal{S}_i\}, i = 1..n$, simultaneously. On each iteration, each learner learns its own set of patterns, and each assigns its own relevance, $Rel^{\mathcal{S}_i}(d)$, to each document. Some documents are "ambiguous"—have high relevance in more than one scenario.

Given multiple learners, we refine the measure of pattern precision in Eq. 4 for scenario $\mathcal{S}_i$, to take into account the *negative* evidence—i.e., how much weight the documents matched by the pattern received in the *other* scenarios:

$$Prec(p) = \frac{1}{|H|} \sum_{d \in H(p)} \left(Rel^{\mathcal{S}_i}(d) - \sum_{j \neq i} Rel^{\mathcal{S}_j}(d) \right) \qquad (6)$$

Eq. 6 implies that the learner disfavors a pattern for scenario $\mathcal{S}_i$ if it has too much opposition from other scenarios. Candidates with $Prec(p) \leq 0$ are not considered.

The algorithm proceeds for as long two or more scenarios continue to learn patterns. Learning terminates when the number of active scenarios drops to one, since, running unopposed, a sole remaining scenario will learn non-relevant patterns and will eventually diverge.

4   Experiments and Results

The corpora used in the experiments are described in Section 2. The texts were pre-processed, as in Section 3.1, to obtain a pattern-based representation.

Figure 1 shows the distribution of patterns in the corpus. The ratio of the number of patterns to the number of documents is about linear, at about 60.

The figure also shows the number of distinct patterns (curve labeled "distinct") vs. the number of all patterns ("actual"). This number grows slower, and although its growth is almost linear, the curve is slightly concave downward, which suggests that as the corpus size grows, there are more repeated patterns.[6]

The ratio of distinct patterns to the number of documents in the smaller IR-retrieved sub-corpus is 39.28, as compared to 26.61 in the complete corpus (referred to as the "IR" corpus and the "AP" corpus from now on). This is the experimental setting in which we applied our variant of Counter-Training.

4.1 Finding Target Scenarios

The question that arises next is: how can one determine which scenarios are prevalent in the IR sub-corpus, and should therefore be counter-trained to extract the semantics for this corpus? We propose the following two-phase procedure:

Phase 1. Run mono-training to discover which scenarios are dominant in the IR corpus, and find some seed patterns for them; then

Phase 2. Counter-Train the dominant scenarios (plus additional scenarios, for enhanced negative evidence) to discover patterns that cover the IR corpus.

The first phase was accomplished by running a single learner in isolation, in "mono-training" mode: a single, ExDisco-like learner was run against the entire AP corpus. However, it was seeded with documents from the IR corpus rather than with patterns: the algorithm was started at step 2, and assigned relevance 1 to all the IR documents, and zero relevance to the remaining AP documents.

Note, that this is somewhat of a departure from the original use of this learning paradigm, since labeling as relevant those documents that match only a keyword is more liberal than insisting that the document match an entire (seed) pattern to be deemed relevant. Therefore, as expected, the algorithm diverged after several dozen iterations. However it yielded an interesting result: the acquired patterns indicated to us that

– the corpus is heavily dominated by two scenarios: *"War"* and *"Sport"*; and
– other scenarios are poorly represented in it.

The War scenario contains events like international or domestic military conflicts, guerrilla warfare, armed insurrections, and abductions. The Sport scenario contains sporting events and athletic competitions. Other topics are clearly also mentioned in the IR corpus, but to a lesser degree, and they do not receive substantial coverage for successful discovery of documents or patterns.

4.2 Counter-Training

Based on this finding, Counter-Training was applied to the two scenarios, plus several others: diseases, political elections, and stock and interest rate fluctuation. Although

---

[6] This effect should help the process of learning by bootstrapping, and should enable us to use larger corpora to get better results.

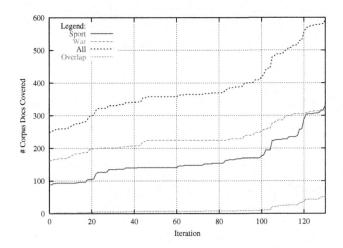

Fig. 2. Coverage of the IR Corpus

these additional scenarios are manifested in the AP corpus, they found little representation in the IR corpus, and therefore, in this experiment, where our focus is on covering the IR corpus, they served as negative scenarios, to steer the counter-training learners from each other's territory.

The corpus coverage in this Counter-Training phase is traced in Figure 2. The Figure shows the War and Sport scenarios, which were able to pick up substantial numbers of patterns that occur within the IR corpus.

The curves labeled "Sport" and "War" show the number of documents in the IR corpus which are covered by these scenarios, as the iterations progressed. The curve labeled "All" shows the total number of IR documents, or the *union* of those in the scenario curves.[7] The "Overlap" curve, shows how many documents received non-zero scores in both target scenarios. (This is an undesirable effect, and it potentially relates to Problem-B, discussed below.)

Table 1 lists the seed patterns for each scenario, followed by some of the patterns acquired by the Counter-Training on the initial iterations. The seed patterns are marked with †.

The concept classes (the capitalized tokens) used in these patterns are:[8]

Location: a proper name of a location;
National: a nationality, e.g., *Kenyan* or *British*;
Person: a name of a person, or a personal pronoun, {*he, she, someone, ...*};
Company/Organization: a name of a commercial/other type of organization;
Name: a proper name of an unidentified type;
Money: a monetary amount, e.g., US$100;

---

[7] The Figure shows that by about 110 iterations, more than 50% of the IR corpus has been covered, with modest overlap. Counter-training terminated at 265 iterations.

[8] These classes are identified by the Named Entity tagger or by the part-of-speech tagger.

Table 1. Sample Acquired Patterns

War	Sport
† rebel abduct.kidnap.kill *	† * win.lose competition.marathon.race
† * support.back rebel	† * win title
† rebel overthrow Person	† * finish Nth
† Location send troop.force.soldier	† * place Nth
† * end war	
rebel.fighter flee Location	Person finish course
Pro.rebel ambush vehicle	Person.Name win division
rebel separate.assemble.round tourist	Location win championship.Name
rebel control.flee Location	Person sweep.beat.lead.win.take Name
Pro release.slaughter tourist	Person.Name defend title
rebel surround.storm.raid camp	Name retain.defend.retake title
plan.accord.agreement call_for cease_fire	Person earn prize
Organization deploy mission.observer.force	winner receive.earn.win Money
rebel reject agreement	Person break.set record
...	...

Pro: impersonal pronoun: {*something, that, ...*};
Nth: an ordinal number: *first, second*, etc.

In the discovered patterns, each entry is a lexical item or a class of items; the members of the class are separated by a dot; e.g., *Separate.Assemble.Round.*

4.3 Pattern Analysis

Before we proceed to the discussion of the pattern quality, we should mention two problems that were observed in the training data.

Problem A: Repeated Articles: Many articles in the corpus were found to be identical, or near-identical, copies of each other. This often happens in a large news corpus when articles are reprinted after initial publication, with small changes: re-wording, corrections of names, or one or two sentences of additional information, as in evolving events.[9]

Repetition affects bootstrapping by skewing pattern frequency scores. Tracking such repetitions is not entirely trivial in itself: its presence is not immediately apparent, e.g., it cannot be inferred from the size of the document alone; documents containing repeated text are not near each other in the chronological sequence; repetition is not dependent on the topic of the text. One approach that might be undertaken to correct for the repetition is to create a hash table of {sentence, article ID} pairs, find sentences appearing multiple times, and then look for documents containing multiple such sentences.

As we saw from the extracted patterns, this phenomenon can affect learning by overstating the weight of otherwise "useless" patterns, simply because they appear

---

[9] In some cases, an article—usually by the same author—reappeared four or more times.

in repeated documents, and cause them to be learned as highly relevant to the target scenario.[10]

Problem B: Mixed-topic Narrative: Some documents in the IR corpus cover multiple topics. This is a natural phenomenon in publishing, and therefore it cannot really be considered a "problem" (in the same sense as "A"). Such texts contain a legitimate mixture of topics. Unfortunately, such mixture confuses the learning process, by telling the system that the patterns appearing in the different topics are correlated, when in reality they are not. Multiple examples of this type of narrative appear in the data, (e.g., the Digest Briefs in the AP corpus).

The extracted patterns were manually analyzed, and patterns that were flawed in some way (not useful for the scenario) were categorized to indicate what type of problem caused the pattern to be acquired:

- "b": a bad pattern, more relevant to a scenario other than the target scenario.
- "u": "useless" pattern; e.g., those acquired due to Problem A.
- "p": a partially bad pattern: some incorrect members in a class in the pattern.
- "g": a pattern that is too general to be used as a trigger for this scenario.
- "d": a dubious pattern, of uncertain utility. It may match relevant facts, but those facts are not expressible as a [s,v,o] tuple, (i.e., it may require syntactic arguments beyond subject and object to make it specific to the scenario).
- "x": a wrong pattern, likely due to a parse error.

Note that patterns marked "p", "g", or "?" may be of some value to an IE system for the target scenario in some way; we do not pursue that possibility in this discussion, and deem these patterns generally incorrect.

The lower bound, i.e., the conservative estimate of the proportion of "good" patterns is $\frac{159}{265} = 60\%$ in the War scenario, and $\frac{114}{157} = 72.6\%$ in Sport. The proportion of patterns deemed definitely bad—not counting those judged too general for the scenario—is $\frac{(230-159)}{265} = 27\%$ for War, $\frac{20}{157} = 12.7\%$ for Sport.

4.4 Scenario Templates

The next natural question is: what templates for describing events in these scenarios may be inferred from the extracted patterns?

A first approximation to a solution is shown in table 2. For each scenario, the table shows the names of principal slots and a brief description of the slot's intended contents. The template structure is intentionally "flat," (as opposed to a nested structure, as, e.g., in MUC-6 or MUC-7) to make it simple to define and fill, yet powerful enough to represent the information in the text.

For the Sport scenario, the principal slot fills are the name, location and date of the competition or event, the name of a participant—a person or a team—and a description of the participant's results in absolute and relative terms.

---

[10] For example, several patterns like ([tourist, observe, gorilla], etc.) were learned in the first few iterations of the War domain, due to a *single* text—which appeared in at least four documents in the IR corpus—about a group of Western tourists who came to Africa to see gorillas, and were abducted or killed by local rebels.

Table 2. Sample Templates Covering the Acquired Patterns

War	Sport
Incident Type: anchoring expression, indicating the type of incident: attack, raid, bombing, etc.	**Name:** Name of competition or sporting event
Damage: Number of casualties, or an indication of severity of damage or injury	**Competitor:** Name of event participant, athlete or team
Primary: Description of primary party in an armed conflict, i.e., attacker/initiator of incident	**Result-Absolute:** The competitor's performance in absolute terms: 1:25:59 (time); 3-0 (score), etc.
Secondary: Description/name of second party in armed conflict, typically, the victim	**Result-Relative:** Performance in relative terms, e.g., world record; lost to or beat other competitor
Location	**Location**
Date	**Date**

Note that a text may describe an event only, without mentioning participants or results, in which case the participant and result slots would be left unfilled.

For the War scenario, the primary information describing an incident is: the date and the location of the engagement, the number and type of casualties, and a description of the parties involved.

In case the text indicates which party had initiated the incident, that is listed as the primary party, and the target of its actions is listed as secondary.[11]

5   Conclusion

We have presented experiments with automatic acquisition of semantic resources useful for IE, in a minimally-supervised fashion. In prior work, Counter-training was shown to be useful for acquisition of large semantic classes of terms. Here we focused on acquisition of semantic patterns and templates for describing events. Several interesting points emerge from these experiments.

We introduced a variation on the original Counter-training approach: whereas in prior published work, to acquire patterns, Counter-training is seeded with patterns, here we in effect used keywords as "seeds."

This modification enables us to start from a set of somewhat "loosely relevant" documents—rather than from a strictly relevant set of seed patterns, as in prior work—and nonetheless arrive at useful results, by a two-phase application of the basic unsupervised learner, with human intervention in between, to select—at a very coarse level—the salient features of a set of documents obtained by a simple IR query.

Another interesting application of this technique, to be explored in future work, is that, in effect, it may allow us, for a given pair of query terms A and B—such as two country names—to quickly answer questions like "how is A like B?" or "how is A unlike B?" To answer the former, one would counter-train A and B together against another set of terms. To answer the latter, one would counter-train them against each other.

---

[11] If the initiating party cannot be determined from context, the order of the parties is not expected to carry useful information.

Difficult questions remain to be addressed in the future: How can the discovered patterns be combined and collapsed to form templates automatically? How can we determine for each pattern, which of the template slots it fills?

Nonetheless, the results indicate that the counter-training approach provides simple, effective methods for exploring the semantics in a corpus.

Acknowledgements

Many thanks to the anonymous reviewers for their thoughtful feedback.

References

1. Lin, W., Yangarber, R., Grishman, R.: Bootstrapped learning of semantic classes from positive and negative examples. In: Proc. ICML Workshop, Washington, DC (2003)
2. Yangarber, R.: Counter-training in discovery of semantic patterns. In: Proc. ACL-2003, Sapporo, Japan (2003)
3. Riloff, E.: Automatically generating extraction patterns from untagged text. In: Proc. 13th Natl. Conf. on AI (AAAI-96). (1996)
4. Califf, M.E., Mooney, R.J.: Bottom-up relational learning of pattern matching rules for information extraction. J. Machine Learning Research 4 (2003)
5. Wilks, Y., Catizone, R.: Can we make information extraction more adaptive? In Pazienza, M., ed.: Information Extraction: Scalable, Adaptable Systems. Springer, LNAI (1999)
6. Yangarber, R., Grishman, R., Tapanainen, P., Huttunen, S.: Automatic acquisition of domain knowledge for information extraction. In: Proc. 18th Intl. Conf. Computational Linguistics (COLING 2000), Saarbrücken (2000)
7. Allan, J.: Relevance feedback with too much data. In: Proc. 18th International ACM SIGIR Conf. on R&D in IR, Seattle, Washington (1995)
8. Thelen, M., Riloff, E.: A bootstrapping method for learning semantic lexicons using extraction pattern contexts. In: Proc. EMNLP. (2002)
9. Tapanainen, P., Järvinen, T.: A non-projective dependency parser. In: Proc. 5th Conf. Applied Natural Language Processing, Washington, D.C. (1997)
10. Meyers, A., Grishman, R., Kosaka, M.: Formal mechanisms for capturing regularizations. In: Proc. Language Resources and Evaluation Conf. (LREC 2002), Las Palmas, Spain (2002)
11. Riloff, E., Jones, R.: Learning dictionaries for information extraction by multi-level bootstrapping. In: Proc. 16th Natl. Conf. on AI (AAAI-99), Orlando, FL (1999)

Minimum Redundancy Cut in Ontologies
for Semantic Indexing*

Florian Seydoux and Jean-Cédric Chappelier

School of Computer and Communication Sciences,
École Polytechnique Fédérale de Lausanne (EPFL),
CH-1015 Lausanne, Switzerland
{florian.seydoux, jean-cedric.chappelier}@epfl.ch

Abstract. This paper presents a new method that aims at improving semantic indexing while reducing the number of indexing terms. Indexing terms are determined using a minimum redundancy cut in a hierarchy of conceptual hypernyms provided by an ontology (e.g. *WordNet*, *EDR*). The results of some information retrieval experiments carried out on several standard document collections using the *EDR* ontology are presented, illustrating the benefit of the method.

1 Introduction

The main idea of semantic indexing is to use word senses rather than, or in addition to the words[1] for indexing documents, in order to improve both recall (by handling synonymy) and precision (by handling homonymy and polysemy). However, the related experiments reported in the Information Retrieval (IR) literature lead to contradicting results: some claim that this substitution (or addition), carried out in an automatic way, degrades the performances [1–4]; for others conversely, the gain seems significant [5–9].

Although it seems desirable for document indexing to take a maximum of semantic information into account, the resulting expansion of the data processed could happen to be counter-productive. Indeed, the growth of the number of indexing terms not only increases the processing time, but could also reduce the precision: discriminating documents by using a very large number of indexing terms is a hard task (*"curse of dimensionality"* effect). This problem is not new, and various techniques aiming at reducing the size of the indexing set already exist: filtering by stoplist, part of speech tags, frequencies, or through statistical techniques such as LSI [10] or PLSI [11]. However, most of these techniques are not adapted to the case where an explicit semantic information is available in the form of an ontology, i.e. with some underlying formal – not statistical – structure.

The focus of the work presented here is to use ontologies to create semantic indexing sets of "sensible" sizes. This relates, but from a different point of

---

* This work was partially supported by the Swiss National Fund for Scientific Research (SNFSR) under grant #200020–103529.
[1] Usually stems or lemmas.

C. Bento, A. Cardoso, and G. Dias (Eds.): EPIA 2005, LNAI 3808, pp. 658–668, 2005.

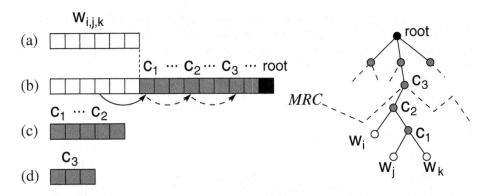

Fig. 1. Different indexing scheme: (a) usual indexing with words (stems or lemmas); (b) using a semantic ontology (displayed on the right), each indexing term is extended with all the concepts that dominate it; this leads to an explosion of the number of indexes for documents; (c) synset (or hypernyms synsets) indexing: each indexing term is replaced with its (hypernyms) synset; this, in principle, can reduce the size of the indexing set since all the indexing terms that are covered by the same hypernym are regrouped in one single indexing feature; (d) Minimum Redundancy Cut (*MRC*) indexing: each indexing term is replaced with its dominating concept defined by *MRC*. This reduces further the size of the indexing set since all the indexing terms that are subsumed by the same concept in the *MRC* are regrouped in one single indexing feature.

view, with experiments reported in [8], [12] or [9], which uses the synsets (or hypernyms synsets [9]) of *WordNet* as indexing terms. Our work goes one step ahead, selecting the indexing set using an information theory based criterion, the *Minimum Redundancy Cut* (*MRC*, see Fig. 1). This criterion is applied to the inclusive "is-a" relation (hypernyms) provided by the *EDR* taxonomy [13].

2   Ontology-Cut Model

2.1   Goals

The choice of the appropriate hypernym (a concept in the ontology) to be used for representing a word is not easy: be it too general, the performances of the system will degrade (lack of precision); be it too specific, the indexing set will not reduce enough, preserving some distinction between words with close senses (lack of recall).

To select the appropriate level of conceptual indexing, we consider cuts in the ontology. A cut is a minimal set[2] of nodes in the ontology defining a coverage of all the leaf nodes (i.e. words). Each node in the cut is used to represent every leaf node it dominates.

The problem is to find a computable strategy to select an optimal cut. For a related task, Li and Abe [14] use the Minimum Description Length principle

---

[2] By "minimal set" we mean that no node can be removed from the set without decreasing it's coverage (i.e. the number of leaves it dominates).

(MDL). Although easy to compute, this criterion has the drawback in practice (with *EDR*) of often selecting as a cut the root of the ontology, which is not really useful for document indexing. We rather propose to use a new criterion, based on information theory, that selects a cut for which the redundancy is minimal, i.e. a cut where the degree of description of the indexing features in the ontology is as balanced as possible (maximum entropy).

2.2   Minimum Redundancy Cut (*MRC*)

Let $\mathcal{N} = \{n_i\}$ and $\mathcal{W}$ respectively be the set of nodes and the set of words in the ontology. A cut Γ is defined as a minimal subset[2] of $\mathcal{N}$ which covers $\mathcal{W}$. A probabilized cut $M = (\Gamma, P)$ consists of a cut Γ with a probability distribution P on it. From now on, the probabilized cut $M = (\Gamma, P_{tf})$ is considered, where P_{tf} is defined by the relative frequencies of the words in the collection:

$$P_{tf}(n_i) = \frac{f(n_i)}{|D|}, \tag{1}$$

$f(n_i)$ being the number of occurrences of the node n_i in a document collection D, and $|D|$ the total number of word occurrences in this collection. To compute $f(n_i)$, we consider that an occurrence of n_i happens whenever some of its hyponym words occurs.

The redundancy $R(M)$ of a probabilized cut $M = (\Gamma, P)$ is defined as [15]:

$$R(M) = 1 - \frac{H(M)}{\log |M|},$$

where $H(M) = -\sum_{n \in \Gamma} P(n) \cdot \log P(n)$ and $|M|$ denotes the number of nodes in the cut Γ.

Minimizing the redundancy is equivalent to maximizing the ratio between the entropy of the cut, $H(M)$, and its maximum possible value, $\log |M|$, i.e. balancing the probabilities of the nodes in the cut so far as it could.

To illustrate *MRC* with a toy example, consider the ontology given in Fig. 2 and an hypothetic dataset for which the frequencies of the words in the ontology are indicated on the same figure. The redundancy of the example cut $\Gamma = [\text{ANIMAL}, \text{PLANT}, \text{TRANSPORT}]$ is 0.272:

n	ANIMAL	PLANT	TRANSPORT
$f(n)$	20	33	2
$P_{tf}(n)$	0.3704	0.5926	0.0370
$-P_{tf}(n) \log_2 P_{tf}(n)$	0.5307	0.4473	0.1761
$R(\Gamma) = 1 - \dfrac{1.1541}{\log_2(3)} = 0.2718$			

In this example, it can checked by examining each of the 2036 possible cuts that the global *MRC* is the one displayed on Fig. 2. Its redundancy is 0.071. It also corresponds to the local *MRC* found (with only 117 evaluations) by the local search algorithm presented in the next section.

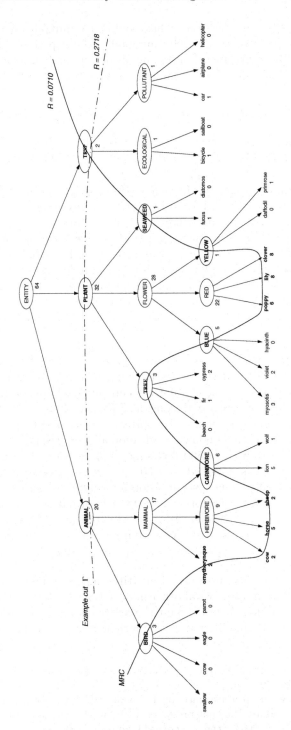

Fig. 2. Example of cuts and their redundancy value

Notice that R does not necessarily have a unique minimum on all possible cuts, but may rather have several equally minimal cuts. In practice, this can easily be overcome, considering for instance any of the minimal cuts or those having a minimal number of nodes, or the minimum average depth of the nodes, etc.

2.3   Finding a *MRC*

In order to identify global *MRC*, the whole set of possible cuts has to be considered. We thus decided to give up global optimality for the sake of tractability and focussed rather on more efficient heuristics.

The algorithm we propose for finding a *MRC* starts from the cut containing all the leaves and iteratively modifies it by systematically choosing the replacement of a node by its parent or its children[3] that minimizes the redundancy. More precisely, for each node n_i in the current cut, we consider on one hand $n_i\downarrow$, the (set of) children of n_i, (see Fig. 3a) and on the other hand $n_i\uparrow$, the (set of) parents of n_i (see Fig. 3b). The cut with minimal redundancy among these new considered cuts (and the current one) is kept, and the search continues as long as better cuts are found. The full algorithm[4] is given on Fig. 3.

3   Experiments

To evaluate the benefit of the *MRC* indexing method, we carried out several experiments with some of the standard document collections of the SMART [16] system[5] and ontologies generated from the *EDR Electronic Dictionary* [13].

EDR gathers information about approximatively $420,000$ "words" of different types (including compounds and idiomatic expressions); organized into $\approx 490,000$ concepts, with $\approx 500,000$ super/sub relations between them. The two different ontologies provided by *EDR* were used: a very large scale general ontology and a smallest one specialized on information science.

For the evaluation, the vector-space SMART information retrieval system and an external lemmatizer[6] (which also acts as a tokenizer) are used. A filtering based on the POS tag is also carried out (but no stoplist, nor frequency filtering). The new indexing sets are produced while preprocessing the data as follow:

1. First of all, the textual information (title and contents) is aggregated for each document and query; all other informations (authors, sources, etc.) are removed; then, documents and queries are tokenized and lemmatized by the third-party tool[6], and filtered based on their POS tag (name, adjective, verb and adverb are kept).

---

[3] Due to the DAG structure of the ontology, this replacement can involve more than one node in the cut.

[4] In practice, several optimizations can be made, which do not conceptually change the algorithm and are thus not presented here for the sake of clarity.

[5] Available online at `ftp://ftp.cs.cornell.edu/pub/smart/`.

[6] Sylex 1.7, © 1993-98 DECAN INGENIA.

Requires: a hierarchy $\mathcal{N}$ (the leaves of which are $\mathcal{W}$).
Provides: a cut Γ with (local) minimal redundancy.

$\Gamma \leftarrow \mathcal{W}$ # *The current cut. We start from the leaves.*
repeat
    $\Gamma' \leftarrow \varnothing$ # *The new best cut.*
    $\Gamma'' \leftarrow \varnothing$ # *The tested candidate.*
    continue $\leftarrow$ false # *Search-loop control flag.*
    for all $n_i \in \Gamma$ **do**
        # *Evaluate the children's cut:*
        $\Gamma'' \leftarrow (\Gamma \setminus \{n_i\}) \cup \left(n_i{}^{\downarrow} \setminus (\Gamma \setminus \{n_i\})^{\Downarrow}\right)$
        $\Gamma' \leftarrow \text{Argmin}\left(R(\Gamma'), R(\Gamma'')\right)$
        # *Evaluate each parent's cut:*
        for all $n_j \in n_i{}^{\uparrow}$ **do**
            $\Gamma'' \leftarrow (\Gamma \cup \{n_j\}) \setminus n_j{}^{\Downarrow}$
            $\Gamma' \leftarrow \text{Argmin}\left(R(\Gamma'), R(\Gamma'')\right)$
    if $R(\Gamma') < R(\Gamma)$ **then**
        $\Gamma \leftarrow \Gamma'$ # *Keep the best cut.*
        continue $\leftarrow$ true # *The search goes on.*
        # *Some watchdog or timer can be put here.*
until continue is false
return Γ

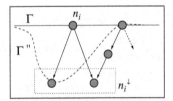
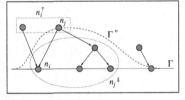

(a) Lower search on $n_i{}^{\downarrow}$: keep only those nodes of $n_i{}^{\downarrow}$ that are not already covered by Γ, i.e. $n_i{}^{\downarrow} \setminus (\Gamma \setminus \{n_i\})^{\Downarrow}$.

(b) Upper search on $n_i{}^{\uparrow}$: if $n_j \in n_i{}^{\uparrow}$ is kept, then remove from Γ the nodes it covers, i.e. those in $(n_j)^{\Downarrow}$.

Fig. 3. *MRC local search algorithm, where $n^{\Downarrow}$ is the transitive closure of $n^{\downarrow}$, and $R(\varnothing) = R(\{c\}) = 1$, by convention. Sub-figures (a) and (b) illustrate the two local search steps of the algorithm.*

2. Then we look for the correspondences between the tokens in a document and the entries (leaves) in the ontology, with the lexical string first and the lemmatized form then, if necessary. Tokens without correspondence in the ontology are indexed in the standard way. The coverage rate[7] of the collections by the ontology was 90% in average.

---

[7] The coverage rate is the number of different words in the collection that are in the ontology, divided by the total number of different words in the collection.

3. Then the hierarchy of concepts related to the tokens found in the ontology is expanded by:
   (a) in a first set of experiments, selecting all possible senses (relying upon the mutual reinforcement induced by collocations to have a sort of disambiguation);
   (b) in a second run of experiments, selecting only one sense, always the same independently of the context, e.g. the most frequent one[8].
4. An *MRC* cut is then computed with the algorithm previously presented (in practice, we limit the cut only to the nodes covering words contained in the documents, but neither the whole ontology, nor the words in the queries are considered).
5. Finally, the tokens in both documents and queries are substituted by the identifiers of the concepts which subordinate them in the cut determined at the preceding step. Tokens of the queries which do not occur in the documents and are not subordinated by a node of the cut are ignored.

Table 1. Indexing sizes and Mean Average Precision (ntn weighting) of several indexing schemes (see Fig. 1); (a): words only; (b): words + concepts; (b1): same with trivial WSD; (c): direct hypernyms; (c1): same with trivial WSD (d): hypernyms from the *MRC*; (d1): same with trivial WSD.

	(a)	(b)	(b1)	(c)	(c1)	(d)	(d1)
	ADI collection (82 documents, 35 topics) [Documents from Information Science]						
$|index|$	1800	14664	5254	10080	2891	5516	**1740**
MAP	0.3431	0.2871	0.3840	0.3140	**0.4071**	0.2976	**0.4071**
	TIME collection (423 documents, 83 topics) [General world news articles from the Time magazine (1963)]						
$|index|$	21815	92117	53142	69354	31583	18949	18404
MAP	0.5349	0.3908	0.4999	0.4284	0.5442	**0.5476**	**0.5471**
	CACM collection (3204 documents, 64 topics) [Titles and abstracts from a computer science journal]						
$|index|$	10053	51712	25208	38524	14696	8410	**8339**
MAP	0.2814	0.1245	0.2324	0.1869	0.2774	0.2532	**0.2950**
	MED collection (1033 documents, 30 topics) [Abstracts from a medical journal]						
$|index|$	11893	56091	30305	41742	18113	**10206**	10306
MAP	**0.4470**	0.2532	0.3984	0.2704	0.4284	0.3679	0.4226
	CISI collection (1460 documents, 112 topics) [Articles from Information science (Library science)]						
$|index|$	10019	53453	26278	39544	14998	8404	**8114**
MAP	0.1535	0.0875	0.1413	0.0959	**0.1632**	0.1300	0.1489

---

[8] In *EDR*, this information is available for each word.

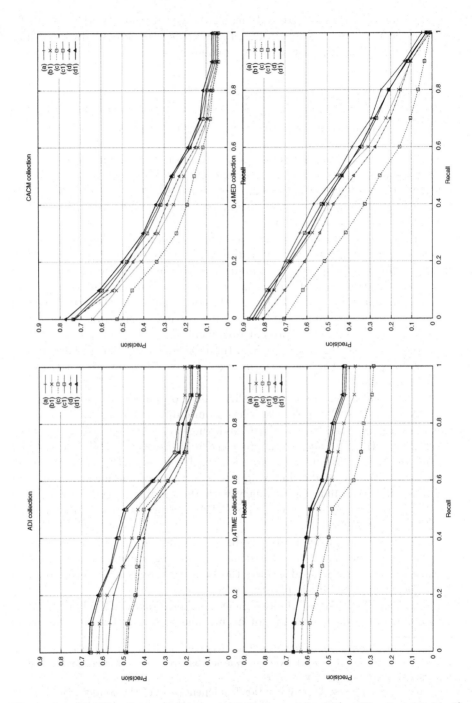

Fig. 4. Precision-Recall curves for several indexing methods (see Fig. 1 and table 1) on the ADI, TIME, CACM and MED collections

Table 1 gathers the index size and Mean Average Precision (MAP)[9] results for the IR experiments carried out. In Fig. 4, we furthermore provide the precision-recall curves for the four most interesting collections.

4   Discussion and Conclusion

Five main conclusions can be drawn out of these experiments:

1. Using *adapted* additional semantic information can enhance the indexing of documents, and thus the performances of a IR system. The results of semantic (ontology-based) indexing (columns (c), (c1), (d) and (d1)) are indeed better than the baseline system for four of the collections, but slightly worse on the MED collection.

   This can be explained by the specificity of the vocabulary of these collections and their adequacy with the semantic resource. ADI and CACM have an important technical vocabulary well covered by the *EDR* ontology, whereas the MED collection has an extremely specific vocabulary, for which the *EDR* ontology is not adapted. Moreover, although the vocabulary of TIME is very general, semantic indexing methods perform well on it. Finally, the CISI collection present documents with a significant number of dates, proper names, etc., for which the POS filtering seems to have annoying consequences; the low performances clearly indicating an initial loss of informations.

   The results presented here confirm those obtained with similar experiments using *WordNet* [17], which has a quite different structure than *EDR*.
2. The overall performance of *MRC* indexing ((d) and (d1)) is better than indexing with direct hypernyms ((c) and (c1)) on ADI, TIME and CACM, both on MAP measure and precision-recall curves. *MRC* is often ahead, with a noticeably smaller indexing set. It furthermore performs better both on specific vocabulary in adequacy with the ontology (ADI, CACM) and on general purpose large documents (TIME), which is a good omen for the future of the method.
3. Semantic disambiguation, even rudimentary, appears to be necessary. Indeed, the simple heuristics consisting in removing semantic ambiguities by choosing, for a given word, always the same of its senses[10] already allows a significant increase in the performances.

   The expected mutual reinforcement of collocations as a kind of "natural" disambiguation does actually not occur. The reason is that the number of

---

[9] The "Mean Average Precision" is the average precision of all relevant documents for a query, averaged over all queries as given by the `trec_eval` system (`http://trec.nist.gov/trec_eval`).

[10] I.e. doing "Word Sense Disambiguation" independently of the context. Notice that this choice is made prior to the computation of a *MRC*. Thus the *MRC* with WSD is not at all related to the one without. It can even be closer to the leaves, having then more nodes as for instance in (d) vs (d1) on the MED collection.

different senses of ambiguous words tends to give more importance to the most ambiguous terms, i.e. increases the cosine measure between queries and documents with ambiguous word, which may not be relevant.

Anyway, these results urge on the use of a proper WSD procedure for further improving the results.

4. The results obtained on the TIME collection are illustrating the benefit of the method quite well: comparing indexing size and performance increase between columns (c) and (c1) on one hand, and (d) and (d1) on the other, clearly shows that choosing one concept among many is of real importance at the level of synset indexing (c), whereas it as much less impact at the level of higher cuts in the hierarchy (d). This shows that the description level chosen by the *MRC* cut (d) has reached a level of generalization which is good enough for the targeted discrimination task, indexing the documents correctly enough so as not to fall into semantically meaningless (polysemic) details.

5. As a final evaluation, we tried different weighting schemes in `trec_eval`. As expected, schemes including idf were always giving better results. For this reason, we had the idea to evaluate the impact of idf weighting early on the computing of *MRC*, i.e. changing P_{tf} of Eq. 1 for

$$P_{tf.idf} = \frac{f(n_i)}{|D|} \cdot \log \frac{|d|}{df(n_i)}$$

Although this is no longer a probability distribution on Γ, this weighting gave better results:

		ADI	TIME	CACM	MED	CISI
(d1) P_{tf}	$|index|$	1740	18404	8339	10306	8114
	MAP	0.4071	0.5471	0.2950	0.4226	0.1489
(d1) $P_{tf.idf}$	$|index|$	1808	19067	8779	10741	8642
	MAP	**0.4155**	**0.5501**	**0.3018**	**0.4300**	**0.1540**

The conclusion is that weighting plays definitely an important role (this is not new!) and should be closely watched. It would for instance certainly be interesting to confront the results presented here with similar experiments using other weighting schemes, such as Lnu weighting for example, which is known to be more reliable for handling noisy data and dealing with long documents.

As another future work, we also plan to generalize this technique with ontologies modelling thematic relationships between terms, in addition to a hierarchical structure of hypernyms. It would be also interesting to use better WSD procedure.

References

1. Salton, G.: Automatic Information Organization and Retrieval. McGraw-Hill (1968)
2. Harman, D.: Towards interactive query expansion. In: Proc. of the 11th Annual Int. ACM-SIGIR Conference on Research and development in information retrieval. (1988) 321–331
3. Voorhees, E.M.: Using WordNet to disambiguate word senses for text retrieval. In: Proc. of 16th Annual International ACM-SIGIR Conference on Research and Development in Information Retrieval. (1993) 171–80
4. Voorhees, E.M.: Using WordNet for text retrieval. In Fellbaum, C., ed.: WordNet: An Electronic Lexical Database. MIT Press (1998) 285–303
5. Richardson, R., Smeaton, A.F.: Using WordNet in a knowledge-based approach to information retrieval. Technical Report CA-0395, Dublin City University, Glasnevin, Dublin 9, Ireland (1995)
6. Smeaton, A.F., Quigley, I.: Experiments on using semantic distances between words in image caption retrieval. In: Proc. of 19th Int. Conf. on Research and Development in Information Retrieval. (1996) 174–180
7. Gonzalo, J., Verdejo, F., Chugur, I., Cigarran, J.: Indexing with WordNet synsets can improve text retrieval. In: Proc. of the COLING/ACL 1998 Workshop on Usage of WordNet for Natural Language Processing. (1998) 38–44
8. Gonzalo, J., Verdejo, F., Peters, C., Calzolari, N.: Applying EuroWordNet to multilingual text retrieval. Journal of Computers and the Humanities **32** (1998) 185–207
9. Mihalcea, R., Moldovan, D.: Semantic indexing using WordNet senses. In: Proc. of ACL Workshop on IR & NLP. (2000)
10. Deerwester, S.C., Dumais, S.T., Landauer, T.K., Furnas, G.W., Harshman, R.A.: Indexing by latent semantic analysis. Journal of the American Society of Information Science **41** (1990) 391–407
11. Hofmann, T.: Probabilistic latent semantic indexing. In: proc. of the 22th International Conference on Research and Development in Information Retrieval (SIGIR). (1999) 50–57
12. Whaley, J.M.: An application of word sense disambiguation to information retrieval. Technical Report PCS-TR99-352, Dartmouth College, Computer Science, Hanover, NH (1999)
13. Miyoshi, H., amd M. Kobayashi, K.S., Ogino, T.: An overview of the EDR electronic dictionary and the current status of its utilization. In: Proc. of COLING. (1996) 1090–1093
14. Li, H.: A probabilistic approach to lexical semantic knowledge acquisition and structural disambiguation. Master's thesis, Graduate School of Science, University of Tokyo (1998)
15. Shannon, C.E.: A mathematical theory of communication. The Bell System Technical Journal **27** (1948) 379–423
16. Salton, G.: The SMART Retrieval System – Experiments in Automatic Document Processing. Prentice Hall (1971)
17. Seydoux, F., Chappelier, J.C.: Semantic indexing using Minimum Redundancy Cut in ontologies. In: Proc. of the International Conference on Recent Advances in Natural Language Processing (RANLP'05), Bulgaria. (2005)

Unsupervised Learning of Multiword Units from Part-of-Speech Tagged Corpora: Does Quantity Mean Quality?

Gaël Dias[1] and Špela Vintar[2]

[1] University of Beira Interior, Computer Science Department,
PT-6200-z001 Covilhã, Portugal
ddg@di.ubi.pt
http://www.di.ubi.pt/~ddg
[2] Faculty of Arts, University of Ljubljana,
SI-1000 Ljubljana, Slovenia
spela.vintar@guest.arnes.si
http://www2.arnes.si/~svinta

Abstract. This paper describes an original hybrid system that extracts multi-word unit candidates from part-of-speech tagged corpora. While classical hybrid systems manually define local part-of-speech patterns that lead to the identification of well-known multiword units (mainly compound nouns), we automatically identify relevant syntactical patterns from the corpus. Word statistics are then combined with the endogenously acquired linguistic information in order to extract the most relevant sequences of words. As a result, (1) human intervention is avoided providing total flexibility of use of the system and (2) different multiword units like phrasal verbs, adverbial locutions and prepositional locutions may be identified. Finally, we propose an exhaustive evaluation of our architecture based on the multi-domain, bilingual Slovene-English IJS-ELAN corpus where surprising results are evidenced. To our knowledge, this challenge has never been attempted before.

1 Introduction

Multiword units (MWUs) include a large range of linguistic phenomena, such as compound nouns (e.g. *interior designer*), phrasal verbs (e.g. *run through*), adverbial locutions (e.g. *on purpose*), compound determinants (e.g. *an amount of*), prepositional locutions (e.g. *in front of*) and institutionalized phrases (e.g. *con carne*). MWUs are frequently used in everyday language, usually to precisely express ideas and concepts that cannot be compressed into a single word. As a consequence, their identification is a crucial issue for applications that require some degree of semantic processing (e.g. machine translation, summarization, information retrieval).

In the last 15 years, there has been a growing awareness in the Natural Language Processing (NLP) community of the problems that MWUs pose and the need for their robust handling [1][2]. For that purpose, syntactical [3], statistical [4] and hybrid semantic-syntactic-statistical methodologies [5] have been proposed[1].

---

[1] We only mention recent works as we assume that the reader is familiar with the field of MWUs extraction.

C. Bento, A. Cardoso, and G. Dias (Eds.): EPIA 2005, LNAI 3808, pp. 669–679, 2005.
© Springer-Verlag Berlin Heidelberg 2005

However, in the recent past years, the field of MWU acquisition has known a decreasing interest as no new architecture has been proposed that allows the systems to generalize over all MWU linguistic phenomena. In fact, most systems only deal with noun phrases and verb phrases and are defined and tuned for specific languages. In order to avoid these problems and propose more flexible systems, some investigation has been carried out in the field of machine learning but so far with mixed results [6][7][8][9].

In this paper, we propose an original hybrid system called HELAS[2] that extracts MWU candidates from part-of-speech tagged corpora. Unlike classical hybrid systems that manually pre-define local part-of-speech patterns of interest like Noun+Noun, our solution automatically identifies relevant syntactical patterns from the corpus. Word statistics are then combined with the endogenously acquired linguistic information in order to extract the most relevant sequences of words i.e. MWU candidates. Technically, we conjugate the Mutual Expectation (ME) association measure with the acquisition process called GenLocalMaxs [10] in a five step process. First, the part-of-speech tagged corpus is divided into two sub-corpora: one containing only words and one containing only part-of-speech tags. Each sub-corpus is then segmented into a set of positional n-grams i.e. ordered vectors of textual units. Third, the ME independently evaluates the degree of cohesiveness of each positional n-gram i.e. any positional n-gram of words and any positional n-gram of part-of-speech tags. A combination of both MEs is then used to evaluate the global degree of cohesiveness of any sequence of words associated with its respective part-of-speech tag sequence. This combination of MEs is called the Combined Association Measure (CAM). Finally, the GenLocalMaxs retrieves all the MWU candidates by evidencing local maxima of association measure values thus avoiding the definition of global thresholds.

Compared to existing hybrid systems, the benefits of HELAS are clear. By avoiding human intervention in the definition of syntactical patterns, it provides total flexibility of use. Indeed, the system can be used for any language without any specific tuning. HELAS also allows the identification of various MWUs like phrasal verbs, adverbial locutions, compound determinants, prepositional locutions and institutionalized phrases. Finally, it responds to some extent to the affirmation of [11] that claim that *"existing hybrid systems do not sufficiently tackle the problem of the interdependency between the filtering stage [the definition of syntactical patterns] and the acquisition process [the scoring and the election of relevant sequences of words] as they propose that these two steps should be independent"*. To our knowledge, no system has ever tried to disclaim this statement.

The paper is divided into four main sections: (1) we present the text corpus segmentation into positional n-grams; (2) we define the Mutual Expectation and the Combined Association Measure; (3) we propose the GenLocalMaxs algorithm as the acquisition process; finally, in (4), we propose an exhaustive evaluation based on the multi-domain bilingual Slovene-English IJS-ELAN corpus [12].

2   Text Segmentation

Positional n-grams are nothing more than ordered vectors of textual units which principles are introduced in the next subsection.

---

[2] HELAS stands for *Hybrid Extraction of Lexical ASsociations*.

2.1 Positional N-Grams

The original idea of the positional n-gram model [10] comes from the lexicographic evidence that most lexical relations associate words separated by at most five other words [13]. As a consequence, lexical relations such as MWUs can be continuous or discontinuous sequences of words in a context of at most eleven words (i.e. 5 words to the left of a pivot word, 5 words to the right of the same pivot word and the pivot word itself). In general terms, a MWU can be defined as a specific continuous or discontinuous sequence of words in a $(2.F+1)$-word size window context (i.e. F words to the left of a pivot word, F words to the right of the same pivot word and the pivot word itself). This situation is illustrated in Figure 1 for the multiword unit Ngram Statistics that fits in the window context of size $2.3+1=7$.

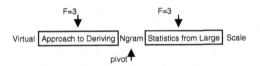

Fig. 1. 7-word size window context

Thus, any substring (continuous or discontinuous) that fits inside the window context and contains the pivot word is called a positional word n-gram. For instance, the vector [Ngram Statistics] is a positional word n-gram as is the discontinuous sequence [Ngram ___ from] where the gap represented by the underline stands for any word occurring between Ngram and from (in this case, Statistics). Generically, any positional word n-gram may be defined as the following vector of words $[p_{11}\ u_1\ p_{12}\ u_2\ \dots\ p_{1n}\ u_n]$ where u_i stands for any word in the positional n-gram and p_{1i} represents the distance that separates words u_1 and u_i[3]. Thus, the positional word n-gram [Ngram Statistics] would be rewritten as [0 Ngram +1 Statistics].

However, in a part-of-speech tagged corpus, each word occurrence is associated to a unique part-of-speech tag. As a consequence, each positional word n-gram is linked to a corresponding positional tag n-gram. A positional tag n-gram is nothing more than an ordered vector of part-of-speech tags exactly in the same way a positional word n-gram is an ordered vector of words. Let's illustrate this situation. Let's consider the following portion of a part-of-speech tagged sentence:

Virtual /JJ Approach /NN to /IN Deriving /VBG Ngram /NN Statistics /NN from /IN Large /JJ
Scale /NN Corpus /NN

It is clear that the corresponding positional tag n-gram of the positional word n-gram [0 Ngram +1 Statistics] is the vector [0 /NN +1 /NN]. Generically, any positional tag n-gram may be defined as a vector of part-of-speech tags $[p_{11}\ t_1\ p_{12}\ t_2\ \dots\ p_{1n}\ t_n]$ where t_i stands for any part-of-speech tag in the positional tag n-gram and p_{1i} represents the distance that separates the part-of-speech tags t_1 and t_i.

---

[3] By statement, any p_{ii} is equal to zero.

So, any sequence of words, in a part-of-speech tagged corpus, is associated to a positional word n-gram and a corresponding positional tag n-gram. In order to introduce the part-of-speech tag factor in any sequence of words of part-of-speech tagged corpus, we present an alternative notation of positional n-grams called positional word-tag n-grams. In order to represent a sequence of words with its associated part-of-speech tags, a positional n-gram may be represented by the following vector of words and part-of-speech tags $[p_{11} \ u_1 \ t_1 \ p_{12} \ u_2 \ t_2 ... \ p_{1n} \ u_n \ t_n]$ where u_i stands for any word in the positional n-gram, t_i stands for the part-of-speech tag of the word u_i and p_{1i} represents the distance that separates words u_1 and u_i. Thus, the positional n-gram [Ngram Statistics] can be represented by the vector [0 Ngram /NN +1 Statistics /NN] given the text corpus above. This alternative notation will allow us to defining, with elegance, our combined association measure, introduced in the next section.

2.2 Data Preparation

The first step of our architecture deals with segmenting the input text corpus into positional n-grams. First, the part-of-speech tagged corpus is divided into two sub-corpora: one sub-corpus of words and one sub-corpus of part-of-speech tags. The word sub-corpus is then segmented into its set of positional word n-grams exactly in the same way the tagged sub-corpus is segmented into its set of positional tag n-grams.

In parallel, each positional word n-gram is associated to its corresponding positional tag n-gram in order to further evaluate the global degree of cohesiveness of any sequence of words in a part-of-speech tagged corpus. Our basic idea is to evaluate the degree of cohesiveness of each positional n-gram independently (i.e. the positional word n-grams on one side and the positional tag n-grams on the other side) in order to calculate the global degree of cohesiveness of any sequence in the part-of-speech tagged corpus by combining its respective degrees of cohesiveness i.e. the degree of cohesiveness of its sequence of words and the degree of cohesiveness of its sequence of part-of-speech tags. In order to evaluate the degree of cohesiveness of any sequence of textual units, we use the association measure called Mutual Expectation and introduce the new Combined Association Measure for the specific case of word-tag n-grams.

3 Association Measures

The Mutual Expectation (ME) has been introduced by [10] and evaluates the degree of cohesiveness that links together all the textual units contained in a positional n-gram ($\forall n, n \geq 2$) based on the concept of Normalized Expectation and relative frequency. In particular, the ME can be seen as an extension to text data of [14]'s support and confidence measures in the context of association rules: the Normalized Expectation representing the confidence of an association rule and the relative frequency the support of an association rule [10].

3.1 Normalized Expectation

The basic idea of the Normalized Expectation (NE) is to evaluate the cost, in terms of cohesiveness, of the loss of one element in a positional n-gram. In fact, it models an average of a combination of n conditional probabilities present inside a given positional n-gram. Thus, the NE is defined in Equation 1 where the function $k(.)$ returns the frequency of any positional n-gram[4].

$$NE\left(\left[\mathrm{p}_{11}\mathrm{u}_1\ldots\mathrm{p}_{1j}\mathrm{u}_j\ldots\mathrm{p}_{1n}\mathrm{u}_n\right]\right)=\frac{k\left(\left[\mathrm{p}_{11}\mathrm{u}_1\ldots\mathrm{p}_{1i}\mathrm{u}_i\ldots\mathrm{p}_{1n}\mathrm{u}_n\right]\right)}{\dfrac{1}{n}\left(k\left(\left[\mathrm{p}_{22}\mathrm{u}_2\ldots\mathrm{p}_{2i}\mathrm{u}_i\ldots\mathrm{p}_{2n}\mathrm{u}_n\right]\right)+\displaystyle\sum_{i=2}^{n}k\left(\left[\mathrm{p}_{11}\mathrm{w}_1\ldots\mathrm{p}_{1i}\hat{\mathrm{u}}_i\ldots\mathrm{p}_{1n}\mathrm{u}_n\right]\right)\right)} \quad (1)$$

3.2 Mutual Expectation

Many applied works in Natural Language Processing have shown that frequency is one of the most relevant statistics to identify relevant textual associations [15][16]. [10] believes that this phenomenon can be enlarged to part-of-speech tags. From this assumption, he poses that between two positional n-grams with the same NE, the most frequent positional n-gram is more likely to be a relevant sequence. The Mutual Expectation is defined in Equation 2 based on its NE and its relative frequency embodied by the function $p(.)$.

$$ME\left(\left[\mathrm{p}_{11}\mathrm{u}_1\ldots\mathrm{p}_{1i}\mathrm{u}_i\ldots\mathrm{p}_{1n}\mathrm{u}_n\right]\right)=p\left(\left[\mathrm{p}_{11}\mathrm{u}_1\ldots\mathrm{p}_{1i}\mathrm{u}_i\ldots\mathrm{p}_{1n}\mathrm{u}_n\right]\right)\times NE\left(\left[\mathrm{p}_{11}\mathrm{u}_1\ldots\mathrm{p}_{1i}\mathrm{u}_i\ldots\mathrm{p}_{1n}\mathrm{u}_n\right]\right) \quad (2)$$

As we said earlier, the ME is going to be used to calculate the degree cohesiveness of any positional word n-gram and any positional tag n-gram. The way we calculate the global degree of cohesiveness of any sequence of words associated to its part-of-speech tag sequence, based on its two MEs, is discussed in the next subsection.

3.3 Combined Association Measure

The drawbacks shown by the statistical methodologies evidence the lack of linguistic information. Indeed, these methodologies can only identify textual associations in the context of their usage. As a consequence, many relevant structures can not be introduced directly into lexical databases as they do not guarantee adequate linguistic structures.

For that purpose, [17] proposed a first attempt to solve this problem without predefining syntactical patterns of interest that bias the extraction process. His idea is simply to combine the strength existing between words in a sequence and the evidenced interdependencies between its part-of-speech tags. We could summarize this idea as follows: the more cohesive the words of a sequence and the more cohesive its part-of-speech tags are, the more likely the sequence may embody a multiword unit.

The degree of cohesiveness of any positional n-gram based on a part-of-speech tagged corpus can then be evaluated by the Combined Association Measure (CAM) defined in Equation 3 where α stands as a parameter that tunes the focus whether on words or on part-of-speech tags.

$$CAM\left(\left[\mathrm{p}_{11}\mathrm{u}_1\mathrm{t}_1\ldots\mathrm{p}_{1i}\mathrm{u}_i\mathrm{t}_i\ldots\mathrm{p}_{1n}\mathrm{u}_n\mathrm{t}_n\right]\right)=$$
$$ME\left(\left[\mathrm{p}_{11}\mathrm{u}_1\ldots\mathrm{p}_{1i}\mathrm{u}_i\ldots\mathrm{p}_{1n}\mathrm{u}_n\right]\right)^{\alpha}\times ME\left(\left[\mathrm{p}_{11}\mathrm{t}_1\ldots\mathrm{p}_{1i}\mathrm{t}_i\ldots\mathrm{p}_{1n}\mathrm{t}_n\right]\right)^{1-\alpha} \quad (3)$$

---

[4] The "^" corresponds to a convention used in Algebra that consists in writing a "^" on the top of the omitted term of a given succession indexed from 1 to n.

In order to illustrate the *CAM* formula, we illustrate its value for the positional 2-gram [0 Ngram /NN +1 Statistics /NN] in Equation 4.

$$CAM([0\,\mathrm{Ngram}\,/\mathrm{NN}+1\,\mathrm{Statistics}\,/\mathrm{NN}]) =$$
$$ME([0\,\mathrm{Ngram}+1\,\mathrm{Statistics}])^{\alpha} \times ME([0\,/\mathrm{NN}+1\,/\mathrm{NN}])^{1-\alpha} \qquad (4)$$

We will see in the final section of this paper that different values of α lead to fundamentally different sets of multiword unit candidates. Indeed, α can go from a total focus on part-of-speech tags (i.e. with $\alpha=0$, the relevance of a word sequence is based only on the relevance of its part-of-speech sequence) to a total focus on words (i.e. with $\alpha=1$, the relevance of a word sequence is defined only by its word dependencies).

It is important to notice that unlike general smoothing methodologies that use linear interpolation, we preferred, in a first step of our experiments, to use a more drastic smoothing technique. Indeed, with our experience in the field, we believe that radical smoothing could lead to better results than weaker techniques such as linear interpolation. However, we are aware that the linear interpolation should be experimented in further work as a baseline for evaluation. We propose the formula of the linear interpolation in Equation 5.

$$CAM([0\,\mathrm{Ngram}\,/\mathrm{NN}+1\,\mathrm{Statistics}\,/\mathrm{NN}]) =$$
$$\alpha \times ME([0\,\mathrm{Ngram}+1\,\mathrm{Statistics}]) + (1-\alpha) \times ME([0\,/\mathrm{NN}+1\,/\mathrm{NN}]) \qquad (5)$$

Before going to experimentation, we need to introduce the used acquisition process which objective is to extract the MWUs candidates in the overall search space.

4   The Acquisition Process

The GenLocalMaxs [10] proposes a flexible and fine-tuned approach for the selection process as it concentrates on the identification of local maxima of association measure values. So, we may deduce that a positional word-tag n-gram is a MWU if its combined association measure value is higher or equal than the combined association measure values of all its sub-groups of (n-1) words and if it is strictly higher than the combined association measure values of all its super-groups of (n+1) words. Let *CAM* be the combined association measure, *W* a positional word-tag ngram, Ω_{n-1} the set of all the positional word-tag (n-1)-grams contained in *W*, Ω_{n+1} the set of all the positional word-tag (n+1)-grams containing *W* and *sizeof(.)* a function that returns the number of words of a positional word-tag ngram. The GenLocalMaxs is defined as:

$\forall x \in \Omega_{n-1}, \ \forall y \in \Omega_{n+1}, \ W$ is a relevant sequence of textual units if

$(sizeof(W){=}2 \ \wedge \ CAM(W) > CAM(y)\,) \vee (sizeof(W){\neq}2 \ \wedge \ CAM(W) \geq CAM(x) \ \wedge \ CAM(W) > CAM(y))$

Algo 1. The GenLocalMaxs algorithm

The GenLocalMaxs evidences three interesting properties. First, it allows the testing of various association measures. Second, the GenLocalMaxs allows extracting multiword units obtained by composition. Indeed, as the algorithm retrieves pertinent units by analysing their immediate context, it may identify multiword units that are composed by one or more other MWUs. Third, the GenLocalMaxs shows one important property: it does not depend on global thresholds. A direct implication of this characteristic is the fact that, as no tuning needs to be made in order to acquire the set of all the MWU candidates, the use of the system remains as flexible as possible. Thus, the GenLocalMaxs proposes an excellent evaluation platform for Multiword Unit extraction.

Finally, we propose an exhaustive evaluation of our architecture based on the multi-domain, bilingual Slovene-English IJS-ELAN corpus [12].

5 Evaluation

The main idea of our evaluation is to verify whether our architecture is capable of extending itself to different language families, domains and corpora sizes. For that purpose, we chose three sub-corpora of the multi-domain bilingual Slovene-English IJS-ELAN corpus [12]: the Annex II (Anx2) to the Europe Agreement about EU legislation and politics of 25.000 words, the Slovenian Economic Mirror (Ecmr) about economics of 239.000 words and the Linux Installation and Getting Started (Ligs) about computing of 173.000 words.

In particular, MWUs of sizes 2 to 6 units were extracted from these texts with α ranging from 0.1 to 1[5] and only contiguous units were taken into account.

The evaluation was performed manually by three native speakers of Slovene and two near-native speakers of English, whereby the evaluators were instructed to mark all MWUs belonging to either of the following categories: set phrases, phrasal verbs, adverbial locutions, compound determinants, prepositional locutions and institutionalized phrases, including domain-specific terms and names based on the work developed by [18]. Candidates were marked simply as correct or incorrect with no classes in between. The global precision results are illustrated in Table 1.

Table 1. Average precision

Alpha	English	Slovene
0.1	0.109	0.139
0.2	0.128	0.151
0.3	0.137	0.168
0.4	0.141	0.168
0.5	0.138	0.167
0.6	0.145	0.177
0.7	0.130	0.191
0.8	0.132	0.209
0.9	0.142	0.296
1	0.144	0.284

---

[5] At the moment of submission, the evaluation for α=0 is still running.

The overall precision regardless of n-gram type and text type shows that the best result for English is obtained with $\alpha = 0.6$, while for Slovene the precision seems to be gradually rising as α increases, with the highest value at $\alpha = 0.9$. The part-of-speech sequence apparently plays a lesser role with a highly inflectional language like Slovene, where on the whole far fewer candidates are extracted due to morphologically reduced frequencies. Although, the results seem to be low, they depend a lot on the corpus size, the type of n-gram and the domain of the corpus. For instance, the best single precision was obtained for Slovene 2grams at $\alpha = 0.8$ for the smallest corpus,

Table 2. Detailed precision

		English					Slovene				
	Alpha	2grams	3grams	4grams	5grams	6grams	2grams	3grams	4grams	5grams	6grams
Anx2	0.1	0.4452	0.2051	0.333	0	0	0.4304	0.1096	0.129	0.0714	0
	0.2	0.4804	0.203	0.5	0	0	0.4336	0.1226	0.1212	0.0909	0.0833
	0.3	0.5166	0.257	0.333	0	0	0.4642	0.1306	0.125	0.166	0.0833
	0.4	0.5298	0.2514	0.333	0	0	0.5168	0.139	0.1142	0.1818	0.0833
	0.5	0.4351	0.2217	0.333	0	0	0.581	0.1616	0.1111	0.1666	0.0833
	0.6	0.5833	0.1947	0.333	0	0	0.6379	0.1666	0.1052	0.1428	0.0833
	0.7	0.4623	0.181	0.25	0	0	0.6595	0.1681	0.1351	0.1428	0.0833
	0.8	0.5	0.188	0.25	0	0	0.7941	0.1637	0.1562	0.1538	0.0833
	0.9	0.5909	0.204	0.25	0	0	0.7037	0.1576	0.1818	0.2	0.07692
	1	0.396	0.1985	0	0	0	0.5714	0.1576	0.2	0.2222	0.07692
Ecmr	0.1	0.1381	0.1308	0	0	0	0.1489	0.1238	0.258	0.125	0
	0.2	0.1432	0.1231	0.0909	0	0	0.1637	0.1337	0.2424	0.125	0
	0.3	0.1597	0.1378	0.1428	0	0	0.1665	0.141	0.2857	0.125	0
	0.4	0.1752	0.1319	0.1463	0	0	0.1801	0.1386	0.2647	0.0625	0
	0.5	0.1764	0.1317	0.1481	0	0	0.2255	0.144	0.2	0	0
	0.6	0.1752	0.1319	0.1463	0	0	0.2866	0.1466	0.2	0	0
	0.7	0.1883	0.132	0.1428	0	0	0.35	0.1555	0.2222	0	0
	0.8	0.1834	0.1336	0.1296	0	0	0.3976	0.1575	0.1904	0	0
	0.9	0.2054	0.1567	0.1228	0	0	0.4015	0.1832	0.2558	0.1538	0.6666
	1	0.2125	0.1865	0.2244	0.1818	0.1	0.4084	0.2012	0.1818	0.1538	0.6666
Ligs	0.1	0.204	0.116	0	0	0.0714	0.159	0.047	0.060	0.108	0.059
	0.2	0.203	0.1603	0.0322	0	0.0714	0.180	0.048	0.058	0.111	0.059
	0.3	0.21	0.2	0.0666	0	0.0714	0.186	0.045	0.061	0.108	0.059
	0.4	0.2084	0.2188	0.0571	0	0.0714	0.183	0.039	0.048	0.111	0.059
	0.5	0.2054	0.2202	0.0957	0.037	0.0666	0.245	0.035	0.054	0.099	0
	0.6	0.2172	0.2086	0.1181	0.0689	0	0.287	0.032	0.049	0.096	0
	0.7	0.2285	0.2032	0.1111	0.0526	0	0.355	0.035	0.047	0.090	0
	0.8	0.2178	0.2046	0.1261	0.0454	0	0.501	0.039	0.045	0.100	0
	0.9	0.1882	0.199	0.1361	0.0847	0	0.462	0.037	0.040	0.099	0
	1	0.2053	0.1933	0.1308	0.0851	0.0487	0.403	0.031	0.033	0.036	0

Annex II, and reached 79% precision. It is clear that a deeper analysis needs to be carried out to really understand the behaviour of our system. A complete evaluation over the three corpora is proposed in Table 2.

In comparing overall precision by n-gram type and by text type it becomes clear that the size of the sub-corpus plays a substantial role. The larger the corpus, the lower the precision is, especially for 2-grams. These results are very interesting as it has always been said in the literature that bigger corpora would automatically lead to better results for statistical methodologies. It seems that this assumption does not stand for our architecture[6]. Indeed, as big corpora evidence large lexical diversity it seems that our system is not as reliable as for small corpora where lexical diversity is small. What could be seen as a problem of scalability is in fact a providential result for many real-world NLP applications which can now integrate a multiword unit recognition "plug-in" that will process texts in real-time[7].

For both English and Slovene, the highest precision is obtained when extracting 2-grams and it then deteriorates with n-gram length, although small differences according to text type may be observed. Moreover, a comparison between English and Slovene shows a constant overall higher precision for Slovene compared to English. The reason for this difference is undoubtedly again the morphological richness of Slovene, which on the one hand results in lower recall, and on the other hand causes for the same phrase to be extracted several times in different cases. However, in order to be extracted at all, an inflected phrase must occur in that form often enough to be spotted, which positively influences precision.

Finally, we evaluated overall precision according to the frequency of the proposed MWUs. As can be expected, precision rapidly increases with frequency, so that for n-grams occurring at least five times, it will almost be increased 50% compared to the precision for n-grams occurring only twice as expressed in Table 3.

Table 3. Overall precision by n-gram frequency

	Slovene					English				
Alpha	2	3	4	5	>5	2	3	4	5	>5
0.1	0.175	0.139	0.135	0.217	0.179	0.091	0.098	0.125	0.121	0.134
0.2	0.161	0.152	0.232	0.195	0.196	0.233	0.243	0.292	0.267	0.328
0.3	0.169	0.169	0.243	0.189	0.223	0.257	0.246	0.331	0.268	0.346
0.4	0.159	0.172	0.224	0.191	0.234	0.236	0.203	0.309	0.253	0.320
0.5	0.171	0.203	0.231	0.203	0.270	0.202	0.178	0.328	0.224	0.322
0.6	0.178	0.165	0.195	0.218	0.259	0.198	0.172	0.293	0.232	0.373
0.7	0.173	0.174	0.182	0.200	0.330	0.177	0.177	0.242	0.242	0.300
0.8	0.161	0.197	0.216	0.204	0.323	0.177	0.171	0.247	0.233	0.286
0.9	0.251	0.304	0.335	0.253	0.345	0.192	0.186	0.220	0.215	0.307
1	0.154	0.226	0.232	0.308	0.326	0.192	0.168	0.248	0.216	0.293

---

[6] In fact, these results stand for other experiments we did with other corpora and do not only stand for this particular experiment.

[7] In particular, we successfully use this module in our different research works on Topic Segmentation [19] and Web search.

6 Conclusion and Future Work

The paper described a system for extracting multiword units from part-of-speech tagged corpora using a hybrid approach that exploits both statistical and linguistic properties. To our knowledge, this experiment had never been attempted before. The evaluation that was performed for three sub-corpora of a multi-domain Slovene-English corpus shows interesting differences between the languages and between the sub-corpora. The general conclusion is however that the combination of these two layers of information works better than purely statistical methods, while still remaining unsupervised in terms of part-of-speech sequence selection.

Future work will focus on several interesting aspects of language specificity that seem to influence performance. Firstly, the implication that part-of-speech information plays a lesser role for highly inflectional languages like Slovene should be reviewed by expanding the set of languages on the one hand, and by simplifying the tag set on the other hand. We believe that certain layers of the morpho-syntactic analysis, such as gender and number, are redundant for the task at hand.

Secondly, the findings that a smaller corpus yields more accurate MWUs than a larger one, and that frequency nevertheless plays a major role in overall precision, are somewhat controversial and should be explored in more detail. Lexical variation is undoubtedly linked to the corpus composition and corpus homogeneity [19], so that the latter must be considered before any final conclusions can be drawn.

References

1. Tanaka, T. and Baldwin, T.: Noun-Noun Compound Machine Translation: A Feasibility Study on Shallow Processing. In Workshop on Multiword Expressions of the 41st ACL meeting. 7-12 July Sapporo Japan (2003) 17-25.
2. Nivre, J. and Nilsson, J.: Multiword Units in Syntactic Parsing. In: Dias, G., Lopes, J.G.L. and Vintar, S. (eds.): Workshop on Methodologies and Evaluation of Multiword Units in Real-world Applications associated with the 4th International Conference on Languages Resources and Evaluation, Lisbon, Portugal, May 25. ISBN: 2-9517408-1-6. EAN: 0782951740815. (2004) 39-47.
3. Bourigault, D.: Analyse syntaxique locale pour le repérage de termes complexes dans un texte. Traitement Automatique des Langues, vol. 34 (2). (1993) 105-117.
4. Tomokiyo, T. and Hurst, M.: A Language Model Approach to Keyphrase Extraction. In Workshop on Multiword Expressions of the 41st ACL meeting. 7-12 July. Sapporo. Japan. (2003) 33-41.
5. Piao, S., Rayson, P., Archer, D., Wilson, A. and McEnery, T.: Extracting Multiword Expressions with a Semantic Tagger. In Workshop on Multiword Expressions of the 41st ACL meeting. 7-12 July. Sapporo. Japan. (2003) 49-57.
6. Yang, S.: Machine Learning for Collocation Identification. International Conference on Natural Language Processing and Knowledge Engineering, Chengqing Zong (eds), Beijing. China, IEEE Press, October 26-29. ISBN: 0-7803-7902-0. 315-321 (2003)
7. Dias, G. and Nunes, S.: Evaluation of Different Similarity Measures for the Extraction of Multiword Units in a Reinforcement Learning Environment. In M.T. Lino, M.F. Xavier, F. Pereira, R. Costa and R. Silva (eds): Proceedings of the 4th International Conference On Languages Resources and Evaluation, M.T. Lino, M.F. Xavier, F. Pereira, R. Costa and R. Silva (eds), Lisbon, Portugal, May 26-28. ISBN: 2-9517408-1-6. EAN: 0782951740815. (2004) 1717-1721.

8. Díaz-Galiano, M.C, Martín-Valdivia, M.T., Martínez-Santiago, F. and Ureña-López, L.A. Multiword Expressions Recognition with the LVQ Algorithm. In: Dias, G., Lopes, J.G.L. and Vintar, S. (eds.): Workshop on Methodologies and Evaluation of Multiword Units in Real-world Applications associated with the 4th International Conference on Languages Resources and Evaluation, Lisbon, Portugal, May 25. ISBN: 2-9517408-1-6. EAN: 0782951740815. (2004) 12-17.

9. Ogata, T., Terao, K. and Umemura, K.: Japanese Multiword Extraction using SVM and Adaptation. In: Dias, G., Lopes, J.G.L. and Vintar, S. (eds.): Workshop on Methodologies and Evaluation of Multiword Units in Real-world Applications associated with the 4th International Conference on Languages Resources and Evaluation, Lisbon, Portugal, May 25. ISBN: 2-9517408-1-6. EAN: 0782951740815. (2004) 8-12.

10. Dias, G.: Extraction Automatique d'Associations Lexicales à partir de Corpora. PhD Thesis. DI/FCT New University of Lisbon (Portugal) and LIFO University of Orléans (France) (2002).

11. Habert, B. and Jacquemin, C.: Noms composés, termes, dénominations complexes: problématiques linguistiques et traitements automatiques. Traitement Automatique des Langues, vol. 34(2). (1993) 5-41.

12. Erjavec, T. The IJS-ELAN Slovene-English Parallel Corpus. International Journal of Corpus Linguistics, 7(1), (2002) 1-20.

13. Sinclair, J.: English Lexical Collocations: A study in computational linguistics. Singapore, reprinted as chapter 2 of Foley, J. A. (ed). 1996, John Sinclair on Lexis and Lexicography, Uni Press. (1974)

14. Agrawal, R., Imielinski, T. and Swami, A.: Mining association rules between sets of items in large databases. In Proceedings of the ACM SIGMOD Conference on Management of Data, Washington, D.C. USA. (1993) 207--216

15. Justeson, J. and Katz, S.: Technical Terminology: some linguistic properties and an algorithm for identification in text. Natural Language Engineering, vol. 1, (1995) 9-27.

16. Daille, B.: Study and Implementation of Combined Techniques for Automatic Extraction of Terminology. The balancing act combining symbolic and statistical approaches to language, MIT Press, (1996) 49-66.

17. Dias, G.: Multiword Unit Hybrid Extraction. Workshop on Multiword Expressions of the 41st ACL meeting. 7-12 July. Sapporo. Japan. (2003) 41-49.

18. Gross, G.: Les expressions figées en français. Paris, Ophrys. (1996)

19. Dias, G. and Alves, E.: Language-Independent Informative Topic Segmentation. In Proceedings of the 9th International Symposium on Social Communication, Santiago de Cuba, Cuba, January 24-28. (Best Award Paper). ISBN: 959-7174-05-7. (2005). 588-592

20. Kilgarriff, A.: Comparing Corpora. International Jounal of Corpus Lingustics, 6(1), (2001) 97-133.

Lappin and Leass' Algorithm for Pronoun Resolution in Portuguese*

Thiago Thomes Coelho and Ariadne Maria Brito Rizzoni Carvalho

Institute of Computing, State University of Campinas,
Mail Box 6176, 13084-971 Campinas (SP), Brazil
{thiago.coelho, ariadne}@ic.unicamp.br

Abstract. This paper presents a variant of Lappin and Leass' Algorithm for pronoun resolution in Portuguese texts; the algorithm resolves third person pronominal anaphora, as well as reflexive and reciprocal pronouns. It relies on salience measures, derived from the syntactic structure of the sentence, and on a simple discourse representation model. The algorithm, as well as its evaluation with legal and literary corpora, are presented.

1 Introduction

The phenomenon of coreference that occurs in natural language is the device of making an abbreviated reference to some entity (or entities) in the expectation that the perceiver of the discourse will be able to disabbreviate the reference and, thereby, determine the identity of the entity. The abbreviated reference is called an anaphor and the entity to which it refers is its referent or antecedent. The process of determining the referent of an anaphor is called resolution [1].

Anaphora resolution can improve significantly the performance of several natural language processing applications, such as automatic translation and summarisation, among others. The main difficult is to identify the proper referent when there exists more than one candidate. Several approaches to anaphora resolution have been proposed, such as Lappin and Leass Algorithm [2], Hobbs Algorithm [3] and Centering Algorithm [4].

Lappin and Leass' Algorithm, or RAP (*Resolution of Anaphora Procedure*), aims at identifying both intra and intersentential antecedents of third person pronouns and lexical anaphors (reflexive and reciprocal), in English. This paper presents a variant of Lappin and Leass' Algorithm for pronoun resolution in Portuguese, as well as its evaluation with legal and literary corpora. This algorithm was chosen because of its good performance with English texts.

The remainder of this paper is organized as follows: in the next section the Lappin and Leass' original algorithm is presented; in section 3 the algorithm built for pronoun resolution in Portuguese is described and an example of its execution is presented; in section 4 the algorithm is evaluated on two different corpora and the results are shown; and finally, in section 5 the conclusions and future work are presented.

---

* The work was partially sponsored by CNPq.

C. Bento, A. Cardoso, and G. Dias (Eds.): EPIA 2005, LNAI 3808, pp. 680–692, 2005.

2   Lappin and Leass' Algorithm

The main components of the Lappin and Leass Algorithm are [2]:

- An intrasentential syntactic filter [5,6] for ruling out anaphoric dependence of a pronoun on a noun phrase, based on syntactic grounds;
- A morphological filter for ruling out anaphoric dependence of a pronoun on a noun phrase due to person, number, or gender non-agreement;
- An anaphor binding algorithm [6] for identifying the possible antecedent binder of a lexical anaphor (reciprocal or reflexive pronoun) within the same sentence;
- A procedure for assigning the suitable salience factors weights to a noun phrase, according to its grammatical role, such as syntactic parallelism, subject, etc.;
- A decision procedure for selecting the preferred element from a list of possible antecedent candidates.

The anaphor binding algorithm identifies the intrasentential candidates for reflexive or reciprocal pronouns; the syntactic filter rules out the intrasentential coreference candidates for third person pronouns that are unlikely to be the antecedent. For the remaining candidates, the value of the salience factors are calculated (as described in section 2.1). The chosen referent will be the one with the highest salience factor. When there is more than one candidate with the same salience factor, the algorithm chooses the candidate which is closer to the pronoun. The syntactic filter and the anaphor binding algorithm analyse the pronoun's sentence syntactic structure to decide if coreference is allowed. The algorithm uses the grammatical representation generated by the parser developed by McCord [7,8].

2.1   Salience Factors

RAP uses a salience weighting system based on syntactic features. There are two types of operations performed by the algorithm: discourse model update and pronoun resolution. When a noun phrase, which introduces a new entity in the discourse is found, a representation for that entity is created and its salience factor is calculated. The salience factor for a given entity is the total of all salience factors applied to that entity. The initial salience factors are presented in Table 1.

Table 1. Salience factors with initial weights [2]

Salience factors	Weights
Sentence recency	100.0
Subject emphasis	80.0
Existential emphasis	70.0
Accusative emphasis	50.0
Indirect object and oblique complement emphasis	40.0
Non-adverbial emphasis	50.0
Head noun emphasis	80.0

The salience factor weights show the preference for choosing a certain antecedent based on its grammatical role, according to the following hierarchy [9]:

subject emphasis>existential emphasis>accusative emphasis>indirect object and oblique complement emphasis>non-adverbial emphasis

The following sentences illustrate the salience factors assignment to the expressions in bold:

- Subject emphasis:
  (1) **Os examinadores** começaram a prova com atraso.
  (**The examiners** *started the exam late.*)
- Existential emphasis:
  (2) Havia **uma casa azul** ao lado da padaria.
  (*There was* **a blue house** *next to the bakery.*)
- Accusative emphasis:
  (3) Mariana mudou **a minha vida**.
  (*Mariana changed* **my life.**)
- Indirect object and oblique complement emphasis:
  (4) Duvidava **da riqueza da terra**.
  (*He doubted* **about the richness of the Earth.**)
- Non-adverbial emphasis:
  (5) Não saímos por causa **da chuva**.
  (*We didn't get out because* **of the rain**).
- Head noun emphasis:
  (6) **Pedro** comprou **um carro**.
  (**Pedro** *bought* **a car.**)

The assignment to the first four sentences is straightforward, but the assignment to the fifth and sixth sentences deserves an additional explanation.

The salience factor *Non-adverbial emphasis* is given to discourse entities which are not contained in an adverbial prepositional phrase demarcated by a separator. Therefore, in sentence (5), the salience factor is assigned to "chuva" because, although it is contained in an adverbial prepositional phrase, it is not demarcated. On the other hand, in sentence (7), below, the salience factor *Non-adverbial emphasis* is not assigned to "da padaria", because it is contained within the demarcated adverbial prepositional phrase "Perto da padaria".

(7) Perto da padaria, Pedro foi roubado.
    (*Next to the bakery, Peter was robbed.*)

The salience factor *Head noun emphasis* is assigned to discourse entities which are not contained in another noun phrase. Therefore, this salience factor is assigned to the noun phrases "Pedro" and "um carro" in sentence (6). On the other hand, in sentence (8), below, the salience factor is not assigned to the noun phrases "usuário do carro" and "carro", because they are part of the noun phrases "O manual de usuário do carro" and "usuário do carro", respectively. Nevertheless, this salience factor is assigned to "O manual de usuário do carro" as a whole, because it is not contained in another noun phrase.

(8) **O manual de usuário do carro** está no banco de trás.
(**The car user manual** *is in the back seat*).

Finally, the salience factor *Sentence recency* is assigned to all noun phrases present in the sentence being processed. The salience factor assigned to every entity in the discourse is divided by two at the beginning of the processing of the current sentence.

The salience factor degradation and the *Sentence recency* aim at giving priority to the most recently mentioned candidates, since the candidates from the current sentence, and from the one next to it, will tend to have the higher salience weights. In the process of finding an antecedent, two more salience factors are considered: *parallelism*, and *cataphora*. The first gives priority to candidates which present syntactic parallelism with the pronoun, as in the text (9), below:

(9) **Pedro** foi à concessionária com Bruno. Ele comprou um carro.
(**Peter** *went to the concessionary with Bruno. He bought a car.*)

The noun phrase "Pedro" will receive the salience factor *parallelism*, during the resolution of pronoun "Ele", because they present a syntactic parallelism, that is, they are both subject noun phrases. The second factor penalizes cataphors, as in sentence (10), below:

(10) Ela estava preparando o almoço quando **Maria** chegou.
(*She was preparing lunch when* **Mary** *arrived.*)

The noun phrase "Maria" is penalized during the resolution of pronoun "Ela" because it occurs after the pronoun in the sentence. The assignment of the last two salience factors depends on the pronoun which is being resolved, since the salience weight is assigned to the discourse entity only during pronoun resolution. These values are presented in Table 2.

Table 2. Additional salience factors [2]

Salience Factors	Weights
Syntactic Parallelism	35.0
Cataphora	-175.0

All salience weights were empirically obtained by Lappin and Leass in order to improve the performance of the algorithm, on a corpus composed of computer manuals in English. It is important to notice that more than one salience factor may be assigned to an entity, according to its syntactic role and to the sentence structure. The pronouns which have the same referent are grouped together in the same equivalence class. The salience factor of a class is given by the sum of all its members. Details about the assignment will be illustrated through an example, presented in section 3.3.

3   Implementation of Lappin and Leass' Algorithm for Portuguese

The algorithm which was developed and evaluated in this work is based on RAP. The main components of Lappin and Leass' Algorithm, presented in section 2, were implemented, with the following differences:

- The syntactic filter and the binding algorithm were substituted by the constraints on coreference proposed by Reinhart [10]. A thorough analysis of the examples presented in [2,5,6] has shown that Reinhart's constraints were sufficient to deal with the cases presented by the authors of the original algorithm;
- The parser used by the system was PALAVRAS [11], a very robust parser for Portuguese;
- A tool called PALAVRAS Xtractor [12] was used to convert the parser's output to XML (*Extensible Markup Language*[1]), in order to improve the linguistic information extraction from the corpora analysed by PALAVRAS. The tool produces three XML files: *words*, which contains a list of the words from the text; *pos*, which contains morfosyntactic information; and *chunks*, which contains information on the text structure;
- The algorithm does not deal with cataphora.

3.1   Reinhart's Constraints

Certain structural sentence properties impose further restrictions on coreference [13]. Reinhart constraints, used and implemented here, are based on the notion of *c-command (constituent-command)*, which is defined as follows [10]:

- *Node A c-commands node B if and only if the first branching node α which dominates*[2] *node A also dominates node B, or α is immediately dominated by a node β which is of the same syntactic category of node α.*

The relevant constraints on pronominal anaphora which have been implemented are [10]:

1. Coreference is forbidden when the pronoun c-commands the noun phrase;
2. Coreference is allowed when the pronoun is either reflexive or reciprocal, the noun phrase c-commands the pronoun, and is within the Minimal Governing Category (MGC)[3] of the pronoun;
3. Coreference is forbidden when the pronoun is non reflexive or reciprocal, the noun phrase c-commands the pronoun, and is within its MGC.

---

[1] Available at http://www.w3.org/XML/.

[2] A node α is dominated by all its ancestral nodes [14].

[3] The Minimal Governing Category of a node α is defined as the root node of the sentence, or the ancestral noun phrase node α which dominates the sentence subject.

Consider the following sentences:

(11) Ele sentou perto de Pedro. (*He seat near Peter.*)
(12) Maria gosta de si. (*Mary likes herself.*)
(13) Maria gosta dela. (*Mary likes her.*)

The simplified derivation trees for sentences (11), (12) and (13), produced by the parser PALAVRAS, are presented in Figures 1(a), 1(b) and 1(c), respectively[4].

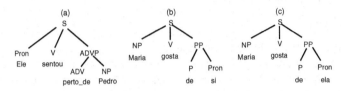

Fig. 1. Derivation trees for (11), (12) and (13)

In sentence (11), according to the first Reinhart's constraint, coreference between noun phrase "Pedro" and pronoun "Ele" is forbidden because the pronoun c-commands the noun phrase, that is, the first branching node which dominates "Ele", the node S, also dominates "Pedro".

On the other hand, in sentence (12), the second constraint allows coreference between the noun phrase "Maria" and the pronoun "si", because the noun phrase c-commands the pronoun, the pronoun is reflexive and the noun phrase is within the MGC of the pronoun.

In sentence (13), the third constraint does not allow coreference between the noun phrase "Maria" and the pronoun "dela", because the noun phrase c-commands the pronoun, the pronoun is not reflexive, and the noun phrase is within the MGC of the pronoun.

3.2   The Resolution Process

The following steps describe the coreference resolution process according to the the algorithm for pronoun resolution in Portuguese:

 – At the beginning of the processing of a new sentence, degradate the salience factor of all equivalence classes, that is, divide the salience factor of all equivalence classes by two;
 – Extract all possible candidates from the sentence;
 – Create equivalence classes for all candidates which do not belong to any of the existing classes. In this case, the appropriate salience factors are assigned to the candidate according to Table 1. The salience factor of a candidate already included in an equivalence class will be the salience factor of the class to whom it belongs;

---

[4] Legend: ADVP: adverbial phrase; ADV: adverb; ART: article; N: noun; NP: noun phrase; PP: prepositional phrase; P: preposition; PRON: pronoun; V: verb.

- For every pronoun of the sentence:
    - Calculate the pronoun salience factor using values from Table 1;
    - Generate the list with the possible candidates for third person pronouns:
        * Extract candidates which agree in gender and number with the pronoun, using a four sentence window;
    - Generate a list with the possible candidates for reflexive and reciprocal pronouns:
        * Extract only intrasentential candidates which agree in gender and number with the pronoun;
    - Apply Reinhart's constraints to the intrasentential remaining candidates; if the candidate is rejected, all entities from its equivalence class are excluded from the list of candidates;
    - Assign additional weights to the candidates according to Table 2;
    - Select the candidate with the highest salience factor; if candidates are tied, choose the candidate closer to the pronoun;
    - Include the pronoun in the equivalence class for the best selected candidate.

3.3   Example

The algorithm's functioning is illustrated through an example. Consider the following sentences:

(14) Pedro bebeu vinho de jabuticaba. (*Peter drank jabuticaba wine.*)
(15) Ele comprou-o no supermercado. (*He bought it in the supermarket.*)

The derivation trees for sentences (14) and (15), produced by PALAVRAS, are presented in Figure 2.

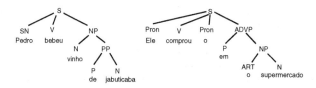

Fig. 2. Derivation trees for sentences (14) and (15)

When sentence (14) is being analysed, first all candidates for referent are selected, that is "Pedro", "vinho de jabuticaba" and "jabuticaba"; next, their salience values are calculated and new equivalence classes are created for them. Salience value 310 is assigned to the first, because "Pedro" is the subject of the sentence (80), it is neither contained in another noun phrase (80), nor in a demarcated adverbial prepositional phrase (50), and it is within the sentence which is being analysed (100). To the second noun phrase, that is "vinho de jabuticaba", the salience factor 280 is assigned, because it is a direct object (50), it is neither

(a)

Referent	Anaphor	Value
Pedro		310
vinho de jabuticaba		280
jabuticaba		150

(b)

Referent	Anaphor	Value
Pedro		155
vinho de jabuticaba		140
jabuticaba		75
supermercado		230

(c)

Referent	Anaphor	Value
Pedro	Ele	465
vinho de jabuticaba		140
jabuticaba		75
supermercado		230

(d)

Referent	Anaphor	Value
Pedro	Ele	465
vinho de jabuticaba	o	420
jabuticaba		75
supermercado		230

Fig. 3. Discourse model evolution as sentences (14) and (15) are analysed

contained in another noun phrase (80), nor in a demarcated adverbial prepositional phrase (50), and it is present in the sentence which is being analysed (100). To the last candidate, that is "jabuticaba", the salience factor 150 is assigned, because it is not contained in a demarcated adverbial prepositional phrase (50), and it is present in the sentence which is being analysed (100). The equivalence classes for sentence (14) are shown in Figure 3(a).

At the beginning of the analysis of the new sentence, that is sentence (15), all previous equivalence classes have their salience factors divided by two. Therefore, the salience factor of the equivalence class for "Pedro" becomes 155, for "vinho de jabuticaba" becomes 140, and for "jabuticaba", 75.

The possible candidate extracted from sentence (15) is "o supermercado", whose salience factor is 230, since it is neither contained in another noun phrase (80), nor in an demarcated adverbial prepositional phrase (50). Also, it is within the sentence which is being processed (100). Figure 3(b) shows the discourse model at this point.

Next, the pronoun references are resolved. For pronoun "Ele", there are no intrasentential candidates, since the noun phrase "o supermercado" comes after the pronoun and its choice would result in cataphora, which is not dealt with by the algorithm. The possible intersentential candidates are "Pedro" and "vinho de jabuticaba", because they both agree with the pronoun in gender and number; also, they are within a four-sentence window. The noun "jabuticaba" is ruled out by the morphological filter since it doesn't agree in gender with the pronoun – the noun gender is female and the pronoun gender is male. The salience factors from Table 2 are used do calculate the candidates' final salience factors. The candidate "Pedro" has 35 added to its salience factor value, because it presents a syntactic parallelism with the pronoun being resolved, the pronoun "Ele" – that is, they are both subject noun phrases. To "vinho de jabuticaba", on the other hand, nothing is added. Note that the salience factor assignment, according to Table 2, is temporary; thus, the salience factor *Syntactic Parallelism*, added to "Pedro", will only be considered during the resolution of pronoun "Ele". Therefore, "Pedro" is chosen as referent of pronoun "Ele", because it has the highest salience factor.

The discourse model is now updated, and the salience factor of the pronoun is calculated. Pronoun "Ele" receives the salience factor 310 because it is subject of the sentence (80), it is neither contained in a demarcated prepositional adverbial phrase (50), nor in another noun phrase (80), and it belongs to the sentence which is being analysed (100). Next, the pronoun is added to the equivalence class of the candidate, and its salience factor is added the to salience factor of the equivalence class of the chosen candidate. Therefore, the salience factor for "Pedro" becomes 465. Figure 3(c) shows the discourse model after the last update.

The next pronoun to be resolved is pronoun "o". The possible candidate for intrasentential referent is "Ele", since it was already resolved and, therefore, it is treated as the noun phrase to whom it refers. Thus, coreference is not allowed according to the third Reinhart's constraint, presented in section 3.1.

The possible intersentential candidates are "vinho de jabuticaba" and "Pedro", because they both agree with the pronoun in gender and number. "Pedro" is eliminated because it belongs to the same equivalence class of the pronoun "Ele", which has already been eliminated according to the third Reinhart's constraint. The noun "jabuticaba" is ruled out by the morphological filter since it doesn't agree in gender with the pronoun. Therefore, the noun phrase "vinho de jabuticaba" is the only candidate and it is chosen. Again, the discourse model is updated and the salience factor of the pronoun is calculated. Pronoun "o" receives salience factor 280, because it is a direct object (50), it is neither contained in another noun phrase (80), nor in a demarcated propositional adverbial phrase (50), and belongs to the sentence which is being analysed (100).

The process of discourse model updating is the same as described before. Figure 3(d) shows the discourse model at the end of the processing.

4   Results

The algorithm was tested and evaluated on two corpora. The first corpus was composed of legal opinions from the *Procuradoria Geral da República de Portugal*[5], and the second was a literary book called *O Alienista*, from a well-known Brazilian author, Machado de Assis[6]. Both corpora were automatically annotated by the parser PALAVRAS, with morfosyntactic information. Pronouns were manually annotated with a tool for discourse annotation, MMAX (*Multi-Modal Annotation in XML*) [15]. Reciprocal and reflexive pronouns were only annotated for the literary corpus.

In our first experiment, with the legal corpus, we considered the resolution process successful if the solution offered by our algorithm was the same as that offered by manual annotation. Therefore, all solutions given by the annotators were later automatically compared with the solutions given by our system.

---

[5] Attorney General's Office of the Republic of Portugal.

[6] Available at http://bibvirt.futuro.usp.br/textos/autores/machadodeassis/alienista/alienista.html

Table 3. Global analysis of the legal corpus

Total of annotated anaphora[7]	297
Anaphora wrongly resolved	190
Anaphora correctly resolved	103
Anaphora not identified[8]	4
Success rate	35.15%

Table 4. Evaluation of the separate files of legal corpus

	2.txt	3.txt	4.txt	7.txt	10.txt	11.txt	12.txt	13.txt	14.txt	15.txt
Total of annotated anaphora	17	21	23	13	5	41	21	32	10	2
Anaphora correctly resolved	5	7	9	6	2	16	6	10	5	1
Anaphora not identified	0	1	0	0	1	1	0	1	0	0
Success rate	29.41%	35%	39.13%	46.15%	50%	40%	28.57%	32.26%	50%	50%

	24.txt	25.txt	28.txt	29.txt	30.txt	36.txt
Total of annotated anaphora	36	4	21	22	13	16
Anaphora correctly resolved	16	0	3	7	4	6
Anaphora not identified	0	0	0	0	0	0
Success rate	44.44%	0%	14.29%	31.82%	30.77%	37.50%

In the second experiment, with the literary corpus, we considered the resolution process successful if the solution offered by our algorithm was the same as that offered by manual annotation, or if it was a noun phrase which corefered with the solution given by the annotators. Therefore, all the algorithm solutions were manually compared with the solution given by the annotators.

The legal corpus was split up into 16 files. Table 3 presents the global results of the analysis, and Table 4 shows the results of the individual files.

As we can see, the success rate is very low if compared with the 86% success rate reported by Lappin and Leass on a corpus composed of computer manuals, in English [2]. For the second corpus, as it was already said, reflexive and reciprocal pronouns were also annotated. The book was split up into four files and the results of the analysis are shown in Tables 5 and 6.

Table 5. Global analysis of the literary corpus

Anaphora correctly resolved	230 (33.05%)
Anaphora wrongly resolved	466 (66.95%)
Total of annotated anaphora	696
Intrasentential anaphors correctly resolved	82 (37.44%)
Intrasentential anaphors wrongly resolved	137 (62.56%)
Total of annotated Intrasentential anaphors	219 (31.46%)
Intersentential anaphors correctly resolved	109 (29.30%)
Intersentential anaphors wrongly resolved	263 (70.70%)
Total of annotated Intersentential anaphors	372 (53.45%)
Anaphors without antecedent correctly resolved	36 (34.29%)
Anaphors without antecedent wrongly resolved	69 (65.71%)
Total of annotated anaphors without antecedent	105 (15.09%)

---

[7] Total of third person pronouns manually annotated; reflexive and reciprocal pronouns were not annotated.

[8] Number of pronouns manually annotated which were not identified by the algorithm.

Table 6. Evaluation of the separated parts of literary corpus

	first	second	third	fourth
Third person pronouns correctly resolved	31	46	30	62
Third person pronouns wrongly resolved	85	136	44	161
Total of annotated third person pronouns	116	182	74	223
Success rate in third person pronouns resolution	26.72%	25.27%	40.54%	27.80%
Reflexive and reciprocal anaphors correctly resolved	7	19	14	21
Reflexive and reciprocal anaphors wrongly resolved	6	9	6	19
Total of annotated reflexive and reciprocal anaphors	13	28	20	40
Success rate in reflexive and reciprocal anaphor resolution	53.85%	67.86%	70%	52.50%
Total of annotated pronouns	129	210	94	263
Total success rate	29.46%	30.95%	46.81%	31.56%

As we can see, there was no improvement on the success rate, and we did not get even closer to the 50% we expected to achieve with the new corpus. The better results with reflexive and reciprocal pronouns were due to their resolution process; since only intrasentential candidates were taken into account, the amount of candidates considered for these pronoun categories was smaller.

The results were worst than the ones reported using different approaches for Portuguese, such as the Centering Algorithm [16], which achieved a success rate of 51% on the same legal corpus used here. A direct comparison with the Centering Algorithm was not possible due to the different annotation used in its evaluation. Lappin and Leass and Centering Algorithms were also evaluated with Spanish texts [17], achieving a success rate of 67.40% and 62.60%, respectively.

Therefore, we came to the conclusion that the problem was neither with the corpora we have chosen, nor with the fact that the legal corpus had not been annotated with reciprocal and reflexive pronouns. A thorough manual analysis of the system's execution has shown that there were several problems with the output of PALAVRAS, such as incorrect morfosyntactic information, and reflexive and reciprocal pronouns incorrectly identified, and duplicated nodes in the syntactic structure of the sentence. We have also noted some problems with the XML generated by the Xtractor, introduced after the correct parsing, such as absent nodes in the syntactic structure of the sentence, and the extraction of incorrect morfosyntactic information. The salience factors, empirically obtained by Lappin and Leass on an English corpus, may also have contributed to the low success rates.

5   Conclusion and Future Work

We have developed and evaluated a variant of Lappin and Leass' Algorithm for pronoun resolution in Portuguese. The algorithm resolves inter and intrasentential third person, and reflexive and reciprocal pronouns. The algorithm was evaluated on two corpora: legal and literary corpora. The evaluation of the algorithm on both corpora showed a performance much lower than the original algorithm, developed for English. There was not a significant improvement with the second corpus, even with the addition of reflexive and reciprocal pronoun evaluation.

The evaluation of the original Lappin and Leass' Algorithm was on a corpus composed of computer manuals, less complex than the corpora we have used, which may have contributed to the discrepancy between the results reported by Lappin and Leass, and the results presented here. Also, the salience factors empirically obtained on an English corpus may not be applicable as such to Portuguese. Nevertheless, the results presented here seem promising, since they were obtained on corpora composed of very complex and long sentences.

As future work, we will evaluate the algorithm on a corpus of newspaper articles and we expect to get closer to the rates reported by Lappin and Leass. A quantification of how many errors were actually introduced by the tools we have used will also be made. Also, we hope to be able to compare the algorithm developed here with the Centering Algorithm, adapted to Portuguese and evaluated in [16], on a corpus composed of newspaper's articles. Finally, we will change the salience factors taking the Portuguese language features into account in order to see if we can obtain a considerable improvement.

Acknowledgements

We thank Ana Margarida Aires, Charlotte Marie Chambelland Galves, Paulo Quaresma, Renata Vieira, Sandra Collovini, and Sheila Morais de Almeida for their valuable help.

References

1. Hirst, G.: Anaphora in natural language understanding: a survey. Lecture notes in computer science : 119. Springer-Verlag (1981)
2. Lappin, S., Leass, H.J.: An algorithm for pronomial anaphora resolution. Computational Linguistics **20** (1994) 535–561
3. Hobbs, J.: Resolving pronoun references. Lingua **44** (1978) 311–338
4. Grosz, B.J., Weinstein, S., Joshi, A.K.: Centering: A framework for modeling the local coherence of discourse. Association for Computational Linguistics **21** (1995) 203–225
5. Lappin, S., McCord, M.: A syntatic filter on pronominal anaphora in slot grammar. In: 28th Annual Meeting of the Association for Computational Linguistics. (1990) 135–142
6. Lappin, S., McCord, M.: Anaphora resolution in slot grammar. Computational Linguistics **16** (1990) 197–212
7. McCord, M.: Slot grammar: A system for simpler construction of practical natural language grammars. In Studer, R., ed.: Natural Language and Logic: International Scientific Symposium. (1990) 118–145
8. McCord, M.: Heuristics for broad-coverage natural language parsing. In: ARPA Human Language Technology Workshop, University of Pennsylvania (1993)
9. Jurafsky, D., H. Martin, J.: Speech and Language Processing: An Introduction to Natural Language Processing, Computational Linguistics and Speech Recognition. 1 edn. Prentice Hall (2000)
10. Reinhart, T.: Anaphora and Semantic Interpretation. Croom Helm Ltd (1983)
11. Bick, E.: The Parsing System PALAVRAS: Automatic Grammatical Analysis of Portuguese in a Constraint Grammar Frammework. PhD thesis, Årthus University (2000)

12. Gasperin, C.V., Vieira, R., Goulart, R.R.V., Quaresma, P.: Extracting xml chunks from Portuguese corpora. In: Proceedings of the Workshop on Traitement automatique des langues minoritaires, Batz-sur-Mer (2003)
13. Carvalho, A.M.B.R.: Logic Grammars and Pronominal Anaphora. PhD thesis, University of Reading (1989)
14. Allen, J.: Natural Language Understanding. The Benjamin/Cummings Publishing Company (1995)
15. Müller, C., Strube, M.: Mmax: A tool for the annotation of multi-modal corpora. In: the 2nd IJCAI Workshop on Knowledge and Reasoning in Practical Dialogue Systems, Washington, USA (2001) 45–50
16. Aires, A.M., Coelho, J.C.B., Collovini, S., Quaresma, P., Vieira, R.: Avaliação de centering em resolução pronominal da língua portuguesa. In: Taller de Herramientas y Recursos Lingüísticos para el Español y el Portugués. Volume 1. (2004) 1–8
17. Palomar, M., Moreno, L., Peral, J., Muñoz, R., Ferrández, A., Martínez-Barco, P., Saiz-Noeda, M.: An algorithm for anaphora resolution in Spanish texts. Computacional Linguistics **27** (2001) 545–567

STEMBR: A Stemming Algorithm for the Brazilian Portuguese Language

Reinaldo Viana Alvares, Ana Cristina Bicharra Garcia, and Inhaúma Ferraz

UFF – Universidade Federal Fluminense, Instituto de Computação,
Rua Passo da Pátria, 156 Bloco E - 3º Andar,
São Domingos, Niterói, RJ 24210-240
{ralvares, bicharra, ferraz}@ic.uff.br

Abstract. Stemming algorithms have traditionally been utilized in information retrieval systems as they generate a more concise word representation. However, the efficiency of these algorithms varies according to the language they are used with. This paper presents STEMBR, a stemmer for Brazilian Portuguese whereby the suffix treatment is based on a statistical study of the frequency of the last letter for words found in Brazilian web pages. The proposed stemmer is compared with another algorithm specifically developed for Portuguese. The results show the efficiency of our stemmer.

1 Introduction

A word is a string of letters organized in such a way that they can represent the meaning of language expression about objects and ideas. It is common in texts to find affixal variations of words. For example, the words "cantores (singers)", "cantora (female singer)" and "canto (song or singing)" represent, in generic terms, the meaning of "cantar (to sing)". Research in the area of information retrieval (IR) aims to find a single representation for such words, thus providing the user with a broader search result. Stemming algorithms are an option for this task.

Stemming is the process of converting variations of a word into a concise and accurate representation. The concept adheres to the annotation principle [10]. The aim of the stemming process is to merge words, that have a common meaning, into a single representation known as a stem. The stem is the result of the process of stemming. In the stemming process, two kinds of error may occur:

- Over stemming: removing too many letters, so that words with different meanings are merged to a single stem. See Table1:

Table 1. Example of over stemming errors

Meaning	Word	Stem
comportamento (behavior)	comportado (well behaved)	comp
comparar (compare)	comparou (compared)	comp

- Under stemming: leaving too many letters, so that words with the same core meaning are merged into different stems. See Table 2:

C. Bento, A. Cardoso, and G. Dias (Eds.): EPIA 2005, LNAI 3808, pp. 693–701, 2005.
© Springer-Verlag Berlin Heidelberg 2005

Table 2. Example of under stemming errors

Meaning	Word	Stem
movimento (movement)	movimentação (moving)	movimentaç
movimento (movement)	movimentar (to move)	movimenta

Various different stemming algorithms have been proposed for the English language [3]. However, few solutions have been put forward regarding the Portuguese language.

Below, we present the approaches most commonly used in the stemming process, the methods for evaluating these algorithms, the STEMBR, a case study, and overall comments regarding the work.

2 Stemming Algorithms

In this section, we present the approaches most commonly used in the stemming process, which are: affix stripping, table lookup and statistical methods.

2.1 Affix Stripping

This approach is dependent on the morphology of the target language. The stem is obtained by stripping some elements (morphemes) from the beginning/end of the word.

We find here the most traditional method of extracting suffixes: the Porter algorithm [9]. Originally developed for the English language, this stemmer is made up of five steps, during which certain rules are applied to the words and the most common suffixes are removed. Based on a specific measurement, relating to the number of vowels/consonants in a word, the algorithm attempts to avoid removing letters when the stem is very short. As it was a pioneering work in this area, the method has been adapted for a variety of languages, including Brazilian Portuguese.

A stemmer specially developed for the Portuguese language is presented in [4], and has shown itself to be more efficient than the Brazilian version of the Porter algorithm. This stemmer, hereon referred to as STEMP, comprises 8 steps (plural, feminine, augmentative, adverb, noun and verb reduction, remove vowel and remove accents) that are performed in a predetermined order. Each step is made up of a set of rules that are sequentially applied, but with only one rule being applied in each instance. Each rule has four elements:

- The suffix to be removed;
- The minimum size of the stem;
- An alternative suffix, if necessary, and;
- A list of exceptions.

To illustrate a rule: *{"ura",4,"",{"acupuntura", "costura"}}*, where "ura" is the suffix to be removed, 4 is the minimum stem size, and the words in inverted commas represent the list of exceptions, in this case because there is no alternative suffix.

2.2 Table Lookup

Under this approach, the stemming process is performed manually, wherein the stems are defined for each word and stored in some kind of structured form. The advantage is that it generates perfect stems. However, the approach is limited to retrieving only those words that have been previously stored. What is more, the space occupied for storage tends to grow as the corpus expands, which can make the search process inefficient.

2.3 Statistical Stemmers

Here, the stemming process involves statistical methods whereby, through a process of inference and based on a corpus, rules are formulated regarding word formation. Some of the methodologies adopted are: frequency counts, n-gram [7], link analysis [1], and Hidden Markov Models (HMM) [6]. This approach does not require any linguistic knowledge whatsoever, being totally independent of the morphological structure of the target language.

3 Evaluation Methods

In this section, we present the methodologies utilized to evaluate the performance of the stemmers, namely: the manual method, vocabulary reduction and Paice's method.

In the manual method, a human being, who decides the correct stem for each word, performs the stemming process. Three evaluation measurements are obtained in this manner: the number of correct results; the number of errors due to over stemming; and the number of errors due to under stemming.

One of the purposes of stemmers is to reduce the size of the vocabulary for indexing purposes. The vocabulary reduction is obtained by dividing the number of words in the corpus by the number of stems generated, excluding repetitions.

In Paice's method [8], three measurements are implemented: the over stemming index (OI); the under stemming index (UI); and the stemming weight (SW). This method requires a word sampling, with no repetitions, separated into conceptual groups in which the words are semantically and morphologically related. The over stemming and under stemming errors are counted for each group and the OI and UI are calculated for all the groups. The SW is given by the ratio OI/UI.

4 STEMBR

Our algorithm composes he classical steps and the affix stripping is adequate to Portuguese language. The rationale, affix treatments and the STEMBR model are presented below.

4.1 The Rationale for the STEMBR

4.1.1 Corpus
Our stemmer is based on a statistical study (the Evaluator module in figure 1) of the LexWeb corpus [5]. The LexWeb is a lexical generator for the Portuguese language, constructed with tools that visit Brazilian web pages and select the most frequently used words. The size of the corpus is approximately 130,000 words.

4.1.2 The Most Common Last Letters

From the statistical study, a list was obtained showing the frequency, in descending order, of the last letter of the words surveyed. The nine most common letters on the list (see figure 2) represent approximately 85% of the total sampling.

4.1.3 Suffix Size Ordering

An important factor in the construction of the stemmer is the way in which each suffix is removed. For example, consider the word "cantávamos (we sang)", and the suffixes "mos" and "ávamos". Either of these suffixes could be stripped from the word, as both represent its substrings. The best choice would be to remove the largest substring, generating the stem "cant".

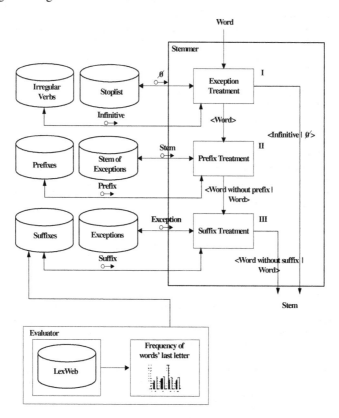

Fig. 1. The STEMBR Model

4.2 Prefix Treatment

The treatment of prefixes is simple. Known prefixes are stripped form the words. The only peculiarity occurs when the substring does not represent a prefix. For example, in the word "impossibilidade (impossibility)", the substring "im" performs the function of a prefix. However, in the word "imagem (image)" this is not the case, so its removal would cause the word to lose all meaning. In order to minimize this problem, the algorithm is given a list of exceptions (25 prefixes), which contains the stems of words whose substrings are not prefixes. Prefixes that generate many exceptions are not treated.

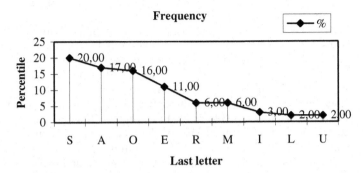

Fig. 2. Last letter frequency for words in the LexWeb corpus

4.3 Suffix Treatment

Our challenge is to obtain a simple and efficient stemmer for the Portuguese language. To this end, the suffix treatment is performed for each subset of words from the list generated by the statistical study (words that have the same last letter). The list of suffixes is organized so as to strip the largest suffix from each word. Nevertheless, the key issue relates to the order in which the suffix treatment is performed, in an attempt to generate the fewest possible errors. With the empirical assistance of a Lexicographical Specialist, and following exhaustive testing, we arrived at a configuration that generated the most satisfactory results. The best order for performing the suffix treatment is: "S", "R", "M", "L", "O", "A", "U", "E" and "I". The reasoning behind this includes:

- In the Portuguese language, with few exceptions, words with suffixes ending in "s" represent the plural form and are generally longer (number of letters) than the singular form;
- After stripping the suffixes ending in "r", "m" or "l", there are cases where the substrings generated still do not represent the correct stem of the word. Some of these cases are resolved after performing suffix treatment for the vowel endings ("a", "e", "o", "i" and "u" – the latter two are considered semi-vowels in Portuguese). Changing the suffix treatment order among the three consonants did not make any significant difference to the results of the process;
- The vowels "o" and "a" represent approximately 33% of the total sampling. Again, no significant differences were noted when their order was changed.

4.4 The STEMBR Model

In the STEMBR model, every word is sequentially submitted to three modules: specific cases; prefix reduction; and suffix reduction.

- Specific cases: at this instance, the word is checked to see if it belongs to some special category, for which prefix and suffix reductions would be inappropriate. Verbs with irregular conjugations are examples of such words. These verbs are merged in their infinitive form. This list was obtained through a Lexographical Specialist's help.
- Prefix reduction: at this point, the prefix treatment is performed. This process strips the prefix from the word, if it is not found on the list of exceptions;
- Suffix reduction: the suffix treatment is the most important process to be performed. The process comprises a set of rules whereby the longest suffix is stripped from the word. Some of these rules were obtained from [4], while others were specially created, through a Lexographical Specialist's help. The stemmer currently has 394 rules. Each rule has three elements: the suffix to be removed; the minimum size of the stem; and a list of exceptions. The minimum stem size is to avoid generating extremely short stems. This technique, utilized in [4], helps to avoid over stemming errors. Meanwhile, the list of exceptions organizes words that, despite ending in a suffix form, should not have this ending removed. In the rule below, the words on the list of exceptions do not have the suffix "mento" removed.

{"mento",{"complemento(complement)","instrumento (instrument)", "departamento (department)"}}

Let us consider the word "irritadíssina" (extremely annoyed, in English). This word is sequentially submitted to three modules:

- Specific cases: If the word is a irregular verb or a stopword it is substituted by the infinitive form or eliminated (stopwords);
  Else the prefix treatment is performed.
- Prefix reduction: If the initial substring of the word is a known prefix the prefix is eliminated;
  Else the suffix treatment is performed.
- Suffix reduction: The suffix treatment begins identifying the final letter of the word. The list of final substrings ending with the encountered letter is classified in length descending order and is used for comparison. The longest suffix is stripped. The "adíssima" substring is eliminated generating the token "irrit" (see figure 3).

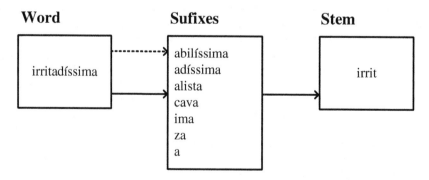

Fig. 3. Suffix reduction for the word "irritadíssima"

5 Case Study

In order to evaluate the quality of the STEMBR model, tests were carried out involving the three evaluation methods presented, comparing the model against the stemmer proposed in [4] and the Brazilian version of the Porter algorithm.

5.1 Corpus

We used two samples, of different sizes and origins, as follows:

- 1,000 words, taken from the electronic dictionary "Aurélio – Século XXI (Twenty-first Century)" [2], hereon referred to as "Sample I";
- 5,000 words, taken from the LexWeb, hereon referred to as "Sample II".

5.2 The Manual Method

A Lexicographical Specialist, being a person with considerable Portuguese language experience, performed the manual stemming procedure. The test results are shown in tables 3 and 4:

Table 3. Results of the test using Sample I

Stemmer	Correct	Over stemming	Under stemming
STEMBR	62.20 %	8.90 %	27.10 %
STEMP	55.30 %	4.70 %	37.70 %
PORTER	43.80 %	1.30 %	51.20 %

Table 4. Resuls of the test using Sample II

Stemmer	Correct	Over stemming	Under stemming
STEMBR	69.02 %	12.05 %	17.96 %
STEMP	67.60 %	8.96 %	22.58 %
PORTER	57.86 %	5.00 %	34.48 %

5.3 Vocabulary Reduction

Tables 5 and 6 show vocabulary reduction of the samples:

Table 5. Vocabulary reduction using Sample I

Stemmer	Reduction to
STEMBR	29.20 %
STEMP	32.70 %
PORTER	40.50 %

Table 6. Vocabulary reduction using Sample II

Stemmer	Reduction to
STEMBR	53.92 %
STEMP	53.90 %
PORTER	60.00 %

5.4 Paice Evaluation

A Lexographical Specialist manually generated a total of 102 and 2,696 semantic groups, respectively, for Sample I and Sample II. The test results are shown in tables 6 and 7:

Table 7. Results of Paice's Method using Sample I

Stemmer	OI	UI	SW
STEMBR	7.30×10^{-4}	0.447	1.60×10^{-3}
STEMP	7.09×10^{-4}	0.492	1.44×10^{-3}
PORTER	3.06×10^{-4}	0.537	0.67×10^{-3}

Table 8. Results of Paice's Method using Sample II

Stemmer	OI	UI	SW
STEMBR	1.01×10^{-4}	0.288	3.50×10^{-4}
STEMP	0.98×10^{-4}	0.295	3.30×10^{-4}
PORTER	0.50×10^{-4}	0.395	1.25×10^{-4}

5.5 Discussion

The test results showed that:

- Using the manual method ("Gold Standard"), with Sample I, the STEMBR model obtained a correct rate approximately 7% higher than the stemmer STEMP and 18.4% higher than the PORTER stemmer. With Sample II, the STEMBR and STEMP were practically equal (the STEMBR having an advantage of 1.42%) and they obtained a correct rate approximately 10% higher than the PORTER stemmer. Our stemmer obtained a lower rate of under stemming and a higher rate of over stemming errors than the STEMP, in both the samples;
- The vocabulary reduction of STEMBR was 3.5% lower than that of STEMP for Sample I and they were practically equal for Sample II;
- Using Paice's method, the rate of under stemming for STEMBR was lower than STEMP and PORTER stemmer, in both the samples;
- Using Paice's method, the rate of over stemming for PORTER stemmer was lower for both samples.

6 Conclusions

This paper presented the development of a stemmer for Brazilian Portuguese, wherein the suffix treatment is performed for each subset of words with a common last letter. The test results show that the STEMBR model is more efficient than the STEMP reference model in terms of under stemming errors, and less so with regard to over stemming errors. In practice, it can be seen that it is a conflicting task to try reducing the two types of error. It is our intention to apply our stemmer on an Information Retrieval system to assess its impact over recall and precision.

References

1. Bacchin, M.., Ferro, N. and Melucci, M.. University of Padua at CLEF 2002: Experiments to evaluate a statistical stemming algorithm. Working Notes for CLEF 2002, pages 161-168: In *Proceedings*, Rome, September 2002.
2. Ferreira, A. B. H.. *Dicionário Aurélio Eletrônico*. CD-ROM (In Portuguese). Nova Fronteira. 1999.
3. Frakes, W. and B. Yates, R.. *Information Retrieval: Data Structures and Algorithms*. Prentice Hall, NJ, 1992.
4. Orengo, V. and Huyck, C.. A Stemming Algorithm for The Portuguese Language. In *Proceedings of Eighth Symposium on String Processing and Information Retrieval (SPIRE 2001)*, pages 186-193, Laguna de San Raphael, Chile, November 2001.
5. Junior, A. M.. *LexWeb: um léxico da língua portuguesa extraído automaticamente da internet*. Master Thesis (in Portuguese). Programa de Pós-Graduação em Engenharia Elétrica. UFPA, November 2004.
6. Melucci, M. and Orio, N. A Novel Method for Stemmer Generation Based on Hidden Markov Models. In *Proceedings of Conference on Information and Knowledge Management (CIKM03)*, pages 131-138, New Orleans, LA, November 2003. ACM Press.
7. Mayfield, J. and McNamee, P.. Single N-gram Stemming. In *Proceedings of the 26th annual international ACM SIGIR conference on Research and development in information retrieval*, pages 415-416, Toronto, Canada, July 2003. ACM Press.
8. Paice, C.: An evaluation method for stemming algorithms, in *Proceedings of the 17th annual international ACM SIGIR conference on Research and development in information retrieval*, pages 42-50, Dublin, Ireland, July 1994. ACM Press.
9. Porter, M.. An Algorithm for Suffix Stripping. *Program*, 14(3), 130-137, July 1980.
10. Stefik, M. *Introduction to Knowledge systems*. Morgan Kaufmann Publishers. 1995.

Author Index

Lecture Notes in Artificial Intelligence (LNAI)